PRICE
THEORY
AND
APPLICATIONS

PRICE
THEORY
AND
APPLICATIONS

B. Peter Pashigian
Graduate School of Business
University of Chicago

McGraw-Hill, Inc.
New York   St. Louis   San Francisco   Auckland   Bogotá   Caracas
Lisbon   London   Madrid   Mexico City   Milan   Montreal
New Delhi   San Juan   Singapore   Sydney   Tokyo   Toronto

PRICE THEORY AND APPLICATIONS

This book is printed on recycled, acid-free paper containing 10% postconsumer waste.

4 5 6 7 8 9 0   AGM   AGM   9 0 9 8 7 6 5

ISBN 0-07-048741-3

This book was set in ITC Century Book by Ruttle, Shaw & Wetherill, Inc. The editors were James A. Bittker and Scott Stratford; the design was done by Keithley and Associates, Inc.; the production supervisor was Friederich W. Schulte.
The cover photographer was Paul Silverman.
The art was rendered by Keithley and Associates, Inc.
Arcata Graphics/Martinsburg was printer and binder.

Acknowledgments
1. Figure 5-5 and Figure 10-11 are reprinted by permission of Harvard University Press, copyright 1955 and 1974, respectively, by the President and Fellows of Harvard College.
2. Table 8-3 and 8-4 are reprinted with the permission of Blackwell Publishers for the Royal Economic Society.
3. Table 10-6 is reprinted with the permission of University of Chicago Press, copyright 1991 by the University of Chicago. All rights reserved.
4. Table 10-9 is reprinted by permission of Mary W. Sullivan, "Brand Extensions: When to Use Them," Management Sciences, vol. 38, June 1992, copyright 1992 by the Institute of Management Sciences, 290 Westminister Street, Providence, RI 02903.
5. Table 11-1 on page 410 and Table 11-4 on page 431 are reprinted with the kind permission of Elsevier Sequoia, Lausanne, Switzerland, publishers of the *Journal of Financial Economics*.
6. Table 12-4 and Table 14-5 are copyrighted in 1991 by the President and Fellows of Harvard College and the Massachusetts Institute of Technology.
7. Figure 17-3 are reprinted with the permission of the *Journal of Law and Economics*, copyright 1986 by the University of Chicago. All rights reserved.

Library of Congress Cataloging-in-Publication Data

Pashigian, B. Peter (Bedros Peter)
    Price theory and applications / B. Peter Pashigian.
        p.   cm.
    Includes bibliographical references.
    ISBN 0-07-048741-3
    1. Microeconomics.   2. Prices.   I. Title.
HB172.P26   1995
338.5'2—dc20   93-36667

ABOUT THE AUTHOR

B. Peter Pashigian is a professor of economics in the Graduate School of Business at the University of Chicago. He received his Ph.D. from the Department of Economics at Massachusetts Institute of Technology. He has published articles in the *American Economic Review*, the *Journal of Political Economy*, the *Journal of Law and Economics*, the *Quarterly Journal of Economics*, and other leading journals on diverse topics such as why firms have sales, farmer opposition to futures markets, political support of and opposition to environmental regulation, the demand for and supply of lawyers, and other topics. He is a coeditor of the *Journal of Business*.

CONTENTS IN BRIEF

CONTENTS

**PART VI INTERTEMPORAL EQUILIBRIUM
AND FACTOR MARKETS**   *583*

PREFACE

Students enrolled in an intermediate price theory class appear to be divided equally between courses offered in departments of economics and those offered in business schools. Only a minority of these students have and take the opportunity to apply the theory in upper-level courses. In most business schools microeconomics is a required course and students seldom take advanced courses where the theory is applied. *Most readers of this book will never take another microeconomics course.* These are the stark facts that each instructor must recognize, adapt to, and somehow contend with.

Given the student's fleeting encounter with economics, how should the essentials of microeconomics be taught? I take the position that a microeconomics course should impart not only an understanding of the theory but also the excitement of using the theory to explain a broad set of behaviors. In my view this can be best accomplished by teaching the course with an artful blend of theory and application.

Product Differentiation

A chorus of reviewers has singled out the intermingling of theory and application as a distinctive feature of this book. This is a source of personal satisfaction to me because that is what I set out to achieve. I made a conscientious effort to motivate the student's interest either in theory or in an application of the theory by using interesting, serious real-world applications. Each chapter includes applications of the theory under discussion, some containing more than others, and most readers will quickly notice the empirical flavor of the book. References to actual behavior of consumers and firms reinforce the theory and make the theoretical material more accessible to the student. The applications are often taken from the business press or from academic journals where interesting illustrations of consumer and firm behavior can be found and related to the theory. Rather than take the somewhat conventional approach of looking at government behavior for applications, I turned more to the private sector. I have refrained from flooding students with short, and probably less informative, applications of the theory, in favor of fewer but more in-depth applications showing how the theory is used to address specific questions and issues. Such applications are intended to prepare students for the end-of-chapter review questions and exercises. I consider these exercises a valuable part of the book because they test students' understanding of the theory by requiring them to apply it in new situations. Applying microeconomic theory to new situations is exactly what many students will be doing for the rest of their lives.

Instructors of microeconomics are fortunate because a consensus exists about what the core material of a course should include. Nevertheless, each author exercises some latitude in deciding how to present the core material and which modern topics to include. The core chapters include many new and different applications that demonstrate the relevance of theory. For example, in Chapter 6, "The Cost Functions of the Firm," regulating plant emissions by requiring emissions from each smokestack to be reduced by the same percentage is shown to be unnecessarily costly. In Chapter 8, "Price Determination in a Competitive Industry," the question is raised whether hurricane victims can get assistance more quickly by allowing prices to rise. In the same chapter the adjustment of a competitive industry to a cost-reducing innovation is given detailed treatment since price reductions appear to be all-pervasive as an industry evolves through stages of development. Chapter 9, "Pricing under Monopoly," shows the inconsistency between the claim that cigarette and oil companies behave like monopolists and the claim that the demand for these products is inelastic. Chapter 10, "Pricing in Oligopoly," shows why a price policy of meeting competition can yield higher, not lower, prices.

A differentiating feature of this book is its systematic examination of several topics either not treated or treated superficially elsewhere. Numerous reviewers have mentioned that the section dealing with pricing practices and policies is one of the strengths of the book. Chapters 12 through 15 develop several models that help explain firms' price policies. Chapter 12, "Price Discrimination," presents an in-depth examination of the different forms of price discrimination. Unlike most books, where the free rider problem is briefly discussed when public goods are introduced, Chapter 13, "The Free Rider Problem and Pricing," highlights free rider problems in private markets and shows how firms use the price system and other methods to circumvent these problems. My classroom experiences and the reviewer comments indicate that students find this topic fascinating, and I urge instructors to include part or all of this chapter in their course outlines if at all possible. Chapter 14, "Market Behavior with Asymmetric Information," discusses how firms acquire a reputation for honesty and how private markets adapt to situations where asymmetric information exists. Finally, Chapter 15, "Pricing under Uncertainty," introduces the topic of uncertainty, showing how the theory of pricing under uncertainty can explain why firms have sales and what kinds of products are placed on sale.

Other chapters also treat subjects that are often ignored. The cost of time is given comprehensive treatment in Chapter 4, "The Cost of Time and the Theory of Consumer Behavior." With more women in the work force and with women's earnings rising faster than men's, time plays an important role in explaining consumer behavior and deserves fuller recognition in microeconomics texts. Another topic that is often ignored is governance of the firm. After a decade of massive hostile takeovers and mergers, can a modern textbook ignore the role of product and capital markets in the way a firm is governed? Much has been learned about the role of the capital market in monitoring management performance in the last 15 years, and this topic receives full treatment in Chapter 11, "The Goals of the Firm."

Alternative Course Designs

What topics to include in a course is always a challenge, and some instructors may look for guidance. This book has been written to give an instructor considerable flexibility with regard to both content and level of difficulty. For a quarter course offered at a business school an instructor will have to select among chapters. One suggestion is to include Chapters 1, 2, 4, and 6 to 9 and then choose from Chapters 10 to 15. Some instructors in business schools do not include production theory, and they can skip to Chapter 6, where the development of cost functions is independently derived. For a quarter course offered in an economics department an instructor can include Chapters 1 to 9, 18, 19, and possibly parts of other chapters. For a semester course at either a business school or department an instructor has greater latitude in supplementing the above chapters with others depending on the interests of the instructor and the students.

Alternative Levels of Rigor

Price Theory and Applications was written to give the instructor the added flexibility of either including or excluding sections marked with an asterisk (*) in the opening outlines; these cover more difficult material. There is also flexibility in the use of mathematics, with all the calculus presented in footnotes or in optional chapter appendixes. Special care was taken to keep the exposition clear without sacrificing rigor. The finished product is appropriate for students with diverse backgrounds and interests.

An Innovative Teaching-Learning Package

Daniel Fuller and Sarah Tinkler of Weber State University have prepared a remarkable Study Guide with software, *Microquest*, to accompany *Price Theory and Applications*. This Study Guide and software package provides an integrated environment to enhance students' understanding of and mastery over the fundamentals of intermediate microeconomics. *Microquest* is designed to be as user-friendly as possible, minimizing student startup time and complaints. While the software is planned primarily to supplement student work, it can also be a valuable classroom supplement given appropriate projection technology. *Microquest* is available for both DOS and Macintosh systems.

The Study Guide follows the textbook, chapter by chapter. It is designed to strengthen comprehension by putting students in problem-solving and other analytical situations. Where possible, the Study Guide makes use of the simulations and exercises contained in *Microquest*.

Microquest takes advantage of the superiority of computer-based graphics to explore central concepts presented in the textbook. In addition to brief textual and graphic analysis of these concepts, *Microquest* seeks to present students with a number of exploratory exercises. These are what-if model situations in which students change the values of key variables and parameters, as well as models in which they must assume the role of an optimizing decision maker. This material includes market simulation models, consumer utility models, profit maximization under perfect competition, profit-maximizing behavior, and models of imperfect competition.

The Instructor's Resource Manual and the Test Bank accompanying *Price Theory and Applications* follow the lead of the textbook in their application of economic concepts to real-world problems. Prepared by Clifford Nowell of Weber State University, with a considerable contribution of test questions from Shane Greenstein of the University of Illinois, the Instructor's Resource Manual and the Test Bank have been closely coordinated with the textbook and the Study Guide with accompanying software. Both the Instructor's Resource Manual and the Test Bank are available in computerized format.

Acknowledgments

While this book was being written, it was pretested at several universities. I have benefited from the pretesting experiences of Tammy Feldman of the W. A. Harriman School of Management and Policy at Stony Brook, and of Rodney Smith and Craig Stubblebine of the Department of Economics at Claremont-McKenna College. I express my gratitude to Tammy, Rodney, Craig, and their students for their helpful suggestions and criticism. In addition I have used many chapters repeatedly in two different courses that I teach at the Graduate School of Business at the University of Chicago. Many belated thanks are extended to those students who patiently completed questionnaires, offered their opinions, and diplomatically pointed out unclear sections, typos, and incomplete arguments. The book is better because of their efforts.

Numerous individuals have contributed to this book. First, I want to single out Jim Bittker and Scott Stratford, economics editors at McGraw-Hill, who guided the book from one stage to another, kept it on a reasonable schedule, and patiently responded to my incessant queries. Accolades go to Marjorie Anderson for playing the role of student reader to perfection, with her constant suggestions to clarify, to delete, and to expand; students will never truly know how much of a friend they had. She deserves much credit for the final product. Thanks are also due to Monica Freedman, editorial assistant, and Laura Warner, editing supervisor.

Many economists across the country read anonymous chapters of the book from the rough first drafts to the later more polished third drafts and offered suggestions and criticisms. These include **Ted Amato,** University of North Carolina–Charlotte; **Howard Beales,** George Washington University; **Roger Betancourt,** University of Maryland–College Park; **Eric Bond,** Pennsylvania State University; **James Brickley,** University of Rochester; **David Butz,** University of California–Los Angeles; **Larry Chenault,** Miami University; **Siddhartha Chib,** University of Missouri–Columbia; **Dennis Coates,** University of North Carolina–Chapel Hill; **Robert Cosbell,** University of Massachusetts–Amherst; **Tammy Feldman,** SUNY–Stony Brook; **Roy Gardner,** Indiana University; **Susan Gilbert,** Emory University; **Robert Gillespie,** University of Illinois–Champaign; **Steve Goldman,** University of California–Berkeley; **Shane Greenstein,** University of

Illinois–Champaign; **Thomas Gresik,** Pennsylvania State University; **Simon Hakim,** Temple University; **Alejandro Hernandez,** University of Wisconsin; **Stephen Kaplan,** University of Chicago; **Stacey Kole,** University of Rochester; **Sarah Lane,** Boston University; **Scott Masten,** University of Michigan; **Thomas Merz,** Michigan Technological University; **John Vincent Nye,** Washington University; **Hyun Park,** SUNY–Buffalo; **Richard Peck,** University of Illinois–Chicago; **Christopher Phelan,** University of Wisconsin; **Craig Pirrong,** University of Michigan; **Kevin Quinn,** University of Illinois–Chicago; **Russell Roberts,** Washington University–St. Louis; **Michael Salinger,** Boston University; **Bruce Seaman,** Georgia State University; **Roger Sherman,** University of Virginia; **Curtis Simon,** Clemson University; **Edward Snyder,** University of Michigan; **Mark Stegeman,** University of North Carolina–Chapel Hill; **Joe Turek,** Lynchburg College; **Lawrence White,** New York University; and **Luigi Zingales,** University of Chicago.

In addition I want to thank **Paul Farnham,** Georgia State University; **Thomas Ireland,** University of Missouri–St. Louis; **Hirschel Kasper,** Oberlin College; **Anthony Krautmann,** DePaul University; **William Schaffer,** Georgia Technological University; and **Valerie Suslow,** University of Michigan; who attended a focus session at the Allied Social Science Meetings in December 1991 and offered different perspectives of what a microeconomics text should and should not include. The discussion was valuable in framing the current book. Thanks are extended to still other economists who, early on, completed questionnaires concerning the proposed outline for the book and who collectively helped shape it by indicating what topics are essential and what topics are of lesser importance. Included in this last group are **Debra Aron,** Northwestern University; **Ann Bartel,** Columbia University; **Robert Becker,** Indiana University; **Arthur Bensal,** Washington University; **Dan Black,** University of Kentucky; **James Brander,** University of British Columbia; **Laurence Chang,** Case Western Reserve University; **Thomas Duchesneau,** University of Maine; **Darwin Hall,** California State University–Long Beach; **Jonathan Hamilton,** University of Florida; **Masanori Hashimoto,** Ohio State University; **Barbara McCutcheon,** University of Iowa; **Richard Mills,** University of New Hampshire; **Mike Moore,** Duke University; **David Pearce,** Yale University; **Charles Plourde,** York University; **James Rakowski,** University of Nortre Dame; **Peter Reiss,** Stanford University; **Rodney Smith,** Claremont-McKenna College; **Daniel Sullivan,** Northwestern University; **Mark Thornton,** Auburn University; and **Maurice Wilkinson,** Columbia University.

There are still others who have made important contributions to this book that I would like to acknowledge. Dan McJohn of Amoco Oil Company supplied useful information and advice on the tanker market, and Brian Bowen provided valuable research help in tracking down statistics and studies. Eric Gould demonstrated an uncanny ability to purge errors from the page proofs. Finally, a special word of gratitude is due my wife, Rose, who exhibited such patience while she shared her husband with *Price Theory and Applications.*

B. Peter Pashigian

PART I

INTRODUCTION: SUPPLY AND DEMAND

CHAPTER 1

PRICING AND THE DEMAND AND SUPPLY MODEL

Among the decisions you make before purchasing a good is whether the price is too high and, if not, how many units to purchase. In either case, the price has a great deal to do with your final decision. Just as price influences consumers, so too does it influence the behavior of firms. The price determines whether a firm will produce a product and, if so, the number of units it will supply. Clearly, price influences the behavior of buyers and suppliers. We want to go beyond this and ask how prices are determined and what causes them to change. The answers to these questions are the subject of this book, and in finding these answers, we will see how prices help allocate the scarce resources used to produce goods and services.

Modern industrial economies produce an incredible array of products and services, and how this all comes about is truly miraculous. How do producers know that consumers want more VCRs and fewer radios, more fashionable and less basic clothing, more fish and less beef, and more prepared foods and fewer home-cooked meals? Prices play a vital role in signaling suppliers that consumers want more of some products and fewer of others. Similarly, prices convey information from suppliers to demanders that the cost of a good is higher or lower than before. After reading this book, you will have a better understanding and a greater appreciation of the way prices transmit messages between consumers and producers.

Economists use **models**—simplifications of reality—to describe the behavior of demanders and suppliers. This chapter introduces the fundamental building blocks of demand and supply that economists use and begins to explain how prices are determined. The demand and supply model is applied repeatedly throughout the book and serves as a powerful tool for demonstrating how markets work. After presenting the concepts of demand and supply and building the basic model, we use the model to predict how market behavior and prices change when conditions change. As you work through the chapter, try to develop a facility in solving problems with the model. The true test of your understanding of demand and supply concepts lies in your ability to apply them in different situations to predict the market behavior of participants and prices.

1-1   THE MEANING OF DEMAND AND SUPPLY

Economists use "demand" and "supply" in a very precise way, and this chapter begins by explaining what these terms mean to an economist. Later in the chapter the economist's usage is contrasted with everyday usage of the terms.

The economist's view of demanders and suppliers rests on one fundamental premise: demanders and suppliers respond to incentives. This means that they respond to price changes. For example, consumers react to a lower price by demanding more units of a good, and a higher price induces producers to supply more units of a good. Consumer and producer responses to incentives imply neither that consumers "need" to consume nor that producers "need" to supply a good. "Need" is a word that economists avoid because it suggests that consumers cannot do without a product no matter what the price. This type of behavior conflicts with the fundamental premise that demanders and suppliers respond to incentives.

Table 1-1 RELATIONSHIP BETWEEN THE NUMBER OF CANS OF FRUIT DRINK DEMANDED PER WEEK AND THE PRICE PER CAN

PRICE PER CAN ($)	CANS DEMANDED PER WEEK
3.00	2
2.00	4
1.00	5
0.50	7

If you are comfortable with the notion that consumers modify demands and producers change supplies in response to price changes, you are already thinking like an economist. If you want to know something about the demand or supply for crude oil, you would not ask, What is the demand for crude oil? or What is the supply of crude oil? Because the demand and supply of crude oil depend on its price, no one can answer these questions without specifying a price. An economist would phrase the question differently: What will be the quantity demanded or the quantity supplied of crude oil if the price is $20 per barrel?

1-2 THE MARKET DEMAND FUNCTION

Let's consider how you might respond as the price per can of your favorite fruit drink declines. Table 1-1 shows how the number of cans of fruit drink per week that you demand changes as the price per can changes.

If the price per can is $3, you might drink only a few cans a week given that it is so expensive. On the other hand, if the price is only 50 cents a can, you might drink a can a day. As the price of your favorite fruit drink decreases, the quantity you demand increases. The relationship between the quantity of cans you demand per week and the price per can is your individual demand function.

Other consumers have individual demand functions for the same fruit drink, and adding up the individual quantities demanded by all individuals at each price results in what economists call the market demand function.[1]

> The **demand function** expresses the relationship between the total quantity demanded and the price of the product.

The relationship between the price and the quantity demanded can be expressed as

$$Q_d = D(P) \qquad \text{(Market Demand Function)} \qquad \textbf{(1-1)}$$

---

[1] Individual demand functions are summed horizontally to derive the market demand function.

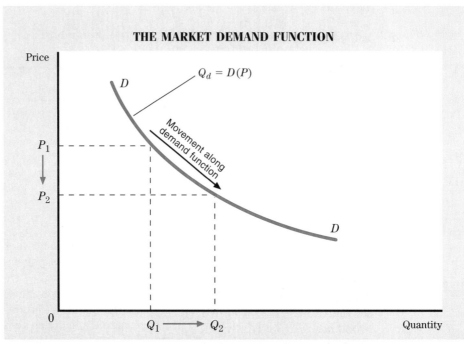

THE MARKET DEMAND FUNCTION

Figure 1-1   The quantity demanded Q_d increases when the price P decreases. At a price of P_1 the quantity demanded is Q_1. When the price is reduced to P_2, the quantity demanded increases to Q_2. This relationship is called the law of demand.

where Q_d is the quantity demanded, P is the price per unit, and D is the notation for a function. Equation 1-1 shows the total quantity demanded at each price, and Figure 1-1 illustrates the market demand function.

Throughout the book we follow the convention of placing price on the vertical axis and quantity demanded on the horizontal axis. Uppercase letters designate market demand, the aggregate quantity demanded by all consumers, and lowercase letters indicate the quantity demanded by a single consumer.

Movement along a Demand Function

The total quantity demanded increases when the price of the product drops. If the price is P_1, the quantity demanded is Q_1 units per period. If the price decreases to P_2, the quantity demanded increases from Q_1 to Q_2 units. This is seen on the graph as a movement along the demand function. A movement along a demand function always involves a change in the *price* of the product in question and a change in the *total quantity demanded* of that product.

The inverse relationship between the price and the quantity demanded is called the law of demand. The increase in the quantity demanded in response to a price decline is due to two effects. First, consumers who are already buying the product increase the quantity demanded when the price falls. Second, new consumers who have never purchased the product before decide to buy it because of the lower price. The behavior of both groups causes the quantity demanded to increase when the price decreases.

> The **law of demand** describes the inverse relationship between the quantity demanded and the price of the product.

APPLICATION 1-1

The Rising Price of Wood and the Demand for Wood

Economist Nathan Rosenberg describes an interesting episode from American economic history that illustrates the law of demand.[2] He notes that the United States possesses vast forest resources in contrast to England's limited timber resources. The price of wood was relatively low in the United States compared with England during the first half of the nineteenth century. Since the price of wood was relatively low and the price of labor relatively high, because of the scarcity of workers, Americans were generous in the use of wood in comparison with the English. In the United States fireplaces were deliberately built large to accommodate large logs, which saved on labor by reducing cutting but wasted wood used for fuel. Americans used timber for all sorts of purposes undreamed of in England. It was employed extensively in the construction of houses and bridges, for the framing of steam engines, for canal locks, and even for plank roads. When the price of wood was low, the quantity demanded was relatively high.

As industrialization during the second half of the nineteenth century used up more forest resources, the price of timber increased rapidly in the United States and the quantity demanded decreased. Before the Civil War, wood was used to power railroad engines, but 20 years later coal had virtually displaced it because the price of timber had increased relative to that of coal. Iron and steel were substituted for wood in the construction of ships, machinery, and bridges. The price of wood continued to rise in the early 1900s and increased fourfold from 1870 to 1950. This resulted in other minerals being substituted for wood. The per capita consumption of mineral products increased 10 times over this period, whereas the per capita consumption of wood peaked at the turn of the century. By 1950 wood consumption was only half of what it had been in 1900. Clearly, the rise in the price of wood reduced the quantity demanded.

Shifts in the Demand Function

So far, we have focused on what happens to the quantity demanded of a product when the price of the item changes. However, the price is only one of several determinants of the total quantity demanded. Changes in the other variables, unlike

[2] Nathan Rosenberg, "Innovative Responses to Materials Shortages," *American Economic Review*, vol. LXIII, no. 2, May 1973, pp. 111–118.

a change in the price of the product, shift the position of the demand function. A shift in the position of the demand function occurs because of a change in (1) the income of consumers, (2) the prices of other goods, or (3) the tastes of consumers. Let's consider each of these changes and show how the demand function shifts.

For many goods and services, a rise in the income of buyers causes the total quantity demanded to increase at each price. As per capita income increases, the demand functions for luxury automobiles like the Mercedes-Benz, BMW, Lexus, and Cadillac shift to the right. The demand function shifts to the right as shown in Figure 1-2. If the price is P_1, the quantity demanded is Q_1 on the original demand function, DD. After household income increases, the demand function shifts to the right and becomes $D'D'$. The aggregate quantity demanded at the price of P_1 increases from Q_1 to Q'_1 because income increases.

For many products, a rise in income causes the demand to shift outward. At each price the quantity demanded increases. However, for a few products the demand function can shift in the direction opposite the income change. For example, during a recession, when income falls, the demand for second-hand clothing increases.

The demand function can shift if the price of another good increases and consumers consider one good a *substitute* for the other. For example, a rise in the

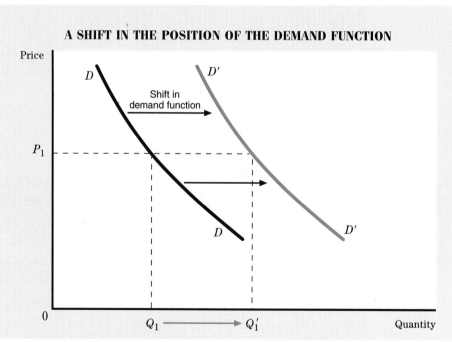

Figure 1-2 The demand curve shifts from DD to $D'D'$ because household income increases, the price of a substitute rises, or tastes change. At each price the quantity demanded increases. For example, at the price of P_1, the quantity demanded increases from Q_1 to Q'_1.

price of riding public transportation shifts the demand for automobiles rightward. A rise in the price of steel shifts the demand function for aluminum to the right because steel and aluminum are considered substitutes in some cases and automobile companies substitute aluminum for steel in producing cars. Likewise, an increase in the price of polyester may shift the demand function for cotton apparel to the right.

It should not be assumed that a change in the price of a related product always shifts the demand function of the product in question in the same direction. When the price of a product changes and the demand function of a related product shifts in the opposite direction, the two goods are called *complements.* Consider the following illustration: In May 1992 American Airlines and other airlines cut passenger fares by 50 percent, and the quantity demanded increased as consumers overwhelmed the airlines for the cheaper tickets. How did the reduction in air fares affect the demand function for rental cars, hotels, and travel agents? Draw a graph showing how the demand for rental cars shifts when the fare for air travel declines. One determinant of the demand for rental cars is the number of airline passengers. A decrease in air fares increases the number of passengers and therefore increases the demand for rental cars. Your graph should relate the daily rate for a rental car to the quantity of rental cars demanded before and after the air fare decreases. It should also show the demand function for rental cars shifting to the right after the reduction in fares. Therefore, passenger trips and rental car use are complements.

Finally, the demand function shifts to the right if tastes change and consumers prefer the product more than before. If income and all prices are constant and the quantity demanded changes, this indicates that a change in tastes has caused the shift in the demand function.

In summary, two different types of changes have been considered, and it is important to distinguish between them when applying the demand and supply model. In the first instance the change involved movement along the demand function when the price of the product changed. We saw how the quantity demanded of that product responded to a change in price. In the second instance, a change shifted the position of the demand function. The change could involve the income of consumers, the price of a related good, or a change in tastes. Any one of these changes causes the demand function of the good in question to shift *either* to the left or to the right.

To test your understanding of the distinction between movement along a demand function and a shift in the position of the demand function, try interpreting the following statements:

1. The demand for automobiles in the United States may not reach 10 million units next year because the prices for new cars will be substantially higher than current prices.

2. I'd buy a Mercedes if they didn't cost so much.

3. A fall in the price of personal computers (PCs) increases the demand for software programs.

4. The demand for new MBAs will increase by 5 percent next year.

The first statement is an example of movement along a demand function. The higher price reduces the quantity demanded. The second statement clearly recognizes the role of price and implies that one consumer's demand for a certain type of automobile vanishes because the price is too high. The third statement says that the demand for software programs depends on the price of PCs and shifts to the right when the price of PCs decreases. The fourth statement could describe a shift to the right in the demand for new MBAs caused by growth of the economy (a rightward shift in the demand function), or it could mean that the quantity demanded will increase by 5 percent if the salary of MBAs decreases by some percentage (movement along the demand function). The statement is so vague that the cause of the increase is not clear.

This concludes our preliminary examination of the market demand function. The fundamental point is that demanders respond to price changes. The quantity demanded is not a constant but changes in the direction opposite the change in the price when other determinants of quantity demanded are held constant. The position of the demand function shifts when the price of a substitute, the income of consumers, or the tastes of consumers change, with the price of the product held constant.

1-3   THE MARKET SUPPLY FUNCTION

The market supply function indicates the total quantity supplied by producers at each price. The quantity supplied is not a fixed amount determined by the physical capabilities of each firm; rather, a higher price acts as an incentive and induces producers to supply larger quantities.

> The **supply function** expresses the relationship between the total quantity supplied and the price received by suppliers.

The market supply function can be expressed symbolically as

$$Q_s = S(P) \qquad \text{(Market Supply Function)} \qquad \textbf{(1-2)}$$

where P is the price that producers receive and Q_s is the total quantity supplied by all producers. Just as the market demand function shows how consumers respond to price changes, the market supply function reflects how producers respond to price changes.

Movements along the Supply Function

Figure 1-3 shows a representative supply function. The price of the product is on the vertical axis, and the quantity supplied is on the horizontal axis. The supply function shows that suppliers offer Q_1 units of a good if the price they receive is P_1, and a larger total quantity of Q_2 units if the price they receive is P_2. The changes in the price and the quantity supplied result in a movement along the supply function.

The slope of the supply function in the figure is positive, but this is not always

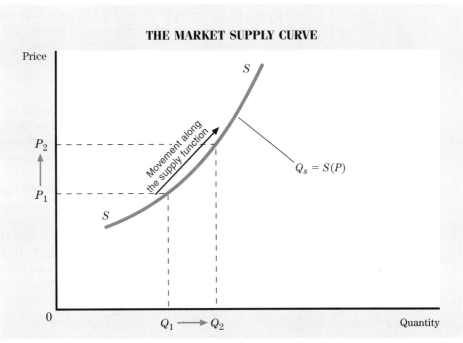

Figure 1-3   Quantity supplied increases from Q_1 to Q_2 when the price that suppliers receive increases from P_1 to P_2.

the case. Later, you will consider other situations where the supply function is flat or can even have a negative slope. When the slope is positive, producers increase the quantity supplied from Q_1 to Q_2 only if the price they receive increases from P_1 to P_2. The total quantity supplied increases at higher prices because (1) existing producers supply a larger quantity at the higher price and (2) some firms that are not particularly efficient at producing this item stay out of the industry when the price is low and enter the market when the price is higher. Both effects increase the quantity supplied at higher prices. The crude oil industry is a good example of an industry with a positively sloped supply function. Many oil wells in the United States and throughout the world are inactive or remain undiscovered when the price of crude oil is only $14 per barrel, but producers pump crude oil or seek new wells when they receive $50 per barrel. This happened in 1974 after crude oil prices shot up because OPEC limited production and the number of wells drilled around the world increased.

Shifts in the Supply Function

The supply function shows the relationship between the price of a product and the total quantity supplied. The position of the supply function shifts when a change occurs in (1) the price of inputs (labor, machinery, raw materials) used to produce the product and (2) the state of technological knowledge that allows firms to combine inputs to produce the good. If the hourly wage rate or the price of raw materials rises, the supply function shifts upward to the left because the cost of producing the product increases. Figure 1-4 shows that producers supplied Q_1 units at a price of P_1 before a rise in wage rates or in the price of raw materials. At the same price P_1, they are willing to supply only Q_2 units when the costs of production increase. The supply function therefore shifts to the left.

> The supply function shifts when the price of a factor of production changes or the state of technology changes.

When a technological breakthrough allows firms to economize on the use of some inputs, the cost of producing the product declines and the supply function shifts to the right. Producers are willing to offer a larger quantity at each price because the technological breakthrough allows them to provide the product at a lower cost than before. The Japanese have cut costs by adopting just-in-time inventory practices. Parts arrive just when they are ready to be used in the final assembly of a product, thereby eliminating the cost of stockpiling inventory. As a result, Japanese manufacturers of automobiles have reduced their production costs and shifted their supply functions to the right. Similarly, Wal-Mart and other major discount retailers have developed intricate conveyor systems that reduce inventory

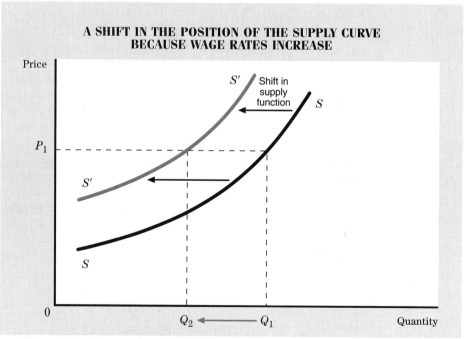

Figure 1-4   The supply curve shifts to the left from *SS* to *S'S'* because the cost of producing the product increases.

costs by shortening the time that merchandise remains in their warehouses. These changes in operational methods cause the supply function to shift to the right.

Technological changes in the United States and throughout the world have lowered production costs and shifted the supply function outward for many products. Japanese firms, for example, have a reputation for translating abstract technological breakthroughs into successful commercial applications. This has shifted the supply function to the right because they can supply greater quantities at each price.

Supply functions also shift because of changes in government regulations. As an example, some regulated public utilities in Ohio, Indiana, and Illinois use high-sulfur, dirty coal to produce electricity. When burned, high-sulfur coal emits pollutants that degrade air quality not only in these states but in other areas as well. Proposed changes in federal environmental legislation will require the utilities to lower emissions, increasing the cost of producing electricity for utilities using high-sulfur coal. As a result the supply function for electricity will shift to the left.

So you can see that the quantity supplied is not a constant determined by some artificial measure of physical productive capacity. Rather, price is an incentive for producers to increase the quantity supplied when they receive a higher price, and to decrease the quantity supplied when the price decreases. The supply function shifts with changes in the cost of producing a product and when the knowledge of production methods expands.

The demand function indicates the quantity demanded if the price is P, and the supply function indicates the quantity supplied if the price is P. The next step, which combines the behavior of consumers and producers, will determine the price in the marketplace.

1-4 MARKET EQUILIBRIUM

To find the market price for a given good, we superimpose the demand and supply functions for a particular product on the same graph (see Figure 1-5). Although there are many prices that might exist in this market, there is only one at which the quantity demanded is equal to the quantity supplied, and only one that is expected to persist in the marketplace. Before identifying that price, the concept of an equilibrium must be introduced.

> A **market equilibrium** exists when the quantity demanded equals the quantity supplied.

This definition of equilibrium emphasizes a balance between the quantity demanded and the quantity supplied. Among the prices on the vertical axis in Figure 1-5, P_e receives special attention because it is the only price where the total quantity demanded equals the total quantity supplied. If the price is P_e, then the quantity demanded *and* supplied is equal to Q_e. P_e is the **equilibrium price,** and Q_e is the **equilibrium quantity.** Economists single out P_e because they believe it has a higher probability of being the market price than any other price. Because the total quantity demanded equals the total quantity supplied at this price, P_e is not likely

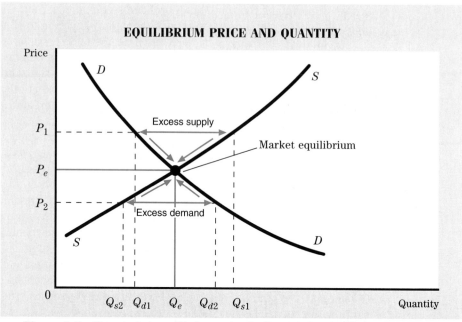

Figure 1-5   The market equilibrium price is P_e, and the equilibrium quantity is Q_e. When the price equals P_e, the quantity demanded and the quantity supplied are the same and are equal to Q_e. When the price equals P_1, the quantity supplied Q_{s1} exceeds the quantity demanded Q_{d1}. When the price equals P_2, the quantity demanded Q_{d2} exceeds the quantity supplied Q_{s2}.

to change once it occurs. Of all the prices on the vertical axis, only P_e satisfies this condition.

At any other price there is a discrepancy between the quantity demanded and the quantity supplied. At the price of P_1 the quantity supplied Q_{s1} exceeds the quantity demanded Q_{d1}. The difference between the quantity supplied and the quantity demanded is the **excess supply.** When too many goods cannot find buyers, stocks of goods soon accumulate in the hands of suppliers who find that they cannot sell all that they have produced at P_1. To reduce the growing inventories, they begin to haggle, offer discounts, and lower prices. As prices fall, two changes occur: The quantity demanded increases, and the quantity supplied decreases. Excess supply shrinks as the difference between the quantity supplied and the quantity demanded diminishes. Both sides of the market work to eliminate the excess supply. Therefore any price above P_e is unlikely to persist because the excess supply causes the price to decrease.

What happens if the price is below P_e? At a price of P_2 the quantity demanded Q_{d2} exceeds the quantity supplied Q_{s2}. There is an **excess demand.** Too many potential buyers cannot find goods to purchase, and stores that have goods have long lines of waiting customers. This is what happens when prices are too low. In many developing countries the government deliberately keeps bread prices low, and waiting lines are an everyday occurrence. For example, the price of a loaf of bread in the former Soviet Union had not changed after World War II until the early 1990s when it increased, and shopping was just one long wait in line.

If the price is below the equilibrium price, what do buyers do to obtain the product? They begin to offer higher prices to purchase the limited supply, and a price like P_2 cannot persist in the marketplace. As the price increases, the quantity demanded decreases, the quantity supplied increases, and the excess demand decreases. Whether the price is above or below the equilibrium price, it moves in the direction of P_e, and any excess demand or excess supply ultimately disappears.

When the price is equal to P_e, there is no reason for it to change unless the position of either the demand or the supply function shifts. Given the demand and supply functions in Figure 1-5, we say that the equilibrium price is P_e and that it is the price more likely to persist in the marketplace than any other price. If the price is not equal to P_e, its movement will be in the direction of P_e.

The equilibrium price and quantity are determined simultaneously. The equilibrium quantity is the one at which the quantity demanded equals the quantity supplied:

$$Q_e = Q_d = Q_s \qquad \text{(Equilibrium Quantity)} \qquad \text{(1-3)}$$

The equilibrium price is the one at which the quantity demanded equals the quantity supplied. We substitute the expressions for the quantity demanded and the quantity supplied for Q_d and Q_s respectively, to determine the equilibrium price:

$$D(P_e) = S(P_e) \qquad \text{(Determination of the Equilibrium Price)} \qquad \text{(1-4)}$$

The equilibrium price can be found by solving equation 1-4 for P. The left-hand side is the quantity demanded, and the right-hand side is the quantity supplied. As Figure 1-5 shows, P_e is the only price where the market is in equilibrium—where Q_d equals Q_s. Given P_e, we can find Q_e by substituting P_e into either the demand function (equation 1-1) or the supply function (equation 1-2).

The Everyday Meaning of Demand and Supply

The economist's usage of the terms "demand" and "supply" is quite different from everyday usage. An important contemporary issue, the impending energy crisis, illustrates the difference. You may have read, perhaps with some trepidation, about the energy crisis some geologists believe to be around the corner. Since the oil embargo in 1974, when the price of crude oil jumped dramatically, the public has begun to heed the warnings of geologists and environmentalists who predict a depletion of petroleum supplies. The dismal prognosis is that world demand for crude oil will continue to grow in the future but that the supply of crude oil is finite or at best only marginally expandable. Although no one can pinpoint the exact year, public policy experts, environmentalists, and others say the United States and the world will face another energy crisis as global oil reserves are depleted. There will come a time, they say, when demand will catch up with and pass supply. With this will come all the inevitable consequences of a shortage— long waits at gasoline stations and irksome allocations placed on industry and consumers to restrict use of the limited supply of crude oil.

This unpleasant scenario is an entirely convincing one to the average person.

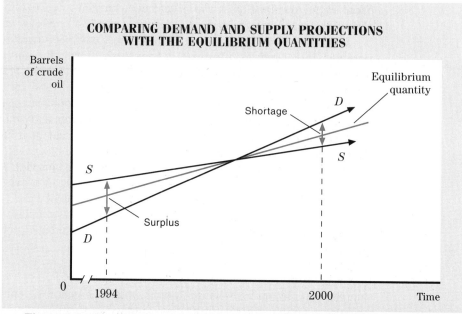

COMPARING DEMAND AND SUPPLY PROJECTIONS WITH THE EQUILIBRIUM QUANTITIES

Figure 1-6   Based on the everyday usage of the terms "demand" and "supply," *DD* represents needs and *SS* represents production capability. During the first half of the 1990s supply is projected to exceed demand and there is a surplus. During the second half of the 1990s demand is projected to exceed supply. In the economist's model price adjusts to equate the quantity demanded with the quantity supplied so that the equilibrium quantity is produced each year. The solid line without the arrow shows how the equilibrium quantity changes over time.

More often than not, he or she thinks of demand as the number of barrels needed to heat houses and factories or to operate automobiles and trucks, and supply as the physical amount of crude oil that can be produced. A graph will illustrate this ordinary interpretation of demand and supply. In Figure 1-6 the predicted demand and supply of barrels of crude oil are on the vertical axis, and time is on the horizontal axis.

Figure 1-6 shows that the demand grows faster than the supply over time. There will be a surplus of crude oil during the first half of the 1990s when supply exceeds demand. If the predictions are accurate, however, this surplus will steadily dwindle and the shortage will begin to hit sometime in the late 1990s.

Problems with the Analysis

Relying on a demand and supply model allows you to identify two problems with this way of looking at how the crude oil market operates. First, the two lines for demand and supply show that demand virtually *never* equals supply. Most of the time there is either a shortage or a surplus because needs and production capabilities are different. This might sound plausible to the average person, but is it true?

Would firms continue to produce a product for which there is less demand? Why should you expect to see a lengthy pattern of surpluses or shortages?

If "demand" means need and "supply" means production capacity, a shortage or a surplus is inevitable because price plays no role in the analysis. Because the average person fails to understand how price equates the quantity demanded with the quantity supplied, he or she believes management is essential to bring a balance to the market and control shortages and surpluses. Balance requires greater reliance on control policies such as rationing, conservation, and other demand-reducing policies or on joint government and industry programs that increase supply by developing new technologies.

This assumed behavior can be contrasted with the behavior of demanders and suppliers in the economist's model where price plays the critical role in equating differences between the quantity demanded and the quantity supplied. Price is constantly changing to bring the market into equilibrium. The economist's model has only one line, rather than two, with each point on the line representing the equilibrium quantity where the quantity demanded equals the quantity supplied. In Figure 1-6 the line without an arrow shows the equilibrium quantity over time, where the price changes each year and the quantity demanded equals the quantity supplied. The projected excess supply during the first half of the 1990s disappears because the price decreases until the quantity demanded is equal to the quantity supplied. The projected shortage disappears because the price increases during the second half of the decade.

The everyday interpretation of demand and supply is limiting because price plays no role. It assumes that the behavior of demanders and suppliers is unresponsive to the price. However, in making buying decisions, demanders use the price to determine how much to purchase, and suppliers use the price to determine how much to supply. The demand and supply model shows how price brings the quantity demanded into equality with the quantity supplied.

1-5   CHANGES IN EQUILIBRIUM: SHIFTS IN MARKET DEMAND AND MARKET SUPPLY FUNCTIONS

The demand and supply model can be used to predict how the equilibrium price and quantity will change when either the demand or the supply function shifts or when both shift.

Shifts in Demand

Figure 1-7 shows what happens to the equilibrium price and quantity when the market demand for the product increases from DD to $D'D'$.

The increase in market demand causes the equilibrium price to increase from P_1 to P_2, and the equilibrium quantity to increase from Q_1 to Q_2. The equilibrium price and quantity increase when the market demand increases because the supply function slopes upward.

This is an appropriate time to return to the initial example involving the crude

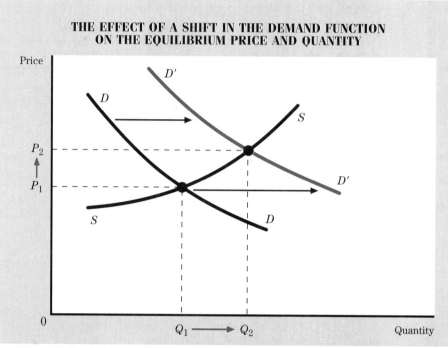

**THE EFFECT OF A SHIFT IN THE DEMAND FUNCTION
ON THE EQUILIBRIUM PRICE AND QUANTITY**

Figure 1-7   A rightward shift in the demand function increases the equilibrium price
and equilibrium quantity when the supply function has a positive slope. The shift in the
market demand curve causes existing suppliers to produce more, and more suppliers
to enter the industry, increasing the quantity supplied from Q_1 to Q_2.

oil market. Figure 1-6 shows separate lines for demand and supply based on
everyday usage of the terms "demand" and "supply." The line without an arrow in
Figure 1-6 shows the equilibrium quantity for each year when the price adjusts to
equate the quantity demanded with the quantity supplied. In Figure 1-7 suppose
DD is the market demand function for crude oil in 1994, $D'D'$ is the market demand
function in 2000, and SS is the market supply function of crude oil which does not
shift. What does the market equilibrium analysis imply about the difference between the quantity demanded and the quantity supplied in the 2 years? By using
the theory of markets—the demand and supply model—you should conclude that
the quantity demanded and the quantity supplied are equal to Q_1 in 1994 and,
although both increase over time, are equal to Q_2 in 2000.

  Q_1 is the equilibrium quantity in 1994 when the market demand function is DD
because the price is P_1. The market is in equilibrium, and the equilibrium quantity
is equal to the quantity demanded *and* the quantity supplied. In 2000 the market
demand function shifts, the equilibrium quantity becomes Q_2, and the equilibrium
price increases to P_2. Each year the price adjusts so that the quantity demanded
equals the quantity supplied. The lines for the quantity demanded and the quantity
supplied are not separate because the price changes to equate the quantity de-

manded to the quantity supplied. The separate solid lines for demand and supply in Figure 1-6 are a result of faulty economic thinking because they assume price has no effect on the behavior of demanders or suppliers.

APPLICATION **1-2**

Demand and Supply on Valentine's Day

Valentine's Day is not only the most romantic day of the year but is also a big business day in some industries. Fifty percent of cut roses sold in February are sold on Valentine's Day. On Valentine's Day in a recent year, the price of a dozen roses jumped from $8.00 to $19.99 at one local store in Chicago. Another bestseller on Valentine's Day is candy. About 13 percent of the annual sales of candy take place on Valentine's Day. Yet the price of a box of chocolates increases modestly if at all on this holiday. Why does the price of roses increase on Valentine's Day but not the price of a box of chocolates?

The behavior of prices tells us about the different shapes of the supply functions for roses and candy. We can use the demand and supply model to explain why the price behavior is different for these two products. In Figure 1-8*a* the demand function for cut roses on an ordinary day is *DD*, and on Valentine's Day it is *D'D'*. To explain the price behavior, we must consider a supply function for roses like *SS*. The quantity of roses supplied on any day increases only if the price rises substantially. When demand shifts on Valentine's Day, the price of roses jumps. Increasing the supply of cut roses for Valentine's Day would require more land devoted to producing roses and less to producing other flowers. Also, it is not possible to produce more cut roses before Valentine's Day and store them until the holiday arrives. In Figure 1-8*b* *DD* is the demand for a box of chocolates on an ordinary day, and *D'D'* is the demand on Valentine's Day. The supply function for a box of chocolates is relatively flat because retailers build up stocks before hand to meet the expected increase in demand. This means that producers of chocolates are able to increase production before the holiday without increasing the unit production cost substantially. Therefore, the price of chocolates increases only modestly on Valentine's Day.

A difference in the *shape* of the supply functions explains why the price of roses increases more than the price of chocolates on Valentine's Day.

An Explanation of Shortages and Surpluses

If the market price each year is the equilibrium price, there is neither an excess demand nor an excess supply and the market moves from one equilibrium position to another when the demand function shifts. It appears, however, that the demand and supply model cannot explain shortages or surpluses. The model can tell you when and why you might expect a shortage or a surplus, and it tells you that the market will correct itself and return to equilibrium. Still, this most basic demand and supply model cannot explain some shortages that last for long periods of time.

To begin, consider the argument that shortages occur whenever the demand

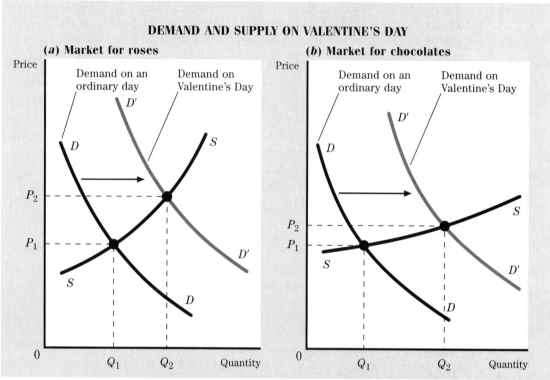

DEMAND AND SUPPLY ON VALENTINE'S DAY

(a) Market for roses

Price

Demand on an ordinary day   Demand on Valentine's Day

D'

D

S

P_2

P_1

S

D'

D

0 Q_1 Q_2 Quantity

(b) Market for chocolates

Price

Demand on an ordinary day   Demand on Valentine's Day

D'

D

S

P_2

P_1

S

D

D'

0 Q_1 Q_2 Quantity

Figure 1-8 (*a*) An increase in demand for roses on Valentine's Day increases the price from P_1 to P_2. (*b*) The price of chocolates changes by less on Valentine's Day because the supply function is flatter.

function shifts to the right at a faster rate than the supply function. In the early phase of a growth industry the demand function can shift to the right by 25 percent per year while the supply function shifts to the right by only 10 percent. Then, you might predict that a shortage will appear because demand is growing more rapidly than supply. Although the argument sounds appealing, it does not stand up to analysis. Differential growth rates for demand and supply functions are not the reason for a shortage or a surplus. If the demand function shifts to the right more rapidly than the supply function, the correct prediction of the model is not that a shortage will appear but that the price will increase. The price increase is what prevents a potential shortage from becoming an actual shortage by reducing the quantity demanded and increasing the quantity supplied so that any excess demand evaporates.

Figure 1-9 shows the demand function shifting to the right more rapidly than the supply function. The initial demand function is DD, the original supply function is SS, and the equilibrium price is P_1. The demand and supply functions shift to the right and become $D'D'$ and $S'S'$, respectively. The equilibrium price increases from P_1 to P_2, and the equilibrium quantity increases from Q_1 to Q_2. If the price does not change but remains at P_1, a shortage will appear as excess demand because the quantity demanded will be Q_{1d} and the quantity supplied will be Q_{1s}. The price increase eliminates a potential shortage of $Q_{1d} - Q_{1s}$ by reducing the quantity demanded to Q_2 and increasing the quantity supplied to Q_2. So it is not true that shortages occur just because the demand and supply functions do not increase or decrease at the same rate.

However, this example indicates when a shortage or a surplus might appear. If the price cannot change because of regulations or if the price adjusts sluggishly to shifts in demand and supply, then a shortage can occur. Thus one reason for a shortage is that the price does not perform the role of increasing the quantity supplied and decreasing the quantity demanded. For example, New York City and a few other cities have placed rent controls on some apartments for decades and created a perpetual excess demand for rental housing since controlled rents are well below what equilibrium rents would be.

Fixed or slowly adjusting prices do not provide a complete explanation of shortages and surpluses. There are notable examples of persistent excess demand

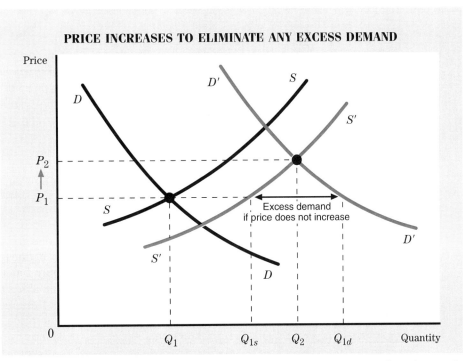

Figure 1-9   The demand function shifts to the right at a faster rate than the supply function. The demand curve shifts from DD to $D'D'$, and the supply curve shifts from SS to $S'S'$. If the price remains at P_1, a shortage will appear because the quantity demanded equals Q_{1d} and is greater than the quantity supplied Q_{1s}. The shortage does not appear because the price rises from P_1 to P_2. Differential rates of growth of the demand and supply functions do not explain why shortages and surpluses exist.

in private markets such as those for sporting events and entertainment that the model does not explain satisfactorily. In these instances there is no government interference in the operation of the market. Well-known rock groups like the Grateful Dead perform periodic outdoor concerts. Their concerts sell out in advance in virtually every city on the tour, and holders of tickets can resell them for considerably more than the initial ticket price. Another classic, if dated, example, was the 1950s hit musical *My Fair Lady*, which played for years on Broadway and was sold out night after night for long stretches of time. Likewise, the Montreal Canadiens have been a very successful hockey team for many decades. Home games sell out consistently, and tickets are difficult to find.[3] Why doesn't management raise prices and eliminate the excess demand? This remains an unanswered question that is beginning to attract the attention of economists.[4]

APPLICATION 1-3

Shifts in Demand and Supply: The Market for Illegal Drugs

The federal government has initiated various programs to reduce the size of the drug market. However, there is considerable disagreement about whether these programs are working and little agreement about what determines whether they are effective.

Suppose you plan to evaluate the effects of the federal programs. You have to decide what measure should be used to determine whether they are working. Your staff has proposed that you look at trends in the street price of drugs. They tell you that it is easier to find out and track the street price of drugs than to determine the total consumption of drugs. They feel that the trend in drug prices will indicate whether the programs are or are not working. If the price of drugs is increasing, then the federal programs have taken hold. If the street price of drugs is unchanged or is decreasing, the federal programs have failed.

Ted Koppel, the host of ABC's *Nightline*, made this point: "Do you know what's happened to the price of drugs in the United States? The price of cocaine, way down, the price of marijuana, way down. You don't have to be an expert in economics to know that when the price goes down, it means more stuff is coming in. That's supply and demand."[5] Clearly, Koppel is interpreting the drop in drug prices as a shift of the supply function of drugs to the right. He concludes from the price evidence that the federal programs are not effective.

We can use the demand and supply model to determine if the success or failure of the federal antidrug programs can be inferred from the trend in prices. Figure 1-10 shows the demand function for drugs as *DD*, and the supply function before the start of federal programs as *SS*. If the federal programs have been unsuccessful and the supply function shifts from *SS* to *S'S'*, the equilibrium price of drugs

---

[3] Season ticket holders often will their tickets to family members.
[4] For an attempted explanation of these pricing practices, the curious reader should wait until completing Chapter 9 and then read Gary S. Becker, "A Note on Restaurant Pricing and Other Examples of Social Influences on Price," *Journal of Political Economy*, vol. 99, October 1991, pp. 1109–1116.
[5] Reported in Kenneth R. Clark, "Legalize Drugs? A Case for Koppel," *Chicago Tribune*, August 30, 1988, section 5, page 8.

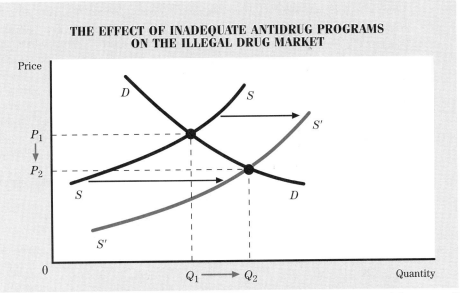

**THE EFFECT OF INADEQUATE ANTIDRUG PROGRAMS
ON THE ILLEGAL DRUG MARKET**

Figure 1-10   The price of drugs declines and the quantity consumed increases if antidrug programs fail to prevent the supply curve from shifting to the right.

decreases from P_1 to P_2 and the quantity of drugs consumed increases from Q_1 to Q_2. The price decline demonstrates the failure of the federal programs to prevent the supply function from shifting to the right—which is Ted Koppel's point.

Yet there is a problem with his explanation. If your staff applied the demand and supply model, they would recognize that trends in drug prices should not be used in isolation to assess the success or failure of government programs. What does the demand and supply model predict if federal and private efforts are successful and reduce the demand for drugs? Figure 1-11 shows that the market demand will decrease from DD to $D'D'$ and the equilibrium price from P_1 to P_2.

In both situations the price decreases. Yet in one case the federal programs are failing and consumption is increasing, whereas in the other case the programs are succeeding and consumption is decreasing. The demand and supply model points out the limits of relying solely on price trends, which could lead to the curtailment of a successful policy. Private and public policies will be more successful if the theory supports the criterion used to evaluate the programs.

The demand and supply model suggests that it is imperative to obtain more information about trends in the quantities consumed as well as in the price changes. Neither you nor your staff should take the easy way out by relying only on price trends. The model suggests that more attention should be paid to trends in consumption, although this information may be more difficult to obtain. It says that you will make fewer policy mistakes if you are aware of the trends in *both* price and in quantity.

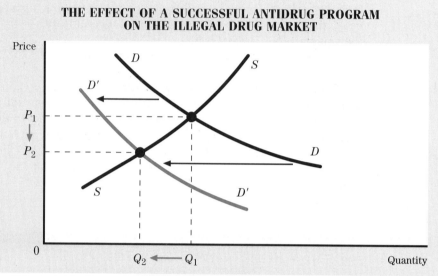

**THE EFFECT OF A SUCCESSFUL ANTIDRUG PROGRAM
ON THE ILLEGAL DRUG MARKET**

Figure 1-11   The price and the quantity of drugs consumed decline if antidrug programs cause the demand curve to shift to the left.

APPLICATION 1-4

Should Your Company Support a Lobbying Effort to Reduce the Price of an Input?

Your company uses a raw material, A, in the production of its main product, X. Over the last 5 years the price of A has been growing much faster than the average price of raw materials. As the price of A has increased, so has the cost of producing X. The CEOs of several leading companies in industry X want to end the upward cost spiral. They propose an intensive lobbying campaign to enlist congressional support for rolling back the price of A. Supporters argue that the cost of producing X will decline if they can obtain congressional approval to lower the price of A. If the cost of producing X declines, the producers of X expect a temporary benefit because the price of X will not decrease immediately by the full amount of the cost reduction. They believe this is one issue that all members of the industry can unite behind. You receive an invitation to join the campaign and support the lobbying effort.

You think the idea sounds good, and you ask your staff to study the possible effects of a price ceiling. The majority of your staff members support the idea. They think that any policy that reduces the cost of X will benefit the company, based on the following reasoning. Before a price ceiling is imposed, the demand and supply functions for A are D_A and S_A in Figure 1-12a, and the equilibrium price of A is P_A. The demand and supply functions for X are D_X and S_X in Figure 1-12b, and the equilibrium price of X is P_X. If the government imposes a price ceiling of P_A' on the price of A, the cost of producing X falls. The majority argue that this will cause the supply function of X to shift to the right from S_X to S_X'. They claim that the equilibrium price of X will decline to P_X' and that the equilibrium quantity will increase to Q_X'. Consequently, they recommend that the firm support the lobbying effort.

There is one dissenter, however. She believes that the argument of the majority, while appearing reasonable on the surface, has a fundamental weakness. (Try to guess what it is.) She thinks that producers of A will react to the price ceiling by supplying only Q_A' (movement along the supply function for A in Figure 1-12a). If the company were offered a guaranteed quota of A at the ceiling price, then she would favor the lobbying effort. But the firm has received no such guarantee. What puzzles her is that the argument of the majority implies that the production of X will increase (the quantity of X will go from Q_X to Q_X') although the production of

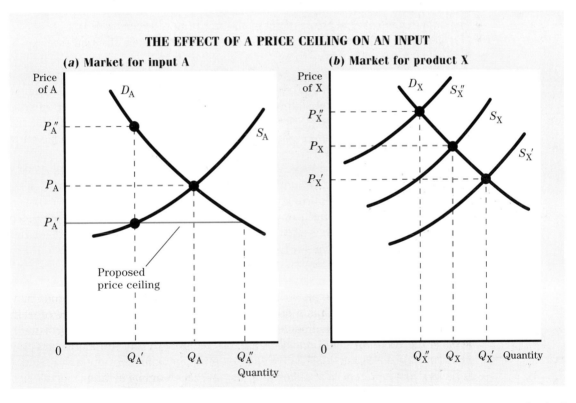

Figure 1-12   The effect of a price ceiling on an input causes the price of the final good to rise, not fall. A price ceiling of P_A' is placed on an input, and the quantity supplied of A decreases to Q_A'. Demanders then incur added costs to acquire the limited supply of Q_A'. The difference between P_A'' and P_A' represents the added cost incurred by firms to acquire Q_A', which increases the cost of producing X. The supply curve of X shifts upward and to the left, and the price of X increases because of the price ceiling.

A declines. How can more X be produced with less A? She does not believe this will happen and thinks the argument of the majority is illogical. She maintains that the firm should not sign on to the lobbying campaign, her basic point being that any policy that reduces the output of an important input will only harm the company.

Would you side with the majority, or are the points raised by the dissenter valid? How can industry X produce more units with less A? What will happen when a price ceiling is introduced? At first the price ceiling creates an excess demand of $Q_A'' - Q_A'$. Then market forces begin to eliminate the excess demand. Let us assume that the government enforces a price ceiling. This means a supplier of A cannot obtain a price higher than P_A'. Clearly, there is a potential for waiting lines to develop. At the ceiling price producers supply only Q_A' units of A. The demand function says that demanders of A are willing to pay up to P_A'' for Q_A' units of A and will adopt all kinds of tactics to increase their chance of getting their hands on Q_A'. They will have their buyers on the telephone, courting the suppliers of A as they try to obtain the limited quantities of A. The entertainment budgets of demanders will soar, and they might even offer bribes.

Of course, these tactics are not cost-free, and they raise the real price of A. Not only do demanders have to pay P_A' to suppliers who have access to the limited supply of A, but they must also incur the added cost of courting suppliers. These practices raise the price of A from the perspective of demanders of A. The intense competition for the limited supply of A could raise the "effective" price of A to P_A'' and in this way ration Q_A' among potential buyers. Under this scenario, the introduction of a price ceiling, far from lowering the price of A, will cause the effective price to increase.

If the effective price of A rises, then the supply function of X shifts to the left to S_X'' and the quantity of X produced declines from Q_X to Q_X'' as the effective price rises to P_X''. Under this scenario a price ceiling on an input, which at first looks so advantageous to the firm, turns out to be harmful. The company should think twice before joining this lobbying effort, and the dissenter deserves a reward for her sophisticated analysis of the problem.

This situation can occur where there are regulated prices. An interesting example is rent control for apartment buildings. These lucky renters find with time that they live in a valuable apartment. Because of rent control, builders may construct fewer apartments, and the stock of rental housing may decline or grow less rapidly. The market-clearing rental price is well above the regulated rent because there are fewer apartments available. Renters receive attractive offers to sublease their apartments—sometimes called "key money." Since the current renter cannot sublease the apartment at a higher rent, the market clears by setting an artificially high price for the apartment key. Of course, landlords oppose rent control since the original renters benefit and not the landlords.

Another example is federal regulation of natural gas prices in interstate commerce. These regulations created a serious excess demand problem after the crude oil prices increased when manufacturers of goods found that they could not obtain supplies of natural gas. Gas producers supplied less natural gas to interstate pipeline companies, and these companies supplied less natural gas to manufacturers with contracts that permitted the pipeline company to interrupt service. Curtailment of natural gas deliveries increased from 1,031 billion cubic feet in 1972–1973 to 3,770 in 1976–1977. Manufacturers not only had more difficulty finding natural gas, but were forced to substitute more expensive energy such as oil or electricity. Manufacturers with interruptible service were worse off because of natural gas price regulations.[6]

1-6   THE PRICE ELASTICITY OF DEMAND AND SUPPLY

Up to this point, the demand and supply model has been used to predict changes in the behavior of demanders and suppliers either when the demand or supply function shifts or when a market is out of equilibrium. Now we return to the demand and supply functions and present a measure that summarizes the shape of either the demand or the supply function.

The shape of the demand function differs from one product to another. If American Airlines increases the air fare from Chicago to Los Angeles and other airlines do not, the number of passengers on American flights will fall precipitously because many travelers will switch to lower-priced airlines. A small price difference can cause a large decrease in the quantity demanded. On the other hand, if a publisher raises the price of a textbook, many instructors continue to assign the book and often are unaware of the price increase until later. Although some teachers may select substitute books, the overall effect is that the quantity demanded will decrease by a relatively small amount when the price increases. The shapes of the two demand functions are different.

Firms want to know how much the quantity demanded changes when the price changes because they want to know whether the total amount consumers spend on the good increases or decreases. If a manager can estimate the shape of the demand function, he or she can determine whether the total revenue received by the firm will increase if the price falls. If the quantity demanded will not increase by enough, a price cut will spell disaster because the total revenue received by the firm will decrease. Whether total revenue increases or decreases depends on the shape of the demand function, that is, on the relative sizes of the change in price and the change in quantity.

Price Elasticity of Demand

Economists have developed a measure called the *price elasticity of demand* to determine the responsiveness of the quantity demanded and total revenue to a price change.

The price elasticity of demand compares the average percentage change in

---

[6] For a discussion of these issues, see W. Kip Viscusi, John M. Vernon, and Joseph E. Harrington, *Economics of Regulation and Antitrust*, D. C. Heath and Co., 1992, pp. 582–593.

quantity to the average percentage change in price. Roughly speaking, if the percentage change in quantity demanded is larger than the percentage change in price, then the total revenue will change in the direction opposite the price change. For example, a price decrease increases total revenue.

> The **price elasticity of demand** measures the responsiveness of the quantity demanded to a price change.

To see this, consider Figure 1-13. Let the demand function for a product that the firm sells be DD. If the price is P_1, the quantity demanded is Q_1. The total revenue R the firm receives equals the price per unit times the quantity demanded:

$$R = PQ \quad \text{(Total Revenue)} \quad (1\text{-}5)$$

If the price is P_1, $R = P_1Q_1$, the sum of areas 1 and 2. When the price falls to P_2, the quantity demanded increases to Q_2. Total revenue is now $R = P_2Q_2$ or the sum of areas 2 and 3. The change in total revenue received by the firm is the net effect of two opposing changes. At the higher price of P_1 the quantity demanded is only Q_1 units. At the lower price of P_2, demanders who would purchase Q_1 units at the

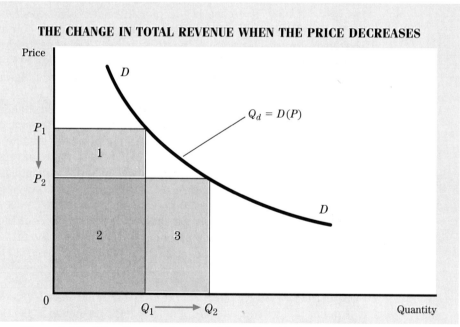

THE CHANGE IN TOTAL REVENUE WHEN THE PRICE DECREASES

Figure 1-13   When the price is reduced from P_1 to P_2, the quantity demanded increases from Q_1 to Q_2. Total revenue may be higher, lower, or the same after the price is reduced. Area 1 represents the loss in revenue because demanders who would have paid P_1 purchase the product at the lower price of P_2. Area 3 represents the increase in revenue because the lower price increases the total quantity demanded from Q_1 to Q_2.

higher price can purchase them at the lower price of P_2. This effect reduces total revenue, and the size of the loss is equal to area 1. At the lower price of P_2 the firm can sell more units because the quantity demanded increases from Q_1 to Q_2. This effect increases total revenue, and the size of the increase is equal to area 3. Whether a price change increases or decreases total revenue depends on the relative sizes of these two opposing effects, area 1 compared to area 3.

Based on this analysis, how revenue changes when price changes can be described as follows:

1. If the total revenue changes in the direction opposite the price change (e.g., total revenue decreases when price increases), the demand is **price-elastic.**

2. If the total revenue does not change when the price changes, the demand has **unitary elasticity.**

3. If the total revenue changes in the same direction that the price changes (e.g., total revenue increases when price increases), the demand is **price-inelastic.**

Now consider a formula that economists use to calculate the numerical value of the price elasticity. By applying this formula, you can determine whether total revenue increases or decreases or stays the same for any price change.

Arc Price Elasticity of Demand

The formula for the arc price elasticity of demand E_P describes the relative responsiveness of the quantity demanded to a price change between two points on the demand function and shows how total revenue changes when price changes. To determine how total revenue changes when the price falls from P_1 to P_2 on the demand function in Figure 1-13, you must know what happens to the quantity demanded. We use the formula for the arc price elasticity of demand:

$$E_P = \frac{\dfrac{\Delta Q}{(Q_1 + Q_2)/2}}{\dfrac{\Delta P}{(P_1 + P_2)/2}} \qquad \text{(Arc Price Elasticity of Demand)} \qquad \text{(1-6)}$$

The arc price elasticity is the ratio of two magnitudes that resemble but are not exactly equal to percentage changes. The numerator in the formula is the change in the quantity demanded (ΔQ) divided by the average of the two quantities demanded at the two prices, $(Q_1 + Q_2)/2$. The numerator is the average percentage change in the quantity demanded, and the denominator is the change in the price (ΔP) divided by the average of the two prices, $(P_1 + P_2)/2$. We call the denominator the average percentage change in price.

The **arc price elasticity** is the average percentage change in the quantity demanded divided by the average percentage change in price.

The fraction in the formula for the arc price elasticity can be simplified for easier calculation:

$$E_P = \frac{\dfrac{\Delta Q}{(Q_1 + Q_2)/2}}{\dfrac{\Delta P}{(P_1 + P_2)/2}} = \frac{\dfrac{2\,\Delta Q}{Q_1 + Q_2}}{\dfrac{2\,\Delta P}{P_1 + P_2}} \qquad (1\text{-}6a)$$

Multiplying the numerator and the denominator by $\frac{1}{2}$ yields

$$E_p = \frac{\Delta Q/(Q_1 + Q_2)}{\Delta P/(P_1 + P_2)} = \frac{\Delta Q}{\Delta P}\frac{P_1 + P_2}{Q_1 + Q_2} \qquad (1\text{-}6b)$$

Two points should be noted about the last expression in equation 1-6b. First, the numerical value of the arc elasticity is always negative because $\Delta Q/\Delta P$ is negative; the quantity demanded changes in the direction opposite the price change. Second, the arc price elasticity is the slope of the demand function between the two points ($\Delta Q/\Delta P$) times a factor equal to the sum of the two prices divided by the sum of the two quantities. Therefore, the arc price elasticity is *not* equal to the slope of the demand function. A straight-line demand function has a constant slope, but the value of the price elasticity changes because $(P_1 + P_2)/(Q_1 + Q_2)$ changes when moving along a straight-line demand function.[7]

There are three possible outcomes for the numerical value of the arc price elasticity:

1. If the value of the arc price elasticity is *less than -1*, the demand is *price-elastic* and the total revenue changes in the direction opposite the price change.[8] A decrease in price increases total revenue.

[7] The expression for a straight-line (linear) demand function is

$$Q = a - bP$$

where a and b are constants. The slope of the demand function is

$$\frac{\Delta Q}{\Delta P} = -b$$

Therefore, the slope of a linear demand function is constant and independent of price. The arc price elasticity for a linear demand function is

$$E_P = -b\,\frac{P_1 + P_2}{Q_1 + Q_2}$$

[8] For example, we want to show that total revenue increases when price decreases if $E_P < -1$. If E_P is less than -1, then

$$E_P = \frac{(Q_2 - Q_1)(P_1 + P_2)}{(P_2 - P_1)(Q_1 + Q_2)} < -1$$

where $\Delta Q = Q_2 - Q_1$ and $\Delta P = P_2 - P_1$. Because $P_2 - P_1$ is negative, multiplying both sides of the inequality by $(P_2 - P_1)(Q_1 + Q_2)$, a negative number, reverses the inequality and yields

$$(Q_2 - Q_1)(P_1 + P_2) > -(P_2 - P_1)(Q_1 + Q_2)$$

Expanding both sides of the inequality results in

$$P_1Q_2 - P_1Q_1 + P_2Q_2 - P_2Q_1 > -P_2Q_1 + P_1Q_1 - P_2Q_2 + P_1Q_2$$

Adding P_2Q_1 and subtracting P_1Q_2 on both sides of the inequality, and dividing both sides by 2, yields

$$P_2Q_2 > P_1Q_1$$

If $E_P < -1$, $P_2Q_2 > P_1Q_1$, and so the total revenue increases when the price falls from P_1 to P_2. Similar derivations would show that $P_2Q_2 = P_1Q_1$ when $E_P = -1$, and $P_2Q_2 < P_1Q_1$ when $E_P > -1$.

Table 1-2   REVENUE CHANGES DUE TO A PRICE CHANGE FOR DIFFERENT VALUES OF ARC PRICE ELASTICITY

PRICE ELASTICITY, E_P	PRICE CHANGE, ΔP	REVENUE CHANGE, ΔR
Price-elastic, $E_P < -1$	$\Delta P > 0$	$\Delta R < 0$
	$\Delta P < 0$	$\Delta R > 0$
Unitary, $E_P = -1$	$\Delta P > 0$	$\Delta R = 0$
	$\Delta P < 0$	$\Delta R = 0$
Price-inelastic, $0 > E_P > -1$	$\Delta P > 0$	$\Delta R > 0$
	$\Delta P < 0$	$\Delta R < 0$

2. If the value of the arc price elasticity is *equal to* -1, the demand has *unitary elasticity*. A price change does not change total revenue.

3. If the value of the arc price elasticity is *between* -1 *and* 0, the demand is *price-inelastic*. This means that total revenue changes in the same direction as the price change. A decrease in price decreases total revenue.

Table 1-2 summarizes how total revenue changes for increases and decreases in price when the demand is price-elastic, has unitary elasticity, or is price-inelastic.

Let's apply the formula for arc price elasticity by working through an example. A car manufacturer wants to know whether the demand for automobile air bags is price-elastic or price-inelastic. Automobile fleet managers were asked in a survey to report how many cars with air bags they would demand at different prices for the air bag. The responses are shown in Table 1-3.

Is the demand for cars with air bags by fleet managers price-elastic or price-inelastic? This question does not have a simple yes or no answer because it depends on which two prices are being compared.

Table 1-3   THE DEMAND FUNCTION FOR AIR BAGS

PRICE OF AIR BAG ($)	QUANTITY OF CARS WITH AIR BAGS DEMANDED (THOUSANDS)
200	14
150	38
100	56
50	66

If the price drops from \$200 to \$150, the quantity demanded of cars with air bags increases from 14,000 to 38,000. When the price is \$200, total revenue is \$200 $\times$ 14,000 = \$2.8 million. If the price is \$150, the total revenue is \$150 $\times$ 38,000 = \$5.7 million. A price cut increases total revenue, and so demand is price-elastic between \$200 and \$150.

We can use the formula for the arc price elasticity in equation 1-6*b* to calculate the numerical value:

$$E_P = \frac{\Delta Q}{\Delta P} \frac{P_1 + P_2}{Q_1 + Q_2}$$

$\Delta Q = 38,000 - 14,000 = 24,000$ units, and $\Delta P = \$150 - \$200 = -\$50$. So, $\Delta Q/\Delta P = 24,000/-\$50$. $P_1 + P_2 = \$350$, and $(Q_1 + Q_2) = 52,000$ units. Therefore, the value of the arc price elasticity is

$$E_P = \frac{24}{-\$50} \times \frac{\$350}{52} = \frac{6}{-\$1} \times \frac{\$7}{13}$$

$$= \frac{\$42}{-\$13} = -3.23$$

Since the estimated arc elasticity of -3.23 is less than -1, demand is price-elastic between \$150 and \$200. Total revenue is higher at the lower price. Just because demand is price-elastic between \$200 and \$150 does not mean that it is price-elastic for all pairs of prices. The price elasticity usually changes in moving along a given demand function. To check this, calculate the arc price elasticity when the price decreases from \$100 to \$50. You should find the estimate of the price elasticity is -0.25. Therefore, total revenue decreases when the price decreases from \$100 to \$50.

When estimating the price elasticity for a product by using observed prices and quantities, you must take care to use only observations from two different points on the *same* demand function. You must be reasonably certain that the price-quantity pairs used to calculate the price elasticity come from the same demand function. If you derive an estimate of the price elasticity from a price-quantity pair on one demand function and from another price-quantity pair on a different demand function, because of shifts in the demand function, your estimate of the price elasticity will be inaccurate. You are erroneously attributing all the increase in the quantity demanded to the price reduction. For example, suppose the demand function for a product shifts because the incomes of consumers increase just when the price decreases. Part of the increase in the quantity demanded is due to the lower price, but part of the increase is due to the increase in income that shifts the demand function to the right. Your estimate of the price elasticity will be wrong because it reflects both changes, whereas the arc price elasticity measures only the effect of the price change on the quantity demanded on a given demand function. You might decide demand is price-elastic and lower the price when demand is price-inelastic. If you rely on the incorrect estimate and decide to reduce the price, you could easily make a fatal pricing mistake. Revenue will not increase but will decrease when you cut the price because demand is price-inelastic.

To sum up, the price elasticity of demand measures the responsiveness of the quantity demanded to a price change. Demand may be either price-elastic, price-inelastic, or unitary, depending on the size of the average percentage change in the quantity demanded relative to the average percentage change in price.

Determinants of the Price Elasticity of Demand

Several factors affect the size of the price elasticity.

1. If each demander spends a small percent of his or her total income on the product, then the demand for the product will be price-inelastic. A consumer may spend much time and effort getting the best price for a $20,000 automobile but later pay virtually the quoted price to have rear mud flaps put on the new car.

2. Another determinant of the price elasticity is the number of equivalent products available. If there are many products that can be substituted for the product, demand will be more price-elastic. A small rise in price will cause massive substitution by consumers toward equivalent products.

3. Luxury goods and goods for which consumers spend an increasing proportion of their income as their income increases also have more elastic demand functions.

4. The price elasticity of demand can change over time as consumers obtain more information about substitute products. Often the demand function becomes more price-elastic over time. An unexpected price increase may not cause the quantity demanded to fall by much immediately. Users of the product will not know of alternative products or suppliers and therefore will not reduce the quantity demanded by much in the short run. Given more time, buyers will search out and find alternative products. So in the long run, the quantity demanded decreases by more because of the initial price increase. A price increase that looks very successful in the short run may prove to be disastrous in the long run.

Figure 1-14 shows how the demand function rotates around the original equilibrium point over time because price increases from P_1 to P_2. Initially the demand function is DD and the price is P_1, and so the quantity demanded is Q_1. Now suppose the price increases from P_1 to P_2. Because of the increase, consumers reduce the quantity demanded modestly to Q_2 at first. If the price increase catches them unprepared, they grin and bear it in the short run. As demanders investigate and find alternatives for this product, the demand function becomes more price-elastic. It changes position and becomes the long-run demand function labeled $D'D'$. The long-run demand function has become price-elastic between the prices of P_1 and P_2. In the long run the price increase causes the quantity demanded to decrease to Q_3.

The events following the quadrupling of oil prices in 1974 demonstrate the difference between immediate and longer-term effects of a price increase. At first, the quantity demanded of gasoline declined modestly. Up until then, statistical models had estimated the demand for gasoline to be price-inelastic, with low price

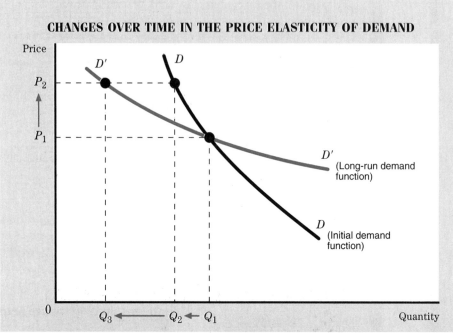

Figure 1-14   The initial demand curve is *DD*. A price increase from P_1 to P_2 causes the quantity demanded to decrease from Q_1 to Q_2. The long-run demand curve is *D'D'* and is more elastic than *DD*. Given sufficient time for demanders to find equivalent products, the demand curve becomes more elastic in the long run and the quantity demanded decreases from Q_2 to Q_3.

elasticities of about -0.2 to -0.4. Oil company executives and economists thought that Americans would never alter their driving habits and many predicted that the quantity demanded would fall only modestly when gasoline prices increased. However, the rise in the price of gasoline resulted in a number of long-run substitutions. The size of cars decreased and mileage per gallon increased. Consumers began to use their automobiles more efficiently by planning fewer shopping trips, economizing on the use of gasoline, and taking shorter vacation trips. Over time, the quantity demanded decreased by a larger percentage, and the size of the decrease surprised even some experts in the oil industry.

Arc Price Elasticity of Supply

The quantity supplied changes when the price changes. For some products the change in the quantity supplied is modest when the price increases, but for others it is larger. The price elasticity of supply measures the sensitivity of the quantity supplied to a price change. You will recall that the price of cut roses increased more than the price of chocolates on Valentine's Day because the supply function of roses was less sensitive to price.

> The **price elasticity of supply** measures the responsiveness of the quantity supplied to a price change.

The formula for the arc price elasticity of supply (N_P) describes the relative responsiveness of the quantity supplied to a price change between two points on the supply function. The same formula is used for the arc price elasticity of supply as for the arc price elasticity of demand:

$$N_P = \frac{\dfrac{\Delta Q}{(Q_1 + Q_2)/2}}{\dfrac{\Delta P}{(P_1 + P_2)/2}} \qquad \text{(Arc Price Elasticity of Supply)} \qquad (1\text{-}7)$$

$$= \frac{\Delta Q}{\Delta P} \frac{P_1 + P_2}{Q_1 + Q_2}$$

Although the formulas for the price elasticities are identical, their application sets the price elasticity of supply apart from the price elasticity of demand. The observations for price and quantity come from two points on the supply function, not on the demand function.

The price elasticity of supply is the ratio of the average percentage change in the quantity supplied to the average percentage change in price. As long as the supply function has a positive slope, the numerical value of the price elasticity of supply is positive. If the quantity supplied barely changes when the price changes, the price elasticity of supply is close to zero. In this case the supply function is steeper—more like the supply function for cut roses in Figure 1-8. As the quantity supplied becomes more sensitive to a price change, the price elasticity of supply becomes a larger positive number—more like the supply function for chocolates in Figure 1-8.

SUMMARY

- The quantity demanded and the quantity supplied depend on the price of the product.
- The demand function shows how the quantity demanded varies with the price of the product. The law of demand states that the quantity demanded is inversely related to the price of the product.
- A change in the income of households, in the price of substitutes or complements, or in the tastes of consumers shifts the position of the demand function.
- The market supply function shows how the quantity supplied changes as the price changes. The supply function shifts if the price of an input changes or if there is a technological innovation.
- Market equilibrium exists when the market price equates the quantity demanded with the quantity supplied. At other prices there is either an excess supply or an excess demand and the price changes in the direction of reducing the excess.

- Shortages or surpluses can exist if prices do not or cannot adjust to excess demand or excess supply.
- The numerical value of the price elasticity of demand determines whether total revenue increases, decreases, or stays the same when the price of a product changes. If the price elasticity is less than -1, demand is price-elastic and total revenue changes in the direction opposite the change in price. If the price elasticity is -1, demand has unitary elasticity and total revenue does not change when the price changes. If the price elasticity is greater than -1, demand is price-inelastic and total revenue changes in the same direction as the change in price.
- The price elasticity of supply shows the sensitivity of the quantity supplied to a price change. As long as the supply function has a positive slope, the price elasticity of supply is positive.

KEY TERMS

Demand and supply model
Quantity demanded and movement
    along a demand function
Substitutes and complements
Quantity supplied and movement
    along a supply function
Equilibrium price and quantity
Price elasticity of demand or supply

Demand function
Shift in the demand function
Supply function
Shift in the supply function
Excess demand and supply
Price-elastic, unitary, and price-
    inelastic demand

REVIEW QUESTIONS

1. Describe what the demand and supply functions represent.
2. What is the meaning of an equilibrium price and quantity?
3. Movement along the demand function involves a change in the price of a product, whereas a shift in the position of the demand function involves a change in the price of another good. Explain why you agree or disagree with this statement.
4. What causes the demand function to shift?
5. What causes the supply function to shift?
6. Because a fall in consumer income shifts the demand function to the left, consumers may nevertheless demand the same quantity of a good if the price of the good falls. Explain why you agree or disagree with this statement.
7. More turkeys are eaten on Thanksgiving Day than on any other day of the year. Yet, the price per pound of turkey barely changes around Thanksgiving; for this to happen, the supply function of turkeys must shift to the right. Explain why you agree or disagree with this statement.
8. Explain why the following events represent movement along a demand function or a shift in the demand function for a box of tissues.
    a. A technological change reduces the cost of paper.

b. The ski season begins when the temperature falls below freezing.

c. The prices of cold remedies increase.

d. A restriction is placed on the number of trees that can be cut.

9. The demand function for electrical engineers has increased relative to the demand function for civil engineers. If the salary of electrical engineers has not increased relative to the salary of civil engineers, what does this say about the shapes of the supply functions of electrical and civil engineers? Can you give some reasons why the supply functions have this shape?

10. If the price of a product increases by 20 percent and the quantity demanded decreases by 20 percent, demand is unit elastic. Use the formula for the arc price elasticity of demand to calculate the price elasticity and explain why you agree or disagree with this statement.

11. If a surplus appears when the supply function decreases less than the demand function at the price paid in the recent past, then a surplus reveals itself by a fall in price and a rise in the quantity consumed. Do you agree or disagree with this statement?

12. It is legal to give permission to *donate* parts of your body to others after death. It is illegal for individuals to *sell* parts of their bodies to others. Use the demand and supply model to predict the consequences of this ban.

13. Toronto, Canada, has a rent ceiling on apartments. Individuals hoping to sublease a rent-controlled apartment advertise or distribute leaflets in a building that they like, offering a cash reward—called key money—for anyone willing to sublease their apartment. Use the demand and supply model to explain this practice. What determines the amount of the key money?

EXERCISES

1. The figure below shows two demand functions, *DD* and *D'D'*. At each price the quantity demanded is greater on *D'D'* than on *DD*. Given these demand functions, can you say that a shortage is more likely if the demand function is *D'D'* and that a surplus is more likely if the demand function is *DD*? Explain why or why not.

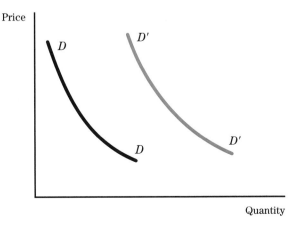

2. A mass transit district is facing a financial crisis. Because no further subsidies are available from either the city or the state, it has increased fares by 75 percent. After the first year of the fare increase, the district reports a revenue increase of 52 percent.
   a. Using these figures, estimate the percentage drop in riders because of the fare increase.
   b. Give an estimate of the arc price elasticity of demand.
3. Because the government held down the price of gasoline during the energy crisis, most grades of gasoline are cheaper than four years earlier at least in real terms, that is, adjusted for inflation. Because gasoline is cheaper, people use more of it, and it should not be surprising that Americans have been burning it up on the highways at record rates. Explain whether you agree or disagree with the logic of this.
4. If the government places a per unit tax on the production of a good, the price of the product will increase and the quantity supplied by producers will increase because the producer will receive a higher price. Explain why you agree or disagree with this statement. (*Hint:* Show what happens to the supply function when the government levies a per unit tax on suppliers. Before the tax, suppliers offer Q at each P. What price must they receive after the government imposes the tax if they are still willing to offer the same Q?)
5. If an antidrug program is effective and causes the price of drugs to increase, it should reduce the quantity of drugs consumed and increase the total amount spent on drugs. Explain why you agree or disagree with this statement.

PROBLEM SET

Estimating the Price Elasticity of Demand

You have just transferred from another division and been appointed manager of a division that sells replacement parts for air conditioners to wholesalers. The division has been losing money during the last 2 years, and your mandate is to turn the situation around quickly.

You decide to examine all aspects of the division's performance. You appoint five members to a pricing committee and ask them to recommend a procedure for reviewing the pricing decisions for major parts sold by the division. The committee is to report back in 2 weeks so that a comprehensive review of the pricing of all parts can begin.

The pricing committee submits the report as requested, but because of the limited amount of time it restricts the review to a few parts whose prices have changed during the last 4 years. The committee members propose the following procedure to determine whether the firm should raise or lower the price of individual parts.

Recommended Methodology

The committee uses part 1006 to illustrate the recommended procedure.

- *Step 1.* Review the past pricing history to determine when the price changed. The price history of part 1006 reveals the price was $20 per unit until April 1, 1988, when it increased by 50 percent to $30.
- *Step 2.* Assemble monthly sales data to determine how the quantity sold responded to the price change. The sales history of part 1006 from 1987 to 1990 is shown in the accompanying table.
- *Step 3.* Calculate a price elasticity of demand.

MONTH	1987	1988	1989	1990
January	12	14	12	7
February	13	13	15	8
March	18	20	16	11
April	25	23	18	14
May	29	27	20	19
June	32	30	23	24
July	42	33	26	26
August	48	31	29	31
September	38	28	24	26
October	38	25	18	23
November	20	14	12	14
December	10	9	5	7

The committee cannot agree on how to implement the procedure. They disagree about which quantity data should be used to calculate the price elasticity. Two different proposals are being considered.

- *Proposal 1.* Three members suggest that the price elasticity should be calculated by comparing cumulative sales during the 6 months before the price increase with cumulative sales during the first 6 months after the price increase. They argue that the figures for less than 6 months may contain too many random effects that will distort the price elasticity estimates. If data for more than 6 months are used to calculate the elasticity, they fear that the assumption that other variables are constant would be violated.
- *Proposal 2.* Two members recommend that cumulative sales for the 12 months before the price increase be compared with cumulative sales for the 12 months after the price increase.

Questions

1. Calculate the price elasticities using the two recommended procedures.
2. Why do the two estimates differ? With the use of demand functions explain what factors determine the estimate obtained by using the first procedure.
3. Which of the two procedures would you favor? Explain why.
4. Did the 1988 price change increase or decrease total revenue? If you were a member of the pricing committee, would you be satisfied with either proposal or would you suggest still another one?
5. What other information, besides that presented in the table, would you like to have to improve your estimate of the price elasticity or, at the very least, to determine any bias in the estimates?

PART II

CONSUMER
BEHAVIOR

■ C H A P T E R 2

CONSUMER BEHAVIOR AND MARKET DEMAND

Chapter 1 showed that the intersection of the market demand and supply functions determines the equilibrium price and quantity. This chapter goes behind the market demand function for a good and shows just where this function comes from. The centerpiece of the analysis is the consumer, and so we build a model that focuses on the behavior of an individual. In this theory the consumer purchases a market basket of goods that makes him or her as well off as possible given the prices paid for the goods and the consumer's income. By working with this model, you will learn how to derive the consumer's demand function for a good and what causes shifts in its position. You will also learn how the price of the product, the price of other goods, and the income of the consumer all affect the quantity demanded.

After developing the theory of consumer behavior and deriving the individual's demand function, we will proceed to the next step and determine the market demand function by adding up the demand functions of all consumers.

2-1   BUILDING THE CONSUMER BEHAVIOR MODEL

Consumers purchase a diverse set of goods ranging from housing to food to movies to fitness equipment, and each individual selects a different market basket of goods. A market basket is a collection of quantities of different goods. Table 2-1 lists possible market baskets having just two goods, chicken and beef. Later, we will consider market baskets with more than two goods.

Each row represents a market basket with so many pounds of chicken and so many pounds of beef.

> A **market basket** specifies the quantities of different goods.

Before we can develop a theory of consumer behavior, some assumptions must be made about the way consumers behave. These assumptions are the foundation of our theory of consumer behavior.

Assumptions about Consumer Behavior

In selecting among market baskets, it is assumed that consumers can distinguish between the benefits of consuming one market basket or another. More specifically,

Table 2-1   EXAMPLES OF MARKET BASKETS

MARKET BASKET	POUNDS OF CHICKEN	POUNDS OF BEEF
1	10	4
2	9	6
3	0	12
4	8	8

it is assumed that they (1) can rank market baskets by the benefits obtained, (2) are consistent in their choices, and (3) satisfy a transitivity condition described as follows:

1. *Completeness.* At the most basic level a consumer must be capable of making decisions. When comparing market baskets 1 and 2 in Table 2-1, he or she can express a preference for market basket 1 (10 pounds of chicken and 4 pounds of beef) over market basket 2 (9 pounds of chicken and 6 pounds of beef), an indifference between the two market baskets, or a preference for market basket 2 over market basket 1. Therefore, an individual must be able to *rank* market baskets. We could, but do not, require the consumer to know how much better off he or she will be by consuming one market basket rather than another. All that is needed is an ability to rank market baskets solely on the basis of the person's own well-being.

2. *Making consistent choices.* Our consumer demonstrates a consistent preference ordering. If market basket 1 is preferred to market basket 2, then he or she demonstrates consistency by maintaining the preference ranking. Throughout this chapter it is assumed that tastes are stable.

3. *Transitivity.* The requirement of transitivity eliminates contradictions in the consumer's preference ordering. An example will illustrate the meaning of "transitivity." If a consumer prefers market basket 1 to market basket 2 in Table 2-1 and prefers market basket 2 to market basket 3, then these preferences satisfy the transitivity assumption if market basket 1 is preferred to market basket 3.

4. *More is preferred to less.* Our consumer prefers more of any good that increases his or her well-being, choosing a market basket that contains more units of at least one good over another with the same number of units of the other goods.

These are the minimal requirements placed on each consumer in developing the consumer behavior model. They are not demanding requirements, and so economists proceed as if most individuals can satisfy these conditions.

2-2   DESCRIBING CONSUMER PREFERENCES

Economists have a very precise concept in mind when referring to consumer preferences or tastes. This section introduces the concept of the indifference curve and illustrates how a consumer's preferences can be described with a set of indifference curves.

Indifference Curves

An indifference curve represents a set of market baskets where the well-being of the consumer is the same. Let's determine which market baskets are in the set. To begin, consider a market basket of just two goods. Let hours attending the movies per year be one good and hours attending sporting events per year be the other.

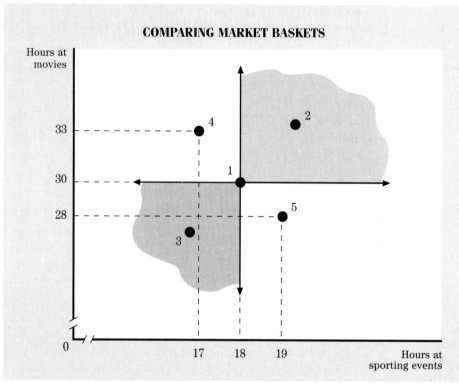

Figure 2-1   The consumer prefers all market baskets in the shaded area to the northeast of market basket 1. Market basket 2 is preferred because more of both goods are included than in market basket 1. All market baskets in the gray area to the southwest of market basket 1 are inferior to market basket 1. The consumer prefers market basket 1 to market basket 3 because market basket 3 has fewer of both goods than market basket 1. The consumer may or may not be better off by consuming market baskets 4 and 5 than by consuming market basket 1.

In Figure 2-1 hours attending movies are on the y or vertical axis, and hours at sporting events on the x or horizontal axis. Each point on the diagram represents a market basket—different quantities of the two goods. For example, market basket 1 includes 30 hours at the movies a year and 18 hours attending sporting events a year.

From the graph, you can make some observations about the well-being of the consumer. Market basket 2 has more of both goods than market basket 1, and so you can conclude that the consumer's well-being or utility is higher with market basket 2. ("Well being" and "utility" are used interchangeably throughout this chapter to describe the level of satisfaction of the purchaser.) The consumer prefers any market basket to the northeast of market basket 1, such as market basket 2. The opposite is true for market basket 3 which includes fewer hours at the movies and at sporting events than market basket 1. Therefore market basket 1 is preferred to market basket 3 and to any market basket southwest of market basket 1. We can sum up by saying that the consumer prefers market basket 2 to market basket 1, and market basket 1 to market basket 3. Clearly, neither market basket 2 nor market basket 3 is on the same indifference curve as market basket 1 because the consumer is not indifferent between these two market baskets.

Now consider market baskets 4 and 5. Market basket 4 includes more movies but fewer sporting events, and market basket 5 includes fewer movies and more sporting events. Suppose our consumer expresses an indifference between market baskets 1 and 4 and 1 and 5. The consumer's utility is the same if market basket 1, 4, or 5 is purchased because they are on the same indifference curve. The consumer expresses indifference among attending (1) 33 hours of movies and 17 hours of sporting events (market basket 4), (2) 30 hours of movies and 18 hours of sporting events (market basket 1), and (3) 28 hours of movies and 19 hours of sporting events (market basket 5).

> An **indifference curve** represents a set of market baskets where the well-being of the consumer is the same.

These are just three of many market baskets among which the consumer professes indifference. In Figure 2-2 the many market baskets are connected with

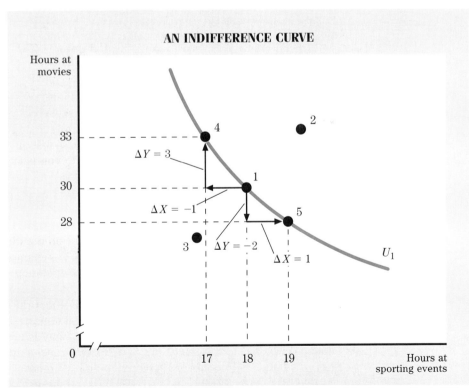

AN INDIFFERENCE CURVE

Figure 2-2   The consumer is indifferent between all market baskets on the indifference curve labeled U_1 and is as well off consuming market basket 1, 4, or 5. Market basket 3 is inferior to any market basket on the indifference curve U_1, and market basket 2 is preferred to any market basket on the indifference curve U_1.

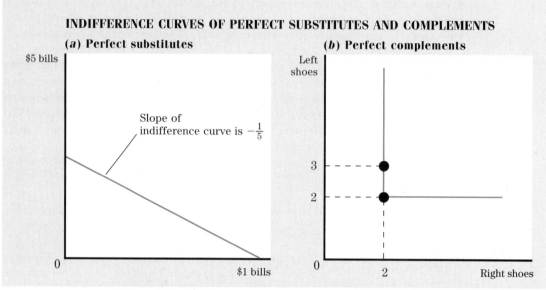

Figure 2-3   (*a*) The consumer is willing to substitute units of Y ($5 bills) for units of X ($1 bills) at a constant rate and still remain indifferent. The two goods are perfect substitutes. (*b*) Right and left shoes are perfect complements. The indifference curve has an L shape because Y (left shoes) and X (right shoes) are used in a fixed proportion.

a curve called an indifference curve. The consumer is indifferent among all market baskets on the curve labeled U_1 because all market baskets on a given indifference curve produce the same level of utility. The concept of substitutability underlies the notion of an indifference curve, which tells us how willing a consumer is to substitute one good for another and still remain indifferent. For example, an individual does not have to attend 18 hours of sporting events per year to reach a certain level of well-being. Even the most avid sports fan receives some enjoyment from seeing the classic film *Gone With the Wind.* Although the shapes of indifference curves differ from one consumer to another, each person is willing to substitute hours at sporting events for hours at the movies at some rate where he or she is indifferent.

Two extreme cases of indifference curves are worth noting. In one case the curve is a straight line, and in the second case it has an L shape. When the indifference curve is a straight line, the consumer substitutes one good for another at a constant rate no matter how many units of a good are purchased. When this occurs, we call the two goods **perfect substitutes.** In Figure 2-3*a* the indifference curve between Y and X is a straight line. For example, your indifference curve between $5 bills and $1 bills always has a slope of $-\frac{1}{5}$ because you are always willing to give up one $5 bill for five $1 bills. If brand names mean little to you, you might be willing to substitute one can of Del Monte corn for one can of a generic brand of corn no matter how many cans of Del Monte corn you consume.

The second special case occurs when two goods are used together in some fixed proportion. Then the indifference curve has an L shape (Figure 2-3*b*), and we call the two goods **perfect complements.** If you have one right shoe, for example, another left shoe does not increase your utility. If you always add two teaspoons of sugar to every cup of coffee and think a third teaspoon adds nothing to the taste, you use coffee and sugar in fixed proportions and the two goods are perfect complements.

Between these two extreme presentations of the shape of indifference curves is the more common indifference curve like the one in Figure 2-2.

The Marginal Rate of Substitution

The slope of the indifference curve at any point measures the personal tradeoff between two goods that keeps the consumer's utility constant. The slope of the indifference curve at any point is called the marginal rate of substitution (MRS).

> The **marginal rate of substitution** is the slope of the indifference curve at any point on the indifference map. It is negative and measures the tradeoff between two goods that keeps the utility of the consumer constant.

The marginal rate of substitution can be expressed as

$$\text{MRS}_{YX} = \left.\frac{\Delta Y}{\Delta X}\right|_{U=\text{constant}} \qquad \text{(Marginal Rate of Substitution)} \qquad \textbf{(2-1)}$$

It indicates how much of one good the consumer is willing to give up for a given increase in another good and is equal to the slope of the indifference curve, $\Delta Y/\Delta X$. The notation $|_{U=\text{constant}}$ means that the utility of the consumer is constant, and so the slope is being measured along a given indifference curve.

As long as an increase in hours at the movies or at sporting events increases the consumer's utility, the slope of an indifference curve must be negative if utility is to remain constant. For example, an individual can remain indifferent between market baskets 1 and 5 in Figure 2-2 only if he or she reduces hours at the movies when spending another hour at a sporting event. This is why the MRS is negative.

Except for the special case of perfect substitutes, the slope of the indifference curve does not remain constant as the consumer moves along the curve. Figure 2-4 is another version of Figure 2-2. Starting with a market basket of 33 hours per year at the movies and 17 hours per year at sporting events (market basket 4), this individual is willing to give up 3 hours at the movies for one more hour at sporting events. Because more time is being spent at sporting events and less time at the movies than before, the consumer is now willing to give up only 2 hours at the movies to spend one more hour at sporting events. The slope of the indifference curve changes at different points along the curve. There is an even sharper distinction between the slopes along the indifference curve when comparing market baskets a and b. Market basket a indicates that the consumer spends 50 hours at the movies and just 8 hours at sporting events per year but is willing to give up 6 hours at the movies for 1 hour at sporting events and remain indifferent. The slope of the indifference curve is $\Delta Y/\Delta X = -\frac{6}{1}$. With market basket b only 18 hours are

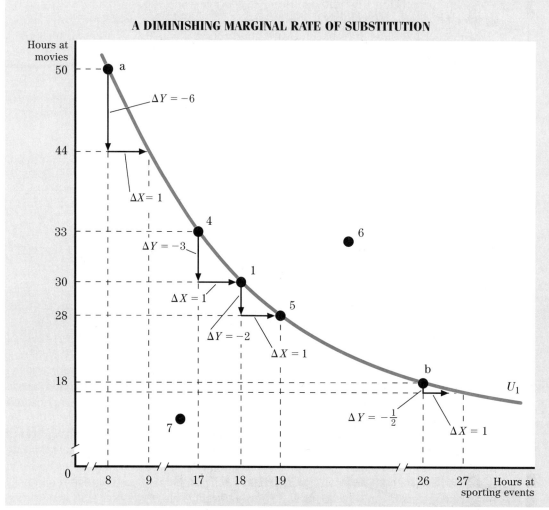

A DIMINISHING MARGINAL RATE OF SUBSTITUTION

Figure 2-4   A diminishing marginal rate of substitution means that the slope of the indifference curve becomes less negative as the consumer spends more time at sporting events. Starting with market basket a, the consumer is willing to spend six fewer hours at the movies for one more hour at sporting events and remain indifferent. The marginal rate of substitution is -6. With market basket b the consumer spends 26 hours at sporting events and is willing to forgo only $\frac{1}{2}$ hour for one more hour at the movies. The marginal rate of substitution is $-\frac{1}{2}$.

spent at the movies and 26 hours at sporting events. The consumer will sacrifice only a half hour of time at the movies for one more hour at sporting events and still remain indifferent. The slope of the indifference curve is $\Delta Y/\Delta X = -\frac{1}{2}/1 = -\frac{1}{2}$. When moving along the indifference curve, the slope of the curve becomes flatter as it increases from -6 for market basket a to $-\frac{1}{2}$ for market basket b. Therefore, indifference curves typically exhibit a diminishing rate of substitution.

A **diminishing marginal rate of substitution** means the slope of the indifference curve becomes flatter as the quantity of X increases.[1]

The consumer is willing to give up fewer and fewer hours of movies for one more hour at sporting events as more time is spent at sporting events. Similarly, anyone who has fruit for breakfast is willing to give up many slices of apples for a few strawberries when spring comes, after eating apple slices all winter long.

The Indifference Map of a Consumer

An **indifference map** includes all indifference curves of a consumer, and every available market basket is on one of these indifference curves. The indifference curve U_1 in Figure 2-4 is just one of several and demonstrates that the same utility is obtained with market basket 4, 1, or 5. Any market basket above U_1, such as market basket 6, is on a different indifference curve and provides more utility than market basket 4, 1, or 5. And any market basket below U_1, such as market basket 7, is on another indifference curve and provides less utility. Each indifference curve represents a certain level of utility. The curves lying above U_1 represent higher levels of utility, and those lying below U_1 represent lower levels. The consumer is indifferent between market baskets on the *same* indifference curve but not between market baskets on *different* indifference curves.

For example, Figure 2-5 shows only three of the many indifference curves of a consumer. Market baskets b and c are on U_3, and so the consumer is indifferent between them. On the other hand, market basket b on indifference curve U_3 is preferred to market basket a on indifference curve U_2 because it includes more of each good. The transitivity requirement says that market basket c is preferred to market basket a since market basket b is preferred to market basket a. To summarize, any market basket on an indifference curve to the northeast of another indifference curve is preferred to any market basket on the original indifference curve.

Assigning Numbers to Indifference Curves

Our consumer does not have to know how much better off he or she will be by purchasing one market basket rather than another but must just rank the market baskets to create an indifference map. Suppose that an individual assigns numbers called utility numbers to indifference curves. All market baskets on the same indifference curve would then have the same utility number, and larger numbers would be assigned to market baskets on higher indifference curves. In this way the consumer could attach a number to each market basket. A function that relates the utility number to the quantity consumed of each good summarizes the preferences of the consumer.

The consumer's **utility function** is

$$U = U(X,Y) \qquad \text{(Utility Function)} \qquad \text{(2-2)}$$

---

[1] The slope of the indifference curve is $\Delta Y/\Delta X$ and changes as the consumer moves along the curve. A diminishing marginal rate of substitution requires $[\Delta(\Delta Y/\Delta X)]/\Delta X > 0$.

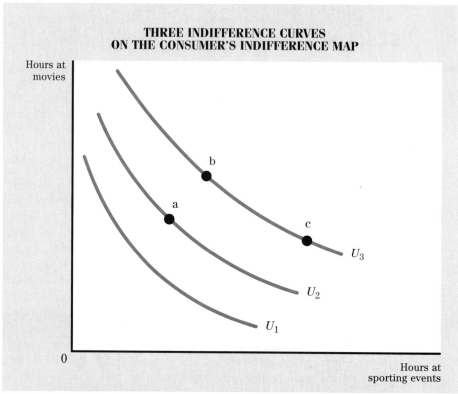

**THREE INDIFFERENCE CURVES
ON THE CONSUMER'S INDIFFERENCE MAP**

Figure 2-5   An indifference map includes all the indifference curves of a consumer. Here three sample indifference curves are shown. The consumer is better off selecting market baskets on higher indifference curves and prefers market baskets b and c to market basket a.

Equation 2-2 says that the utility (as represented by the assigned number) of the consumer depends on the quantities of X and Y consumed. Utility is measured in subjective units called **utils.** Because the numbers assigned to indifference curves by the consumer are arbitrary, they can be replaced by another number system as long as the consumer's ranking of the indifference curves is preserved. The theory of consumer behavior does not depend on any particular assignment of numbers to the indifference curves but only on the ranking of these curves.

To summarize, each consumer has a utility function that expresses his or her well-being or utility as a function of the quantity consumed of each good.

2-3   PROPERTIES OF INDIFFERENCE CURVES

The indifference map for a consumer describes the individual's tastes or preferences. Although personal tastes may differ, the indifference curves of each purchaser must satisfy the following conditions:

1. *The slope of an indifference curve must be negative.* You have already learned why indifference curves must have a negative slope if the consumption of more of each good increases the well-being of the consumer.

2. *Indifference curves must not touch.* The transitivity assumption prevents indifference curves from touching or intersecting. Two indifference curves of a consumer intersect in Figure 2-6. This individual prefers market basket b to market basket a because more of each good is obtained with market basket b. However, market baskets a and c are equivalent since they are on U_1. Therefore, market basket b should be preferred to market basket c if the transitivity condition is satisfied. However, market baskets b and c are on U_0, and so the consumer is indifferent between them and therefore between market baskets a and b. This cannot be because market basket b contains more goods. Therefore, indifference curves cannot intersect.

This completes our examination of consumer preferences as expressed by the consumer's indifference map. Now we bring the consumer back to reality by identifying which market baskets are affordable.

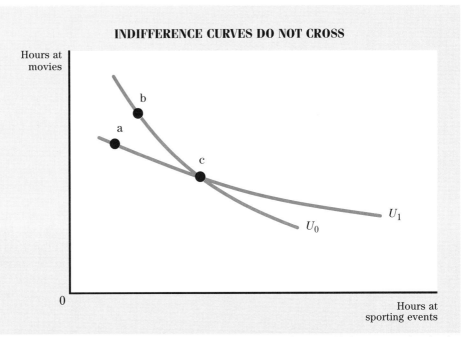

Figure 2-6   When two indifference curves cross, the transitivity assumption is violated. A consumer professes an indifference between market baskets a and c and also expresses a preference for market basket b over market basket a. Therefore, the consumer should prefer market basket b over market basket c. However, the consumer expresses an indifference between market baskets b and c. He or she will express a preference for market basket b to c only if the indifference curves do not cross.

2-4 BUDGET CONSTRAINT

Although each individual has a distinct ordering of market baskets, income and the price of each good limit the choice of market baskets. Consumers can afford only a subset of all possible market baskets because each one faces a **budget constraint** that limits the number of affordable market baskets. Such limitations are familiar to everyone: You might like to drive an expensive Mercedes-Benz or have a house in the south of France, but your budget constraint forces you to make more modest selections.

Affordable Market Baskets

This chapter considers a single-period model of consumption in which the consumer has no reason to save. (Later, Chapter 16 describes the consumption decision where the consumer may decide to save in the present in order to consume more in the future.) In this chapter a person's total expenditure for goods and services is equal to income. To demonstrate how income and market prices determine what market baskets the consumer can afford, let's continue to assume that the individual purchases just two goods, X and Y. Income is I, the price of a unit of X is P_X, and the price of each unit of Y is P_Y. It is also assumed that the buyer can purchase each unit of either good at these market prices.

The budget constraint is expressed as

$$P_X X + P_Y Y = I \qquad \text{(Budget Constraint)} \tag{2-3}$$

where $P_X X$ is total expenditure for X, and $P_Y Y$ is total expenditure for Y. Equation 2-3 says that total expenditure for goods is equal to income. Initially, we will assume that the prices are constant and do not vary with the quantity purchased. The consumer selects from the market baskets of X and Y that satisfy his or her budget constraint (equation 2-3).

> The **budget constraint** shows which market baskets the consumer can afford.

By rearranging the budget constraint equation, we can tell just how many units of Y can be consumed for any given quantity of X. Equation 2-3 can be rearranged to show this by subtracting $P_X X$ from both sides and then dividing both sides by P_Y to obtain

$$Y = \frac{I}{P_Y} - \frac{P_X}{P_Y} X \qquad \text{(Tradeoff between Y and X)} \tag{2-4}$$

Equation 2-4 is an equation of a straight line. Figure 2-7 is the graph of equation 2-4, where Y is hours at the movies and X is hours at sporting events. The quantity of Y and the quantity of X are the two variables, I/P_Y is the y intercept of the straight line, and $-P_X/P_Y$ is the slope of the straight line. If the consumer does not purchase any units of X ($X = 0$), he spends all income on Y and is able to purchase I/P_Y units of Y. Dividing income by the price of Y yields the maximum

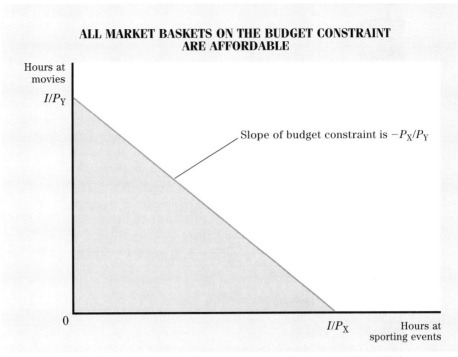

**ALL MARKET BASKETS ON THE BUDGET CONSTRAINT
ARE AFFORDABLE**

Hours at movies

I/P_Y

Slope of budget constraint is $-P_X/P_Y$

0

I/P_X Hours at sporting events

Figure 2-7 Given the income of the consumer and the prices of X and Y, the consumer can purchase any market basket on or below the budget constraint in the shaded area. Each point on the budget line represents an affordable market basket of so many units of Y and so many units of X. If all income is spent on Y, the consumer purchases I/P_Y units of Y. If all income is spent on X, the consumer purchases I/P_X units of X. The slope of the budget constraint is $-P_X/P_Y$ and shows how many fewer units of Y are purchased for each unit increase in X.

number of units of Y that can be purchased, Consequently, one affordable market basket is zero units of X and I/P_Y units of Y. Now suppose the consumer purchases only X ($Y = 0$). How many units of X can he purchase? If you set $Y = 0$ in equation 2-4 and solve for X, you will find that $X = I/P_X$. Dividing income by the price of X gives the maximum quantity of X that the individual can consume. So another affordable market basket is I/P_X units of X and no units of Y. These are the ends or the intercepts of the budget line. An example will make the calculation of these end points clearer. Suppose the monthly income of the consumer is $2,000. The price of X is $50, and the price of Y is $10. Then, the budget constraint becomes

$$Y = 200 - 5X$$

The consumer can buy $2000/$10 = 200 units of Y by spending all income on Y, and $2000/$50 = 40 units of X by spending all income on X.

The slope of equation 2-4 is $-P_X/P_Y$, the negative of the price of X divided by the price of Y. The slope of the budget constraint is negative because more units of Y can be purchased only if fewer units of X are bought. It measures the rate at which the consumption of Y must be reduced for each unit increase in X. In our numerical example $-P_X/P_Y = -\$50/\$10 = -5$. By purchasing one less unit of X (reducing the expenditure for X by $50), the buyer can purchase five more units of Y (increasing the expenditure for Y by $50). Sometimes, students find it useful to think of the slope of the budget constraint as the marginal rate of substitution of the market, and the slope of the indifference curve as the consumer's personal marginal rate of substitution.

We have assumed that the consumer pays the same price regardless of the number of units purchased. What happens to the shape of the budget line if the price depends on the quantity purchased? For example, firms offer quantity discounts. A store advertisement that says "Buy one dress at the regular price and get 50 percent off the second dress" is offering a quantity discount on every second dress purchased. Let's see how the shape of the budget constraint changes under two different discount policies. In the first case the firm offers a 50 percent discount on only the *second* unit purchased. An individual who buys three or more units does not receive a price discount on every second unit. In the second case the firm offers a discount of 50 percent on *every second* item purchased.

Let's return to our example of movies and sporting events and assume that the consumer gets 50 percent off for every second sporting event when full price is paid for the first event. Furthermore, it is assumed that each sporting event takes 1 hour. In Figure 2-8a and b the hourly price of a sporting event is P_r, and the dashed line aa' is the budget constraint when no discount is available. When a 50 percent discount becomes available on only the second unit, the budget constraint becomes $abcd$ in Figure 2-8a. The cost of the first unit is P_r, and when buying the second unit, the consumer pays only 50 percent of P_r. If more than two units are purchased, each unit costs P_r. This is why the slope of line segment cd is the same as the slope of line segment ab.

When a 50 percent discount is available on every second event, the budget constraint becomes a series of connected segments with every other segment having the same slope. Although the second sporting event can be purchased at a discount, the price for the first event remains at P_r, the hourly rate for the first hour. For the second sporting event, hour 2, the hourly price declines to $0.5P_r$. In Figure 2.8b the slope of the segment bc is half the slope of the segment ab because the hourly rate decreases by 50 percent. For the third sporting event, hour 3, the buyer pays the full hourly rate of P_r, and so the slope of segment cd is equal to the slope of ab and is steeper than that of segment bc. The consumer qualifies for the 50 percent discount on the fourth sporting event, hour 4, and so the slope of segment de is the same as the slope of bc. A numerical example illustrates how the budget line shifts outward. If the regular hourly rate is $8, the first sports event costs $8 and the second event costs $4. The consumer pays $12 for the two events. Without the discount the two events would cost a total of $16. Therefore, the 50 percent discount offers a total saving of 25 percent off the regular price for an individual who attends two sporting events.

There are many different types of quantity discounts, but for all of them the price depends in some way on the quantity purchased. With a quantity discount the budget line is no longer a straight line. Quantity discounts offer the buyer a

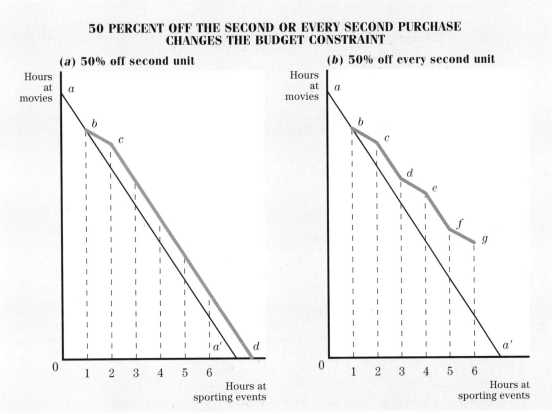

Figure 2-8   (*a*) The consumer receives 50 percent off on only the second unit purchased. When the hourly price for a sporting event is P_r, the budget constraint is the line aa'. A pricing promotion that reduces the price for only the second sporting event by 50 percent changes the budget constraint to ab, bc, cd. The slope of the segment bc is half the slope of ab because of the 50 percent discount. The price is P_r for subsequent sporting events. (*b*) The consumer receives a 50 percent discount on every second purchase. The price of the first, third, and fifth sporting events is P_r. The price of the second, fourth, sixth, and so on, is $\frac{1}{2}P_r$. The budget contraint becomes ab, bc, cd, de, ef, fg.

larger set of affordable opportunities by shifting some portion of the budget line outward.

Shifts in the Budget Constraint

Let's return to the original budget line where the price is constant and determine how the position of the budget constraint shifts when the income of the consumer or the price of X or Y changes. Observe what happens when income increases from I to I^*. The y intercept increases from I/P_Y to I^*/P_Y, but the slope of the budget constraint, $-P_X/P_Y$, is unaffected. Therefore, an increase in income causes a par-

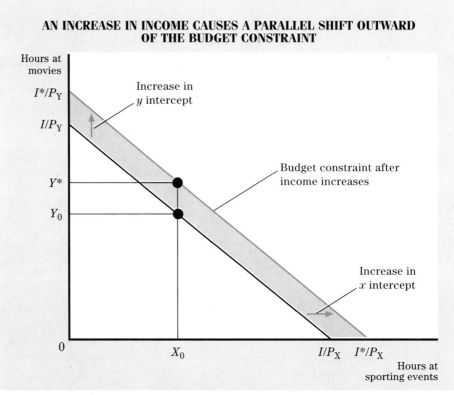

**AN INCREASE IN INCOME CAUSES A PARALLEL SHIFT OUTWARD
OF THE BUDGET CONSTRAINT**

Figure 2-9   An increase in income from I to I^* causes a parallel outward shift in the
budget constraint. The slope of the budget constraint is $-P_X/P_Y$ and is unaffected when
income increases. After income increases to I^*, the consumer has more affordable
opportunities. If the individual consumes X_0 units, he or she can now consume Y^* units
rather than Y_0 units.

allel shift to the right for the budget constraint in Figure 2-9. The shaded area
shows the expanded set of affordable market baskets. Before the increase in
income, the consumer could spend Y_0 hours at the movies when X_0 hours were
spent at sporting events. After an increase in income, the consumer can spend Y^*
hours at the movies while still spending X_0 hours at sporting events.

A decrease in the price of either good allows the buyer to purchase some
market baskets that were not affordable before. A fall in the price of X from P_X to
P_X^* does not change the intercept on the vertical axis because the intercept is
I/P_Y, but it makes the budget constraint flatter. The new slope is $-P_X^*/P_Y$, increasing in value from some initial negative number to a smaller negative number. When
the price of X is \$50 and the price of Y is \$10, the consumer must purchase five
fewer units of Y to consume one more unit of X. When the price of X drops to \$20,
the consumer sacrifices two units of Y to consume another unit of X. Therefore,
as the budget constraint becomes flatter, the slope increases from -5 to -2. Figure

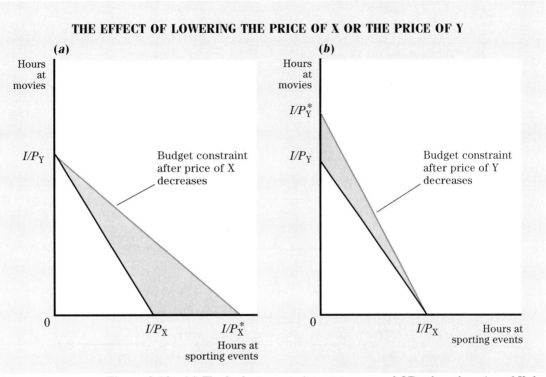

Figure 2-10   (*a*) The budget constraint rotates around I/P_Y when the price of X decreases. (*b*) The budget constraint rotates around I/P_X when the price of Y decreases. A reduction in the price of X or of Y increases the affordable opportunities available to the consumer.

2-10*a* shows the budget line rotating outward around I/P_Y. The buyer can still purchase I/P_Y hours of movies after the price of an hour of sporting events decreases if all income is spent on movies. On the other hand, the consumer can now purchase I/P_X^* hours of sporting events if all income is spent on X. The shaded area shows the expanded set of opportunities when the price of X decreases.

A fall in the price of Y also allows the purchaser to select from a larger set of affordable market baskets. Equation 2-4 shows that the *y* intercept increases and the slope decreases. If the price of Y decreases from P_Y to P_Y^*, the *y* intercept increases to I/P_Y^* and makes the budget line steeper. The slope of the budget constraint becomes $-P_X/P_Y^*$, which is smaller than $-P_X/P_Y$. In our example, the slope of the budget constraint decreases from -5 to -10 if the price of X is $50 and the price of Y decreases from $10 to $5. Now the consumer can buy 10 more units of Y by choosing 1 less unit of X. A decrease in the price of Y does not affect the quantity of X if all income is spent on X. Figure 2-10*b* shows the budget line rotating around the *x* intercept as the price of Y decreases. Here again, the shaded area shows the expanded set of market baskets that can be purchased when the price of Y decreases.

If all prices and income change by a common percentage, then equation 2-4 indicates that the budget constraint is unaffected and does not change position. If inflation increases consumer income by 10 percent a year but raises the price of all goods by the same percentage, affordable opportunities do not change and the budget constraint stays put. The percentage increase in income offsets the equivalent percentage increase in all prices. The consumer is not any richer if income increases by 10 percent and prices also increase by 10 percent.

2-5   THE CONSUMER'S CONSUMPTION DECISION

The two essential components of the consumer behavior model have been introduced. The first is the indifference map of the consumer that describes the person's preferences and comparative likes and dislikes. The second is the budget constraint that brings a sense of reality to the consumer by defining which market baskets are affordable. Now we bring the two components together and explain how the consumer determines which one of the many affordable market baskets to purchase.

Finding the Market Basket That Maximizes Utility and Satisfies the Budget Constraint

The goal of the consumer is to maximize utility while satisfying the budget constraint. Although all market baskets on the budget constraint are affordable, the buyer wants to select the one that places him on the highest indifference curve.

> The goal of the consumer is to maximize utility while satisfying the budget constraint.

How does the consumer achieve this goal? In Figure 2-11 the budget constraint is superimposed on the indifference map, but only three of the many indifference curves are shown. Because the consumer must satisfy the budget constraint, he can purchase any market basket on the budget line. Market basket a with Y_0 hours at the movies and X_0 hours at sporting events is affordable because it is on the budget constraint. If the consumer purchases X_0 and Y_0 units, he is on indifference curve U_0.

Is this the best the consumer can do? Suppose he decides to spend fewer hours at the movies and more hours at sporting events while remaining on the budget constraint by spending X_1 hours at the movies and Y_1 hours at sporting events. By moving along the budget constraint from market basket a to market basket b, the consumer moves from U_0 to a higher indifference curve, U_1. Market basket b is a better buy from the consumer's perspective. To remain indifferent, starting with market basket a, the consumer is willing to give up more hours at the movies than the budget constraint requires in order to obtain another hour at sporting events. The marginal rate of substitution of the market is different from the consumer's

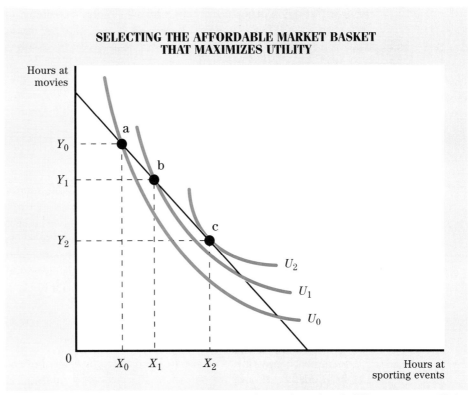

**SELECTING THE AFFORDABLE MARKET BASKET
THAT MAXIMIZES UTILITY**

Figure 2-11   The consumer maximizes utility and reaches indifference curve U_2 by selecting market basket c where the marginal rate of substitution equals the slope of the budget constraint. By purchasing the market basket of X_2 and Y_2 units, the consumer not only satisfies the budget constraint but reaches the highest affordable indifference curve.

marginal rate of substitution. This is why market basket b is a better buy than market basket a. Utility increases when fewer hours are spent at the movies and more at sporting events. An important point to take note of is that the slope of the indifference curve is less than the slope of the budget constraint when the consumer purchases market basket a. When this is true, the buyer prefers a different available market basket.

What market basket allows the buyer to reach the highest indifference curve while satisyfing the budget constraint? With market basket c, the highest possible indifference curve, U_2, can be reached by purchasing a market basket of X_2 units of X and Y_2 units of Y while satisfying the budget constraint. Market basket c is a best buy. The distinguishing feature of this market basket is that the slope of the budget line and the slope of the indifference curve U_2 are equal. In contrast, the indifference curve is steeper than the budget line with market basket a or b. Therefore, the slope of the budget line is not equal to the slope of the indifference curve with market basket a or b. Only with market basket c is the budget line tangent to an indifference curve. A necessary condition for the consumer to maximize utility subject to the budget constraint is

$$\text{MRS}_{YX} = -\frac{P_X}{P_Y} \qquad \begin{array}{l}\text{(Condition for Maximizing Utility} \\ \text{Subject to Budget Constraint)}\end{array} \qquad \textbf{(2-5)}$$

Equation 2-5 says the consumer divides total income between the two goods so that the marginal rate of substitution between Y and X equals the negative of the price ratio, the slope of the budget line.

> When maximizing utility by purchasing both goods, the consumer makes the marginal rate of substitution equal to the slope of the budget constraint.

Notice that the consumer purchases a market basket consisting of X_2 and Y_2 units—not just one type but a portfolio of goods. This is surely the more common case since most studies of consumer behavior show that people purchase a variety of goods, not just one. Still, consumers do not purchase all possible goods in the marketplace. The diet of most millionaires includes caviar but not turnips, and few middle-class families have $50,000 automobiles parked in their garages.

Specialization of Consumption

The consumer behavior model can be used to explain why buyers do not purchase certain goods. To do so, we return to the two-good model. Figure 2-12a and b shows the indifference curves of two consumers. Consumer 1 in Figure 2-12a has indifference curves labeled U_1 to U_3, and consumer 2 in Figure 2-12b has different indifference curves labeled U_1 to U_3. Consumer 1 has a penchant for movies and will remain indifferent by requiring a larger increase in hours at sporting events in place of one less hour at the movies. Her indifference curves are relatively flat, and the marginal rate of substitution is numerically large. Consumer 2 is just the opposite. To be indifferent, he requires many more hours at the movies in place of one less hour at a sporting event.

Let's suppose the budget constraint is the same for the two consumers. In Figure 2-12 the budget line is superimposed on the indifference curves of the two consumers. Consumer 1 maximizes utility and reaches indifference curve U_2 by selecting market basket a and consuming only movies. In contrast, consumer 2 maximizes utility and reaches U_2 by selecting market basket b and attending only sporting events. The different *tastes* of the two consumers explain the different market baskets they select. These solutions are called **corner solutions** because both consumers are at one boundary of the budget constraint or the other.

Both market baskets show specialization of consumption. Consumer 1 does not purchase any hours of sporting events because the marginal rate of substitution is greater than the slope of the budget line, $\text{MRS}_{YX} > -P_X/P_Y$, when she selects market basket a. If she purchases a market basket that includes some hours at sporting events, her well-being declines. For consumer 2 the marginal

MAXIMIZING UTILITY BY PURCHASING ONLY ONE GOOD

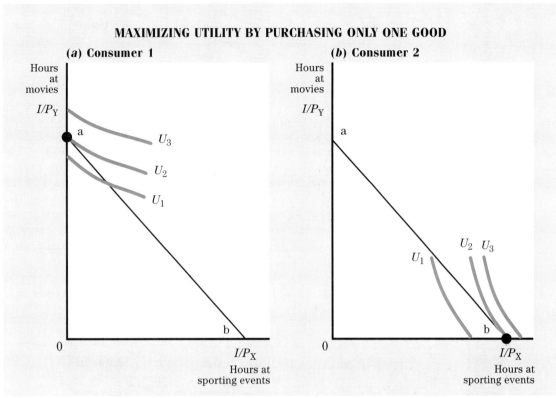

Figure 2-12   (*a*) Consumer 1 maximizes utility by specializing and going only to the movies. She purchases market basket a. The slope of her indifference curve at point *a* is flatter than the slope of the budget constraint. (*b*) Consumer 2 maximizes utility by attending only sporting events. He purchases market basket b. The slope of his indifference curve at point *b* is steeper than the slope of the budget constraint.

rate of substitution is numerically less than the slope of the budget line, $MRS_{YX} < -P_X/P_Y$, when he selects market basket b. If he spends one less hour at a sporting event, the market allows him to purchase fewer hours at the movies than he requires to be indifferent. This is why he specializes and attends only sporting events.

Consumer 1 can truthfully say she never goes to sporting events, and consumer 2 can truthfully say he never goes to the movies. This does not mean that he hates movies or that she hates sporting events. Their decisions are not etched in stone but depend on the budget constraint. If the budget constraint shifts because of a change in the price of either good, then both consumers will change their behavior and begin purchasing a market basket that includes both goods. If the price of movies falls or the price of sporting events increases, his market basket might change and include both movies and sporting events.

Pricing to Break into an Established Market

Your company is planning to introduce a new frozen gourmet meal into the market. An outside market research firm has conducted focus group sessions with many consumers to see how well the new product stands up against brand A, the market leader, and has developed consumer preference maps for brand A and for your product. The market research firm summarizes the indifference map for a typical respondent in Figure 2-13.

The number of gourmet meals per year of brand A is on the y axis, and the number of gourmet meals per year of the new product is on the x axis. The indifference curves are fairly flat and show that a representative consumer remains indifferent when several of your gourmet dinners are substituted for one brand A gourmet meal. These are discouraging findings. Your new product is clearly not a perfect substitute for brand A since consumers are not willing to trade one of your dinners for one brand A meal. Let's assume that a consumer spends a certain amount on gourmet meals during the year, and so the budget line of the consumer

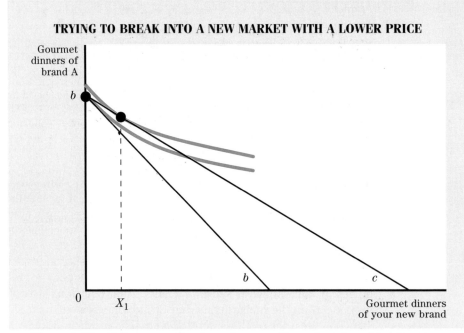

Figure 2-13   At the same price the consumer will purchase brand A rather than your new gourmet dinner. If your price is 15 percent lower, the consumer will purchase X_1 dinners per year of your new product. The success of the new product depends on whether the cost of producing it is lower.

is *bb* if you match brand A's price. The budget line has a slope of -1. If the market research firm has accurately reported the preferences of consumers, your new product will fail if you introduce it at this price because consumers will buy brand A rather than your product if the prices are equal. They will maximize utility by purchasing only brand A because $\mathrm{MRS}_{YX} > -P_X/P_Y$.

What are your alternatives? You can introduce the new product at a lower price if you still hope to break into the market. The budget line *bc* assumes you introduce your product at a 15 percent discount. At this price the estimated quantity demanded is X_1 units per year per consumer. So, a 15 percent price discount will allow you to enter the market. Given the features of your new product, the success of the project now depends critically on your ability to produce the item at a lower cost than your competitor can. Otherwise, you will never be able to sell it at the lower price. If your costs cannot be lowered, you have the choice of (1) starting again by redeveloping the product in hopes of changing the consumers' indifference maps, or (2) scrapping the project.

2-6   INTRODUCING A COMPOSITE GOOD INTO THE CONSUMER BEHAVIOR MODEL

A typical consumer purchases many goods and services, not just two. As you can imagine, it would be next to impossible to show the quantity of n goods purchased on a two-dimensional graph. This raises the question of whether the consumer behavior theory applies to only two goods or whether it can be extended to cover more. Fortunately, we can reduce the more complicated problem of many goods to one of just two goods and apply the two-good model of consumer behavior. This can be done by introducing a pseudo good called a composite good. Let's assume a market basket consists of n goods, one of which is X. A **composite good** is defined as the number of dollars spent on the other $n-1$ goods. The two goods in the consumer's utility function become units of X and units of S, where S is total spending on all goods other than X.[2] You can think of the composite good as having a price of $1.

[2] When there are n goods, x_1 through x_n, the utility function of the consumer is

$$U = U(x_1, x_2, x_3, \ldots, x_n)$$

The budget constraint is

$$P_1x_1 + P_2x_2 + \cdots + P_nx_n = I$$

We fix x_1 at some quantity and then maximize U with respect to x_2 through x_n. Let S equal spending on goods other than x_1

$$S = I - P_1x_1 = P_2x_2 + P_3x_3 + \cdots + P_nx_n$$

We can express x_2 through x_n as a function of $P_2, P_3, \ldots, P_n$ and x_1. After substituting these equations into the utility function, we reduce the problem to one of maximizing

$$U = U[V(x_1,S)] \qquad \text{subject to } P_1x_1 + S = I$$

This is now a two-good problem where the two goods are x_1 and S. We have reduced the n good problem to a two-good problem, and we can directly apply the consumer behavior theory.

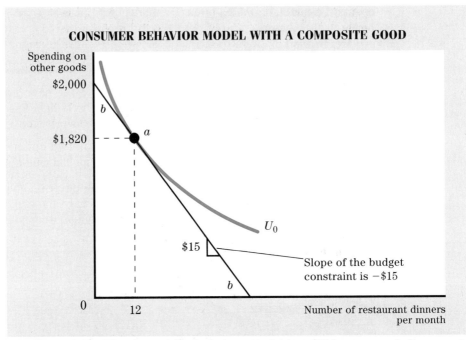

Figure 2-14   The slope of the budget constraint is $-\$15$ because each dinner costs $15. Market basket a maximizes the consumer's utility and satisfies the budget constraint. The marginal rate of substitution between the composite good and the frequency of eating out is $-\$15$. The consumer purchases 12 meals out, spending $180 per month on restaurant meals and $1,820 on other goods.

Let's apply the composite good concept in explaining how frequently a consumer eats out at a restaurant. In Figure 2.14 total spending on all goods other than dinners eaten at a restaurant is on the y axis, and the frequency of dining out each month is on the x axis. If the consumer's monthly income is $2,000, the y intercept of the budget constraint is at $2,000. The y intercept shows the total amount spent on other goods when the individual always eats in. Suppose the price of dinner at the consumer's favorite restaurant is $15. Then the slope of the budget constraint is -15. Each dinner costs $15 and reduces the amount that can be spent on other goods by $15. The budget constraint in Figure 2-14 shows the affordable market baskets between spending on other goods during the month and the frequency of eating out per month.

The indifference curve U_0 shows the tradeoff between spending on other goods and eating out so that the consumer is indifferent. The budget constraint is bb in Figure 2-14. The consumer maximizes utility subject to the budget constraint by selecting a market basket where the marginal rate of substitution of the indifference curve is -15, the slope of the budget constraint. Assume that utility is maximized by eating out 12 evenings per month and spending $180 on restaurant dinners and therefore $1,820 on other goods. The distance between $2,000 and the amount spent on other goods on the y axis measures the amount spent on restaurant meals per month—$180.

By using a composite good, we can allow for the purchase of n goods and still retain the simplicity of the two-good model.

APPLICATION 2-2

Should a Golfer Join a Golf Club?[3]

Suppose you are a golfer and a golf club offers you two options. You can either play a round of golf at a price of P_r or you pay a special annual golf membership fee of F and pay just 40 percent of P_r for each round you play. Which option should you take?

To find a solution that maximizes your utility, we have to derive a budget constraint. In Figure 2-15 spending on goods other than golf is on the vertical axis, and rounds of golf per year are on the horizontal axis. Let's first consider the budget constraint if you pay as you golf. Your income is I. Each round costs P_r, and so the slope of the budget constraint bb is $-P_r$. If you join the club, you must pay an up-front fee of F, and so the amount that you can spend on other goods is $I - F$. Each round costs only $0.4P_r$, and so the slope of the budget constraint cc is $-0.4P_r$.

An infrequent golfer will find the cost of joining the club prohibitive, whereas a frequent golfer will find the club membership a bargain. Let's find out how many rounds you would have to play to be indifferent between joining and not joining. If you join, the total cost is $F + 0.4P_rR$, where R is the number of rounds played per year. If you do not join, the cost is P_rR. Costs are equal when

$$F + 0.4P_rR = P_rR$$

This equation can be solved for R^*, the number of rounds at which the costs are equal, by collecting terms and dividing both sides of the equation by $0.6P_r$:

$$R^* = \frac{F}{0.6P_r}$$

The two budget constraints cross at R^*.

Although we know that a golfer who plays more than R^* rounds of golf will want to join the club, we cannot tell whether any one golfer will join without knowing the person's tastes. Which of the two budget constraints would you take? The budget constraint you pick depends on which one maximizes your utility. If you maximize utility by playing fewer than R^* rounds, then you will choose not to join the club and the budget constraint will be bb. The budget constraint will be cc if you maximize utility by playing more than R^* rounds per year. Clearly, the option you select depends on your tastes.

Figure 2-15*a* and *b* shows the indifference curve of two different golfers with

[3] For a similar discussion and other applications, consult W. Keith Bryant, *The Economic Organization of the Household*, Cambridge University Press, New York, 1990, pp. 61–69.

DECIDING TO JOIN A GOLF CLUB

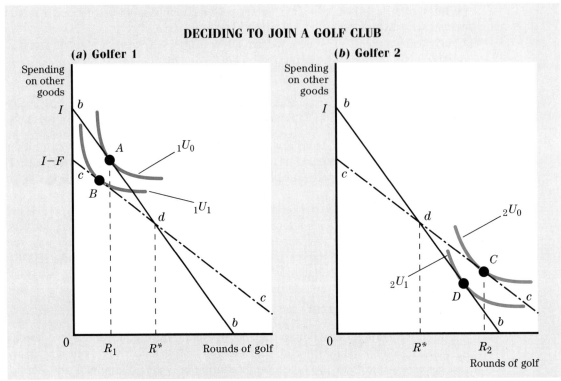

Figure 2-15 A golfer who has the option of joining a golf club or not must select one of two budget constraints. (*a*) Golfer 1 maximizes utility at point *A* by playing less than R^* rounds and does not join the club. (*b*) Golfer 2 maximizes utility at point *C* by playing more than R^* rounds and joins the club.

the same income. In Figure 2-15*a* golfer 1 maximizes utility by playing R_1 rounds per year, and his indifference curve $_1U_0$ is tangent to the budget line *bb* at point *A*. If golfer 1 joins the club, his maximum utility will be only $_1U_1$ at point *B*. In Figure 2-15*b* golfer 2 maximizes utility by playing R_2 rounds per year, and her indifference curve $_2U_0$ is tangent to the budget line *cc* at point *C*. If golfer 2 does not join the club, the maximum utility she will receive is $_2U_1$ at point *D*. Golfer 2 joins the club, while golfer 1 chooses the golf-and-pay option.

2-7 THE MARKET DEMAND FUNCTION

The ultimate goal of this chapter is to derive the market demand function for a good—the relationship between the price and the quantity demanded by all consumers. In order to derive the market demand function, we must know how to determine each consumer's demand function, and for this we rely on the utility maximization model of consumer behavior. After this function is obtained, you will see how easy it is to derive the market demand function. Then, we will have a theory of market demand that is firmly anchored to the utility-maximizing behavior of each consumer.

The Consumer's Demand Function

Let's start with a given budget line for a consumer. We take as given the person's income I, the price of Y, P_Y^1, and the price of X, P_X^1. In Figure 2-16a the budget line is aa, and market basket A maximizes the consumer's utility. Market basket A includes X_1 units of X and Y_1 units of Y. Therefore, this consumer will demand X_1 units of X if the price of X is P_X^1, given that income is I and the price of Y is P_Y^1.

Holding the consumer's income and the price of Y constant, we can determine which market basket will be selected if the price of X decreases to P_X^2. The budget constraint rotates around point a on the y-axis and becomes budget line ab. The consumer maximizes utility by selecting market basket B, which has X_2 units of X and Y_2 units of Y. This consumer demands X_2 units of X when the price of X is P_X^2, given an income of I and a price of P_Y^1. We find the quantity demanded at P_X^1 and at P_X^2 by determining which market basket maximizes utility at each price of X. Figure 2-16a shows three points of tangency of the budget line to the corresponding indifference curves. Each point determines the optimum market basket for the consumer and has a different price of X associated with it. These points of tangency identify market baskets A, B, and C. As the price of X decreases, with the price of Y and income held constant, the consumer changes the optimum market basket and therefore the quantity demanded of X.

We have all the information needed to derive the consumer's demand function $d_X d_X$ in Figure 2-16b, which differs from Figure 2-16a in that the price of X rather than the number of units of Y is on the vertical axis. The buyer demands X_1 units if the price is P_X^1. The quantity demanded is X_2 if the price is P_X^2, and X_3 units if the price is P_X^3. You should have a clear understanding about what is constant and what changes as we move along $d_X d_X$. Consumer income and the price of Y are constant, and the price of X and the quantities of X and of Y change as the individual selects different market baskets that maximize his or her utility at each price of X.

APPLICATION 2-3

Measuring Brand Loyalty by Relative Frequency of Purchase

Market researchers often measure brand loyalty by the relative frequency with which a consumer purchases a particular brand.[4] Over a year, one person may buy a given brand more than 90 percent of the time, whereas another may buy it only 10 percent of the time. For some products consumers buy only one brand to the exclusion of all others. They drink either Coke or Pepsi, but not both, or purchase

---

[4] This example is motivated by the discussion in a more technical paper by Greg M. Allensby and Peter E. Rossi, "Quality Perceptions and Asymmetric Switching Between Brands," *Marketing Science*, vol. 10, no. 3, Summer 1991, pp. 185–204.

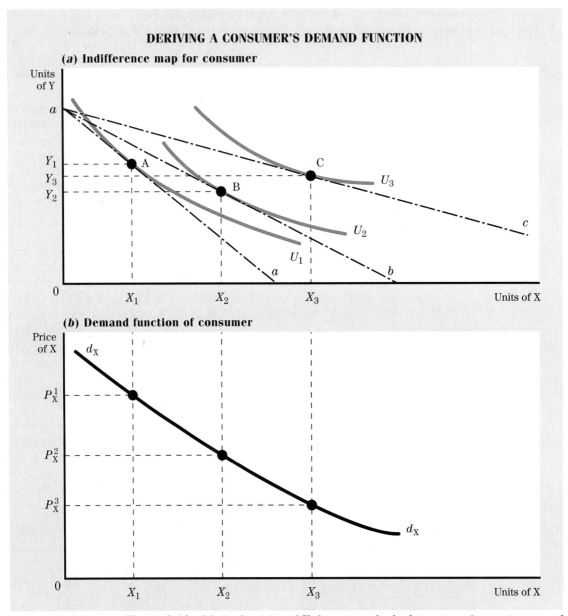

DERIVING A CONSUMER'S DEMAND FUNCTION

(a) Indifference map for consumer

(b) Demand function of consumer

Figure 2-16   (*a*) As the price of X decreases, the budget constraint rotates around point *a* and the consumer selects different market baskets. (*b*) The consumer's demand function relates the price to the quantity demanded of X.

only one brand of coffee. A popular measure of brand loyalty is **relative frequency of purchase.** Market researchers who use relative frequency of purchase to measure brand loyalty feel that individuals who repeatedly purchase a product value the characteristics of the product so much that they consider only one brand when making a purchase.

Let's critically assess the advantages and limitations of this measure of brand loyalty using the theory of consumer behavior. Since we are interested in explaining why consumers are loyal to one brand, we assume that two brands are perfect substitutes, although the same point can be made with indifference curves that display a diminishing marginal rate of substitution. In Figure 2-17a units of brand A are on the Y axis and units of brand B are on the x axis. Consumer 1 is willing to give up one unit of brand B for two units of brand A. His indifference curves, labeled $_1U_0$ and $_1U_1$, are solid straight lines with a slope of -2. In Figure 2-17b consumer 2 is willing to give up one unit of brand A for one unit of brand B and remain indifferent. Her indifference curves are solid straight lines with a slope of

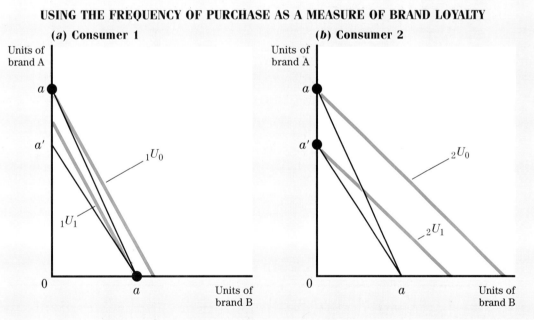

Figure 2-17 When the budget line is aa, both consumer 1 and consumer 2 maximize utility by always buying brand A. However, they respond differently if the price of brand A increases. An increase in the price shifts the budget line to $a'a$. Consumer 1 switches to brand B, but consumer 2 continues to purchase brand A. Although both consumers have a history of purchasing brand A, they exhibit different consumption responses to an increase in the price.

−1. When the indifference curves are straight lines, the consumer selects one brand or the other. (This is an extreme example of the specialization in consumption discussed earlier in the chapter.)

The initial budget line is *aa* for both consumers, and maximal utility is obtained by selecting market basket a and purchasing only brand A. Both consumers will have a history of purchasing only brand A and will exhibit brand loyalty to brand A for that reason.

By looking at the purchasing behavior of these two customers, a marketing manager might conclude that they are so loyal to brand A that it is the only one they consider when shopping and that they will continue to buy it even if its price increases. When the price of brand A increases, the budget line becomes *a′a*. Consumer 1 switches to brand B, whereas consumer 2 continues to purchase brand A. Although both consumers have identical histories of brand loyalty, their responses to a price cut are different. Therefore, a history of making repeat purchases does not mean that brand selection by all such consumers is independent of price.

Market Demand: Adding Up the Individual Demand Functions

The market demand function shows the total quantity demanded of a product by all consumers at each price. It is derived by summing the demand curve of each consumer horizontally. For each price, the quantity demanded by each consumer is added to derive the total quantity demanded in the market. Individual demand functions differ because income and tastes differ across consumers. Figure 2-18 shows the individual demand curves for X for three of a large number of consumers. The market demand function is *DD* and is a horizontal summation of the individual demand curves of all consumers in the market. Consumer 1 has a positive demand for X only if the price is less than P_1. The quantity demanded by consumers 2 and 3 becomes positive at prices less than P_2 and P_3, respectively.

> The **market demand function** is a horizontal summation of all individual consumer demand functions.

We refer to prices P_1, P_2, and P_3 as reservation prices for each of the consumers. A **reservation price** is the lowest price at which the consumer's quantity demanded is zero. Because the demand functions of consumers differ, they have different reservation prices.

Let us step back for a moment and review our progress. We have used the theory of consumer behavior to derive the individual consumer's demand function and the market demand function. The theory of consumer behavior is the cornerstone of the theory of market demand. In turn, the assumption of utility maximization is the cornerstone of the theory of consumer behavior.

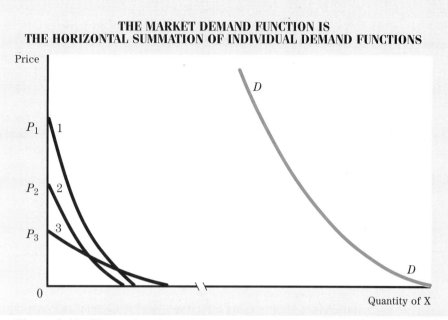

Figure 2-18   The market demand function is obtained by summing horizontally the demand curves of all consumers. The demand functions of only three among many consumers are shown. The quantity demanded by consumer 1 is positive only if the price of X is less than P_1. The quantity demanded by consumer 2 is positive if the price is less than P_2. Consumer 3 will not demand any units of X unless the price is less than P_3.

APPLICATION **2-4**

Why Are Americans Eating More Poultry and Less Red Meat?

In this application we investigate the causes of a shift in the eating habits of Americans. We want to determine the relative importance of price versus health concerns in explaining why Americans are consuming more chicken and turkey and less beef, pork, and other red meat. If the changes are due to increased health concerns, then we can treat this as a change in tastes caused by new information about meat consumption and health that shifts the demand function to the right for poultry and to the left for red meat. If price is the main reason for the increase in poultry consumption, then we are considering movement along a consumer's demand function.

Table 2-2 shows estimates of the per capita consumption of poultry (chicken and turkey) and of red meat (beef, pork, veal, and lamb) from 1970 to 1990. These are only estimates because the U.S. Department of Agriculture (USDA) takes the total production of poultry, converts it to the equivalent of boneless, trimmed meat,

Table 2-2   ESTIMATED PER CAPITA CONSUMPTION OF POULTRY AND RED MEAT

YEAR	PER CAPITA CONSUMPTION OF POULTRY (LB)	PER CAPITA CONSUMPTION OF RED MEAT (LB)
1970	33.8	132.3
1975	32.9	126.2
1980	40.6	126.4
1985	45.2	124.9
1990	55.4	112.4

Source: Judith Jones Putnam and Jane E. Allshouse, *Food Consumption, Prices, and Expenditures, 1970–1990*, SB-840, Economic Research Service, USDA, August 1992.

and divides by the total population. Per capita poultry consumption has increased, while red meat consumption has declined. Are health concerns the primary cause of the change, or can consumer selection be explained as a response to price changes?

Researchers at the USDA studied this question and came up with some interesting answers. Their findings suggest that price plays the dominant role. Figure 2-19 is a diagram of the inflation-adjusted retail price per pound of chicken and per capita pounds of chicken consumed from 1950 to 1990. Each point on the figure represents a yearly observation. From the figure you can see that the inflation-adjusted price of poultry declined dramatically over this period—by about 75 percent. Because the price of chicken has declined absolutely and relative to the prices of red meat, the per capita quantity demanded has increased.

It appears that the yearly observations made between 1950 and 1983 are the consequence of a stable per capita demand function and a supply function that has shifted downward over time. Figure 2-20 illustrates this process with a hypothetical supply function that shifts downward over time and a hypothetical stable demand function. The observations of price and per capita quantity consumed trace out the demand function of a representative consumer. This is one way of explaining the decline in the price of chicken and the increase in the quantities consumed over time. Because the price declines started in the 1950s, well before concerns about diet and health surfaced, it appears that changes in relative prices are primarily responsible for the changes in the type of meat Americans eat.

There is a hint that the demand function may have shifted to the right since 1983 because the inflation-adjusted price has not changed appreciably although per capita consumption has increased. However, the USDA researchers suggest that this is an artifact of the data. Per capita human consumption is not really growing as rapidly as Figure 2-19 indicates because of the growing use of chicken in pet foods.

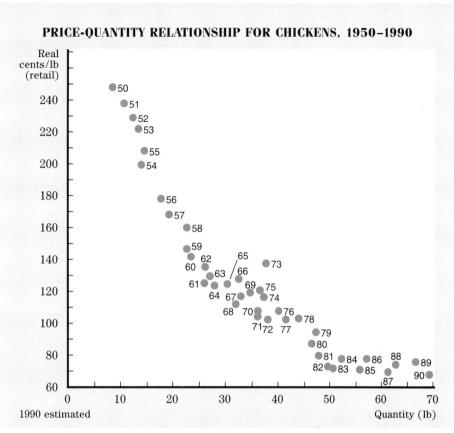

Figure 2-19   Annual observations of real retail chicken price and the number of gross pounds consumed appear to trace out the consumer's demand function. [*After Mark R. Weimar and Richard P. Stillman, "Market Trends Driving Broiler Consumption,"* Livestock and Poultry Situation and Outlook Report, *LPS-44, Economic Research Service, USDA, November 1990.*]

It appears that changes in the selection of meat by American consumers are largely explained by changes in the relative prices of the different types of meat and that health concerns play a secondary role in causing these changes.

2-8   GROSS SUBSTITUTES AND COMPLEMENTS

Chapter 1 described how the demand function for a good shifts when the price of another good changes. When air fares decrease, the market demand function for rental cars shifts to the right. On the other hand, the market demand function for 100 percent cotton shirts falls when the price of polyester shirts decreases. The demand for a good can either increase or decrease when the price of another good changes. The theory of consumer behavior can explain these different reactions.

Let's see how the quantity demanded of X by a utility-maximizing consumer

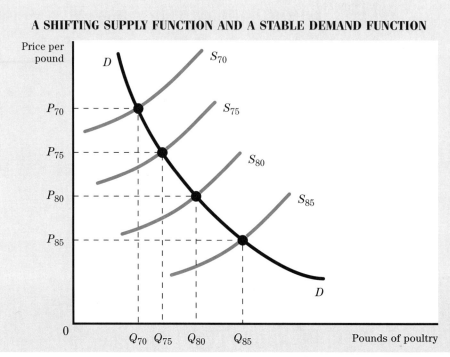

Figure 2-20   The demand function for poultry is stable, but the supply function shifts to the right because it becomes cheaper to produce poultry over time. The equilibrium prices and quantities trace out the demand function. This appears to be what has been happening in the poultry market.

changes when the price of Y, another good, changes. Suppose the price of X is P_X^1, consumer income is I, and both are constant. If the price of Y *decreases*, the consumer's budget constraint rotates around the x intercept and the individual selects a new market basket. Figure 2-21*a* shows that market basket A is purchased before and market basket B after the price of Y decreases. Market basket B includes more units of X. Given income and the price of X, a decrease in the price of Y *increases* the quantity demanded of X from X_1 to X_2. This is what happens to the demand function for rental cars when air fares fall, or to the demand function for software programs when prices of personal computers fall. Figure 2-21*b* shows that the demand function for rental cars shifts to the right from D to D' when air fares fall. At a price of P_X^1, the demand function for rental cars shifts to the right and the quantity demanded of rental cars increases from X_1 to X_2 when air fares decrease. When the demand function for X shifts to the right because the price of Y decreases, X and Y are called gross complements.

When the price of Y changes and the quantity demanded of X changes in the opposite direction, with the price of X held constant, X and Y are called **gross complements.**

GROSS COMPLEMENTS AND SUBSTITUTES

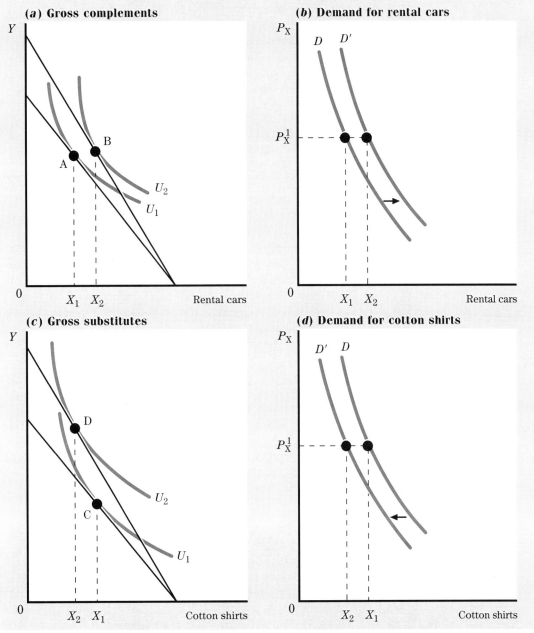

(a) Gross complements

(b) Demand for rental cars

(c) Gross substitutes

(d) Demand for cotton shirts

Figure 2-21 When the price of Y decreases, the demand function for X can shift outward (*b*) or shift inward (*d*). When a change in the price of Y changes the quantity demanded of X in the opposite direction, X and Y are called gross complements. (*b*) A decrease in air fares increases the quantity demanded of rental cars at the price of P_X^1. When a change in the price of Y changes the quantity demanded of X in the same direction at a given price of X, X and Y are called gross substitutes. (*d*) A decrease in the price of polyester shirts decreases the quantity demanded of cotton shirts at the price of P_X^1.

In Figure 2-21c the price of Y decreases, the price of X remains at P_X^1, and income is I. Before the price of Y changes, the consumer purchases market basket C. The budget constraint rotates around the intercept on the horizontal axis when the price of Y decreases, and the consumer purchases market basket D. The quantity demanded of X decreases from X_1 to X_2 when the price of Y decreases. This is what happens when the price of polyester shirts falls and the demand for cotton shirts shifts to the left. Figure 2-21d shows that the demand function for cotton shirts shifts to the left from D to D' when the price of polyester shirts falls. The quantity demanded decreases from X_1 to X_2 when the price of X is P_X^1. If a decrease in the price of Y causes the demand function of X to shift to the left and the quantity demanded of X to decrease, X and Y are called gross substitutes.

> When the price of Y changes and the quantity demanded of X changes in the same direction, with the price of X held constant, X and Y are called **gross substitutes.**

We can determine whether two goods are gross substitutes or complements by the sign of the cross arc elasticity of demand. The **cross arc elasticity of demand** measures the average percentage change in the quantity of one good relative to the average percentage change in the price of another. If the two goods are X and Y, the cross arc elasticity of demand is

$$E_{YP_X} = \frac{\Delta Y}{\Delta P_X} \frac{P_X^1 + P_X^2}{Y_1 + Y_2} \qquad \text{(Cross Arc Price Elasticity of Demand)} \qquad \textbf{(2-6)}$$

This expression is similar to the equation for the price elasticity of demand. The only difference is that the change in the quantity of X has been replaced by the change in the quantity of Y, and the sum of the units of X by the sum of the units of Y. Equation 2-6 measures the response of Y to a change in the price of X. If X and Y are gross complements, then $\Delta Y/\Delta P_X$ is negative and the arc cross price elasticity of demand is negative. If they are gross substitutes, then $\Delta Y/\Delta P_X$ is positive and the arc cross price elasticity of demand is positive.

2-9 APPLYING THE CONSUMER BEHAVIOR MODEL

This section applies the theory of consumer behavior by comparing the responses of consumers when they must spend a subsidy on a particular good or when the subsidy is unrestricted. This public policy question is treated in some detail to give you some practice in applying the consumer behavior model. It is hoped you will then be able to apply the theory successfully to other problems.

APPLICATION 2-5

Earmarked versus General-Purpose Grants

Governments provide grants to some of their citizens, and the often stated purpose of a grant program is to increase the well-being of the recipients. Frequently, grants are earmarked for spending on a specific good. For example, recipients of food stamps must spend them on food. What are the consequences of giving earmarked grants rather than unrestricted money grants?

Let's analyze a public program for providing decent housing to low-income families. Suppose the government issues a voucher of H dollars per month that must be spent on housing. The public expects the recipient to spend the earmarked grant on housing so that total spending on housing increases by the amount of the grant.

We can use the model of consumer behavior to analyze the consequences of providing an earmarked rather than a general-purpose grant of the same amount. Let's begin by showing the market basket the consumer selects before any grant is available. In Figure 2-22a and b total spending on all goods other than housing is on the vertical axis, and square footage of an apartment is on the horizontal axis. Without a grant program, consumers 1 and 2 each have an income of I^* and a budget constraint of BB', where the slope of the budget line is equal to the price

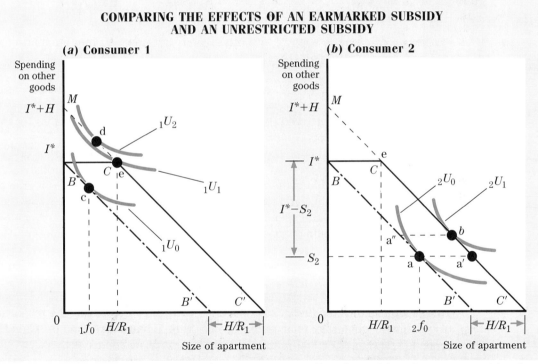

Figure 2-22 An earmarked subsidy offers the recipient fewer opportunities than a money subsidy with no strings attached. With an earmarked subsidy the budget constraint shifts horizontally from BB' to CC', and with a money subsidy it shifts outward from BB' to MCC'. (a) With a money subsidy consumer 1 can spend less than H dollars on additional rent if he so desires. Without a subsidy consumer 1 purchases market basket c. With a money subsidy he can reach the indifference curve $_1U_2$ by purchasing market basket d. With an earmarked subsidy consumer 1 reaches only indifference curve $_1U_1$ by purchasing market basket e. (b) Without a subsidy consumer 2 purchases market basket a. She purchases market basket b under either form of subsidy.

COMPARING THE EFFECTS OF AN EARMARKED SUBSIDY AND AN UNRESTRICTED SUBSIDY

per 100 square feet of living space. Let R_1 be the rent per 100 square feet of living space, assuming that an apartment with 400 square feet rents for half the amount of an apartment with 800 square feet. Let's consider consumer 2 first. Her indifference curves are $_2U_0$ and $_2U_1$ in Figure 2-22b. She maximizes utility by selecting market basket a which includes an apartment with $_2f_0$ square feet, spending S_2 on other goods, and spending $I^* - S_2$ on housing.

When an earmarked grant is made available, the government gives the recipient a voucher for H dollars per month and the landlord deposits the voucher and receives payment from the government. What we must do is determine how the budget constraint shifts when an earmarked grant is provided. By dividing H by R_1, we find out how many more square feet the recipient can rent with the earmarked subsidy. If the voucher is worth \$400 a month and R_1 equals \$200 per 100 square feet, the consumer can afford to rent an apartment that is larger by 200 square feet. For example, if she continues to spend S_2 on other goods, a larger apartment with $_2f_0 + 200$ square feet can be rented for a monthly rent of $I^* - S_2 + H$. With the earmarked grant, market basket a' becomes an affordable market basket. If the consumer was homeless before the grant became available and spent nothing on housing and I^* on other goods (the market basket at point B), she can continue to spend I^* on other goods but now can rent an apartment of 200 hundred square feet. Therefore, she can purchase market basket e on the solid line CC'. With the earmarked grant, apartment size can be increased by H/R_1 for every market basket on BB'. A grant that earmarks spending on housing shifts BB' horizontally, and so the consumer's new budget line becomes the line CC'. Not surprisingly, an earmarked grant expands the affordable opportunities for the recipient, but only in a particular way.

However, an unrestricted grant of H dollars opens up still more opportunities for the recipient. If she receives an unrestricted money grant of H dollars, BB' shifts outward and becomes the new budget line MCC'. The consumer is free to spend *all* the money grant on other goods. Therefore, she has the option of spending $I^* + H$ on other goods and spending nothing on housing. An unrestricted grant is similar to an increase in income, and the budget constraint shifts out parallel. The difference between the budget line with a money grant and with an earmarked grant is the segment MC. This segment becomes affordable with a money grant but not with an earmarked grant. All other things being equal, the recipient will prefer a money grant to an earmarked grant because she can afford more market baskets with an unrestricted money grant.

For some consumers utility will be lower with an earmarked grant than with a money grant, and for others there will be no effect on utility. We can use the model to illustrate the two cases: If the recipient of an unrestricted grant rents an apartment smaller than H/R_1 feet, utility can be lower with an earmarked grant. In Figure 2-22a consumer 1's indifference curves are $_1U_0$, $_1U_1$, and $_1U_2$. Without a grant, he purchases market basket c where the indifference curve $_1U_0$ is tangent to the budget line BB'. This individual rents a very small apartment of size $_1f_0$ and spends little on housing. When a money grant becomes available, he purchases market basket d where the indifference curve $_1U_2$ is tangent to MCC'. With an earmarked grant he maximizes utility by purchasing market basket e where the indifference curve $_1U_2$ touches the edge of the budget line CC' and rents a larger apartment of size H/R_1 than with a money grant. However, he reaches only $_1U_1$ with an earmarked grant and so is worse off with an earmarked than with an unrestricted grant.

On the other hand, in Figure 2-22*b* consumer 2 starts with market basket a and purchases market basket b when either an earmarked or a money grant becomes available. Market basket b is affordable with either type of grant; however, consumer 2 does not increase spending on housing by the full amount of the grant. That would occur only if she continued to spend the same amount as before on other goods and spent all the grant on housing. However, this does not happen because she is better off by increasing spending on other goods when she receives a grant. What she does is spend less of I^* on housing than before and more on other goods by purchasing market basket a″ with I^* and then uses the earmarked grant to increase spending on housing so that she ends up with market basket b. With either grant the recipient responds by not spending as much of her private income on housing as before and more on other goods. Although total spending on housing increases, so does total spending on other goods. Therefore, total spending on housing does not increase by the amount of the grant. The intuition behind this result goes something like this. If your monthly income increased by $500 a month, would you spend all the increase on housing? Chances are you would spend some of it on housing, some on food, some on clothing, and so on. The grant would raise your income, and you will maximize utility by spending the higher income on all goods, not just on housing.

If the goal of a grant program is to maximize the utility of the recipient, then an earmarked grant program does not achieve that goal. If maximizing utility is the goal, grants should take the form of unrestricted money grants. To explain the nature of these subsidy programs, we have to assume that the well-being of the givers is also important. They appear to be saying that *their* utility is higher if they know or think they know that the subsidy is being spent in particular ways and on particular goods. The givers believe that recipients must spend the grant on housing or food and not on other goods that the givers consider less essential.

SUMMARY

- A consumer ranks all market baskets while satisfying the consistency and transitivity conditions.
- An indifference curve represents a set of market baskets where the well-being of the consumer is the same.
- The marginal rate of substitution is the slope of the indifference curve. It is negative and measures the subjective tradeoff between two goods such that the consumer remains indifferent.
- Indifference curves have negative slopes if more of each good increases well-being and the curves do not touch.
- The budget constraint of a consumer determines what market baskets the individual can afford.
- The goal of a consumer is to reach the highest indifference curve while satisfying the budget constraint.

- A consumer who purchases two goods maximizes utility by making the marginal rate of substitution equal to the slope of the budget line. The personal tradeoff between the two goods is equal to the market's tradeoff.
- The consumer's demand function for a good is derived by determining the quantity demanded at each price of the good, holding other prices and consumer income constant.
- The market demand function is the horizontal sum of the individual demand functions.
- When the price of a related product changes and the quantity demanded of this product changes in the opposite direction, the two products are gross complements.
- When the price of a related product changes and the quantity demanded of this product changes in the same direction, the two products are gross substitutes.

KEY TERMS

Market basket	Transitivity
Indifference curve	Marginal rate of substitution
Diminishing marginal rate of substitution	Perfect substitutes and perfect complements
Indifference map	Budget constraint
Affordable market baskets	Maximal utility
Specialization in consumption	Composite good
Consumer demand function	Market demand function
Gross substitutes and gross complements	Earmarked and unrestricted subsidies

REVIEW QUESTIONS

1. What is the marginal rate of substitution? What is the marginal rate of substitution between nickels and dimes?
2. What happens to the budget constraint if the price of X and Y both increase by K percent?
3. What happens to the budget constraint if income and the price of X both increase by K percent?
4. If the price of Y is $8, the price of X is $4, and the marginal rate of substitution with my current market basket is -2, will my utility increase if I purchase more X and less Y?
5. If I maximize utility by purchasing X and Y, what must be the relationship between my marginal rate of substitution and the slope of the budget constraint?
6. If I maximize utility by purchasing only Y, what must be the relationship between my marginal rate of substitution and the slope of the budget constraint?
7. When the price of X is $10 and the price of Y is $30, a consumer purchases 100 units of X and 50 units of Y. Because 100 units of X and 50 units of Y are

purchased, the consumer must be willing to substitute 2 units of X for 1 unit of Y to remain indifferent. Given the prices, 3 units of X can be substituted for each unit of Y along the budget constraint. Therefore, the consumer is not maximizing utility. Explain why you agree or disagree with this statement.

8. If the price of X falls and I purchase more units of X while spending more on all other goods, my demand function for X can be either price-elastic or price-inelastic. Explain why you agree or disagree with this statement.

9. A firm is considering two price policies. The first policy will reduce the price from the current price of P_r to 75 percent of P_r for every unit purchased. The second will reduce the price of every second unit purchased to 50 percent of P_r. Draw the consumer's budget constraint for the two price policies.

10. According to the terms of a buying club, a consumer with income I who joins will save 5 percent on the price of every good purchased. Using a graph, show the largest membership fee M the buying club can charge and still convince the consumer to join.

11. What does a consumer's utility function look like if X and Y are perfect substitutes?

12. What does a consumer's utility function look like if X and Y are perfect complements?

13. This question refers to Figure 2-15. At the break-even cost, the slope of the budget constraint is $-0.4P_r$ if the golfer joins the golf club. What must the slope of the consumer's indifference curve be at this point if the individual maximizes utility by joining the club?

EXERCISES

1. Suppose you buy two goods, beef and fish. As the price of beef falls relative to the price of fish, you buy slightly more beef than formerly. Show this behavior with indifference curves and locate your approximate position.

2. The following data show the prices of X and Y, the annual income of the consumer, and the quantities of X consumed during the last 6 years.

YEAR	PRICE OF X ($)	QUANTITY OF X	PRICE OF Y ($)	ANNUAL INCOME ($)
1987	100	80	50	20,000
1988	110	90	40	18,000
1989	90	100	40	18,000
1990	100	100	50	20,000
1991	100	90	40	20,000
1992	100	110	40	25,000

a. What pair of years would you use to calculate the price elasticity of the demand for X? Explain why you selected this pair. What is the arc price elasticity of demand for X?

b. The calculation of the price elasticity of the demand for X is biased because of a change in preference for X and Y if you use which two years to calculate the price elasticity?

c. Given your answer to question *b*, what two years would you use to determine if X and Y are gross complements or gross substitutes?

d. What pair of years would you use to calculate the price elasticity of the demand for Y? Explain why you selected this pair of years.

3. What does the consumer's demand function for X look like if X and Y are perfect substitutes?

4. What is the consumer's demand function for X if X and Y are perfect complements?

5. By accumulating miles on business trips, an employee can convert mileage into "free" leisure trips for personal use. Consider a consumer whose utility depends on (*a*) spending on other goods and (*b*) T airplane trips for leisure travel. In the absence of a frequent flyer program the consumer has an income of I and the price of a trip is P_a.

a. On a graph find the market basket that maximizes the utility of the consumer. Suppose the employee maximizes utility by taking T_1 leisure trips.

b. Show how the frequent flyer program shifts the budget line of the consumer. Assume that the employee flies enough miles to qualify for T^* additional leisure trips.

c. Will the total number of leisure trips the employee takes increase from T_1 to $T_1 + T^*$? Explain why or why not.

d. Assume that the employer requires all reservations for business trips be made by the company, so that the employee does not receive any leisure trips from frequent flyer programs, but increases the compensation of the employee by $P_r T^*$. If the employee pays 28 percent of income in taxes, what will the individual's budget constraint look like? Explain why taxes on income cause the employee to prefer benefits from the frequent flyer program over an increase in income.

6. Absenteeism is a costly problem for many firms. It disrupts production and reduces labor productivity. Suppose a firm plans to reward attendance. Currently, the firm pays production workers a wage of D dollars per day.

   Assume that the "two" goods in the utility function of a worker are spending on other goods and days of leisure (L). The worker will consume more of both "goods" if the budget constraint shifts outward parallel. Let days of leisure of a worker be $L = 365 - W$, where W is the number of days worked. The income earned by a worker is spent on goods.

   A review of the attendance records of all production workers employed by the firm reveals the average number of days worked per year was 210. Some worked as many as 250 days per year, whereas others showed up for work as few as 180 days. Dissatisfied with this performance, management would like to raise the average to 220 days per year. To reduce absenteeism, it is considering this proposal: Offer a flat annual bonus of B dollars to each production worker who works at least 220 days a year.

   a. Write out an expression for the income of the worker. Draw the budget constraint for a typical production worker.

   b. With the aid of a graph show how the employer's proposal changes the budget constraint of the worker.
   c. Show the effect of the proposal on the total days worked by employees who were initially (1) working less than 220 days per year; (2) working 220 or more days per year.
   d. Will the proposal raise the average days worked to 220? Explain why or why not.
7. When a firm charges a price P' for each unit, some consumers do not purchase the product. To induce these individuals to buy, the firm offers a discount of 25 percent on just the second unit. Even with a discount on just the second unit (*a*) some consumers still do not try the product, (*b*) others purchase one unit, and (*c*) still others purchase two units. Are all three responses to the quantity discount consistent with utility maximization? Use indifference curves to explain your answer.
8. To encourage more spending on education by local school districts, the state government plans to offer aid. Suppose that within each district all families are alike but that districts differ because of differences in income and spend different amounts on education. A particular district is currently spending $500 per student, and the state would like to raise this amount to $550 per student. The utility function of each family in the district includes two goods, spending on other goods and spending on education. The state is considering two proposals:

   ▪ *Lump sum grant 1.* The state will pay $50 per child toward educational expenditures if the district spends more than $100 per child.
   ▪ *Lump sum grant 2.* The state will pay $50 per child toward educational expenditures if the district spends more than $550 per child.

   a. Show the indifference curves of a representative family in the district that spends $500 per child. Show how each proposal would alter the budget constraint of the family.
   b. With the aid of graphs, indicate whether the families in a district are more likely to increase per pupil expenditure (i.e., total per pupil expenditure less per pupil state aid) under proposal 1 or under proposal 2.
   c. Is it possible to determine if total spending on education per pupil (i.e., local plus state spending) will be higher under proposal 1 or under proposal 2? Explain your answer.

PROBLEM SET

Will a Challenge Grant Increase Alumni Contributions?

The year is 2021. You received your undergraduate degree in the early 1990s and have had a successful and financially rewarding career. Over the years you have made annual contributions to your university and are aware of its progress and its problems. Because you hold a warm spot in your heart for your alma mater, you decide to do something special by giving it a major donation.

During a recent conversation, the president of the university expressed a desire to expand the science building, to find a new home for the social sciences faculty, and to improve the facilities for intramural athletics. High on the president's wish list is a major donation and an increase in the percentage of contributors donating at least $100 per year from the current 35 percent to 50 percent (column 2 in Table 2-3 indicates 65 percent of donors give less than $100). She reports that most alumni increase their contributions as their income increases.

You decide that the time is right to make a large donation to the university, but you want to create an incentive mechanism that will raise alumni contributions. A challenge grant seems to be the perfect solution. You will donate $100 to the university for any alumni gift between $100 and $299. You hope the challenge grant will stimulate those giving less than $100 to increase their contribution to $100, and some of those giving between $100 and $299 to increase their contribution also.

You ask the alumni office to estimate how the challenge grant will change the distribution of contributions. The predicted distribution in column 3 of Table 2-3 shows that the percentage giving $100 or more will increase to 50 percent. The alumni office also predicts that the percentage giving between $100 and $299 will increase and that those who give more than $299 will give with or without a challenge grant.

You hire an economist to evaluate the predictions made by the alumni office. In particular, you ask about the effect of the challenge grant on (1) those currently contributing less than $100, (2) those contributing between $100 and $299, and (3) those contributing more than $300.

To analyze the effects of the challenge grant, the economist builds a simple model of the behavior of an individual donor. Suppose the two goods in the utility function of an individual donor are (1) a composite good that represents spending on other goods and (2) the total donation to the university that is due to the individual's contribution. This assumes that each contributor receives utility from

Table 2-3   ACTUAL AND PREDICTED DISTRIBUTION OF CONTRIBUTORS BY AMOUNT CONTRIBUTED

AMOUNT CONTRIBUTED BY EACH INDIVIDUAL IN 2020 ($) (1)	PERCENT OF THOSE GIVING IN 2020 (2)	PREDICTED PERCENT OF THOSE GIVING IN 2021 BECAUSE OF CHALLENGE GRANT (3)
$0–$49	40	35
$50–$99	25	15
$100–$149	13	27
$150–$199	10	10
$200–$299	7	8
$300–	5	5

THE EFFECT OF A CHALLENGE GRANT ON ALUMNI DONATING LESS THAN $100

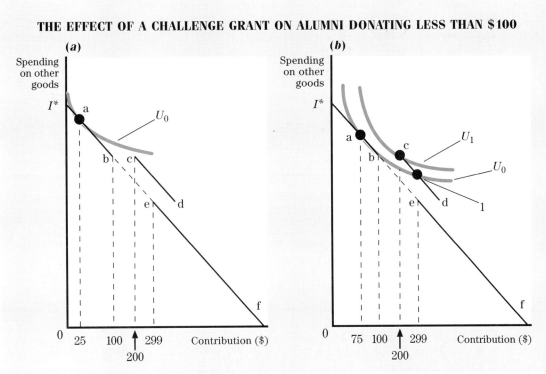

Figure 2-23 (*a*) The consumer is unaffected by the challenge grant and continues to donate $25 to the university. (*b*) The consumer purchases market basket c and increases his or her donation from $75 to $100 because of the challenge grant.

the sum of his or her contribution and the contribution from the challenge grant that is triggered by the individual's contribution. If the utility of the donor depends *only* on the individual's direct contribution, the challenge grant will have no incentive effect.

The economist first considers the effect of the challenge grant on donors currently contributing less than $100. The donor in Figure 2-23*a* is unaffected by the challenge grant. Total spending on other goods is on the vertical axis, and the total contribution that results from the individual's donation is on the horizontal axis. The income of this donor is I^*, and the budget constraint is the line I^*f. Without a challenge grant every dollar contributed to the university by this individual reduces the amount spent on other goods by a corresponding dollar. Therefore the slope of the budget constraint equals -1. Market basket a maximizes the donor's utility because it makes the marginal rate of substitution equal to the slope of the budget constraint. The individual in Figure 2-23*a* has a modest income and contributes just $25 per year.

How does the challenge grant change the budget constraint of this consumer? If the individual contributes less than $100, the budget constraint remains the same. If the individual contributes between $100 and $299, the contribution triggers another $100. Hypothetically, you could think of the donor as receiving a check for $100 from the challenge grant, forwarded to the university with a solemn promise to contribute any amount from $100 to $299. Therefore, for gifts between $100 and $299, the budget constraint shifts horizontally to the right by $100. For example, the donor's contribution of $100 is augmented by $100 from the challenge grant, so that the total contribution is $200. If any amount between $100 and $299 is contributed, the donation triggers another $100 contribution. Any gift of more than $299 does not qualify for a challenge grant. With the challenge grant the new budget constraint of the donor becomes the line segments I^* to b, c to d, and e to f. There is a discontinuity between points b and c and between points d and e. Because the indifference curve U_0 in Figure 2-23a does not intersect the new budget line, the consumer maximizes utility by continuing to donate $25 to the university. The challenge grant has no effect on the consumer's decision.

The consumer in Figure 2-23b has a different preference map but the same income. Without the challenge grant the indifference curve U_0 is tangent to the budget constraint with market basket a when the individual donates $75 to the university. With the challenge grant this donor's contribution increases from $75 to $100 and the donor reaches U_1 by contributing $100 per year. This case differs from the previous one because U_0 cuts through the new budget constraint at point 1. The utility of this individual is increased by the purchase of market basket c. He or she contributes $100 and thereby triggers a $100 challenge contribution. The challenge grant induces this individual to contribute $25 more and increases the total amount donated by $125, that is, $25 from the individual and $100 from the challenge grant. Without the challenge grant the donor must reduce spending on other goods by $25 to donate $25 more. With the challenge grant the opportunity cost of giving declines because a $25 reduction in spending on other goods increases total contributions to the university by $125, not $25. For this donor, the challenge grant has reduced the price of giving to the university.

Donors who contributed amounts slightly less than $100 are more likely to respond to the challenge grant than those giving substantially less than $100, although some of these alumni could also be affected. The predictions of the alumni office look reasonable. Of those giving less than $50 a smaller fraction respond to the challenge grant (the percentage drops by only five percentage points) than in the group giving between $50 and $99 (the percentage giving drops by 10 percentage points).

Use the model of consumer behavior to explain why you do or do not agree with the remaining predictions of the alumni office concerning the effect of the challenge grant.

1. Will donors who give between $100 and $299 increase their individual contributions?

2. Are donors who give more than $299 unaffected by the challenge grant?

3. Comment on the incentive effects of a challenge grant in view of your answers to questions 1 and 2.

4. Will the challenge grant increase total private contributions? Explain why or why not.

CHAPTER 3

EXTENDING THE THEORY OF CONSUMER BEHAVIOR

* More difficult material.

Section 3-1 expands on the theory of consumer behavior and explains why a price cut causes the quantity demanded to increase more for one consumer than for another. To improve your understanding of the different consumer responses to a price cut, each consumer's change in the quantity demanded can be separated into two parts. One part of the increase occurs because a price cut releases income that can be used to purchase more of the product. This effect is called the income effect. The other part of the increase occurs because the good whose price has fallen is now cheaper relative to other goods and the consumer substitutes toward the lower-priced good and demands more units. This effect is called the substitution effect. By working with the income and substitution effects, we can identify those situations when a price change will cause a larger change in the quantity demanded.

A consumer's utility is increased by purchasing rather than doing without a product. Consumer surplus is a dollar measure of how much more an individual would be willing to pay for the product rather than do without it. Because consumer surplus measures how much more the buyer would be willing to pay for so many units of a good, it is of considerable interest to a seller because it represents a potential source of extra revenue. The second part of the chapter shows how to derive consumer surplus from the consumer's indifference curve and to determine when a seller can accurately estimate consumer surplus from the buyer's demand function.

In the last section of the chapter the consumer is placed in an uncertain environment where his or her decision does not lead to a known outcome but to multiple possible outcomes. Of interest is how decisions are made in an uncertain environment. Why do some individuals go out of their way to avoid risky situations, whereas others take risks and flourish in risky environments? Some choose to go into industries where there is considerable uncertainty about what they will earn, whereas others choose a more secure existence by selecting employment where their income is more predictable. We will explain why some people are willing to pay an insurance premium that lowers their wealth to convert a risky situation into a more certain one.

3-1   THE SHAPE OF THE CONSUMER'S DEMAND FUNCTION

Since consumers respond differently to a price cut, they must have different demand functions. A price reduction can cause the quantity demanded to increase more for one consumer than for another. Figure 3-1a and b shows the indifference curves for two consumers. Spending on other goods is on the vertical axis, and units of X are on the horizontal axis. Although both consumers purchase goods at the same prices, they have different tastes and incomes. Initially, consumer 1 maximizes utility by selecting market basket A, while consumer 2 purchases market basket C. When the price of X decreases, the budget line rotates around the intercept on the y axis and consumer 1 purchases market basket B while consumer 2 selects market basket D. The different demand functions dd of the two consumers are shown in Figure 3-1c and d. When the price changes by ΔP, the quantity

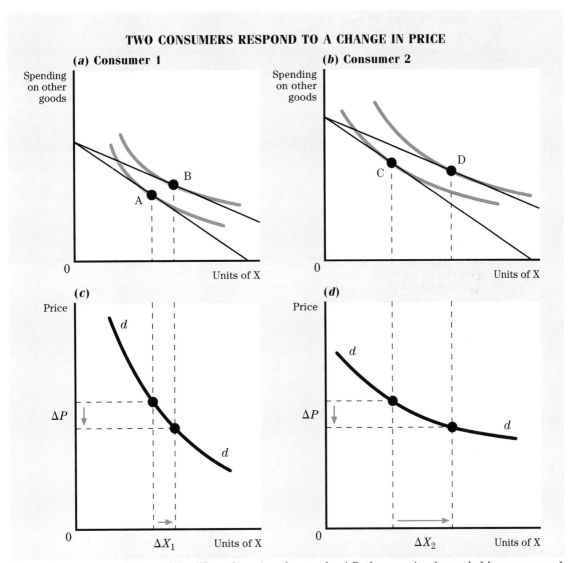

Figure 3-1   When the price changes by ΔP, the quantity demanded by consumer 1 increases by only ΔX_1. It increases by ΔX_2, a larger amount, for consumer 2.

demanded by consumer 1 increases by only ΔX_1, whereas the quantity demanded by consumer 2 increases by ΔX_2. The two consumers respond differently to the price cut.

This section identifies the factors that determine the different responses to a price change. To start this investigation, consider someone who purchases X and a composite good. How does a change in the price of X affect the consumer's behavior? From the buyer's perspective, a price reduction of X immediately releases income that was formerly spent to purchase X. For example, you are richer by $10 if you are consuming 10 units of X and the price of X falls by $1. You can use these funds by purchasing more units of X or by spending more on the composite good, or both. So, a price reduction creates an increase in disposable funds that the consumer can use to purchase more of some or all goods. If the price decreases by ΔP and X equals the number of units initially consumed, the individual now has $-(\Delta P)X$ more income to spend on X and the composite good. Because a price cut releases income, it resembles a parallel shift outward in the budget constraint, and so the consumer can select a new market basket on a higher indifference curve.

> The change in quantity demanded of X due to the change in money income is the **income effect.**

However, a price cut does more than simply release income so that the consumer can increase the demand for some or all goods. A price cut makes X cheaper relative to other goods. What is measured with the substitution effect is the change in the number of units that the consumer demands because the relative price of X falls when the consumer's utility remains constant. If the consumer remains on the same indifference curve, he or she can be expected to purchase more units of X than before because X is now cheaper relative to other goods. The substitution effect measures the change in the quantity demanded of X when the relative price of X changes and utility remains constant.

Hypothetically, we view the consumer as separating the total change in the quantity demanded of X because of a price change into changes caused by the income and by the substitution effect. This introduction to these effects is altogether too brief. We need to discuss each effect in greater detail and show how to measure each one. Then, we will join the two effects and describe situations where the consumer's response to a price change will be large or small.

Measuring the Income Effect

Let's take up the income effect first. Figure 3-2a shows two of the consumer's indifference curves, U_0 and U_1. Total spending S on other goods is on the vertical axis, and units of X are on the horizontal axis. Consider a situation where the income of the consumer is I_0 and the price of X is P_X. The initial budget constraint of this individual is aa', and it has a slope of $-P_X$ because spending on the composite good declines by $-P_X$ for each unit of X consumed. The buyer maximizes utility subject to the budget constraint aa' by purchasing market basket A. The marginal rate of substitution equals the slope of the budget constraint when the consumer purchases X_0 units of X and spends S_0 dollars on other goods. If income increases to I_1, the budget constraint shifts outward parallel and becomes bb'. The consumer purchases market basket B, which includes X_1 units of X, and spends S_1 dollars on other goods. This consumer demands more units of X and spends more on other goods because income increases and prices remain constant. Only two points of tangency between the budget constraint and an indifference

NORMAL AND INFERIOR GOODS

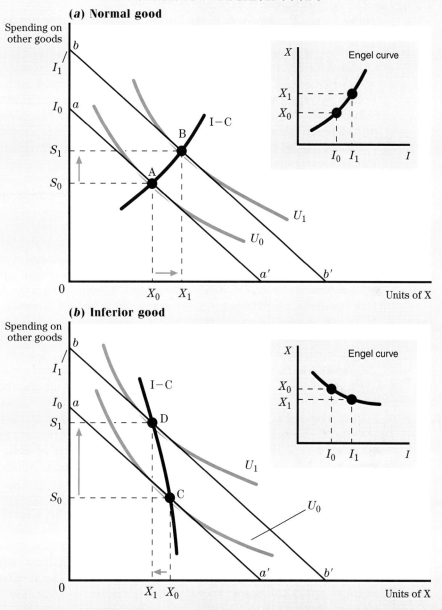

Figure 3-2 (*a*) An increase in income shifts the budget constraint from aa' to bb'. The consumer increases the consumption of X from X_0 to X_1 units. The income-consumption curve connects all points of tangency between the budget constraint and the indifference curve as income increases. When an increase in income increases the number of units consumed, the good is a normal good. The Engel curve shows the relationship between the quantity demanded and the income of the consumer and has a positive slope when the good is a normal good. The utility function in (*b*) is different from the utility function in (*a*). (*b*) An increase in income reduces the number of units consumed from X_0 to X_1. When an increase in income reduces the number of units consumed, the good is an inferior good and the Engel curve has a negative slope.

curve are shown, but there is one for every level of income. All points of tangency between successive budget constraints and the appropriate indifference curves can be connected to form the **income-consumption curve,** I-C.

An **Engel curve** shows the relationship between the quantity demanded of X and the income of the consumer with prices held constant. In the smaller graph in Figure 3-2*a* consumer income is on the horizontal axis and units of X are on the vertical axis. The Engel curve for X has a positive slope when X is a normal good and shows that the quantity demanded increases from X_0 to X_1 units when income increases from I_0 to I_1.

> When the quantity demanded of a good changes in the same direction as the change in income, we call the good a **normal good** and the Engel curve has a positive slope.

Some examples of normal goods are housing, durable goods, eating out, and vacations. Chances are that your first house will be a starter house with limited square footage, but that you will move to larger quarters with greater privacy when your income increases. Durable goods are often normal goods. When income is low, families opt for a lower-priced economy car that provides basic transportation, but when income increases, they may purchase a larger automobile with a better and quieter ride and more safety features. As another example, vacation days usually increase with family income.

An increase in income does not always increase the quantity consumed, however. In Figure 3-2*b* the indifference curves are such that an increase in income *decreases* the quantity of X consumed. Initially, the budget constraint of the consumer is *aa'* when income is I_0. She purchases market basket C with X_0 units of X and spends S_0 on other goods. After income increases to I_1, the budget constraint becomes *bb'* and the consumer prefers market basket D, and so the quantity demanded of X decreases fom X_0 to X_1 and spending on other goods increases from S_0 to S_1. The utility of the consumer is higher, although she purchases fewer units of X. An increase in income of $I_1 - I_0$ decreases the quantity demanded by $X_1 - X_0 < 0$. When the quantity demanded changes in the direction *opposite* the income change, the good is called an inferior good. The smaller graph in Figure 3-2*b* shows the Engel curve has a negative slope when the good is an inferior good because the quantity demanded decreases when income increases and prices are held constant. As an aside, it should be noted that inferior goods are not inferior in the everyday use of the word.

> When the quantity demanded of a good changes in the direction opposite the change in income, the good is an **inferior good** and the Engel curve has a negative slope.

An example of an inferior good might be hamburger meat, polyester clothing, or shopping at second-hand clothing stores. Although it is common to classify a product as either a normal or an inferior good, this does not mean that everyone treats the product in the same way at all income levels. A consumer might consider a good a normal good for some changes in income and an inferior good for other changes in income. Another point to keep in mind is the heterogeneity among consumers. Some consumers may treat a product as an inferior good, whereas others treat it as a normal good. Peanut butter may be an inferior good for you but a normal good for your younger sister or brother.

Income Elasticity of Demand

Income elasticity is a measure that economists use to compare the percentage change in the quantity demanded relative to a percentage change in income. The expression for the arc income elasticity is

$$E_I = \frac{\dfrac{\Delta X}{(X_0 + X_1)/2}}{\dfrac{\Delta I}{(I_0 + I_1)/2}} = \frac{\Delta X}{\Delta I}\frac{I_0 + I_1}{X_0 + X_1} \qquad \text{(Arc Income Elasticity of Demand)} \qquad \text{(3-1)}$$

$$= \frac{X_1 - X_0}{I_1 - I_0}\frac{I_0 + I_1}{X_0 + X_1}$$

Equation 3-1 shows the arc income elasticity of demand as the ratio of the change in the quantity demanded to the average quantity demanded at the two income levels, divided by the change in income relative to the average income when prices are held constant. E_I is positive for a normal good because the quantity demanded increases when income increases, and is negative for an inferior good because the quantity demanded decreases when income increases.

> The **arc income elasticity of demand** measures the average percentage change in the quantity demanded relative to the average percentage change in income.

Even if a good is a normal good, that does not necessarily mean that a consumer will spend an increasing share of income on it as income increases. This occurs only if E_I is greater than 1. Then the percentage increase in the quantity demanded exceeds the percentage increase in income, and so the share of income spent on X increases when income increases because prices are constant. If $0 < E_I < 1$, a good is a normal good but the consumer spends a decreasing share of income on it as income rises because prices are constant. After you receive your degree, your income will increase and you will consume more units per year of most food items, although the share of income spent on food will probably go down. On the other hand, the share of income spent on leisure time activities will probably increase.

Measuring the Substitution Effect

The substitution effect focuses on how a consumer responds when the relative price of X changes in such a way that his or her utility remains constant.

The **substitution effect** measures the change in the quantity demanded of X due to a change in the relative price of X with utility held constant.

How can we measure the substitution effect? From Chapter 2 you have learned that the budget constraint rotates around the intercept on the vertical axis when the price of X changes while income and other prices remain constant. If the price of X falls and the budget constraint rotates outward, the consumer purchases a different market basket on a higher indifference curve, and so the consumer's utility increases. However, the substitution effect measures the change in the quantity demanded when relative prices change with utility held constant. To keep the consumer on the original indifference curve so that utility is unchanged, we change money income as the price changes by just enough so that the consumer finds a new market basket on the original indifference curve where the slope of the new budget constraint equals the slope of the indifference curve. The substitution effect measures the change in the quantity demanded of X after a change in relative prices with utility held constant.

Figure 3-3 shows how the substitution effect can be found when the initial price of X is P_X. The consumer starts with market basket A on indifference curve U_0 and purchases X_0 units of X while spending S_0 dollars on other goods on budget line aa. If the price of X falls to P'_X, the budget line aa in Figure 3-3 will rotate outward around point a and become the dashed budget line ab. If nothing else changes, the consumer will reach a higher indifference curve. To prevent utility from increasing, we decrease income by enough to shift the budget line ab back toward U_0 until it becomes cc where it is tangent to indifference curve U_0 at market basket B. In this way we see that the reduction in the relative price of X causes the consumer to substitute market basket B for market basket A and therefore to increase the quantity demanded from X_0 to X_1. The relative price of X is lower, and so cc is flatter than aa. The consumer responds to a fall in the relative price of X by purchasing more units of X and spending less on other goods. Therefore, the sign of the substitution effect is negative because a change in the relative price of X changes the quantity demanded in the opposite direction.[1]

Combining the Two Effects

Let's combine the income and substitution effects and show how an increase or decrease in price changes the quantity demanded. The resulting change is the sum of the two effects. We can express this as

Change in quantity demanded	=	Change in quantity demanded due to substitution effect	+	Change in quantity demanded due to income effect

---

[1] The substitution effect is zero in the special case when X is a perfect complement and the indifference curve is L-shaped.

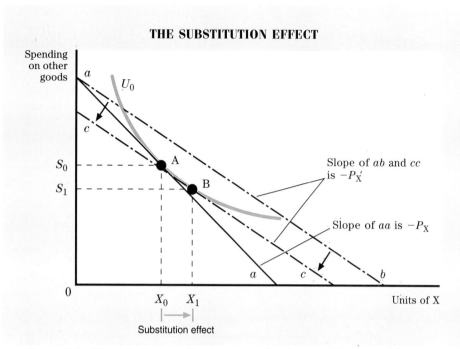

Figure 3-3   The substitution effect measures the change in the quantity demanded of X when the relative price of X changes and utility is constant. A decrease in the price of X offset by a decrease in income keeps the consumer on the same indifference curve. The consumer moves from the original market basket A to market basket B. The quantity demanded increases from X_0 to X_1 because of a fall in the relative price of X. The substitution effect is negative. A change in the relative price of X changes the quantity demanded in the opposite direction.

Figure 3-4 shows how both effects cause the quantity demanded to change. The initial budget constraint is aa when income is I_0 and the price of X is P_X. The consumer maximizes utility by selecting market basket A, purchasing X_0 units, and spending S_0 dollars on other goods. When the price of X decreases to P_X', the budget line becomes ab. The slope of ab equals the slope of the indifference curve U_1 when the consumer selects market basket B, purchases X_2 units of X, and spends S_2 dollars on other goods. The total quantity demanded increases from X_0 to X_2 when the price falls, and so the demand function in Figure 3-4b has a negative slope.

The increase in the quantity demanded caused by the price cut, $X_2 - X_0$, is partly due to the substitution effect and partly due to the income effect. Recall that the substitution effect measures the change in the quantity demanded when the relative price of X changes with utility held constant. To find this quantity, we shift the budget constraint to cc by decreasing the relative price of X and changing income so that utility is unchanged. The consumer selects market basket C where

COMBINING THE INCOME EFFECT AND THE SUBSTITUTION EFFECT

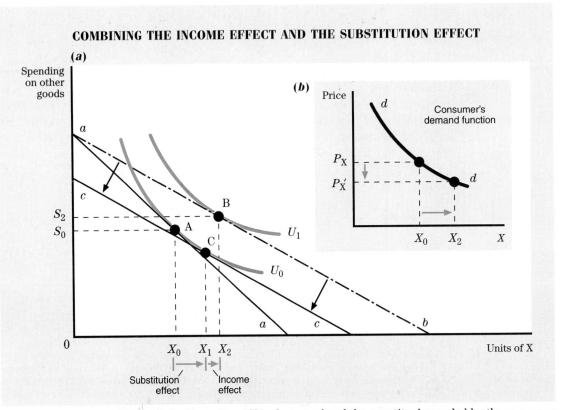

Figure 3-4   The price of X is decreased and the quantity demanded by the consumer increases from X_0 to X_2. The total change can be separated into the sum of the quantity demanded because of the substitution effect and because of the income effect. The change in the quantity demanded because of the substitution effect is $X_1 - X_0$. The change in the quantity demanded because of the income effect is $X_2 - X_1$. Because the good is a normal good, an increase in income increases the quantity demanded. (*b*) The demand function of this consumer has a negative slope.

the slope of *cc* equals the slope of indifference curve U_0. The substitution effect is the increase in the quantity demanded from X_0 to X_1 units. The income effect shifts the budget line parallel from *cc* to *ab* because the price reduction makes income available to spend on X and on the composite good. The consumer moves from market basket C to market basket B, and the income effect increases the quantity demanded by $X_2 - X_1$. Combining the two effects, we find the quantity demanded increases from X_0 to X_2.

When the good is a normal good, the income effect augments the substitution effect, and so the quantity demanded must increase when the price falls and the demand function has a negative slope.

A consumer demands more units at a lower price if the good is a normal good, and so the demand function of the consumer has a negative slope.

We cannot predict the slope of the consumer's demand function when the good is an inferior good. Figure 3-5 shows a case where the good is an inferior good *and* the income effect is larger than the substitution effect. In this case a decrease in the price of X *decreases* the quantity demanded. The initial budget constraint is *aa*. The consumer purchases X_0 units of X with market basket A in Figure 3-5a. When the price falls from P_X to P_X', the budget constraint becomes *ab*, the consumer selects market basket B, and the total quantity demanded decreases from X_0 to X_2. Figure 3-5b shows the demand curve has a positive slope. The quantity demanded

AN INFERIOR GOOD WITH A LARGER INCOME THAN SUBSTITUTION EFFECT

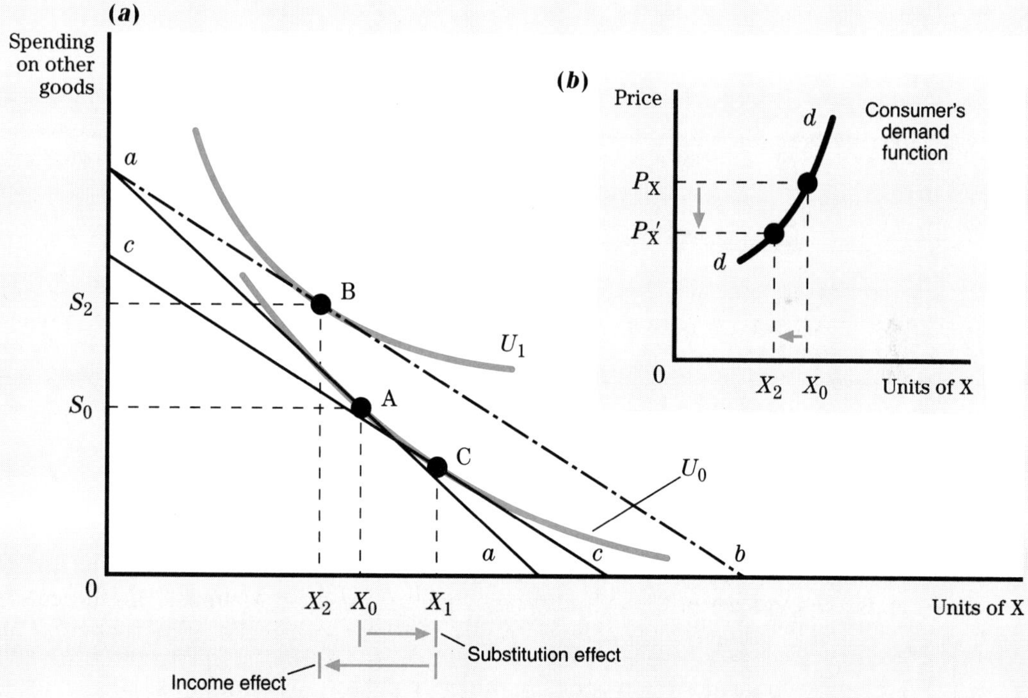

Figure 3-5   When the income effect is larger than the substitution effect and the good is an inferior good, the demand function has a positive slope. When the price decreases to P_X', the quantity demanded by the consumer decreases from X_0 to X_2. (b) The demand function has a positive slope. The substitution effect is $X_1 - X_0$, and the income effect is $X_2 - X_1$. The income effect is negative and swamps the substitution effect.

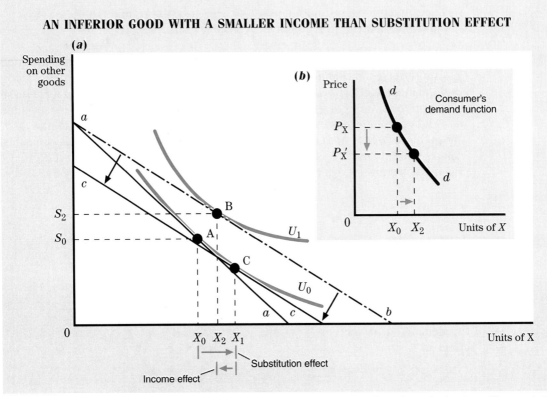

Figure 3-6 When the income effect is smaller than the substitution effect and the good is an inferior good, the demand function has a negative slope. When the price decreases to P_X', the quantity demanded by the consumer increases from X_0 to X_2. (b) The demand function has a negative slope. The substitution effect is $X_1 - X_0$ and the income effect is $X_2 - X_1$. The income effect is negative but is smaller than the substitution effect.

decreases when the price falls from P_X to P_X'. A utility-maximizing consumer can have a positively sloped demand function.

Again, we separate the total change in the quantity demanded from X_0 to X_2 into a change caused by the substitution effect and a change caused by the income effect. The substitution effect is $X_1 - X_0$. As always, the quantity demanded changes in the direction opposite the price change. What makes this case different from the previous one is the sign and the size of the income effect. An increase in income shifts the budget constraint from cc to ab. Since X is an inferior good, the quantity demanded decreases from X_1 to X_2 when income increases. The net effect of the two opposing changes is $X_2 - X_0$ and is negative. The income effect not only decreases the quantity demanded but swamps the substitution effect. The consumer's demand function in Figure 3-5b has a *positive* slope. When this event occurs, economists refer to the good as a **Giffen good**.

Sometimes students mistakenly conclude that the demand curve has a positive slope if the good is an inferior good. Try to avoid this mistake. Although a good is an inferior good, the demand function will still have a negative slope if the substitution effect is larger than the income effect. In Figure 3-6 the substitution effect, $X_1 - X_0$, is larger than the income effect, $X_2 - X_1$, and so the demand function has a negative slope although the good is an inferior good. To summarize, the slope of the demand function can be either positive or negative if the good is an inferior good.

> If a good is an inferior good, the consumer may demand more or fewer units when the price decreases. The slope of the demand function can be positive or negative.

The Effect of a Price Change on the Quantity Demanded

Table 3-1 summarizes the different cases and shows the effects of a price increase or decrease on the quantity demanded for a normal good and an inferior good.

The substitution and income effects augment each other when the good is a normal good. For example, column 1 shows that a price increase causes the quantity demanded to decrease $(-)$ because of the substitution effect. The income effect also decreases the quantity demanded $(-)$. Therefore, the quantity de-

Table 3-1   CHANGE IN QUANTITY DEMANDED FOR NORMAL AND INFERIOR GOODS

	Normal Good		Inferior Good	
	PRICE INCREASE (1)	PRICE DECREASE (2)	PRICE INCREASE (3)	PRICE DECREASE (4)
Change due to substitution effect (holding utility constant)	$(-)$	$(+)$	$(-)$	$(+)$
Change due to income effect (holding prices constant)	$(-)$	$(+)$	$(+)$	$(-)$
Total change	$(-)$	$(+)$	$(+)$ or $(-)$	$(+)$ or $(-)$
Slope of demand function	$(-)$	$(-)$	$(+)$ or $(-)$	$(+)$ or $(-)$

manded decreases when the price increases. Column 2 summarizes the effects of a price decrease on the quantity demanded. If the good is an inferior good, the slope of the demand function can be either positive or negative. Column 3 shows that the substitution effect decreases the quantity demanded ($-$) when the price increases. On the other hand, the income effect is positive ($+$). Whether the quantity demanded increases or decreases depends on whether the substitution effect is larger or smaller than the income effect. The net effect on the quantity demanded cannot be predicted when the good is an inferior good. Consequently, the slope of the consumer's demand curve can be either positive or negative.

You must also be careful not to infer that the *market* demand function has a positive slope just because a few consumer demand functions have a positive slope. In Chapter 2 the negatively sloped market demand function was derived by summing the individual demand functions horizontally. Although some consumers may have a positively sloped demand function over a range of prices, it is improbable that all of them will have demand functions that slope upward over the same range of prices. If a few consumers have a positively sloped demand function while most have the more common negatively sloped demand functions, the market demand function will have a negative slope. Therefore, economists do not expect to observe and have not observed positively sloped market demand functions.

APPLICATION 3-1

Subsidizing Day Care

We can apply the analysis of income and substitution effects to study how the demand for day care is affected by a price subsidy as compared to a lump sum subsidy. Day care is a serious problem for many families. Legislators are aware of the increasing demand by working parents of young children to do something about day care. Assume they are evaluating two subsidy programs.

- *Program 1.* A family receives a subsidy of *s dollars per day* for each day a child attends an authorized day care facility.
- *Program 2.* Each family with a child registered in an authorized day care facility receives a *lump sum* subsidy.

A trade association of day care providers and groups representing day care users both favor a subsidy but cannot agree on which program to support. The trade association actively lobbies for the per day subsidy, whereas users of child care favor the lump sum program. The opposition of the trade association to program 2 exasperates several members of Congress. They have repeatedly assured the trade association that government spending on day care will be the same no matter which program is adopted. Therefore, they cannot understand why the trade association is being so obstinate.

Is the disagreement between the providers and the users much ado about nothing? Let's see how the two programs affect a representative family. In Figure 3-7 a composite good is on the vertical axis, and the number of days of care is on the horizontal axis. Suppose a family with an income of I_0 currently purchases day care services for a child at a price of P_0 per day. I_0a is the initial budget constraint of the family and has a slope of $-P_0$. The family maximizes utility by selecting market basket 0 on U_0, purchasing D_0 days of day care, and spending S_0 dollars on other goods. Under program 1 the family receives a daily subsidy of s dollars, and so the daily price of day care falls from P_0 to $P_0 - s$. The price reduction rotates the budget constraint to $I_0 b$. The family selects market basket 1 on U_1, where the slope of U_1 equals the slope of $I_0 b$. The family purchases D_1 days of care and spends S_1 on the composite good. The subsidy lowers the effective price of child care, and the family purchases more.

Now let's calculate the total subsidy received by the family. For any given

DOES A PER UNIT OR A LUMP SUM DAY CARE SUBSIDY COST TAXPAYERS MORE?

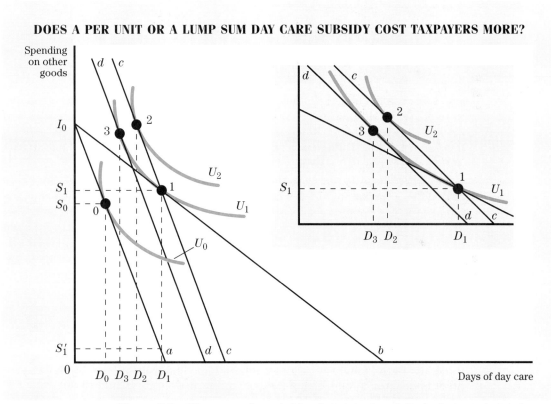

Figure 3-7   When a per day subsidy of s is introduced, the budget constraint changes from $I_0 a$ to $I_0 b$. The family increases the number of days of child care from D_0 to D_1. The subsidy received by the family is $S_1 - S_1'$, the difference between $I_0 b$ and $I_0 a$ when the family uses D_1 days. A lump sum subsidy shifts the budget constraint from $I_0 a$ to cc. The budget line cc intersects U_1 at market basket 1. Under a lump sum subsidy the family selects market basket 2 on the indifference curve U_2. A smaller lump sum subsidy is necessary if the family is permitted to reach only indifference curve U_1. The budget constraint dd is tangent to U_1 with market basket 3. The move from market basket 3 to market basket 1 is the substitution effect. The family prefers a lump sum subsidy because it reaches a higher indifference curve. The day care industry prefers a per unit subsidy because the quantity demanded will be higher.

number of days of child care, the distance between the budget constraint I_0b and the budget constraint I_0a is the total amount of the subsidy received by the family. When the family purchases D_1 days, the total dollar subsidy is equal to the distance $S_1 - S_1'$ between I_0b and I_0a. Remember that S denotes total spending on the composite good and s is the daily subsidy. If the family had purchased D_1 days of child care without the subsidy, it could only spend S_1' dollars on the composite good. With a per day subsidy, the family spends S_1 dollars on the composite good while still using D_1 days of child care. The family can spend more on the composite good because it is given a per day subsidy. It receives a total subsidy of sD_1 that equals the increase in spending on other goods from S_1' to S_1. To review, $S_1 - S_1'$ is the total dollar subsidy received by the family when it purchases D_1 days of child care with a per day subsidy of s.

Will the family respond differently to a lump sum subsidy? The lump sum subsidy is determined so that the per family cost to taxpayers for the two programs is the same. We already know that the total subsidy received by the family is $S_1 - S_1'$ under the per day subsidy. The lump sum subsidy program must cost taxpayers the same amount. To make the total cost the same, the family's lump sum subsidy must be large enough so that the new budget line cc allows the family to purchase market basket 1. The distance between the two budget lines cc and I_0a is $S_1 - S_1'$ no matter how many days of day care the family selects under a lump sum subsidy. Therefore, a lump sum subsidy of $S_1 - S_1'$ makes the total cost of the two programs the same.

You can begin to see why the trade association and the users of child care have different points of view. When the two subsidy programs cost the same, the family prefers a lump sum subsidy. The family will move along cc to market basket 2 and reach a higher indifference curve U_2 by contracting for only D_2 days of child care under a lump sum subsidy. Although the parents could select D_1 days under a lump sum subsidy, they prefer not to because the relative price of day care has not changed. The slope of cc equals $-P_0$ which is numerically smaller than $-(P_0 - s)$, the slope of I_0b. The lump sum subsidy does not affect relative prices, whereas the per day subsidy does. Since the slope of I_0b equals the slope of the indifference curve U_1 with market basket 1, the slope of the budget constraint cc cannot equal the slope of the indifference curve U_1 with market basket 1. By reducing the number of child care days and increasing spending on other goods, the utility of the family increases. Under a lump sum subsidy the family is better off by purchasing less day care because the relative price is unaffected.

The change from D_1 to D_2 approximates but does not equal the substitution effect. Although the relative price of day care increases by switching from the per day subsidy to the lump sum subsidy, the family moves to a higher indifference curve by decreasing day care from D_1 to D_2 days.

How much would the lump sum subsidy program cost if the lump sum subsidy just allowed the family to reach indifference curve U_1 with market basket 3? The budget line dd in the inset is just tangent to U_1. Because dd lies below cc, a lump sum subsidy that makes the family indifferent between a per day subsidy of s and a lump sum subsidy costs the taxpayers less. The difference between cc and dd at any D represents the lower cost of the lump sum program. Starting from market basket 1, the price of day care can be raised by eliminating the per day subsidy and then offering a lump sum subsidy so that the family selects market basket 3 on U_1. The change from D_1 to D_3 is the true substitution effect. Therefore, offering a lump sum payment for child care that makes the family as well off as a daily subsidy would cost taxpayers less.

In summary, the welfare of the family improves more if it receives a lump sum subsidy that costs the same as a per day subsidy. The day care trade association probably opposes the lump sum subsidy program because the days of child care demanded by the family will be lower under the lump sum proposal than under the per day subsidy program. The different positions taken by the trade association and by the users of day care are not due to faulty reasoning on the part of either party. Both sides know which side their bread is buttered on.

The Slope of the Demand Function

In the introduction to this chapter we asked why the quantity demanded increases more for some consumers than for others. Some individuals have more elastic demand functions than others, and the income and substitution effects can be used to explain when and why the responses of consumers differ. We can draw up a convenient checklist that tells us when either the substitution or the income effect is large so that the change in the quantity demanded caused by a price change is large. Although the analysis focuses on the slope of the demand curve, much of what we say applies to the consumer's price elasticity of demand as well.

The consumer's demand function expresses the quantity demanded as a function of the price of the product with income and other prices held constant. The demand function is expressed as

$$X = d(P) \qquad \text{(Consumer's Demand Function)} \qquad (3\text{-}2)$$

where the symbol d denotes the consumer's demand function. The slope of the demand function is $\Delta X/\Delta P$. The size of the slope of the demand function depends on the magnitude of the substitution and income effects. So, we want to know when the size of the income or substitution effect is large to determine when a price change causes a large change in the quantity demanded.

The substitution effect measures the change in the quantity demanded due to a price change when the consumer remains on the original indifference curve. The expression $(\Delta X/\Delta P)|_{U=c}$ represents the substitution effect. The expresson $|_{U=c}$ means "utility is constant." So, we can determine $\Delta X/\Delta P$ by measuring how the quantity demanded changes along a given indifference curve as the relative price of X changes. We know that the sign of $(\Delta X/\Delta P)|_{U=c}$ is always negative because the consumer demands more units of X when the price falls.

However, the slope of the demand curve depends not only on the substitution effect but also on the income effect. We already know that the income effect is positive for a normal good. Now we want to investigate when will the income effect be large.

The explanation of the size of the income effect is a little more involved. This effect depends on two factors: (1) how much income becomes available when the price of X decreases, and (2) how many more units of X the consumer demands because income has increased. The income that becomes available per dollar change in price depends on the number of units the individual is currently consuming. A price decrease releases income to be spent on goods equal to $\Delta I = -(\Delta P)X$ (the negative sign is required because a decrease in the price of X releases more income to purchase more of all goods). For a price decrease of ΔP, more funds become available to the consumer the larger the number of units of X the individual consumes. The change in income per dollar decrease in price $(\Delta I/\Delta P)$ is equal to $-X$, and $\Delta X/\Delta I$ represents the increase in the quantity demanded of X per dollar increase in income. Therefore, the change in the quantity demanded because of the income effect is $-X(\Delta X/\Delta I)$.

A numerical example will clarify how to calculate the income effect. If you rent a movie for home viewing on your VCR 30 times a year and the rental price decreases by $1, you will have $30 more to spend each year on movies and other goods. In this case $\Delta I/\Delta P = -X = -30$. So, $-X$ represents the additional dollars released when the price decreases by $1. Furthermore, assume that you demand one more movie per $10 increase in income, and so $\Delta X/\Delta I = 0.1$ unit per dollar increase in income. Then, the change in the quantity demanded because of the income effect is $30 \times 0.1 = 3$ more movies per year per dollar decrease in price.

Our graphical analysis of the income and substitution effects showed that the change in the quantity demanded due to a price change is the sum of the changes caused by the substitution and income effects. Therefore, we can express the slope of the consumer's demand function as

$$\frac{\Delta X}{\Delta P} = \frac{\Delta X}{\Delta P}\bigg|_{U=c} - X\left(\frac{\Delta X}{\Delta I}\right) \qquad \text{(Slope of Consumer's Demand Function)} \qquad \textbf{(3-3)}$$

Equation 3-3 is called the Slutsky equation and is named after the economist who first derived it. The **Slutsky equation** simply says that the slope of the demand function equals the sum of the contributions of the substitution and income effects.[2] The first term on the right-hand side of equation 3-3 is the substitution effect, and the second term is the income effect. The sign of the substitution effect is always negative. When the income effect is zero, the slope of the demand function is negative because the substitution effect is always negative. If the good is a normal good, the income effect is also negative because $-X(\Delta X/\Delta I)$ is negative since $\Delta X/\Delta I$ is positive, and therefore the demand function must have a negative slope. If the good is an inferior good, then the income effect is $-X(\Delta X/\Delta I)$ and is positive. Therefore, the slope of the demand curve can be either positive or negative.

[2] Strictly speaking, equation 3-3 holds exactly for infinitesimal changes in price; that is,

$$\frac{\partial X}{\partial P} = \frac{\partial X}{\partial P}\bigg|_{U=c} - X\frac{\partial X}{\partial I}$$

where $\partial X/\partial P$ represents an infinitesimal change in X with respect to an infinitesimal change in the price of X with all other prices held constant and $\partial X/\partial I$ is the infinitesimal change in the quantity demanded with respect to an infinitesimal change in I.

The Size of Each Effect

Equation 3-3 shows how the slope of the demand function depends on the substitution and income effects. By carefully considering each effect separately, we can discover situations when the substitution of income effect will be large or small.[3] The two determinants are the size of the substitution and income effects.

The Size of the Substitution Effect The substitution effect is larger if the consumer considers X a close rather than a distant substitute for other goods. If X is a close substitute for other goods, the quantity demanded will increase by a larger amount when the price falls, holding the consumer's utility constant. In Figure 3-8a units of Y, another good, are on the y axis, and units of X are on the x axis. You may remember from Chapter 2 that the indifference curve is a straight line when two goods are perfect substitutes. The indifference curve of the consumer in Figure 3-8 resembles but is not quite a straight line. The shape of the indifference curve between Y and X indicates that the consumer is just about willing to give up the same number of units of Y for each unit of X no matter how many units of X he or she consumes.

If two goods are close to being perfect complements, each indifference curve looks more like an L. In Chapter 2 it was noted that one right shoe and one left shoe are perfect complements. The indifference curve in Figure 3-8b resembles but is not quite a right angle. For a given decrease in Y, the consumer requires still larger increases in X at lower levels of Y to remain indifferent.

Figure 3-8 shows how the size of the substitution effect depends on whether the two goods are close substitutes or close complements. In Figure 3-8a the substitution effect is larger when the two goods are close substitutes and is ΔX_1 when the price decreases from P_X to P'_X. This is more like the case where the consumer considers Green Giant peas a close substitute for Del Monte peas and

---

[3] The equation in footnote 2 can be converted into an expression for the point price elasticity of demand.

$$\frac{\partial X}{\partial P} = \frac{\partial X}{\partial P}\bigg|_{U=c} - X\frac{\partial X}{\partial I}$$

Multiplying both sides of the equation by the ratio of P/X results in

$$\frac{P}{X}\frac{\partial X}{\partial P} = \frac{P}{X}\frac{\partial X}{\partial P}\bigg|_{U=c} - \frac{P}{X}X\frac{\partial X}{\partial I}$$

Multiplying the numerator and the denominator of the last term by I yields

$$\frac{P}{X}\frac{\partial X}{\partial P} = \frac{P}{X}\frac{\partial X}{\partial P}\bigg|_{U=c} - \frac{PX}{I}\left(\frac{I}{X}\frac{\partial X}{\partial I}\right)$$

$$E_p = E_p^c - (s)(E_I)$$

The left-hand side is the point price elasticity of demand E_p. The point price elasticity equals the percentage change in the quantity demanded for an infinitesimal percentage change in price. The first term on the right-hand side is called the compensated price elasticity of demand E_p^c and measures the price elasticity of demand with utility held constant. The second term on the right-hand side is the product of the share of income spent on the good, $s = PX/I$, and the point income elasticity of demand, $E_I = (I/X)(\partial X/\partial I)$. The point income elasticity of demand can be interpreted as the percentage change in the quantity demand due to an infinitesimal percentage change in income.

THE SIZE OF THE SUBSTITUTION EFFECT

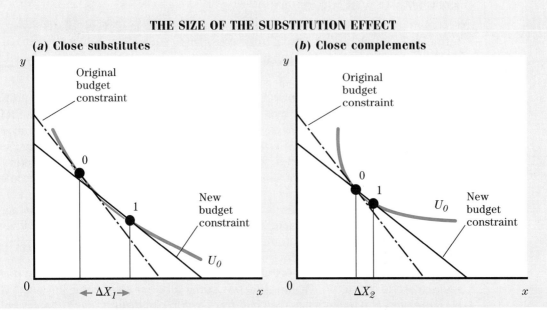

Figure 3-8 The indifference curve in (*a*) appears more like a straight line than the indifference curve in (*b*) which appears more like a right angle. In each case the consumer starts with market basket 0 and selects market basket 1 because of the substitution effect. The substitution effect is ΔX_1 in (*a*) and ΔX_2 in (*b*). The substitution effect is larger in (*a*), when the two goods are close substitutes, than in (*b*), when the two goods are close complements.

so will purchase Green Giant if the price decreases. The substitution effect in Figure 3-8*b* is smaller when the two goods are close complements and is ΔX_2.

The Size of the Income Effect   When the price of X falls, the consumer finds $-(\Delta P)X$ dollars available to spend on X and other goods. For a given change in price, more funds become available the larger X is. If I buy just a few units of X and spend only a small percentage of my income on X, only a few dollars become available for me to spend on X and other goods when the price of X falls. A fall in the price of mangoes is not likely to cause a large income effect for most individuals because most consumers eat only a few, if any, mangoes per year. If I consume many units of X and spend a large percentage of my income on a good, for example, housing, a price reduction on a house will release a considerable sum that I might use to purchase a still larger house, an automobile, clothing, or more vacations. The income effect is larger because the budget line shifts outward parallel by a larger amount when the price of X decreases.

The second component of the income effect is the responsiveness of the quantity demanded to a change in income ($\Delta X/\Delta I$). The consumer's demand for different goods responds differently when income increases. For example, a 10 percent increase in consumer income may increase an individual's demand for vacation days by 20 percent because the income elasticity of demand exceeds 1. On the other hand, a 10 percent increase in income may increase his or her demand for soft drinks by only 1 percent.

Observing the Effect of Each Determinant

To sum up, $\Delta X/\Delta P$, the slope of the demand function, depends on (1) whether X is a close or an imperfect substitute for some other good, (2) whether a large or a small percentage of income is spent on X, and (3) how much the consumer's demand for X increases when income increases. These three items jointly determine the slope of the demand function and the consumer's price elasticity of demand.

Keep this checklist of determinants in mind as you look at the following analysis. Some business decisions depend on an estimate of the price elasticity of demand. Often, speed is essential and decisions are made with limited information. Suppose you need to estimate the price elasticity of demand for a product you are selling. You do not have the luxury of hiring a high-priced consultant to complete an elaborate statistical study. More often than not, business managers have to make decisions with very little hard information available. In these situations you will have to guess about the likely size of the price elasticity of demand. Let's illustrate how our checklist might help organize your thinking.

Would you expect that the demand function for a given brand in a product category is more price-elastic than the demand for all brands within a product category? For example, we may want to estimate the price elasticity of demand for Christian Dior shirts or for all expensive shirts. Would you expect the price elasticity of demand for Christian Dior dress shirts to be more elastic or less elastic than the price elasticity of demand for all brands in the same price class? You might use the following argument. There are probably more close substitutes for a single brand within a product category than there are close substitutes between product categories. If so, you could plausibly argue that the demand for an individual brand would be more elastic than the demand for the whole category. If the price of Christian Dior shirts is increased, how will consumers react? Some consumers will purchase a Giorgio Armani shirt or a Perry Ellis shirt which they consider a close substitute.

On the other hand, suppose the prices of all expensive dress shirts increase. Many consumers may find the shirts in middle- and low-price classes more distant substitutes for shirts in the higher-price class. You can make a plausible argument that shirts within a price class are closer substitutes than shirts in different price classes. The size of the substitution effect between brands within a price class will be larger than between shirts in different price classes. Therefore, if you are considering an independent price increase for your higher-priced brand name dress shirt, you should expect a larger decrease in the quantity demanded because there are many available close substitutes. Your demand function will be more price-elastic than the demand for all higher-priced shirts. The theory of consumer behavior suggests that the substitution effect between goods that are closer substitutes will be larger. The demand function for Christian Dior dress shirts will be more elastic than the demand function for all expensive dress shirts.

In this example the comparative assessment of price elasticities depends on the comparative size of the substitution effects. Income effects are ignored because the share of total income spent on dress shirts is trivial and the fraction of income spent on shirts of a particular brand is still smaller.

Consider another example. Although the market is changing rapidly, there currently are fewer substitute automobiles in the luxury price class (Lincoln, Cadillac, Acura, Lexus, etc.) than in the middle- and lower-price classes (Taurus, Accord, Maxima, Camry, Lumina, etc.). The product space appears more densely filled in the middle- and lower-price classes than in the luxury field. If so, the theory of consumer behavior predicts that the demand function for a specific make in the luxury price class will be less elastic than the demand function for a specific make in the middle-price class. Here again, income effects are ignored.

Finally, the income effect and therefore the slope of the consumer's demand function depend on the quantity purchased and on $\Delta X/\Delta I$. Suppose consumers could be classified into two groups. Members of one group purchase a few units per year, whereas each member of the other group purchases a large volume each year. If you are planning to reduce the price to members in one of the two groups, which group will increase the quantity demanded by a larger amount? Would you offer the price cut to the group with members who individually purchase a small quantity or to the group with members who individually purchase a large quantity? When other factors are held constant, a consumer who purchases a large quantity will have a more elastic demand function because the income effect is larger. A price reduction will cause a larger increase in the quantity demanded if the price cut is offered to members of this group with other factors held constant. The analysis says that when all other factors are held constant, the demand function will be more elastic the larger the percentage of income spent on the good.

*3-2 CONSUMER SURPLUS

An individual buys a product at a given price because he or she is better off consuming the product than doing without it. It is expected that every purchased product or service, whether it is a soft drink, carrots, medical care, or listening to a rock concert, will leave the consumer better off given the price of the good or service. If we ignore fraud and misrepresentation, every purchase made by the consumer is a bargain. This claim may surprise you, but it is true. Because the consumer's utility is higher, he or she receives a surplus by consuming a good and, if forced to, is willing to pay more than is actually paid rather than go without the good.

> **Consumer surplus** is the difference between the maximum amount the purchaser would pay to consume a given quantity and the actual amount paid.

In this section two issues are considered: how to derive the maximum amount that a consumer is willing to pay for a given quantity of a good and how someone other than the consumer can estimate consumer surplus.

Why would anyone want to know what the consumer surplus is? If you are a marketing manager, you would like to know because you want to know how much more revenue you may be able to collect from the consumer. If you are negotiating a contract with a buyer, you would like to know how much more you can charge for the contract before the buyer will terminate the negotiations. If you are a public official, you may want to know how much consumer surplus will decline and how much political opposition will increase when a tariff of 10 percent is placed on imports of sugar or automobiles, or you may want to know how much consumer surplus will increase if a new public park is built.

Marginal Willingness to Pay Function

Let's begin by determining the maximum amount a buyer is willing to pay to consume a certain quantity of a good. In Figure 3-9 spending on a composite good is on the vertical axis and units of X are on the horizontal axis. When the income of the consumer is I_0 and the price of X is P^*, the consumer's budget line I_0a has a slope of $-P^*$. If the consumer does not purchase any units of X, he or she spends all income on other goods and is on indifference curve U_0 at point I_0 on the vertical axis. The consumer maximizes utility by purchasing X^* units and spending S^* on other goods where the budget line I_0a is tangent to the indifference curve U_1. The total amount spent on X is P^*X^* and is equal to $I_0 - S^*$.

By purchasing X^* units, the consumer moves from indifference curve U_0 to indifference curve U_1 and is better off than if he goes without X. This is why every purchase is considered a bargain. Whether the consumer is paying a higher monopoly price or a competitive price, his utility increases. Of course, utility increases by more if the buyer pays a lower price, but it increases even if a higher monopoly price is paid. A local cable company may be charging you a monopoly price for basic service, but you are still better off using the service than doing without it.

Because the consumer's utility increases, he is willing to pay more for the right to purchase X^* units at a per unit price of P^*. We want to derive a measure of the maximum dollar amount the consumer would be willing to pay for this option. This maximum amount is the sum of the maximum amounts he would pay for each successive unit from the first to the X^*th unit. Suppose the consumer spends all income on other goods and therefore is on U_0. What is the *most* this individual would be willing to pay for the first unit of X? The most that he would be willing to reduce spending on other goods to purchase the first unit of X is an amount that keeps the consumer on indifference curve U_0.

Define W_1 as the maximum amount the individual is willing to pay for the first unit of X. In Figure 3-9 W_1 is determined so that the consumer remains on U_0. Spending on other goods falls by $\Delta S = -W_1$, and consumption of X increases by one unit. The slope of the indifference curve U_0 when X increases by one unit is $\Delta S/\Delta X = -W_1/1 = -W_1$. The absolute value of the slope of the indifference curve U_0 when $X = 1$ is the consumer's marginal willingness to pay for the first unit.

The **marginal willingness to pay** for the first unit is the amount that keeps the consumer on the same indifference curve.

Given that the consumer pays W_1 dollars for the first unit, he is willing to reduce spending on other goods by at most W_2 to consume the second unit. W_2 is the marginal willingness to pay for the second unit and is determined so that the consumer remains on U_0. Here again, the slope of the indifference curve U_0 when X increases from one unit to two units is $\Delta S/\Delta X = -W_2/1 = -W_2$. Therefore, the maximum amount the consumer is willing to pay for the first two units of X is the sum of the two values for marginal willingness to pay, or $W_1 + W_2$.

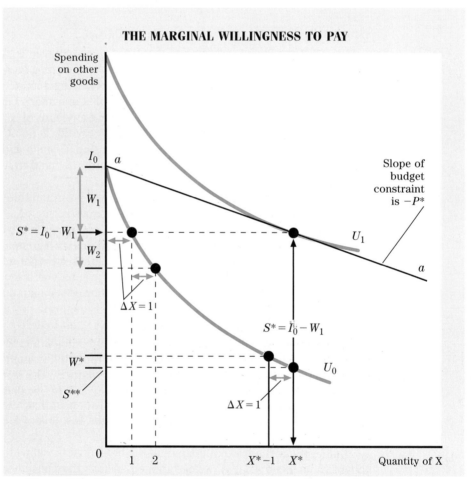

THE MARGINAL WILLINGNESS TO PAY

Figure 3-9   The consumer is willing to reduce spending on other goods by at most W_1 to purchase the first unit of X. Given the payment of W_1, he or she will pay at most W_2 for the second unit. The consumer will pay at most W^* to consume the X^*th unit. The marginal willingness to pay for successive units decreases as the quantity of X increases because of the diminishing marginal rate of substitution.

THE MARGINAL WILLINGNESS TO PAY FUNCTION

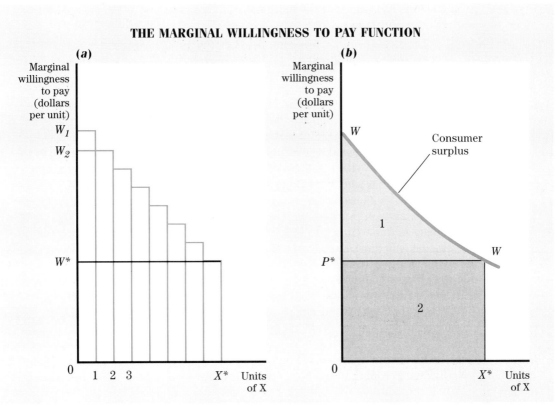

Figure 3-10   (*a*) The marginal willingness to pay function for successive units of X is represented by the rectangles. The consumer is willing to pay at most W_1 for the first unit, W_2 for the second unit, and W^* for the X^*th unit. (*b*) WW is the continuous marginal willingness to pay function. The maximum amount the consumer will pay for X^* units is the sum of areas 1 and 2. The actual amount paid is area 2. Consumer surplus is the difference, or area 1.

This procedure can be repeated for successive units until X^* is reached. For the X^*th unit, the consumer is willing to pay at most W^*, a smaller dollar amount. The marginal willingness to pay for successive units on the y axis of Figure 3-9 decreases with successive units of X because the indifference curve U_0 exhibits a diminishing marginal rate of substitution. If we sum the W values from W_1 to W^*, we get the most the purchaser is willing to pay for X^* units. Let $S^{**} = I_0 - (W_1 + W_2 + \cdots + W^*)$ or income spent on other goods if the consumer spends the maximum amount on successive units up to X^* units. So, another measure of the maximum amount the consumer is willing to pay for X^* units is $I_0 - S^{**}$.

We can derive a marginal willingness to pay function by graphing the marginal willingness to pay for each unit of X. A step function of the marginal willingness to pay is shown in Figure 3-10*a*. The buyer is willing to pay at most W_1 for the first unit; given the payment of W_1, he or she is willing to pay W_2 for the second unit;

and so on. The values of the marginal willingness to pay are the absolute value of the successive slopes along the consumer's indifference curve U_0.

> A **marginal willingness to pay function** shows the maximum amount the consumer is willing to pay for additional units of a good.

Until now, we have assumed that the consumer purchases X in discrete single units. Considerable analytical simplicity can be obtained by assuming the individual consumes X in infinitesimal amounts instead of in single units. By allowing for infinitesimal changes in X, we can derive a continuous marginal willingness to pay function (Figure 3-10b). At each point on the indifference curve we determine what the consumer would be willing to pay for an infinitesimal increase in X. The marginal willingness to pay is the absolute value of the slope of the indifference curve U_0 at each point along the curve. The corresponding continuous marginal willingness to pay function is *WW* in Figure 3-10b. The area under the continuous marginal willingness to pay function is the *maximum* dollar amount the consumer is willing to pay for X^* units.

Figure 3-9 showed a dollar measure of the surplus the consumer receives. When purchasing each unit at P^*, the consumer would be willing to pay $I_0 - S^{**}$ for X^* units but has to pay only $I_0 - S^*$. Consumer surplus is the difference between the maximum amount the consumer is willing to pay and the amount paid, or $(I_0 - S^{**}) - (I_0 - S^*) = S^* - S^{**}$. It can also be measured from the areas under the marginal willingness to pay function. The maximum amount the individual is willing to pay for X^* units is the sum of areas 1 and 2 in Figure 3-10b. When the price is P^*, the consumer purchases X^* units and pays only area 2. Consumer surplus is the difference between these two areas, or area 1.

When the consumer can vary X continuously, his marginal willingness to pay becomes the absolute value of the slope of the indifference curve. This is shown in Figure 3-11 for two points when $X = 2$ and $X = X^*$. When $X = 2$, the slope of the indifference curve U_0 at point 1 equals the slope of the tangent *bb*. The absolute value of the slope of *bb* is the marginal willingness to pay for an infinitesimal increase in X when $X = 2$. Similarly, when $X = X^*$, the slope of the indifference curve at point 2 equals the slope of the tangent *cc*, and the absolute value of the slope of *cc* equals the marginal willingness to pay for an infinitesimal increase in X when $X = X^*$. Therefore, we can interpret the slope of the consumer's indifference curve (after changing the sign) as his marginal willingness to pay for an infinitesimal increase in X.

Estimating Consumer Surplus
from the Consumer's Demand Function

While the consumer receives a surplus by purchasing X^* units at a price of P^*, only the consumer knows the value of this surplus. As noted above, a marketing manager or a public official would like to know the value of consumer surplus, but this appears nearly impossible without knowing the shapes of the consumer's indifference curves, which are seldom known.

Fortunately, there is a way to estimate consumer surplus if the demand func-

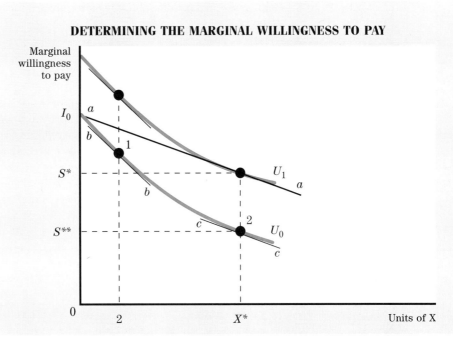

DETERMINING THE MARGINAL WILLINGNESS TO PAY

Figure 3-11 The marginal willingness to pay is the absolute value of the slope of the indifference curve U_0. The tangent bb equals the slope of the indifference curve when $X = 2$. The negative of the slope of bb measures the marginal willingness to pay for an infinitesimal increase in X when $X = 2$. The line cc is tangent to U_0 when $X = X^*$. The absolute value of the slope of cc measures the marginal willingness to pay for an infinitesimal increase in X when $X = X^*$.

tion is known or can be estimated. Information about the consumer's demand function, though not easy to obtain, is easier to come by than information about the shapes of the consumer's indifference curves. Sometimes economists estimate the demand curve of an individual by observing the quantities bought at alternative prices or from consumer purchase diaries that report prices and quantities purchased.

If the demand function of the consumer is known, how can we use this information to estimate consumer surplus? The consumer's demand curve is dd in Figure 3-12. This individual demands X^* units if the price is P^*. Area 2 represents the total amount paid for X^* units and is equal to $I_0 - S^*$ in Figure 3-11. Assuming the consumer's demand function is known, will the demand function coincide with the marginal willingness to pay functions? Figure 3-12 shows the buyer demands X^* units when the price is P^* while Figure 3-9 shows that the consumer is willing to pay W^* for the X^*th unit. We can show that the two functions are identical when there are no income effects. This occurs when the indifference curves are vertical displacements of each other—in other words, when the slope of every indifference curve is the same for each X. The slope changes as X changes but, for a given X, all the consumer's indifference curves have the same slope. For example, Figure 3-11 shows two indifference curves of a consumer. When the

THE DEMAND FUNCTION OF A CONSUMER

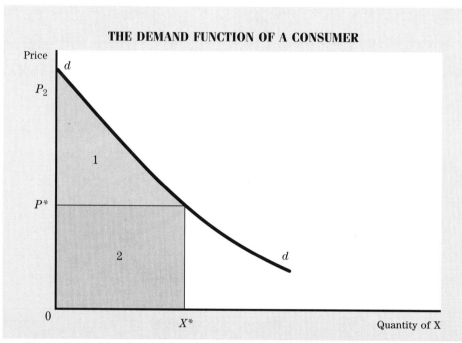

Figure 3-12   The demand function of a consumer is dd. The quantity demanded is X^* if the price is P^*. Area 2 represents the total expenditure for X by this consumer. When there are no income effects, area 1 is the consumer surplus.

consumer purchases two units, the slope of the indifference curve U_0 equals the slope of bb which equals the slope of U_1. Similarly, the slope of U_0 is the same as the slope of U_1 when $X = X^*$ and equals the slope of tangent cc which equals the slope of I_0a. When there are no income effects, a parallel shift in the tangent cc to I_0a does not change the consumer's quantity demanded and so the income effect is zero.

Let's consider the full implications of this assumption of no income effects. We know that the consumer determines the quantity demanded of X where the slope of the indifference curve equals the slope of the budget line. When the price is P^*, the budget constraint is I_0a in Figure 3-13 and has a slope of $-P^*$. The consumer maximizes utility by demanding X^* units of X (market basket 2). This is one point on the demand function. The slope of I_0a equals the slope of the indifference curve U_2 at $X = X^*$. So we have

$$\text{Slope of indifference curve } U_2 = -P^* \qquad \text{when } X = X^*$$

Now let's find the consumer's marginal willingness to pay for the X^*th unit on the indifference curve U_0. It is the absolute value of the slope of the tangent cc to U_0, and the slope of U_0 is the same as the slope of U_2 when $X = X^*$ because income effects are zero. The consumer is willing to pay W^* for the X^*th unit, and $-W^*$ equals $-P^*$, the price of the product. So we have

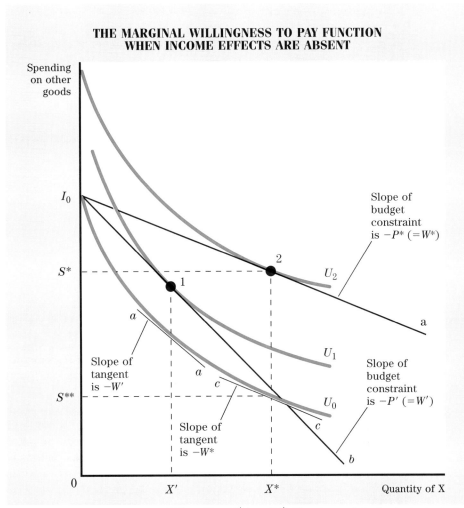

**THE MARGINAL WILLINGNESS TO PAY FUNCTION
WHEN INCOME EFFECTS ARE ABSENT**

Figure 3-13   The slope of U_0 at $X = X^*$ is $-W^*$. The slope of the budget constraint I_0a is $-P^*$. The tangent to the indifference curve when $X = X^*$ is parallel to I_0a. An increase in income will shift the tangent upward to I_0a. The consumer will continue to demand X^* units of X. Therefore, the income effect is zero. When $X = X'$, the tangent to U_0 has a slope of $-W'$. The slope of the budget constraint I_0b is $-P'$ which is equal to $-W'$. An increase in income shifts the tangent upward parallel to I_0b, and the quantity demanded remains X' units. The income effect is zero. When income effects are absent, the demand function is identical to the willingness to pay function.

$$-W^* = \text{Slope of indifference curve } U_0$$

$$= \text{Slope of indifference curve } U_2 = -P^* \qquad \text{when } X = X^*$$

W^* is the consumer's marginal willingness to pay for the X^*th unit in Figure 3-13, a point on the marginal willingness to pay function. P^* is the price when the consumer demands X^* total units, a point on the consumer's demand function.

Because income effects are zero, the marginal willingness to pay function and the demand function have a point in common. Similarly, for X' we can show that $-W'$ equals the slope of U_0 which in turn equals the slope of U_1 which equals $-P'$. Therefore, the marginal willingness to pay function and the demand function have another point in common. By repeating this argument it can be shown that the demand function is identical to the marginal willingness to pay function when income effects are zero.

> The demand function is the same as the marginal willingness to pay function when there are no income effects.

When there are no income effects, the demand function is identical to the marginal willingness to pay function and consumer surplus can be estimated directly from the consumer's demand function. In Figure 3-12 consumer surplus is equal to area 1, the difference between the area under the demand function and the area representing the amount paid by the buyer. The area under the demand function up to X^* is equal to the sum of areas 1 and 2, or $I_0 - S^{**}$ in Figure 3-13, and area 2 is equal to the amount paid for X^* units, or $I_0 - S^*$ in Figure 3-13. Consumer surplus is equal to area 1, or $S^* - S^{**}$. To summarize, consumer surplus is the area under the demand function and above the price line of P^* when income effects are zero.

When the indifference curves are not vertical displacements of each other, there are income effects and the demand function is no longer identical to the marginal willingness to pay function. The appendix to this chapter explains why consumer surplus estimated from the demand function overestimates consumer surplus when the good is a normal good. For many goods, economists ignore income effects because the consumer spends a tiny fraction of income on them. In these cases the area under the demand function can be used to estimate consumer surplus with tolerable accuracy. Throughout most of this book it is assumed that the area under the demand function and above the price line is equal to or closely approximates consumer surplus.

Economists use the consumer surplus concept to evaluate the consequences of public policies. For example, the United States has a sugar quota that prevents foreign suppliers from selling as much sugar as they would like to in the United States. The quota increases the U.S. price of a pound of sugar by shifting the supply function of domestic and imported sugar to the left and reduces consumer surplus. In Figure 3-14 the market demand curve for sugar is DD. Without the quota the U.S. price of a pound of sugar would be P_0 and consumers would purchase Q_0 pounds of sugar. With the quota the price of sugar increases to P_1 and the quantity of sugar consumed falls to only Q_1 pounds. Without a quota, consumer surplus is equal to the sum of areas 1, 2, and 3. With a quota, it falls by the sum of areas 1 and 2 and becomes area 3. The price received by suppliers increases by $P_1 - P_0$, and Q_1 pounds are sold at the higher price. Area 1 represents a transfer from consumers to producers as the incomes of domestic suppliers of sugar increase because of the quota. What about area 2? It represents part of the loss in consumer

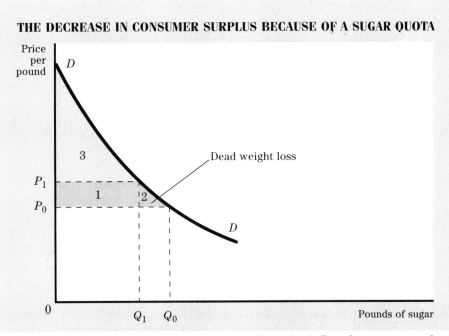

THE DECREASE IN CONSUMER SURPLUS BECAUSE OF A SUGAR QUOTA

Figure 3-14   Without the sugar quota the market price is P_0 and consumer surplus is the sum of areas 1, 2, and 3. The sugar quota increases the price per pound to P_1. Consumer surplus decreases by the sum of areas 1 and 2 and now equals area 3. Area 1 is transferred from consumers to suppliers. Area 2 represents a loss to consumers with no offsetting gain to any other group and is referred to as a dead weight loss.

surplus. No other group receives an offsetting benefit from this loss which occurs because the industry contracts in size when the price of sugar increases and is called a dead weight loss.

> A **dead weight loss** represents the decrease in consumer surplus that is not transferred to some other group.

As alluded to above, consumer surplus is a useful concept because it measures how much more the consumer is willing to pay for any quantity purchased. Obviously, firms have an incentive to capture some or all of the consumer surplus by adopting ingenious pricing policies that increase the amount paid for a product. For example, suppose you operate an amusement park. Instead of just charging for each ride, you can raise more revenue by charging an entrance fee equal to consumer surplus in addition to a per ride fee. When firms adopt these types of pricing policies is a fascinating topic and will be discussed later in Chapter 12 on price discrimination.

3-3 UNCERTAINTY AND CONSUMER DECISION MAKING

In the first two sections of this chapter it was assumed that the consumer makes decisions under certainty. When an individual consumes a tomato, he or she knows the outcome and has a clear idea of the benefits of consumption. If the consumer purchases a house, the individual knows what benefits come with ownership. However, there are situations where the consequences of a decision are not known with certainty. An individual who has just received an MBA and enters an industry still faces considerable uncertainty concerning how much she will earn. Are her talents a good match or a poor match for the requirements of the position? As a consumer or as a worker, an individual will make some important decisions where the outcome of the decision is uncertain. This section considers decision making under uncertainty.

When uncertainty exists, a decision does not lead to a single outcome but to several possible outcomes that occur with different probabilities. If you decide to purchase a house in the Los Angeles metropolitan area, you are not certain of enjoying all its benefits. You are taking a gamble. One remote but distinct outcome is that your dream home will be leveled or damaged extensively by an earthquake. Or, consider another example. You have invested in a college education and look forward to a prosperous career. Still, you may not receive the benefits of the education that you worked for so diligently. There is a small probability that you will be killed in an automobile accident. Each of these dismal events has a small probability of occurring, but the consequence of each outcome is devastating. In each example an individual makes a decision where multiple outcomes are possible. After a house is purchased, there are two outcomes or states of nature—an earthquake either does or does not occur. Either the owner suffers a large loss or the house retains its market value.

Because more than a single outcome is associated with a decision, it makes little sense to say that the individual maximizes utility, because each decision leads to multiple outcomes and therefore multiple utilities corresponding to these outcomes. To analyze decision making under uncertainty, utility maximization must be replaced with some other objective. This section considers two competing models of what an individual maximizes: the expected income and the expected utility hypotheses.

The Expected Income Hypothesis

The expected income hypothesis states that an individual selects from among possible uncertain situations to maximize expected income. The following example is used to illustrate and derive some implications of the expected income hypothesis. Let's assume that you plan to start your own business and have narrowed your choice to industry A or industry B. You believe that you can earn $75,000 a year in industry A. Given your talents, industry A is the safe industry for you to enter. Industry B is the other possibility attracting your attention, but many newcomers are unsuccessful in industry B. In industry B the probability is .75 that you will not do well and will earn only $25,000 a year, and the probability is .25 that you will be a success and earn $225,000. Which industry would you enter?

This appears to be a relatively simple problem. The only complication occurs because there are two possible outcomes in industry B. If you knew you would be a success in industry B, you would definitely enter industry B. But if you knew you would be a colossal failure in industry B, you would enter industry A. A problem exists because you do not know whether you are going to be successful or unsuccessful.

The expected income hypothesis states that an individual enters the industry with the highest expected income. Expected income weights the income of each outcome by its probability of occurrence and sums this product over all possible outcomes or states of nature.

> **Expected income** is a probability-weighted average of income over all outcomes.

The expression for expected income is

$$EI = \Sigma \, p_i I_i \qquad \text{(Expected Income)} \tag{3-4}$$

where p_i is the probability that the ith outcome or state of nature will occur (earthquake or no earthquake) and I_i is the resulting income under that outcome. The symbol Σ means that we add up all products of the probability and income for all states of nature.

Let's calculate the expected income of the two choices and see whether industry A or industry B has the higher expected income. Expected income in industry A is $EI_A = 1(\$75,000) = \$75,000$ because the probability of earning $75,000 is 1. On the other hand, if you enter industry B, there are two possible outcomes. Your expected income is

$$EI_B = 0.75(\$25,000) + 0.25(\$225,000) = \$75,000$$

One way of interpreting expected income in industry B is to think of a large number of individuals with similar backgrounds entering industry B. We can expect that about 75 percent will be failures and earn only $25,000 a year and that 25 percent will earn $225,000 a year. Averaging the income of all entrants, we find the average income is $75,000.

So, it turns out that expected income in the two industries is the same. If each individual based the entry decision solely on maximizing expected income, each should be indifferent between industries A and B and be willing to flip a coin to decide.

The Expected Utility Hypothesis

Chances are that most individuals would not express an indifference between entering the two industries. Although the expected income of the two choices is the same, many would prefer to enter industry A and only a minority would select industry B. Those favoring industry A would express concern over the different

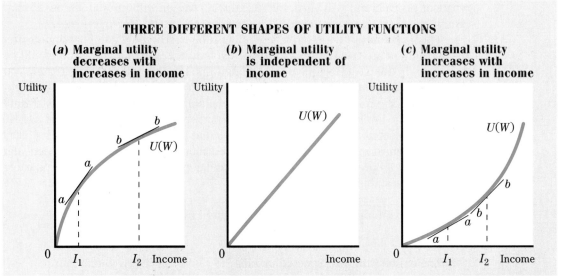

Figure 3-15   The effect of income on the marginal utility of income differentiates the three utility of income functions. (*a*) Marginal utility decreases with increases in income. (*b*) Marginal utility is independent of income. (*c*) Finally, marginal utility increases with increases in income.

possible outcomes in industry B and view the diverse outcomes as something to avoid. To them, industry B is a risky business where you might struggle by with only $25,000 annually or receive a handsome yearly income of $225,000. Whether you react favorably or unfavorably to these extreme outcomes depends on how much more utility you receive from $225,000 and how much less utility you receive from $25,000. Somehow, the analysis of decision making under uncertainty must take account of the *utility* that the consumer derives from higher- and lower-income outcomes.

Assuming this approach has some merit, we need to consider the utility of income. We must know how much better off or worse off the individual will be if income is higher or lower. To do this, we introduce the consumer's utility of income function:

$$U = U(I) \qquad \text{(Utility of Income Function)} \qquad \text{(3-5)}$$

where U is the individual's utility (in personal units called utils) and I is income. Figure 3-15a to c shows the utility of the consumer as a function of income. In all three cases utility increases with increases in income, and so $\Delta U/\Delta I > 0$. The slope of the utility function is marginal utility. What differentiates the three cases is how marginal utility changes with changes in income. In Figure 3-15a marginal utility *decreases* with increases in income. Each dollar increase in income causes successively smaller increases in marginal utility. The slope of the utility function in Figure 3-15a decreases with increases in I. Notice that the slope of the tangent aa when $I = I_1$ is steeper than the slope of the tangent bb when $I = I_2$. Mathematically, this means the second derivative of the utility function is negative because the slope decreases, $[\Delta(\Delta U/\Delta I)]/\Delta I = \Delta^2 U/\Delta I^2 < 0$. In Figure 3-15*b* the marginal utility of incomes does not change with changes in income. Marginal utility, the slope of the utility function, is *constant* and independent of *I*. In Figure 3-15*c* the slope of the utility function increases with *I*. The slope of the tangent *aa* is less than the slope of the tangent *bb*. Marginal utility *increases* with increases in the income of the consumer, and so $\Delta^2 U/\Delta I^2 > 0$. We distinguish between the different shapes of the utility function because it has much to do with the degree of risk an individual is comfortable with.

Now that the utility of income function has been introduced, we can consider the expected utility hypothesis. Some economists have proposed that consumers select from among uncertain situations so that expected utility is maximized. Expected utility weights the utility of income by the probability of that outcome or state of nature and sums the product over all possible outcomes.

$$EU = \Sigma p_i U(I_i) \qquad \text{(Expected Utility)} \qquad \text{(3-6)}$$

Under the expected utility hypothesis it is the utility of income that counts.

> **Expected utility** is a probability-weighted average of the utilities of the consumer over all outcomes.

Let's compare the predictions of the expected income and the expected utility hypotheses in the situation involving industries A and B. Table 3-2 shows the outcomes (income) in column 1, and columns 2 and 3 indicate the probability of each outcome. Column 4 lists the utility of income for each outcome and shows a utility function that corresponds to the utility function in Figure 3-15*a*. Finally,

Table 3-2 EXPECTED INCOME AND EXPECTED UTILITY OF ENTERING INDUSTRY A OR B

INCOME ($) (1)	PROBABILITY OF OUTCOME IN INDUSTRY A, (p_i) (2)	PROBABILITY OF OUTCOME IN INDUSTRY B, (p_i) (3)	UTILITY OF INCOME, $U(I_i)$ (4)	CONTRIBUTION TO EXPECTED UTILITY FOR INDUSTRY A, $(p_i U(I_i))$ (5)	CONTRIBUTION TO EXPECTED UTILITY FOR INDUSTRY B, $(p_i U(I_i))$ (6)
25,000		.75	4 utils		3 utils
75,000	1		10	10 utils	
225,000		.25	16		4 utils
Expected income	$75,000	$75,000			
Expected utility				10 utils	7 utils

columns 5 and 6 indicate the expected utility of each outcome. Row 4 shows the expected income of each decision, and row 5 the expected utility of each decision. In Table 3-2 the expected income of the two choices is the same and is equal to $75,000, but the expected utilities of the two industries are different. Column 5 shows the individual contributions to expected utility of each outcome if you enter industry A and earn $75,000: the contribution to expected utility is $pU(\$75,000) = 1(10) = 10$ utils. On the other hand, if you enter industry B, the expected utility is only 7 utils. If you are maximizing expected utility, you will enter industry A.

The shape of your utility function determines your choice of employment. Note that utility increases, but at a decreasing rate, as income increases. A tripling of income from $25,000 to $75,000 does not triple utility. An increase from $25,000 to $75,000 increases utility from 4 to 10 utils or only $2\frac{1}{2}$ times. An increase in income from $75,000 to $225,000, a threefold increase, increases utility by less than twofold. So, a relatively high income does not add that much more utility, and a relatively low income causes a comparatively large decrease in utility compared to the certain outcome in industry A. This is the reason many individuals would be reluctant to enter industry B.

Risk Aversion and Risk Taking

Let's show how the decision made by the individual depends on the shape of the utility function. Some people are risk-averse and avoid risky situations, whereas others are risk takers and flourish in uncertain environments. The expected utility hypothesis explains this difference in behavior by the different shapes of the individuals' utility functions. We consider two individuals with different utility functions. The first has the utility function $U_1(I_i)$ in Figure 3-16a, and the second has the utility function $U_2(I_i)$ in Figure 3-16b. Utility is measured in utils on the vertical axis, and income on the horizontal axis. The marginal utility of $U_1(I_i)$ decreases and the marginal utility of $U_2(I_i)$ increases with increases in income. How do these two individuals decide which industry to enter? In industry A each receives a certain income of I^*, while in industry B each receives $I^* - k$ with probability p and $I^* + k$ with probability $1 - p$. Industry A might be a large insurance company or the government, and industry B might be a new biotechnology firm. If the firm is unsuccessful, k might be equal to I^* and so you will end up with nothing, or it might be a success and you will end up earning twice I^*. If the individual enters industry B, expected income EI_B is

$$EI_B = p(I^* - k) + (1 - p)(I^* + k)$$

Collecting terms, we have

$$EI_B = [p + (1 - p)]I^* + [-p + (1 - p)]k$$

$$= I^* + (1 - 2p)k$$

If $p = \frac{1}{2}$, $EI_B = I^*$. Therefore, the expected income in the two industries is the same. Although the expected income is the same, this does not mean that the

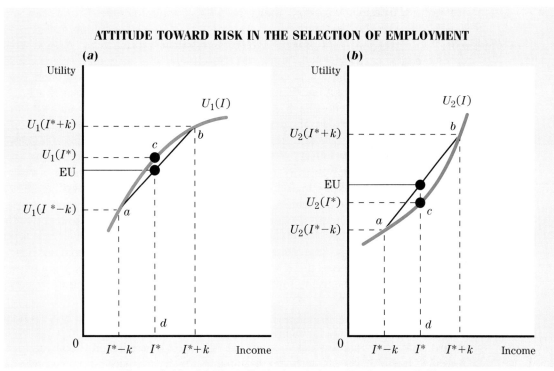

Figure 3-16   (*a*) The individual with the utility function $U_1(I)$ prefers industry A with the certain earnings of I^* and $U_1(I^*)$ rather than the EU in industry B. (*b*) The individual with $U_2(I)$ is a risk taker and prefers industry B with its uncertain prospects because EU is greater than $U_2(I^*)$.

expected utility is the same. Now let's compare the expected utility of the two industries. For the first individual the expected utility from entering industry A is simply $U_1(I^*)$, and for the second individual it is $U_2(I^*)$. For the first individual the expected utility of entering industry B is

$$\text{EU}_B = .5U_1(I^* - k) + .5U_1(I^* + k) = \frac{U_1(I^* - k) + U_1(I^* + k)}{2}$$

or the average of the two utilities. The same is true for the second individual because the expected utility is

$$\text{EU}_B = .5U_2(I^* - k) + .5U_2(I^* + k) = \frac{U_2(I^* - k) + U_2(I^* + k)}{2}$$

Expected utility is the average of the two utilities of each individual when $p = \frac{1}{2}$.

Figure 3-16 shows that the expected utility in industry A is $U_1(I^*)$ for the first individual and $U_2(I^*)$ for the second individual because each individual is certain of earning I^*. Because expected utility in industry B is the average of utilities for both individuals, expected utility is the midpoint between $U_1(I^* - k)$ and $U_1(I^* + k)$ for the first individual (Figure 3-16a), and the midpoint between $U_2(I^* - k)$ and $U_2(I^* + k)$ for the second individual (Figure 3-16b).

Now it is clear why individual 1 prefers industry A to industry B, because the utility from the certain income of I^* in industry A (point c) is greater than the expected utility of entering industry B; that is, $U_1(I^*) > .5U_1(I^* - k) + .5U_1(I^* + k)$. On the other hand, individual 2 prefers industry B because expected utility is higher than the utility of the certain income of I^* in industry A (point c); that is, $.5U_2(I^* - k) + .5U_2(I^* + k) > U_2(I^*)$. The different choices are due to the different shapes of the utility functions. Marginal utility of income decreases with income for individual 1. Individual 1 receives a relatively small increase in utility when income is relatively high and loses relatively more utility when income is relatively low. Just the opposite is true for individual 2. Individual 2 receives relatively large increases in utility when income is relatively high and suffers a relatively small decrease in utility when income is relatively low. We can say that individual 1 is risk-averse because he avoids uncertain situations, while individual 2 is a risk taker because she prefers the uncertain situation. The basic point of the analysis is that the shape of the utility function determines whether an individual is a risk taker or a risk avoider.

Everyday behavior indicates that people differ in their attitudes toward risk. If you always fasten your seat belt when you enter your automobile, your behavior reflects risk aversion. Fastening your seat belt each time you enter your car is a nuisance for most people, although in some states driving without a seat belt is a violation of the law. For other drivers, it is a small cost to incur each time they enter an automobile because of the smaller loss if an accident does happen. They incur this cost to purchase more certainty. A person who does not use a seat belt avoids this cost but faces greater uncertainty. The seat belt user's utility function resembles $U_1(I)$.

A young aspiring baseball player who enters the minor leagues illustrates the risk taker because there is a very small probability that he will ever reach the major leagues. In the minor leagues night baseball is played under less-than-ideal lighting conditions, travel by bus from town to town is wearing, and the pay is often low. An aspiring ball player enters the minor leagues because he is a risk taker and prefers to take a gamble. There is a very high probability that he will fail and that his earnings will be less than if he had accepted the certain and higher salary of a nine-to-five job, but there is also a tiny probability that he will succeed and earn a major league salary of more than a million dollars. The aspiring ball player is obviously willing to take the gamble, and his utility function resembles utility function $U_2(I)$.

It has been shown that expected utility is the average of the two utilities when $p = \frac{1}{2}$. However, a graphic measure of expected utility can be obtained for any value of p, not only for $p = \frac{1}{2}$, by following three steps.

   1. Construct a chord from $U(I^* - k)$ to $U(I^* + k)$. In Figure 13-16 the chord is the line ab.

   2. Calculate expected income from the expression EI $= I^* + (1 - 2p)k$. As

Table 3-3   RESPONSE OF RISK-AVERSE, RISK-NEUTRAL, AND RISK-TAKING INDIVIDUALS TO AN UNCERTAIN SITUATION

TYPE OF INDIVIDUAL	SECOND DERIVATIVE OF UTILITY FUNCTION		CHOICE
Risk avoider	$\dfrac{\Delta^2 U}{\Delta I^2} < 0$	Marginal utility decreases with income.	Prefers certainty
Risk-neutral individual	$\dfrac{\Delta^2 U}{\Delta I^2} = 0$	Marginal utility is constant.	Indifferent
Risk taker	$\dfrac{\Delta^2 U}{\Delta I^2} > 0$	Marginal utility increases with income.	Prefers uncertain situation

p increases from 0 to 1, EI decreases from $I^* + k$ to $I^* - k$. If $p = p^*$, then $EI^* = p^*(I^* - k) + (1 - p^*)(I^* + k)$.

3. Determine expected utility by working directly up to the chord ab at EI = EI*. In Figure 3-16 expected income is I^* because $p = \frac{1}{2}$, and expected utility of an uncertain event is a point on the chord ab at the value of expected income on the horizontal axis. When p is closer to 0, expected utility is on ab but closer to point b. When p is closer to 1, expected utility is closer to point a on the chord ab.

Table 3-3 reviews the decisions made by a risk avoider, a risk-neutral individual, and a risk taker when comparing an uncertain situation and a certain one with the same expected income. The risk avoider has utility function where $\Delta^2 U/\Delta I^2 < 0$ and prefers certainty. The risk-neutral individual has a linear utility function where $\Delta^2 U/\Delta I^2 = 0$ and so is indifferent. The risk taker has a utility function where $\Delta^2 U/\Delta I^2 > 0$ and prefers to gamble.

Buying Insurance

Many individuals avoid risky situations. They seek ways of insuring against a loss. Let's assume that you own a house in the Los Angeles metropolitan area with a market value of V dollars. The probability of an earthquake is p, and the loss is L if an earthquake occurs. Your expected wealth is

$$EW = p(V - L) + (1 - p)V = V - pL$$

Suppose you decide to purchase earthquake insurance. The insurance company agrees to restore the value of the house if there is an earthquake, and you pay a premium of P. The premium is made up of two components. The first component equals the expected loss of the insurance company, or pL. From the company's point of view there is a probability p of an earthquake that causes a loss of L. Therefore, the expected loss is pL. For example, if the probability of an earthquake is .01 and a house suffers a $1 million loss, then the expected loss is $10,000. The second component of the premium is called the load factor or O. It represents the cost of running the insurance company and any profit earned by the company.

The premium charged by the insurance company for coverage equal to L is

$$P = pL + O \qquad \text{(Premium of Insurance Company)} \qquad (3\text{-}7)$$

If you purchase insurance and an earthquake occurs, your wealth is equal to $V - L + L - P = V - P$. Your loss L is covered by the insurance company's payment of L, and so your wealth decreases by the amount of the premium. If no earthquake occurs, your wealth is equal to $V - P$ because you pay a premium of P. Purchasing an insurance policy shows that you are willing to pay a premium of P in exchange for a certain outcome of $V - P$ and a certain utility of $U(V - P)$. If you purchase insurance, your expected wealth, EW, is

$$\text{EW} = p(V - P) + (1 - p)(V - P) = V - P = V - pL - O$$

We know that expected wealth is $V - pL$ if the individual does not purchase insurance. Purchasing insurance shows that this individual is willing to settle for a lower expected wealth in exchange for a certain utility.

Let's determine when a risk-averse consumer will purchase insurance. Figure 3-17 shows the utility function of such an individual. Without insurance wealth is

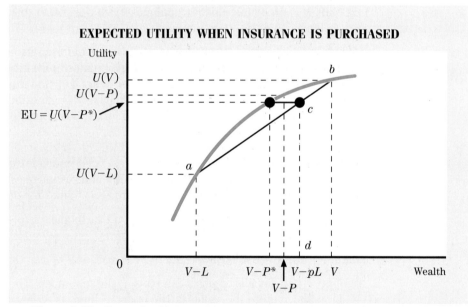

Figure 3-17   If an individual purchases insurance, the expected utility of the individual is $U(V - P)$, where P is the premium. As long as the premium is not too large, so that $P < P^*$, the expected utility from purchasing insurance is greater than the expected utility of not purchasing insurance.

either V, if no loss occurs, or $V - L$, if a loss occurs. The chord connecting $U(V - L)$ and $U(V)$ is ab, and expected wealth is EW $= p(V - L) + (1 - p)V = V - pL$. With insurance, the expected utility of the individual is $U(V - P)$. The consumer prefers insurance if the utility of the certain outcome, $U(V - P)$, is greater than the expected utility, EU, which is equal to cd if insurance is not purchased. With an insurance policy the expected wealth of the individual is $V - P = V - pL - O$. If the loading fee is not too large, a risk-averse individual will purchase insurance because $U(V - P)$ is greater than the expected utility without an insurance policy.

As the loading charge increases, the consumer will at some point decide not to purchase insurance. We can determine what premium makes a risk-averse individual indifferent between buying and not buying insurance. The premium P^* must be large enough so that $U(V - P^*) = $ EU in Figure 3-17. Then, the individual is indifferent between the utility of a certain wealth of $V - P^*$ and the expected utility of owning a home without insurance. If the premium exceeds P^*, even a risk-averse individual will not purchase insurance.

In summary, a risk-averse individual will pay a premium that exceeds the expected loss in order to get some peace of mind. This is an acceptable tradeoff for a risk-averse individual who maximizes expected utility. However, even a risk-averse individual will not purchase insurance if the premium is too large and exceeds P^*.

APPLICATION 3-2

Why Is Earthquake Insurance a Slow Seller in California?

On October 17, 1989, at 5:04 P.M. a major earthquake registering 6.9 on the Richter scale struck the San Francisco Bay Area. The tremor set off many fires and caused extensive damage to houses and apartments throughout the Bay Area. Highway pillars collapsed, crushing cars on lower-level ramps, and a section of the Bay Bridge connecting San Francisco and Oakland collapsed.

Periodic warnings have been and continue to be issued to Californians that the "big one" is yet to come. Yet only 20 percent of the houses in California have earthquake insurance. On the other hand, most Californians insure their automobiles for comprehensive damage. This raises the interesting question of why they don't heed the warnings of experts and insure their homes for damage caused by earthquakes.

By working with the expected utility hypothesis we can come up with two explanations of why many Californians refuse to purchase earthquake insurance. The first reason is that it is too expensive. If the loading charge is sufficiently large on earthquake insurance, a risk-averse individual will not buy it. In 1989 earthquake insurance for a brick home cost about $6,000 a year for $500,000 coverage. For a frame house, the cost was $630 a year for similar coverage because a frame house is more flexible and can better withstand the stresses caused by an earthquake.[4]

[4] Robert J. Cole, "Who Pays? Insurers Tallying, But Policies on Houses Are Few," *New York Times*, October 19, 1989.

These cost estimates do not indicate if the loading charge is sufficiently high to discourage purchase of earthquake insurance, but the expense probably does deter some individuals from becoming insured.

A second reason is that homeowners without insurance expect to receive aid from the rest of the country through federal government disaster programs when the "big one" hits. California is a large state with considerable political influence, and it is likely that federal disaster aid will be forthcoming if a major earthquake occurs. After all, Alaska received disaster aid after a major earthquake, and owners of oceanfront properties along the path of hurricanes have received assistance.

Let's see how the expectation of aid alters the decision to purchase insurance. Figure 3-18 shows that an individual will purchase earthquake insurance and pay a premium of P if no aid is expected. The expected utility of this homeowner is $U(V - P)$ at point a, where P is the premium and the expected wealth of the individual is $V - P = V - pL - O$, whereas the expected utility is lower if the individual does not purchase insurance (point e). Suppose the individual expects the government to supply aid in the form of a grant G, where $G \leq L$, to cover some fraction of the earthquake loss if the residence is *not* covered by insurance. If an earthquake occurs, the wealth of this homeowner without insurance is $V - L + G$. Therefore, the expected utility is

$$EU = pU(V - L + G) + (1 - p)U(V)$$

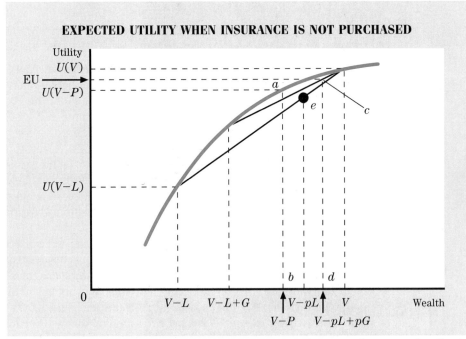

Figure 3-18 If an individual purchases insurance, the person's expected utility is $U(V - P)$, where P is the premium. If the government grants aid equal to G to all those without insurance, the expected utility of not buying insurance is EU which is greater than $U(V - P)$, expected utility with insurance.

when the individual qualifies for aid because he does not have insurance. The expected wealth of the individual is $EW = p(V - L + G) + (1 - p)V = V - pL + pG$ and is higher if the homeowner does not purchase insurance. Expected utility may be higher depending on the value of G. If $G = L$, the expected utility of not purchasing insurance is $U(V)$, which is greater than the expected utility of buying insurance. The government provides full insurance and does not charge a premium. If $G = 0$, we already know that the individual prefers to purchase insurance. Therefore, there is some value of G between 0 and L where the homeowner will decide not to purchase insurance. Figure 3-18 shows a case where G is large enough so that the individual does not purchase earthquake insurance. Expected utility is cd when the homeowner does not purchase insurance but receives aid, and ab when he purchases insurance and does not qualify for aid.

By providing disaster aid the government discourages the purchase of insurance and encourages individuals to take risks. On the Atlantic and Gulf coasts many people build summer homes along the oceanfront directly in the path of hurricanes and vulnerable to damage. Periodically, hurricanes cause extensive damage to oceanfront properties. The homes are rebuilt along the same oceanfront with federal disaster aid, and so by providing disaster aid the government subsidizes this type of risk-taking behavior.

In summary, the expected utility hypothesis offers two possible explanations for the reluctance of Californians to purchase earthquake insurance.

SUMMARY

- The income effect measures the change in the quantity demanded caused by a change in income when prices are held constant.
- The quantity demanded changes in the same direction as the change in income for a normal good and in the opposite direction for an inferior good.
- The substitution effect measures the change in the quantity demanded caused by a relative price change with the utility of the consumer held constant.
- The demand function of a consumer has a negative slope if the good is a normal good.
- The slope of the demand function can be either positive or negative if the good is an inferior good.
- The combined effect of the substitution and income effects determines the slope of the demand function.
- The demand function will be more elastic if (a) the product is a close substitute for another product, (b) the consumer spends a higher percentage of income on the good, and (c) the income elasticity of demand is large.
- The marginal willingness to pay function shows the maximum amount a consumer will pay for successive units of a good.
- Consumer surplus is the difference between the maximum amount the consumer would pay and the actual amount paid.
- The demand function is identical to the marginal willingness to pay function if the income effect is zero.

- Expected income is a probability-weighted average of incomes for all outcomes.
- Expected utility is a probability-weighted average of utility for all outcomes.
- A risk-averse individual prefers to purchase insurance if the premium is not too high.
- A risk taker prefers an uncertain situation and will not purchase insurance.

KEY TERMS

Income and substitution effects

Income elasticity of demand

Giffen good

Positively sloped demand function

Marginal willingness to pay function

Probability

Utility of income function

Expected utility

Insurance

Load factor

Normal and inferior goods

Income consumption curve

Negatively sloped demand function

Consumer surplus

Dead weight loss

Expected income

Marginal utility

Risk-taking, risk-neutral, and risk-averse individuals

Premium

REVIEW QUESTIONS

1. If a good is a normal good, the consumer spends an increasing fraction of total income on it as income increases. Explain why you agree or disagree with this statement.

2. Explain why you agree or disagree with the following statements:
   a. If a good is a normal good, the demand function has a negative slope.
   b. If a demand curve has a negative slope, the good is a normal good.
   c. If a good is an inferior good, the demand curve has a positive slope.
   d. If a demand curve has a positive slope in the relevant price range, the good is a normal good.
   e. If a demand function has a positive slope in the relative price range, the good is an inferior good.
   f. If an increase in income does not change the demand for a good, the demand function can have either a positive or a negative slope.

3. When a good is a close substitute for other goods, the dead weight loss of a price support program is small. Explain why you agree or disagree with this statement.

4. If two goods are perfect complements, the substitution effect is zero. Explain why you agree or disagree with this statement.

5. If two goods are perfect substitutes, the substitution effect is zero. Explain why you agree or disagree with this statement.

6. If two goods are perfect complements, the income effect is positive. Explain why you agree or disagree with this statement.

7. A consumer does not subscribe to cable television service. Draw the indifference curve and the budget constraint of this individual. What is his or her consumer surplus?

8. After cable service was deregulated, cable companies raised the rates for basic service. Draw a graph and show how the consumer surplus of demanders changed. Can you measure the loss in consumer surplus by multiplying the increase in the basic rate by the number of subscribers to basic service after rates were increased? Explain why or why not.

9. A risk-averse individual always prefers to be insured rather than uninsured. Explain why you agree or disagree with this statement.

10. A risk-neutral individual never purchases insurance that includes a loading charge. Explain why you agree or disagree with this statement.

EXERCISES

1. A consumer participates in an experiment. First, the price of Y is $5 and the price of X is $10. Then, the income of the consumer changes, and a record is made of the units of X and Y that he or she purchases.

INCOME ($)	UNITS OF X	UNITS OF Y		PRICE OF X ($)	UNITS OF X
200	11	18		20	4
220	12	20		15	6
240	13	22		10	12
260	14	24		5	10

The same consumer participates in a second experiment. This time income is held constant at $220 and the price of Y is $5. The price of X is changed, and the number of units of X consumed is recorded. The results of the second experiment are shown in the right-hand table above.

The experimenter notices that the consumer buys fewer units of X when the price declines from $P_X = \$10$ to $P_X = \$5$ and claims the consumer is not acting irrationally. Do you agree or disagree? Explain your answer.

2. The income-consumption line of a consumer is derived with prices held constant. After the price of X falls, a second income-consumption line is derived. Explain why the two income-consumption lines cannot cross.

3. The slope of the demand function is -1.2 for a consumer currently purchasing three units of a good. A $1 increase in income increases the quantity demanded by five units. Is the behavior of the consumer consistent with rational behavior? Explain why or why not.

4. What does the opposition of the day care industry to a lump sum subsidy tell you about the sign of the income effect?

5. Explain why a wealthy individual's demand function for a good is or is not more elastic than the demand function of a less wealthy consumer.

6. Suppose you are operating an amusement park that offers different rides. Assume the typical patron has a downward sloping demand function for rides.
   a. With a graph show what is the maximum amount you can charge a consumer to enter the park if the rides are free.
   b. What is the maximum amount you can charge a consumer to enter the park if the price per ride is $4?

7. An individual with a current wealth of $100,000 is planning to enter one of two occupations:

   ▪ If the individual enters occupation 1, wealth will either increase to 1.333($100,000) with probability $p = .6$ or decrease to .5($100,000) with $1 - p = .4$.
   ▪ If the individual enters occupation 2, wealth will either increase to 1.8($100,000) with probability $p = .5$ or decrease to .2($100,000) with probability $1 - p = .5$.

   a. If the individual maximizes expected wealth, which occupation will he or she prefer?
   b. Write out an expression for expected utility.
   c. If the individual enters occupation 1, what can you infer about the shape of his or her utility function? With the aid of a graph explain why the person chooses occupation 1.

8. A risk taker hopes to rebuild a house on a Gulf Coast beach after it has been destroyed by a hurricane. The government hopes to discourage rebuilding on the beach. How much would the government have to pay the homeowner to prevent the individual from rebuilding?

CHAPTER 3 APPENDIX

Measuring Consumer Surplus with Income Effects

This appendix demonstrates why the demand function of the consumer cannot be used to estimate consumer surplus when income effects are large. If a good is a normal good, the income effect is positive and an increase in income increases the quantity demanded. For a normal good, the area under the demand function overestimates the maximum amount a consumer would pay for any given quantity. Figure 3-19 shows the two indifference curves, U_0 and U_1. The marginal willingness to pay function is derived as before by determining the maximum amount the consumer would pay for successive units along the indifference curve U_0. When an individual consumes X' units of X, the slope of tangent aa to U_0 is $-W'$ and the absolute value of the slope of U_0 represents the maximum amount the consumer would be willing to reduce spending on other goods for an infinitesimal increase in X. Let the slope of the budget constraint I_0a be $-P'$ and assume P' equals W'. Therefore, the tangent aa is parallel to the budget constraint I_0a. The budget constraint I_0a is tangent to the indifference curve U_1 when $X = X^* > X'$ with market basket 1 because X is a normal good. What makes this case different is that X^* is greater than X'. Because the tangent aa and I_0a have the same slope, $X^* - X'$ is the income effect when the tangent aa shifts upward to I_0b.

In Figure 3-20 the consumer's demand function is dd and the marginal willingness to pay function is ww. When the price is P', the quantity demanded is X^*, one point on the

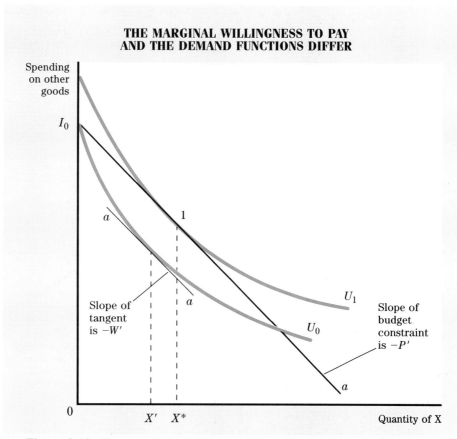

Figure 3-19   The slope of the U_0 is equal to $-W'$ when $X = X'$. The slope of the budget constraint $I_0 a$ equals $-P'$ which equals $-W'$. Because the slope of the tangent aa is equal to the slope of $I_0 a$, the increase in the quantity demanded of $X^* - X'$ is the income effect.

consumer's demand function. When $X = X'$, the most that the consumer is willing to pay for an infinitesimal increase in X is W', a point on the consumer's willingness to pay function. Because $W' = P'$ but $X^* > X'$, the demand function lies to the right of the willingness to pay function.

> The demand function differs from the marginal willingness to pay function if the income effect is not zero.

By repeating this argument for different values of W, it can be shown that the demand function lies to the right of the marginal willingness to pay function. Therefore, the area under the demand function in Figure 3-20 clearly overestimates the maximum amount that this consumer is willing to pay for a given quantity, which is the area under ww up to the specified quantity.

The main point of this analysis is that the demand function overestimates consumer surplus. If a firm used advanced statistical or experimental methods to estimate the shape

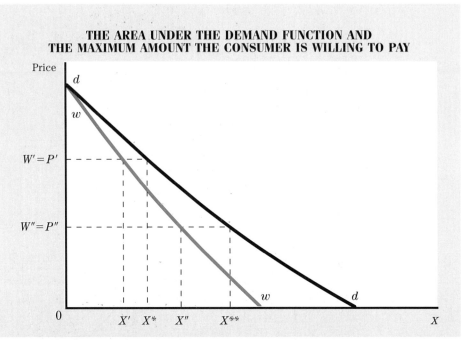

Figure 3-20 When the income effect is positive, the marginal willingness to pay function lies to the left of the demand function of the consumer. For any quantity, the area under the demand function is larger than the maximum amount the consumer would be willing to pay for that quantity.

of the consumer's demand curve, it would take the area under the demand function as an estimate of the maximum amount the individual will pay for a given quantity. For example, the firm could offer to sell X^{**} units to the consumer for a sum equal to the area under the demand curve up to X^{**} and would expect to sell X^{**} units. Because this is a normal good, the consumer would refuse to purchase any units because he or she would be better off without it rather than pay the amount required.

The firm has failed to recognize that this is a normal good, and so the area under the demand function overestimates the maximum amount the consumer will pay for each unit. The area under the demand curves measures the maximum amount the consumer will pay only if the income effect is negligible. However, the income effect will be small either if the consumer spends a small share of income on the good or if the income elasticity of demand is small.

This is a convenient place to stop and reexamine the marginal willingness to pay function. All points on this function are derived as the consumer moves along U_0. Utility is constant as the consumer moves along the indifference curve or down the marginal willingness to pay function. The movement from one point to another point on a given indifference curve measures the substitution effect. So, movements along the marginal willingness to pay function measure just the substitution effect. Curve ww is sometimes referred to as the (income) compensated demand function. This function measures the substitution effect, and the demand function measures the substitution and income effects. The compensated demand function differs from the demand function whenever the income effect is not zero.

CHAPTER 4

THE COST OF TIME AND THE THEORY OF CONSUMER BEHAVIOR

In Chapters 2 and 3 it was assumed that the the price paid by the consumer is the only cost of consuming a good. For some goods, this is an accurate estimate of the cost of consumption. For others, the market price is only a small fraction of the total cost of consuming the product. What would you say is the cost of reading the novel *War and Peace?* It certainly is not the price of the book. A dedicated reader will set aside many hours for reading, hours that he or she might apply to earning income. On the other hand, what would you say is the price of consuming a hamburger at a fast food outlet? Here the market price of the product comes closer to the total cost of consumption. It takes just a few minutes to order and eat a hamburger. These two extreme examples illustrate that for some products consumption is more time-intensive than for others. Therefore, the "price" of some goods is not the market price but must include the time required for consumption.

Not only does consumption take more time for some goods than for others, but the value of time differs from one person to another. Two individuals with the same tastes make different decisions about how many units of a good to consume although they can purchase the good at the same market price. Suppose the earnings of one person depend on hours of work and his hourly wage, while another more fortunate person sits back and receives the same income from dividends and interest. The cost of consuming is different for the two individuals. For the individual whose earnings depend on hours of work, time devoted to consuming is lost income. The higher the wage rate, the greater the income loss. For the individual who receives dividend and interest income, time spent on consumption has little effect on income. She receives dividend checks regardless of how she spends her time, and so she can use time in any way without losing income. While one individual may be well-read and a great conversationalist, the other has barely enough time to read the daily newspaper. The value of time also affects the types of goods that a consumer purchases.

This chapter modifies the theory of consumer behavior presented in Chapter 2 by including a more comprehensive measure of the price of a good. In Chapter 2 the income of the consumer and the prices of the goods determined what market baskets the consumer could afford. Chapter 4 expands the theory to include time as a scarce resource that a consumer allocates to consumption and work activities. Nobel Prize winner Gary Becker is the foremost proponent of incorporating time explicitly into the theory.[1] He suggests that a deeper understanding of consumer behavior can be gained by recognizing that consumers not only allocate income between different products but also allocate time between earning and consuming activities. These views are included in this analysis of the consumption decision by adding the cost of time to the consumer behavior model.

4-1   AFFORDABLE MARKET BASKETS

Time is another constraint that determines what market baskets the consumer can afford. For example, it takes time to sleep, to shop, to watch TV, to eat, or to daydream. The familiar lament "Where did all the time go?" expresses the time

[1] Gary S. Becker, "A Theory of the Allocation of Time," *Economic Journal*, vol. 75, September 1965, pp. 493–517.

constraint. A consumer allocates time to an array of activities, just as he or she spends income on a range of goods. To observe the impact of time on the consumption decision, we look at the effects of limited time on the choice of goods. Again, the useful two-good model simplifies the situation confronting the consumer and still allows us to identify the effect of a scarce resource on the consumer's behavior.

The Limits of Time

To include time in the analysis, some fundamental relationships between time and consumption behavior must be established. In the model total time available to the consumer is T hours per period, where a period can be a day, a week, or a month. T is a constant and outside the control of the individual. In our simplified model the consumer spends time either *working* or *consuming X and Y*, the two goods in the model. The individual decides how much time to allocate to work and to the consumption of each unit of X or Y. This interpretation of "consuming" includes the time spent shopping for and preparing the good for consumption, as well as the time used to consume it. For example, consuming a steak includes the time required to shop at a supermarket, to prepare and cook the steak, and to eat the steak and clean up afterward. Reading a book includes the total time required to purchase, read, and think about the book.

Because the consumption of goods requires time, it is necessary to specify how much time is used to consume each unit of X and Y. Initially, it is assumed that the consumer uses t_X hours to consume each unit of X and t_Y hours to consume each unit of Y, where both t_X and t_Y are constants outside the individual's control. Work is the other activity that requires time in this simplified model where T_w is the hours of work per period. In the model the individual manages time by determining how much time to allocate for the consumption of each good and for work.

The consumer satisfies the time constraint

$$\frac{\text{Time spent}}{\text{consuming X}} + \frac{\text{Time spent}}{\text{consuming Y}} + \frac{\text{Time}}{\text{working}} = \frac{\text{Total}}{\text{time}}$$

$$t_X X + t_Y Y + T_w = T \qquad \text{(Time Constraint)} \qquad \text{(4-1)}$$

Equation 4-1 says that time spent consuming goods X and Y and working equals the total time available. The time used to consume X units of X is $t_X X$ because it takes t_X hours to consume each unit of X. Similarly, the time needed to consume Y units of Y is $t_Y Y$. For example, if each movie you see lasts 2 hours and you see 30 movies a year, then the time involved is 60 hours.

In the model the individual picks the number of hours to work per period, although you may wonder if each person really has this choice. In the model the individual can pick from industries and firms within industries to determine the optimal number of hours of work. Anyone who works in either the consulting or the investment banking industry puts in many hours per year. Other industries require fewer hours per year, and so there is considerable variation in work time in the economy. If you are self-employed, you decide how much effort and time to put into your business. Throughout this discussion of the model, it is assumed that the individual can decide the number of hours to work per year.

The Budget Constraint

Chapter 2 took the income of the consumer and the prices of goods as given. The purchaser managed the budget constraint by matching expenditures to income. When time is introduced, the individual manages time as well by allocating it to consumption and to work. Consequently, income is no longer a constant but depends on how many hours are spent at work. Total earned income increases as work time increases.

The budget constraint of the consumer is slightly more complicated when time is included in the consumer behavior model. Earned income is equal to hours worked per period times the hourly wage w. In addition the consumer may receive nonwage income V which includes pensions, dividends, social security payments, and so on.[2] So, total income is the sum of wage and nonwage income or $wT_w + V$. As before, the market price is P_X for each unit of X and P_Y for each unit of Y. Total expenditures for X and Y are $P_X X$ and $P_Y Y$, respectively.

The budget constraint requires that total spending on X and Y equal total income. The revised budget constraint is written as

Total spending = Total income

$$P_X X + P_Y Y = wT_w + V \qquad \text{(Revised Budget Constraint)} \qquad \textbf{(4-2)}$$

Deriving the Full Price Budget Constraint

Let's determine which market baskets satisfy the time and the budget constraints of the consumer. First, you will learn how to find these market baskets and then you will combine the time and budget constraints to find all affordable market baskets. Given hours worked, the consumer earns income of $wT_w + V$ and spends it on X and Y such that the time constraint (equation 4-1) and the budget constraint (equation 4-2) are satisfied. Only one market basket of X and Y will satisfy both constraints. By repeating this procedure for each T_w, different market baskets of X and Y that satisfy the time and budget constraints can be determined.

How many units of Y the consumer can purchase for each quantity of X can be determined by combining the time and income constraints. First, solve equation 4-2 for T_w by subtracting V from both sides of the equation and then dividing both sides by w to get

$$T_w = \frac{P_X X + P_Y Y - V}{w}$$

Then substitute the expression for T_w into equation 4-1 to obtain the full price budget constraint:[3]

---

[2] It is assumed that the consumer does not spend time collecting nonwage income.

[3] This expression is derived by substituting the expression for T_w into equation 4-1 to obtain

$$t_X X + t_Y Y + \frac{P_X X + P_Y Y - V}{w} = T$$

To simplify the fraction, multiply both sides of the equation by w and add V to both sides to get

$$wt_X X + wt_Y Y + P_X X + P_Y Y = wT + V$$

After collecting terms, we derive equation 4-3.

$$(P_X + wt_X)X + (P_Y + wt_Y)Y = wT + V \qquad \text{(Full Price Budget Constraint)} \quad \text{(4-3)}$$

Full income F_I is on the right-hand side and is equal to $wT + V$.[4]

Full income is the consumer's income if all time is work time.

Full Prices

A useful measure of the cost of consuming a unit of X or Y can be obtained by examining the expressions in parentheses on the left-hand side of equation 4-3. These terms are the full price of consuming a unit of either good. The full price of X or Y is defined as

$$\text{Full price} = \text{Market price} + \text{Opportunity cost of time}$$

$$F_X = P_X + wt_X \qquad \text{(Full Price of X)} \tag{4-4}$$

$$F_Y = P_Y + wt_Y \qquad \text{(Full Price of Y)} \tag{4-5}$$

where F_X and F_Y are the symbols for the full prices of X and Y. The full price of either good is the market price plus the opportunity cost of consuming a good. Because you use t_X hours to consume each unit of X, your forgone income is wt_X, and so wt_X is the opportunity cost of time.

The **full price** of a good is equal to the market price of the good plus the consumer's opportunity cost of time required to consume the good.

As mentioned in the introduction to this chapter, the full price depends on the time required to consume a good and the wage rate. The full price of a good reflects the expression "time is money." With this interpretation of full prices equation 4-3 can be reinterpreted as saying total money expenditure plus forgone income of consuming goods X and Y must equal full income.

In setting prices and understanding consumer behavior, firms must realize that the consumer uses full prices and not simply market prices to determine how many units of each good to purchase. Full prices, not market prices, guide consumer behavior. One firm may set a very low market price but provide very little service, or it may be located a long distance from the consumer. A buyer could decide to purchase the product from another seller who charges a higher market price but offers quicker service and a lower full price. You might very well purchase a higher-priced graphics or drawing software program that has few bugs in it and a complete, elaborate, well-written manual rather than a lower-priced graphics or drawing program with an incomplete or confusing manual because of the extra time you would have to spend trying to decipher the manual or to recover data lost as a result of program glitches.

Because the full price has two components, a firm can reduce the price to consumers in either of two ways. Firms can compete with each other by lowering

---

[4] It is assumed that both the time and budget constraints can be satisfied with nonnegative values for *X* and *Y*.

the market price or by reducing the consumption time of the consumer, both of which decrease the full price. Although businesspeople do not use the term "full price," they are constantly thinking about full prices when they design pricing and marketing strategies. They often talk about offering more convenience to the consumer. What they are thinking about are ways to reduce consumption time. For example, firms offer convenience by locating items where consumers can easily find them, by eliminating stock shortages, providing checkout and sales staff, reducing shipping time, and providing one-stop shopping.

APPLICATION 4-1

Walgreens Offers Convenience[5]

Walgreens is one of the fastest growing major drugstore chains with outlets located primarily in the Midwest. The firm relies on a nationwide computer system for ordering and stocking merchandise and for filling prescriptions and is dedicated to customer convenience. The company firmly believes that consumers value convenience as much as good price when shopping for prescriptions and other drugstore merchandise. Management feels that providing convenience is critical to the success of the company, and the stores are laid out so that the consumer can enter, purchase, and leave quickly. The average Walgreens customer buys two items in less than 10 minutes. The company has adopted a policy of establishing most stores as isolated units, rather than as parts of shopping centers. In this way, the managers believe, consumers are better able to save time by parking near each Walgreens outlet, which is not always possible if units are located in shopping centers.

The prices charged by the company are not the lowest in the industry. Deep discount drug outlets and some supermarkets charge lower prices, but Walgreens has successfully competed with these low-price competitors by offering convenience. Ease of access and quick, reliable service are what the firm strives for. The president of Walgreens aptly summarized the company's philosophy at the 1990 annual meeting: "We believe the retailer who wastes consumers' time in the 90's is committing competitive suicide."

Using the Full Price Budget Constraint to Find Affordable Market Baskets

Equation 4-3 combined the separate time and budget constraints into a single full price budget constraint. If the consumer satisfies the full price budget constraint, then he or she satisfies the separate time and budget contraints. Using the full price budget constraint, we can find those market baskets of X and Y that the consumer can afford. A linear equation derived in Chapter 2 showed the units of

[5] Based on Eben Shapiro, "A Drugstore Industry Leader Raises the Level of Its Game," *New York Times*, August 26, 1990, p. F16. See also Nancy Ryan, "Simplicity Is Walgreens' Cure for the '90's," *Chicago Tribune*, January 21, 1991, Section 4, p. 1.

Y that the consumer could afford for each quantity of X. The same thing can be done with the full price budget constraint.

Equation 4-3 can be rearranged to show how many units of Y can be consumed for any quantity of X. It is solved for Y by subtracting $(P_X + wt_X)X$ from both sides and dividing both sides by $P_Y + wt_Y$:

$$Y = \frac{wT + V}{P_Y + wt_Y} - \left(\frac{P_X + wt_X}{P_Y + wt_Y}\right)X$$

$$= \frac{\text{Full income}}{\text{Full price of Y}} - \left(\frac{\text{Full price of X}}{\text{Full price of Y}}\right)X \qquad \begin{array}{l}\text{(Full Price Budget} \\ \text{Constraint Rearranged)}\end{array} \qquad \textbf{(4-6)}$$

Equation 4-6 is the equation of a straight line between Y and X. The y intercept is $(wT + V)/(P_Y + wt_Y)$, and the slope of the equation is $(P_X + wt_X)/(P_Y + wt_Y)$. Before graphing equation 4-6, let's provide an interpretation of the intercept and the slope of this linear equation in Y and X. If the consumer does not purchase any X, equation 4-6 says the number of units of Y that she can purchase is equal to full income divided by the full price of Y, or $(wT + V)/(P_Y + wt_Y)$. Let's see why this is true. If the individual consumes just Y, her money income is equal to full income less income forgone because Y units are consumed, or $wT + V - wt_Y Y$. The expression $wt_Y Y$ represents the income forgone because the consumer purchases Y units. Because she spends all her money income on Y and the market price of each unit of Y is P_Y, the number of units of Y that can be purchased is equal to total money income divided by P_Y:

$$Y = \frac{wT + V - wt_Y Y}{P_Y} \qquad \textbf{(4-7)}$$

Solving equation 4-7 for Y yields the maximum number of units of Y that the consumer can purchase:[6]

$$Y = \frac{wT + V}{P_Y + wt_Y} \qquad \textbf{(4-8)}$$

This explains why the y intercept is $(wT + V)/(P_Y + wt_Y)$ units of Y. The x intercept is the number of units of X that can be consumed if nothing is spent on Y and is equal to full income divided by the full price of X:

$$X = \frac{wT + V}{P_X + wt_X} \qquad \textbf{(4-9)}$$

Let's consider a numerical example and show how the full price budget constraint can be derived. In rows 1 to 7 of Table 4-1 numerical values are assigned for each of the constants.

---

[6] This result is obtained by multiplying both sides of equation 4-7 by P_Y:

$$P_Y Y = wt + V - wt_Y Y$$

After adding $wt_Y Y$ to both sides of the equation and collecting terms, we have

$$(P_Y + wt_Y)Y = wt + V$$

Dividing both sides by $P_Y + wt_Y$ yields equation 4-8.

Table 4-1   THE FULL PRICE BUDGET CONSTRAINT

1. Hours to consume a unit of X $t_X = 0.5$ or 30 minutes

2. Hours to consume a unit of Y $t_Y = 1$

3. Total time $T = 60$ hours

4. Price of X $P_X = \$20$ per unit

5. Price of Y $P_Y = \$15$ per unit

6. Hourly wage rate $w = \$10$ per hour

7. Nonwage income $V = 0$

8. Full price of X $F_X = P_X + w_X t_X = \$20 + \$10(0.5) = \$25$

9. Full price of Y $F_Y = P_Y + w t_Y = \$15 + \$10(1) = \$25$

10. Full income $F_I = \$10(60) = \$600$

Figure 4-1 shows the full price budget constraint. Equation 4-8 indicates that the y intercept is equal to full income divided by the full price of Y. Row 10 shows that full income is $600, and row 9 shows that the full price of Y is $25, and so the individual can consume $600/\$25 = 24$ units of Y if nothing is spent on X. If 24 units of Y are consumed, money income is equal to $wT - wt_Y Y$, or $600 - \$240 = \$360$. Since the price of Y is $15, total spending on Y is $15(24) = \$360$. So, expenditures match income. Since the individual consumes 24 units of Y and each takes 1 hour, he or she spends 24 hours consuming Y and works $60 - 24 = 36$ hours.

If the consumer purchases only X, she can also buy 24 units of X (equation 4-9). Full income is $600, and the full price of X is $20 + \$10(0.5) = \$25$. The market price is higher for X than for Y, but the consumption time is low enough so that the full price of each good happens to be the same. The ratio of full income to the full price of X is 24 units. Another way of reaching the same conclusion is to recognize that income is $wT - wt_X X = \$600 - \$120 = \$480$ if 24 units of X are purchased. Since the price of X is $20, total expenditure is $20(24) = \$480$. T_w equals $60 - 0.5(24) = 48$ hours. Total income is higher if the buyer consumes only X rather than only Y.

Because the slope of the full price budget constraint is $-F_X/F_Y$ and the full prices are equal, the slope of the full price budget constraint is -1 in this example. Because full income is a constant, each unit of X increases expenditure by $20 and lowers money income by $5 for a total of $25. The change in the number of units of Y times the full price of Y must exactly offset this and therefore must decrease by $25. If the consumer purchases one less unit of Y, spending on Y is reduced by $P_Y = \$15$ and wage income increases by $10. The reduction in spending resulting from purchasing one less unit of Y plus the additional income totals $25 and just offsets the $25 additional cost of purchasing one more unit of X.

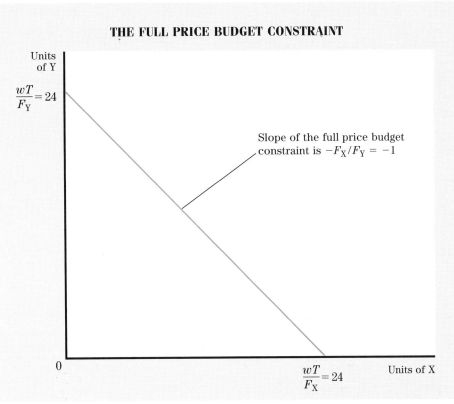

Figure 4-1   The full price budget constraint shows how many units of Y the individual can consume for a given number of units of X while satisfying the time and the budget constraints. In the numerical example the consumer can purchase 24 units of either Y or X if he or she purchases only Y or only X. Although the market price of X is greater than the market price of Y, the full price of X equals the full price of Y and the slope of the full price budget constraint equals -1.

Shifts in the Full Price Budget Constraint

In the numerical example we assumed that nonwage income is zero. If the consumer has nonwage income and receives an increase in dividend income, nonwage income increases from V to V'. The intercept on the vertical axis increases from $(wT + V)/(P_Y + wt_Y)$ to $(wT + V')/(P_Y + wt_Y)$, but $-F_X/F_Y$, the slope of the full price budget constraint, does not change when V changes. Figure 4-2 shows a parallel outward shift in the full price budget just as an increase in income caused a parallel shift in the budget line in Chapter 2. The easiest way to observe the effect of changes in the wage rate is to assume that the consumer has no nonwage income ($V = 0$) and to look at how an increase in w shifts the full price budget constraint. The full price budget constraint is rewritten as

$$Y = \frac{wT}{P_Y + wt_Y} - \left(\frac{P_X + wt_X}{P_Y + wt_Y}\right)X \qquad (4\text{-}10)$$

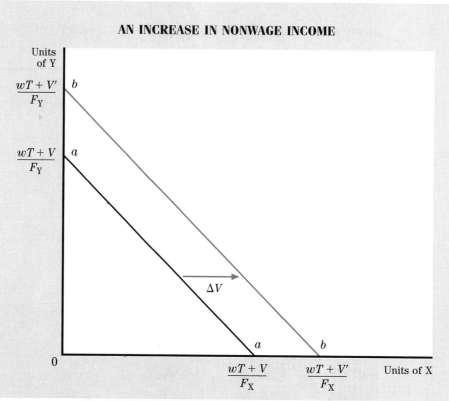

Figure 4-2   The full price budget constraint shifts outward when nonwage income increases. Because the full prices of the goods are unaffected, the slope of the full price budget constraint does not change.

and then rearranged:

$$Y = \frac{T}{(P_Y/w) + t_Y} - \left[\frac{(P_X/w) + t_X}{(P_Y/w) + t_Y}\right]X \qquad \textbf{(4-10a)}$$

Equation 4-10a is derived by multiplying and dividing both sides of equation 4-10 by $1/w$. It shows that the intercept increases when w increases because P_Y/w decreases. The consumer can purchase more units of Y when the wage increases. For example, if the wage rate increases from \$10 to \$15 an hour, the full income of the consumer increases from \$600 to \$900 and the full price of Y increases from \$25 to \$30 and so the consumer can now purchase \$900/\$30 = 30 units of Y.

From equation 4-10a we can see that the slope of the full price budget constraint may change depending on whether the full price of X changes proportionately more or less than the full price of Y. To determine when the percentage change in the full price of X is less than the percentage change in the full price of Y, we derive an expression of the percentage change in each full price. Let's start with F_X. Given P_X and t_X, a change of Δw does not change P_X or t_X but changes the full price of X by $t_X \Delta w$. The change in the full price is the change in the opportunity cost of time:

$$\Delta F_x = t_X \Delta w$$

where ΔF_X is the change in the full price of X.

The percentage change in the full price of X equals the change in the full price divided by the full price of X.

$$\% \, \Delta F_X = \frac{\Delta F_X}{F_X} = \frac{t_X \Delta w}{P_X + wt_X}$$

The percentage change in the full price of Y is, correspondingly,

$$\% \, \Delta F_Y = \frac{t_Y \Delta w}{P_Y + wt_Y}$$

The percentage change in the full price of X is less than the percentage change in the full price of Y if

$$\frac{t_X \Delta w}{P_X + wt_X} < \frac{t_Y \Delta w}{P_Y + wt_Y}$$

This inequality simplifies to[7]

$$\frac{t_X}{P_X} < \frac{t_Y}{P_Y} \qquad \text{(Time per Dollar of Expenditure Inequality)} \qquad \text{(4-11)}$$

An increase in the wage rate will lower the full price of X relative to the full price of Y if the t/P ratio of X is less than the t/P ratio of Y.

The ratio on the left-hand side of equation 4-11 is the number of hours (in minutes) used to consume X per dollar spent on a unit of X. It measures the time intensity of X per dollar expenditure for a unit of X. Similarly, the ratio on the right-hand side is the time intensity of Y per dollar expenditure for a unit of Y. In our numerical example, t_X/P_X is 30 minutes divided by \$20, or $1\frac{1}{2}$ minutes per dollar. Every dollar expenditure for X requires a time commitment of $1\frac{1}{2}$ minutes. For Y, t_Y/P_Y equals 60 minutes divided by \$15, or 4 minutes per dollar. Every dollar expenditure for Y requires a 4-minute time commitment. X is less time-intensive per dollar of expenditure than Y. Because Y uses more time per dollar than X, a rise in the wage rate increases the full cost of Y proportionately more than that of

---

[7] The inequality is derived by multiplying both sides by the full price of X and then by the full price of Y:

$$t_X \Delta w (P_Y + wt_Y) < t_Y \Delta w (P_X + wt_X)$$
$$\Delta w (t_X P_Y) < \Delta w (t_Y P_X)$$
$$\frac{t_X}{P_X} < \frac{t_Y}{P_Y}$$

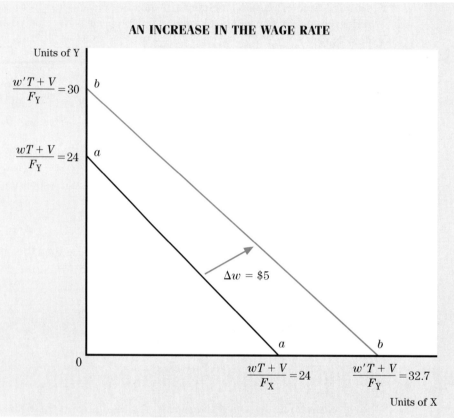

AN INCREASE IN THE WAGE RATE

Figure 4-3 When the wage rate increases from $10 to $15 per hour, the full price budget constraint shifts from *aa* to *bb*. It becomes flatter when the wage rate increases if X is less time-intensive per dollar expenditure than Y. Because the full price of X increases by less than the full price of Y, the full price budget constraint becomes flatter. X becomes cheaper relative to Y when *w* increases.

X. When the wage rate increases, the full price of X increases by a smaller percentage than the full price of Y. In our new terminology the full price of X falls relative to the full price of Y. As the wage rate increases, the consumer finds that X is becoming cheaper relative to Y although the market prices of X and Y are *constant*.

Figure 4-3 shows how the full price budget constraint shifts outward and becomes flatter when *w* increases. The full price budget constraint is the line *aa* when the wage rate is $10 per hour and becomes *bb* when the wage rate increases to $15 per hour. The increase in the wage rate shifts the full price budget constraint outward to the northeast *and* changes the slope of the budget constraint. In our numerical example, the *y* intercept increases to 30 units when the wage rate increases from $10 to $15 an hour. The slope of the full price budget constraint increases from −1 to −$27.5/$30 = −0.917, and the full price budget constraint becomes flatter.

To summarize, a rise in nonwage income has no effect on the slope of the full price budget constraint. On the other hand, a rise in the wage rate can affect relative full prices if the t/P ratios differ among goods. If the t/P ratios differ, the purchaser will substitute toward goods that are less time-intensive per dollar of expenditure. Therefore, a consumer's response to an increase in income is different depending on the source of the increased income.

4-2 THE REVISED CONSUMER BEHAVIOR MODEL

In Chapter 2 the goal of the consumer was to select a market basket that maximized utility subject to the constraint that expenditures match income. Now, the full price budget constraint has been included that takes account of the time and the budget constraints. As before, the consumer's indifference map is defined over all market baskets of X and Y. The goal of the consumer is to find one that maximizes utility subject to the full price budget constraint.

Choosing a Market Basket

Figure 4-4 shows one indifference curve of a consumer and the full price budget constraint. The marginal rate of substitution between Y and X is the slope of the

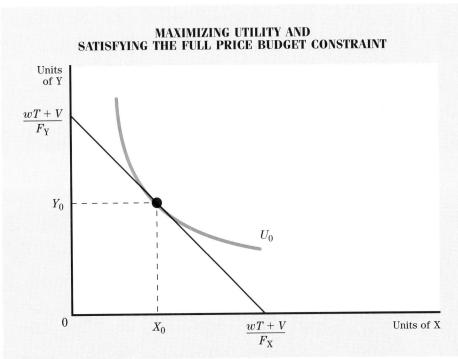

Figure 4-4   The consumer maximizes utility by selecting a market basket of X_0 and Y_0 where the marginal rate of substitution is equal to the slope of the full price budget constraint.

indifference curve at each point on the curve. The consumer selects a market basket on the full price budget constraint where the marginal rate of substitution between Y and X is equal to the slope of the full price budget constraint:

$$\text{MRS}_{YX} = -\frac{F_X}{F_Y} \qquad \begin{array}{l}\text{(Condition for Maximizing Utility}\\ \text{Subject to the Full Price Budget Constraint)}\end{array} \qquad \textbf{(4-12)}$$

where MRS_{YX} denotes the marginal rate of substitution between Y and X. The consumer satisfies this condition by selecting a market basket containing X_0 units of X and Y_0 units of Y.

> If the consumer purchases both goods, he or she selects a market basket where the marginal rate of substitution is equal to the slope of the full price budget constraint.

The Effects of a Change in Income

How does the market basket change when the income of the consumer changes? The market basket selected depends on the source of the income increase. It has been shown that an increase in nonwage income shifts the full price budget constraint outward without changing its slope. On the other hand, a rise in the wage rate shifts the full price budget constraint outward but can change its slope as well. So, we need to keep track of the source of the increased income to predict how the consumer reacts.

Figure 4-5 shows how an increase in nonwage income shifts the full price budget constraint parallel from *aa* to *bb* so that the consumer can reach indifference curve U_1. When nonwage income increases, the consumer moves from market basket A to market basket B and increases purchases of X from X_0 to X_1 and of Y from Y_0 to Y_1.

Now consider an increase in the wage rate that allows the consumer to reach indifference curve U_1. The budget constraint becomes *cc* and is tangent to the indifference curve U_1 with market basket C. If X is less time-intensive per dollar than Y, the full price of X falls relative to the full price of Y and the budget constraint *cc* becomes flatter. The consumer selects market basket C and purchases X_2 units of X and Y_2 units of Y because of the increase in the wage rate. The increase in the wage rate encourages the consumer to substitute toward X and away from Y because X has a lower t/P ratio. When wage rate increases, the consumer buys relatively fewer units of goods with higher t/P ratios and may even stop consuming some of these goods.

When the wage rate increases, the consumer substitutes toward good X because X is less time-intensive per dollar of expenditure. This version of the consumer behavior theory tells us that a person with a lower wage rate faces a different ratio of full prices than a person with a higher wage rate. When other factors are held constant, the types of goods that individuals with lower wage rates purchase are more time-intensive per dollar of expenditure. The mix of goods bought shifts in the direction of goods with lower t/P ratios when the wage rate increases over time.

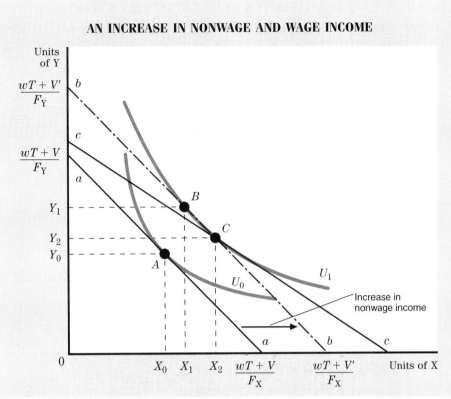

AN INCREASE IN NONWAGE AND WAGE INCOME

Figure 4-5   An increase in nonwage income does not change the slope of the full price budget constraint and therefore shifts the full price budget constraint from *aa* to *bb*. With market basket B the consumer purchases X_1 and Y_1 units. An increase in the wage rate makes the full price budget constraint flatter if X is less time-intensive per dollar than Y. The consumer substitutes toward X and purchases market basket C. The market basket purchased depends on the source of the increased income.

Here are some examples of how the cost of time affects consumer behavior: Some restaurants do not accept reservations and are generally frequented by younger adults who have a lower opportunity cost of time and are willing to stand in line for up to 2 hours to eat at a popular, moderately priced restaurant. When they reach their thirties and their wage rates and cost of time increase, they decline to stand in line and are more likely to patronize restaurants that accept reservations. This difference in behavior is due in part to changes in the cost of time.

   The cost of time affects when individuals shop. For working men and women, the relative cost of time is higher during the work week than during the weekend, and they respond by shopping less during weekdays after work and concentrate more on weekend shopping. In contrast the relative cost of time of shopping for nonworking men and women is lower during the week than on the weekend. Another advantage of shopping during the weekday is that there are fewer people in the stores and the sales staff can offer more help than on the weekend. Figure

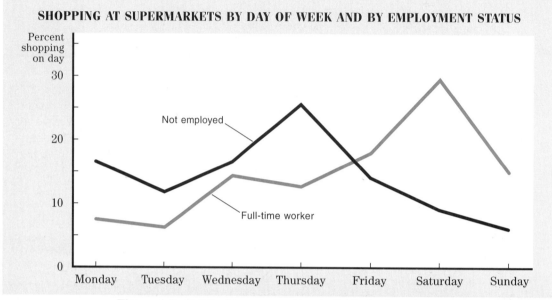

SHOPPING AT SUPERMARKETS BY DAY OF WEEK AND BY EMPLOYMENT STATUS

Figure 4-6   Relatively more working individuals shop for groceries on weekends, whereas relatively more nonworking people shop during the week. [*From* Progressive Grocer, *April 1989.*]

4-6 shows that more full-time workers than nonworking individuals shop for groceries on the weekend.

As the cost of time increases, people also guard their time more carefully. Not wanting to be interrupted by telephone calls, many use telephone answering machines to screen calls. Walker Research in Indianapolis reports that more than half of the 32 million households with answering machines screen calls and resent receiving calls from automatic dialers on Saturday mornings or during the dinner hour.[8]

College students often debate and argue among themselves, an activity with a high t/P ratio. Bull sessions in dorms are commonplace on most campuses. The propensity to argue and the length of debates diminish with age in part because the opportunity cost of time increases with age.

APPLICATION 4-2

Which Consumers Purchase Gasoline at Below Market Price?[9]

In 1980 company-owned Chevron stations in California were mandated to reduce the price of gasoline by 16 to 21 cents per gallon below the current market price

[8] Lena Williams, "Consumers vs Callers: The Lines Are Busier," *New York Times*, June 20, 1991, p. B1.
[9] Based on Robert T. Deacon and Jon Sonstelie, "Rationing by Waiting and the Value of Time: Results from a Natural Experiment," *Journal of Political Economy*, 1985, vol. 93, no. 4, pp. 627–647.

because of a violation of ceiling price regulations. Other independently owned stations selling Chevron gasoline were unaffected and continued to sell Chevron at the market price. Economists Robert Deacon and Jon Sonstelie surveyed the customers who purchased gasoline at the lower-priced company-owned stations as well as those who purchased gasoline at the higher-priced independently owned stations.

The lower-priced stations attracted so many more customers that waiting lines formed. Deacon and Sonstelie found that customers at Chevron-owned stations waited on average an extra 14.6 minutes to purchase gasoline at an average discount of 18.5 cents per gallon. Since the average purchase was 10.5 gallons, the economists estimated that anyone with a wage rate of less than $7.98 per hour would prefer to buy gasoline at the lower-priced station. Economists derive this estimated wage rate by noting that a customer would be indifferent between stations if

$$(P_i - P_c)g = w(t_c - t_i)$$

where P_c and P_i are the prices at the company-owned and independently owned stations, respectively, t_c and t_i are the waiting times at the company-owned and independently owned stations, respectively, g is the number of gallons purchased, and w is the individual's wage rate. Since the average difference in price was 18.5 cents per gallon, the average difference in waiting time was 14.6 minutes and the average number of gallons bought at all stations was 10.5 gallons, the authors calculated that a wage of $7.98 per hour just made the consumer indifferent between the two types of stations. A consumer with a wage rate of less than $7.98 would be more likely to wait in line to purchase gasoline at a company-owned station.

Although Deacon and Sonstelie didn't confirm the estimated wage rate, their predictions were supported by the behavior of gas station patrons. The lower-priced stations attracted more automobiles with larger tank capacities and sold more gallons per transaction. The cars waiting in line at company-owned stations had fewer adult passengers in them. The total opportunity cost of time of all the passengers in a car was lower at company-owned stations. It was also discovered that a higher percentage of unemployed workers and a lower percentage of full-time employed workers were in line at company-owned stations.

This imaginative study shows how the opportunity cost of time of consumers affects the choice of gas station.

4-3   FINDING THE LOWEST FULL PRICE

Up to now, it has been assumed that a consumer uses a fixed amount of time to consume each unit of a good. In the model, the consumer uses t_X hours to consume each unit of X. Often the amount of time used to consume a unit of a good is not a constant but is under the control of the consumer. There are many everyday illustrations where the individual determines the amount of time used to consume a unit of a good.

1. You can select a dentist who charges a high hourly rate but takes patients on time, or you can go to another dentist who charges a low hourly rate but keeps you waiting for your appointment. If you are willing to pay a higher fee, you can save time.

2. You can fly on the Concorde from New York to London at a cost of $4,013 one way, or you can fly first class on a Boeing 747 that takes 3 hours longer for a fare of $3,205. Some consumers and firms are willing to pay about $800 to save about 3 hours of flying time.

3. You can live in the suburbs and spend more time commuting, or you can live in the central city and pay a higher rent but save on commuting time. If you are willing to pay more for housing, you can save time.

4. You can shop at a higher-priced store that employs knowledgeable salespeople and is seldom out of stock. Or, you can run from one low-priced store to another, each of which has fewer salespeople and frequent shortages of merchandise.

5. You can purchase a chicken at a relatively low price at the supermarket and spend time preparing a delicious meal at home, or you can purchase chicken cut up in parts or in boneless form or a more expensive gourmet chicken dinner and spend less time preparing the meal. In 1960 Americans bought whole chickens and prepared them for cooking at home. Today, they buy packages of more expensive cut-up or boneless chicken and save on preparation time.

These illustrations show that individuals have a choice between paying a higher price and saving time or paying a lower price and using more time. The consumer has some control over t_X and t_Y, and so these values are really not constant. To see how the consumer balances the tradeoff between the price paid and the time saved, the theory must be modified.

Dependence of the Full Price on the Market Price

This section examines the price-time tradeoff to see how the consumer determines the full price of a product. Let us concentrate on good X. We assume that the consumer can shop for X at different stores. Some stores offer more service and charge higher prices, and a consumer who decides to shop at these stores pays a higher price but spends less time shopping. Other stores offer less service and charge lower prices, and an individual who shops at these stores pays a lower price but spends more time shopping.

By paying a higher price P_X, the consumer reduces consumption time t_X. So there is an inverse relationship between the price paid and t_X. It is assumed that the consumer can choose from a continuous array of price-time combinations. Let the function

$$t_X = g(P_X) \qquad \text{(Price-Time Tradeoff)} \qquad \textbf{(4-13)}$$

describe the price-time choices in the marketplace. The consumer can select a high P_X–low t_X store or a low P_X–high t_X store. In other words, the slope of the price-time function is negative.

$$\frac{\Delta t_X}{\Delta P_X} = \frac{\Delta[g(P_X)]}{\Delta P_X} < 0$$

In Figure 4-7 the price at one store is P_X^1, but the consumer has to shop for only t_X^1 hours. The price at another store is only P_X^2, but shopping time is t_X^2 hours. Substituting the expression for t_X in equation 4-13 into the expression for the full price of X yields

$$F_X = P_X + wt_X = P_X + wg(P_X) \qquad \text{(4-14)}$$

Equation 4-14 says that the full price of X paid by the consumer depends on the market price, which in turn depends on the type of store the consumer patronizes.

Before the consumer selects a market basket, he or she has to know the full prices of X and Y. However, there is not a single full price of X, but many. By shopping at a higher-price store, the consumer pays a higher market price but

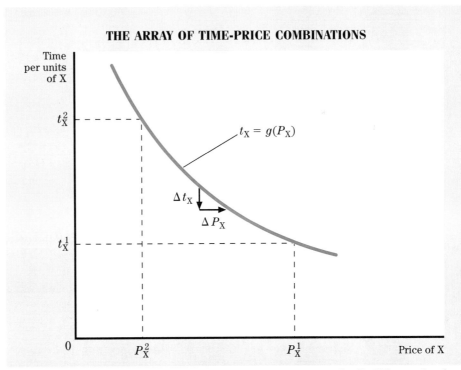

THE ARRAY OF TIME-PRICE COMBINATIONS

Figure 4-7 The consumer faces an array of price-time tradeoffs. If he or she shops at a higher-price store and pays P_X^1, the individual saves on time and only uses t_X^1 hours per unit of X. If the consumer pays a lower price of P_X^2, he or she uses t_X^2 hours per unit of X.

saves on shopping time. We assume that each individual selects the type of store that minimizes the full price. To achieve this minimum full price, he or she balances the increase in the price paid for the good and the decrease in the opportunity cost of time.

Figure 4-8 shows the optimal solution for a consumer. Dollars per unit of X are on the vertical axis, and the price of X is on the horizontal axis. The full price of X is $P_X + wt_X = P_X + wg(P_X)$ and can be derived as a function of P_X by adding the two components vertically. The 45-degree line labeled aa represents the first component, P_X, the market price paid by the consumer. The 45-degree line merely transposes the price the consumer pays from the x axis to the y axis. The second component of the full price is $wg(P_X)$, which in Figure 4-8 is the curve bb. Curve bb slopes downward because shopping time decreases when the consumer pays a higher price; $\Delta t_X/\Delta P_X < 0$. The full price curve cc is formed by summing the aa and bb functions vertically. An important point to realize is that the full price of X

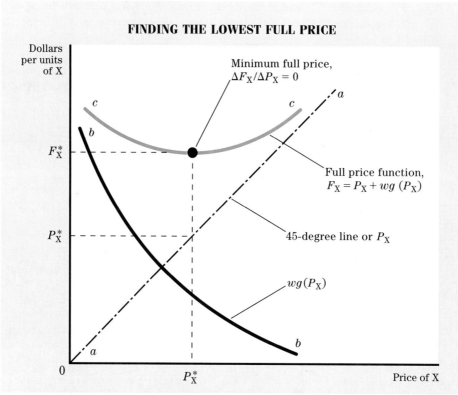

FINDING THE LOWEST FULL PRICE

Figure 4-8   The full price equals the market price plus the opportunity cost of time. The function aa is a 45-degree line and shows the price paid by the consumer. The function bb shows the opportunity cost of time $wg(P_X)$ decreases if the consumer pays a higher price. The full price function is cc and is the vertical sum of the aa and bb functions. The minimum full price for this individual occurs when the consumer shops at a store that charges a price of P_X^*.

changes as P_X changes. At first, as P_X increases, the full price decreases because the decrease in the opportunity cost of time is greater than the increase in the market price paid for the product. At some price of X the increase in the price paid just matches the savings in opportunity cost of time and the consumer minimizes the full price of X.

In Figure 4-8 the minimum full price of X is F_X^* and occurs when $P_X = P_X^*$. The consumer minimizes the full price when a dollar increase in the price of X equals the savings in time.[10]

$$1 = -w \frac{\Delta t_X}{\Delta P_X} \qquad \text{(Condition for the Minimum Full Price)} \qquad \text{(4-15)}$$

The left-hand side of equation 4-15 represents a dollar increase in the price of X. The dollar savings obtained from the reduced time spent shopping is on the right-hand side of the equation and is $-w\,\Delta t_X/\Delta P_X$.

We can use this model showing how a consumer minimizes the full price to determine how an increase in w changes the market price an individual is willing to pay. Equation 4-15 indicates that the opportunity cost of time increases when w increases. The curve bb in Figure 4-9 shifts up and becomes $b'b'$ when the wage increases. The distance between $b'b'$ and bb diminishes as P_X increases.[11] Because bb shifts upward, the full price curve shifts upward and becomes $c'c'$. The minimum of the new full price curve occurs at P_X^{**}, a higher price. What this means is that an increase in w causes the consumer to shop at a more expensive store where he or she can save still more valuable time. Higher-wage consumers are more willing to pay higher prices to save more time per purchase than are lower-wage consumers. Holding other things constant, higher-wage consumers will pay higher prices to economize still more on consumption time.

APPLICATION 4-3

How Much More Will Some Consumers Pay?[12]

Here are some specific comparisons of how much some consumers are willing to pay to save time in the kitchen.

The food industry has been very responsive to the cost of time of consumers. Surveys report that consumers in most age and income brackets are willing to pay more for packaged and processed foods than their counterparts in past decades.

More of today's shoppers buy food that is easy to prepare. The *Wall Street Journal* reports that consumers are willing to pay for processed food if they feel

---

[10] The full price is minimized when the slope of the full price function is zero. Using calculus, this condition requires

$$\frac{dF_X}{dP_X} = 1 + w\frac{dt_X}{dP_X} = 0$$

[11] When $\Delta t_X/\Delta P_X$ is close to zero, a rise in w increases the value of the time savings by less when $\Delta t_X/\Delta P_X$ is far different from zero.

[12] Betsy Morris, "How Much Will People Pay To Save a Few Minutes of Cooking? Plenty," *Wall Street Journal*, July 25, 1985.

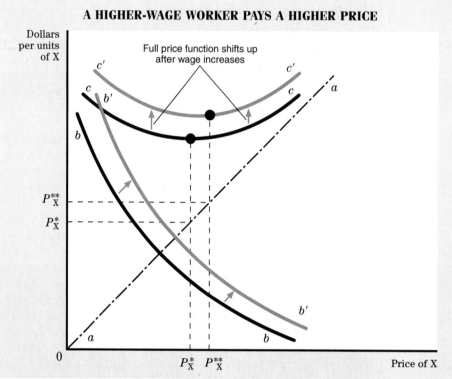

Figure 4-9   An increase in the wage rate increases the value of the savings in time. The *bb* function shifts up and becomes $b'b'$. The distance between the $b'b'$ function and the *bb* function is smaller when P_X is larger. The full price function shifts up and becomes the function labeled $c'c'$. The price that minimizes the full price increases from P_X^* to P_X^{**}.

that they can get something equivalent to home cooking. For many years, food companies worried about making their food so convenient that cooks would lose their sense of creativity. A few years ago, the Pillsbury Company introduced its yeast bread mix which cut the time needed to make bread from $2\frac{1}{2}$ hours to $1\frac{1}{2}$ hours while still giving people the satisfaction of making their own bread. It didn't sell, and Pillsbury replaced it with a bread that can be popped right into the oven, taking even less time.

Table 4-2 lists the 1985 price of prepared items compared to the cost of the basic ingredient required to make a comparable meal.

In 1985 a consumer could purchase 15 Pillsbury's microwave pancakes for $1.59 that could be prepared in 90 seconds with no standing over the griddle. A 2-pound box of Pillsbury's pancake mix cost about $1.27 and, with a few eggs, milk, and oil, could make 80 pancakes.

In addition to citing the cost comparisons between processed and unprocessed

Table 4-2   THE PRICE OF CONVENIENCE

ITEM PURCHASED	TIME-CONSUMING METHOD	COST PER POUND ($)	TIME-SAVING METHOD	COST PER POUND ($)
Chicken	Whole fryer	0.79	Swanson fried chicken entree with whipped potatoes	2.58
			Swift chicken Cordon Blue	3.99
			Tyson frozen breaded breast fillets	4.92
Potatoes	5 lb of potatoes	0.40	Ore-Ida frozen cottage fries	0.85
			Frozen Stouffer's potatoes au gratin	1.93
			Betty Crocker au gratin potatoes	2.88

food, the *Wall Street Journal* article described the problems facing a newly married woman who tried to cook everything from scratch and run her own consulting firm—a nearly impossible task. After a time, she recognized that her expectations were too high. She now cooks just two nights a week while relying more on restaurants, frozen foods, and fancy prepared items to feed her family even if she must pay more.

4-4   THE RISING COST OF WOMEN'S TIME

The revised model of consumer behavior can help us understand some of the behavior of working women and the marketing policies of firms as they adjust to the changing role of females. Since the outbreak of World War II women have entered the labor force in increasing numbers, and since the mid-1970s their earnings have increased relative to those of men although they still earn less than men. Both trends have placed increasing demands on their use of time and increased the demand for time-saving products. This section illustrates some of the changes that have occurred because of an increase in the cost of time.

The Increasing Number of Working Women

As women have entered the work force, increasing their cost of time, demand has increased for such time-saving innovations as microwave ovens, frozen foods, videocassette recorders (as a substitute for going to the movies), dishwashers, automatic washers and dryers, and blenders.

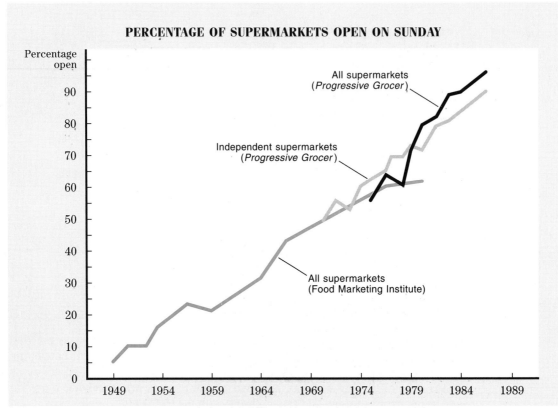

Figure 4-10   The percentage of supermarkets that stay open on Sundays has increased since World War II. [*From Food Marketing Institute and* Progressive Grocer, *various years.*]

Manufacturers and retailers are well aware of these changes and have altered their marketing practices in response to the growth of the female labor force. One such change is the increase in the hours that stores stay open. The business hours of all types of stores have increased over time because the cost of shopping during the workday has increased. Figure 4-10 shows a dramatic increase in the percentage of supermarkets that are open on Sunday. At the end of World War II in 1945 few stores opened on Sunday, which was considered a day of rest. Now Sunday openings are commonplace. Much of this change is due to the growth of the female work force. Working women increase the demand for longer store hours per day and for openings on more days per week.

Differences in the Cost of Time for Females and Males

Historically, women's wages have always been lower than men's wages. This means that the cost of time is lower for women than for men. Because of these differences,

**Table 4-3   NONWHITE DRESS SHIRTS BOUGHT ON SALE AND MARKDOWN OF DRESS SHIRTS BOUGHT ON SALE, BY SEX OF BUYER
(Two-Member Households)**

TYPE OF SHIRT	Percentage Bought on Sale		Percentage Markdown	
	FEMALE BUYER	MALE BUYER	FEMALE BUYER	MALE BUYER
Domestically produced	63.7	60.9	25.3	24.8
Imported	72.5	66.0	30.1	26.7

Source: Based on data supplied by Market Research Corporation of America.

the shopping behavior of women is different from that of men. For example, women are willing to search more intensively before they decide what to purchase and to spend more time finding bargains. Men take less time to shop, are more likely to purchase at the first opportunity, and are less likely to look for sales or to time their purchases to take advantage of sales.

The different behavior toward shopping shows up in the data. Both males and females buy men's dress shirts, with women purchasing about 60 percent of these shirts in husband-and-wife households in 1986. Table 4-3 shows the percentage of shirts bought on sale and the percentage markdown of shirts bought on sale by sex of the buyer. For each category of dress shirt, women purchase a larger percentage on sale and receive a higher percentage markdown off the original price. The sex of the buyer is an important determinant of the probability that the buyer will purchase a dress shirt on sale.

The economics explanation for the observed shopping behavior can be contrasted with the stereotypical view that women are somehow "shoppers" and men are not. The model explains why women are better shoppers than men (for some goods) but not because of some genetic or even cultural reason but because of economic incentives. The economics explanation predicts differences in shopping behavior will change if women's earnings continue to rise relative to men's.

The Increase in Female Earnings
Relative to Male Earnings

Over approximately the last 15 years women's earnings have risen relative to men's earnings. Table 4-4 shows trends from 1960 to 1988 in the ratio of female-to-male earnings of full-time workers by age of worker. The ratios declined from 1960 to 1970 and have increased in virtually all age groups since 1970. In 1960 the earnings of women between the years of 25 and 34 were 65 percent of men's earnings. In 1988 the ratio was 76 percent. The cost of time is lower for women than for men but is rising faster for women than for men.

The rise in the cost of time of women means that women will increasingly look for ways to reduce time-intensive activities. If this trend continues, the roles played

Table 4-4   FEMALE EARNINGS AS A PERCENTAGE OF MALE EARNINGS

AGE (YR)	1960	1970	1980	1988
20–24	80.6	74.0	77.7	88.5
25–34	65.1	64.9	68.6	76.1
35–44	57.6	53.9	56.2	64.8
45–54	58.0	56.3	54.3	61.7
55–64	64.5	60.3	56.7	58.0

Source: June O'Neil, "Women and Wages," *The American Enterprise,* November/December 1990, pp. 25–31.

by males and females in household activities will continue to change. We can expect greater use of the marketplace by women to purchase services that save time. The growth of day care and purchasing food away from home reflects the increasing cost of time of women. In addition we can expect the allocation of responsibilities for shopping, household duties, and so on, among the members of a household to change as women's wages rise relative to men's.

The rise in the cost of time of females has far-reaching effects on the way goods are marketed. A person with a higher cost of time is less likely to spend time searching for goods with unknown brand names. To economize on time, consumers having a higher cost of time are more likely to rely on well-known brand names. The female shopper will favor brand name goods for herself and for other members of the family. As women's cost of time increases, the demand for brand name merchandise will continue to grow.

Another industry that has grown rapidly is the catalog industry. Much of the growth is related to the increasing cost of time of consumers. The development of new inventory systems and decreases in the cost of shipping have reduced the cost of meeting the increased demand for goods ordered by telephone. The full price of ordering over the telephone has decreased relative to the full price of personal shopping. Consumers are more willing to place telephone orders when purchasing well-known brand name merchandise than when buying unknown names. So, the increase in the cost of time has not only increased the demand for brand names but has also helped the catalog industry to expand by merchandising branded merchandise.

This section has touched on only some of the changes in the merchandising of goods that have occurred because of the increasing cost of time of workers. Nevertheless, they appear to be permanent. The change in the economic position of females in the work force is a long-run change and is likely to continue into the future unless there is an unforeseen change in economic conditions. This means that the cost of time will continue to rise, and that we can expect to see continued significant changes in the marketing of goods as firms respond.

SUMMARY

▪ For some products the price paid by an individual represents only a fraction of the cost of the good because consuming a good takes time.

▪ A consumer must manage not only the budget constraint but also the total time constraint.

▪ The full price budget constraint shows the number of units of Y a consumer can purchase for a given quantity of X given the consumer's time and budget constraints.

▪ Full income is the consumer's maximum income if all time is spent working.

▪ The full price of a good equals the market price plus the opportunity cost of time.

▪ An increase in nonwage income shifts the full price budget constraint outward but does not change its slope.

▪ An increase in the wage rate shifts the full budget constraint outward and lowers the full price of X relative to the full price of Y if the time intensity per dollar spent on X is less than the time intensity per dollar spent on Y.

▪ Consumers with higher wage rates will substitute more toward goods with lower time-price ratios than consumers with lower wage rates.

▪ All other things being equal, consumers with higher wage rates will pay higher prices to economize more on their time than will consumers with lower wage rates.

KEY TERMS

Time constraint	**Budget constraint**
Full price budget constraint	**Full price**
Full income	**Wage and nonwage income**
Opportunity cost of time	**Affordable market basket**
Ratio of full prices	**Maximizing utility**
Minimizing full price	**Effects of a change in nonwage**
Effects of a change in wage rate	**income**

REVIEW QUESTIONS

1. What is the "full price" of a product?
2. Explain what the expression "full income" means.
3. When the price of X increases by 10 percent and the price of Y increases by 15 percent, the full price budget constraint becomes flatter; that is, the slope of the full-price budget line increases in value. Explain why you agree or disagree with this statement.
4. When the price of X, the price of Y, and w each increase by 10 percent, the slope of the full price budget constraint does not change. Do you agree or disagree with this statement?
5. How do the types of goods and services purchased change for a person who takes early retirement?

6. Describe how the goods that you purchase depend on whether your income is mostly nonwage income or wage income.

7. During a recession many workers are temporarily unemployed. They spend more time painting and fixing up their houses when unemployed than when employed. Can you use the modified theory of consumer behavior to explain this type of behavior?

EXERCISES

1. The consumer will substitute toward the good with the lower per unit time requirement. Is this statement correct? Explain why or why not.

2. Suppose good X has a higher t/P ratio than good Y. Show how an increase in (*a*) nonwage income and (*b*) wage income affects the quantity of X consumed.

3. Suppose Y is hours of leisure. Let P_Y equal zero and t_Y equal 1. How does the full price of X change relative to the full price of Y if the wage rate increases? Will the consumer consume more or less leisure?

4. Suppose it takes a consumer a fixed amount of time C_X to travel to a store, as well as t_X to consume each unit of X. The total time needed to consume X units is $C_X + t_X X$. For Y, the time required to consume a unit of Y is t_Y. How does this change the full price budget constraint?

5. If the cost of time is increasing, would you expect the quality of retail services to improve? Do you think it has? If so, give examples. If not, why not? Can you speculate why discount stores have become so much more popular?

6. Can you explain why some restaurants guarantee to deliver lunches within a specified amount of time or why more companies are guaranteeing that they can change your oil in a certain number of minutes?

7. Some communities have many convenience stores located nearby, while others do not. Suppose you are asked to study the characteristics of communities with and without convenience stores. Use your understanding of the theory of consumer behavior to answer the following questions.

   a. In what way would you expect consumers in communities with convenience stores to differ from consumers in communities without convenience stores?

   b. How would the average price paid for convenience products differ in the two types of communities?

THE FIRM: ITS TECHNOLOGY AND COSTS

THE PRODUCTION
FUNCTION AND
COSTS OF THE FIRM

Like consumers who must decide which market basket to consume, a firm must decide what quantity to produce and how to produce that quantity. Before we can determine what quantity the firm supplies, we must start at a more basic level and investigate how firms use inputs to produce output. A relationship called the production function links these inputs to firm output and is the basis of the theory of production. Inputs are called factors of production, and they include such resources as the number of workers, raw materials, and machinery. This chapter examines the production function and shows how the firm minimizes the cost of producing each rate of output given the price of each factor of production.

5-1 THE PRODUCTION FUNCTION

Labor, capital, and raw materials, among other inputs, are the factors of production that a firm combines to produce output. The relationship between inputs and outputs, called the production function, describes how a firm organizes the factors of production to produce goods or services.

The quantity that a firm can produce with its factors of production depends on the state of technology. The **state of technology** encompasses existing knowledge about methods of production. For example, it includes knowledge of the heat-resistant properties of metals, chemical reactions among carbon atoms, methods of networking personal computers, sequencing tasks, and store layouts. Therefore, when economists express the production function of a firm, they are assuming a given state of technology in an industry. When new advances change the state of technology, the production function changes as well.

> The **production function** describes the maximum quantity that can be produced with each combination of factors of production given a certain state of technology.

The production function can be represented as

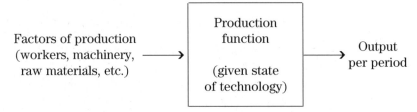

For a given state of technology, the production function describes the physical relationship between the quantities of different inputs and the resulting quantity of output. The management of the firm organizes and combines the factors within the box to produce units of output per period. For example, the production function for wheat describes the number of bushels of wheat a farmer grows per period with so many acres of land, days of labor, gallons of water, tons of fertilizer, and pounds of seed.

This schematic diagram of the production process sidesteps some important questions, however. It assumes that the tasks performed within the firm are given, although in reality firms decide what tasks to perform. For example, an automobile manufacturer can produce cars by building the bodies, transmissions, suspension systems, and air bags at its own plants, or it can purchase bodies, suspension systems, or air bags from other firms and be just a final assembler. For many years the General Motors Corporation manufactured its own automobile bodies, whereas the Chrysler Corporation purchased bodies from an outside supplier. McDonald's and other fast food companies own and operate some outlets and franchise others. Each firm decides which tasks to perform within the firm and which not to.

Nobel Prize winner Ronald Coase studied the options that firms have in producing a good.[1] He contrasted the decisions of some firms to produce components themselves with other firms' decisions to use the marketplace and purchase ready-made components. Each choice has different costs, which Coase identified. Each firm must compare these costs when it decides to manufacture everything itself or to rely on suppliers for some or all of the components. For example, the costs of purchasing components in the marketplace include finding reliable and flexible suppliers, determining the market price for each quality of product, and negotiating contracts. Acquiring reliable and accurate information about supplier reputation and market prices is costly. On the other hand, the costs of manufacturing all parts used in the product require monitoring of the efforts of workers and managers and rewarding desirable performance. It is costly to measure worker and manager performance and to control shirking by employees. Using the marketplace is not free, nor is circumventing the marketplace.

Managers face make-or-buy decisions daily, and economists have begun to study the determinants of a firm's boundaries. More advanced courses discuss how companies make these decisions,[2] but here the tasks performed by a firm are considered given.

By using an equation for a production function, we can determine the combinations of factors of production, L and K, that the firm selects to produce a particular level of output.[3] Our introduction to the production function is similar to the two-good model used to illustrate how the consumer selects a particular market basket (see Chapter 2). In this analysis, and throughout this chapter, a similar convention is followed in working with a production function that has two inputs, demonstrating the combination of factors the firm uses to produce each quantity. The quantity produced per period is q, and the two factors of production are labor and capital. L can represent the number of workers or aggregate hours of work, and K can be the number of machines or machine hours, the area of a plant, or the number of plants. Throughout most of the chapter L is the number of

---

[1] R. H. Coase, "The Nature of the Firm," *Economic Journal*, vol. IV, 1937, pp. 386–405.
[2] For a discussion of these make-or-buy questions, see Paul Milgrom and John Roberts, *Economics, Organization and Management*, Prentice-Hall, Englewood Cliffs, N.J., 1992, especially chaps. 1, 2, and 16.
[3] Throughout this chapter it is assumed that each unit of an input has the same quality.

Table 5-1 · UNITS OF OUTPUT FROM DIFFERENT COMBINATIONS OF FACTORS OF PRODUCTION

NUMBER OF MACHINES, K	Number of Workers, L					
	10	20	30	40	50	60
1	220	390	470	540	600	620
2	320	470	560	605	635	660
3	400	530	600	635	665	685
4	460	550	630	670	690	700
5	490	600	655	685	705	710
6	510	630	665	690	710	712

workers and K is the number of machines; however, it should be understood that this is for illustrative purposes only.

We can write the production function symbolically as

$$q = f(L, K) \qquad \text{(Production Function of the Firm)} \qquad \textbf{(5-1)}$$

The function f describes how the inputs L and K are combined to produce units of output per period. For each combination of workers and machines, there is a corresponding quantity of output per period.

Table 5-1 shows the quantity produced with different combinations of the two factors of production. Each entry represents the quantity produced when the firm uses a particular combination of workers and machines. For example, 3 machines and 30 workers produce 600 units per period.

5-2 CHANGING FACTORS OF PRODUCTION IN THE SHORT AND LONG RUNS

Table 5-1 shows what quantity the firm produces when it can vary both L and K. However, sometimes one factor is fixed, and so the firm can change output only by changing the other variable factor.

When airfares were lowered during the summer of 1992 and the demand for flights increased, airlines were overwhelmed by the increase in calls from potential travelers seeking low-priced tickets. They could not instantly increase the number of telephone lines or their computer processing capabilities, and so people who called were forced to wait impatiently for an operator. The airlines had only so many telephone lines and operators in the short run, and they had to make do with the existing equipment although they could have put more operators on overtime to meet the overload partially. If the higher demand had persisted, they would have increased the number of lines and their computer processing capabilities over a longer period of time. Firms cannot change one or several factors of production in the short run but can do so with the passage of time.

A distinction is made between the short and long runs in this chapter and throughout this book because firms do adjust their behavior over time. In the short run, a company can change some factors of production but has at least one fixed factor. In the long run, it can change all factors of production. The model developed here has just two factors of production—labor and capital. Therefore, it is assumed that the firm can adjust only one factor of production—labor—in the short run.

5-3   THE SHORT-RUN PRODUCTION FUNCTION

In the short run the firm cannot change the number of machines quickly without incurring an unacceptably high cost, and so it treats the number of machines as fixed. With one fixed factor the short-run production function of the company shows how total output changes as the number of workers changes. Suppose the firm must work with 4 machines until it orders and receives more. In the meantime it can increase output only by increasing the number of workers. The accompanying table reproduces the portion of Table 5-1 where the firm has 4 machines and shows output and output per worker at different employment levels. Total output of the firm increases by 80 units from 550 to 630 units if the company increases employment from 20 to 30 workers. The firm can increase total output by only an additional 40 units, to 670 units, as the number of workers increases from 30 to 40. The table shows that output per worker decreases from 46 units to 27.5 units when the number of workers increases from 10 to 20. Each addition of 10 workers produces smaller and smaller increases in output, and so output per worker falls as more workers are employed.

NUMBER OF WORKERS	10	20	30	40	50	60
OUTPUT	460	550	630	670	690	700
OUTPUT PER WORKER	46	27.5	21	16.75	13.8	11.7

Let's examine in a more general way this property of diminishing increases in output with increases in one factor and the other factor fixed. To do this we return to the general specification of the production function given in equation 5-1 and define different production relationships to be used later when the firm employs each factor in the short and long runs.

The Total, Average, and Marginal Product of Labor

To express the relationship between the variable factor and the total output in a more general way, economists use a function called the total product function. In our model, the total product function of labor TP_L merely shows the output that is produced with L workers and a fixed number of machines. It is a function that relates total quantity produced to the number of workers when K is fixed at K^*.

$$\text{TP}_L(L,K^*) = f(L,K^*) \qquad \text{(Total Product of Labor)} \qquad \textbf{(5-2)}$$

The total product of labor shows that the output produced changes as the number of workers changes with capital held constant at K^*. Equation 5-2 is a simplified production function because capital (machines) is held constant at K^*. The output produced by the workers is called the total product of labor because we are observing how output changes when the firm hires more workers. An analogous total product function of machines can be defined if the number of workers is fixed and the number of machines is variable.

Figure 5-1 shows how the total product (output) increases when the number of workers increases with the number of machines fixed at K^*. Quantity increases at an increasing rate at first, and then at a diminishing rate when more workers are employed. After some point, adding workers to the existing number of machines no longer increases output. The total product function is only suggestive. For example, it is possible for the total product to decrease when the number of

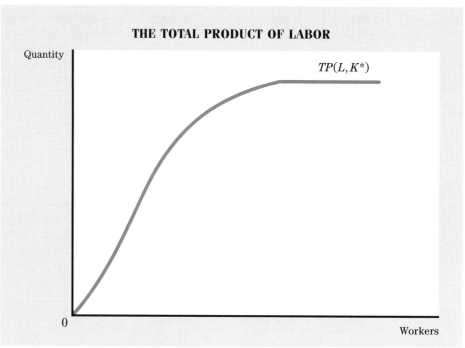

THE TOTAL PRODUCT OF LABOR

Quantity

$TP(L,K^*)$

0

Workers

Figure 5-1 The total product of labor shows the relationship between the quantity produced and the quantity of the variable factor with the other factor held constant. With the number of machines fixed at K^*, output increases as the number of workers increases, but after some point at a decreasing rate.

workers becomes so large that worker productivity falls because workers get in the way of one another.

We can derive the average and marginal product functions of labor from the total product function. The average product function of labor AP_L measures output per worker, and is defined as

$$\text{Average product of labor} = \frac{\text{Total product of labor}}{\text{Number of workers}}$$

$$AP_L(L,K^*) = \frac{TP_L(L,K^*)}{L} \qquad \text{(Average Product of Labor)} \qquad \textbf{(5-3)}$$

The average product of labor is the measure of productivity reported in newspaper articles that compare U.S. workers with foreign workers.

The marginal product of labor MP_L measures the change in quantity due to a change in the labor input, or the slope of the total product function of labor. For discrete changes in the number of workers, the marginal product of labor is defined as

$$\text{Marginal product of labor} = \frac{\Delta \text{ in total product of labor}}{\Delta \text{ in number of workers}}$$

$$MP_L(L,K^*) = \frac{\Delta TP_L(L,K^*)}{\Delta L} \qquad \text{(Marginal Product of Labor)} \qquad \textbf{(5-4)}$$

If we consider the number of workers fixed at L^* and allow the number of machines to be variable, we can define the marginal product of capital in an analogous way.

$$MP_K(L^*,K) = \frac{\Delta TP_K(L^*,K)}{\Delta K} \qquad \text{(Marginal Product of Capital)}$$

Returning to the case where the fixed factor is capital, we reproduce the total product function in Figure 5-2a and derive the average and marginal product functions of labor in Figure 5-2b. The shape of the total product function of labor determines the shape of the average and marginal product functions, and we derive the average and marginal product functions of labor from the total product function of labor. AP_L measures output per worker and is the slope of a straight line drawn from the origin to any point on the TP_L function. When the firm employs L_1 workers, it produces q_1 units. $AP_L = q_1/L_1$ or the ratio $ab/0L_1$. The slope of the dashed line from the origin to point b is equal to $ab/0L_1$ or the average product of labor. The average product of labor for any given level of employment is equal to the slope of a straight line drawn from the origin to the total product function at that employment level. Remember that the steeper the straight line, the greater the slope.

As the number of workers increases, AP_L increases at first. For example, compare AP_L when the firm employs L_1 versus L_2 workers. The slope of the straight line from the origin to point b is less (i.e., flatter) than the slope of the straight line from the origin to point d. When the firm increases employment from L_1 to L_2 workers, AP_L, or output per worker, increases because the slope increases to

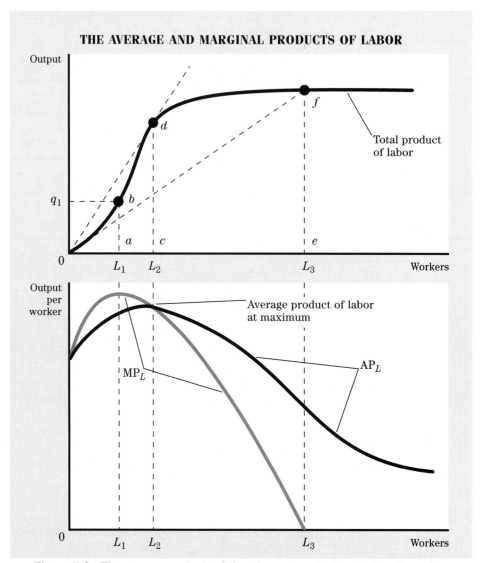

THE AVERAGE AND MARGINAL PRODUCTS OF LABOR

Figure 5-2   The average product of labor decreases when more than L_2 workers are added to a fixed amount of capital. As more workers are employed with a given number of machines, output per worker eventually decreases. The law of diminishing returns means that MP_L eventually falls as more workers are employed with the number of machines fixed. When the marginal product exceeds, equals, or is less than the average product, the average product increases, remains the same, or decreases, respectively.

$cd/0L_2$ from $ab/0L_1$. With a fixed number of machines, the firm can add workers and finds output per worker increases initially. What may be happening here is that workers can perform more specialized tasks as more are employed, and this raises the average product of labor. For example, instead of having a machine operator obtain raw materials as well as operate a machine, one worker can be a machine operator while another supplies the material.

Further increases in employment reduce AP_L. We can verify that AP_L decreases when employment increases from L_2 to L_3. With L_3 workers total output is equal to the distance *ef*, and the number of workers is equal to the distance $0L_3$. The slope of ray $0f$ is $ef/0L_3$ and is smaller than the slope of ray $0d$. Therefore, AP_L declines when employment increases to L_3 workers. As the firm adds more workers to the production line, this eventually may cause more machine stoppages for maintenance and a higher defect rate, both of which contribute to the declining AP_L.

Figure 5-2*b* shows that AP_L initially increases, reaches a maximum when the firm hires L_2 workers, and then declines as the firm hires more workers. The slope of the ray $0d$ is larger than the slope of any other ray from the origin to any other point on the total product function. Therefore, AP_L reaches a maximum when the firm hires L_2 workers and decreases when it employs fewer or more than L_2 workers.

There is a fundamental relationship between MP_L and AP_L. When MP_L is greater than, equal to, or less than AP_L, AP_L is increasing, constant, or decreasing, respectively.[4] A simple example may clarify this relationship between the marginal product and the average product. Let's say that you have a B or 3.0 average after completing 24 undergraduate courses. Put differently, you average 3 points per course and this is your average product. By the end of your junior year you are thinking seriously of attending graduate school. To improve your chances of acceptance, you decide to improve your grade point average, and so you apply yourself seriously during the first semester of your senior year and receive all A's. For the four courses you take during the semester, your marginal product for each course is 4.0 points. Because your marginal product (4.0) for each course in your senior year is greater than your average product (3.0), your average product increases above 3.0. This example just illustrates the principle that the average product increases whenever the marginal product is greater than the average product.

---

[4] The total product equals the product of the average product times the number of workers:

$$TP_L = AP_L(L)L$$

The marginal product is the slope of the total product function. Differentiating this equation with respect to L yields

$$\frac{d(TP_L)}{dL} = MP_L = AP_L + L\frac{d(AP_L)}{dL}$$

This equation says that $MP_L = AP_L$ plus a correction factor that depends on the slope of the AP_L function. When $d(AP_L)/dL = 0$, $AP_L = MP_L$ and AP_L is at a maximum. When $d(AP_L)/dL > 0$, MP_L is greater than AP_L and AP_L is increasing. When $d(AP_L)/dL < 0$, MP_L is less than AP_L and AP_L is decreasing.

Figure 5-2 illustrates the same principle. In Figure 5-2*b* the marginal product of an extra worker is greater than the average product when L_1 workers are employed, and so the average product function increases (the slope of AP_L is positive). When the number of workers is L_2, $MP_L = AP_L$ and AP_L reaches a maximum. With L_3 workers MP_L is less than AP_L, and so output per worker is decreasing and the slope of the AP_L function is negative.

The law of diminishing returns describes the eventual decline in the marginal product as more workers are employed with a given number of machines. As the company employs an increasing quantity of the variable factor (labor), with other factors held constant (machines), the increase in output due to an increase in ΔL eventually declines.

> The **law of diminishing returns** describes the eventual decline in the marginal product of the variable factor as the variable factor increases with other factors held constant.

The law of diminishing returns applies *only* to situations where one factor is increasing and other factors are fixed. For example, applying more fertilizer to a farm of a given size will after some point reduce the marginal product of pounds of fertilizer. In an industrial context the law of diminishing returns means an increase in labor hours, given a certain number of machines, will after some point reduce MP_L.

APPLICATION 5-1

Distinguishing between Marginal and Average Productivity

Michael Jordan is an exciting, well-known professional basketball player for the Chicago Bulls. But even though they had the highest-scoring player in the National Basketball Association, the Bulls failed to win the league championship until the 1990–1991 season when they finally were successful. Critics complained that Jordan shot too frequently and so opposing teams planned special defenses to guard him and ignored his teammates.

Let's compare his shooting performance with that of his teammates and see if you can conclude whether Michael Jordan shoots too frequently or not enough. As a measure of shooting efficiency, we use points per shot.[5] Table 5-2 shows the points per shot for Jordan and for the other Bulls from the 1987–1988 season to the 1990–1991 season.

Columns 1 and 2 of Table 5-2 show that Michael Jordan's points per shot exceed the points per shot of the other members of the team although the difference narrows over time. A shot by Jordan produces more points than a shot by one of his teammates. The third column shows that Michael Jordan's share of total shots was lowest during the 1990–1991 championship season. If the Chicago Bulls

[5] Two free throws are considered a single shot.

Table 5-2   AVERAGE POINTS PER SHOT BY MICHAEL JORDAN AND TEAMMATES

SEASON	POINTS PER SHOT BY JORDAN (1)	POINTS PER SHOT BY OTHER BULLS (2)	JORDAN'S SHARE OF TOTAL SHOTS (3)
1987–1988	1.060	1.008	0.299
1988–1989	1.088	1.045	0.273
1989–1990	1.100	1.065	0.284
1990–1991	1.103	1.073	0.266

Source: Raw data obtained from the *Chicago Tribune.*

are using Jordan's talents optimally, shouldn't his share of total shots be increasing and not decreasing given that he scores more points per shot than his teammates?

To analyze this question, you must distinguish between the AP and the MP of a player. The figures in columns 1 and 2 measure the average point productivity or AP of Jordan and his teammates and show that Jordan's AP is larger than that of the other Bulls. However, this does not mean that Jordan's MP is greater than that of his teammates.

What do you think would happen if the total shots were redistributed so that Jordan made one more shot per game and his teammates made one less shot?[6] Would the total points scored by his team increase or decrease? To answer this question, you must know the MPs of Jordan and his teammates. How many additional points would Jordan score if he took one more shot per game throughout the season and his teammates took one less shot. We can call this the marginal points per shot. You cannot assume that the marginal points per shot equal the average points per shot. Each player's marginal points per shot are likely to be less than his average points per shot. As Jordan's share of shots increases, the opposing team assigns more players to guard him, changes its defense, and forces him to take still more difficult shots. By using these tactics, opposing teams can reduce his effectiveness, and his marginal points per shot will be lower than his average points per shot.[7]

---

[6] It is assumed that a redistribution of shots does not affect defensive performance.

[7] Why is Michael Jordan shooting a smaller percentage of shots over time? The results in column 2 suggest that his teammates are improving over time. As they improve, Jordan passes to them more frequently rather than shooting himself. As he involves the other players on the team in scoring, the defense adjusts by guarding the other Bulls more closely and guarding Jordan less closely. Because the other teams begin to guard Jordan's teammates more closely, we would normally expect their average points per shot to *decrease* as Jordan's share of shots decreases. Since their average points per shot have increased, we can conclude that the other players have become even better offensive players over time. The improved play of his teammates appears to be the best explanation of why Jordan's share of total shots has decreased.

To determine whether Michael Jordan should shoot more frequently, you have to compare the marginal points per shot for Jordan with those for his teammates. If Jordan's marginal points exceed those of his teammates, then total team points will increase if he shoots more frequently. If his marginal points equal those of his teammates, then the Bull's coach is using his talents optimally although the APs differ. The team maximizes total team points when the marginal points per shot are equal across players. Although the *average* points differ, the *marginal* points can still be equal across players.

In summary, the higher average point productivity of Michael Jordan does not imply that he should shoot more or less frequently.

Our investigation of the properties of the production function is complete, and so we now turn to the long run where the firm can vary all factors of production.

5-4   THE LONG-RUN PRODUCTION FUNCTION

The production function described in Table 5-1 shows the quantity produced for different combinations of factors when both factors are variable. The relationships observed can be expressed more broadly. In the remainder of this section, we develop general expressions for the substitution of factors of production and the returns to scale when all factors are variable. We use these general relationships later in the chapter to learn more about the firm's production and output decisions.

Substitution among Factors

Like a consumer who receives the same utility by substituting between goods, the firm can produce the same quantity by substituting between factors of production. Suppose a company decides to produce q_1 units per year. What combination of factors should it use to produce q_1 units? You might think the answer can be found by asking production experts—those on the engineering staff with specialized expertise and on-the-job experience. However, they cannot answer this question because there simply is no single way to produce the product.

Figure 5-3 shows why. The number of machines is on the vertical axis, and the number of workers is on the horizontal axis. The curve with an output of q_1 is called an isoquant (*iso* means "equal," and *quant* signifies "quantity").[8] Output is constant along the isoquant, and the points along the isoquant $q = q_1$ represent the different combination of factors that can produce q_1 units per period. For example, the firm builds a capital-intensive plant, with many robots and few workers, to produce q_1 units. In Figure 5-3 the combination of K_1 machines and L_1 workers will produce q_1 units per period. However, this is just one way to produce q_1 units. The isoquant shows a menu of technical options: The company can use a more labor-intensive method of production to produce q_1 by substituting labor for

[8] Table 5-1 shows three points on the isoquant $q = 600$ units. The firm can produce 600 units with 1 machine and 50 workers, 2 machines and 30 workers, or 5 machines and 20 workers.

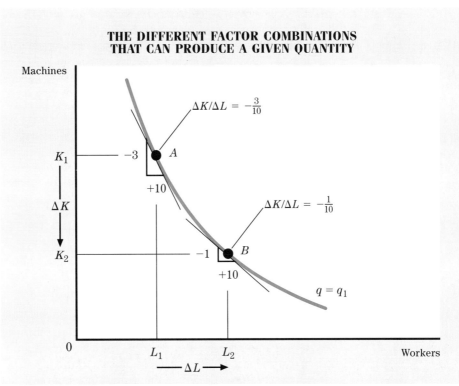

Figure 5-3 Isoquant q_1 shows the different combinations of factors of production for producing q_1 units. At point A the firm produces q_1 units per period with a more capital-intensive method of production. It uses K_1 machines and L_1 workers. At point B the firm produces q_1 units per period with a more labor-intensive method. It hires L_2 workers and uses only K_2 machines.

machinery, or it can reduce capital input by $\Delta K = K_2 - K_1$ and increase labor input by $\Delta L = L_2 - L_1$.

An **isoquant** shows the different combinations of factors of production that can produce a given quantity of output.

The fundamental point is that there seldom is only one way to do something. The state of technology often offers alternative methods of production. To illustrate this point, consider the following examples.

1. A perceptive visitor from a developed country traveling in a less developed country is immediately struck by the different methods firms use abroad to produce goods and services. Labor substitutes for capital to supply domestic help, provide service in restaurants, and construct and maintain roads more than in developed countries. Workers substitute for bulldozers, and in factories labor is used instead of forklifts and conveyer belts to move material and inventories from one location to another. Companies in both types of economies are aware of the production options even though they adopt far different methods. Firms in less developed countries use more labor-intensive production methods, whereas those in developed countries use more equipment- or capital-intensive methods because labor is scarce and has a higher relative resource cost compared to capital goods.

2. Steel plants produce steel and undesirable by-products such as dust. Firms control dust particle emissions from smokestacks by installing filters. The larger the filter, the smaller the volume of dust emissions. Reducing emissions requires more filters or more sophisticated filters and a larger capital investment in filters. However, firms can control dust emissions by changing and maintaining filters more frequently. This is a more labor-intensive method of reducing air emissions. A company can attain a given volume of emissions by using either more capital-intensive methods (larger and more sophisticated filters) or more labor-intensive methods (maintaining filters). The firm faces a tradeoff between capital- and labor-intensive methods.[9]

3. When you step into the shower in the morning, the last thing you are thinking about is the production function for hot water. Yet a production function produces water of a given temperature. The temperature of the water at the showerhead depends on the temperature of the water as it leaves the water heater and the heat loss as it travels through the pipe to the showerhead. The more insulation around the pipe, the smaller the heat loss and therefore the lower the required temperature of the water as it leaves the water heater. The water temperature at the showerhead will be the same by substituting between the water temperature at the water heater and the amount of insulation surrounding the pipe. The thicker the insulation, the lower the required initial temperature at the water heater to achieve a given temperature at the showerhead.

We can develop a measure that shows the technical options of producing the same output with different combinations of factors of production.

The Marginal Rate of Technical Substitution

The marginal rate of technical substitution (MRTS) measures the rate of substitution of one factor for another along an isoquant.

> The **marginal rate of technical substitution** shows how a firm can substitute capital and labor for one another so that the output is constant.

For a discrete change in each factor of production, the definition of the marginal rate of technical substitution is

[9] For a more extended discussion of this situation and the general problem of controlling pollution, see Paul Downing, *Environmental Economics and Policy*, Little, Brown, Boston, 1984, chap. 4.

$$\text{MRTS}_{KL} = \left.\frac{\Delta K}{\Delta L}\right|_{q=c} \qquad \text{(Marginal Rate of Technical Substitution)} \qquad (5\text{-}5)$$

where $\Delta K/\Delta L$ is the slope between two points on a given isoquant.[10] The expression $\big|_{q=c}$ means output is constant at some level c.

An isoquant *cannot* have a positive slope because an increase in one factor that causes output to increase must be offset by a decrease in the other to keep output the same.[11] In the usual case the MRTS_{KL}, the slope of the isoquant, is not constant but changes as the firm shifts from capital-intensive to labor-intensive methods of production. It uses more capital-intensive methods at point A than at point B on the isoquant in Figure 5-3 where it has more machines relative to workers. The firm must reduce the number of machines by a larger quantity for a given increase of ΔL starting at point A than at point B while keeping output constant. At point A the firm reduces the number of machines by 3 given an increase of 10 workers and still keeps output constant. For discrete changes in the number of workers and machines, the slope of the isoquant is $\Delta K/\Delta L = -\frac{3}{10}$. At point B the firm has far fewer machines relative to workers. If it increases the number of workers by 10, it can reduce the number of machines by only 1 if the firm continues to produce q_1 units. At point B, $\Delta K/\Delta L$ equals $-\frac{1}{10}$.

As the firm moves along the isoquant from the upper left to the lower right, the numerical value of the slope increases from $-\frac{3}{10}$ to $-\frac{1}{10}$. The firm substitutes labor for capital, but at a diminishing rate, as the firm moves along the isoquant. When this occurs, there is a diminishing marginal rate of technical substitution.[12] Throughout this chapter it is assumed that the production function exhibits a diminishing marginal rate of substitution.

Returns to Scale

As you study a firm's output decisions, you will see how the productivity of the firm changes as the quantity produced by the firm changes. **Returns to scale** compare the percentage change in output with the percentage change in inputs.[13] We distinguish among three cases.

---

[10] For infinitesimal changes in each factor, the marginal rate of technical substitution is dK/dL, the slope of the isoquant at each point on the isoquant.

[11] When there are many units of one factor relative to the quantity of another, it is possible for factors to get in each other's way and cause output to fall. The MP of a factor can then become negative.

[12] Given the production function $q = f(L,K)$, a diminishing marginal rate of technical substitution requires that

$$\frac{d(dK/dL)}{dL} > 0$$

The slope of the isoquant increases as the number of workers increases.

[13] In Table 5-1 output more than doubles from 220 to 470 units when the firm increases the number of workers from 10 to 20 and the number of machines from 1 to 2. There are increasing returns to scale. Output increases from 470 to 670 units, less than twofold, when the number of workers increases from 20 to 40 and the number of machines increases from 2 to 4. In this range there are decreasing returns to scale.

1. When both inputs increase by m percent and output increases by more than m percent, there are *increasing* returns to scale.

2. When both inputs increase by m percent and output increases by m percent, there are *constant* returns to scale.

3. When both inputs increase by m percent and output increases by less than m percent, there are *decreasing* returns to scale.[14]

The ratio of capital to labor is constant along a ray from the origin like ray RR in Figure 5-4. We measure returns to scale for a given ratio of capital to labor.

How do returns to scale affect the spacing of isoquants? That is, how does the percentage change in q relate to the percentage changes in L and K? The six isoquants in Figure 5-4 correspond to total quantities of 200, 400, 500, 750, 850, and 1,000 units produced per year. The firm produces 200 units per year with 5 machines and 10 workers (point a). Quantity increases by 100 percent from 200 units to 400 units (point b) when both inputs increase by only 60 percent, workers increase from 10 to 16 and machines increase from 5 to 8. When there are increasing returns to scale, the isoquants are closer together. If there were constant returns to scale, the isoquant with 400 units would have to be displaced to the northeast and go through point c so that output doubles when both inputs double relative to point a. However, a doubling of both inputs more than doubles output because output increases from 200 to 500 units.

When the firm combines 10 machines and 20 workers, it produces 500 units per year (point c). By combining 15 machines with 30 workers, output increases to 750 units per year (point d). Output and both inputs increase by 50 percent from point c to point d, and so there are constant returns to scale.

Between points d and e there are decreasing returns to scale. Both inputs increase by 33.3 percent, from 15 to 20 machines and from 30 to 40 workers, but firm output increases only from 750 to 850 units or by 13.3 percent. In this instance the percentage increase in both factors of production is greater than the percentage increase in output, and the space between isoquants is farther apart. If the isoquant with 1,000 units went through point e instead of point f, output and inputs would increase by 33.3 percent and there would be constant returns to scale. But the isoquant with 1,000 units goes through point f, where the percentage increase in inputs is greater than 33.3 percent.

When there are increasing returns to scale, a firm that produces a larger output

---

[14] There are constant returns to scale when

$$mf(L,K) = f(mL,mK)$$

An m percent increase in each factor increases total output by m percent. Geometrically, this condition says output increases by m percentage points, or $mf(L,K)$, when each factor increases by m percentage points. For example, if $m = 2$, the quantity of each factor doubles. If there are constant returns to scale, then $f(2L,2K) = 2f(L,K)$. A doubling of each input doubles total output. There are increasing returns to scale when $mf(L,K) < f(mL,mK)$ and decreasing returns to scale when $mf(L,K) > f(mL,mK)$. If there are increasing returns to scale, an m percent increase in each input increases output by more than m percent. If there are decreasing returns to scale, an m percent increase in each input increases output by less than m percent.

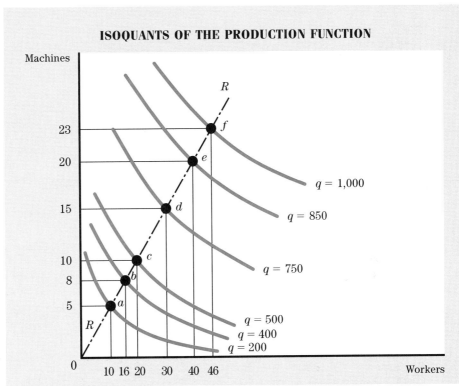

Figure 5-4   Between points *a* and *c* there are increasing returns to scale because inputs are doubled and output is more than doubled by increasing from 200 units to 500 units. To double output, the firm needs to have only 16 workers and 8 machines at point *b*. Between points *c* and *d* there are constant returns to scale since inputs increase by 50 percent and output increases by 50 percent from 500 units to 750 units. There are decreasing returns to scale between points *d* and *e*. Both inputs increase by 33.3 percent, but the increase in output is less than 33.3 percent from 750 units to 850 units. To increase output by 33.3 percent, the firm must employ 46 workers and 23 machines at point *f*.

requires fewer inputs relative to output than a smaller firm does. The larger firm is physically more productive than the smaller one. When there are constant returns to scale, the physical productivity of a larger firm is no greater than that of a smaller firm. Although the output of the larger firm is *m* times larger than that of the smaller one, so too are the input requirements of the larger firm. In this situation the smaller firm is just as productive as the larger firm. When there are decreasing returns to scale, a larger firm is physically less productive than a smaller firm. The larger firm must increase inputs by more than *m* percent just to produce *m* percent more output. The extent of return to scale plays a key role in determining whether large or small firms are more productive.

APPLICATION 5-2

Substitution and Returns to Scale
for a Pipeline Production Function

In some industries engineering principles establish the link between inputs and output and help to identify the production function. As an example, consider the inputs and the output of an oil pipeline between two points.

The output of an oil pipeline is the number of barrels of oil per day that flow

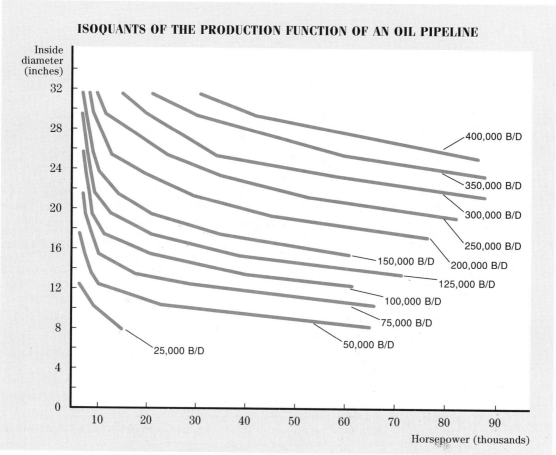

ISOQUANTS OF THE PRODUCTION FUNCTION OF AN OIL PIPELINE

Figure 5-5   The isoquants of a pipeline production function show that the number of barrels of oil per day (B/D) that flow out of the pipeline depends on the inside diameter of the pipeline and the hydraulic horsepower. Pipelines with larger diameters require less horsepower to maintain a given flow of barrels of oil per day. [*After Leslie Cookenboo, Jr.*, Crude Oil Pipelines and Competition in the Oil Industry, *Harvard University Press, Cambridge, Mass., 1955, p. 15.*]

through it. The inputs are the pipeline diameter and the amount of horsepower required to pump the oil through the pipeline. For a given pipeline diameter, more barrels of oil flow through the pipeline per day as the horsepower of the pump increases. For a given horsepower, more barrels of oil flow through the pipeline per day as the pipeline diameter gets larger. As expected, the same number of barrels of oil per day flow through the pipeline with different combinations of diameter and horsepower. The firm can substitute a larger pipeline diameter for a larger pump horsepower, and when planning a pipeline, must be familiar with the marginal rate of technical substitution between the diameter of the pipeline and horsepower.

In a study by economist Leslie Cookenboo, the equation for the production function of an oil pipeline was[15]

$$T = AH^a D^b$$

where A, a, and b are constants, T is the number of barrels of oil per day, H is the horsepower, and D is the inside diameter of the pipeline.[16] The numerical values of the constants depend on variables like the length of the pipeline, terrain variability from location A to location B, and the viscosity of the oil. Although technological advances will change the value of these constants over time, they do not alter the fundamental fact that the firm can substitute diameter for horsepower to produce a given flow through a pipeline.

Figure 5-5 shows the isoquants of the production function presented in Cookenboo's study. The firm can choose among several diameter-horsepower combinations to produce a given flow. In the figure selected isoquants of the production function correspond to different numbers of barrels of oil per day.[17] Each isoquant indicates how the marginal rate of technical substitution between pipeline diameter and horsepower changes as the firm substitutes between inputs. Like all isoquants, these isoquants have negative slopes and exhibit a diminishing marginal rate of technical substitution. Only selected combinations of inputs are shown in Figure 5-5, and so it is not possible to hold the ratio of pipeline diameter to horsepower

---

[15] Leslie Cookenboo, *Crude Oil Pipelines and Competition in the Oil Industry*, Harvard University Press, Cambridge, Mass., 1955.

[16] The returns to scale of a pipeline depend on the numerical value of $a + b$. Suppose H and D change by m percent; then

$$A(mH)^a (mD)^b = Am^a H^a m^b D^b$$
$$Am^a m^b H^a D^b = m^{a+b} AH^a D^b$$

This shows that an m percent increase in both factors increases total output T by a factor m^{a+b}. If $a + b > 1$, there are increasing returns to scale; if $a + b = 1$, there are constant returns to scale; and if $a + b < 1$, there are decreasing returns to scale.

[17] The exact production function is $T = 5.4H^{0.37} D^{1.73}$. The production function exhibits increasing returns to scale.

$$T = 5.4(mH)^{0.37}(mD)^{1.73} = 5.4m^{0.37}H^{0.37}m^{1.73} D^{1.73}$$
$$= m^{2.1}(5.4H^{0.37}D^{1.73})$$

Because the exponent of m is greater than 1, an increase of m percent in each factor increases output by more than m percent. If $m = 2$, each input doubles. Output increases by $2^{2.1}$, or by slightly more than 3 times.

strictly constant. Still, Figure 5-5 indicates the presence of increasing returns to scale. When the diameter is approximately 13 inches and horsepower is approximately 7.5 (in thousands), 50,000 barrels of oil per day flow through the pipeline. The ratio of inches to horsepower (in thousands) is 1.73. When the diameter is 20 inches and horsepower is approximately 13, 125,000 barrels of oil per day flow through the pipeline. The ratio of inches to horsepower is 1.54. Although the two ratios are not equal, they are close enough for our purposes. The inside diameter increases from about 13 to 20 inches or by 54 percent. Horsepower (in thousands) increases from 7.5 to 13 or by 73 percent. Total output increases from 50,000 to 125,000 barrels of oil per day or by 150 percent. Consequently there are increasing returns to scale.

The Marginal Rate of Technical Substitution and the Marginal Product of Both Factors

The marginal rate of technical substitution and the marginal product of labor and capital may appear to be independent entities. However, it turns out that knowing any two allows us to predict the third because the slope of the isoquant is related to the marginal products of the two factors. We can relate the marginal rate of technical substitution to the marginal product of labor and the marginal product of capital in a precise way.

We start at some point on an isoquant. Because a movement along an isoquant is being considered, we allow the firm to change both factors as it considers different ways of producing a given quantity. Suppose it decides to substitute toward a more capital-intensive method of production by increasing the number of machines by ΔK and decreasing the number of workers by ΔL. What determines the size of the change in the numbers of machines and workers so that output is constant?

Let's begin by increasing the number of machines by ΔK with the number of workers fixed. Output will increase by Δq_K because the number of machines increases by ΔK. The increase in output is approximated by

$$\Delta q_K = \text{MP}_K \, \Delta K$$

Δq_K is approximately equal to the marginal product of another machine times the change in the number of machines. If the marginal product of a machine, holding the number of workers constant, is 120 units per year and the firm adds one more machine, then total output increases by 120 units.

Now let's hold the number of machines constant and decrease the number of workers by ΔL. For a given number of machines, output decreases by Δq_L when the number of workers decreases by ΔL. The decrease in output is approximated by

$$\Delta q_L = \text{MP}_L \, \Delta L$$

Δq_L is approximately equal to the marginal product of labor multiplied by ΔL. Let's say the marginal product of a worker, given the number of machines, is 60 units per year. Therefore, the loss of 2 workers decreases output by 120 units.

Since we are considering movements along a given isoquant, output must be constant and the increase in output because of a ΔK increase in machines must equal the decrease in output because of the ΔL decrease in workers. Therefore,

$$\Delta q_K + \Delta q_L = 0$$

After substituting the expressions for Δq_K and Δq_L, the condition becomes

$$\text{MP}_K \, \Delta K + \text{MP}_L \, \Delta L = 0$$

We solve for $\Delta K/\Delta L$,[18] which gives us an expression for the slope of an isoquant in terms of the marginal products of the two factors.[19]

$$\frac{\Delta K}{\Delta L} = -\frac{\text{MP}_L}{\text{MP}_K} \qquad \text{(Marginal Rate of Technical Substitution)} \qquad \textbf{(5-6)}$$

Since the marginal rate of technical substitution is equal to the slope of the isoquant,

$$\text{MRTS}_{KL} = -\frac{\text{MP}_L}{\text{MP}_K}$$

The marginal rate of technical substitution is the negative of the ratio of the two marginal products. If the marginal product of a machine is 120 units and the marginal product of a worker is 60 units, equation 5-6 says that the marginal rate of technical substitution is $-\frac{60}{120} = -\frac{1}{2}$. An increase in quantity because the firm adds one more machine just offsets the decrease in quantity caused when the firm hires two fewer workers. In review, the slope of the isoquant equals the negative of the ratio of MP_L to MP_K.

5-5   THE ISOCOST FUNCTION

The production function describes the technological options facing the firm. In the long run, the company is free to change all factors of production to produce a given level of output. But what specific combination of labor and capital does the firm select to produce any given output in the long run? To determine its choice of factors, it must know the prices of the factors of production. In this analysis we assume that the firm selects the factors of production that minimize the total cost of producing a given output. Once you learn how to include production costs in the analysis of the firm's decision to use factors, you will see how a relationship

---

[18] Subtracting $\text{MP}_L \, \Delta L$ from both sides of the equation yields $\text{MP}_K \, \Delta K = -\text{MP}_L \, \Delta L$. Then, dividing both sides by ΔL and by MP_K produces the expression in the text.

[19] The production function is $q = f(L,K)$. Consider only those changes dL and dK such that output does not change, and so $dq = 0$.

$$0 = dq = \frac{\partial q}{\partial L} \, dL + \frac{\partial q}{\partial K} \, dK$$

Solve for dK/dL to obtain

$$\frac{dK}{dL} = -\frac{\partial q/\partial L}{\partial q/\partial K} = -\frac{\text{MP}_L}{\text{MP}_K}$$

between total cost for the firm and the quantity produced in the long and the short runs is derived in Sections 5-6 and 5-7.

To find the production cost of a given output, the firm must know how much it costs to hire workers and machines. Assume that the annual earnings of each worker are w, and so the annual cost of a worker to the firm is w. What is the annual cost of the services of a machine? There are different ways of assessing this cost. If an organized rental market for machines exists, the annual cost of the machine is the rental value. There are rental markets for cars, workstations, large computers, office equipment, and so on; however, organized rental markets do not exist for many capital goods. For example, there is no organized market for specialized machinery that manufactures and dyes rugs. In such cases we use a different method to determine the cost of maintaining the machine in production.

Assume the price of a machine with an infinite life is M. Suppose the firm borrows funds and pays annual interest of i dollars per \$100 of the amount borrowed. The cost of maintaining one machine in production for a year is the annual interest paid by the firm or i times M. Still another interpretation is possible. Suppose the firm has the funds to purchase the machine but chooses not to buy it and can earn a rate of return of i per \$100 invested in the next best investment. If the firm purchases the machine, it forgoes an annual rate of return of i. The cost of maintaining one machine in production of the product for 1 year is iM. Let $r = iM$ be the opportunity cost of maintaining one machine in production. The opportunity cost is \$18,000 if the rate of return is 5 percent and the price of a machine is \$360,000.

To summarize, the cost of each worker is w, the earnings of the worker, and the cost of a unit of capital equipment is r, the opportunity cost of purchasing a machine.

The expression for the total annual cost C is

$$\text{Total cost} = \text{Cost of labor} + \text{Cost of capital}$$

$$C = wL + rK \qquad \text{(Total Cost of Production)} \qquad (5\text{-}7)$$

The firm can substitute machines for labor, or vice versa, in only a restrictive way if the total cost is constant. The tradeoff between machines and workers can be seen more clearly by solving equation 5-7 for K:[20]

$$K = \frac{C}{r} - \frac{w}{r}L \qquad \text{(Isocost Line)} \qquad (5\text{-}8)$$

For a given C, equation 5-8 shows that the firm can substitute machines for workers. Equation 5-8 is an isocost line because the total cost is constant for all machine-worker combinations satisfying the equation. Hereafter, we will refer to total cost with the understanding that we mean total cost per period.

Equation 5-8 is a straight line with the familiar form $y = b + mx$. K and L represent the two variables, and r and w are constants. For a given total cost C, the intercept (b) of this straight line is C/r and is the number of machines the

[20] This equation is derived by subtracting wL from both sides of equation 5-7 to obtain $C - wL = rK$. Then, divide both sides of the equation by r and rearrange the equation to obtain equation 5-8.

firm can purchase when it hires no workers. The slope (m) of the straight line is $-w/r$ and, ignoring the sign, is equal to the factor price ratio, the annual cost of a worker divided by the cost of a machine. The slope is negative because, given a fixed total cost, the firm cannot afford to hire more of one input without cutting back on the other.

To illustrate the isocost line of equation 5-8, consider the following example. Suppose the annual earnings of each worker are $36,000. The price of each machine is $360,000, and i equals 5 percent. Then, the annual cost of a machine (r) is $18,000. How many machines can the firm purchase and how many workers can it employ if its total cost of production is $180,000? The y intercept of equation 5-8 is $180,000 divided by $18,000, or 10 machines. The x intercept is $180,000 divided by $36,000, or 5 units. Since the cost of a worker is $36,000 and the annual cost of a machine is only $18,000, the slope of the isocost line is -2. For each additional worker hired by the firm, it purchases two fewer machines, and so the total annual cost of production remains at $180,000. The isocost line ab in Figure 5-6 has an intercept of 10 machines and a slope of -2.

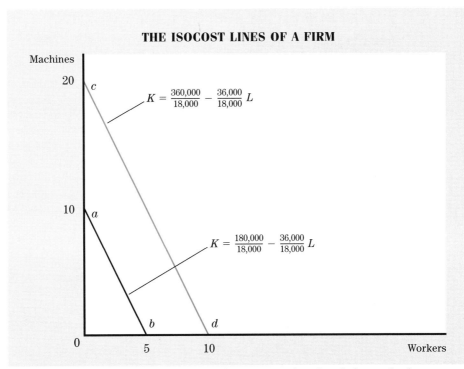

THE ISOCOST LINES OF A FIRM

$$K = \frac{360,000}{18,000} - \frac{36,000}{18,000} L$$

$$K = \frac{180,000}{18,000} - \frac{36,000}{18,000} L$$

Figure 5-6   The isocost lines show how many units of each factor the firm can use while incurring the same total cost. If the total cost for the firm is $180,000, it can substitute machines for labor along the isocost line labeled ab. The firm could purchase 10 machines if it did not hire any workers, and it could employ 5 workers if it did not purchase any machines. If the total cost is $360,000, the firm can substitute machines for workers along the isocost line cd. It can now purchase 20 machines if it employs no workers and hire 10 workers if it purchases no machines.

Now that we know how to derive the isocost line, let's consider shifts in the isocost line. Equation 5-8 shows that a higher value of C increases the intercept but does not affect the slope of the isocost line. Therefore, the isocost line shifts outward parallel and becomes the isocost line cd. To continue the example, suppose the total cost increases from \$180,000 to \$360,000. Any combination of factors on the new isocost line cd in Figure 5-6 will cost \$360,000. The firm can still substitute 2 machines for 1 worker. Therefore, a change in total cost causes a parallel shift in the isocost line.

5-6   MINIMIZING THE TOTAL COST OF PRODUCING A GIVEN QUANTITY

To find which factor combination produces a given quantity at the lowest total cost, the isoquants of the production function and the isocost lines are displayed on the same diagram. Figure 5-7 shows the isoquant q_1 and three isocost lines, aa, bb, and cc. Total cost increases by moving from aa to bb to cc. We know that the firm can produce q_1 units in many ways, and the firm's total cost depends on which combination of factors is chosen. The firm can produce q_1 units at a total cost of C' on cc by using either L_0 workers and K_0 machines or L_2 workers and K_2 machines. Either of these combinations of factors will produce q_1 units with a total cost of C'.

The total cost of the different factor combinations along the isocost line bb equals C_1, which is less than C'. The firm can produce q_1 units if it employs K_1 machines and L_1 workers (point 1). This factor combination produces q_1 units at a minimum total cost of C_1. There is no other way of producing q_1 units at a lower total cost. The total cost on the isocost line aa is C'', which is less than C_1, but no machine-labor combination on aa can produce q_1 units. Therefore, the total cost of producing q_1 units cannot be less than C_1.

If the firm is producing q_1 units at minimum total cost, the slope of the isoquant equals the slope of the isocost line:

$$\text{MRTS}_{LK} = -\frac{w}{r} \qquad \text{(Minimum Cost Condition)} \qquad \textbf{(5-9)}$$

Equation 5-9 says that the marginal rate of technical substitution equals the negative of the ratio of the cost of a worker to the cost of a machine when the firm minimizes the total cost of producing q_1 units.

> A firm minimizes the total cost of producing a given quantity by selecting a combination of factors where the slope of the isoquant equals the slope of the isocost line.

There is another commonsense interpretation of the minimum cost condition. Earlier we showed that the marginal rate of technical substitution is equal to the

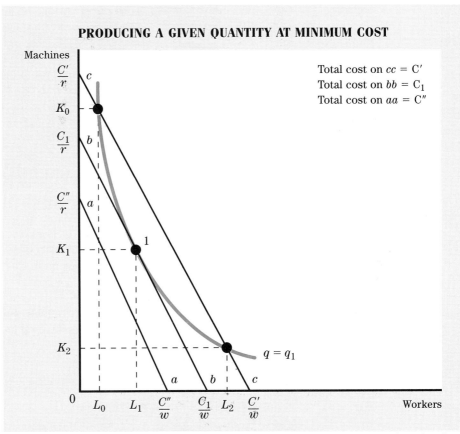

Figure 5-7   The minimum cost of producing a given quantity occurs when the slope of the isoquant equals the slope of the isocost line. At point 1 the slope of the isoquant for $q = q_1$ equals the slope of the isocost line bb. If the firm employs L_1 workers and purchases K_1 machines, it can produce q_1 units at the minimum total cost C_1. The firm could produce q_1 units by employing L_0 workers and using K_0 machines or by hiring L_2 workers and buying K_2 machines. However, the total cost will equal C', which is greater than C_1.

negative of the ratio of the marginal products of the two factors. Let's replace the marginal rate of technical substitution in equation 5-9 by the negative of the marginal product of labor divided by the marginal product of capital:

$$-\frac{\mathrm{MP}_L}{\mathrm{MP}_K} = -\frac{w}{r}$$

If both sides of this equation are divided by $-w$ and both sides of the equation are then multiplied by MP_K, the equation becomes

$$\frac{\mathrm{MP}_L}{w} = \frac{\mathrm{MP}_K}{r} \qquad \text{(Minimum Cost Condition)} \qquad \text{(5-10)}$$

Equation 5-10 says that the firm minimizes the total cost of producing a given quantity if the ratio of the marginal product to the price of a factor is the same for all factors.

The ratio of the marginal product of labor to the price of labor represents the increase in output due to the last dollar spent on labor. To minimize total cost, the additional output due to the last dollar spent on labor must be equal to the additional output due to the last dollar spent on capital. If they are not equal, it pays the firm to reallocate its expenditure from one factor to another. The firm should spend more money on the factor with the higher marginal product per additional dollar spent on the factor because that factor gives the firm a greater boost in output for the extra dollar spent. Total output will increase while total cost does not change. If the last dollar spent on labor increases output by 3 units and the last dollar spent on capital increases output by just 1 unit, then the firm produces more output for the same total cost by transferring the last dollar spent on capital to labor. Total cost does not change, but total output increases by 2 units. Geometrically, this experiment is equivalent to moving along a given isocost line because total cost is constant in such a way that output increases as the machine-worker ratio decreases.

> The lowest total cost of producing a given quantity occurs when the ratio of the marginal product to the last dollar spent on the factor is equal for all factors of production.

The following example illustrates this situation. Suppose $MP_L = 30{,}000$ units per period and the earnings of a worker are \$20,000. For capital, assume that $MP_K = 60{,}000$ units per period and $r = \$60{,}000$. The marginal product of the last worker divided by the price of a worker is equal to 30,000 units divided by \$20,000, or 1.5 units per additional dollar spent on a worker, and 60,000 units divided by \$60,000, or 1.0 unit per additional dollar spent on capital. Therefore, we have

$$\frac{MP_L}{w} > \frac{MP_K}{r} \qquad 1.5 > 1.0$$

On a per dollar basis, the last dollar spent on a worker produces a larger increase in output than the last dollar spent on capital. Therefore, the firm has not found the minimum cost solution. By spending more on workers and less on machines so that total cost remains constant, the firm can produce a larger quantity.

Now that you know how the firm selects the combination of factors that minimizes the total cost of producing a given quantity, you can use this information to derive the different cost functions of the firm. This investigation of the long- and short-run total costs begins in the next section.

5-7 THE LONG- AND SHORT-RUN TOTAL COST FUNCTIONS

A firm produces a given output at minimum total cost by finding a factor combination where the slope of the isoquant equals the slope of the isocost line. By satisfying this condition for each quantity the firm produces, we can observe how minimum total cost varies with quantity. The firm cannot determine how many units to produce in the long run without knowing this relationship, which explains its interest in the shape of the long-run total cost function. We will derive a relationship between total cost and the quantity when both factors of production are variable and when capital is the fixed factor and only the number of workers is variable.

The Long-Run Total Cost Function

The long-run total cost function indicates the lowest total cost of producing each quantity. Figure 5-8 shows two points of tangency of isocost lines with two isoquants. If the firm wants to produce q' units, it minimizes total cost by employing L' workers and purchasing K' machines so that total cost is C'. If the firm wants to produce q^* units at minimum cost, it combines L^* workers with K^* machines so that total cost is C^*.

Economists call the curve ee an expansion path. The **expansion path** includes all points of tangency between an isoquant and an isocost line. Each point on the

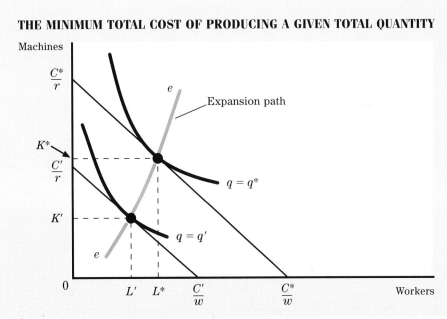

THE MINIMUM TOTAL COST OF PRODUCING A GIVEN TOTAL QUANTITY

Figure 5-8 The point of tangency between an isocost line and the isoquant determines the minimum total cost of producing a given quantity. The lowest total cost of producing q' units is C'. By hiring L' workers and purchasing K' machines the firm produces q' units at a minimum total cost of C'. The lowest total cost of producing q^* is C^*. The firm employs L^* workers and uses K^* machines. The expansion path ee is formed by connecting all points of tangency between the isoquant and the isocost line. Associated with any total quantity is a minimum total cost of producing that quantity.

path relates a quantity with a minimum total cost. For example, one point on *ee* pairs q' units with C'. The minimum total cost of producing q' units is C'. Another point on *ee* pairs q^* with C^* so that the minimum total cost of producing q^* units is C^*. Although it does not have to, the ratio of machines to workers can change at different points along *ee*. Consumers can purchase dresses at a small store that provides more service and is labor-intensive, or from a large discount store that sells dresses by using more capital-intensive methods—offering more square feet and less sales help.

Notice that there is no graph of the total cost function in Figure 5-8 because the axes measure units of capital and units of labor. To find the long-run total cost function, a different graph is needed where total cost is on the vertical axis and quantity is on the horizontal axis. If we take the many pairs of total cost and quantity on the expansion path *ee* and relate them on a different graph, we will have the firm's long-run total cost function, which shows the lowest total cost of producing each quantity. Figure 5-9 shows the relationship between the quantity produced by a firm and minimum total cost. The long-run total cost function is

$$C_L = C_L(q) \qquad \text{(Long-Run Total Cost Function)} \qquad \textbf{(5-11)}$$

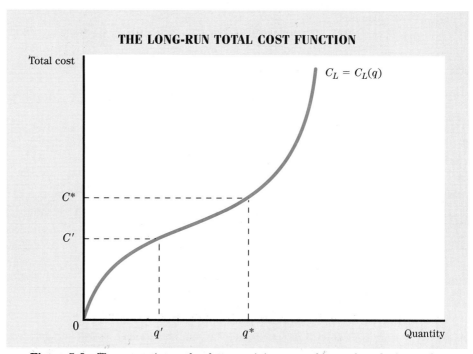

THE LONG-RUN TOTAL COST FUNCTION

Figure 5-9   The expansion path relates a minimum total cost of producing each quantity. The long-run total cost function shows the lowest total cost of producing each quantity when all factors of production can be changed. The lowest total cost of producing q' units is C'. The lowest total cost of producing q^* units is C^*.

Equation 5-11 indicates that the long-run total cost depends on the quantity produced. This is a long-run total cost function because the firm varies all factors of production to produce each quantity at the lowest total cost.

> The **long-run total cost function** shows the lowest total cost of producing each quantity when all factors of production are variable.

The long-run total cost function has a positive slope throughout. The total cost of producing q^* units is larger than the total cost of producing q' units in Figure 5-9.

Returns to Scale and the Shape of the Long-Run Average Cost Function

The long-run total cost increases initially at a moderate rate as the quantity increases. This moderate increase indicates that the firm is operating in a region of the production function where there are increasing returns to scale. Although output increases by m percentage points, total long-run cost increases by less than m percentage points. As the quantity of output becomes still larger, long-run total cost increases more rapidly than output and the firm experiences decreasing returns to scale.

When there are increasing returns to scale, an m percent increase in output increases total cost by less than m percent. This means that the percentage increase in total cost is less than the percentage increase in quantity, and so long-run average cost declines as the firm produces a larger output.

The long-run average cost or cost per unit is equal to the long-run total cost divided by quantity:

$$AC_L(q) = \frac{C_L}{q} \qquad \text{(Long-Run Average Cost Function)} \qquad \textbf{(5-12)}$$

When there are increasing returns to scale, a firm that produces a larger quantity has a lower long-run average cost than a firm that produces a smaller quantity. Figure 5-10a shows the shape of the long-run average cost function when there are increasing returns to scale. Notice that the larger the quantity produced, the lower the long-run average cost. In contrast, the long-run average cost function is U-shaped in Figure 5-10b. The long-run average cost decreases because of increasing returns and reaches a minimum where there are constant returns to scale; then decreasing returns to scale set in.

APPLICATION 5-3

The Long-Run Average Cost Function of a Pipeline

Figure 5-5 showed the production function of a pipeline with two factors of production: pipeline inside diameter and horsepower. The relative position of the isoquants in Figure 5-5 indicates that there are increasing returns to scale. Cookenboo calculated long-run average cost (in cents per barrel) as a function of the flow of barrels of oil per day per thousand miles of pipeline. Figure 5-11 shows that long-run average cost decreases at a decreasing rate as the number of barrels per day increases. The decline in long-run average cost demonstrates the presence of increasing returns to scale.

The Short-Run Total Cost Function

Since one factor is fixed in the short run, the cost of this factor does not vary with the quantity produced by the firm. The short-run total cost function of the firm includes a fixed cost plus the cost of the variable factor.

Short-run total cost = Fixed cost + Variable cost

$$C_s = F + V(q) \qquad \text{(Short-Run Total Cost Function)} \qquad \text{(5-13)}$$

The **short-run total cost function** shows the lowest total cost of producing each quantity when one factor is fixed.

The total short-run cost is equal to the sum of a fixed cost component and a variable cost component. The fixed cost component is the total annual cost of the fixed factor. In this case the firm has K^* machines in place and must pay interest of iMK^* on the amount borrowed to pay for the machines. Total fixed cost is $F = rK^*$. We assume that the firm must meet this expense even if it shuts its doors

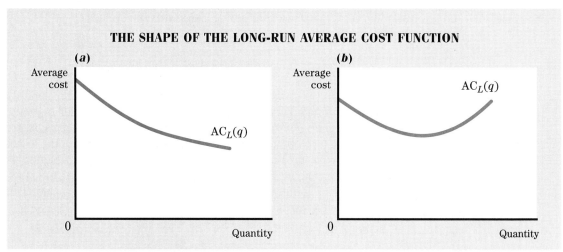

THE SHAPE OF THE LONG-RUN AVERAGE COST FUNCTION

Figure 5-10   (*a*) There are increasing returns to scale, so the long-run average cost is lower for a firm that produces a larger quantity than for a firm that produces a smaller quantity. (*b*) There are increasing returns to scale initially, and the long-run average cost decreases as the quantity produced by the firm increases. Long-run average cost reaches a minimum and then increases when there are decreasing returns to scale.

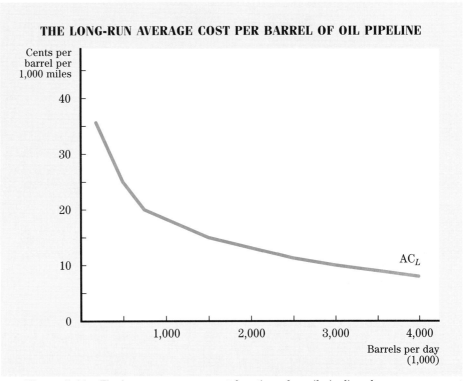

Figure 5-11   The long-run average cost function of an oil pipeline shows average cost decreases at a decreasing rate as the number of barrels of oil per day increases. The larger the throughput, the lower the long-run average cost. [*Graph is an approximation of chart 6 in Leslie Cookenboo*, Crude Oil Pipelines and Competition in the Oil Industry, *Harvard University Press, Cambridge, Mass., 1955.*]

and stops production. The variable cost component $V(q)$ represents costs that increase when the quantity produced increases. When there are just two factors with fixed capital, variable cost equals total labor cost.

Let's see how the short-run total cost function is derived from the isoquants of the firm's production function by looking at Figure 5-12. In the long run the firm selects the factor combinations along the expansion path *ee* to produce any output at minimum cost (Figure 5-12*a*). It can produce q^* units at lowest cost C^* by selecting K^* machines and L^* workers. If the firm produces q' units, it combines K' machines with L' workers at a minimum total cost of C'.

In the short run the firm does not have the luxury of varying both factors because it has K^* machines. In the short run the company's expansion path is the horizontal dashed line *ss* because the number of machines is fixed at K^* (Figure 5-12*b*).

If the firm wants to produce q' units in the short run with the number of

DERIVING THE LONG- AND SHORT-RUN COST FUNCTIONS

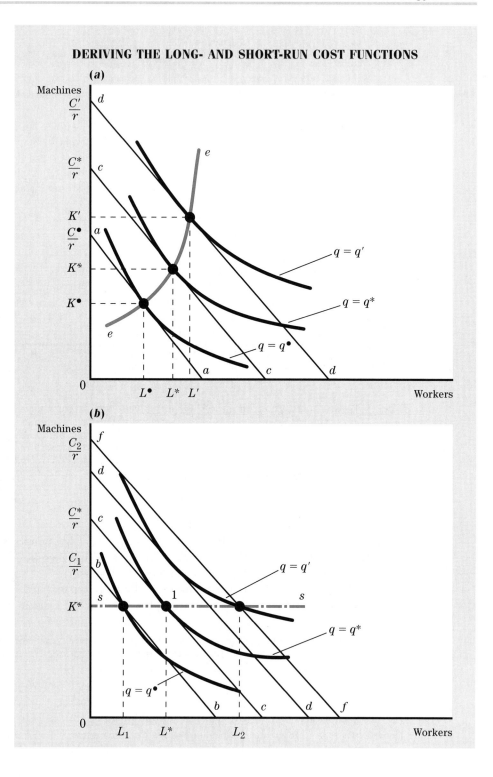

machines fixed at K^*, it must employ L_2 workers and incurs a total cost of C_2 (Figure 5-12b). The factor combination of L_2 and K^* is on the isocost line *ff*. The lowest total cost of producing q' is along the isocost line *dd* where total cost is C' (Figure 5-12a). Because the isocost line *ff* is to the northeast of the isocost line *dd*, C_2 is greater than C'. It is more expensive to produce q' units in the short run when the number of machines is fixed at K^* than in the long run.

While it is assumed that the firm has just K^* machines, we need to know why it cannot speed up the delivery of machines so that the cost of producing q' units can be reduced from C_2 to C'. Presumably, a priority shipment of machines will cost the firm more than the cost savings of $C_2 - C'$. Therefore the cost of rapidly adjusting the number of machines is what prevents it from increasing the number of machines quickly.

Figure 5-13 reproduces the long-run total cost function in Figure 5-9 and includes the short-run total cost function when the number of machines equals K^*. Figure 5-13 shows that the short-run total cost of producing q' units with K^* machines is C_2, while the long-run total cost of producing q' is only C'. If the firm wants to produce q^* units in the short run, it hires L^* workers and incurs a total cost of C^* along the isocost line *cc* in Figure 5-12. While the company has K^* machines in the short run, this is the exact number it would select in the long run to produce q^* at the lowest cost. It just so happens that the number of machines the firm has is exactly the number it would need to produce q^* units at the lowest total cost. Therefore, the total cost of producing q^* units in the short run is equal to the total long-run cost. In other words, being constrained to K^* machines is no constraint at all because the firm would use K^* machines to produce q^* units at the lowest cost anyway. Figure 5-13 shows that long-run total cost and short-run total cost are equal when the firm produces q^* units with K^* machines.

What happens if the number of machines is fixed at K^* and the firm wants to produce the smaller quantity $q^\bullet$? The firm employs L_1 workers to produce $q^\bullet$ units. The isocost curve *bb* in Figure 5-12b goes through the point where the firm has K^* machines and L_1 workers and incurs a total cost of C_1. The minimum total cost of producing $q^\bullet$ units is $C^\bullet$ on the isocost line *aa* in Figure 5-12a and requires a combination of $K^\bullet$ machines and $L^\bullet$ workers. Because C_1 is greater than $C^\bullet$, the short-run total cost of producing $q^\bullet$ units with K^* machines is greater than the total long-run cost $C^\bullet$. Figure 5-13 shows that the total short-run cost of producing $q^\bullet$ units is C_1 and is greater than the total long-run cost $C^\bullet$.

Let's pause here and restate some of our findings. We used the firm's production function and its isocost lines to derive the long-run cost function from the expan-

Figure 5-12   (*Opposite page*) In the short run the number of machines is K^*. If the firm wants to produce q' units, it employs L_2 workers (b). The short-run total cost of producing q' units is C_2. If the firm wants to produce q^* units, it employs L^* workers, the number it would employ in the long run if it wanted to produce q^* units at lowest total cost (a). The short-run total cost of producing q^* units is C^*, which also is equal to the long-run total cost of producing q^* units. If the firm produces $q^\bullet$ units, it employs L_1 workers in the short run and incurs a total cost of C_1 (b). In the long run it would produce $q^\bullet$ units with $K^\bullet$ machines and $L^\bullet$ workers at a lower total cost of $C^\bullet$ (a).

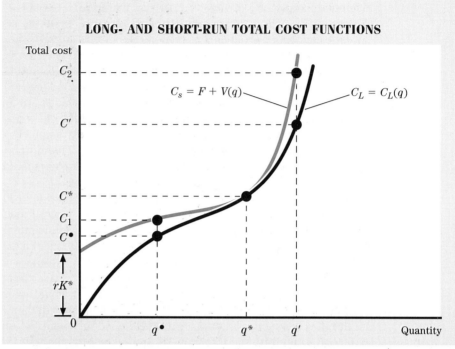

LONG- AND SHORT-RUN TOTAL COST FUNCTIONS

Figure 5-13   In the short run the number of machines is fixed at K^*. The firm can increase output only by increasing the number of workers. The total cost of producing any given rate of output will be greater in the short run than in the long run, except when the firm produces q^* units because q^* units can be produced at lowest cost by using K^* machines. Therefore, the short-run cost curve lies above the long-run total cost curve at all outputs except $q = q^*$. When the firm produces $q^\bullet$ in the short run, the short-run total cost is C_1, which is greater than the long-run total cost $C^\bullet$.

sion path. In the short run the number of machines is the fixed factor, and so the firm's expansion path is reduced to a horizontal line. The firm can increase output only by increasing the number of workers. We traced out the short-run total cost function when the number of machines is fixed at K^*. The short-run total cost function lies above the long-run total cost function for all quantities except one. At the quantity where the short-run expansion path *ss* intersects the expansion path *ee* (point 1) in Figure 5-12*b*, short-run total cost equals long-run total cost (Figure 5-13).

5-8   SHIFTS IN THE LONG-RUN TOTAL COST FUNCTION

In analyzing consumer behavior we first derived the consumer's demand function from the consumer's utility function and budget constraint. Then we investigated what causes the demand function to shift. Something similar can be done on the cost side. Now that you know how to derive the long-run average cost function from the production function and the prices of the factors of production, you can ask what causes the long-run cost function to shift position. Such shifts in the long-run total cost function can affect the survival of firms in an industry and of firms in different industries. Differential shifts in the cost of producing a good in different regions of the country can explain why the textile industry moved from New England during the 1930s and 1940s and relocated to North and South Carolina and Georgia. The displacement of textile jobs from these states to Mexico is due to differential shifts in the cost of production and to changes in tariff barriers. The displacement of steel by aluminum in automobiles and in soft drink containers provides other illustrations of the effects of differential shifts in the cost of production.

The position of the long-run total cost function shifts whenever the price of a factor changes or when technological change creates new ways of producing a product and shifts the position of the production function. This section shows how decreases in the prices of the factors of production and new production methods shift the long-run cost function downward.

A Change in the Price of a Factor

Suppose the price of a factor of production decreases. How does this decrease affect the behavior of the firm? In the long run the firm has an incentive to select a different factor combination and produce each quantity at a lower total cost than before. If the firm continues to employ the same machine-worker combination as before, it can produce any given quantity at a lower total cost than before because the price of one factor is lower. It can reduce total cost even more by selecting a different machine-worker combination to produce the same output.

To demonstrate this change, let's assume that the market price of a machine decreases. Before the price decreases, the expansion path is ee in Figure 5-14. The firm produces q^* units at lowest total cost C^* by employing L^* workers and buying K^* machines. The slope of the isocost line aa equals the slope of the isoquant at point 1. After the price of a machine decreases from m to m', the original isocost line aa becomes ab in Figure 5-14. Because the annual cost of a worker is unchanged and the price of a machine falls, each isocost line rotates around the horizontal intercept. The cost of a machine decreases relative to the cost of a worker. Before the price of a machine decreases, the firm incurs a total cost of C^* if it purchases C^*/r machines and does not hire any workers. After the price of a machine is reduced, its annual cost falls and becomes $r' = iM'$, where M' is the lower price of a machine. All the firm's isocost lines now have the same slope as isocost line ab.

Therefore, the new expansion path of the firm becomes EE in Figure 5-14. The new expansion path is formed by connecting all points of tangency between the slope of each new isocost line and the slope of the isoquant. Because the price of a machine falls relative to the price of a worker, the new isocost lines are steeper and the ratio of machines to workers is higher than before at the new point of tangency for a given quantity. If the firm produces q^* units after the price of a

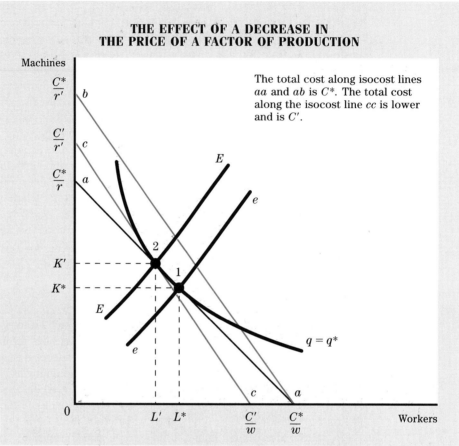

**THE EFFECT OF A DECREASE IN
THE PRICE OF A FACTOR OF PRODUCTION**

The total cost along isocost lines
aa and *ab* is C^*. The total cost
along the isocost line *cc* is lower
and is C'.

Figure 5-14   When the price of a machine decreases, the firm will substitute more
capital for fewer workers to produce any given quantity. Initially, the firm uses K^* and
L^* to produce q^* units (point 1). The slope of the isocost line *aa* equals the slope of
the isoquant at point 1. The expansion path is the curve *ee*. After the price of a machine
decreases, the isocost line becomes steeper and shifts from *aa* to *ab*. If the firm produces q^* units, it uses K' and L' to produce q^* units. A fall in the price of capital
encourages the firm to substitute capital for labor. The new equilibrium is at point 2,
where the slope of the new isocost line equals the slope of the isoquant. The new
expansion path becomes *EE*.

machine decreases, it combines K' machines with L' workers and incurs a total
cost of C'. The slope of the isocost line *cc* is tangent to the isoquant at point 2. The
firm substitutes more capital for labor when the price of capital falls relative to
the price of labor.

Because the isocost line *cc* lies below the isocost line *ab*, the total cost C'
associated with isocost line *cc* is less than the total cost C^* associated with isocost
lines *ab* and *aa*. Therefore, the total cost of producing q^* units is lower after the
price of a machine decreases. By tracing along the new expansion path *EE*, we

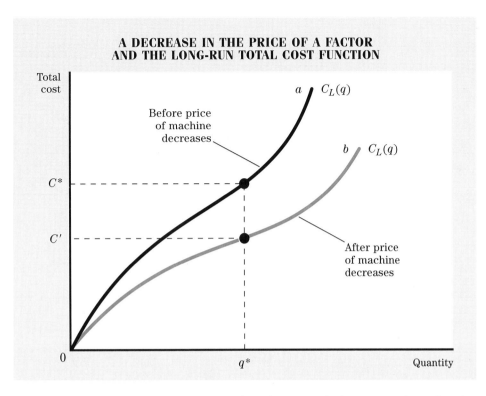

**A DECREASE IN THE PRICE OF A FACTOR
AND THE LONG-RUN TOTAL COST FUNCTION**

Figure 5-15 Before the price of a machine decreases, the long-run total cost function of the firm is the upper curve $0a$. After the price of a machine decreases, the new long-run total cost function is $0b$. At each quantity, the firm can produce that quantity at a lower total cost. If the firm produces q^* units, the total cost is C^* before the price of a machine decreases and C' after the price of a machine decreases.

can relate the total cost of production to each quantity. Figure 5-15 shows that the new long-run total cost function lies below the original total cost function. Therefore, the total cost of producing each rate of output falls after the price of a machine decreases.

Technological Change

The long-run total cost function shifts downward when there are technological advances that allow the firm to produce a larger quantity with any given combination of factors. New ways of organizing factors of production permit it to produce a larger quantity with each combination of factors. The technological advance may cause the company to shift to more or less capital-intensive methods depending on how the production function changes. What happens is that the technological advances allow the firm to produce a given quantity at a lower cost. Figure 5-16 shows the new long-run total cost function after a technological change. At each quantity the long-run total cost is lower after the technological change.

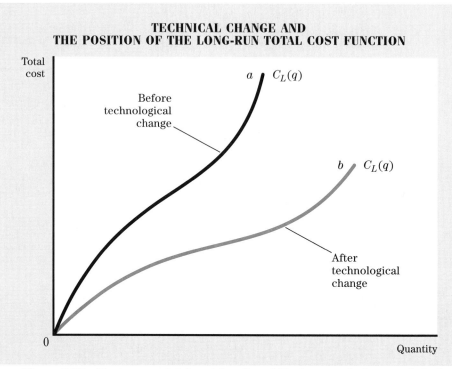

**TECHNICAL CHANGE AND
THE POSITION OF THE LONG-RUN TOTAL COST FUNCTION**

Figure 5-16   The long-run total cost function shifts downward after a technical advance shifts the position of the production function. Each quantity can be produced at a lower total cost after the technical advance than before. The technical advance allows the firm to produce a larger quantity for each combination of factors.

5-9   THE PRODUCTION FUNCTION AND LEARNING BY DOING

The production function relates the quantity of each factor to the output of the firm. Some researchers suggest that firm output of some goods depends not only on the quantity of each factor but also on the total production history of the firm. They argue that the productivity of a firm also depends on the knowledge gained by producing the good. In some industries, companies learn by doing. The cumulative experience of the firm is a separate determinant of the quantity produced in addition to the quantity of each factor.

We can modify the production function to take into account the effect of learning by doing by adding the cumulative output of the firm as another input in the production function.

$$q = f(L, K, \Sigma q) \qquad \text{(Modified Production Function)} \qquad (5\text{-}14)$$

where Σq represents the cumulative quantity produced during the lifetime of the firm. In this formulation the production history of the firm is important.

Two firms may currently employ the same number of workers and have the same amount of capital equipment. However, the cumulative production over the years is greater for one firm than for the other. According to this modified production theory, the quantity produced in the current period by the more experienced firm will be higher than that produced by the other firm because of the difference in production experience. Learning by doing means that one firm can be physically more productive than another because it has produced more in the past. Other firms can duplicate the productive efficiency of this firm only over time and by producing more and learning more.

The learning-by-doing hypothesis appears to explain some of the differences in the efficiency of firms in selected industries, but some interesting questions about the hypothesis remain unanswered. Can other firms catch up to a firm with a larger cumulative output by hiring away some of its employees? Is learning at one firm transferable to another firm or is learning by doing firm-specific? Is learning by doing determined by cumulative firm output or is it related to cumulative industry output? For example, the cost of constructing an industrial plant may depend on the number of plants that have been built by all construction firms. In other words, all construction firms may gain information when a single construction firm builds another plant. If this does occur, each firm will have a tendency to wait and learn from the experience of others.

APPLICATION 5-4

Learning While Building More Nuclear Power Plants

Martin Zimmerman investigated how construction costs relative to plant capacity changed as construction firms built more nuclear power plants, at a time when building nuclear power plants was a new technology.[21] Zimmerman's study focused on what determined learning by doing. Did actual construction cost per kilowatt of plant capacity depend on the total number of plants built by a construction firm (firm experience), or did it depend on the number of plants built by the industry (industry experience)? The answer to this question is of considerable importance. If construction cost per kilowatt depends on industry experience, the case for a government subsidy is stronger, for otherwise each firm will delay in order to learn from the experience of another builder. On the other hand, if construction cost per kilowatt depends more on the cumulative experience of the construction firm, other construction firms do not benefit from what a particular construction firm learns by building another nuclear plant.

Zimmerman found greater learning effects for a construction firm's experience than for industry experience, holding other variables constant. So, the more nuclear plants a particular construction firm constructed, the lower the construction cost per kilowatt. It appears that internal learning is more important in this industry.

---

[21] Martin Zimmerman, "Learning Effects and the Commercialization of New Energy Technologies: The Case of Nuclear Power," *Bell Journal of Economics*, vol. 13, no. 2, 1988, pp. 297–310.

APPLICATION 5-5

Learning by Doing at the Indianapolis 500

An interesting example of the benefits of learning by doing comes from an unlikely source, the Indianapolis 500, an annual car race held on Memorial Day weekend. Consider miles per hour of the winner as the output of the race. Does learning by doing affect the miles per hour of the winner? Learning by doing could depend on the number of times the winner has raced; however, this information is not readily available. Still, we can determine if the cumulative number of times the Indianapolis 500 has been held affects the miles per hour of the winner. In other words, we can test to see how miles per hour depends on the cumulative frequency of the race.

Figure 5-17 shows the miles per hour of the winner of the Indianapolis 500 race from 1911 to 1972,[22] and there is a clear upward trend over time. Among the

---

[22] Restrictions were placed on racing cars after 1972, so that comparisons are more difficult to make after this year.

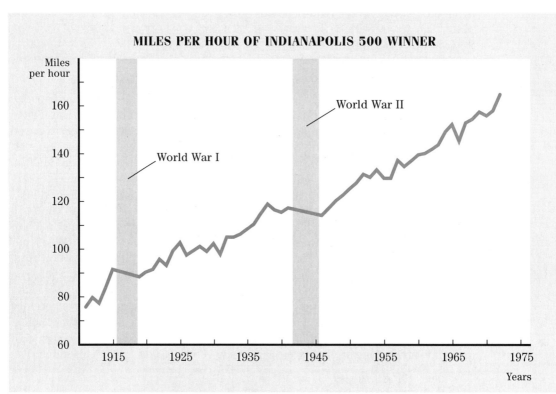

Figure 5-17   Miles per hour of the Indianapolis 500 winner did not increase between the beginning and the end of the two world wars.

factors responsible for the increase are improvements in engine performance, better car design, better suspensions, and improved gasoline quality. There is another interesting feature in Figure 5-17. Racing stopped during World War I and World War II. Note that a striking feature of the graph is that these improvements apparently stopped during each war. Miles per hour was not higher when racing resumed after each war. Racing stopped in 1942 because of World War II and did not resume until 1946, and Figure 5-17 indicates that learning stopped when racing stopped. Miles per hour of the winner at the end of the war is about the same as miles per hour of the winner before the war. If learning depends simply on time and not on experience, then the miles per hour of the winner would be higher at the end of each war than at the beginning.

Miles per hour could have increased over time because racing expands learning about the design of race cars and engine performance. Another explanation is that learning occurs in other industries during peacetime and that this learning benefits racing and increases racing performance during such times. Perhaps both factors are at work. The data do indicate that learning stops when racing stops, and so learning by doing appears to be an important determinant of performance in this sport.

This chapter developed the theory of production and introduced the total cost functions of the firm. With this as background information we will examine the different relationships between the long- and short-run cost functions of the firm in Chapter 6.

SUMMARY

- The production function describes how a firm combines factors of production, given the current state of technology, to produce goods or services.
- When capital is the fixed factor, it cannot be changed in the short run. The average product of labor is output per worker and, after some point, decreases as more workers are employed. The marginal product of labor measures the increase in output due to an increase in the number of workers. The law of diminishing returns means that the marginal product of labor eventually decreases as the firm hires more workers.
- An isoquant shows the different methods of producing a given quantity.
- The marginal rate of technical substitution is the slope of an isoquant and measures the required substitution between two factors of production so that the quantity produced is constant.
- Returns to scale describe the relationship between inputs and output for a given ratio of the two factors. A firm may experience increasing, constant, or decreasing returns to scale.
- In the long run a firm can vary each factor of production to the desired quantity. In the short run one factor is fixed and output can be increased only by increasing the other factor.

■ The isocost line shows how a firm can substitute one factor for another with total cost held constant.

■ The minimum total cost of producing a given quantity requires the slope of an isocost line to equal the slope of the isoquant. The minimum total cost of producing a given quantity occurs when the ratio of the marginal product of a factor to the price of the factor is equal for all factors.

■ The long-run total cost function shows the lowest total cost of producing each quantity. If there are increasing returns, the long-run average cost decreases as the quantity increases.

■ The position of the long-run total cost function shifts downward if the price of a factor decreases or if there is a technical advance.

■ The short-run total cost function shows the cost of producing each quantity when one factor is fixed.

■ In some industries firms learn to be more productive through experience gained by producing. The cumulative output of the firm is a separate determinant in the production function.

KEY TERMS

Production function
Short and long runs
Total product of labor
The law of diminishing returns
Marginal rate of technical substitution
Isocost function
Minimizing cost of producing a given output
Expansion path
Short-run total cost function
Learning by doing

Factors of production
Short-run production function
Average and marginal product of a factor
Long-run production function
Returns to scale
Price of a factor
Slope of an isoquant and slope of the isocost line
Long-run total cost function
Shifts in the long-run cost function

REVIEW QUESTIONS

1. Explain the concepts marginal and average product of labor. How are they related to each other?
2. What is the law of diminishing returns?
3. If the marginal product of labor is decreasing, the average product of labor is decreasing. Explain why you agree or disagree with this statement.
4. If the average product of labor is decreasing, then the marginal product of labor is decreasing. Explain why you agree or disagree with this statement.
5. If there are increasing returns to scale, an m percentage point increase in output will require a less than m percentage point increase in the factors of production. Explain why you agree or disagree with this statement.
6. Give two examples of substitution among factors of production.

7. If a firm has 6 machines and 4 workers and the marginal rate of technical substitution is -6, would you expect the marginal rate of technical substitution to be -12 when the firm has 2 machines and 8 workers and is still producing the same output? Explain why or why not.

8. If the price of capital is $40 per period and the price of labor is $10, write an expression for the firm's isocost line. Show how the isocost line changes when (*a*) both prices increase by 10 percent, (*b*) the price of labor decreases to $9, and (*c*) the price of capital increases to $50.

9. If the price of labor decreases by $2 per worker and the firm has 10 workers, the firm will take the savings of $20 and spend it to hire more workers. By doing this, the firm hires more labor relative to capital and can still produce the same output. Explain why you agree or disagree with this statement.

10. Two factors in the production of a good are unskilled labor and skilled labor. Suppose the price of skilled labor is 50 percent higher than the price of unskilled labor. Explain why you agree or disagree with each of the following conclusions.
    a. The firm will hire 50 percent fewer skilled workers than unskilled workers.
    b. The firm will hire 50 percent more skilled workers than unskilled workers.
    c. The marginal product of a skilled worker will be one-half the marginal product of an unskilled worker.
    d. The marginal product of a skilled worker will be twice the marginal product of an unskilled worker.

11. What is the expansion path of a firm? What information is needed to derive an expansion path?

12. If there are learning-by-doing effects, what should happen to the quantity produced for a given quantity of labor and capital over time?

EXERCISES

1. In the short run a firm can increase output by increasing the number of workers. The average product of labor is shown in the accompanying table.

NUMBER OF WORKERS	1	2	3	4	5	6
AVERAGE PRODUCT OF LABOR	5	7	8	6	4	2

    a. Derive the marginal product of labor.
    b. Present an explanation of why the marginal product of labor increases and then decreases and becomes negative.

2. If the price of factor A is $20 per unit and the price of factor B is $300 per unit and the marginal product of factor A is 40 units and the marginal product of factor B is 60 units, the firm should increase the employment of A and decrease

the employment of B to minimize the total long-run cost of producing existing output. Explain why you agree or disagree with this statement.

3. Given the prices of the factors, the expansion path of a firm is *ee*. After the wage of workers increases, the new expansion path becomes *EE*. Can *EE* intersect *ee*? Explain why or why not.

4. A recent study estimated total farm output would remain constant if 20 tons of fertilizer were substituted for 1 acre of land. If the price of 1 ton of fertilizer is $175, what must be the lowest rental price of 1 acre of land before farmers will substitute fertilizer for land?

5. The isocost line of a firm is *aa* in the accompanying figure. If the firm moves from point *B* to point *A* in (*a*), what is the relationship between MP_L/P_L and MP_K/P_K? If the firm moves from point *A* to point *B* in (*b*), what can you say about the relationship between MP_L/P_L and MP_K/P_K?

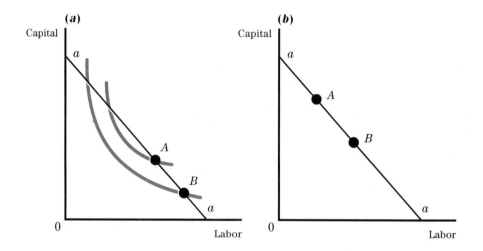

6. Currently a firm uses 100 personal computers and employs 30 workers. To help the domestic computer industry the government gives a subsidy of 10 percent off the price for every *extra* computer the firm purchases from a domestic computer company. With the aid of graphs show how this subsidy affects the firm's isocost line.

7. A firm cannot change a fixed factor in the short run. Therefore, its total cost in the short run must exceed its total cost in the long run when it can vary all of its factors of production. Explain why you agree or disagree with this statement.

8. If there are constant returns to scale, the long-run total cost function will increase linearly with increases in output. Explain why you agree or disagree with this statement.

9. When a new way of producing a good becomes available, the long-run total cost function of the firm shifts downward by the same dollar amount for each quantity. Explain why you agree or disagree with this statement.

CHAPTER 6

THE COST FUNCTIONS OF THE FIRM

The last chapter showed how to derive the long- and short-run total cost functions from a firm's production and isocost functions. This chapter examines the firm's short- and long-run cost functions in more detail. After identifying the short-run cost functions, we demonstrate how the long-run cost function emanates from the many short-run cost functions as we find the minimum total cost of producing each quantity in the long run. A new and important cost concept is also introduced—marginal or incremental cost. As part of the investigation we show how a firm that thinks incrementally is more likely to produce an output that minimizes cost. The chapter closes with a discussion of how the shape of the firm's long-run cost function affects the number of companies that can exist in an industry.

This chapter is an essential building block in developing a theory of firm supply that will be taken up in Chapter 7. Studying this more technical material is like going to the dentist—most of us don't look forward to the visit but go because it is the lesser of two evils. You will have to master a new vocabulary and work with some new cost concepts. The material on the relationships between the different cost functions can be challenging. Nevertheless, it is important that you have a complete understanding of the different cost concepts and of the relationships between the different cost functions before you go on to Chapter 7.

6-1   DEFINING COSTS

Before studying the firm's cost functions, we must decide precisely what to include as a cost for the firm. Most people would agree to including payments for raw materials and labor and rent paid for land and buildings as costs of the firm. We call these explicit costs.

> **Explicit costs** are payments for factors of production, such as wages and rents, and purchases of goods and services.

Besides explicit costs, opportunity costs are also part of the cost functions of the firm.

> **Opportunity costs** represent the forgone earnings or income when a firm employs a resource for a specific use.

To demonstrate what economists include in opportunity cost, let's assume that you start your own business by opening a bookstore near a university. If you hadn't gone into business for yourself, you could have earned a salary in some capacity, perhaps managing someone else's bookstore, and this forgone salary is an opportunity cost. However, your decision to start your own business is even more costly. When you own and manage your own bookstore, you not only forgo the salary you could have earned but also the earnings on funds you would have invested elsewhere had you not invested in the bookstore. Another opportunity cost is the return on investment that you forgo by investing in the bookstore.

In summary, the total cost for the firm encompasses all explicit and opportunity costs.[1] Hereafter, we assume that the cost functions of the firm include all explicit and opportunity costs.

You may wonder why economists include opportunity costs as part of the total cost of the firm. Suppose the firm's cost did not include opportunity costs and total revenue from the bookstore just equaled total explicit costs. The bookstore would appear to have neither earned a profit nor incurred a loss. However, this is an unwarranted conclusion because you are not as well off as you would have been had you worked for someone else. You would have received a salary and earned a rate of return on the funds that you invested in the bookstore, and so you are worse off operating your own bookstore. Economists argue that the firm breaks even only if total revenue equals the sum of all explicit and opportunity costs and earns profits only if total revenue exceeds total explicit and opportunity costs.

6-2   THE SHORT AND LONG RUNS

The cost that the firm incurs is different in the short run than in the long run. In the long run, all factors of production are variable, and so the firm can change the amount of labor and capital it employs. In the short run, it operates under a constraint because it cannot change at least one factor of production. We retain this simplification of distinguishing between the long run and the short run, as well as treating capital as the fixed factor. Likewise, the number of machines or the size of plant is still considered the fixed factor.

> In the short run at least one factor of production is fixed.

In reality the distinction between the long run and the short run is not quite so clear-cut. There is not only a single short run but a variety of short runs, each of a different length. As time elapses, the firm is able to change more factors of production. At this instant, all factors of production are fixed because the firm cannot change any factor. In a week's time the firm may be able to hire more unskilled workers and purchase more supplies, and by the end of the month it may find and hire more skilled workers. By the end of a year the firm may receive delivery on more machines, and in 2 years' time, it may expand the size of the plant. More factors of production become variable as time passes, and fewer and

---

[1] Accountants treat some costs differently than economists do. They consider advertising and research and development expenses as costs in the year incurred, although this practice is changing. Economists suggest that some types of advertising expenditures have long-term effects and contribute to the goodwill of the firm, providing an intangible asset. In short, some types of advertising create goodwill, and goodwill is an asset just as expenditures on plant and equipment are. Just as the cost of a physical asset is a depreciation in its value, the cost of intangible goodwill is its depreciation. For example, Coca Cola has built considerable goodwill by advertising its name. The value of the name is enormous. But suppose Coca Cola completely stopped advertising for 1 year. An accountant would say that the cost of advertising is zero. An economist would say that the firm incurs a cost equal to the decline in the value of goodwill because Coca Cola did not maintain the intangible asset by continuing to advertise. Many accountants agree with economists in principle but are quick to point out the practical difficulties of estimating a decline in the value of goodwill.

fewer constraints are binding on the firm. For the purpose of analysis, however, the simpler distinction between the short and the long run allows us to study the firm's behavior when at least one factor is fixed and all factors are variable.

The duration of the short run depends on how long it takes or how expensive it is to change capital and differs from one industry to another. In one industry the short run could span just a few months, while it might extend over several years in another. If the capital good is a personal computer, delivery of a new computer may take no more than a week. If the capital good is a specialized die, it may take 6 months before the die becomes available. If the capital good is a nuclear generating plant, the short run could involve a decade or more before the plant becomes operational.

6-3   THE SHORT-RUN COST FUNCTIONS OF THE FIRM

Suppose the fixed factor is the size of plant so that the firm cannot change plant size in the short run. For example, suppose the company signs a 5-year lease to rent a specialized factory. It is committed to this production facility for the duration of the lease and cannot change the terms of the lease.[2] Alternatively, if the firm finances the construction of a plant by borrowing, it incurs a fixed annual interest cost. It pays interest regardless of the number of units it produces. These fixed costs do not change with the quantity produced, but they are also sunk in the sense that the firm cannot escape them. On the other hand, if you rent a building and include a clause in the rental agreement allowing you to break the lease, the rent is a fixed cost because it is independent of output but not a sunk cost because you can break the lease at no cost. For the most part throughout this book, it is assumed that a fixed cost is also a sunk cost.

> A **sunk cost** is a past expenditure or a contracted expenditure that a firm cannot avoid.

As noted in Chapter 5, the short-run total cost function $C_s(q)$ shows the total cost of producing each quantity with a given plant size. The short-run total cost function is the sum of the fixed and variable cost functions.

$$C_s(q) = F + V(q) \qquad \text{(Short-Run Total Cost Function)} \qquad \textbf{(6-1)}$$

> The **short-run total cost function** shows the lowest total cost of producing each quantity when at least one factor is fixed.

The subscript s in equation 6-1 refers to the short run. F is a constant amount and equals the total cost of the fixed factor. The firm pays F per period no matter

---

[2] We assume the firm leases a specialized production facility and cannot subcontract the lease to some other firm.

what, if any, output it produces. $V(q)$ represents the variable cost function and includes those costs that change with the quantity produced. If labor is the only variable factor, variable cost equals total cost of labor. As the firm hires more workers, output and variable cost increase.

Graphing the Short-Run Cost Functions

We can graph the fixed and variable cost functions and then sum these two functions vertically to derive the short-run total cost function. Figure 6-1*a* shows the variable and fixed cost functions and the derived short-run total cost function. Total cost is on the vertical axis, and quantity is on the horizontal axis. F is a horizontal line since it does not change with quantity produced. Variable cost $V(q)$ increases at first at a decreasing rate as quantity increases but then at an increasing rate. The vertical sum of the fixed cost and variable cost functions forms the short-run total cost function.

From the short-run total cost, the variable and fixed cost functions, we can derive several average cost functions and a new cost function called marginal cost. The different short-run cost functions are dealt with extensively in this and following chapters. Here, we discuss what each cost function represents and explain the relationships among these functions. The seven basic cost functions are:

- Short-run total cost function, $C_s(q)$
- Short-run variable cost function, $V(q)$
- Fixed cost, F
- Short-run marginal cost, $MC_s(q)$
- Short-run average cost function, $AC_s(q)$
- Average variable cost function, $AVC(q)$
- Average fixed cost function, $AFC(q)$

Figure 6-1*b* shows the firm's short-run average cost function $AC_s(q)$, average variable cost function $AVC(q)$, average fixed cost $AFC(q)$, and short-run marginal cost function $MC_s(q)$. Each of these functions can be derived from the cost functions in Figure 6-1*a*. After defining each of these functions, we will explain how to graph each one.

The short-run average cost function of the firm is defined as

$$\text{Short-run average cost} = \frac{\text{Short-run total cost}}{\text{Quantity}}$$

$$AC_s(q) = \frac{C_s(q)}{q} \qquad \text{(Short-Run Average Cost Function)} \qquad \textbf{(6-2)}$$

$$= \frac{F}{q} + \frac{V(q)}{q}$$

$$= AFC + AVC$$

At each quantity short-run average cost is the sum of average fixed cost F/q and average variable cost V/q.

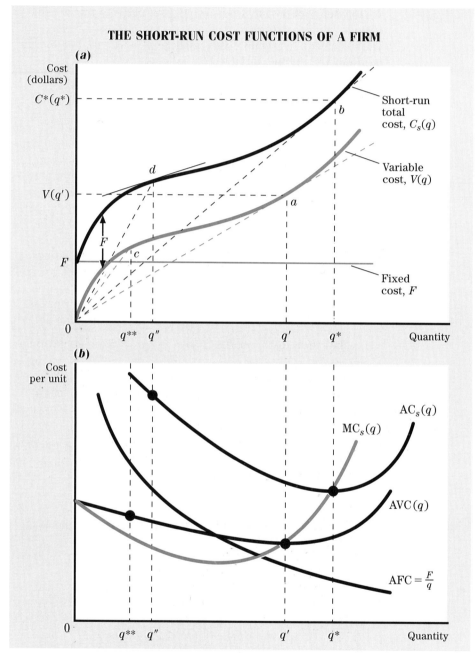

Figure 6-1   (*a*) The short-run fixed cost, variable cost, and short-run total cost functions of the firm. (*b*) The average variable, short-run average and marginal costs, average variable and average fixed cost functions of the firm.

The average variable cost function is

$$\text{Average variable cost} = \frac{\text{Variable cost}}{\text{Quantity}}$$

$$\text{AVC}(q) = \frac{V(q)}{q} \qquad \text{(Average Variable Cost)} \qquad \textbf{(6-3)}$$

The short-run marginal cost is the change in total cost when quantity changes by Δq. For discrete changes in quantity,

$$\text{Short-run marginal cost} = \frac{\text{Change in short-run total cost}}{\text{Change in quantity}}$$

$$\text{MC}_s(q) = \frac{\Delta C_s(q)}{\Delta q} \qquad \text{(Short-Run Marginal Cost)} \qquad \textbf{(6-4)}$$

$\Delta C_s(q)$ is the change in fixed cost plus the change in variable cost, but since fixed cost is constant, we can express marginal cost as

$$\text{MC}_s(q) = \frac{\Delta V(q)}{\Delta q}$$

The short-run marginal cost is the slope of either the short-run total cost function or the variable cost function since the two functions differ by F, a constant.

Just how are the short-run average and marginal cost functions derived from the short-run total cost function? The short-run average cost at any quantity is the slope of a straight line drawn from the origin to the point on $C_s(q)$ associated with that quantity. For example, short-run total cost of producing q^* units is C^*. The ray $0b$ from the origin has a slope equal to total cost, the distance between b and q^*, or q^*b, divided by the quantity produced, the distance from the origin to q^*, or $0q^*$. The slope of the ray is $\text{AC}_s(q^*)$, or C^*/q^*. To recapitulate, the slope of the straight line from the origin to any point on the short-run total cost function is $\text{AC}_s(q)$ for that quantity.

You can tell whether $\text{AC}_s(q)$ increases or decreases when quantity changes by determining how the slopes of the successive rays to different points on the total cost curve change. You can see that the slope of the ray $0b$ is smaller (flatter) than the slope of the ray $0d$ in Figure 6-1a. Therefore, the average cost of producing q^* units is less than the average cost of producing q'' units.

What makes the ray $0b$ unique is that it alone is tangent to the short-run total cost function. The slope of ray $0b$ is smaller than the slopes of all other rays from the origin to points on the short-run total cost function. Therefore, short-run average cost reaches a minimum when the firm produces q^* and is higher for smaller or larger quantities.

There is now enough information to describe the general shape of the short-run average cost function.[3] As output increases, the short-run average cost function

---

[3] The graph in Figure 6-1b is meant to be illustrative. The shapes of AC_s, AVC, and MC_s will depend on the shape of C_s.

decreases until it reaches a minimum when the firm produces $q*$ units and then increases when output exceeds $q*$.[4]

Now consider the shape of the average variable cost function. For a given quantity, AVC is the slope of a ray from the origin to the variable cost function. In Figure 6-1a the ray $0a$ is just tangent to $V(q)$ and the slope of the ray $0a$ is $q'a/0q'$. The slope of ray $0a$ is smaller than that of any other ray from the origin to any other point on the variable cost function. For example, ray $0c$ is steeper than ray $0a$. Thus, its slope is larger than the slope of ray $0a$. Figure 6-1b shows that AVC decreases as quantity increases, reaches a minimum value when the firm produces q' units, and increases as output expands beyond q' units. Given $V(q)$, AVC reaches a minimum at a smaller quantity than the quantity where $AC_s(q)$ reaches a minimum. The reason that average variable cost increases at quantities above q' is that labor becomes relatively less productive as the firm adds more workers with a given amount of capital.[5]

The Marginal and Average Cost Functions

You will recall that Chapter 5 derived a fundamental relationship between marginal and average products of a factor of production. The same quantitative statements apply to the relationship between the marginal and average cost functions.

1. When marginal cost is less than average cost, average cost decreases.

2. When marginal cost equals average cost, average cost is constant.

3. When marginal cost is greater than average cost, average cost increases.[6]

These relationships may appear more complicated than they actually are. In reality, they are something any baseball fan from 7 to 77 understands. To borrow an example from America's favorite pastime, let's consider a baseball player who

---

[4] As q approaches 0, $AC_s(q)$ approaches infinity since F/q becomes ever larger.

[5] Short-run marginal cost is equal to the wage of the variable factor (labor) divided by the marginal product of labor. As in Chapter 5, the marginal product of labor is $MP_L = \Delta q/\Delta L$ and measures the increase in output that the firm produces when another worker is added. If the firm hires another worker, it pays a wage of w. Therefore w/MP_L measures the additional cost incurred by the firm per unit increase in output, or short-run marginal cost with capital constant.

[6] Although the relationship between the marginal and average cost functions holds in both the short and long runs, the relationship for the short-run cost functions is shown here. Short-run total cost equals short-run average cost times quantity: $C_s(q) = AC_s(q)q$.

Marginal cost equals the slope of the total cost function. If we consider an infinitesimal change in q, the change in total cost is given by

$$\frac{dC(q)}{dq} = MC_s(q) = AC_s(q) + q\frac{dAC_s(q)}{dq}$$

This equation says that $MC_s(q) = AC_s(q)$ plus a correction factor that is the product of quantity and the slope of the $AC_s(q)$ function. When $dAC_s(q)/dq = 0$, the slope of the short-run average cost function is zero, and so $AC(q)$ is at a minimum and the equation indicates $AC(q) = MC_s(q)$. When $dAC_s(q)/dq > 0$, the slope of the short-run average cost function is positive, and so $AC_s(q)$ is increasing and $MC_s(q)$ is greater than $AC_s(q)$. When $dAC_s(q)/dL < 0$, the slope of the short-run average cost function is negative, and so $AC_s(q)$ is decreasing and $MC_s(q)$ is less than $AC_s(q)$.

has a season batting average of .300. What this means is that he gets 3 hits on average for each 10 times at bat. Let's suppose the player gets 1 hit in 3 times at bat in the next game. For this one game, his *marginal* batting average is .333. Because his marginal batting average of .333 is greater than his season or *average* batting average of .300, his season batting average rises to over .300. When the marginal exceeds the average, the average increases. This example covers the last of the three cases.

Returning to our discussion of the short-run cost functions, we know that marginal cost is equal to the slope of the short-run total cost function. In Figure 6-2 short-run marginal cost is less than short-run average cost when the firm produces q_1 units, and so short-run average cost is declining. When the firm produces q_2 units, short-run marginal cost equals short-run average cost, and so the slope of the short-run average cost function is zero in Figure 6-2. For any quantity larger than q_2, the slope of the short-run average cost function is positive, and so short-run marginal cost is *greater* than short-run average cost. For example, short-run marginal cost exceeds short-run average cost when the firm produces q_3 units, and so short-run average cost is increasing. There is a corresponding relationship

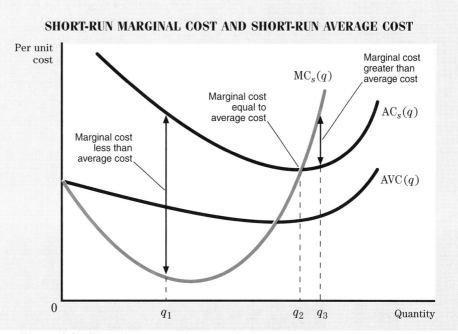

Figure 6-2   When the firm produces q_1, short-run marginal cost is less than short-run average cost, and so short-run average cost declines. At output q_2 short-run marginal cost equals short-run average cost, and so the average is constant. At output q_3 short-run marginal cost is greater than short-run average cost, and so short-run average cost increases.

between the marginal and average variable costs,[7] and when marginal cost is less than average variable cost, average variable cost decreases. The slope of the average variable cost function is zero when marginal cost equals average variable cost and it is positive when marginal cost exceeds average variable cost.

When drawing the short-run average cost, average variable, and marginal cost functions, you need to exercise care so that your graphs meet the conditions that we have described. You will be using graphs of these cost functions to solve problems, and so you must learn to draw these curves accurately. At the risk of being repetitive, let's restate the salient points. Your graphs of the short-run cost functions should meet the following five conditions, and you should be able to explain to yourself why the curves in Figure 6-1*b* satisfy each of these conditions.

1. *Short-run average cost approaches infinity when q approaches zero because F/q becomes very large.*

2. *Short-run average cost declines as quantity increases until it reaches a minimum, and then it increases.*

3. *The difference between $AC_s(q)$ and AVC decreases as the quantity increases because AFC decreases.*

4. *Average variable cost normally reaches a minimum at a smaller quantity than the quantity where short-run average cost reaches a minimum.[8]*

5. *The marginal cost function goes through the minimum points of the average variable cost and short-run average cost functions.*

The Area under the Marginal Cost Function

Before we use the short-run cost functions to solve some problems, we want to establish that the area under the marginal cost function between any two quantities is equal to the increase in variable cost when the firm's output increases from one quantity to the other.

---

[7] Total variable cost is equal to average variable cost times quantity: $V(q) = \text{AVC}(q)q$. Short-run marginal cost equals the slope of the total variable cost function. Differentiating this equation with respect to q yields

$$\frac{dV(q)}{dq} = \text{MC}_s(q) = \text{AVC}(q) + q\frac{d\text{AVC}(q)}{dq}$$

$\text{MC}_s(q) = \text{AVC}(q)$ plus a correction factor equal to the product of quantity and the slope of the $\text{AVC}(q)$ function. When $d[\text{AVC}(q)]/dq = 0$, $\text{AVC}(q)$ is at a minimum and $\text{AVC}(q) = \text{MC}_s(q)$. If $d[\text{AVC}(q)]/dq > 0$, $\text{AVC}(q)$ is increasing and $\text{MC}_s(q)$ is greater than $\text{AVC}(q)$. When $d\text{AVC}(q)/dL < 0$, $\text{AVC}(q)$ is decreasing and $\text{MC}_s(q)$ is less than $\text{AVC}(q)$.

[8] $\text{AVC}(q) = V(q)/q$. As q approaches zero, $V(q)$ gets smaller and smaller, as does q. Therefore, the ratio of $v(q)$ to q is indeterminate. To evaluate this indeterminate form, we differentiate both the numerator and the denominator and evaluate each as q approaches zero. The numerator is $dV/dq = \text{MC}_s(q)$ or marginal cost as q approaches zero, and the denominator is 1. As q gets smaller and smaller, $\text{AVC}(q)$ approaches marginal cost. Because the slope of the total variable cost function approaches some limiting finite value as q approaches zero, AVC approaches that value as q approaches zero. $\text{AVC} = \text{MC}_s$ as q approaches zero. If the short-run total cost function is linear up to a well-defined capacity output, AVC is constant up to capacity output where AC_s reaches a minimum.

Table 6-1   VARIABLE COST AND THE SUM OF MARGINAL COSTS

QUANTITY PRODUCED (1)	VARIABLE COST($) (2)	SHORT-RUN MARGINAL COST($) (3)	SUM OF SHORT-RUN MARGINAL COSTS ($) (4)
1	80	80	80
2	140	60	140
3	240	100	240
4	380	140	380

Let's show this first by way of a numerical example. Table 6-1 lists the quantity produced in column 1, variable cost in column 2, and short-run marginal cost in column 3. Column 4 shows the sum of the marginal costs for each unit up to and including the last unit produced.

Figure 6-3*a* shows the marginal cost of increasing output by 1 unit. Variable cost is $80 when the firm produces 1 unit, and the marginal cost of producing the first unit is also $80. When the firm produces 1 unit, the sum of the marginal cost in column 4 is just $80. If the firm produces 2 units, column 2 shows that variable cost equals $140. Figure 6-3*a* shows that the marginal cost of the second unit is $60, and so the sum of the two values of marginal cost is $80 + $60 or $140. The marginal cost of the first unit plus the marginal cost of the second unit is equal to the variable cost of producing 2 units or $140. Geometrically, taking the sum of the values of marginal cost in this manner is equivalent to calculating the area under the marginal cost function up to 2 units. Now skip to the fourth unit. The variable cost of producing 4 units is $380, and the marginal cost of producing the fourth unit is $140. The sum of the marginal costs is $380 ($80 + $60 + $100 + $140). Here again, the sum of the marginal costs is equal to the variable cost of producing 4 units.

This numerical example can be extended one step further. The area under the marginal cost function between any two quantities, say q' and q^*, where $q^* > q'$, is equal to the incremental cost the firm incurs by producing the increased quantity. Suppose that you want to determine the incremental cost the firm incurs by increasing production from 2 to 4 units. Column 1 in Table 6-1 shows variable cost increases from $140 to $380 or by $240. However, we reach the same conclusion by taking the area under the marginal cost function between 2 and 4 units, the shaded area in Figure 6-3*a*. The area under the marginal cost function is equal to $100 + $140 = $240. Therefore, the increase in variable cost equals the area under the marginal cost function between 2 and 4 units.

Figure 6-3*b* shows the average variable and the marginal cost functions when the quantity variable is continuous. To calculate the increase in variable cost from increasing production from q' to q^*, we take the area under the marginal cost function from q' to q^*, or area 2. To measure the increase in variable cost caused

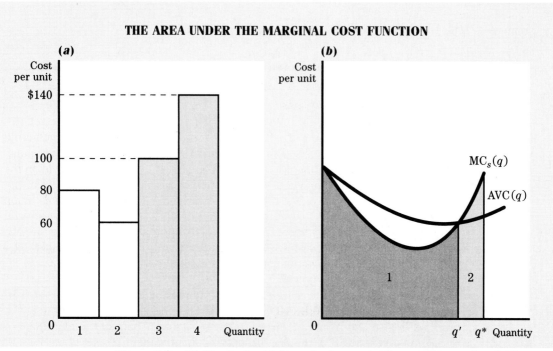

Figure 6-3   (*a*) Marginal cost for unit changes in the quantity produced. The area under the rectangles up to any quantity is the variable cost of producing that quantity. In (*b*) quantity is assumed to be continuous. The increase in variable cost from increasing output from q' to q^* is the area under the marginal cost function between q' and q^*, or area 2. The variable cost of producing q' is the area under the marginal cost function up to the quantity q', or area 1.

by increasing the production from zero to q', we take the area under the marginal cost function from $q = 0$ to $q = q'$, or area 1.

> The area under the marginal cost function between q' and q^* units is equal to the increase in variable cost from increasing output from q' to q^* units.

In summary, the area under the marginal cost function between two quantities measures the change in variable cost. The variable cost of producing any quantity equals the entire area under the marginal cost function up to that quantity.

6-4   IDENTIFYING THE RELEVANT COSTS WHEN SOLVING SHORT-RUN COST PROBLEMS

With these preliminaries established, we can use the short-run cost functions to show how a firm that uses incremental analysis is more likely to minimize cost than one that does not.

APPLICATION 6-1

How to Schedule Production
between a New Plant and an Old Plant

A firm has two plants. We assume that, like many manufacturing companies, it constructed the plants at different times and that they have different cost functions. Plant 1 is 30 years old and located in a northern city. Plant 2 is only 3 years old and located in the South. The short-run average cost functions of the two plants are shown in Figure 6-4. Cost per unit is on the vertical axis, and quantity is on the horizontal axis. Plant 2, the younger plant, has a lower average cost at each rate of output. The management is justifiably proud of this plant because it is so much more efficient than plant 1. The responsibility of the production manager is to minimize the total cost of producing the monthly quota, which for the next month is q^* units as shown on the horizontal axis of Figure 6-4. The top management team

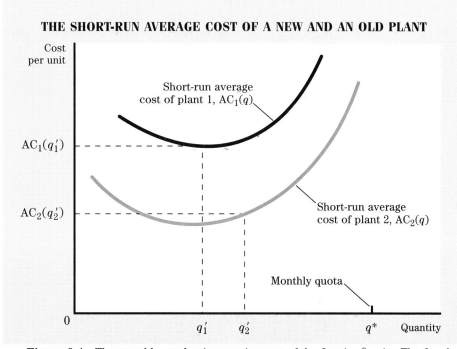

THE SHORT-RUN AVERAGE COST OF A NEW AND AN OLD PLANT

Figure 6-4   The monthly production requirement of the firm is q^* units. The firm has an old plant with a short-run average cost function AC_1 and a new plant with a short-run average cost function AC_2. The production manager schedules q_1' units at plant 1 and thereby guarantees that the average cost at plant 1 is at a minimum. The remainder of the monthly requirement, q_2', is scheduled for plant 2. The production manager says this schedule will minimize the simple average of the short-run average costs and meet the production quota. Does this schedule minimize total cost?

urges the production manager to use plant 2 fully since it is more efficient than plant 1. But the manager realizes that he cannot minimize total cost by producing the entire quota at plant 2 because short-run average cost would be much too high. Given the monthly quota, the production manager recognizes that he must use both plants. To minimize total cost, he schedules production at both to minimize the simple average of the short-run average cost for the two.

To achieve this objective, the production manager reduces the amount produced at plant 2 from q^* and increases the quantity produced at plant 1, in this way reducing the average cost of production at each plant. Ultimately, he decides to assign q_1' units to plant 1, minimizing its average cost, and to assign q_2' units to plant 2 so that $q_1' + q_2' = q^*$. The production manager believes this production schedule lowers the simple average of the short-run average cost of the two plants as much as possible and meets the monthly quota.

Some members of the management team are very upset when they learn about the production schedule. By scheduling q_1' units at plant 1 and only q_2' units at plant 2, the firm ends up with a production schedule where short-run average cost at plant 1, $AC_1(q_1')$, is greater than short-run average cost at plant 2, $AC_2(q_2')$. They cannot fathom how this can be the cost-minimizing solution and why the new plant is not producing more since its average cost is less than the average cost for plant 1. During several heated meetings, the production manager defends his policy by noting that average cost at both plants will increase if plant 2 produces more and plant 1 less. He asks his critics, "How can total cost decrease if average cost increases at each plant?" He points out that his responsibility is to produce the monthly quota at the lowest total cost—not to show a special preference for plant 2.

Has the production manager found the cost-minimizing solution or do the members of the management team have a valid point in advocating greater output at plant 2? The first step in finding the lowest cost solution is to identify the costs that the manager's decision affects. The production manager should totally ignore fixed cost because the fixed cost at each plant is a bygone that the firm incurs no matter what the production manager decides. The production schedule affects only the variable cost of each plant. Therefore, the production manager should find a schedule that minimizes Z, the sum of total variable costs,

$$\text{Minimize } Z = V_1(q_1) + V_2(q_2)$$

and meets the monthly quota.

What condition must the manager satisfy if he minimizes the sum of total variable costs? Shifting production from one plant to another will raise the variable cost at the plant where output rises and lower the variable cost at the plant where output falls. The marginal cost of producing Δq_2 units at plant 2 is $\Delta V_2 / \Delta q_2$, and the marginal cost of producing Δq_1 units at plant 1 is $\Delta V_1 / \Delta q_1$. Suppose the production manager schedules production so that the marginal costs for the two plants are not equal.

$$MC_1 = \frac{\Delta V_1}{\Delta q_1} \neq \frac{\Delta V_2}{\Delta q_2} = MC_2$$

Then, the firm does not produce q^* units at the lowest cost. For example, suppose the marginal cost of producing another unit is $6 at plant 1 and $3 at plant 2. By producing one more unit at plant 2, the firm incurs an additional cost of $3. By producing one less unit at plant 1 the firm saves $6. The sum of variable costs falls by $3, although the firm is still meeting the production quota. Thus, this is not the lowest cost solution because we can find a lower one. As long as marginal cost differs across plants, the firm does not minimize the sum of total variable costs. The cost-minimizing solution requires *marginal cost* (not average cost) to be the same at all plants.

Minimum total cost occurs when marginal costs are equal at all plants.

Let's use a graph to show why the equality of marginal costs minimizes the sum of variable costs.[9] In Figure 6-5 the length of the horizontal axis is q^* units, the total production quota. The origin for plant 1 is 0 on the left-hand side of the graph. The output of plant 1 increases on moving from left to right. The marginal cost function of this plant goes through the minimum point of its short-run average cost function. The quantity of plant 2 increases from right to left with $0'$ as the origin. Plant 2's short-run average and marginal cost functions start with $0'$ as the origin. Each point on the horizontal axis in Figure 6-5 represents an allocation of production between the two plants that satisfies the monthly quota of q^* units.

Now we can analyze the proposed schedule of the production manager. With the proposed schedule, he assigns q_1' units for plant 1 and thereby minimizes the short-run average cost of this plant. When plant 1 produces q_1', plant 2 produces q_2', and Figure 6-5 shows that the marginal cost of plant 1 exceeds the marginal cost of plant 2. Clearly, the production manager's schedule does not minimize the sum of variable costs. Plant 2 should be producing more and plant 1 less, although this will increase the average cost of production at both plants.

Figure 6-6 reproduces the marginal cost functions of the two plants. The firm minimizes total production cost when marginal costs are the same at both plants and plant 1 produces q_1'' while plant 2 produces q_2''. We can prove this by showing that the variable cost of plant 1 decreases by more than the variable cost increases when plant 2 produces more and plant 1 less. Area 2, the area under the marginal cost function of plant 2 between q_2' and q_2'', is equal to the increase in variable cost when plant 2 produces more. The sum of areas 1 and 2, the area under the marginal cost function of plant 1 between q_1' and q_1'', is equal to the decrease in variable cost at plant 1. The net cost saving is equal to area 1. Therefore, there is merit to the management team's suggestion that plant 2 should produce more.

What led the production manager astray and why did he fail to find the cost-minimizing solution? His first mistake was to focus on average cost at each plant. This proved to be a serious error because the average cost includes average fixed cost and the production manager has no control over fixed cost. He should have completely ignored fixed cost and just concentrated on minimizing the sum of

[9] The appendix to this chapter presents a mathematical derivation of the conditions for cost minimization.

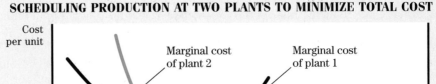

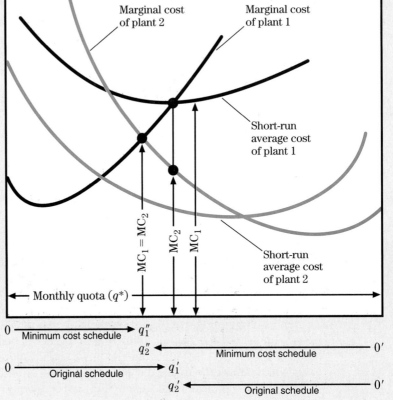

Figure 6-5 The total cost of scheduling q^* units at two plants is minimized if the firm schedules production so that marginal costs are equal. The schedule proposed by the production manager underutilizes plant 2 and overutilizes plant 1. The marginal costs of the two plants are not equal. By expanding the quantity produced at plant 2 to q_2'' and reducing the quantity at plant 1 to q_1'', total cost decreases although the average cost of both plants increases.

variable costs. The production manager was looking backward by allowing past decisions that determined fixed cost to influence future decisions. This example shows why it is critical for a manager to identify costs that are affected by his decision and concentrate on minimizing these costs. His second mistake was not thinking in incremental terms. By failing to do this, the production manager advanced the superficially plausible but defective criterion of minimizing the average of the two short-run average costs. If he had thought in terms of incremental cost, he would have recognized why this criterion was defective.

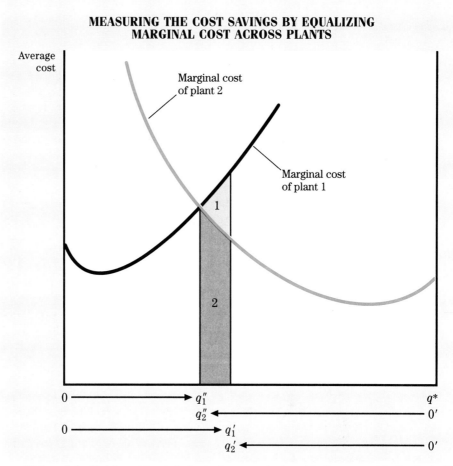

**MEASURING THE COST SAVINGS BY EQUALIZING
MARGINAL COST ACROSS PLANTS**

Figure 6-6   Total cost is minimized when marginal cost is the same at both plants. By increasing the quantity from q_2' to q_2'' at plant 2, total cost increases by area 2. By decreasing the quantity from q_1' to q_1'' at plant 1, the cost savings become equal to the sum of areas 1 and 2. Therefore, the cost savings from equalizing marginal costs equal area 1.

The top management team deserves only faint praise. They are so enamored of the new plant that they want to produce everything at it. It is true that the new plant is more efficient than the old one *at each quantity*. The marginal cost at plant 2 is less than the marginal cost at plant 1 if each plant produces the same quantity. However, this is an irrelevant consideration as well because the plants do not have to produce the same quantity. At the cost-minimizing solution the two plants are equally efficient *at the margin* since marginal costs at both plants are equal.

APPLICATION 6-2

Why "Never Give Up" Is Not Always the Best Advice[10]

Everyone has received advice at some time from a friend or a parent to never give up. Such advice involves the "fixed cost fallacy." Suppose you plan to major in engineering, perhaps because one of your parents did. However, after you have completed several engineering courses, you find the subject uninteresting and wonder if history is more your calling. You may receive advice from your friends or parents to keep working and not to give up because you have put so much time into the engineering courses. This advice is based on the sunk cost fallacy. The time that you have spent in successfully completing the engineering courses is a sunk cost that you cannot recover. It is a bygone and should not affect your future decisions. Saying "Never give up" says that you should let past decisions affect your current decision.

Richard Nesbett and two colleagues surveyed University of Michigan faculty members and seniors and asked them whether they had ever walked out of a bad movie, refused to finish a bad meal, or terminated a bad research project with less promising prospects. Those students and faculty who had not let past decisions affect their future behavior avoided the sunk cost fallacy. If you walk out of a bad movie, you are saying that there are better things to do with your time than sit through the rest of the film. Moreover, your decision to walk out should not depend on how much you paid: the price of admission is a sunk cost and should not affect your decision to leave.

Nesbett et al. found that faculty members who used cost-benefit reasoning had higher salaries relative to their age and department and that economics faculty members used this reasoning more often than faculty members in the humanities or in biology. Interestingly, they also found that seniors who used this reasoning had higher SAT scores and had taken more economics courses.

APPLICATION 6-3

Inefficient or Efficient Environmental Regulation

The Environmental Protection Agency imposes detailed emission standards on manufacturing plants. These standards, designed to improve air quality, require pollution limits on emission sources within a plant. At first glance this regulatory policy sounds eminently sensible and even reasonable. To improve air quality, each source should contribute to the effort.

Let's examine the economic consequences of this source-by-source regulation for a plant that has two sources of dust emissions. In Figure 6-7*a* the total tons of

[10] Based on Alan L. Otten, "Economic Perspective Produces Steady Yields," *Wall Street Journal*, March 31, 1992, B1.

emissions from source 1 are plotted on the horizontal axis, and the marginal cost
of reducing emissions from source 1 on the vertical axis. Figure 6-7*b* shows the
relationship between total emissions and the marginal cost of reducing emissions
from source 2 at the same plant. (The two sources could be two smokestacks at
the same plant.) We assume that source 1 would emit q_1^* tons of dust per day and
source 2 would emit q_2^* tons without any regulation. Suppose a source-by-source
regulatory program requires source 1 to reduce emissions from q_1^* tons per day to
q_1' tons per day, and source 2 to reduce emissions from q_2^* tons per day to q_2' tons
per day. The total cost of reducing emissions by $q_1^* - q_1'$ tons of dust per day is
equal to the area under the marginal cost function for source 1, or area 1. The total
cost of reducing emissions by $q_2^* - q_2'$ tons per day from source 2 is equal to the
area under the marginal cost function for source 2, or area 2.

Source-by-source regulation of emissions can be very costly because it ignores
the different marginal cost functions for pollution abatement. The marginal cost of

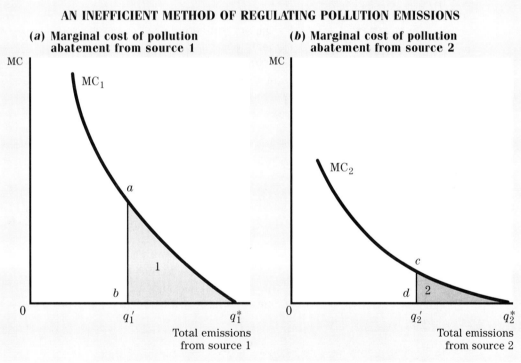

AN INEFFICIENT METHOD OF REGULATING POLLUTION EMISSIONS

Figure 6-7   Dust is emitted from two sources in a plant. Source 1 emits q_1^* tons of
dust per day and source 2 would emit q_2^* tons of dust per day without regulation.
Source-by-source regulation requires source 1 to reduce emissions to q_1' and source 2
to reduce emissions to q_2'. The incremental cost of reducing emissions from source 1 is
equal to area 1, and the incremental cost of reducing emissions from source 2 is equal
to area 2. The source-by-source regulation does not equate the marginal cost of reducing
emissions across sources.

reducing the last ounce of dust at source 1 when the plant removes q_1' tons is ab in Figure 6-7a and is greater than cd in Figure 6-7b, the marginal cost of removing the last ounce of dust from source 2 when the plant removes q_2' tons. Differences in marginal cost occur because source-by-source regulation mandates that the plant reduce emissions to q_1' tons from source 1 and to q_2' tons from source 2.

Regulatory authorities require total emissions of the plant to be reduced by $(q_1^* - q_1') + (q_2^* - q_2')$ tons. Is there a more cost-efficient way of reducing emissions by the same amount? Instead of using command and control regulations and specifying how much to remove from each source, suppose the firm is instructed to reduce emissions by the same total amount as before, but that the management can decide what is the most cost-efficient method. This method of regulation is called the **bubble concept** because it is as if a giant bubble surrounds the plant so that the regulator does not know how many sources there are. The regulator's only concern is with the total emissions escaping from the bubble.

How would the management of the plant respond under the bubble concept? They would find the solution where the marginal cost of reducing a ton of dust from source 1 equals the marginal cost of reducing a ton of dust from source 2. In Figure 6-8 the total mandated reduction of emissions for this plant is on the horizontal axis. The marginal cost of reducing tons of dust per day from source 1 is on the left vertical axis, and from source 2, on the right vertical axis. MC_1 and MC_2 are the marginal cost functions of reducing emissions from the two sources. The marginal cost of reducing a ton of dust emissions from each source increases as the plant removes more tons of dust, and it becomes increasingly expensive to remove dust from a given source as the amount removed increases. It is in the self-interest of management to minimize the cost of removing emissions. Management must find a solution where the marginal cost of dust removal at both sources is the same. The firm removes q_1'' tons of dust from source 1 and q_2'' tons of dust from source 2. Because the marginal cost of reducing emissions is equal for all sources, the bubble concept results in a more cost-efficient solution for a *given* reduction of emissions than the more detailed source-by-source method of regulation. Check your understanding of the analysis by presenting a geometric measure of the firm's cost savings if the regulator shifts from source-by-source regulation to the bubble concept.

Are the cost savings from implementing the bubble concept likely to be large? Robert Hahn has studied innovative environmental policies like the bubble concept and estimates that 40 bubble plans that have received federal approval have saved firms about $300 million.[11]

Marginal analysis is useful not only for firms but also for regulatory authorities. Inefficient regulatory programs just create more political opposition to these programs. Some but not all environmental organizations recognize this fundamental point and support efforts to introduce more efficiency into the enforcement of regulations. The bubble concept and other innovative regulatory policies are gradually gaining more acceptance as preferable forms of regulation.

---

[11] For a summary of incentive-based mechanisms in the implementation of environmental policies, see Robert W. Hahn, "Economic Presciptions for Environmental Problems: How the Patient Followed the Doctor's Orders," *Journal of Economic Perspectives*, vol. 3, no. 2, Spring 1989, pp. 95–114.

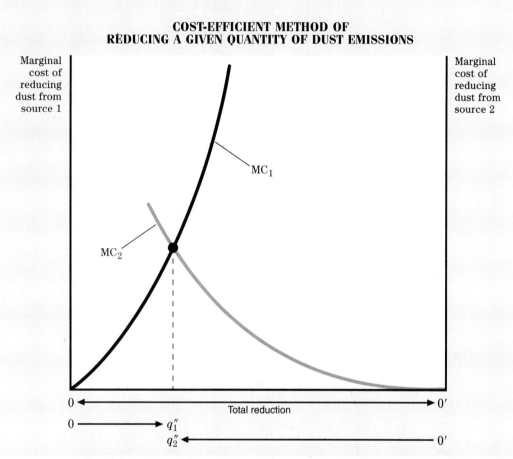

**COST-EFFICIENT METHOD OF
REDUCING A GIVEN QUANTITY OF DUST EMISSIONS**

Figure 6-8   The lowest cost of reducing a given amount of emissions is to equalize the marginal costs across all sources. Source 1 reduces emissions by q_1'' tons of dust per day. Source 2 reduces emissions by q_2'' tons of dust per day. The bubble concept allows each firm to decide what is the cost-efficient method to achieve a given reduction in the total quantity of emissions.

6-5   DERIVING THE LONG-RUN AVERAGE COST FUNCTION FROM THE SHORT-RUN AVERAGE COST FUNCTIONS

In the long run a firm selects a plant size and a number of workers such that it produces each quantity at the lowest total and average costs. How does the company determine which plant size produces a given quantity at the lowest long-run total and average costs?

Let's begin with a description of how the firm identifies the long-run average cost function when it has a choice of just three plant sizes. Then we will demonstrate how to derive the long-run average cost function when the firm selects from a continuum of plant sizes.

The Long-Run Average Cost Function with a Limited Choice of Plants

The graphs of the short-run average cost functions for three different sizes of plants are shown in Figure 6-9. AC_1 is the average cost function of the smallest plant, AC_2 is the average cost function of the medium-sized plant, and AC_3 is the average cost function of the largest plant. If the firm expects to produce any quantity between 0 and q_1 units indefinitely, it will build the smallest plant with the short-run average cost of AC_1 because this plant has the lowest short-run average cost for producing any quantity less than q_1. The firm will build a medium-sized plant with AC_2 if it expects to produce any output between q_1 and q_2 indefinitely, and the largest plant with AC_3 if it plans to produce an output greater than q_2.

Although all three plants can produce any quantity less than q_1, the smallest

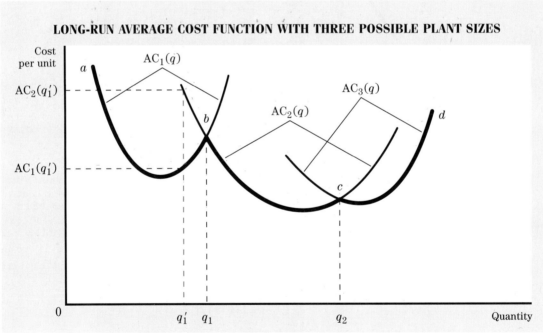

LONG-RUN AVERAGE COST FUNCTION WITH THREE POSSIBLE PLANT SIZES

Figure 6-9 The long-run average cost function shows the lowest average cost of producing each quantity. If the firm can select among only three plant sizes, the long-run average cost function becomes the scalloped curve *abcd*. Plant 1 with AC_1 has the lowest average cost of producing any quantity less than q_1. Plant 2 with AC_2 has the lowest average cost of producing any quantity between q_1 and q_2. Plant 3 has the lowest average cost of producing any quantity greater than q_2.

plant produces it at the lowest short-run average cost. For example, if the firm decides to produce q_1' in Figure 6-9, the average cost of producing q_1' with the smallest plant is $AC_1(q_1')$, the short-run average cost. If the firm errs and builds the medium-sized plant, the mistake is costly because the short-run average cost is higher and is $AC_2(q_1')$, the short-run average cost of producing q_1' units with plant 2. Clearly the smallest plant has a lower short-run average cost and is the cost-efficient plant for producing q_1'.

The procedure for finding the long-run average cost function from the firm's short-run average cost functions is relatively simple. For each quantity on the horizontal axis, move up vertically until you reach the first short-run average cost function. The plant with that average cost function produces that quantity at the lowest average and total costs in the long run. In the present case the firm has just three choices for plant size, and so the long-run average cost function becomes the scalloped average cost function *abcd* in Figure 6-9.

The Long-Run Average Cost Function with a Continuum of Plant Sizes

Let's give the firm more choices of plant sizes. Suppose it can choose from a continuum of plant sizes. How does the shape of the long-run average cost function change? For each plant size, there is a corresponding short-run total and average cost function. Perhaps you can visualize the consequences of having a continuum of plant sizes to select from. Figure 6-10*a* shows just three of *many* short-run total cost functions. The short-run total cost function of one plant is $C_1(q)$. This plant produces the quantity q_1^* and only q_1^* at the lowest total cost. A larger plant with the cost function $C_2(q)$ produces the quantity q_2^* at the lowest total cost. Finally, the plant with the short-run total cost function $C_3(q)$ produces q_3^* at the lowest total cost. Other short-run total cost functions exist, but we do not draw them to keep Figure 6-10 from becoming totally incomprehensible. Each plant would have the lowest total cost for producing some specific quantity. The long-run total cost function $C_L(q)$ is formed by connecting all the points that identify the minimum total cost of producing each quantity.

Given the long-run total cost function, we derive the long-run average and marginal cost functions and include them in Figure 6-10*b*. The long-run average cost function becomes the smooth U-shaped function labeled $AC_L(q)$, and the long-run marginal cost function is $MC_L(q)$. When there is a continuum of plant sizes, each plant has the lowest average cost for producing a unique quantity—not a range of quantities. If the firm expects to produce q_1^*, the plant with the short-run average cost function $AC_1(q)$ produces q_1^* and only q_1^* at the lowest average and total costs. This means that the short-run average cost function $AC_1(q)$ touches the long-run average cost function only when the firm produces q_1^* units. At any other quantity the short-run average cost function $AC_1(q)$ lies above the long-run average cost function. The significance of this point is that other plant sizes can produce these other quantities at a lower average cost than plant 1 can. Plant 1 can produce only q_1^* at the *lowest* average and total costs. If the firm wants to produce q_2^*, the plant with the average cost function $AC_2(q)$ produces q_2^* and only q_2^* at the lowest

THE LONG-RUN TOTAL AVERAGE COST FUNCTIONS WHEN PLANT SIZE IS CONTINUOUS

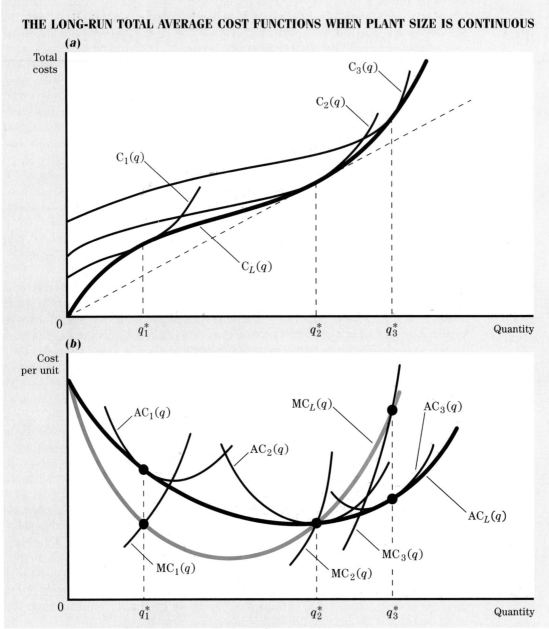

Figure 6-10 The long-run average cost function is derived by finding the plant size that can produce each quantity at the lowest average cost. Each plant size can produce a specific quantity at the lowest average cost. For example, the plant with $AC_1(q)$ can produce q_1^* at the lowest average cost.

total and average costs. The average cost function labeled $AC_2(q)$ touches the long-run average cost function only when the quantity is q_2^*. Here again, plant 2 cannot produce any other output at lowest average cost. Finally, the plant with the short-run average cost function $AC_3(q)$ can produce q_3^* at the lowest average cost.

The procedure for deriving the long-run average cost function remains the same. For each quantity, find the plant with the lowest short-run average cost. There is a minimum average cost for each quantity. We form the long-run average cost function by connecting all such points. The long-run average cost function shows the lowest average cost of producing each quantity. The long-run marginal cost function in Figure 6-10*b* shows the incremental cost of producing another unit when both plant size and the number of workers are variable.

We have already described the relationship that must exist between the short-run average and marginal cost functions and between the long-run average and marginal cost functions. However, we have not discussed how to relate the short- and long-run marginal and average costs to each other.

When the firm produces q_2^*, Figure 6-10*b* shows that the long-run average cost is at a minimum and $AC_L = MC_L = AC_s = MC_s$. This set of equalities holds only at the minimum point of a U-shaped long-run average cost function.

At all other quantities two separate sets of equalities hold: $AC_L = AC_s$ $\neq MC_L = MC_s$. At any quantity other than q_2^* the two separate equalities are (1) short-run average cost equals long-run average cost because the particular plant produces that output at the lowest average cost and (2) short-run marginal cost equals long-run marginal cost because the marginal cost of expanding output is the short-run marginal cost of that plant. However, the average cost does not equal the marginal cost.

The three situations can be summarized as follows.

1. If $q < q_2^*$, $AC_L = AC_s > MC_L = MC_s$.

2. If $q = q_2^*$, $AC_L = AC_s = MC_L = MC_s$.

3. If $q > q_2^*$, $AC_L = AC_s < MC_L = MC_s$.

For example, in Figure 6-10*b* the short-run average cost function $AC_1(q)$ is tangent to the long-run average cost function when the firm produces q_1^*, and so short-run average cost equals long-run average cost. Because the slope of the short-run total cost function equals the slope of the long-run total cost function when $q = q_1^*$, long-run marginal cost equals short-run marginal cost. However, short- and long-run marginal costs are less than short- and long-run average costs.

6-6   THE NUMBER OF FIRMS AND THE LONG-RUN COST FUNCTION

This section will explain why the shape of the long-run average cost function places some limitations on the number of firms that can exist in an industry.

The long-run average cost function in Figure 6-10 is U-shaped. When long-run average cost decreases, the firm experiences internal economies of scale.[12] When all factors are variable, a k percent increase in output increases total cost by less than k percent. After the firm reaches a certain size, long-run average cost increases and the firm experiences internal diseconomies of scale. A k percent increase in output increases costs by more than k percent.

The shape of the long-run average cost function plays an important role in explaining why there are many firms in some industries and only a few in other industries. The number of firms is large when the long-run average cost function is U-shaped and the market size is large. With a U-shaped long-run average cost function internal diseconomies of scale place a limit on the size of a firm. A company that is too large will have higher average cost than a smaller firm. Why are there many and not just a few farms producing wheat? It may be that internal diseconomies of scale set in after a firm reaches a certain size. Just imagine the severe management problems that would emerge if all wheat farms in the United States became one huge collective farm. How could such a large farm be managed? The existence of many companies in an industry is an indicator of internal diseconomies of scale.

Diseconomies of Scale and Industries with Many Firms

How do economists know that there are internal diseconomies of scale? Usually they draw this inference by looking at the number of firms and the size distribution of firms in industries. Many industries have a large number of producers, and so the market share of even the largest is quite small. For example, in 1982 there were 1824 firms producing women's blouses and 853 producing fluid milk. The large number of firms in these industries suggests that diseconomies of scale limit their size.[13]

Economies of Scale and Industries with Few Firms

In some industries the technology creates persistent economies of scale. The larger the output produced by a firm, the lower the long-run per unit cost. The sources of these economies usually spring from the indivisibility of a factor of production. There may be a minimum size so that plant size cannot be scaled down to produce one unit of a product. Advertisers buying time on network television used to face this situation because a company would have to purchase a network package rather than air time in specific broadcast areas. A small regional firm that sold its product in only one region of the country had to pay the national rate and was at a substantial cost disadvantage compared to a national company that sold its product in all regions of the country. Another example of indivisibility involves the mini-

[12] The expression "internal economies of scale" as used here is synonymous with the expression "internal returns to scale" used in Chapter 5. Given factor prices, the two expressions refer to the same phenomena—a k percent increase in output requires a less than k percent in the increase in both inputs. Therefore, long-run average cost decreases as the firm produces a larger quantity.

[13] Nobel Prize winner George Stigler applied this idea of survival of the fittest to firms in George Stigler, "The Economies of Scale," *Journal of Law and Economics*, vol. 1, October 1958, pp. 54–71.

mum size of an automobile dealership. In small rural local markets only the largest manufacturers have automobile dealerships. Not every brand exists in these markets because of the indivisibility of the size of a dealership.

Another source of internal economies of scale is the relationship between a volume and an area. In Chapter 5 we saw that the long-run average cost of a pipeline decreased with quantity and so there were internal economies of scale. The cost of the materials for the construction of a pipeline increases with the diameter of the pipeline. The output of the pipeline depends on the area of its cross section, which increases with the square of the diameter. As the diameter increases, total cost increases less than proportionally with output, and these physical relationships create internal returns to scale.

Finally, specialization of functions fosters economies of scale. In large firms there is greater specialization of functions than in smaller firms. Specialists perform such diverse functions as advertising, quality control, welding, and purchasing within the firm, and specialization is less extensive within smaller firms.

Industries with continual internal economies of scale are natural monopolies which exist when the total cost of producing a given quantity is lowest if only one firm produces the product.

> A **natural monopoly** exists when a single firm can produce a given quantity at lowest total cost.

Many public utilities have this type of cost structure. Where there are persistent internal economies of scale, the lowest total cost of producing any quantity requires just one firm in the industry. The total cost of producing a given quantity increases when there is more than one firm. An industry in which there are continual internal economies of scale evolves into a single-firm industry. In some industries internal economies of scale exist but become less important and disappear beyond a certain quantity. In some industries the number of firms in the industry is typically small. For example, there were only 9 chewing gum manufacturers in 1982 and the leading 4 companies accounted for 95 percent of sales. The breakfast cereal industry had 32 producers but the leading 4 companies accounted for 86 percent of sales. It is not an accident that the number of firms is relatively small in these industries. The internal economies of scale in the manufacture, promotion, and distribution of these products limit the number of firms that are cost-efficient. It is quite likely that the shape of the long-run average cost function explains the small number of producers in these cases.

Now that we have introduced the concept of the long-run average cost function, let's see what can and cannot be explained by the shape of this function.

APPLICATION 6-4

The Emergence of the Standard Oil Company

One of the most prosperous firms in the history of American business was the Standard Oil Company of New Jersey. Standard Oil and its founder, the much vilified John D. Rockefeller, were so successful that the government sued the company in 1911 in a landmark antitrust case for monopolizing the market for refined petroleum products. At the time of the antitrust suit Standard Oil's market share exceeded 75 percent.[14] Standard Oil lost the case, and the firm was subdivided into several smaller regional companies.

Many historians and economists view John D. Rockefeller as an unscrupulous businessman who used unfair methods to eliminate competitors. We do not want to enter the long-standing debate over the competitive methods employed by Rockefeller. However you choose to view his behavior, the question we want to answer is: Why was this company so successful and why did this industry change so much in such a short time? Why didn't firms in other industries have as much success? Surely, there were other businessmen in America at the time whose desire for wealth was as intense as Rockefeller's and who would have been willing to adopt unscrupulous methods of competition. Why didn't they succeed?

One interesting fact uncovered by John McGee in his study of the antitrust case is that Standard Oil was not always a dominant player in the refining market. McGee reports that the company was one of many in the industry and had only about 10 percent of the market in 1870. Between 1870 and 1890 the company went on a merger binge. The government claimed that Standard Oil acquired 123 refineries from 1870 to 1890 or 1900, although there is some disagreement as to when these acquisitions occurred.

Standard Oil had only a small share of the refining market in 1870, but 20 years later the industry was far different. A dominant leader had emerged with more than 75 percent of the market. Increasing any company's market share from 10 to 75+ percent over 20 years is a remarkable feat, a rare event in the annals of American business. How can we explain this transformation?

One hypothesis that might explain this change is the presence of economies of scale in oil refining. Figure 6-11a shows the long-run average cost function of a firm in the refining business, and the shape of this function indicates that there are economies of scale. One could argue that the average cost of most firms was relatively high in 1870 because the typical refiner was small and produced only (say) q_1^* units. Suppose Rockefeller was the first to understand and take advantage of economies of scale. Expanding through acquisitions, he achieved internal economies of scale in the industry, and by 1890 many other firms had disappeared.

What does the internal economies of scale hypothesis leave unexplained? It does not explain why so many firms were in the industry in 1870. If there are internal economies of scale, one would not expect to observe so many firms in an industry because they would be unable to minimize the total cost of producing any given quantity. A few firms can produce any given industry output at a lower total cost than a large number of small firms can. If there are internal economies of scale, just a few firms would be in the industry from the very beginning.

Let's consider an alternative hypothesis. Suppose firms in the industry up to 1870 had U-shaped long-run average cost functions. Therefore, no company could be too large because long-run average cost increases if a firm becomes too large. In that era no firm could control a large share of the market because it would

[14] John S. McGee, "Predatory Price Cutting: The Standard Oil (NJ) Case," *Journal of Law and Economics*, vol. I, October 1958.

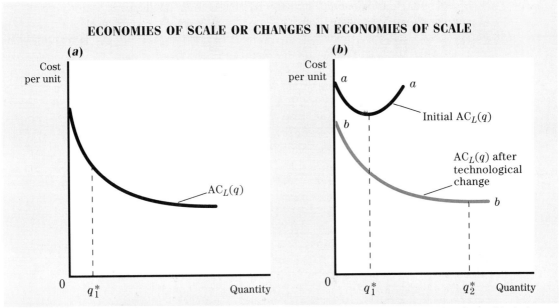

Figure 6-11   In (a) it can be seen that there are economies of scale in this industry. Few firms should exist in the industry if there are economies of scale. In (b) a change in technology shifts the long-run average cost function down and increases the extent of economies of scale. The optimal size of the firm increases from q_1^* to q_2^*.

become an inefficient high-average-cost producer. Figure 6-11b shows the long-run average cost function aa is U-shaped and that the lowest average cost occurs when the firm produces q_1^*.

Now assume that one or several technological changes occurred in the refining and transportation of crude oil. The long-run average cost function of the firm shifted down, and the extent of economies of scale became more pronounced. Because internal economies of scale are more important now, there is a greater incentive to merge and grow to q_2^*. In the past the U-shaped average cost function discouraged such mergers and growth.

How did the industry evolve? The technological changes caused firms to merge, output to become more concentrated, and the real prices of refined products to decline. Do we have any evidence that technological changes occurred? Alfred Chandler reports that the reorganization of Standard Oil Trust's refining facilities and coordination of the flow of raw materials from the oil field to the refinery to the consumer brought a sharp reduction in the average cost of producing a gallon of kerosene, the major product of the time. In 1880 the average cost of kerosene was 2.5 cents per gallon, and by 1885 it had fallen to 1.5 cents, a 40 percent reduction.[15] It appears that significant cost reductions occurred in this industry.

[15] Alfred D. Chandler, Jr., *Scale and Scope: The Dynamics of Industrial Capitalism*, Harvard University Press, Cambridge, Mass., 1990, p. 25.

The technological and managerial change hypothesis gives a more consistent explanation of the facts than the simple economies of scale hypothesis does. It is probably one reason John D. Rockefeller was so successful. He was the first to recognize the significance of the changes in the industry and to understand the implications of these changes for firm size. According to this hypothesis, the industry would have evolved in this manner even if Rockefeller had not lived. Technological changes converted this industry from one with many producers to one dominated by one or a few firms. According to this hypothesis, if not Rockefeller, some other entrepreneur would have become the titan of this industry. Clearly, this hypothesis is at variance with the great man theory of industry, which attributes to Rockefeller many of the traits of a shrewd and talented entrepreneur and organizer. The truth is probably somewhere in between. The dominance of the Standard Oil Company of New Jersey was due to technological changes that favored size and the rare managerial talents possessed by John D. Rockefeller. We examine the effect of unique managerial talent on a firm's cost functions in Chapter 8.

SUMMARY

- In the short run a firm has at least one fixed factor of production. All factors are variable in the long run.
- The short-run total cost function shows the lowest total cost of producing each quantity when at least one factor is fixed. The short-run total cost function is equal to the sum of fixed and variable costs.
- Short-run average cost declines with increases in quantity, reaches a minimum, and then increases. Average variable cost also declines with increases in quantity, reaches a minimum, and then increases.
- Short-run marginal cost goes through the minimum points of the average variable cost function and the short-run average cost function.
- A necessary condition for efficient production of a given total quantity by a multiplant firm is that all plants have the same marginal cost.
- In the long run a firm selects each factor of production so that it can produce each quantity at the lowest total and average costs.
- The shape of the long-run average cost function determines whether there are many or a few firms in an industry. When there are diseconomies of scale, there are a large number of firms in the industry when the size of market is large. When there are economies of scale, there will be one or few firms in an industry.

KEY TERMS

Explicit cost

Fixed factor

Short and long runs

Opportunity cost

Variable factor

Fixed cost

Variable cost
Short-run average and marginal
   costs
Equating marginal cost at all plants
Internal economies and
   diseconomies of scale

Short-run marginal cost
Area under marginal cost function
Long-run average and marginal cost
   functions

REVIEW QUESTIONS

1. How does a fixed cost differ from a sunk cost?
2. Suppose a firm purchases a specialized die for $20,000 to manufacture a prod-
   uct. The die will last 1 year, and the manufacturer can sell it to another manufacturer for only $500 within the year. What is the opportunity cost of the die
   before purchase? What is the opportunity cost of the die after the firm purchases
   it?
3. You enter into a contract with a franchisor to pay a royalty fee of $5,000 per
   year if you sell at least one unit of the franchisor's product. Is the franchise fee
   a fixed cost? Is the franchise fee a sunk cost?
4. To determine marginal cost, you must know the variable cost and fixed cost
   functions. Explain why you agree or disagree with this statement.
5. If short-run marginal cost is increasing, then short-run average cost is increasing. If short-run average cost is increasing, short-run marginal cost is increasing.
   Explain why you agree or disagree with these two statements.
6. Average cost decreases as output rises because a firm can spread a fixed cost
   over more units. Explain why you agree or disagree with this statement. Does
   this statement apply to the short or to the long run?
7. The area under the average variable cost function up to a prespecified quantity
   is equal to the variable cost of producing that quantity. Explain why you agree
   or disagree with this statement.
8. The area under the marginal cost function up to a prespecified quantity is equal
   to the variable cost of producing that quantity. Explain why you agree or disagree with this statement.
9. If AFC is declining and AC is declining, then AVC is declining. Explain why you
   agree or disagree with this statement.

EXERCISES

1. At each quantity the marginal cost at plant 1 is 20 percent lower than the
   marginal cost at plant 2. Total cost will be minimized if total output is produced
   at plant 1. Explain why you agree or disagree with this statement.
2. The accompanying table shows the fixed cost (F), variable cost (V), total cost
   (C), average cost (AC), and marginal cost (MC) at two plants. The average cost
   at plant 1 is greater than the average cost at plant 2 at each quantity.

	Plant 1					Plant 2				
QUANTITY	F_1 (1)	V_1 (2)	C_1 (3)	AC_1 (4)	MC_1 (5)	F_2 (6)	V_2 (7)	C_2 (8)	AC_2 (9)	MC_2 (10)
1	300	10	310	310	10	50	5	55	55	5
2	300	15	315	158	5	50	8	58	29	3
3	300	35	335	112	20	50	12	62	21	4
4	300	60	360	90	35	50	18	68	17	6
5	300	180	480	96	120	50	26	76	15	8
6	300	340	640	107	140	50	46	96	16	20
7	300	500	800	118	180	50	90	140	20	44

Suppose the monthly quota of the firm is 9 units. The production manager schedules 4 units at plant 1 because she minimizes AC_1 at $90 per unit, and plant 2 provides the remaining 5 units at an average cost of $76.

a. Fill in the values in the following table and show whether the production manager's solution minimizes the total cost of production.

$q_1 + q_2 = 9$	AVERAGE COST AT PLANT	SUM OF VARIABLE COST, $V_1 + V_2$	SUM OF TOTAL COST, $C_1 + C_2$
$q_1 = 4, q_2 = 5$	AC_1 = ?, AC_2 = ?		
$q_1 = 3, q_2 = 6$	AC_1 = ?, AC_2 = ?		
$q_1 = 2, q_2 = 7$	AC_1 = ?, AC_2 = ?		

b. Explain why the simple average of the average cost at each plant does or does not minimize total cost.

3. A firm has two plants. The objective of the production manager is to minimize total cost and meet a monthly production schedule.
   a. If the firm schedules production optimally, what condition does it satisfy?
   b. Suppose a strike closes plant 2 for a month. Construct a graph showing the increase in total cost the firm incurs during the month because of the strike.

4. A company operates two oil wells in a state. Well A is capable of producing 1,000 barrels per day, and well B is capable of producing a maximum of 900 barrels a day. The state government regulates the rate of oil extraction from each well in the state. These restrictions are expressed in terms of the percentage of the maximum flow of oil from each well (method 1). Currently, the government restricts output of each well to 50 percent of maximum output, and so the total allocation for the company is 950 barrels a day. Suppose the government is considering a different method of regulating the industry. Under method 2 it simply restricts the company's output to 950 barrels per day. Compare the two methods of regulation and explain whether they would result in the same rate of utilization of the two wells.

5. At the end of August, a manufacturing firm receives an order from a retailing firm for q^* units that the firm must deliver to the store on November 1 for the Christmas season. Let $C = C(q_t)$ be the total cost of producing q_t units in either September or October. Let h be the per unit monthly inventory cost of storing one unit for a single month.

   a. How many units should the manufacturing firm produce in September and October so that the firm ships q^* units on November 1 and minimizes the sum of production and storage costs?

   b. If the firm minimizes total production and storage costs, what condition must it satisfy?

   c. Explain why it will not be efficient to produce one-half of the order in September and one-half in October.

   d. How will the firm change its production decision if h increases?

6. The short-run total cost function is shown in figure a. The short-run average, average variable, and marginal cost functions are shown in figure b. Using figure a as a standard of reference, point out three errors in figure b.

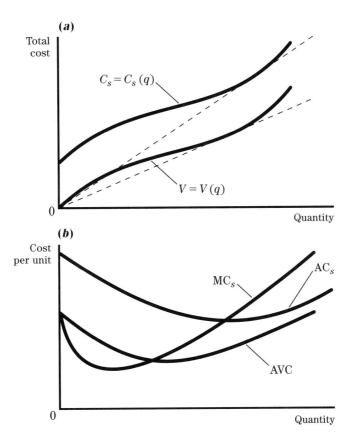

7. Although long-run average cost involves the full cost of all factors of production while average variable cost involves the cost of only those factors that are

variable, average variable cost may exceed long-run average cost. Explain why you agree or disagree with this statement.

8. The number of U.S. beer manufacturers has declined over time. The accompanying table shows the number of manufacturers from 1947 to 1987.

YEAR	NUMBER OF COMPANIES	YEAR	NUMBER OF COMPANIES
1947	404	1972	108
1954	263	1977	81
1958	211	1982	67
1963	171	1987	101
1967	125		

a. How would you explain the 83 percent decline in the number of companies between 1947 and 1982?

b. How would you explain the growth of companies between 1982 and 1987?

CHAPTER 6 APPENDIX

Mathematical Analysis of Minimizing Total Cost with Two Plants

This appendix presents a mathematical analysis of the cost minimization problem. It presumes a familiarity with differential calculus.

The production manager wants to minimize

$$V = V_1(q_1) + V_2(q_2) \qquad \text{(6A-1)}$$

and satisfy the production quota of

$$q_1 + q_2 = q^* \qquad \text{(6A-2)}$$

The condition for a cost minimization can be found by first solving the quota constraint for $q_2 = q^* - q_1$ and substituting this expression for q_2 into equation 6A-1. V depends solely on q_1.

$$V = V_1(q_1) + V_2(q^* - q_1)$$

The first-order condition for a minimum requires

$$\frac{dV}{dq_1} = \frac{dV_1}{dq_1} + \frac{dV_2}{dq_2}\frac{dq_2}{dq_1} = \frac{dV_1}{dq_1} - \frac{dV_2}{dq_2} = 0 \qquad \text{(6A-3)}$$

since $dq_2/dq_1 = -1$. With a fixed total quantity a unit increase in q_1 must be offset by a unit decrease in q_2. The firm wants to schedule production so that the marginal cost is the same at the two plants.

The second-order condition for a cost minimum requires

$$\frac{d^2V}{dq_1^2} = \frac{d^2V_1}{dq_1^2} - \frac{d^2V_2}{dq_2^2}\frac{dq_2}{dq_1} = \frac{d^2V_1}{dq_1^2} + \frac{d^2V_2}{dq_2^2} > 0 \qquad \text{(6A-4)}$$

d^2V_1/dq_1^2 and d^2V_2/dq_2^2 can be interpreted as the slopes of the marginal cost function of plants 1 and 2, respectively. At the cost-minimizing solution ($dV_1/dq_1 = dV_2/dq_2$), the sum of the slopes of the marginal cost functions must be positive.

We apply these ideas with a numerical example. Let the marginal cost functions of the two firms be

$$MC_1(q_1) = \$50 + \$5q_1$$

$$MC_2(q_2) = \$25 + \$5q_2$$

Suppose the monthly quota is 25 units, and so $q_1 + q_2 = 25$. What quantity should the firm produce at plant 1 and at plant 2 so that it minimizes total cost?

Because the marginal cost functions slope upward—marginal cost increases as the plant produces more—the slope of the marginal cost function is positive. Therefore, $d^2V_1/dq_1^2 + d^2V_2/dq_2^2 > 0$ since the slope of the marginal cost function is the second derivative of the total cost function of a plant.

We can find the solution by equating marginal costs.

$$MC_1(q_1) = MC_2(q_2)$$

$$\$50 + \$5q_1 = \$25 + \$5q_2$$

After substituting $25 - q_1$ for q_2, we have

$$\$50 + \$5q_1 = \$25 + \$5(25 - q_1)$$

After collecting terms, we have

$$\$10q_1 = \$100$$

So, $q_1 = 10$ units and $q_2 = 15$ units. The plant with the lower marginal cost function produces more.

FIRM AND MARKET BEHAVIOR

CHAPTER 7

THE SUPPLY FUNCTIONS OF A COMPETITIVE FIRM

One main topic of interest in this book is the pricing and output decisions of firms. This chapter focuses on the quantity a price-taking firm supplies at each price and derives the firm's short- and long-run supply functions. To derive these supply functions, we assume the firm strives to maximize profits. While the justification of this assumption is briefly examined in this chapter, the profit maximization assumption is discussed in more depth in Chapter 11.

As you will see in future chapters, some firms are price makers, setting price and output. A competitive firm cannot do this, however. Since price is outside its control, the decision a competitive firm has to make is how much to produce. A competitive firm can produce as much as it wants without affecting the market price, and this is why a competitive firm is called a price taker.

Most of this chapter is spent developing the tools that are used in Chapter 8. The firm's supply functions derived here are needed to construct the market supply functions in Chapter 8. Then the market demand and supply functions are used to show how the market price, the quantity supplied and demanded, and the number of firms are determined in a competitive industry and how a competitive industry adjusts to changes in demand and supply conditions.

7-1 THE COMPETITIVE FIRM
The Price-Taking Assumption

Before developing a theory of supply for a competitive firm, it is necessary to define precisely what a price-taking firm is. This section describes the characteristics of a competitive firm and gives some background for understanding the output decisions that a competitive firm makes.

The trademark of a competitive firm is that the quantity supplied by the firm has no effect on the market price. A competitive firm behaves as if the market price is independent of the number of units sold by the firm, which explains why it is called a price taker.

> A competitive firm acts as if the market price is independent of the number of units sold by the firm.

The price taker assumption implies that the firm's demand function is a horizontal line. Figure 7-1a shows the market demand function, where the horizontal scale is in millions of units. If the market price is P_1, the horizontal line dd in Figure 7-1b is the firm's demand function, where the horizontal scale is in thousands of units. The horizontal shape of dd means that a competitive firm can sell as much as it desires without affecting the market price P_1. The slope of the demand function of a competitive firm is therefore zero, so that $\Delta P/\Delta q = 0$.

A competitive firm responds to but does not singularly determine the market price. Therefore, it cannot affect the fortunes of any other firm in the industry. As a result, rivalry between any two competitive firms is not immediate but distant and impersonal. If this sounds surprising or paradoxical, it is only because competition is usually associated with rivalry. To an economist, a competitive firm is

MARKET AND FIRM DEMAND FUNCTIONS

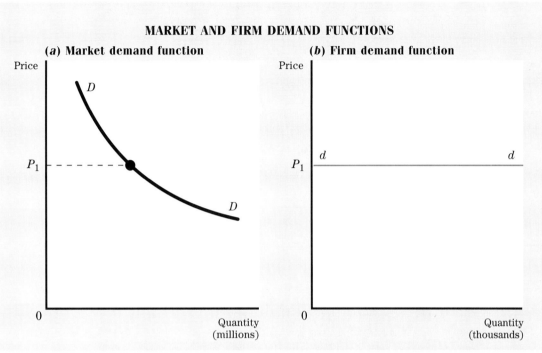

Figure 7-1   (*a*) The market demand function. The horizontal scale is in millions of units. When the market price is P_1, *dd* in (*b*) is the demand curve facing a competitive firm. The horizontal scale in (*b*) is in thousands of units. A competitive firm is a price taker and acts as if the quantity sold has no effect on the market price. The firm sells each unit at the existing market price of P_1.

just a firm that is a price taker. It then follows that rivalry among price-taking firms must be impersonal.

For example, there are thousands of wheat farmers. If we ask a farmer why the price of wheat is low, a knowledgeable one will not claim that a neighbor is producing too much wheat and flooding the market. The price of wheat is unaffected by the quantity a neighbor produces because the neighbor is only one of thousands of wheat farmers. Similarly, if a tornado destroys a paint factory and puts the company out of commission for a year, the increase in the price of a gallon of paint will be imperceptible. The same argument applies to restaurants, video stores, car washes, and other industries with many firms.

In contrast to a price-taking firm, a price-making firm makes supply decisions that affect the market price and therefore the profits of other firms in the industry. In these kinds of industries an individual firm can be the object of intense private condemnation for producing too much and driving the market price down. This is quite different from the impersonal competition among firms in a competitive industry.

Since the market price is unaffected by the quantity supplied by a competitive

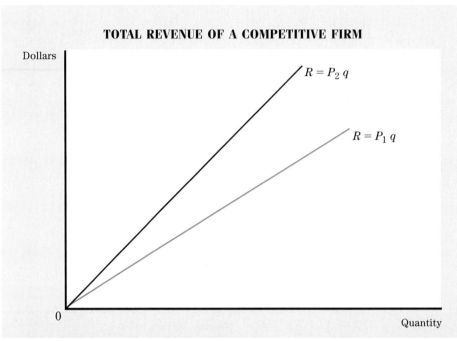

Figure 7-2   Because a competitive firm is a price taker, total revenue increases linearly with the quantity sold. The firm can sell each additional unit at the market price. If the price is P_1, total revenue function is $R = P_1 q$. If the price rises to P_2, the total revenue function becomes $R = P_2 q$.

firm, the company's total revenue increases proportionally with the quantity sold. The expression for total revenue of a competitive firm is

$$R = Pq \qquad \text{(Total Revenue of a Price-Taking Firm)} \qquad \text{(7-1)}$$

where R is total revenue received by the firm, P is market price, and q represents units sold by the firm.

Figure 7-2 shows two total revenue functions, one for each price. Dollars are on the vertical axis, and quantity is on the horizontal axis. The total revenue function is a straight line for a given price. If the price is P_1, the total revenue function is $R = P_1 q$. Each unit sold increases total revenue by P_1. At a higher price of P_2, the firm's total revenue function becomes $R = P_2 q$. Now, each unit sold increases total revenue by still more since P_2 is greater than P_1. The total revenue function rotates upward around the origin in Figure 7-2 when the price is higher.

For a price-taking firm, the additional revenue from selling another unit equals the market price. If a video store rents cassettes at $3 per cassette, the rental of each additional cassette brings in additional revenue of $3. **Marginal revenue** (MR) is defined as the change in total revenue, ΔR, due to a change in quantity sold, Δq. The increased revenue of a competitive firm per unit increase in quantity sold equals the price of the product. Therefore,

$$\text{MR} = \frac{\Delta R}{\Delta q} = P \qquad \text{(Marginal Revenue for a Competitive Firm)} \qquad (7\text{-}2)$$

$\Delta R/\Delta q$ is the symbol for marginal revenue, and for a price-taking firm, $\Delta R/\Delta q$ equals price.[1] For example, marginal revenue is the slope of the colored line in Figure 7-2, when the price is P_1.

The Price Elasticity of Demand of a Competitive Firm

As noted above, the demand function of a competitive firm is virtually flat with a slope approaching zero. A change in the quantity demanded, Δq, barely changes the market price, ΔP. Therefore, $\Delta P/\Delta q$ is slightly negative but very close to zero and, consequently, $\Delta q/\Delta P$ approaches negative infinity. The arc price elasticity of demand for a firm's demand function, E_d, approaches negative infinity. Economists say the price elasticity of demand of a price-taking firm is infinitely elastic.

$$E_d = \frac{\Delta q}{\Delta P} \frac{P_1 + P_2}{q_1 + q_2} = -\infty$$

since $\Delta q/\Delta P$ approaches negative infinity.

The price elasticity of demand for a competitive firm is infinitely elastic.

The appendix to this chapter presents a mathematical analysis demonstrating that the firm's price elasticity of demand depends on three factors:

1. *Market share.* As the number of firms increases and the market share of a firm declines, a given percentage increase in the quantity produced by the firm causes a smaller percentage increase in the total quantity supplied and therefore a smaller percentage decrease in the market price. If a firm with 1 percent of the market supplies 10 units and increases output by 10 percent, it increases the quantity by 1 unit. If the firm has 2 percent of the market and therefore supplies 20 units and increases output by 10 percent, the increase in the quantity supplied of 2 units causes a larger percentage, though still small, decline in the market price. So, the smaller the firm's market share, the more elastic the firm's demand function.

2. *Price elasticity of market demand function.* In the vicinity of the current market price, the more elastic the market demand function, the smaller the decrease in market price caused by an increase in the quantity produced by a competitive firm. When the industry demand function is more elastic,

---

[1] Marginal revenue is derived from the total revenue function, $R = Pq$. For a given P, the revenue equation is a straight line. Define the derivative of the total revenue function as marginal revenue. The change in total revenue due to a change in q is

$$\text{MR} = \frac{dR}{dq} = P$$

This equation says that the slope of the total revenue function is equal to the price of the product.

an increase in the quantity produced by one firm causes an even smaller decline in the market price.

3. *Supply elasticity of other firms.* When a competitive firm produces more units, the size of the price decline depends on the change in quantity supplied by *all* other firms in the industry. If the other firms partially offset the increase in the quantity produced by a single firm by reducing their combined output, the decline in the market price will be smaller than if they keep producing the original amount. For example, the price decrease will be smaller when a firm increases output if total imports into a country decrease when the domestic price falls. The supply elasticity of other firms measures the percentage change in the quantity supplied by other producers for a given percentage change in the market price. The larger the supply elasticity, the larger the percentage decrease in the output of other firms, the smaller the price decline due to the increase in the firm's quantity, and therefore the more elastic the firm's demand function.

These three factors are determinants of the firm's price elasticity of demand.

APPLICATION 7-1

The Price Elasticity of Demand of Firms in Eastern Europe and the Former Soviet Union

This identification of the three determinants of the firm's price elasticity of demand has a direct bearing on the restructuring of industry in the former Soviet Union and in Eastern European countries. One important concern is what will keep prices under control if new firms are free to set any price during the transition from a centrally controlled economy toward more of a market-driven economy.

In some Eastern European countries and in the former Soviet Union there is a deep distrust of capitalism. Some think that a market system will merely replace the monopoly and bureaucracy of the Communist party with firms that will raise prices because of the absence of competitors. There is considerable fear that the new firms will exploit consumers by charging high prices. This is not an empty concern, especially in certain industries. In the past, Soviet planning authorities preferred to build a few massive industrial complexes and factories rather than many smaller plants.

A critical question concerns the price elasticity of demand for each of the new firms. The larger the elasticity of competitive supply, the more elastic the demand function of a firm will become. If a price increase causes a large percentage increase in the supply offered by others, firm demand will be more price-elastic. Because the number of current domestic competitors in Eastern Europe and the former Soviet Union is relatively small, the supply from other firms must come from the rest of the world. If Eastern European countries and the Soviet states keep tariffs low so that imports can enter their markets, and if they allow other domestic firms and firms from other countries to enter and to establish plants, the demand curve facing the existing domestic firms will be more elastic. These firms will behave more as competitive firms than as the sole suppliers of a product. Competitive supply from abroad and, perhaps later, from within will prevent domestic firms from setting higher prices in domestic markets. However, there is no assurance of this. The established domestic firms will probably use their considerable political power to gain protection, as has occurred in many Western economies. If they succeed in gaining protective tariffs, the concern about high prices will not be an empty one.

7-2   THE SHORT-RUN SUPPLY FUNCTION OF A COMPETITIVE FIRM

The short-run supply function of a competitive firm shows the quantity supplied by the firm at each price when at least one factor of production is fixed. In this discussion capital is still the fixed factor, so the firm cannot change plant size in the short run, and the cost of the fixed factor is a sunk cost.

To determine what quantity a competitive firm will supply, the firm's goal must be specified. This chapter assumes that the management of the firm attempts to maximize total profits. There are two reasons why a competitive firm will have difficulty surviving if it does not maximize profits. First, if other firms in the industry find ways to reduce costs and to increase profits, a company that does not will earn lower profits and ultimately suffer losses. A nonmaximizing firm has a lower probability of surviving in the industry. The second reason is more subtle: A management that does not maximize profits invites a takeover. Other firms or shareholders will seek to acquire the inefficiently run company and improve its performance. A takeover attempt could either so weaken the position of the firm's top management that they resign or change managerial policies, reduce costs, and increase firm profits. The possibility of a takeover serves as a disciplinary club and circumscribes the behavior of management. Because of these two reasons, we adopt the assumption of profit maximization, and our derivation of the firm's short- and long-run supply functions rests on this assumption.

The expression for the short-run profits of the firm is

Profits = Revenues − Costs   (Short-Run Profits of a Competitive Firm)

$$\pi(q) = Pq - V(q) - F \qquad \text{(7-3)}$$

In the short-run, total cost equals variable cost, which depends on the quantity produced, plus fixed cost, which is independent of the quantity produced. $V(q)$ represents variable cost, and F is fixed cost. If the company doesn't produce anything, $q = 0$. When $q = 0$, the firm loses $-F$; that is, $\pi = -F$. If the firm decides to produce any quantity, it will do so only because it expects $\pi(q) > -F$. If it produces q units, revenue is Pq and the variable cost of producing q units is $V(q)$. The firm would be foolish to produce these q units if Pq is less than $V(q)$ because its losses would be larger than F. Therefore, in the short run, the firm will operate only if total revenue either equals or exceeds variable cost. Because fixed cost is sunk, a bygone, the quantity produced in the short run does not depend on the size of fixed cost.

> In the short run the firm produces only if $Pq \geq V(q)$.

For example, the market price might be so low that the firm receives only $50,000 from selling 5,000 units and incurs $60,000 in variable cost. The firm would rather shut down and incur losses of $-F$ than produce 5,000 units and increase losses to $-(F + \$10,000)$.

Finding an Output That Maximizes Total Short-Run Profits

Let's derive a rule that a competitive firm follows when it determines the quantity to produce in the short run and then apply this rule to find the quantity supplied at any price.

In the short run, the firm must make do with its current plant. The company's short-run marginal cost function shows the incremental cost of producing another unit with a given plant. To maximize short-run profits, the firm selects an output at which price equals short-run marginal cost.[2]

$$MR = P = MC_S(q) \qquad \text{(Determination of Quantity in the Short Run)} \qquad (7\text{-}4)$$

where $MC_S(q)$ is short-run marginal cost. When the firm maximizes profits, it determines the quantity where price, the additional revenue from selling the last unit, equals short-run marginal cost, the additional cost of producing the last unit.

> A competitive firm determines the quantity produced where price equals short-run marginal cost.

Figure 7-3 shows the firm's horizontal demand function dd when the market price is P_1, the average variable cost (AVC) function, and the short-run marginal cost (MC_S) function. The firm maximizes short-run profits by producing q_1 units where $MR = P_1 = MC_S$. Total profits will decrease if the firm produces either a larger or a smaller output than q_1. In either case price will no longer equal short-run marginal cost, and so the firm will not earn maximum profits. For example, if the firm is producing q_0 units and increases output to q_1, the marginal revenue from selling $q_1 - q_0$ more units is area abq_1q_0 under the firm's demand function, while

---

[2] The firm would like to find a quantity that maximizes short-run total profits. If the profit function is differentiated with respect to q, a necessary first-order condition for profit maximum is

$$\frac{d[\pi(q)]}{dq} = P - \frac{d[C_S(q)]}{dq} = 0$$

The firm selects an output where market price equals short-run marginal cost. The second-order condition for a profit maximum requires

$$\frac{d^2[\pi(q)]}{dq^2} = -\frac{d^2[C_S(q)]}{dq^2} < 0$$

The slope of the marginal cost curve must be positive at the output at which price equals short-run marginal cost.

SHORT-RUN PROFIT-MAXIMIZING OUTPUT OF A COMPETITIVE FIRM

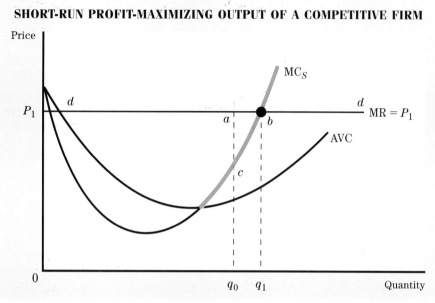

Figure 7-3 The firm maximizes profit by producing q_1 units, where P_1 equals short-run marginal cost. By increasing output from q_0 to q_1, the firm increases total profits.

the marginal cost of producing $q_1 - q_0$ more units is area cbq_1q_0 under the marginal cost function. Since the increase in revenue is greater than the increase in total cost, total profits increase.

The Short-Run Supply Function of a Competitive Firm

We have found one point on the firm's short-run supply function since the firm supplies q_1 units when the price is P_1. By applying the price equals marginal cost rule, the quantity the firm supplies at any price can also be found. What we discover is that the firm's short-run marginal cost function is the firm's short-run supply function as long as revenue equals or exceeds variable cost.

> The firm's short-run marginal cost function is the firm's short-run supply function as long as revenue ≥ variable cost.

Figure 7-4 shows the firm's demand functions for three possible prices, P_1, P_2, and P_3, as well as the firm's short-run average variable and marginal cost functions. You may wonder why Figure 7-4 does not show the short-run average cost curve. In order to determine whether the firm is making a profit or incurring a loss in the short run, you need to know the position of the short-run average cost curve. However, the firm can determine its short-run profit-maximizing output *without* knowing whether it is earning a profit or suffering a loss. The size of fixed cost

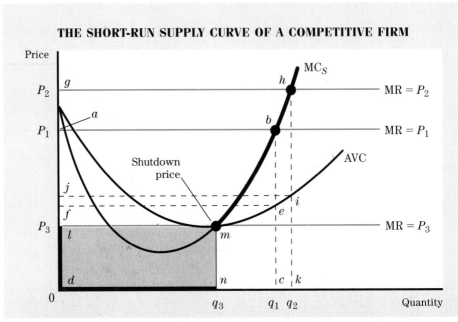

THE SHORT-RUN SUPPLY CURVE OF A COMPETITIVE FIRM

Figure 7-4   In the short run firm profits are maximized at an output where price equals short-run marginal cost. The firm supplies q_2 units if the price is P_2 and q_3 if the price is P_3. The firm will not supply any quantity if the price is less than the minimum average variable cost. The short-run marginal cost function is the firm's short-run supply curve for prices equal to or above P_3. The thick lines are the firm's short-run supply function.

determines whether profits are high or low but has no bearing on what output the firm produces in the short run. If the firm sets output where price equals short-run marginal cost, it is doing as well as it can, given the price at which it can sell its product. Whether it ends up losing \$10 or \$10 million will have no effect on the quantity it produces in the short run as long as total revenue equals or exceeds variable cost.

By considering different prices, we can determine when revenue equals or exceeds variable cost. When the price equals or exceeds minimum average variable cost, the firm maximizes profits by producing an output at which price equals short-run marginal cost. When the market price is P_1, the firm supplies q_1 units. P_1 exceeds average variable cost which is equal to the distance ec. Therefore, total revenue is equal to the area $abcd$ and is greater than variable cost which is equal to the area $fecd$. At the higher price of P_2, the firm maximizes profits by producing q_2 units, where $P_2 = MC_S$. P_2 exceeds average variable cost which is equal to the distance ik. Total revenue is equal to the area $ghkd$ and exceeds variable cost which is equal to the area $jikd$. At a lower price of P_3 the firm supplies only q_3 units. P_3 equals short-run marginal cost *and* minimum average variable cost. Therefore, total revenue (the shaded area $lmnd$) just equals variable cost.

If the market price is less than P_3, total revenue is less than variable cost.

Therefore, the firm would rather close its doors and lose F in the short run than produce any amount and incur still larger losses. At any price less than P_3, the firm supplies nothing. In Figure 7-4, P_3 is the shutdown price because the firm will not produce anything in the short run if the price is less than P_3.

The firm's short-run supply function has two segments. Since the company supplies zero for prices less than P_3, the first segment is the thick vertical line centered on zero for all prices less than P_3. Then, the short-run supply curve jumps across horizontally to q_3 units when the price is P_3. The second segment of the firm's short-run supply curve is the short-run marginal cost curve for prices above P_3.

APPLICATION 7-2

Short-Run Costs and Break-Even Analysis

Managers of firms often use a planning tool called break-even analysis to estimate how many units they must sell to break even, that is, how many units the firm must sell so that revenue covers total cost. Break-even analysis projects revenue and total cost at different levels of production to find the break-even quantity. After demonstrating the use to which break-even analysis is put, we point out some of the underlying assumptions and indicate some important reservations concerning its utility as a planning tool.

Typically, break-even analysis applies to a situation where a firm considers some costs sunk and others variable. On the revenue side, the firm takes the market price as given and projects total revenue as a linear function of the quantity sold. On the cost side, total cost is divided into fixed and variable costs. A common simplifying assumption is that variable cost increases linearly with the quantity produced up to plant capacity. This linear function can be expressed as $V(q) = vq$, where v is a constant.[3] For example, if $v = \$100$, variable cost increases by $\$100$ a unit no matter how many units the firm produces, and so short-run marginal cost is $\$100$. Another assumption of break-even analysis is that the firm has a fixed capacity that prevents it from producing more than q_c units per period.

Figure 7-5 shows total revenue, total cost, and variable cost as a function of the quantity produced. Initially, we assume the market price is $\$150$, and so total revenue is $R = \$150q$. Total cost is $C_S = F + \$100q$, where F is fixed cost. The break-even quantity is q_1 units where total revenue equals total cost. The firm must sell more than q_1 units before total revenue exceeds total cost—before profit is positive.

Break-even analysis simplifies the variable cost function by assuming that (1) variable cost increases linearly with the quantity produced and (2) capacity production is well defined. Both of these planning assumptions are crude approximations designed to simplify the analysis. The assumption of a linear variable cost function is not easy to defend. As the firm produces more output at a given plant per period, defect rates begin to increase and overtime hours increase. Maintenance

---

[3] When $V = vq$, AVC $= V/q = v$. Therefore, average variable cost is constant up to capacity output.

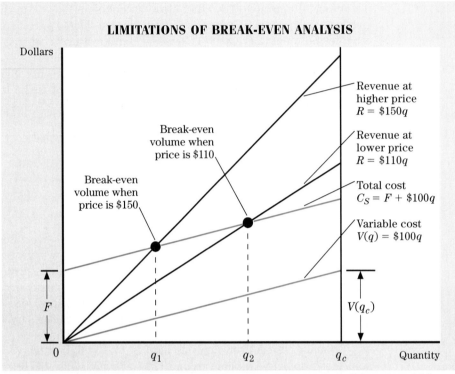

LIMITATIONS OF BREAK-EVEN ANALYSIS

Dollars

Revenue at
higher price
$R = \$150q$

Break-even
volume when
price is \$110

Revenue at
lower price
$R = \$110q$

Break-even
volume when
price is \$150

Total cost
$C_S = F + \$100q$

Variable cost
$V(q) = \$100q$

F

$V(q_c)$

0   q_1 q_2 q_c Quantity

Figure 7-5   Total revenue increases linearly with quantity sold, and variable cost increases linearly with quantity produced. If the price is \$150, the break-even volume is q_1, where total revenue equals total short-run cost. Total profits are maximized when the firm produces q_c. If the price falls to \$110, breakeven volume increases to q_2, but the firm continues to produce q_c.

expenditures increase to keep the equipment running at faster rates and for longer periods. For these and other reasons, variable cost increases faster than the projected linear rate, and so average variable cost and marginal cost will increase.

The assumption of a rigid limit on capacity is also a crude estimate. The firm can produce more, but only by producing successive units at increasing marginal cost. There is seldom an absolute maximum rate of output.

Break-even analysis appears to be a more impressive tool than it really is. If the firm is truly a price taker, it maximizes profits by producing the capacity output. Every unit sells for \$150, the market price, and the short-run marginal cost is only \$100. Since price exceeds short-run marginal cost, the firm wants to sell as much as it can produce in order to maximize short-run profits. If the firm produces q_c units, variable cost will total $\$100q_c$ and profit will be $\$50q_c$. Note that the decision to produce the profit-maximizing quantity, q_c, does not depend on knowing the break-even quantity q_1.

Sometimes the claim is made that firms find break-even analysis useful in deciding by how much variable cost should be cut when the price declines and the break-even quantity increases. Suppose market conditions worsen and the market price falls to $110. The break-even point increases to q_2. How does knowing the new break-even point help the firm determine the quantity to produce and by how much to reduce variable cost? Since marginal revenue is now only $110 but is still greater than the short-run marginal cost of $100, the firm still maximizes short-run profits by producing capacity output. Although the price has declined, the firm will still produce q_c units and will still incur variable cost of $100q_c$. Although price falls, variable cost does not decrease because the firm maximizes profits by producing q_c units. Fixed cost cannot change because it is a sunk cost. So, the assumptions underlying break-even analysis imply that the firm will not reduce variable cost when the price falls. Break-even analysis indicates that the firm should not reduce variable cost if the market price declines. The firm either produces q_c or shuts down if the price is less than $100 a unit. If it continues to produce q_c, variable cost will still be $100q_c$. Break-even analysis is of limited value for a firm because it does not provide answers to the important questions the firm faces.

APPLICATION 7-3

When to Lay Up an Oil Tanker

When charter rates fall, an owner of an oil tanker must decide whether the vessel should be kept in operation or laid up. The owner must project whether the revenues from chartering the tanker will cover variable cost. This prediction is difficult to make because tanker charter rates are volatile and are very sensitive to world economic and political events. When charter rates decline and stay low, owners will place some tankers in dry dock. How do the theoretical principles that determine the shutdown point in the short run apply in the tanker market?

To answer this question, let's classify the costs of a tanker into capital and operating costs. Huge capital costs are incurred in constructing a large tanker, and once built, it may have a useful lifetime of about 20 years. In the short run, we treat the capital cost of a tanker as a sunk cost and concentrate only on the operating cost. The position of the average variable cost function of a tanker depends on the age and size of the vessel, whether it is powered by steam or by a diesel engine, the cost of the crew, the insurance for the cargo, etc. New tankers with larger deadweight tons of rated capacity tend to be more capital-intensive and to have a lower average variable cost function. Many older tankers were built in the 1970s, are usually smaller, and are more likely to be steam-powered. Steam-powered tankers use more fuel for a given trip length, and therefore older tankers have a higher average variable cost function than newer, larger ones. Figure 7-6 shows the hypothetical average variable and short-run marginal cost functions of an old and a new tanker. The minimum average variable cost of the old vessel is higher than the minimum average variable cost of the newer one. The thick curves represent the short-run supply functions of the two tankers. Because of the differ-

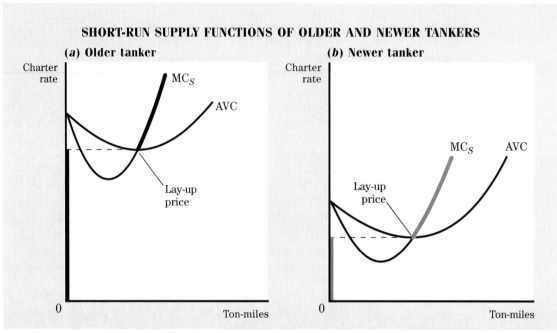

Figure 7-6   (*a*) An older tanker has a higher lay-up price than a newer one. When rates decline, the tanker with the higher minimum average variable cost will be the first to be taken out of service.

ences in the average variable cost functions of the two types of tankers, the older tankers with higher average variable cost would probably be the first ones withdrawn from the fleet and placed in dry dock when charter rates fall.

An interesting situation occurred during and after the Persian Gulf crisis. Following the invasion of Kuwait in July 1990, charter rates rose—reaching a peak in February 1991. After rates increased, only 5 of the 50 tankers that remained in dry dock were the new very large or ultralarge tankers.[4] What makes the period between February 1991 and July 1992 especially interesting is the large 54 percent fall in charter rates, a large percentage drop even for the volatile charter market. By July 1992, 14 of the 74 tankers laid up were very large or ultralarge tankers.

To minimize short-run fluctuations in charter rates, a simple average of charter rates during the last three months was calculated. Figure 7-7 shows the average charter rates by month for a trip from the Arabian Gulf to northwestern Europe by a very large tanker and the number of tankers of all sizes laid up. Because charter rates were so high at the beginning of 1991, the fall in rates that began in February 1991 and continued to May 1992 did not initially cause a large increase in the number of ships in dry dock until March 1993 when the number of ships withdrawn from the fleet rose rapidly. As charter rates fell, owners first withdrew

---

[4] These were American-flagged vessels that transport Alaskan oil to U.S. gulf ports and must use higher-paid American crews and conform to higher American safety standards.

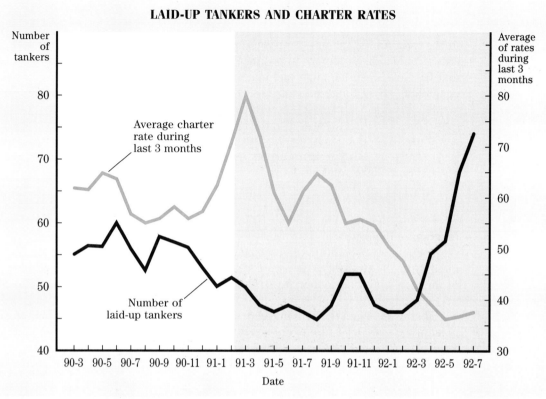

Figure 7-7   When charter rates fall, owners withdraw higher variable cost tankers. [*From Lloyds' of London*, Lloyds' Monthly Shipping Economist.]

tankers with higher minimum average variable cost, just as the theory predicts. The older steam-driven tankers with higher minimum average variable cost were placed in dry dock. As charter rates continued to fall, owners then placed newer tankers with somewhat lower minimum average variable cost in dry dock.

This analysis of the tanker market shows that owners are aware of the different shapes of the variable cost functions for the different types of tankers and respond as the theory predicts. As a first approximation, the short-run model of the behavior of a competitive firm seems to explain firm behavior in the tanker market. Yet, this short-run model has its limitations. First, it does not take into account the one-time lay-up cost that an owner incurs when placing a tanker in dry dock. The owner might keep the tanker operating although the current charter rate is less than the minimum average variable cost if he thinks the rate will increase or will not fall much below minimum average variable cost. In this way the lay-up cost can be avoided. A second limitation of this short-run analysis of the tanker situation is that it does not consider the option to break up a tanker and sell it as scrap metal. More advanced analyses account for these possibilities.

7-3 THE LONG-RUN SUPPLY FUNCTION OF A COMPETITIVE FIRM

In the long run all factors of production are variable, and so the firm can select any combination of factors to produce a given quantity. We continue to assume that the firm is a price taker and maximizes profits in the long run. A useful way of thinking about long-run decisions of the firm is to visualize it as starting from scratch. It devises a plan that describes (1) the profit-maximizing quantity at each market price that might prevail in the long run and (2) what combination of factors it will use to produce that quantity at the lowest total cost.

In the long run the firm's profits equal total revenue less long-run total cost. The expression for total profits is

$$\pi(q) = Pq - C_L(q) \qquad \text{(Profits of a Competitive Firm in the Long Run)} \qquad \textbf{(7-5)}$$

where $\pi(q)$ denotes the profits of the firm and $C_L(q)$ is the long-run total cost function of the firm.

A company would never enter an industry in the long run if it expected to incur a loss. If revenues are less than total long-run costs, the potential shareholders of the firm would not expect to earn as much as they would earn from the next best investment.

Therefore, when the firm makes a decision to enter the industry by building a plant, it expects profits to be nonnegative.

$$\pi(q) \geq 0 \qquad \text{(Nonnegative Profit Constraint in the Long Run)}$$

Finding an Output That Maximizes Long-Run Profits

A price-taking firm maximizes profits by producing the quantity at which marginal revenue equals long-run marginal cost. Since MR = P, the condition for profit maximization becomes

$$\text{MR} = P = \text{MC}_L(q) \qquad \text{(Determining Quantity in the Long Run)} \qquad \textbf{(7-6)}$$

where $\text{MC}_L(q)$ is long-run marginal cost.[5] If the firm produces a quantity where price is greater than marginal cost, it should produce more units since the last unit sold brings more revenue than it costs to produce, and so profits increase. If price

---

[5] The firm selects an output that maximizes its profits. The firm's profits are $\pi(q) = Pq - C_L(q)$. The first-order condition for profit maximization is

$$\frac{d[\pi(q)]}{dq} = P - \frac{d[C_L(q)]}{dq} = 0 \qquad \text{or} \qquad \text{MR} \equiv P = \text{MC}_L(q)$$

A necessary condition for profit maximization is that the firm selects an output where price equals long-run marginal cost. The second-order condition for profit maximization is

$$\frac{d^2[\pi(q)]}{dq^2} = -\frac{d^2[C_L(q)]}{dq^2} < 0$$

For this condition to be satisfied, the slope of the marginal cost curve, $d^2C_L(q)/dq^2$, must be positive at the output where price equals long-run marginal cost.

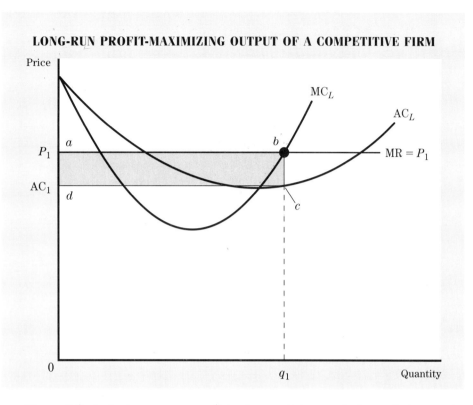

LONG-RUN PROFIT-MAXIMIZING OUTPUT OF A COMPETITIVE FIRM

Figure 7-8   In the long run a competitive firm maximizes profits by producing q_1 units where price equals long-run marginal cost. The firm produces q_1 units at lowest cost by building a plant that produces q_1 units at a long-run average cost of AC_1. Total profits equal the area *abcd*.

is less than marginal cost, the last unit sold brings less revenue than it costs to produce and causes profits to decrease.

In Figure 7-8 price is on the vertical axis, and quantity is on the horizontal axis. The firm's demand function is the horizontal line labeled $MR = P_1$ if P_1 is the market price. The long-run average (AC_L) and marginal cost (MC_L) functions are included in Figure 7-8. Total profits are equal to area *abcd* when the firm produces q_1 units and $P_1 = MC_L$.

The Long-Run Supply Function of a Competitive Firm

The firm's long-run supply function can be derived by repeating the method used to find the short-run supply function. At each price the firm maximizes profits at a quantity where price equals long-run marginal cost. We have already derived one point on the long-run supply curve of a competitive firm because we know the firm supplies q_1 units when the price is P_1.

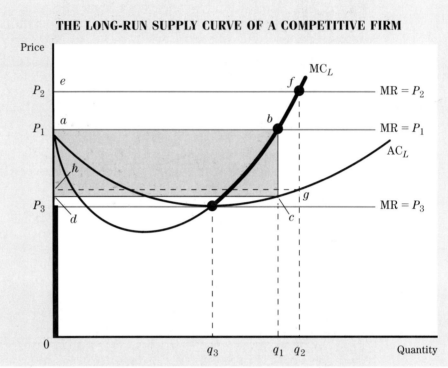

THE LONG-RUN SUPPLY CURVE OF A COMPETITIVE FIRM

Figure 7-9   The thick lines show the long-run supply curve of a competitive firm. If the price is P_2, the firm supplies q_2 units where P_2 equals long-run marginal cost. Total profits equal the area *efgh*. If the price is P_3, the firm supplies q_3 units and does not earn profits.

Figure 7-9 shows the quantity supplied at each of three prices. If price equals P_2, the firm supplies a larger quantity of q_2 units. Total profits are equal to the area *efgh*. At the lower price P_3, the firm will supply only q_3 units. When the firm produces q_3 units, long-run marginal cost equals long-run average cost, and long-run average cost is at a minimum. This is the firm's break-even output in the long run. Therefore, profits are zero and the firm earns the same return on the capital invested as the shareholders would have earned from the next best investment. Shareholders are neither better nor worse off. If the price is less than P_3, the firm does not supply any output because it would incur losses at any quantity and so would not remain in the industry in the long run.

Like its short-run supply function, the firm's long-run supply function has two segments. The first segment is the vertical line in Figure 7-9 centered on zero for prices less than P_3. When the price is P_3, the supply curve jumps across horizontally to the second segment at q_3 units, and the second segment is the firm's long-run marginal cost function for higher prices.

The firm's long-run marginal cost function is the firm's long-run supply function for prices above minimum long-run average cost.

We can draw an important implication from the firm's long-run supply function. The analysis implies that a competitive firm exhausts all internal economies of scale in the long run. A profit-maximizing competitive firm never knowingly produces an output between zero and q_3 units in the long run, and therefore a competitive firm exhausts all internal economies of scale. This model of a profit-maximizing competitive firm cannot logically explain falling prices in a competitive industry by saying that the firms in the industry are achieving greater economies of scale. This explanation implies that a price-taking firm was not maximizing profit before. If a firm is a price taker and maximizes profits, it will produce q_3 or more units and exhaust all internal economies of scale. Therefore, economies of scale are not the reason for declining prices in a competitive industry. Chapter 8 will show how technological change or a fall in the price of a factor of production shifts the firm's cost functions downward and could explain why prices fall in a competitive industry.

This chapter has described the supply decisions of a competitive firm in both the short and long runs. The firm's quest for profits is what makes it produce an output where price equals marginal cost, the hallmark of a competitive firm. By applying the price equals marginal cost rule, we derived the short- and long-run supply functions. Chapter 8 will derive the industry supply functions from the firm's supply functions and show how the equilibrium price is determined in a competitive industry.

SUMMARY

- A firm in a competitive industry faces a horizontal demand curve. The market price is unaffected by the quantity sold by a competitive firm.
- The price elasticity of demand facing a firm depends on (1) the market share of the firm, (2) the price elasticity of market demand, and (3) the supply elasticity of the other firms in the industry.
- When the firm is a price taker, the marginal revenue equals the market price.
- In the short run a competitive firm determines output where price equals short-run marginal cost.
- The short-run marginal cost curve of a competitive firm becomes the short-run supply curve of a competitive firm for prices equal to or above minimum average variable cost.
- In the long run a competitive firm determines output where price equals long-run marginal cost.
- The long-run marginal cost curve is the long-run supply curve of a profit-maximizing competitive firm for prices equal to or above minimum long-run average cost.

■   A profit-maximizing competitive firm completely exhausts all internal economies of scale.

KEY TERMS

Price-taking firm
Supply elasticity of competitive
    firms
Revenues cover variable cost
The firm's short-run supply function
Exhaustion of economies of scale in
    the long run

Price elasticity of demand for a
    competitive firm
Setting price to marginal cost
Shutdown price
The firm's long-run supply function
Nonnegative profits in the long run

REVIEW QUESTIONS

1. What are the three factors that determine a firm's price elasticity of demand?
2. Explain why a competitive firm determines output so that price equals marginal cost.
3. In the short run a firm determines output where price equals short-run marginal cost as long as revenue exceeds fixed cost. Explain why you agree or disagree with this statement.
4. If a price-taking firm determines output where price equals marginal cost but marginal cost is decreasing, the firm is not maximizing profits. Explain why you agree or disagree with this statement.
5. Draw a graph and present a geometric measure of the decrease in profits if a competitive firm increases output by Δq above the profit-maximizing quantity.
6. A profit-maximizing competitive firm will never produce in the region where short-run marginal cost is declining. Explain why you agree or disagree with this statement.
7. A profit-maximizing competitive firm will never produce in the region where average variable cost is declining. Explain why you agree or disagree with this statement.
8. A profit-maximizing competitive firm will never produce in the region where short-run average cost is declining. Explain why you agree or disagree with this statement.
9. To determine the profit-maximizing quantity in the short run, a firm must equate price to short-run marginal cost but does not need to know its average cost function. To determine output in the long run, the firm equates price to long-run marginal cost but must know its long-run average cost function. Explain why you agree or disagree with these statements
10. As the production of television sets has increased over time, the price of a television set has fallen. This implies that producers of television sets have not as yet exhausted all the economies of scale. Explain why you agree or disagree with this conclusion.

EXERCISES

1. Explain why you would expect the price elasticity of demand facing a firm to be more elastic in the long run than in the short run. Clearly specify the factors that would increase the price elasticity of demand in the long run.

2. Suppose you purchase a raw material at a price of M per unit. After you make your purchase, the price falls by 25 percent. What raw-material price should you use to derive the firm's cost functions?

3. If a profit-maximizing competitive firm equates price to long-run marginal cost and produces in the range where long-run marginal cost is increasing, it is maximizing total profits. Explain why you agree or disagree with this statement.

4. The variable cost function of a firm is shown in the following table.

QUANTITY	VARIABLE COST ($)	QUANTITY	VARIABLE COST ($)
1	6	4	20
2	10	5	28
3	12	6	40

The market prices for the next 6 years are as follows:

YEAR	1	2	3	4	5	6
MARKET PRICE ($)	8	6	3	2	5	1

In which years will a profit-maximizing firm produce, and what quantity will it produce each year?

5. Suppose the price is $40 per unit and the short-run cost function of a firm is $1,000 + $20q$ where the firm has a capacity to produce 100 units per period.
    a. What is the firm's break-even point?
    b. What is the profit-maximizing output?

6. A firm that maximizes profit per unit will maximize total profit. Explain when this statement is correct and when it is incorrect.

7. Recently, a newspaper reported that a number of farmers shot and killed young calves in their herds: Waste of this kind is inconsistent with profit-maximizing behavior. Explain why you agree or disagree with this statement.

8. Will break-even analysis tell a firm by how much variable cost should fall when price falls if marginal cost is not constant but decreases and then increases with the quantity produced? Explain.

9. A price-taking firm signs a 5-year contract to lease a building. The owner of the building requires annual rent increases based on the rate of inflation. Suppose inflation increases the general price level by 5 percent in the last year and so the annual rent increases by 5 percent. How will this affect the price of the product made by the firm that leases the building?

PROBLEM SET

Should Your Company Honor a Contract?

In July of this year, your company signed a contract to deliver q_c units by the end of December of next year at a per unit price of P''. The contract will occupy all of your production capacity for next year. The cost function of your firm is

$$C = F + V(q) = F + aq \qquad q \le q_c$$

where F denotes fixed cost and variable cost is aq, where a is a constant and equals short-run marginal cost. Variable cost increases linearly with quantity up to capacity output q_c. Your company must pay a franchise tax of T dollars per year to the local government if it receives any revenue during the year. The firm can waive the franchise tax if it does not receive any revenue during the year.

Between July and the end of December of the current year, the price of a critical raw material the firm uses to manufacture the product soars, and average variable (=marginal) cost increases from a to b, with $b > a$. Variable cost becomes $V(q) = bq$. Much to your horror, you learn that the contract does not include an inflation clause which would have allowed you to increase the price if the price of the raw material increased. Now b is greater than P''. If your company fulfills the contract, the per unit price, P'', will be less than the marginal cost of producing the last unit, b. You face a quandary. Should you fulfill the contract or not?

You ask your attorney what liability you will face if your company does not fulfill the contract. She says that your company will be liable to the tune of any excess the customer will have to pay to purchase the product elsewhere. Your market research people say that a buyer who searches carefully probably could find a price of P^* in the current market but that there is little incentive to search that diligently. The customer is therefore more likely to get a price of P' that is well above P'' and above P^*, that is $P' > P^* > P''$. Your attorney advises you that you will probably be liable for a penalty of $P' - P''$ for each unit not delivered.

In December of the current year another customer approaches you and asks you whether you would be willing to allocate all of your capacity to supply his firm with q_c units in the coming year. He is willing to pay you a price of P^*, where $P' > P^* > b$. Because you have only enough plant capacity to fulfill one of the contracts, you can satisfy the original contract or the new contract, but not both.

Review Questions

1. Write out an expression for the losses your company will incur if it fulfills the original contract.
2. Write out an expression for the losses your company will incur if it does not fulfill the original contract and rejects the new contract.
3. Write out an expression for the losses your company will incur if it does not fulfill the original contract but fulfills the new contract.
4. If you do not fulfill the original contract, under what conditions will you sign and fulfill the new contract?

5. Should you decide not to fulfill the original contract and to sign the new contract? How will F and T affect your decision?

CHAPTER 7 APPENDIX

The Firm's Price Elasticity of Demand

In this mathematical appendix calculus is used to derive the three determinants of a firm's price elasticity of demand.

Let the inverse market demand curve be

$$P = D(Q) \qquad (7A\text{-}1)$$

where Q represents quantity demanded.

Total supply Q_s is the total quantity supplied by all other firms in the industry, and q is the quantity supplied by a new firm entering the industry. In equilibrium total supply equals quantity demanded

$$Q_s + q = Q \qquad (7A\text{-}2)$$

Q_s increases as the market price increases, which simply means that the other firms will supply larger quantities to the market if the price increases.

$$Q_s = S(P) \qquad (7A\text{-}3)$$

where $dQ_s/dP > 0$.

Consider a new firm that plans to enter the market. What will the elasticity of demand be for this new firm? If q is the number of units sold by the new firm, the market price is

$$P = D(Q_s + q) = D[S(P) + q] \qquad (7A\text{-}4)$$

Consider how the market price changes as the new firm adds quantity to the market. If it sells no units, the market price is $P = D(Q_s)$. If it supplies q units, the market price is $P = D(Q_s + q)$, where Q_s depends on price.

An expression can be derived for the price elasticity of demand for the new firm by first differentiating equation 7A-4 totally. An expression for the slope of the new firm's demand function is

$$\frac{dP}{dq} = \frac{dP/dQ}{1 - (dP/dQ)(dQ_s/dP)} \qquad (7A\text{-}5)$$

The left-hand side of equation 7A-5 is the slope of the demand curve facing a competitive firm. On the right-hand side, the numerator dP/dQ is the slope of the market demand curve. The denominator is $1 - (dP/dQ)(dQ_s/dP)$, where dQ_s/dP is the slope of the supply curve.

The point price elasticity of demand function facing a new firm is defined as

$$E_d = \frac{dq}{dP}\frac{P}{q} \qquad (7A\text{-}6)$$

To determine dq/dP, note that the inverse function rule says that $dq/dP = 1/(dP/dq)$ if dP/dq is continuous and not equal to zero. Therefore, equation 7A-5 can be inverted to yield

$$\frac{dq}{dP} = \frac{1 - (dP/dQ)(dQ_s/dP)}{dP/dQ} \tag{7A-7}$$

If each side is multiplied by P/q, the left-hand side of equation 7A-7 becomes $(dq/dP)(P/q)$, which is the point price elasticity of demand of the new firm, E_d. The point price elasticity is the price elasticity of demand at a point on the firm's demand function. The right-hand side of equation 7A-7 yields

$$E_d = \frac{dq}{dP}\frac{P}{q} = \frac{P}{q}\frac{1 - (dP/dQ)(dQ_s/dP)}{dP/dQ} \tag{7A-8}$$

$$= \frac{P}{q}\left(\frac{dQ}{dP} - \frac{dQ_s}{dP}\right) = \frac{Q}{q}\frac{P}{Q}\frac{dQ}{dP} - \frac{Q_s}{q}\frac{P}{Q_s}\frac{dQ_s}{dP}$$

The left-hand side of the equation represents the point price elasticity of the demand curve facing the firm, E_d. The market share (MS) of the new firm is q/Q. Therefore, $Q/q = 1/\text{MS}$. $(P/Q)(dQ/dP)$ is the price elasticity of market demand or E_P. $Q_s/q = (Q - q)/q = (1/\text{MS}) - 1$. $(P/Q_s)(dQ_s/dP)$ is the elasticity of supply of the other firms in the market, E_s, and has a positive value because an increase in the price of the product increases the quantity supplied by the other suppliers. It represents the percentage change in the quantity supplied by the other firms divided by the percentage change in price.

The price elasticity of demand for a competitive firm is

$$E_d = \frac{1}{\text{MS}}E_P - \left(\frac{1}{\text{MS}} - 1\right)E_s \tag{7A-9}$$

and depends on (1) the firm's market share, (2) the price elasticity of the market demand function, and (3) the price elasticity of supply by other firms.

If all the firms in the industry are the same size, $1/\text{MS} = n$, the number of firms in the industry. $(1/\text{MS}) - 1 = n - 1$. The expression for the elasticity of demand for a competitive firm becomes

$$E_d = nE_P - (n - 1)E_s \tag{7A-10}$$

The price elasticity of demand facing a competitive firm depends on (1) the market share of the firm as reflected by n, (2) the price elasticity of market demand, E_P, and (3) the supply elasticity of the other $n - 1$ firms in the industry, E_s.

Suppose that E_s is zero; then the price elasticity of demand facing the firm is n times the price elasticity of market demand. If the price elasticity of market demand is -1 and there are 100 firms in the industry, the firm's price elasticity of demand is -100. Assuming that E_s is not 0 but 1, the firm's price elasticity of demand is -199. As an approximation, we can say that a 1 percent price decrease would increase the firm's quantity demanded by 199 percent. These are large numerical values, and a price elasticity of this magnitude is difficult to distinguish from $-\infty$. Of course, if the price elasticity of market demand were lower in value so that market demand was price-elastic and the supply elasticity was larger, the numerical value of the price elasticity would be still lower. When E_P is -3 and E_s is 3, the price elasticity for the firm is -597, and so the firm's demand curve is virtually flat.

PRICE DETERMINATION IN A COMPETITIVE INDUSTRY

The price-taking firm was the main topic in Chapter 7, but in this chapter it must share the limelight with the competitive industry. This chapter first relies on the theory of firm supply to derive the industry supply functions. Then, it uses the market demand and industry supply functions to predict the market price when a competitive industry is in either long- or short-run equilibrium. After deriving the industry supply functions in the first section of the chapter, we develop a baseline model of a competitive industry and show what the price and industry output must be if an industry is in long-run industry equilibrium. This model is then used to show how an unexpected shift in market demand disrupts an industry equilibrium and causes the industry to pass through a series of short-run equilibria before a new long-run equilibrium emerges.

After completing this initial investigation, we make the analysis more descriptive of reality by relaxing some supply side assumptions of the baseline model and analyzing (1) how a competitive industry performs when managers of firms differ in ability, (2) when firms decide to adopt a cost-reducing innovation, (3) how established suppliers benefit when entry barriers slow or prevent new firms from entering the industry, and (4) how a competitive industry adjusts when the government imposes a per unit tax.

After reading this chapter, you should have a better understanding of how price is determined in a competitive industry and the role that profits and losses play in causing resources to flow into or out of an industry in response to demand or cost changes. In all the models analyzed in this chapter, the entry or exit of firms plays a critical role in limiting the magnitude and duration of firm profits or reducing the magnitude of losses suffered by firms. Throughout, the analysis highlights the role that price plays in transmitting messages from consumers to producers that consumers are demanding more or less of a product and how producers respond to these price signals.

8-1   REQUIREMENTS FOR LONG- AND SHORT-RUN INDUSTRY EQUILIBRIA

This chapter examines the price when a competitive industry is in either a long- or a short-run equilibrium. Before beginning this analysis of prices, you must understand the meaning of the term "long- or short-run industry equilibrium." When economists speak of an industry equilibrium, they are referring to a situation where an industry is at rest—where price and quantity are stable given the market demand and supply functions. We make up a short list of requirements for an industry to be in a long- or short-run equilibrium.

Long-Run Industry Equilibrium

First let's consider the long-run industry equilibrium. As noted repeatedly, all factors of production are variable in the long run. To this statement we append the condition that firms can enter or exit from the industry in the long run. It's as if every firm is starting from scratch in the long run and can decide what product to produce, how much to produce, and how to produce that quantity.

Therefore, a competitive industry is in long-run equilibrium if:

1. Each firm in the industry has no incentive to change its method or its scale of production.

2. Profits are zero, and so no firm desires to enter or exit the industry.

Since no firm inside or outside the industry desires to change its behavior, the industry is said to be in long-run equilibrium.

Short-Run Industry Equilibrium

The short-run industry equilibrium differs from the long-run industry equilibrium because two restrictions apply in the short run. In the short run no more firms than are currently in the industry can enter *and* current producers cannot change one or more factors of production. Therefore, an analysis of the short run examines the behavior of firms already in the industry. A competitive industry has reached a short-run industry equilibrium if the firms currently in the industry have no incentive to change the quantity produced.

Typical Competitive Industries

It is perhaps redundant to point out that the supply behavior of price-taking firms will be analyzed throughout this chapter. Each firm's price elasticity of demand is infinitely elastic, and this condition is more likely to occur if each firm's market share is relatively low. As Chapter 7 demonstrated, the lower the firm's market share, the more elastic its demand function, and so this analysis is more applicable to industries where the market share of firms is small.

Let's consider some examples that might fit the price-taking assumption of a competitive industry. Sometimes there are many firms in an industry, and no firm has a large share of the market; many retailing and wholesaling industries satisfy these conditions. Table 8-1 lists some less glamorous, little-known manufacturing industries comprising more than 100 firms, where the concentration ratio (the combined market share of the four largest firms) is less than 20 percent of the market. Not only are there many firms in these industries, but the industry leaders do not command a large share of the total market.

The results discussed in this chapter apply directly to industries like these but can be extended to other industries as well. The competitive model is applicable to any industry where firms behave as if the firm's market demand function is flat and where entry into the industry is free.

8-2   PRICE DETERMINATION IN A CONSTANT-COST INDUSTRY

The baseline model is that of a constant-cost industry. This model is used to illustrate how the equilibrium price is determined in a long-run industry equilibrium and how a competitive industry progresses through a succession of short-run equilibria after a demand shift before reaching a new long-run industry equilibrium.

Table 8-1 NUMBER OF FIRMS AND MARKET SHARE OF THE LEADING FOUR FIRMS

INDUSTRY	NUMBER OF FIRMS IN 1987	CONCEN- TRATION RATIO (%)	INDUSTRY	NUMBER OF FIRMS IN 1987	CONCEN- TRATION RATIO (%)
Women's, misses, and juniors' dresses	1,406	6	Plastic foam products	653	19
Sawmills and planning mills, general	5,252	15	Aluminum foundries	557	16
Metal heat- treating	631	20	Metal doors	1,428	13
Bolts, nuts, rivets, and forgings	834	16	Conveyers and conveying equipment	703	17
Textile machinery	475	20	Printed circuit boards	950	14
Blowers and fans	445	14	Fresh and frozen prepared fish	579	18

Source: 1987 Census of Manufacturers, "Concentration Ratios in Manufacturing," Subject Series, MC87-S-6.

Two Assumptions of a Constant-Cost Industry

The baseline model makes the following two strong supply-side assumptions, and these two assumptions lead to a horizontal long-run industry supply function.

1. All firms in the industry have the same long-run total cost function and therefore the same long-run average and marginal cost functions.

2. The position of the long-run average cost function of the firm does not shift as industry output changes.

Assumption 1 says that all firms are alike—each one is a clone of another. New firms entering the industry have the same cost functions as existing firms.

Assumption 2 requires a somewhat longer explanation. It implies that a change in industry output does not (*a*) change the prices of factors of production used to produce the product or (*b*) alter the firm's production function. Assumption 2 applies when an industry is small relative to the size of the economy and purchases general-purpose factors that many industries use. For example, the match industry no doubt satisfies assumption 2. If the total production of matches increases, the price of lumber, a factor in the production of matches, is probably unaffected because the match industry accounts for only a tiny fraction of the total demand for wood products. The match industry can expand or contract without affecting the price of lumber. Assumption 2 also applies when the industry employs factors

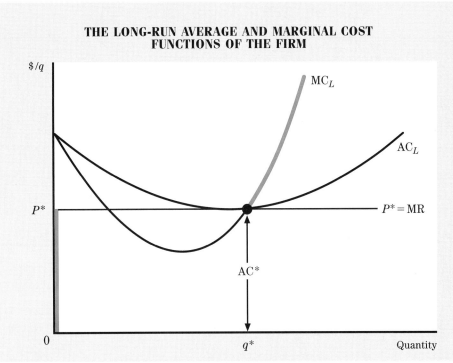

Figure 8-1   The firm experiences internal economies of scale and then internal dis-economies of scale. Minimum long-run average cost equals AC* when the firm produces $q*$ units. The heavy lines show the long-run supply function of a competitive firm.

of production in the same proportion that the other firms in the economy do. Then, a change in an industry's output causes the industry either to employ or to release factors of production just as other industries employ or release the factors without affecting prices of factors.[1]

The Long-Run Industry Supply Function in a Constant-Cost Industry

From the two assumptions of a constant-cost industry, we can deduce that the long-run industry supply function is horizontal. Let's explain why this conclusion follows from these two assumptions. The first assumption states that existing firms and new entrants have the same long-run average and marginal cost functions as those in Figure 8-1. This figure shows the long-run average (AC_L) and marginal

---

[1] We also rule out the possibility that a change in industry output alters the production function of the firm and causes the firm's long-run average cost function to change position. For example, as the total catch in a fishery increases because more boats are plying the waters, each boat finds that its catch declines and its long-run average cost function shifts upward. More fishing leads to a smaller catch per boat. This type of industry is excluded from this analysis.

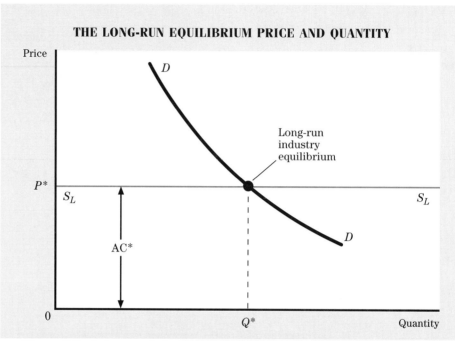

Figure 8-2   In long-run industry equilibrium the market price is P^* and the industry produces Q^* units. No existing producer wants to change the amount produced, and no firm wants to enter the industry if the market price is P^*.

cost (MC_L) functions of a representative firm in a competitive industry. The long-run average cost function of the firm has a typical U-shape, and minimum long-run average cost is AC^* when the firm produces q^* units. If the market price is P^*, the firm maximizes profits by producing q^* units.

The second assumption means that the position of the firm's long-run average cost function does not shift upward or downward as industry output changes. In the long run many new firms can enter, and each firm will be willing to supply q^* units at a price of P^*. In this industry an indefinite quantity will be supplied at this price because equally efficient firms are each ready to supply q^* units at a price of P^*. In Figure 8-2 the long-run supply function is the horizontal line $S_L S_L$. At any price less than P^* the quantity supplied drops to zero in the long run because price is less than minimum long-run average cost.

> The long-run industry supply function is horizontal in a constant-cost industry.

Long-Run Industry Equilibrium in a Constant-Cost Industry

Now that you know what the long-run industry supply function looks like in a constant-cost industry, let's determine what the equilibrium price and quantity are if the industry is in long-run equilibrium. In Figure 8-2 the long-run industry supply function is $S_L S_L$, and the market demand function is DD. The long-run equilibrium price is P^*, and the equilibrium quantity is Q^* units. Given P^*, each competitive firm maximizes profits by producing q^* units, the level of output at which $P^* = \mathrm{MR} = \mathrm{MC}_L = \mathrm{AC}_L$. When the price is P^*, no firm earns profits in long-run equilibrium.

How many firms are in the industry if it is in long-run equilibrium? If the industry supplies Q^* units and each firm produces q^* units, the number of firms in the industry must be $N^* = Q^*/q^*$. If the equilibrium industry quantity is 800,000 units and each firm produces 8,000 units, then 100 firms will be in the industry when it is in long-run equilibrium.

It's fairly easy to check that this is a long-run industry equilibrium. First, none of the N^* firms in the industry desires to change the quantity produced because each one is producing q^* units where $P^* = \mathrm{MC}_L$ and would suffer losses by producing any other quantity.

$$P^* = \mathrm{MC}_L = \mathrm{AC}_L^* \qquad \text{(Long-Run Equilibrium of the Firm)} \qquad \textbf{(8-1)}$$

Second, no firm desires to enter the industry since no firm in the industry is earning profits.

8-3 MOVING FROM ONE LONG-RUN EQUILIBRIUM TO ANOTHER

So far, this analysis has been rather mechanical. You are probably asking yourself why any firm would want to be in an industry where profits are zero. What attracted these firms to this industry in the first place? We can enrich the analysis by disrupting the initial long-run industry equilibrium because demand increases and by tracing the entry of firms into the industry.

When market demand increases, consumers are sending signals to producers that they will pay a higher price for each quantity demanded or are demanding more units at each price than before. How do firms inside and outside the industry know that consumers now value the product more highly? To answer this question, let's frame our analysis in two steps. First, let's determine how the existing firms in the industry respond to a demand increase to create a new short-run industry equilibrium before new firms enter the industry. Then, we can trace the supply behavior of existing firms as new firms gradually enter the industry and the industry passes through a series of short-run equilibrium positions before a new long-run equilibrium is established.

The Short-Run Industry Supply Function and Equilibrium Price

Before market demand increases, each one of N^* firms has a plant that produces q^* units at minimum long-run average cost of AC^*. This plant is the only one that can produce q^* at AC^*. Figure 8-3 shows the short-run average cost function AC_S

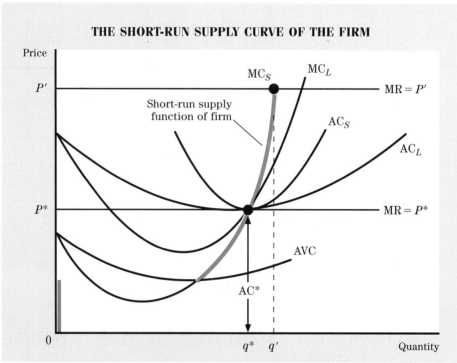

Figure 8-3   The short-run marginal cost function above the average variable cost curve is the short-run supply curve of the firm. In the short run the firm supplies q' units if the price is P'. The heavy lines trace out the firm's short-run supply function.

and the short-run marginal cost function MC_S of a plant that can produce q^* units at minimum cost.

As Chapter 7 demonstrated, each firm maximizes short-run profits by producing q' units if the price is P', and q^* units if the price is P^*. Therefore, the firm's short-run marginal cost function is the firm's short-run supply function. The short-run industry supply function is the horizontal sum of the short-run supply functions of the N^* firms. The short-run industry supply function is *ss* in Figure 8-4[2] and shows the quantity that existing firms in the industry supply at each price. For example, the total quantity supplied in the short run is $Q^* = q^*N^*$ when the price is P^*. Therefore, the short-run industry supply function intersects the long-run industry supply function at $Q = Q^*$.

> The industry's short-run supply function is the horizontal summation of each firm's short-run function.

---

[2] The short-run industry supply function has a horizontal segment because the short-run price cannot fall below minimum average variable cost. Enough firms stop producing so that the price does not fall below minimum average variable cost, and the remaining firms in the industry produce at minimum average variable cost.

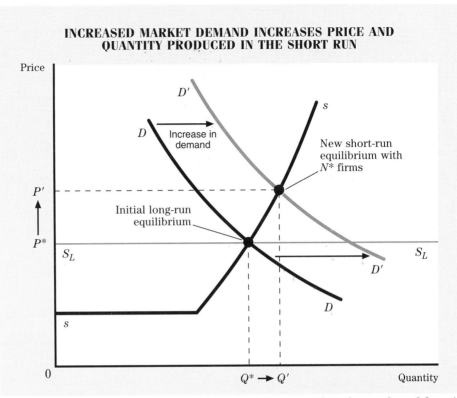

INCREASED MARKET DEMAND INCREASES PRICE AND QUANTITY PRODUCED IN THE SHORT RUN

Figure 8-4   The short-run industry supply curve is *ss* when the number of firms is fixed at N^*. Because demand increases from *DD* to $D'D'$, the initial long-run equilibrium is disrupted and price rises to P' in the short run so that quantity demanded equals quantity supplied by the N^* firms.

Notice the difference between the price elasticity of supply in the short and the long runs. The short-run supply function *ss* is less elastic (steeper) than the long-run supply function $S_L S_L$. In other words, the short-run response of quantity supplied to a price increase is smaller than the long-run response because the number of firms can change in the long run. This implies that any demand shift will cause price to change more in the short than in the long run.

Figure 8-4 shows the original and the new market demand functions and the short- and long-run industry supply functions. Because the market demand increases from *DD* to $D'D'$, price rises to P' to establish a new short-run equlibrium. At P', the existing N^* firms are willing to supply Q' units, and the quantity demanded on $D'D'$ is equal to the quantity supplied on the short-run industry supply function.

How does this increase in demand affect each competitive firm? At the higher price of P' each firm maximizes its profits by producing q' units (see Figure 8-5). The firm's short-run average cost increases from AC^* to AC'_S when the firm increases output from q^* to q' units. The firm's profits rise and are equal to area 1,

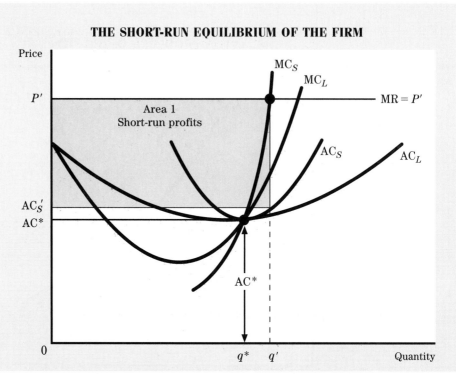

Figure 8-5 The increase in market demand increases the market price to P' in the short run. The firm increases output to q' where P' equals short-run marginal cost. Area 1 measures the short-run profits of the firm.

or $(P' - AC_S')q'$. Although short-run profits do not last indefinitely, they can create enormous wealth before new firms enter the industry.

An unexpected increase in market demand increases price, firm and industry output, and firm profits in the short run.

Adjustment to a New Long-Run Industry Equilibrium

The increase in market demand has made this a profitable industry to enter and sets off alarms throughout the economy. Because the industry is now profitable, new firms contract to build plants so that they can enter and sell at the currently attractive price. How long short-run profits persist depends on how long it takes new firms to enter the industry.

After a time, the duration of which differs from industry to industry, new firms enter the industry and price declines. As these firms build comparable plants, the short-run industry supply function shifts to the right and becomes *ss''*. Figure 8-6 shows that the rightward shift in the short-run supply function causes price to fall to P''.

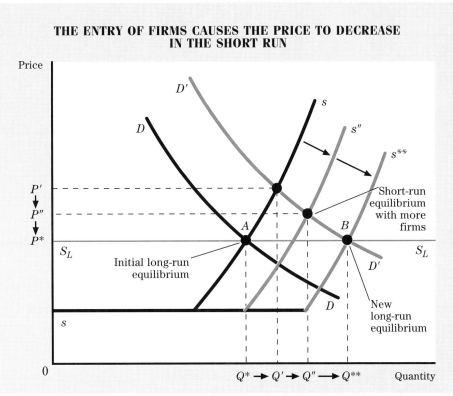

**THE ENTRY OF FIRMS CAUSES THE PRICE TO DECREASE
IN THE SHORT RUN**

Figure 8-6   The short-run profits of firms in the industry attract more firms to the industry. As more firms enter, the short-run supply shifts to the right and becomes ss''. The market price decreases to P'', and quantity produced increases to Q''. As still more firms enter, the short-run supply curve becomes ss^{**}, the price decreases to P^*, total output increases to Q^{**}, and a new long-run equilibrium is reached.

Figure 8-7 indicates that each existing firm reduces output from q' to q'' when the price declines from P' to P''. Firm profits decline as price falls and are now only equal to area 2 in Figure 8-7. The total quantity supplied increases from Q' to Q'' in Figure 8-6 because the additional output supplied by the new firms more than offsets the lower output by the existing firms.

> The entry of firms shifts the short-run supply function to the right and causes price and firm profits to decline.

Later, as still more firms build plants and enter the industry, the short-run supply function shifts further to the right until it becomes ss^{**} in Figure 8-6 and price drops back to the long-run equilibrium price of P^*. The entry of new firms ultimately competes away the profits of the firms in the industry. There are more firms in the industry now, but each one of the larger number is producing only q^* units.

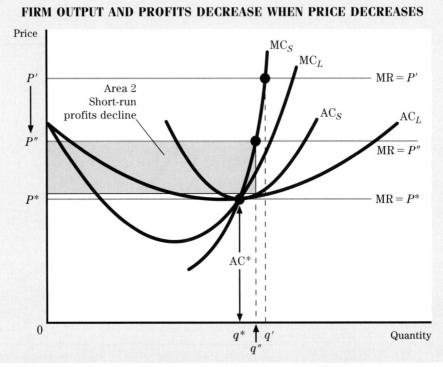

FIRM OUTPUT AND PROFITS DECREASE WHEN PRICE DECREASES

Figure 8-7   The entry of firms reduces the price from P' to P''. The firm reduces output from q' to q'' where P'' equals short-run marginal cost. The firm's profits decline and are equal to area 2.

> An increase in market demand causes equilibrium industry output to increase but does not change the long-run equilibrium price in a constant-cost industry.

Now that our description of the adjustment process to a new long-run equilibrium is complete, let's pause here for several general comments about the constant-cost model and the adjustment process. This explanation of the adjustment process gives some clues how firms in the industry and throughout the economy learn that consumers are demanding more units of the product. It is through the behavior of prices and profits that companies learn of the increased demand. Higher prices and resulting profits attract firms to the industry and increase the supply of the product that consumers are now demanding in larger quantities than before. A search for profits motivates firms to enter the industry and causes price to fall back to the original long-run value where $P = \mathrm{MC}_L = \mathrm{AC}_L$.[3]

---

[3] Chapter 18 discusses the socially optimal properties of an economy where firms are price takers and entry into all industries is free.

Price returns to the long-run equilibrium value in a constant-cost industry because of the two assumptions we started with. Before demand increased, the industry was supplying Q^* units at point A in Figure 8-6. The industry is now supplying Q^{**} units at point B at the same per unit cost as before because (1) firms similar to the existing firms have entered the industry and (2) each firm's long-run average cost function does not shift upward or downward because the industry is producing more. It is because of these two assumptions that the long-run industry supply function is horizontal at the price of P^*, the long-run equilibrium price, and why price must ultimately fall back to P^*.

One conclusion of the constant-cost model is that the growth in market demand cannot explain the growth of the firm. In a constant-cost industry the increase in market demand causes the number of firms to increase but not firm size. The constant-cost model cannot explain why firms grow in size over time. Since firms do grow over time, however, a different model is needed to explain firm growth. Later in this chapter you will see how a firm can grow when a technological innovation increases the quantity at which long-run average cost reaches a minimum.

The Role of Profits

The increase in market demand is the reason that price and profits suddenly increase and ultimately causes more resources to shift into an industry from elsewhere in the economy. While the profits are only transitory, they serve an important function in enticing more firms to enter the industry and in shifting resources into the industry. If an edict prevented price from rising or if profits were hypothetically subject to a 100 percent tax, then there would be little incentive to enter the industry. The increase in demand would not trigger the entry of firms and the supply response. A firm might do just as well by remaining in the industry it is already in.[4] If a market system is to respond to the changing demands of consumers, then the profit motive must reallocate economic resources from industries where demand is decreasing to industries where demand is increasing. Calls to eliminate profits reflect a misunderstanding of the critical role that they play in causing resources throughout the economy to respond to changes in consumer demands.

APPLICATION 8-1

Helping the Victims of Hurricane Andrew

On August 24, 1992, Hurricane Andrew ripped through southern Florida, causing severe flooding, blocked roads, and damage to houses, businesses, and telephone and public utility services. The disruption in electric service kept refrigerators from functioning, and fresh and frozen food spoiled. Residents could not purchase food and ice from grocery stores or plywood from hardware stores to repair their

---

[4] Chapter 10 discusses the incentive for firms to let costs increase when regulation limits profits.

damaged houses and roofs because many stores closed. After the hurricane had passed, the demand for ice, flashlights, food, and plywood increased.

Out of the wreckage came opportunity. Many individuals from outside the area hit by the hurricane set up roadside stands selling food, flashlights, generators, etc. Many came from out of state—some to help and some to help and earn income. Florida officials became incensed when they learned of price increases throughout the damaged area. Bags of ice that normally cost $1 suddenly were being sold for $5. Motel rooms that ordinarily were $35 a night went for over $100 a night. Plywood prices doubled. Some restaurants raised prices. Some officials said that there was no difference between a looter and a price gouger. The Attorney General's office issued subpoenas for the records of firms, including those of seven plywood manufacturers.

Let's try to analyze this bleak situation objectively. After any major hurricane, private and public agencies begin to organize relief efforts. Typically, these agencies respond sluggishly and require several days to a week to take action. The victims have immediate needs, however, and they must fend for themselves during the first week after a hurricane. Will a more flexible and rapid response occur if prices are prevented from increasing or if prices are allowed to increase?

The demand for many goods increases after a hurricane is over, and the supply of these goods provided by local merchants decreases because of the damage caused by the storm. The increase in market demand and the decrease in market supply are the root causes of the price increases. Higher prices make it attractive for outsiders to come into the area and increase the supplies of ice, flashlights, chain saws, work gloves, etc. Especially during the first few days of the hurricane when public and private relief is not yet organized, the profit incentive can be the most effective way to expand supply quickly. It may appear callous to allow price increases after victims have already suffered substantial losses, but it is even more callous to prevent supplies from increasing, thereby preventing prices from falling just when victims are demanding and purchasing essential goods.

If the threat of prosecution holds prices down, some outsiders will have less incentive to increase the supply of badly needed goods. If firms expect lawsuits when prices increase, they will have less incentive to ship goods into the state. The profit motive encourages suppliers to offer goods that are in greater demand and to allocate badly needed goods among different locations. Prices are reduced by increasing supplies, not by preventing supplies from increasing.

You have already seen how a competitive industry moves from one long-run equilibrium to another after market demand increases. Demand can shift to the left, as the makers of typewriters learned when the personal computer arrived. A competitive industry goes through a similar adjustment process after market demand decreases. You can test your understanding of the equilibrating process by drawing graphs for the industry and the firm after market demand decreases and demonstrating why the short-run market price falls and later increases as firms suffer losses and leave the industry.

8-4   PRICE DETERMINATION
IN AN INCREASING-COST INDUSTRY

The two assumptions of the baseline model of a constant-cost industry do not apply in many industries, particularly in those where firms differ in efficiency and size. For example, some firms have more capable managers or chief executive officers (CEOs) than others and can manufacture a product at a lower minimum long-run average cost than others can. Less efficient firms must receive a higher price if they are to enter the industry and increase the quantity supplied.

The second assumption will not apply in an industry that is a relatively large user of a specialized factor of production. Then, an increase in industry output drives up the prices of some factors of production and causes the firm's long-run average and marginal cost functions to shift upward. While the firm is a price taker, the industry is not because an increase in its demand for the specialized factor causes the price of the factor to increase. In an increasing-cost industry the quantity supplied will increase in the long run only if firms receive a higher price. For example, an increase in auto industry output increases the demand for potassium and raises its price because firms use it in catalytic converters for automobiles.

> The long-run industry supply function has a positive slope in an increasing-cost industry.

A Rising Factor Price When Industry Output Expands

In an increasing-cost industry the price of a factor of production increases as industry output expands, and so the industry's long-run supply function slopes upward. When factor prices increase, economists say there is an external pecuniary diseconomy of scale. The growth in industry output, not firm output, causes factor prices to rise, and this growth is external to the firm. The industry is not a price taker in one or more factor markets. The change in price is a pecuniary or monetary change, and there is a diseconomy because the factor price increases. Let's analyze the case of an external pecuniary diseconomy of scale since it is more common than an external pecuniary economy of scale—where an increase in industry output causes a factor price to decrease.

Figure 8-8a shows two pairs of long-run average and marginal cost functions of a competitive firm. AC_L is the firm's long-run average cost function when industry output is Q^* units (Figure 8-8b), while AC'_L is the firm's long-run average cost function when industry output increases to Q' units. The number of firms is large enough so that the short-run industry supply function S_S intersects the long-run supply function at point A. After demand increases, the firm's long-run average cost function shifts upward because a rise in industry output increases the price of a factor of production and causes every firm's long-run average and marginal cost functions to shift upward. In Figure 8-8a the quantity where long-run average cost reaches a minimum increases from q^* to q' because of the increase in the

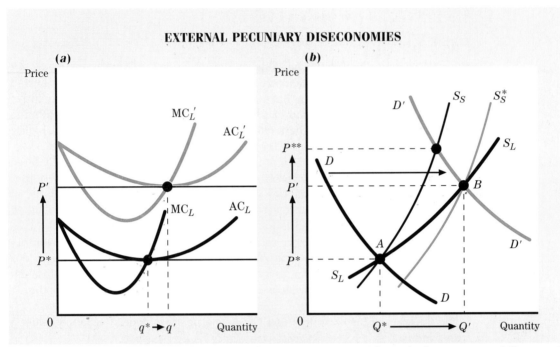

Figure 8-8 (a) The firm's long-run average and marginal cost curves shift upward when the industry output increases from Q^* to Q' because factor prices increase. (b) The equilibrium price and industry output increase in the long run after market demand increases. The increase in industry output causes the price of a factor of production to rise and shifts the firm's cost functions upward.

price of a factor. However, this is a special case. The quantity where long-run average cost reaches a minimum may increase, stay the same, or decrease.

> The price of a factor increases as the industry expands output when there are external pecuniary diseconomies of scale.

Let's trace out the effects of an increase in demand when there is an external pecuniary diseconomy. Initially, market demand is DD, and so the long-run equilibrium price is P^* and the total quantity supplied is Q^* in Figure 8-8b. Each firm produces q^* units, and there are N^* firms in the industry. After market demand increases from DD to $D'D'$, the price increases to the new short-run equilibrium price of P^{**} and the existing firms earn profits. This causes more firms to enter the industry, and the short-run supply function shifts to the right and becomes S_S^*. The price falls from P^{**} to P'. The new short-run supply function intersects the long-run supply function at point B where the new long-run equilibrium price is P', industry output increases to Q', and firm output increases to q' units. When there are external pecuniary diseconomies, an increase in market demand increases the long-run equilibrium price and industry output. In both the old and the new long-run industry equilibria the firms in the industry earn zero profits because the higher price of P' is equal to long-run marginal cost and the minimum average cost of the firm's new long-run average cost function.

The principal difference between a constant-cost industry and this example of an increasing-cost industry is that the equilibrium price increases when market demand increases. Price necessarily increases because the cost of production increases when industry output expands.

When is an industry likely to be an increasing-cost industry? External pecuniary diseconomies are more likely to appear when production requires the use of a specialized factor of production. Land is often considered a specialized factor because the quality of land varies from one acre to another or where natural resources are found. Natural resources and agricultural products require the use of land, and they are likely to be produced under external pecuniary diseconomies.

The Price of a Factor and Economic Rent

You have seen that firm profits are zero in long-run industry equilibrium in an increasing-cost industry. While the profits of firms increase temporarily, entry of new firms competes these profits away in the long run. The main beneficiaries of an increase in market demand are the owners of the specialized factor of production who benefit because the price of the factor increases. If the specialized factor is land, land owners benefit because they can now rent out their land at a higher price. For example, an increase in the demand for wine benefits the owners of the specialized land on which the grapes grow. When the demand for gasoline increases, the owners of crude oil deposits benefit.

The benefits received by the owners of a scarce resource can be measured by studying the market for a scarce factor of production. In Figure 8-9 the supply function of a scarce factor of production, $S_f S_f$, has a positive slope. The quantity supplied of this factor increases at higher prices. Therefore, an increase in the market demand for the good shifts the demand function for the factor from $D_f D_f$ to $D_f' D_f'$ and raises price from P_f^* to P_f'.

When the supply function of a factor of production has a positive slope, the factor earns an economic rent and has a price above the minimum price required for it to be supplied. In Figure 8-9 the equilibrium price and quantity of the factor are P_f^* and F^*, respectively. The total amount paid to employ F^* units is $P_f^* F^*$. To simplify the explanation, assume that single units of the factor are supplied at different prices. The first unit of the factor will be supplied if the factor price is only P_1, the second unit at a slightly higher price of P_2, etc. The difference between the price of the first unit and the minimum price required before that unit will be supplied is $P_f^* - P_1$ in Figure 8-9. The excess of $P_f^* - P_1$ is the economic rent for the first unit. The difference is $P_f^* - P_2$ and is the economic rent for the second unit. Summing these differences for all units up to F^* units produces the total economic rent which is equal to the shaded area in Figure 8-9.

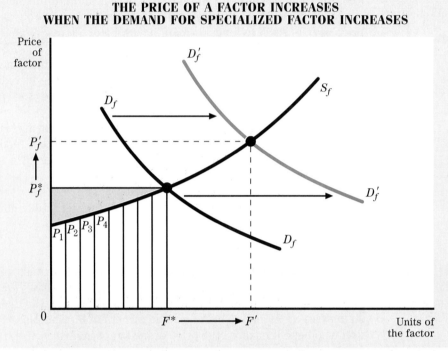

**THE PRICE OF A FACTOR INCREASES
WHEN THE DEMAND FOR SPECIALIZED FACTOR INCREASES**

Figure 8-9   An increase in the demand for the product increases the demand for a specialized factor of production. The price of the factor and total employment of the factor increase. The total rent received by the owners of the factor equals the price received less the minimum price at which each unit would be supplied. When F^* units of the factor are used to produce the product, total rent is equal to the shaded area.

> An economic rent exists when the price received for a factor exceeds the minimum price required to employ the factor.

Some noteworthy examples of economic rent come from professional sports. In a recent interview a quarterback for a professional football team, who had recently signed a long-term contract paying him approximately $3 million annually, mentioned how much he enjoys playing football and how fortunate he is that someone is willing to pay him $3 million a year to play a game that he might be willing to play for perhaps $30,000 a year—his opportunity cost or what he could earn annually in another occupation. The rent he earns is the difference between his compensation and what he would earn in another occupation, or $2,970,000!

To sum up, the long-run industry supply function of the product slopes upward in an increasing-cost industry. An increase in market demand increases the price of the product and industry output, and the resulting increase in the price of the factor benefits the owners of such factors.

Differences in Firm Costs Due to Differences in Managerial Ability

Thus far it has been assumed that all firms are alike, but now it is time to modify this assumption. Here we assume the long-run average cost functions of firms differ because of differences in managerial ability. In the model the position of a firm's long-run average cost function depends on who manages the firm. Some CEOs are skillful at keeping a firm's costs low, whereas others manage companies that are in a perpetual struggle to survive. Because of differences in managerial ability, firms with less efficient managers can supply the product only at higher prices.

Figure 8-10 shows the long-run average cost functions of three of many firms from left to right according to the firm's minimum long-run average cost. The dif-

FIRMS WITH DIFFERENT LONG-RUN AVERAGE AND MARGINAL COST FUNCTIONS

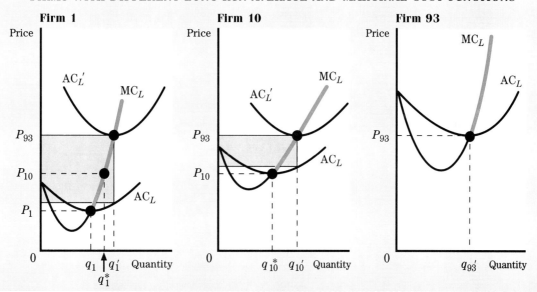

Figure 8-10   The long-run average and marginal cost curves of the three firms differ because of differences in managerial ability. Each firm's long-run supply function is the thick segment of the long-run marginal cost function. Each firm supplies more at a higher price. If the price is P_{93}, firm 1 supplies q_1', firm 10 supplies q_{10}', and firm 93 supplies q_{93}'. Competition for managers will increase managerial compensation above opportunity cost. The shaded area represents the increase in managerial compensation. After managerial compensation increases, the average cost curve of the firm shifts upward and becomes AC_L'.

ferent positions of the long-run average cost functions are due to the different abilities of the firms' managers. When a particular manager runs firm 1, it has the lowest minimum long-run average cost in the industry. Firm 1 enters this industry if the price of the product equals or exceeds P_1. Firm 10 has the tenth lowest minimum long-run average cost and enters the industry if the market price equals or exceeds P_{10}. Firm 93 has the ninety-third lowest minimum long-run average cost in the industry and enters the industry if the price equals or exceeds P_{93}.

Because the firm's long-run marginal cost function is its long-run supply function, the industry's long-run supply function can be derived by summing the individual firms' long-run supply functions horizontally. For example, at a price of P_{10}, firms 1 through 10 supply the product, with firm 1 producing q_1^* units and firm 10 producing q_{10}^* units. If the price is P_{93}, firm 1 produces q_1', firm 10 produces q_{10}', and firm 93 enters the industry and produces q_{93}'. When the price of the good increases, the total quantity supplied increases because (1) each existing firm in the industry is willing to supply more units in the long run and (2) less efficient firms enter the industry and increase the total quantity supplied. The long-run industry supply function $S_L S_L$ in Figure 8-11 has a positive slope.

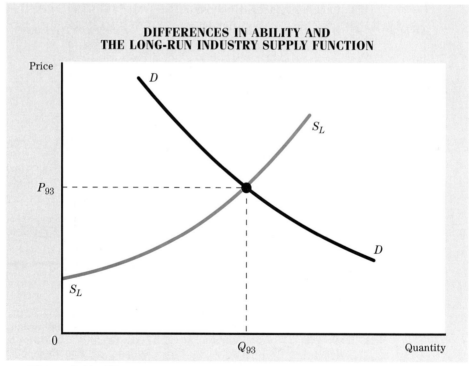

**DIFFERENCES IN ABILITY AND
THE LONG-RUN INDUSTRY SUPPLY FUNCTION**

Figure 8-11   When managers have different abilities, the long-run industry supply curve has a positive slope. As the price increases, each existing firm supplies more units and less efficient firms enter the industry. When market demand is DD, the long-run equilibrium price is P_{93} and firms 1 through 93 supply the product.

> The long-run industry supply function has a positive slope when managers differ in ability.

Long-Run Industry Equilibrium
When Managerial Ability Differs

Given the market demand function DD and the long-run supply function $S_L S_L$, the long-run equilibrium price is P_{93}, the equilibrium quantity is Q_{93}, and there are 93 firms in the industry. Firm 1 produces q_1', firm 10 produces q_{10}', and firm 93 produces q_{93}'. Each firm builds a plant that allows it to produce its profit-maximizing output at lowest total cost.

At a price of P_{93} it appears that all firms except firm 93 earn profits. For the moment, let's think of the two shaded color areas in Figure 8-10 as the profits of the respective firms. Firm 1 is very profitable and the envy of other companies in the industry. What is the profitability of firm 1 due to? The ability of the manager to run a tight ship and keep costs down. Who benefits from these unique talents? This analysis appears to say that the shareholders of the firm are the beneficiaries of the manager's successful cost-reducing efforts.

Would this situation persist if it occurred? Suppose you are the manager of firm 1 and your compensation is currently $150,000 a year, the salary that you would earn managing a firm in another industry. What is likely to happen? You receive phone calls from headhunters who want to know what it would take for you to switch to another firm in the industry. Each firm is willing to offer you a more attractive compensation package because each expects you to reduce the costs of their firm so that it can earn profits. Clearly, firm 1 must match the competing offers if it is to retain your services, or the costs of the firm will increase. You have some special talents, and so you are in an enviable position. How high can your salary go? If there is a competitive market for managers, your compensation will increase until the "apparent" profits of firm 1 in Figure 8-10 disappear. If you received less for your services, whichever firm that employed you would earn profits and other firms would bid more for your services. Competition in the market for managerial talent will increase your salary by the shaded color area for firm 1 in Figure 8-10. The same forces are at work for firm 10. The salary of the manager of firm 10 will increase by the shaded color area for firm 10.

If the market for managers is competitive and managerial compensation increases, the profits of each firm numbered from 1 to 92 will disappear. The average cost function of each firm shifts upward in a certain way when managerial compensation increases, but the firm's marginal cost function does not change. The rise in salary shifts the firm's total cost function upward by the amount of the higher compensation. Figure 8-12 shows the total cost function of the firm before and after salary increases. The difference between the two total cost functions is the increased compensation paid to the manager, which resembles an increase in fixed cost and therefore does not affect the slope of the total cost function. At each quantity the slopes of the two long-run cost functions are the same, and so

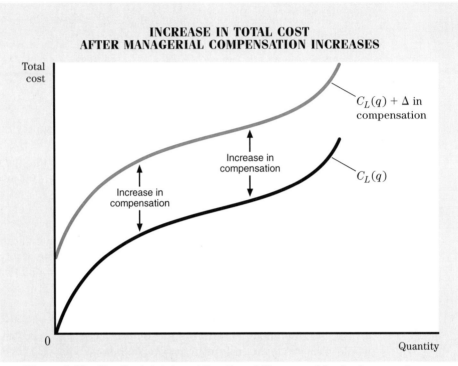

**INCREASE IN TOTAL COST
AFTER MANAGERIAL COMPENSATION INCREASES**

Total cost

$C_L(q) + \Delta$ in compensation

Increase in compensation

Increase in compensation

$C_L(q)$

Increase in compensation

0   Quantity

Figure 8-12   The firm's total cost function shifts upward by the increase in compensation of the manager. The slope of each total cost function for a given quantity is the same. This means the two total cost curves have the same marginal cost function. Therefore, the marginal cost of increasing output does not change when the compensation of the manager increases.

the two total cost functions have the same marginal cost function. Therefore, the marginal cost function does not shift when the compensation of the manager increases.

In Figure 8-10 the average cost functions of firms 1 and 10 shift upward and become AC_L' when executive compensation increases. Minimum average cost on the new average cost function occurs at q_1' for firm 1. Because the marginal cost function does not shift, the firm produces q_1' units before and after compensation increases since P_{93} is still equal to the firm's long-run marginal cost. The same is true for firm 10. Minimum long-run average cost including the higher salary still occurs when the firm produces q_{10}'.

There is a subtle message that you should understand from this analysis. The average cost of the firm *does not* determine the price of the product. When a scarce factor earns rents, the price of the product determines the average cost of the firm, and not the other way around. A higher average cost does not cause price to rise, but the increase in demand raises price and causes the firm's average cost to rise.

The market price of the good does not change when compensation increases because the long-run industry supply function is the horizontal sum of the firms' long-run marginal cost functions. Since each firm's long-run marginal cost function does not shift when managerial compensation increases, the industry's long-run supply function does not shift.

> When there are differences in managerial ability, an increase in market demand benefits managers with scarce talents and not the shareholders of the firms.

APPLICATION 8-2

Cholesterol and the Long-Run Supply Function of Psyllium

In recent years several research studies have reported that psyllium, a tiny seed grown almost exclusively in a small region in western India, may lower blood cholesterol levels and reduce the incidence of heart attacks.[5] Not all of the research studies agree; however, the reports have triggered a demand by Americans for breakfast cereals with psyllium. General Mills and Kellogg introduced new breakfast cereals with psyllium soon after the announcement of the research findings.

What is particularly interesting about this situation is that psyllium is produced only in a small region of India because of the unique climate of the region. As of this writing, it is unknown whether it is possible to produce it elsewhere. If further testing documents the initial findings and if psyllium ultimately becomes a substitute for oat bran, two *big* "ifs," the demand for psyllium will grow.

If the demand for this seed does increase, what will be the effect on its price and on the incomes of the farmers who cultivate it? You can apply the preceding analysis to answer this question. Instead of having managers of different abilities, you now have farms with different productivity in growing psyllium. The cost functions of farms in this region of India will differ from the cost functions of farms in other countries that might produce psyllium.

What will the main effects be if the demand for psyllium increases? Such an increase will raise the price if the production of psyllium is an increasing-cost industry. A rise in the price of psyllium will increase the value of the scarce factor, land. The rental value of the land will rise until any profits from farming psyllium disappear. The possible beneficiaries of the new discovery include the owners of land and not the farmers who work the land. The earnings of the farmers may not change at all. If other regions in India and elsewhere in the world can produce psyllium, an increase in market demand may not cause much of a price increase because the long-run supply function could be relatively flat.

[5] Anthony Spaeth, "Flea Seed Helps Make Area in India a New Heartland," *Wall Street Journal*, October 30, 1989.

*8-5   ADOPTION OF A COST-REDUCING INNOVATION[6]

Like an unexpected increase in demand, costs can change unexpectedly. Technological change is often unforeseen and creates new production methods that reduce the cost of production and shift the supply functions to the right. This section investigates how a competitive industry reacts to a technological change that lowers the firm's long-run average cost function. We will assume that firms outside the industry are the first to adopt the cost-reducing innovation and to begin supplying the product to the market. Once the new firms adopt the new technique, there are two sources of supply—companies using the old technology and companies using the new technology. For example, consider a situation where the technology is first developed abroad and foreign firms begin to supply the domestic market. If all firms can adopt the new production method, the existing firms in the industry will face a critical decision: Should they junk plants that use the old technology immediately or switch over to the new technology later after their old equipment and plants wear out?

Before considering a graphical treatment of the problem, let's look at a numerical example. A competitive firm already has an existing plant that uses the old technology. Table 8-2 shows the fixed (sunk) cost of a firm with a plant that uses the old technology in column 2, the variable cost in column 3, and the short-run marginal cost of the old plant in column 4. If the firm builds a plant that uses the new technology, the long-run total cost is in column 5 and long-run marginal cost is in column 6. One point to notice is that the firm's variable cost is less than the long-run total cost of the plant that uses the new technology at each quantity. Another is that the firm will incur the sunk cost of the old plant whether it uses this plant or builds a new one. Therefore, sunk cost can be ignored.

If the market price is $32 and the firm builds a new plant with the new technology, it will produce 4 units of output where price equals the firm's long-run marginal cost. At a price of $32 revenues are $128 ($32 × 4) and the total cost of producing 4 units with the plant using the new technology is $128, and so the profits of the firm are zero (ignoring sunk cost). On the other hand, if the firm does not build a new plant but produces 4 units with the old plant, its variable cost would be only $80. Therefore, the firm's profits must be higher because the variable cost of the old plant is less than the long-run total cost of using the new plant. If the firm does not build a new plant but continues to use the old plant, it will produce 6 units where the price of $32 equals the short-run marginal cost of the old plant. Total profits will be $192 − $138 = $54 (ignoring sunk cost). The profits of the firm will be higher if the firm continues to use the plant with the old technology whenever the variable cost of the old plant is less than the long-run total cost of the new plant. Equivalently, we can say that the firm will keep the old plant when its average variable cost is less than the long-run average cost of the new plant.

This numerical illustration brings out the importance of comparing the average variable cost of the plant using the old technology with the long-run average cost

---

[6] This section borrows from unpublished writings of R. L. Bishop.

Table 8-2   COMPARING THE VARIABLE COST OF AN OLD PLANT WITH THE TOTAL LONG-RUN COST OF A NEW PLANT

QUANTITY (1)	SUNK COST OF OLD PLANT ($) (2)	VARIABLE COST OF OLD PLANT ($) (3)	MARGINAL COST OF OLD PLANT ($) (4)	LONG-RUN TOTAL COST OF NEW PLANT ($) (5)	LONG-RUN MARGINAL COST OF NEW PLANT ($) (6)
1	200	35	35	65	65
2	200	44	9	80	40
3	200	60	16	90	30
4	200	80	20	128	32
5	200	106	26	180	36
6	200	138	32	240	40

of the plant using the new technology when making the switch-over decision. Now let's consider a graphical analysis of the switch-over decision. To illustrate the theory in its simplest form, our analysis starts with a constant-cost industry in long-run industry equilibrium. Figure 8-13a shows the long-run average cost function of an established firm using the existing technology. The firm has built a plant with a short-run average cost function (AC_S) and a short-run marginal cost function (MC_S). In Figure 8-13c the market demand function is DD and the horizontal long-run industry supply function is S_L, with all firms using the old technology. There are N^* firms in the industry, and the short-run industry supply function is ss. The initial equilibrium price and quantity are P^* and Q^*, respectively, and each firm produces q^* units.

Figure 8-13b shows the long-run average and marginal cost functions of a new firm that uses the new technology. At each quantity the long-run average cost function of this firm is lower than the long-run average cost function of a firm that uses the older technology. Any firm starting from scratch prefers to use the new lower-cost technology.

A cost-reducing innovation lowers the firm's long-run average cost function.

Given the current price of P^*, new firms will quickly enter the industry with plants that use the new technology because they expect to earn profits. As they build new plants, the short-run industry supply function shifts to the right and becomes ss' in Figure 8-13c. The rightward shift in the short-run supply function causes price to fall to P' and total industry output to rise to Q'.

Figure 8-13a shows that each existing firm reduces output to q' where the lower price P' is equal to the firm's short-run marginal cost. Total output supplied by all existing firms still using the older technology decreases from Q^* to Q'_o in

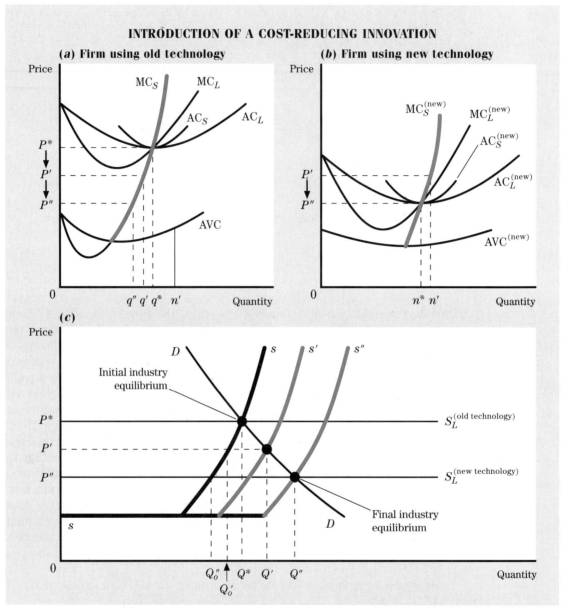

Figure 8-13   A cost-reducing technology is introduced by a new entrant (*b*). The price falls from P^* to P' as the short-run supply function shifts to the right (*c*) and becomes ss'. As more firms enter with the new cost-reducing technology, the price falls to P''. Later, the firms using the old technology (*a*) adopt the new technology when their old plants and equipment must be replaced.

Figure 8-13c. The entry of firms using the new technology lowers the price from P^* to P' and causes existing firms to incur losses. To keep the graph simple, the losses sustained by an existing firm are not shown in Figure 8-13a. The early entrants earn profits after entering the industry with the new technology. Later, as still more firms enter, the short-run supply function shifts further to the right and becomes ss''. The equilibrium falls to P'', the equilibrium industry quantity increases to Q'', and the firms using the new technology no longer earn profits. Each firm using the old technology reduces output by still more to q'', and the total quantity supplied by firms using the old technology falls to Q''_o. The losses of these firms mount.

You might be wondering why the firms using the old technology don't shift over to the new technology immediately since they are suffering losses. The reason is that an existing firm can produce each quantity at a lower average variable cost with the old plant. Consider the problem faced by a firm using the old technology. With this technology, it incurs only the average variable cost of the old plant when it produces any given quantity since fixed cost of the old plant is a sunk cost. If it adopts the new technology, the cost that it will incur to produce any given quantity will be the long-run average cost using the new technology plus the sunk cost of the old plants, because the firm is starting from scratch. The firm should compare the average variable cost of the old plant with the long-run average cost of the new plant using the new technology before deciding whether to continue to use the old technology or to shift immediately to the new.

If a firm adopts the new technology, the profit-maximizing output is n' when the price is P', or n^* when the price is P''. Assume that the firm's average variable cost when using the old technology lies below the long-run average cost function if it chooses to produce n^* or n' units with the new technology. Therefore, it can produce either quantity at a lower average variable cost with the old technology than at the long-run average cost of the new technology. Consequently, the firm will not be maximizing profits if it immediately switches to the new technology.

On the other hand, if the innovation causes such a large downward shift in the long-run average cost function that the old plant's average variable cost function lies above the new long-run average cost function, the firm should switch over immediately. Consequently, firms cannot be expected to switch over immediately unless the change will result in a large cost reduction. It is not because they are not maximizing profits but because they are maximizing profits that firms do not immediately adopt the new technology.

Making a decision on when to switch over involves looking ahead and not allowing sunk costs to influence a firm's decision. The switch-over decision requires a comparison of the average variable cost of the older technology and the long-run average cost of the new technology since these are the costs that the firm can affect. Sunk cost of the older technology is a bygone.

> A firm will continue to use old technology if the average variable cost function of the old plant lies below the long-run average cost function of the new plant.

If the average variable cost of a plant with the old technology is lower than the long-run average cost of one with the new technology, established firms do not immediately switch over and adopt the new technology. After a time, as the old plants wear out, the firms that remain in the industry adopt the new technology since the long-run average cost of the new technology is less than the long-run average cost of the old technology. When the firm makes the reinvestment decision, all costs are variable and none are sunk. The theory predicts that the proportion of industry output that firms supply with the new technology will gradually increase until all firms are using the new technology. During this conversion process the price remains at P'' since the reduction in output by firms that were using the old technology is offset by the added output of firms adopting the new technology.

This analysis says that immediate adoption of a new technology is typically not a rational decision. Although a firm using the old technology is suffering losses and firms using the new technology are earning profits, at least temporarily, it is irrational for a firm to copy the behavior of the profitable firms immediately. It should compare the variable cost of using the old technology with the total cost of using the new technology when making its decision.

How does a cost-reducing innovation affect the size of a firm? It is possible for the cost-reducing method to increase or decrease the quantity where long-run average cost reaches a minimum. In Figure 8-13b, n^* could be substantially larger than q^*. If so, an innovation would increase firm size after the industry reaches the new long-run equilibrium. One way of explaining why firms grow as equilibrium industry output increases is to assume that technological change favors larger firms and increases the quantity at which long-run average cost reaches a minimum.

You can get a better sense of the impact of cost reductions on industry price and quantity by tracing the evolution of industries over time and by examining the rate of price decline. Cost-reducing innovations cause prices to decline. Looking at the *rate* of decline in prices, especially in mature industries, can provide an indication of the frequency with which firms introduce cost-reducing innovations.

APPLICATION 8-3

Regularities in the Evolution of Industries

Michael Gort and Steven Klepper examined the evolution of 46 industries after a firm introduced a major innovation in each one.[7] Although these major changes were made in different decades, the authors hoped to discover a pattern in the way industries evolve after an initial major innovation. How did prices behave over time? Did the innovator maintain its market share and charge a relatively high price, or was the more common pattern one of declining prices and the entry of competitors? Did the number of firms grow steadily over time, or more rapidly in different stages as the industry evolved? Did major cost reductions occur primarily

[7] Michael Gort and Stephen Klepper, "Time Paths in the Diffusion of Product Innovations," *Economic Journal*, vol. 92, September 1982, pp. 630–653.

Table 8-3   REGULARITIES IN THE EVOLUTION OF INDUSTRIES

STAGE OF INDUSTRY DEVELOPMENT	RATE OF DECREASE IN REAL PRICE FOR 23 INDUSTRIES	RATE OF INCREASE IN TOTAL OUTPUT FOR 25 INDUSTRIES	NUMBER OF ENTRANTS PER YEAR FOR 46 INDUSTRIES
First	− 13.6	56.6	0.5
Second	− 13.0	35.1	5.67
Third	− 7.2	12.3	0.13
Fourth	− 9.0	8.1	− 4.84
Fifth	− 5.2	1.0	− 0.47

early in the development of these industries or did they continue to occur as the industry evolved? What happened to the number of firms and total industry output as the industry matured? These are some of the questions raised in this interesting study.

While there was considerable variability among the industries, Gort and Klepper did identify five stages in the evolution of a representative industry. Table 8-3 shows the average percentage change in the inflation-adjusted price, output, and entry in each of the five stages.

In the first stage, industry output grows rapidly and price declines at a rapid annual rate although the number of firms grows modestly. In the second stage, entry of firms increases dramatically, price continues to drop rapidly, and the growth rate of output, while still substantial, begins to decline. During the third stage there is virtually no growth in the number of firms, prices continue to decline, but at a slower rate, and the growth rate of output declines. The fourth stage is the shake-out stage. From the end of the third stage to the end of the fourth stage the authors report that the number of firms in the industry declines by an average of 40 percent, a dramatic decline, even though industry output continues to grow, but at a slower rate. In the fourth stage prices fall at a faster rate than in the third stage. In the last stage, the number of firms has stabilized again, but at a lower level, prices decline at the slowest rate, and industry output has virtually stabilized.

Change continues in these industries after the initial major innovation. There is not simply one major innovation which firms then adapt to. The evidence is not at all consistent with a "big bang" theory of industry development. Prices decline continually, at a faster rate at first but nevertheless continually. Following the initial major innovation, it appears that firms continue to introduce cost-reducing innovations and learn to produce the product more efficiently in all stages. In the shake-out stage these cost-reducing innovations are of sufficient importance that the rate of price declines increases, the size of firms increases, and the number of firms in the industry decreases dramatically.

Table 8-4   DURATION OF FIRST STAGE

YEAR WHEN MAJOR INNOVATION OCCURRED	DURATION OF FIRST STAGE (YEARS)
Before 1930	23
Between 1930 and 1939	10
After 1939	5

Entry of firms was discontinuous in these industries. What is somewhat surprising is that the number of entrants per year did not peak in the first stage. Some new firms did enter during this stage; however, it was not until the second stage that the number increased rapidly. In a particularly interesting finding the authors report that the duration of the first stage has been decreasing over time (see Table 8-4). In industries where the major innovation occurred before 1930, the first stage lasted about 23 years, a lengthy period. In industries where major innovations occurred from 1930 to 1939, the first stage lasted about 10 years. And in industries where the innovation occurred after 1940, the first stage lasted only 5 years. So, the length of the period before the entry rate of competitors speeds up is shortening. Assuming short-run profits from an innovation are higher in the early stages of development of an industry, the Gort and Klepper results suggest that the time period over which firms earn these short-run profits is decreasing.

Perhaps one of the most important lessons of this study is the persistence of price reductions throughout the evolution of an industry. This pattern of declining prices indicates that large and small cost reductions are occurring continually as an industry grows and matures.

8-6   RAISING THE COSTS FOR NEW ENTRANTS

These analyses of a competitive industry have shown that the entry of firms competes away short-run profits of firms in the industry. By limiting the entry of firms into the industry, established firms can prevent their profits from being competed away. The next question is: What are the economic consequences of raising barriers to entry? To answer this question, we first consider the economic effects of licensing that prevent firms from entering a profitable industry. Then, we examine a less extreme case where the established firms benefit when regulation forces new entrants to use a more expensive technology but does not prevent them from entering the industry.

How Licensing Changes the Shape of
the Long-Run Industry Supply Function

Entry into some industries is blocked. In most cities, new firms cannot enter the taxicab business legally. Likewise, not anyone can open a retail establishment that serves alcoholic beverages. In most cities you must have a license, and the license is valuable—very valuable in some cases. In this section the constant-cost model is used to analyze the impact of licensing on long-run equilibrium price and quantity in a competitive industry.

Figure 8-14a shows that a price-taking firm produces q^* units when the equilibrium price is P^*. Figure 8-14b shows the market demand function DD and the horizontal long-run industry supply function $S_L S_L$. The long-run equilibrium price and quantity are P^* and Q^*, and there are N^* firms in the industry.

Assume that a regulatory commission issues a license to each existing firm in the industry and decides that only a firm with a license can supply the product. In effect, this decision blocks entry into the industry.

To determine how licensing affects the long-run equilibrium price and quantity, let's first determine how licensing alters the long-run industry supply function. In the long run each price-taking firm determines output where price equals long-run marginal cost. In Figure 8-14a the heavier portion of the long-run marginal cost function above the long-run average cost function is the firm's long-run supply function. If the price is P', the firm will supply q' units in the long run at a long-run average cost of AC'. Figure 8-14b shows that the new long-run industry supply function has the same horizontal segment as before, running from S_L to point b. Industry output can expand from zero to Q^* by adding more firms that have licenses, where each firm supplies q^* units in the long run. When the industry supplies Q^* units at a price of P^*, all N^* licensed firms are producing in the industry. Further expansion of industry output can occur only if each firm produces more units. It does this by supplying output along its long-run marginal cost function. Consequently, the long-run industry supply function includes the horizontal segment from S_L to point b and the segment from point b to S_L'.

The simple act of licensing the existing N^* firms does not change the equilibrium price P^*. If each of the N^* firms continues to act as a price taker, no firm can increase price just because new firms cannot enter. Each firm knows that consumers will shift to the perfect substitutes supplied by competitors if it alone raises price.

Matters get more interesting when demand increases from DD to $D'D'$. In Figure 8-14b the equilibrium price increases to P' and total quantity supplied increases to Q' when demand increases to $D'D'$. Figure 8-14a shows that the long-run output of each firm increases from q^* to q'. The increase in market demand creates long-run firm profits equal to the shaded area in Figure 8-14a. Normally, the entry of firms would compete these profits away, but with entry restricted the profits of the license holders persist. Each firm produces q' at the lowest long-run average cost of AC' by building a larger plant. The larger plant has a short-run average cost function AC_S that is just tangent to the long-run average cost function at q'. For example, the owner of a taxi may purchase a more expensive and more

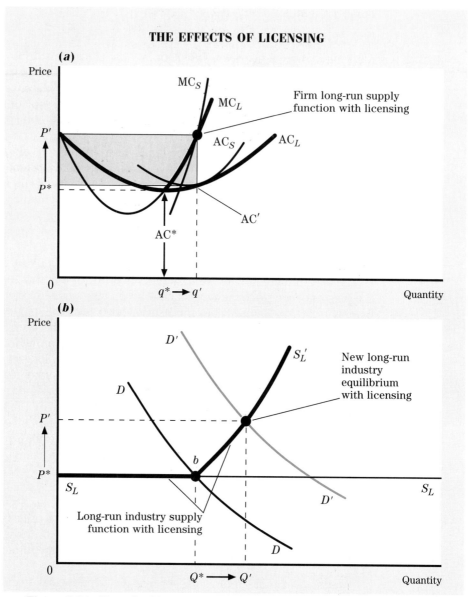

Figure 8-14   Licensing blocks the entry of firms into the industry. The market price increases to P' and the quantity supplied increases to Q' when demand increases to $D'D'$. (*a*) Each firm increases output from q^* to q'. The shaded area represents firm profits. The firm no longer produces at the minimum point of the long-run average cost function. Limiting entry causes a cost inefficiency since Q' is not produced at the lowest total cost.

durable automobile so that he can remain on the road longer and is less likely to break down. A restaurant owner with a license to serve alcoholic beverages may build a larger retail establishment so she can serve more customers even if long-run average cost increases.

The restriction on entry creates a cost inefficiency. Total output of Q' is no longer being produced at the lowest total cost. The lowest total cost of producing Q' units would have each firm produce q^* units at AC^* but have more than N^* firms in the industry. If each of the N^* firms reduces output by $q' - q^*$ units but more firms enter the industry so that all firms produce q^* units, then Q' units will be produced at a lower total cost than under licensing. Therefore, licensing not only raises the price to consumers but creates a cost inefficiency by raising the total cost of producing Q'.

> Licensing prevents new firms from entering, can create profits, and does not minimize the cost of producing industry output.

APPLICATION 8-4

The Value of a License

You must own a medallion (license) to operate a taxicab legally in New York City. Medallions sell for considerable sums, sometimes more than $140,000. The reason that they are so valuable is that new firms cannot enter the industry and the demand for taxi services in New York has increased to the point where the price of the service is well above the long-run minimum average cost of operating a taxi. In contrast, if market demand equaled DD or there was free entry into the industry, the long-run equilibrium price would be P^* in Figure 8-14a. Profits would vanish, and the medallion would be worthless. This is exactly what has happened in Washington, D.C., where entry into the taxicab industry is free and profits are competed away. The medallions in New York City are valuable because entry is restricted and demand is greater than DD.

The theory predicts that a decrease in the demand for the product will reduce the value of the license. Consider this supporting evidence. California has limited the number of licenses permitting the sale of alcoholic beverages in local bars and hotels. In Los Angeles County, the value of a license to sell alcoholic beverages in local bars or in hotels declined to $12,000–$13,000 in 1989 from $23,000–$30,000 in 1984.[8] In San Francisco the value of a license dropped to $16,000 from $32,000 over the same period. The decrease in the value of the license is due in part to the declining popularity of bar hopping and the increased concern about the liability incurred by bar owners.

The value of a license is the most sensitive barometer of changes in demand, cost, and entry conditions.

---

[8] Lawrence M. Fisher, "Old Standby, the Corner Bar, Falling Victim to New Values," *New York Times*, November 18, 1989.

APPLICATION 8-5

Raising Profits by Working with Regulators

You have seen how established firms benefit from licensing. Other mechanisms can benefit these firms by raising the costs to newcomers. Officials can write and interpret regulations that impose more demanding standards on those entering the industry. For example, environmental regulations require newly constructed plants to meet higher pollution abatement standards than existing plants. The average cost of production will be higher for new firms and for new plants built by established firms.

Let's analyze this type of regulation. In Figure 8-15c the market demand function is DD and the horizontal long-run industry supply function is $S_L S_L$ in a constant-cost industry before passage of pollution abatement legislation. The long-run equilibrium price is P^*, total output is Q^*, and there are N^* firms in the industry. Figure 8-15a shows that each of the N^* firms produces q_0^* units at the lowest long-run average cost. The short-run average and marginal cost functions of the firm are AC_S and MC_S, respectively.

Now suppose that the new law mandates that all new firms adopt a new and more expensive technology that produces fewer emissions per unit of output. The long-run average cost function of a firm that uses the mandated technology is AC_L' in Figure 8-15b. A new firm that uses the new technology minimizes long-run average cost when it produces q_n^* units. All new firms must use the new technology, but all established firms are exempt until their old plants wear out, at which time they must use the new technology.

We can derive a new "pseudo" long-run industry supply function before the established firms replace their old plants but when new firms can enter and use the new technology. This is a pseudo long-run supply function because established firms continue to use old plants although ultimately they too will have to adopt the new technology.

The industry supply function becomes the heavy line $S_S abS_L'$ in Figure 8-15c. At any price less than P', the quantity supplied comes only from the N^* established producers using the older technology along the segment $S_S ab$. The supply function of each established firm is its short-run marginal cost function. New firms will not enter the industry when the price is less than P' but will enter if the price is P' or higher. Because this is a constant-cost industry, there are many new firms who are willing to supply q_n^* units at a price of P'.

If demand increases to $D'D'$, new firms enter, the price increases to P', and the equilibrium quantity increases to Q'. In Figure 8-15a each of the N^* established firms expands output to q_o' after the price increases to P', and the established producers supply an aggregate of Q'' units. Enough new firms enter the industry to produce $Q' - Q''$. Again, we have not described the rise in the short-run price to P^{**} before the new firms enter and reduce the price to P'. You can probably fill in the details by now. Once the price equals P', the new firms are in long-run

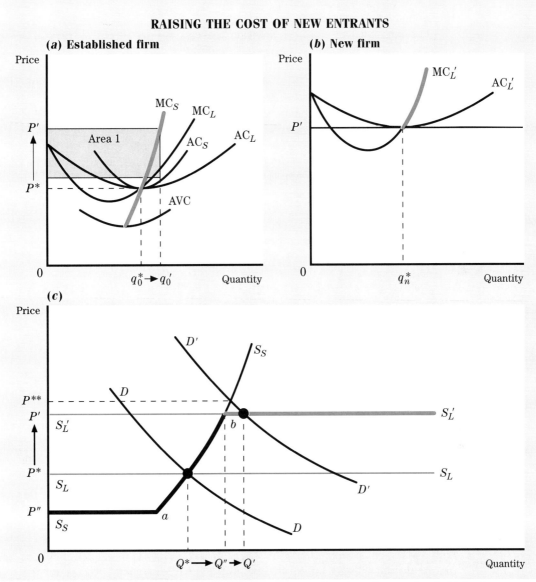

Figure 8-15   The long-run average cost function of a new firm is higher because new firms must use a more expensive but less polluting technology (*b*). (*c*) When demand increases to $D'D'$, the price increases to P'. (*a*) Existing firms earn profits equal to area 1. Established firms produce Q'', and the new firms produce $Q' - Q''$. The established firms benefit from regulations that impose a higher cost on new entrants.

equilibrium and earn no profits. However, the established firms are now earning profits equal to area 1 in Figure 8-15*a*.

Although the N^* established firms are earning profits, these profits persist because all new entrants must use the mandated technology with a higher long-run average cost function. The profits of the established firms will continue until they must replace their plants and adopt the mandated technology. When this happens, the long-run industry supply function becomes $S_L'S_L'$.

The established firms have even less incentive to replace their plants because they must adopt the new higher-cost technology. They will delay by continuing to maintain the old plants. This is one of the undesirable effects of this form of regulation. The same problem exists with the regulation of auto emissions. Older cars are exempt from the emissions regulations and remain on the road still longer, creating still more pollutants.

The frequent railing of business organizations against government regulation may convince some that business always opposes government controls. This example shows how established firms benefit from regulation when new firms must incur higher costs. Companies recognize the importance of influencing the form that legislation takes so that they can obtain some slight advantage over existing or potential competitors. This example should persuade you, if you needed any persuasion, that firms are quite selective, favoring regulation when it serves their interests.

8-7 TAXING A COMPETITIVE INDUSTRY

Governments commonly tax the output of industries to raise revenue for government programs. Governments levy taxes on many goods including cigarettes, liquor, and wine. Sales taxes are placed on food, clothing, and durable goods. This section investigates the economic effects of a per unit tax on the long-run equilibrium price and output.

Imposing a Per Unit Tax on a Competitive Industry

Suppose the government imposes a per unit tax of t dollars on each unit sold by a firm. How will this tax affect the equilibrium price, firm and industry output, firm profits, and number of firms in the industry? In Figure 8-16 the initial equilibrium price and output in a constant-cost industry are P^* and Q^*, respectively. Each firm produces q^* units, and the number of firms in the industry is $N^* = Q^*/q^*$.

After the government levies a per unit tax of t, the firm's profit function becomes

Total profits = Total revenue − Total long-run cost − Total taxes

$$\pi(q) = Pq - C_L(q) - tq \tag{8-2}$$

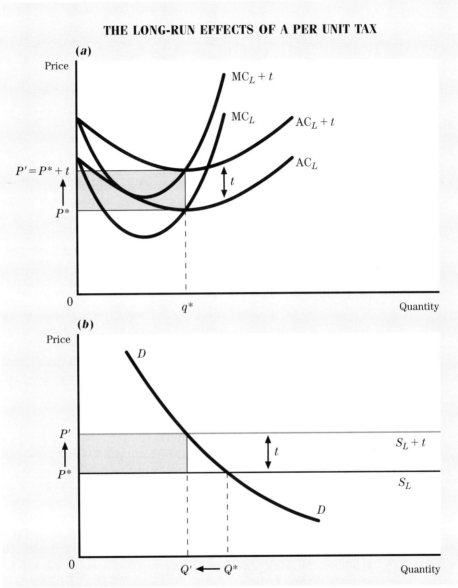

Figure 8-16   (*a*) The firm's long-run average and marginal cost functions shift upward by the per unit tax. The minimum long-run average cost is reached when q^* units are produced before and after the tax is assessed. (*b*) The per unit tax shifts the long-run industry supply function upward by the tax. The long-run equilibrium price increases from P^* to P', the amount of the tax, and total quantity decreases from Q^* to Q'.

Total taxes paid by the firm to the government are tq. The firm's output that maximizes profits must satisfy the following condition.[9]

$$P = \frac{\Delta C_L(q)}{\Delta q} + t \qquad\qquad (8\text{-}3)$$

The firm considers the per unit tax a cost of doing business, and so it determines output where price equals the sum of long-run marginal cost and t. The marginal cost of producing and selling another unit equals the pretax marginal cost of production plus the per unit tax paid to the government.

When the firm considers the per unit tax as another cost of the firm, the long-run average cost of the firm including the tax t becomes $AC_L + t$. The new long-run average cost function of the firm is the firm's pretax long-run average cost function shifted upward by the per unit tax. If the long-run average cost of producing a million units is $67 and the per unit tax is $8, then the new long-run average cost will be $67 + $8 = $75. The marginal cost function also shifts upward and becomes $MC_L + t$. If the marginal cost of producing the last unit was $5, it is now $13 with the tax included. Figure 8-16a shows the initial average and marginal cost functions and the new average and marginal cost functions with the per unit tax included.

Because the average and marginal cost functions shift upward by t, the new and the old long-run average cost functions reach a minimum at the same quantity. In Figure 8-16a long-run average cost reaches a minimum at $q = q^*$ before and after the government levies the per unit tax. Figure 8-16b shows that the long-run industry supply function, S_L, shifts upward by t to become $S_L + t$.

Long-Run Effects of a Per Unit Tax

It is easy to trace the long-run effects of a per unit tax. Figure 8-16b shows that the long-run equilibrium price increases from P^* to P', or by the tax t, in a constant-cost industry. The equilibrium quantity declines from Q^* to Q'. By raising the per unit tax, the government increases the price of the product and decreases the quantity demanded. This confirms the old adage, "The power to tax is the power to destroy." Total tax paid by the firm is equal to the shaded color area in Figure 8-16a, and total tax collections are $T = tQ'$, the shaded color area in Figure 8-16b. Each firm in the industry produces q^* units at the initial and at the new long-run equilibria. Therefore, the tax drives some firms out of the industry since the total quantity decreases to Q'.

> In the long run, price increases by the amount of the tax in a constant-cost industry.

---

[9] The profit-maximizing quantity satisfies

$$\frac{d\pi(q)}{dq} = P - \frac{dC_L(q)}{dq} - t = 0$$

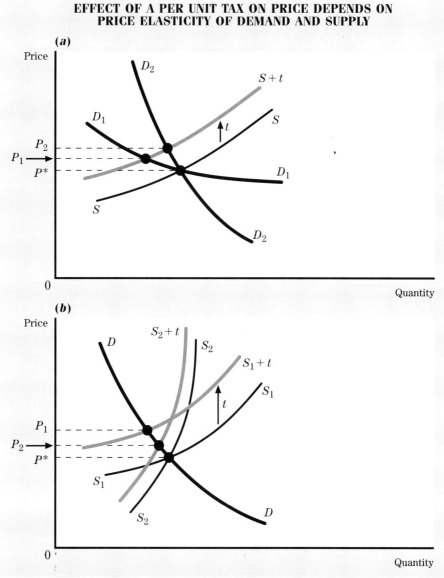

EFFECT OF A PER UNIT TAX ON PRICE DEPENDS ON PRICE ELASTICITY OF DEMAND AND SUPPLY

Figure 8-17   (*a*) When a per unit tax is imposed on a competitive industry, the more elastic the price elasticity of demand, the less the price increases. (*b*) The less elastic the price elasticity of supply, the less the price increases.

While the price increases by the amount of the tax in a constant-cost industry, how much price increases depends on the price elasticity of demand and supply. Let's first consider how the price elasticity of demand affects the effect of the tax on price. Figure 8-17a compares the effect of imposing a per unit tax when the two market demand functions are D_1D_1 and D_2D_2. The initial long-run equilibrium price is P^*. In the immediate neighborhood of the initial equilibrium price of P^*, D_1D_1 is more elastic than D_2D_2. After the government levies the tax and the long-run supply function shifts upward by t, the equilibrium price increases by only $P_1 - P^*$ when the demand function is D_1D_1, and from P^* to P_2 when the demand function is D_2D_2. This shows that the greater the price elasticity of demand, the smaller the price increase caused by a per unit tax.

> The greater the price elasticity of demand, the smaller the price increase caused by a per unit tax.

The effect of the per unit tax is to force more consumers to buy nontaxed substitutes when the market demand function is more elastic. Because this is an increasing-cost industry, the tax reduces industry output and the fall in industry output reduces the demand for the scarce factor and lowers the price of a factor. Because industry output falls, the production cost of the remaining sellers also falls. Therefore, some of the effects of the tax are borne by the owners of the scarce factor of production.

The effect of a per unit tax on price and on industry output also depends on the price elasticity of supply in the neighborhood of the initial equilibrium price. In Figure 8-17b the two supply functions are S_1S_1 and S_2S_2. Starting from the initial equilibrium price of P^*, the greater the price elasticity of supply, the greater the price increase caused by a per unit tax. The price increases from P^* to P_1 if the supply function is S_1S_1, and by a smaller amount to P_2 if the supply function is S_2S_2.

> The greater the price elasticity of supply, the greater the price rise caused by a per unit tax.

As the industry supply function becomes more elastic, it begins to resemble that for the constant-cost case. In the latter case, the price rises by the amount of the tax. Although industry output falls and the number of firms in the industry decreases, factor prices do not change when industry output falls in a constant-cost case. Since the cost functions of the firm do not shift, the price of the good must increase by the amount of the tax if the industry is to reach a new long-run equilibrium. In contrast, when the industry supply function is almost vertical, a small change in industry output causes a larger change in the price of at least one specialized factor. As industry output decreases, its demand for specialized factors falls, as do the prices of those specialized factors. Because the per unit tax causes a decrease in industry output, factor prices fall, and this lowers the firm's long-run average cost function. Therefore, the price of the good does not rise as much as the supply elasticity becomes less elastic. Here again, the tax lowers the rent earned by the owners of specialized factors.

This analysis indicates that a per unit tax is not necessarily paid by the agent that collects it or that only consumers pay the per unit tax. A per unit tax can be completely shifted to consumers so that the price rises by the amount of the tax (constant-cost case), or it can fall entirely on a factor of production if the industry's supply function is perfectly inelastic. The next section examines how a per unit tax affects consumer and producer surplus.

The Effect of a Per Unit Tax on Consumer and Producer Surplus

Taxes alter the behavior of consumers and producers. The concepts of consumer and producer surplus can be used to evaluate the social consequences of imposing a per unit tax.

Before the government levies a per unit tax, the long-run equilibrium price and quantity in a competitive industry are P^* and Q^*, respectively, in Figure 8-18. At

CONSUMER AND PRODUCER SURPLUSES IN LONG-RUN EQUILIBRIUM

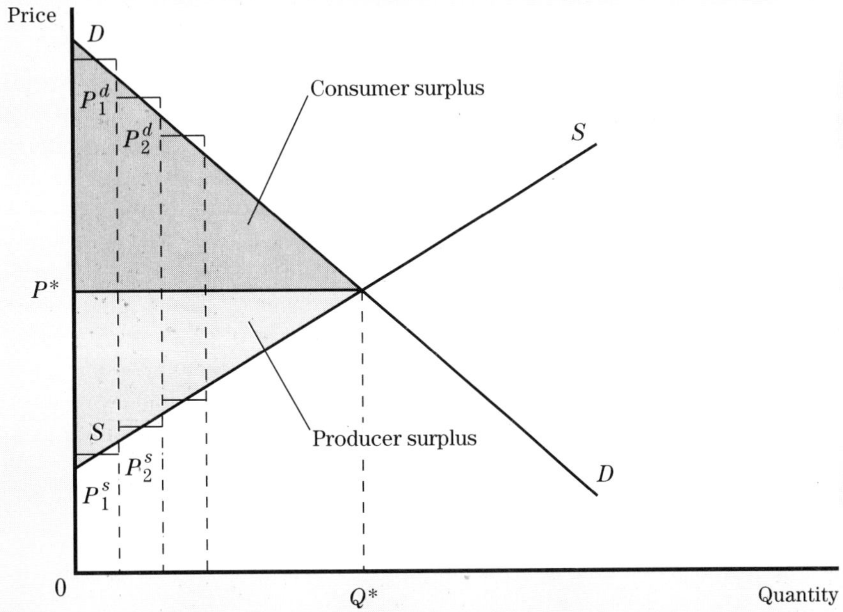

Figure 8-18   The long-run equilibrium price and quantity are P^* and Q^*, respectively. Consumer surplus equals the gray area between the demand function and the price line P^*. Producer surplus equals the shaded color area between the price line P^* and the supply function.

this long-run equilibrium, consumers benefit because they are willing to pay more than P^* for each unit up to the Q^*th. Chapter 3 showed that the area between the market demand function and the price line P^* measures consumer surplus. To refresh your memory, let's review how consumer surplus is determined. The demand function in Figure 8-18 shows that consumers are willing to pay P_1^d for the first unit, P_2^d for the second unit, and so on up to the Q^*th unit. The price paid is P^* for all units, although consumers are willing to pay more. The surplus on the first unit is $P_1^d - P^*$, on the second unit $P_2^d - P^*$, etc. Each consumer receives a surplus because the market price is only P^* for each unit. Therefore, the gray area under the demand function and above the price line represents consumer surplus.[10]

There is a close analogy between consumer surplus and producer surplus. Producers are willing to supply units at different prices. For example, a producer is willing to supply the first unit in Figure 8-18 at a price of P_1^s, another is willing to supply the second unit at a price of P_2^s, and so on up to the Q^*th unit. Producers receive P^* for all the units they sell, although they are willing to supply all units up to the Q^*th unit at lower prices. Therefore, the area between the price line P^* and the industry supply function, or the shaded color area, represents producer surplus when producers sell Q^* units at P^*.

Let's see how the sum of consumer and producer surpluses decreases when the government levies a per unit tax on a competitive industry. The market price increases to P', and the equilibrium quantity decreases to Q' in Figure 8-19. In the pretax situation consumer surplus is equal to the sum of areas 1, 2, and 3. The reason for dividing consumer surplus into these different areas will soon be evident. Producer surplus is the sum of areas 4, 5, and 6.

Because the price increases to P' and the quantity demanded falls to Q' after the tax is imposed, consumer surplus decreases to area 1. The decrease in consumer surplus is area 2 (the rectangle) plus area 3 (the triangle). What happens to producer surplus? Producer surplus is equal to area 6. Producers receive P' for all Q' units, but they must pay the sum of area 2 and area 4 to the government in taxes. Area 2 plus area 4 represents a transfer from consumers to the government with producers acting as tax collectors. Therefore, producer surplus is equal to area 6, and producer surplus decreases by area 4 plus area 5.

To sum up, the consumer surplus is now equal to area 1. The government receives a transfer from producers and consumers equal to area 2 plus area 4, and producers receive a surplus equal to area 6. Area 3 represents the loss in consumer surplus because it is not matched by a corresponding increase in tax payments, and area 5 represents the loss in producer surplus. The two triangles are a deadweight loss and are equal to the loss in value that is not offset by an increase in value to some other group. A deadweight loss occurs because the tax reduces output from Q^* to Q'.

A per unit tax reduces the sum of consumer and producer surpluses.

---

[10] Assuming that income effects are negligible.

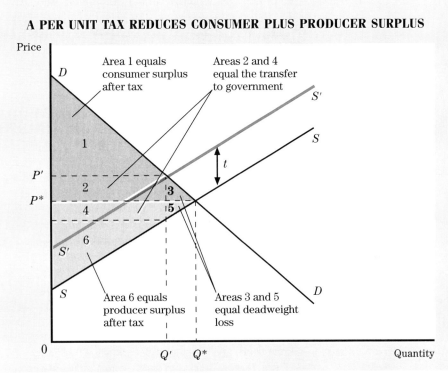

A PER UNIT TAX REDUCES CONSUMER PLUS PRODUCER SURPLUS

Figure 8-19   A per unit tax shifts the supply function and increases the market price to P'. Consumer surplus decreases to area 1. Producer surplus is equal to area 6 since the government collects the sum of areas 2 and 4 from producers. Areas 3 and 5 represent the deadweight loss of a per unit tax.

This analysis indicates that the sum of consumer and producer surpluses is largest when firms act as price takers and there is free entry into and exit from the industry. Under these circumstances the areas between the market demand and supply functions measure the total surplus achieved when the market is competitive.

SUMMARY

- In long-run industry equilibrium each firm has no incentive to change the method and scale of production and no firm has an incentive to enter the industry.
- In short-run industry equilibrium no existing firm desires to produce a different quantity.
- In a constant-cost industry all firms have the same cost functions and the cost function does not shift when industry output changes. The long-run industry

supply function is horizontal in a constant-cost industry. An increase in demand increases industry output but not the long-run equilibrium price.

- An unexpected shift in demand causes short-run profits or losses in the industry. In the short run each firm maximizes profits by equating price to short-run marginal cost. The profits or losses encourage new firms to enter or existing firms to leave the industry. Price and profits decline as new firms enter, or price increases and losses decrease as firms leave.

- The industry supply function has a positive slope in an increasing-cost industry. An increase in market demand increases the long-run equilibrium price and industry output.

- If there are differences in managerial ability, an increase in market demand increases managerial compensation so that each manager captures an economic rent. The firm earns zero profits.

- A cost-reducing innovation causes price to fall as new firms enter the industry using the new technology. Existing firms will not adopt the innovation immediately if the average variable cost function of the old technology lies below the long-run average cost function of the new technology.

- Restricting the entry of firms into an industry through licensing changes the shape of the long-run supply function. A subsequent increase in market demand increases the profits of the holders of licenses. Market price and industry output increase, and each firm produces a larger output at the higher price. A firm will build a larger plant to produce the larger output and operates in the region where there are internal diseconomies of scale.

- A per unit tax increases the market price and reduces industry output. The less elastic the demand function and the more elastic the supply function, the greater the increase in equilibrium price.

- The sum of consumer and producer surpluses is largest when firms act as price takers and there is free entry into and exit out of an industry. Total surplus decreases when the government levies a per unit tax.

KEY TERMS

Long-run industry equilibrium
Constant-cost industry
Short-run industry supply function
The role of profits and losses
External pecuniary economies
Differences in managerial ability
Changing the shape of the supply function through licensing and entry barriers
Maximizing the sum of consumer and producer surpluses

Short-run industry equilibrium
Horizontal industry supply function
Adjustment of an industry to a shift in market demand
Increasing cost industry
Economic rent
Switching over to a new technology
Placing a per unit tax on a competitive industry

REVIEW QUESTIONS

1. What two conditions must be satisfied for an industry to be in long-run equilibrium?
2. What two conditions characterize a constant-cost industry?
3. In the short run a given increase in demand will cause the market price to increase; if the industry is competitive, the magnitude of the price increase will be larger if the firms in the industry were suffering losses before demand increased. Explain why you agree or disagree with this statement.
4. The equilibrium long-run price in a competitive industry must occur in the region where market demand is price-elastic; if market demand is price-inelastic, each firm in the industry can reduce output and increase its total revenue. Explain why you agree or disagree with this statement.
5. The theory of a competitive firm predicts that companies with more efficient managers will operate larger firms than less efficient managers. Explain why you agree or disagree with this statement.
6. Under what conditions will existing firms in an industry immediately adopt a cost-reducing innovation?
7. Placing a per unit tax on an industry or reducing the number of sellers through licensing raises the price of the product and decreases the number of firms in the industry but has no effect on firm size. Explain why you agree or disagree with this statement.
8. When a per unit tax is imposed, the equilibrium price increases, while industry equilibrium and firm output decrease. Explain why you agree or disagree with this statement.
9. The price elasticity of demand is -1.3 in industry A and -4.2 in industry B. The price elasticity of supply is 8.2 in industry A and 0.5 in industry B. If the government levies the same per unit tax in the two industries, in which industry will the price increase be larger?

EXERCISES

1. Use graphs to show how the existing firms in a constant-cost industry adjust in the short and long runs when the market demand function decreases.
2. Managerial ability differs among the firms in an industry. Show the long-run equilibrium price, industry output, and output of the most efficient and the least efficient firms currently operating in the industry. Show the profits of the firm and the compensation of the manager for these two firms.
3. There are two types of firms in a competitive industry: either they are large and produce 1,000 or more units or they are small and produce less than 500 units per year. As a group, the small firms account for 20 percent of industry output.

   Industry observers disagree about the relative efficiency of large and small firms. A recent cost study concluded that differences between the per unit cost of large and small firms are negligible. On the other hand, small firms

drop out of the industry when market demand falls during recessions, while
large firms continue to produce but at somewhat lower volumes. Some industry observers think this indicates that small firms are not as efficient.

The government plans to regulate pollution emissions of large and small
firms by requiring all companies to use equipment that will decrease pollution
emissions. Small firms have petitioned for an exemption, claiming that the
added cost of compliance will drive them out of business. A recent survey of
large companies estimates that total output supplied by large firms will decline
by 15 percent at each price under the new regulations.

   a. Explain why small firms drop out of the industry when market demand
      drops even though large and small firms have the same per unit cost. With
      the aid of graphs show the industry supply functions of (1) large and (2)
      small firms.
   b. If the new regulation applies only to large firms, will the total output of
      large firms be 15 percent smaller than it would be in the absence of the
      new regulation? Explain why or why not. Show how the price of the
      product is determined.
   c. If the new regulation applies only to large firms, total industry output will
      decrease by less than 15 percent because small firms will continue to
      produce what they were producing before. Explain why you agree or dis-
      agree with this statement.

4. A local government passes a law that prohibits additional firms from entering
   a constant-cost industry. Assume that the firms in the industry have U-shaped
   long-run average cost functions and that the industry was in long-run equilibrium before entry was blocked. Show the new long-run equilibrium of the
   industry and a representative firm after market demand increases.

5. An economist suggests that firms are exploiting stockholders by overcompen-
   sating their executives. He claims that the ratio of CEO compensation to the
   compensation of the least skilled worker is higher in a certain industry than
   in other industries. He proposes that all increases in CEO compensation be
   taxed at 39 percent for all firms above a minimum size of q'. His argument is
   that the decrease in compensation will lower the production cost of firms in
   the industry and lower the price of the product. Predict the effects of this
   proposal in an industry where managers differ in ability and show the effect
   of the proposal on price and quantity in the industry.

6. A competitive constant-cost industry is in long-run equilibrium. The firms in
   this industry manufacture a product essential for national security. In response
   to complaints of excess competition, the government announces it will
   purchase only from the existing firms in the industry except under the following conditions: If demand increases so that the price of the product would
   otherwise increase by more than 10 percent, the government will allow
   enough firms to enter so that the price will not increase by more than 10
   percent.

   A congressional committee investigates the firms in the industry and finds
   the profits are excessive. It proposes that a per unit tax equal to the recent 10
   percent price increase be imposed on the industry. It concludes that a per unit

tax of this magnitude will only eliminate the excess profits of firms and will not raise the price of the product.

   a. Suppose demand increases and the government permits enough new firms to enter the industry so that price cannot increase by more than 10 percent. Show the long-run equilibrium position of a representative firm and of the industry and the new long-run industry supply function.

   b. With the use of graphs, show the long-run effects of the proposed per unit tax on the price, industry output, and profits of a representative firm. Do you agree with the claims of the congressional committee?

7. Price declines when demand decreases in an increasing-cost industry or when a technological change occurs. Can you name another variable that decreases when demand declines and increases when a technological change occurs?

8. Suppose that a per unit subsidy of S dollars per unit is offered to manufacturers of a product. Show how the subsidy affects the sum of consumer and producer surpluses.

9. A recent study has found that the average size of a firm increases when the price of a product declines. Which of the models of competitive behavior can explain this?

10. When the yen rises relative to the dollar, the price of cars imported from Japan increases. Because of the rise of the yen against the dollar, U.S. auto companies will be slower to automate factories because they believe they're getting a breather from Japanese competition. Explain why you agree or disagree with this statement.

11. A domestic competitive industry produces a product under increasing cost. Foreign suppliers produce under constant cost and are willing to supply an indefinite amount at the world price of P_w. The price elasticity of demand in the domestic market was recently estimated to be -1. With the aid of graphs show the equilibrium output, q, of a representative domestic supplier, total domestic output, Q_D, and total imports, Q_I.

12. The dependence on foreign imports of a product is a growing political issue. Continuing Exercise 11, two plans are being considered to reduce domestic consumption and total imports by 20 percent each:

   ▪ *Plan 1.* Permit no imports unless accompanied by an import ticket and issue only $0.8Q_I$ import tickets to importers.

   ▪ *Plan 2.* Impose an import duty of t dollars per imported unit.

   a. With the aid of graphs, show how plan 1 affects the combined supply function of domestic and foreign producers, total units consumed, total imports, and domestic output. Will this plan reduce imports and domestic consumption by 20 percent?

   b. How large should the import duty in plan 2 be relative to P_w if total consumption declines by 20 percent?

   c. With the aid of graphs show the effect of plan 2 on the combined supply function of domestic and foreign producers, total units consumed, total imports, and domestic output. Which plan will reduce total imports by a larger amount?

CHAPTER 9

PRICING
UNDER MONOPOLY

* More difficult material.

Unlike Chapter 8, which analyzed a competitive industry with many firms, this chapter considers the price and output in an industry with a single supplier—a pure monopolist. A pure monopolist is not only the sole producer of a product but also sets the price without worrying about the entry of other firms into the market. Consequently, the price policy of a monopolist is not constrained by competition but by the law of demand: The monopolist sells fewer units at a higher price.

This chapter first states the assumptions of the monopoly model and then moves on to explain how a monopolist sets price and output to maximize profits. After presenting the basic theory of monopoly pricing, we extend the theory in several directions, among which are how a monopolist responds to a demand shock and to a cost-reducing innovation and how competition to become a monopolist eliminates profits. We also study the effect of product durability and reach a surprising conclusion about what a monopolist can charge for the durable good. The chapter ends with a comparison of price and output under monopoly and under competition and discusses the social objection to monopoly.

9-1 ASSUMPTIONS OF THE PURE MONOPOLY MODEL

This chapter begins by specifying two rather stringent assumptions if a firm is to behave as a pure monopolist.

1. *Competitors cannot enter the industry.* A pure monopolist has no immediate rivals and determines the quantity and price without fear of attracting other firms to the industry.

2. *No close substitutes.* There are no close substitutes for the product produced by a monopolist. Under the theory of pure monopoly the monopolist does not worry about the effect of its price policy on the price response of firms producing other goods because the other goods are distant substitutes for the monopolist's product.

Pure monopoly rarely occurs, because few industries satisfy these two stringent assumptions completely. Nevertheless, the theory of pure monopoly is useful as a standard or point of reference. The theory indicates what price a monopolist would charge, what quantity it would produce, and the profits it would earn. Chapter 10 considers situations where there are a few firms in a market and why these firms aspire to duplicate the monopolist's price and output policies.

In some industries a firm has a short-run monopoly, but the monopoly erodes eventually with the entry of other firms. Some examples of a short-run monopoly position that eroded with time include DuPont (nylon), Alcoa (aluminum), and the German joint sales agencies of the nineteenth century that permitted firms to coordinate output and price through legally enforced contracts. Another is the New York Stock Exchange which for many years controlled over 90 percent of stock trading on organized exchanges but has lost market share in recent years.

Professional sports provide other examples of monopoly. In each major sport—

baseball, football, hockey, and basketball—there is a single organization that determines the number of teams in each league, competition for players, and other important matters. Infrequently, new leagues are formed and attempt to enter the football, hockey, and basketball markets, but after a time either fail or are merged into a single league. Some economists consider the National Collegiate Athletic Association a monopoly organization because it prevents bidding for high school athletics and prohibits member schools from independently negotiating television contracts.

In some instances, monopoly is a by-product of patent policy. The purpose of patent policy is to foster inventive activity by granting a monopoly for a limited duration—17 years in the United States. Because patent policy prevents firms from quickly copying the inventions of others, a firm is more likely to invest in research and development when the prospects of enjoying the fruits of the effort are greater. In the pharmaceutical industry patent protection is important because drug research is expensive and companies would not make an investment if they could not expect to profit from it. While patent policy promotes innovative activity, it also has a down side—monopoly pricing.

This chapter will have much more to say about the consequences of monopoly than why a monopoly emerges in a particular industry. A theory as to why monopoly emerges is still in the embryonic stage, with much research yet to be completed. Most economists believe monopoly emerges when there are perpetual internal economies of scale, a situation where one firm can produce any output at a lower total cost than two or more firms can, as in a so-called natural monopoly. A monopoly can also emerge when one firm has a large cost advantage over others, so that it can set a profit-maximizing price without attracting other firms to the industry.

9-2   THE MONOPOLIST AS A PRICE MAKER

Because a monopolist is the sole supplier of the product, the monopolist's demand function is the market demand function. Unlike a competitive firm, which takes the market price as given, the monopolist is fully aware that price affects the quantity demanded. The mind-set of a monopolist is completely different from that of a competitive firm. A monopolist is always considering whether the tradeoff between a lower price and a larger quantity demanded will increase or decrease revenue, something a competitive firm never considers. Before determining how a monopolist sets the price and determines quantity, let's explore this mind-set and determine how total revenue changes as the monopolist sells more units.

The Demand Function of a Monopolist

Our starting point is the inverse market demand function of a monopolist. This demand function corresponds to the industry demand function discussed in Chapter 8 since the monopolist supplies the whole market. The monopolist's inverse demand function shows what consumers are willing to pay for each quantity.

$$P = D(Q) \qquad \text{(Inverse Demand Function of a Monopolist)} \qquad \textbf{(9-1a)}$$

The slope of the monopolist's demand function is negative since the quantity demanded increases as the price falls.

$$\frac{\Delta P}{\Delta Q} = \frac{\Delta[D(Q)]}{\Delta Q} < 0 \qquad \textbf{(9-1b)}$$

Figure 9-1 shows that the monopolist can sell more units but only by lowering the price along the demand curve DD. Throughout this chapter it is assumed that the monopolist sells all units at a single price. This means that the monopolist can increase the total units sold only by selling all the units at the lower price. For instance, the monopolist sells Q_1 units at a price of P_1 (point a) and receives P_1Q_1 in total revenue, or the sum of areas 1 and 2 in Figure 9-1. To sell Q_2 units (point b), the monopolist lowers the price to P_2 and receives P_2Q_2 in total revenue, or the sum of areas 2 and 3.

Figure 9-1 illustrates the perpetual tug-of-war that a monopolist faces. Areas 1 and 3 are the source of this tug-of-war. By lowering the price, the monopolist is trading off the additional revenue it receives by selling $Q_2 - Q_1$ more units, because

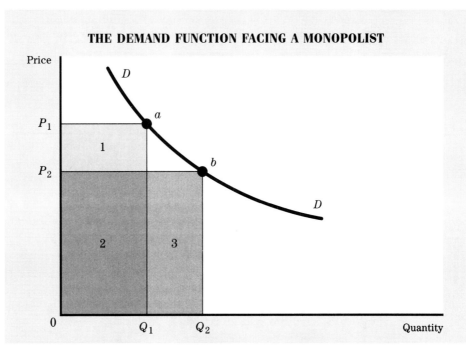

THE DEMAND FUNCTION FACING A MONOPOLIST

Figure 9-1   Because a monopolist faces a downward-sloping demand function, it can increase the quantity demanded from Q_1 to Q_2 by lowering the price from P_1 to P_2. Area 1 measures the loss in revenue because the price is reduced, and area 3 represents the gain in revenue because more units are sold.

more units are sold, against the lower revenue received, because all Q_1 units (which the monopolist could sell at the higher price of P_1) sell for P_2. Area 1 measures the loss in revenue from the Q_1 units because price falls from P_1 to P_2, and area 3 is the gain in revenue from selling $Q_2 - Q_1$ more units at a price of P_2.

Areas 1 and 3 change size as the monopolist lowers price and moves down the demand function. Over one range of prices area 1 wins the tug-of-war, and over another, area 3 wins. Starting with a high price, area 3 is usually greater than area 1, and so total revenue increases when price falls. As the price falls further, there will usually be some price change where area 1 just equals area 3, at which point total revenue does not change. At still lower prices area 1 becomes larger than area 3, and so total revenue decreases. By lowering price and moving down the demand function, a monopolist's total revenue usually changes, first increasing and then decreasing.

The Total and Marginal Revenue Functions

It would be very tedious to determine how total revenue changes by repeatedly comparing the sizes of different rectangles. Fortunately, there is a quicker and more effective way of finding out how total revenue changes when the monopolist sells more units. Economists rely on the marginal revenue function for this determination when more units are sold at a lower price.

You can derive the marginal revenue function by starting with the monopolist's total revenue function. The total revenue received by the monopolist is

$$R = PQ \qquad \text{(Total Revenue of Monopolist)} \qquad (9\text{-}2a)$$

where R is total revenue. Substituting $D(Q)$ for P yields

$$R = D(Q)Q \qquad (9\text{-}2b)$$

$D(Q)$ is the price charged by the monopolist when Q units are sold. Figure 9-2 shows the total revenue function of a monopolist. Initially, total revenue increases as the monopolist lowers the price and sells more units, reaches a maximum when the monopolist sells Q^* units, and then declines when the monopolist lowers price and sells more than Q^* units. As you can see, the monopolist's revenue function is completely different from the linear revenue function of a price-taking competitive firm shown in Figure 7-2. Unlike a competitive firm, a monopolist can spoil the market by selling too many units and reducing total revenue.

Marginal revenue is the slope of the total revenue function, the change in the monopolist's total revenue ΔR when the quantity sold increases by ΔQ, or $\Delta R/\Delta Q$. Figure 9-2 shows that the slope of the total revenue function is positive as long as the quantity sold is less than Q^*, is zero when the quantity sold is Q^* units, and is negative if the firm sells more than Q^* units.

The marginal revenue function shows the change in revenue ΔR when the quantity sold changes by ΔQ.

An expression can be derived for marginal revenue MR at each point on the demand function that relates marginal revenue to the price of the product and the

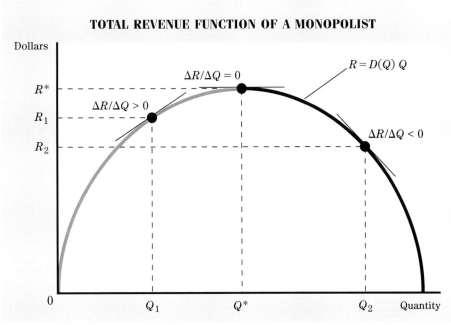

Figure 9-2   Total revenue increases, reaches a maximum, and then declines as the monopolist sells more units. The slope of the total revenue function equals marginal revenue. Marginal revenue is positive when the quantity is less than Q^*, is zero when the quantity sold is Q^*, and is negative when the quantity sold exceeds Q^*.

point price elasticity of demand.[1] To begin, suppose the monopolist changes output by ΔQ so that total revenue changes by

$$\Delta R = P \, \Delta Q + Q \, \Delta P \qquad \text{(Change in Revenue)} \qquad \textbf{(9-3a)}$$

Change in total revenue equals price times change in quantity (or area 3 in Figure 9-1) plus quantity times change in price (or area 1 in Figure 9-1). Dividing both

---

[1] Total revenue equals price times quantity: $R = D(Q)Q$. Marginal revenue is the slope of the total revenue function.

$$\frac{dR}{dQ} = D(Q) + Q\frac{d[D(Q)]}{dQ} = P + Q\frac{dP}{dQ}$$

Multiplying and dividing the right side of P and rearranging the equation for marginal revenue yields

$$\frac{dR}{dQ} = P\left(1 + \frac{Q}{P}\frac{dP}{dQ}\right) = P\left[1 + \frac{1}{(P/Q)(dQ/dP)}\right]$$

The expression for marginal revenue becomes

$$\frac{dR}{dQ} = P\left(1 + \frac{1}{E_P}\right)$$

This equation says that marginal revenue equals the price of the product times a correction factor of $1 + (1/E_P)$ which depends on the point price elasticity of demand.

sides of equation 9-3 by ΔQ results in an expression for $\Delta R/\Delta Q$, or marginal revenue, MR(Q).

$$MR(Q) = P + Q\frac{\Delta P}{\Delta Q} \tag{9-3b}$$

Equation 9-3b says that marginal revenue is $P + Q(\Delta P/\Delta Q)$. The last term is negative since $\Delta P/\Delta Q < 0$ unless $Q = 0$ when MR $= P$. Therefore, marginal revenue is less than the price when $Q > 0$.

$$P > MR \qquad \text{(Price Is Greater than Marginal Revenue)} \tag{9-4}$$

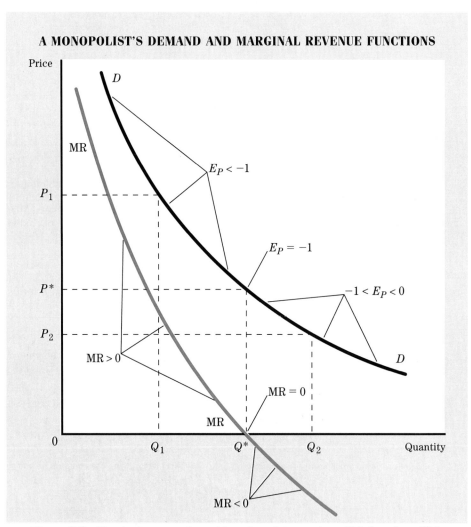

A MONOPOLIST'S DEMAND AND MARGINAL REVENUE FUNCTIONS

Figure 9-3   Marginal revenue is positive when the quantity sold is less than Q^*, is zero when the quantity sold equals Q^*, and is negative when the quantity sold exceeds Q^*. If demand is price-elastic, then marginal revenue is positive. If demand is unit-elastic, marginal revenue is zero and, if demand is price-inelastic, marginal revenue is negative.

Multiplying the right-hand side by P/P and rearranging yields

$$\text{MR}(Q) = P\left(1 + \frac{Q}{P}\frac{\Delta P}{\Delta Q}\right) = P\left[1 + \frac{1}{(P/Q)(\Delta Q/\Delta P)}\right] \qquad \text{(9-5)}$$

Marginal revenue can then be expressed as[2]

$$\text{MR}(Q) = P\left(1 + \frac{1}{E_P}\right) \qquad \text{(9-6)}$$

Equation 9-6 says that marginal revenue can be calculated at each point on the demand function from the price and the price elasticity of demand at a point on the demand function. Marginal revenue equals the price of the product times a correction factor of $1 + (1/E_P)$ which depends on the point price elasticity of demand.

Figure 9-3 shows the demand and the marginal revenue functions. For any Q less than Q^*, demand is price-elastic, and so $E_P < -1$ and $1 + (1/E_P) > 0$. Therefore, equation 9-6 indicates that marginal revenue is positive when demand is price-elastic. Notice that the marginal revenue function in Figure 9-3 lies above the horizontal axis for $Q < Q^*$ because demand is price-elastic. When price is P^*, $E = -1$, and so $1 + (1/E_P) = 0$ and marginal revenue is zero. The marginal revenue function intersects the x axis when $Q = Q^*$ and $P = P^*$. Finally, if the firm sells more than Q^* units, demand becomes price-inelastic, and so $-1 < E_P < 0$ and $1 + (1/E_P) < 0$. Marginal revenue is negative, and so the marginal revenue function lies below the x axis in Figure 9-3 when $Q > Q^*$.

Table 9-1 summarizes the relationship between the price elasticity of demand and marginal revenue for different ranges of the price elasticity.

Measuring the Change in Revenue by the Area under the Marginal Revenue Function

The marginal revenue function is a shorthand way of determining how revenue changes when the quantity sold changes. The area under the marginal revenue function between any two quantities measures the change in the monopolist's revenue when the quantity sold changes from one quantity to another.

For example, the *change* in the firm's revenue resulting from an increase in the quantity sold from Q_1 to Q_2 units is equal to the area under the marginal revenue function between Q_1 and Q_2 or the colored area in Figure 9-4.[3]

---

[2] $E_P = (dQ/dP)(P/Q)$ is the point price elasticity of demand.

[3] The integral of the marginal revenue curve between two quantities, say Q_0 and Q_1, is the area under the marginal revenue function.

$$R(Q_2) - R(Q_1) = \int_{Q_1}^{Q_2} \frac{dR(Q)}{dQ}\, dQ$$

The area under the marginal revenue function from Q_1 to Q_2 is the difference between the total revenue from selling Q_2 units and the total revenue from selling Q_1 units, or the increase in total revenue due to the increase in units sold from Q_1 to Q_2 units. If $Q_1 = 0$, then $R(Q_1) = R(0) = 0$. Integrating from 0 to Q_2 gives the total revenue from selling Q_2 units.

Table 9-1   PRICE ELASTICITY AND MARGINAL REVENUE

PRICE ELASTICITY OF DEMAND, E_P (1)	VALUE OF PRICE ELASTICITY (2)	SIGN OF CORRECTION FACTOR, $1 + (1/E_P)$ (3)	MARGINAL REVENUE, $\Delta R/\Delta Q$ OR SLOPE OF TOTAL REVENUE FUNCTION (4)
Price-elastic	$E_P < -1$	> 0	MR > 0
Unitary	$E_P = -1$	$= 0$	MR $= 0$
Price-inelastic	$-1 < E_P < 0$	< 0	MR < 0

> The change in total revenue resulting from increasing the quantity sold from Q_1 to Q_2 units is equal to the area under the marginal revenue function between Q_1 and Q_2 units.

A simple numerical example demonstrates why the area under the marginal revenue function between any two quantities is equal to the change in total revenue. Consider unit changes in the quantity sold. Table 9-2 shows quantity demanded in column 1, price in column 2, total revenue in column 3, marginal revenue in column 4, and sum of marginal revenues up to and including the last unit sold in column 5. Summing the marginal revenue values is equivalent to adding the areas under the marginal revenue function.

If the firm sells just 1 unit, it charges a price of $100 and receives $100 in total revenue. Marginal revenue obviously equals $100. Column 5 shows the marginal revenue of the first unit sold. The firm sells 2 units if the price is $90, and total revenue is $180. Marginal revenue from selling the second unit is only $80. Summing the marginal revenue from selling the first unit ($100) and the second unit ($80) yields the total revenue of selling 2 units, or $180. The area under the marginal revenue function between $Q = 0$ and $Q = 2$ is equal to the increase in the firm's revenue when the quantity sold increases from 0 to 2 units. We multiply and add, $(1 \times \$100) + (1 \times \$80)$, to obtain $180.

The area under the marginal revenue function between 2 and 4 units represents the additional revenue received when the sales of the firm increase from 2 to 4 units. In Table 9-2 the increase in total revenue by increasing the quantity sold from 2 to 4 units is $45 + $15 = $60. The $45 represents the area under the marginal revenue function when the quantity sold increases from 2 to 3 units, and the $15 represents the area under the marginal revenue function when the quantity sold increases from 3 to 4 units. The monopolist's revenues increase by $60 when the quantity sold increases from 2 to 4 units.

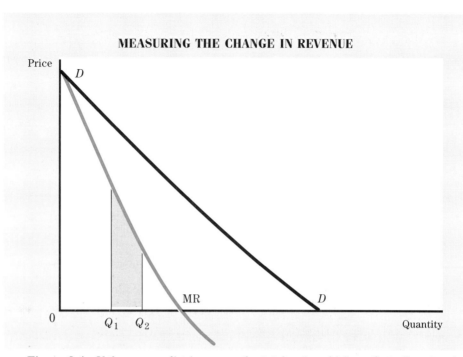

MEASURING THE CHANGE IN REVENUE

Figure 9-4   If the monopolist increases the total units sold from Q_1 to Q_2 units, the shaded area under the marginal revenue function between the two quantities represents the increase in total revenue.

In summary, the area under the marginal revenue function measures the change in the firm's revenue resulting from increasing the quantity sold from Q_1 to Q_2 units. This result will be used shortly to determine how the profits of a monopolist change when it sells another unit.

9-3   THE THEORY OF MONOPOLY PRICING

With these preliminaries out of the way, let us now consider how a profit-maximizing monopolist determines which price and quantity maximize total profits. As in the analysis of a competitive firm, the goal of the firm is to maximize profits. For the present this assumption can be justified, as in the analysis of a competitive firm, by noting that an effective capital market disciplines any management that strays from profit maximization. Management practices and the performance of the firm are under scrutiny by other firms and substantial shareholders who hope to purchase inefficiently operated firms, replace the existing managers with more efficient management, and eventually raise profits. For the moment let's simply assume that the monopolist maximizes profits and defer discussing this question until Chapter 11.

Table 9-2   USING THE AREA UNDER THE MARGINAL REVENUE FUNCTION TO MEASURE THE CHANGE IN REVENUE

QUANTITY DEMANDED, Q (1)	PRICE, P ($) (2)	TOTAL REVENUE, PQ ($) (3)	MARGINAL REVENUE, MR ($) (4)	SUM OF MARGINAL REVENUES ($) (5)
1	100	100	100	100
2	90	180	80	180
3	75	225	45	225
4	60	240	15	240

The expression for long-run total profits of a monopolist is

$$\text{Total profit} = \text{Revenue} - \text{Long-run total cost}$$

$$\pi(Q) = D(Q)Q - C_L(Q) \qquad \text{(Total Profits of Monopolist)} \qquad \textbf{(9-7)}$$

where $\pi(Q)$ represents total profits. Total profit equals total revenue less long-run total cost. The monopolist selects output Q (and indirectly price P through the inverse demand function) to maximize total profits.

We can find the quantity that maximizes total profits from either Figure 9-5a or 9-5b. In Figure 9-5a total revenue and total cost are on the vertical axis, and quantity is on the horizontal axis. As you can see, total profits, $\pi(Q)$, increase at first, reach a maximum, decline, and eventually turn into losses.

To find the profit-maximizing output, the monopolist compares the marginal revenue from selling another unit with the marginal cost of producing the last unit. How much more revenue does the monopolist receive from selling one more unit and how much more cost does the monopolist incur in producing one more unit? If MR $>$ MC$_L$, then profits increase, but decrease if MR $<$ MC$_L$. A profit-maximizing monopolist expands output until marginal revenue equals long-run marginal cost.[4]

---

[4] A profit maximum requires

$$\frac{d[\pi(Q)]}{dQ} = D(Q) + Q\frac{d[D(Q)]}{dQ} - \frac{d[C_L(Q)]}{dQ} = 0$$

or $\qquad D(Q) + Q\frac{d[D(Q)]}{dQ} = \frac{d[C_L(Q)]}{dQ} \qquad$ or $\qquad \text{MR}(Q) = \text{MC}_L(Q)$

For a profit maximum, the second derivative of profits with respect to Q must be negative.

$$\frac{d^2[\pi(Q)]}{dQ^2} = 2\frac{d[D(Q)]}{dQ} + Q\frac{d^2[D(Q)]}{dQ^2} - \frac{d^2[C_L(Q)]}{dQ^2} < 0$$

The first two terms on the right-hand side of the equation represent the slope of the marginal revenue function. The last term on the right-hand side is the slope of the marginal cost curve. The difference between the slope of the marginal revenue function and the slope of the marginal cost curve must be negative at the output where marginal revenue equals marginal cost. The marginal revenue function must cut through the marginal cost function from above.

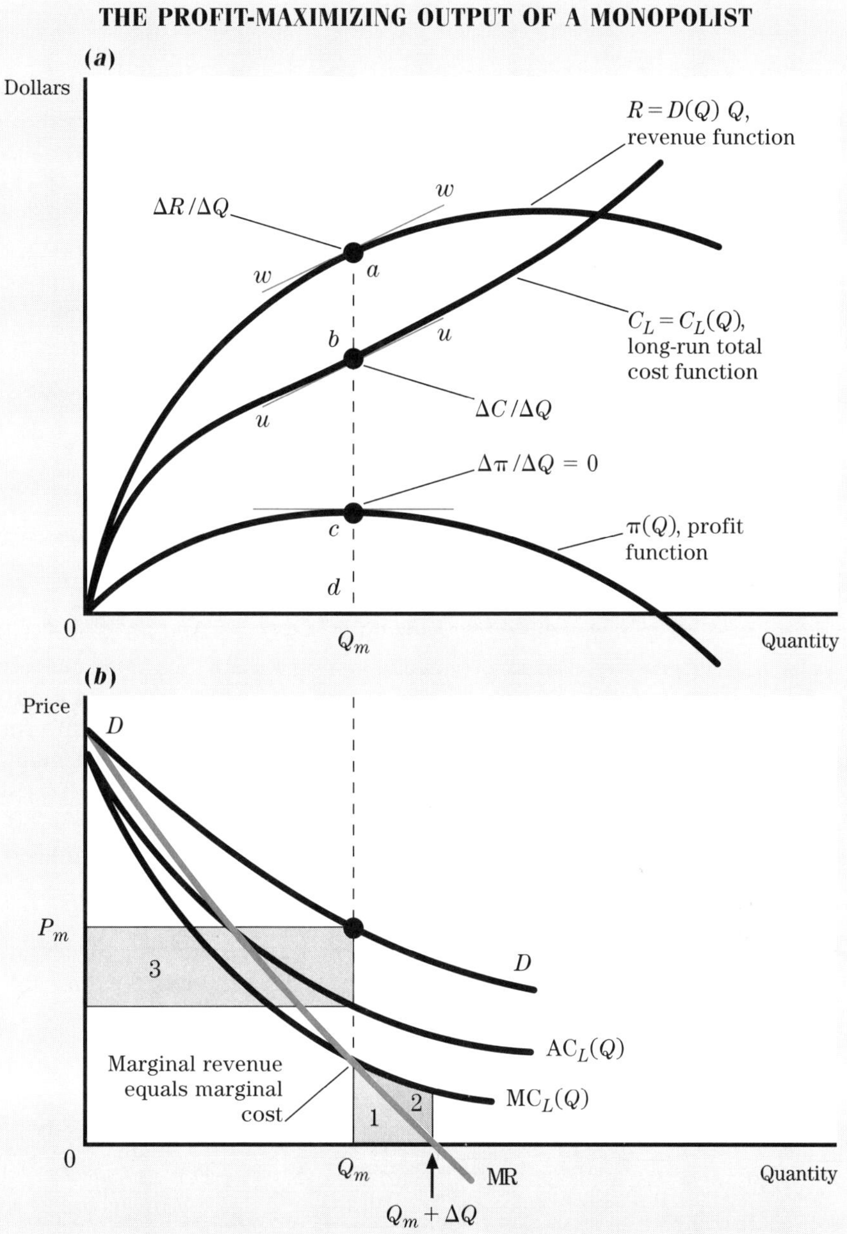

THE PROFIT-MAXIMIZING OUTPUT OF A MONOPOLIST

(a)

(b)

Figure 9-5 A monopolist maximizes profits by producing Q_m where marginal revenue equals marginal cost. In (a) marginal revenue equals the slope of the total revenue function and marginal cost equals the slope of the total cost function. The tangents ww and uu have the same slopes. In (b) the monopolist's total profits decrease if the monopolist increases output to $Q_m + \Delta Q$. The additional cost of producing ΔQ equals the sum of areas 1 and 2, the area under the marginal cost function. The additional revenue from the sale of ΔQ units equals area 1, the area under the marginal revenue function.

$$MR(Q) = \frac{\Delta C_L(Q)}{\Delta Q} = MC_L(Q) \qquad\qquad \textbf{(9-8)}$$

A monopolist selects an output where the marginal revenue obtained from selling the last unit equals the marginal cost of producing the last unit.

In Figure 9-5a a monopolist maximizes profits by producing Q_m units where marginal revenue equals marginal cost. The equality of MR and MC means that the slope of the total revenue function equals the slope of the total cost function when $Q = Q_m$. Therefore, the tangent ww to the total revenue function has the same slope as the tangent uu to the total cost function when $Q = Q_m$. If the monopolist produces Q_m units, monopoly profit equals either the distance ab or the distance cd on the profit function.

The same conclusion can be reached from the information in Figure 9-5b which shows the monopolist's demand, marginal revenue, and long-run average and marginal cost functions. The monopolist reaps maximum profits equal to area 3 by producing Q_m units where marginal revenue equals marginal cost.

If the monopolist maximizes total profits by producing Q_m units, then profits decline if output is increased from Q_m to $Q_m + \Delta Q$. To demonstrate this, we must show that the additional revenue received is less than the additional cost incurred when output increases by ΔQ. Area 1 measures the additional revenue received, and the sum of areas 1 and 2 measures the additional cost of producing ΔQ units. Since the additional cost is greater than the additional revenue, total profits decrease by area 2 when the monopolist increases output by ΔQ. By using a similar argument, you should be able to show that profits decrease if the monopolist produces less than Q_m. Consequently, the monopolist maximizes total profits by producing an output where $MR = MC_L$.

The condition in which maximum profits occur when marginal revenue equals marginal cost has two hidden implications. To uncover these hidden implications first substitute $P[1 + (1/E_P)]$ for marginal revenue in equation 9-8:

$$MR = \frac{\Delta C_L(Q)}{\Delta Q} = MC_L \qquad\qquad \textbf{(9-9a)}$$

$$P\left(1 + \frac{1}{E_P}\right) = MC_L$$

By dividing both sides by MC_L and then by $1 + (1/E_P)$, the rearranged equation becomes

$$\frac{P}{MC_L} = \frac{1}{1 + (1/E_P)} \qquad\qquad \textbf{(9-9b)}$$

Equation 9-9b says that the ratio of monopoly price to marginal cost depends on the price elasticity of demand. The more elastic the demand function at the profit-maximizing price, the smaller the ratio of price to marginal cost. For example, suppose there are two demand functions where one demand function has a price elasticity of -50 and the other has a price elasticity of -2 at the monopoly price. The accompanying table shows the ratio of monopoly price to marginal cost in the two industries.

PRICE ELASTICITY	$1/E_P$	P/MC_L
-50	-0.02	1.02
-2	-0.5	2.0

The price policies of the monopolists in the two industries are quite different. When the market demand function is very price-elastic ($E_P = -50$), the profit-maximizing monopoly price is just 2 percentage points above marginal cost. In the other industry, where demand is less elastic ($E_P = -2$), the monopoly price is twice the marginal cost. The monopolist is able to elevate price well above the marginal cost. Therefore, the more elastic the monopolist's demand function in the vicinity of the monopoly price, the smaller the percentage markup over marginal cost. These two situations can be illustrated with graphs. Figure 9-6*a* shows a market where de-

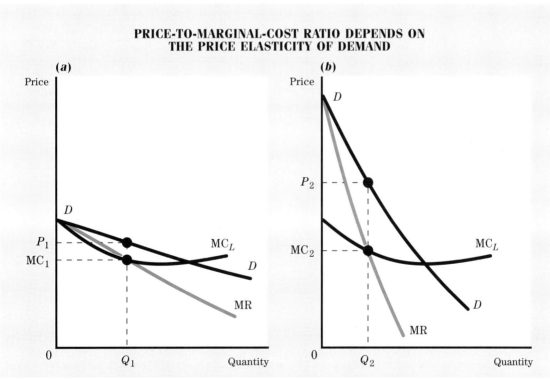

PRICE-TO-MARGINAL-COST RATIO DEPENDS ON THE PRICE ELASTICITY OF DEMAND

Figure 9-6   The price-to-marginal-cost ratio is lower in (*a*) because demand is more price-elastic at the price of P_1 in (*a*) than at the price of P_2 in (*b*).

mand is more price-elastic at the monopoly price and where the markup over marginal cost is smaller than in the market shown in Figure 9-6*b*.

> The greater the price elasticity of demand, the smaller the markup of price over marginal cost.

The second hidden implication is that a monopolist will set the monopoly price at a point along the demand function where demand is price-elastic. The right-hand side of equation 9-6 is marginal cost which must be positive. For marginal revenue to be positive, $1 + (1/E_P)$ must be positive, and this requires that E_P be less than -1. Therefore, the theory of monopoly pricing implies that a pure monopolist will set a price on the demand function where demand is price-elastic. This point is often unappreciated by the student who casually and mistakenly refers to an inelastic demand of a monopolist. Demand is price-elastic at the profit-maximizing monopoly price.

> A profit-maximizing monopolist always operates along the demand function where demand is price-elastic.

APPLICATION 9-1

Are Firms in the Cigarette and Oil Industries Monopolists?

Many individuals, industry experts or otherwise, believe the demand for cigarettes and gasoline is price-inelastic. A reasonable inference is that the average percentage reduction in the quantity demanded will be less than the average percentage

Table 9-3   ESTIMATES OF THE LONG-RUN PRICE ELASTICITY OF DEMAND

INDUSTRY	SOURCE OF ESTIMATE	ESTIMATED VALUE OF LONG-RUN PRICE ELASTICITY
Cigarettes	Becker, Grossman and Murphy (1991)	-0.7 to -0.8
Oil	MacAvoy (1982)	-0.29
	Griffin (1979)	-0.71 to -0.85
	Marquez (1984)	-0.25

Source: Cigarettes: Gary Becker, Michael Grossman, and Kevin M. Murphy, "Rational Addiction and the Effect of Price on Consumption," Center for the Study of the Economy and the State, Working Paper No. 68, February, 1991. Oil: Paul MacAvoy, *Crude Oil Prices as Determined by OPEC and Market Fundamentals*, Balinger Press, Cambridge, Mass., 1982; James Griffin, *Energy Conservation in the OECD: 1980 to 2000*, Balinger Press, Cambridge, Mass., 1979; Jaime R. Marquez, *Oil Price Effects and OPEC's Pricing Policy*, Lexington Books, Lexington, Mass., 1984.

increase in price if the price of either a pack of cigarettes or a gallon of gasoline increases. There is considerable statistical support for these beliefs. Table 9-3 shows estimates of the long-run price elasticity of demand for cigarettes and oil from recent studies.

Demand studies by economists find that the long-run price elasticity of demand is between -1 and 0, and so demand is price-inelastic in the vicinity of the market price for these goods.

Along with the conviction that the demand for these products is price-inelastic is the strongly held view that the firms in these two industries act like a monopolist, by coordinating their price and output policies to raise price and to maximize profits. Since demand is price-inelastic, the cigarette and oil firms get together in each industry and raise price to the monopoly price without suffering a large relative decline in quantity demanded.

What is wrong with this type of reasoning? We concluded that a profit-maximizing monopolist never operates in a region of the demand function where demand is price-inelastic because this implies that marginal revenue is negative. Figure 9-7 shows a monopolist's total revenue function. When the monopolist sells Q_2 units, total revenue is R^*. Envision the total revenue function as being shaped

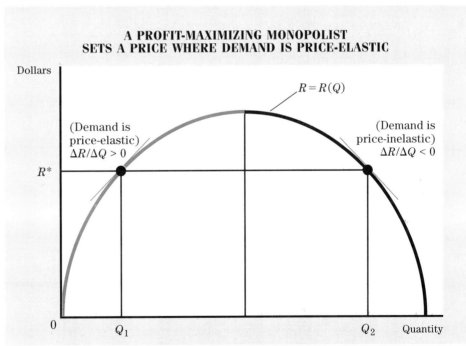

Figure 9-7 If the monopolist produces Q_2 units, total revenue equals R^*, and demand is price-inelastic. The monopolist could receive the same total revenue by producing only Q_1 units. Total profits are higher when the monopolist sells only Q_1 units because total cost of producing a smaller quantity must be lower.

like a hill with the monopolist producing a quantity on the right side of the hill. Because the slope of the total revenue function is negative when the firm is selling Q_2 units, demand is price-inelastic and marginal revenue is negative. Total revenue decreases when quantity sold increases. The monopolist can receive the same revenue R^* by producing Q_1 units, a smaller quantity. While total revenue is the same whether the monopolist produces Q_1 or Q_2, the total cost is smaller when Q_1 units are produced and total profit is higher. Therefore, a profit-maximizing monopolist will operate on the left side of the hill where total revenue increases when more units are sold by lowering the price. Demand is price-elastic, and marginal revenue is positive on the left-hand side of the hill.

If the firms in the cigarette and oil industries behave collectively as a profit-maximizing monopolist would, the price elasticity of demand should not be inelastic, for that is inconsistent with profit-maximizing behavior. One cannot claim that the demand for each of these products is price-inelastic and that the firms in each of these industries get together and act like a profit-maximizing monopolist. It appears that the oil and cigarette firms are unable to coordinate their policies effectively and to charge a monopoly price. If they do get together, they do so imperfectly. They appear to be operating on the right side of the revenue hill. Chapter 10 examines why this might be so.

APPLICATION 9-2

Using a Quota to Create a Partial Monopolist

In a market that would be monopolized except for the discipline of import competition, the sole domestic producer would like to limit imports and thereby become a partial monopoly.

The theory of a competitive industry and that of simple monopoly can be used to analyze this situation and show how a quota affects price and output. Assume a sole domestic producer has the long-run average and marginal cost functions shown in Figure 9-8a. Figure 9-8b shows that foreign suppliers are capable of supplying indefinite quantities of the product to the American market at a price of P_I. It is this foreign supply that prevents the sole domestic supplier from raising the price in the American market. In Figure 9-8c the market demand in the United States is DD, and the long-run supply function of the American producer and the foreign suppliers is $S_L a S_L$. For any price between the minimum long-run average cost function of the domestic producer and P_I, the domestic firm would be the only supplier. At P_I foreign suppliers are willing to supply an indefinite quantity. In a competitive market the equilibrium price is P_I, and total consumption is Q_c. The sole domestic producer supplies Q_d units, and total imports are $Q_c - Q_d$.

Suppose the domestic producer persuades Congress to impose a quota equal to the current quantity of imports, $Q_c - Q_d$. How does the quota change the demand function facing the domestic firm? Figure 9-8b shows that the foreign supply func-

USING A QUOTA TO CREATE A PARTIAL MONOPOLY

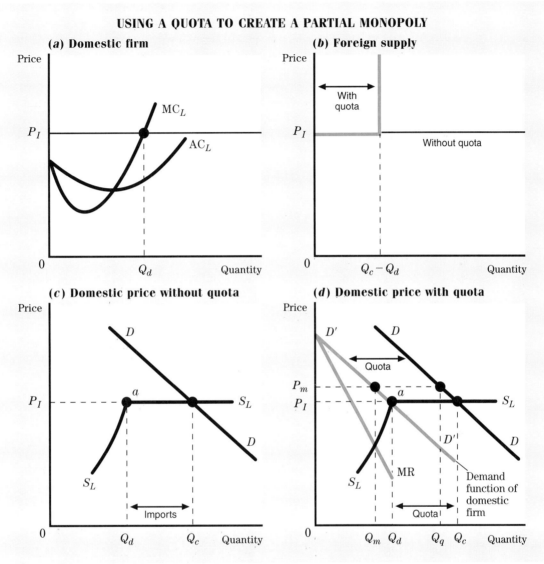

Figure 9-8   The government converts a competitive industry into a partial monopoly by imposing a quota on imports. When imports are unrestricted, the domestic firm produces Q_d. When imports are limited to $Q_c - Q_d$, the demand facing the domestic firm becomes $D'D'$. The domestic firm maximizes profits by producing Q_m units and increases the price to P_m. The total quantity sold by the domestic firm plus foreign firms is Q_q.

tion becomes vertical because foreign firms can only supply $Q_c - Q_d$ units if the price is P_I or higher. In Figure 9-8d the demand function facing the domestic firm is $D'D'$ up to the quantity Q_d, or the quantity demanded less the quota. $D'D'$ shows the quantity the domestic firm can sell at each price. For example, if the price is P_m, the residual quantity demanded is Q_m units, the difference between the total quantity demanded and the import quota. Therefore, the domestic firm knows the quantity demanded for its product will be Q_m units when the price is P_m, and this is one point on its demand function $D'D'$. At any price less than P_I, the foreign supply drops to zero, and so the firm's demand function jumps across and becomes DD at prices less than P_I.

The domestic firm behaves as a partial monopolist and maximizes profits by selling Q_m units at a price of P_m where the marginal revenue from its demand function intersects its marginal cost function. Notice that the foreign producers who have a quota sell their quantity at P_m and are better off with the quota than without it, as is the domestic firm. For example, because American automobile companies raised the domestic price, Japanese auto companies who were already selling in the United States benefited when the Japanese government, at the urging of the Reagan administration, imposed a voluntary export restraint that resembles a quota. In terms of this analysis a quota transforms the domestic market from a competitive industry into a partial monopoly where the price and profits of the foreign suppliers and the domestic producer increase immediately.

9-4 ADJUSTING FROM ONE LONG-RUN EQUILIBRIUM TO ANOTHER

Just as a competitive industry adapts to a shift in demand, so too will a monopolist. Unlike a competitive firm, a monopolist influences the adjustment through its price and output policy. To illustrate the short- and long-run adjustments, let's trace out the monopolist response to an increase in demand.

Initially, the monopolist is selling Q_1 units at a price of P_1 as shown in Figure 9-9. The monopolist produces Q_1 units at lowest cost using a plant with a short-run average cost function AC_S and a marginal cost function MC_S. Here AC_S is tangent to the long-run average cost function AC_L when $Q = Q_1$. The monopolist's profits are equal to area 1. When demand increases from DD to $D'D'$, the monopolist makes do with its existing plant in the short run. It increases output to Q_S units where the new marginal revenue function MR' intersects the short-run marginal cost function. Price increases to P_S, and short-run profits are equal to area *efgh*.

The monopolist can increase profits by still more in the long run by expanding plant size. Figure 9-10 shows that the new marginal revenue function MR' intersects the long-run marginal cost function at a quantity of Q_2 units. Therefore, when the monopolist expands, it builds a larger plant that produces Q_2 units at lowest total cost. Figure 9-10 shows the new short-run average cost function AC_S' and the short-

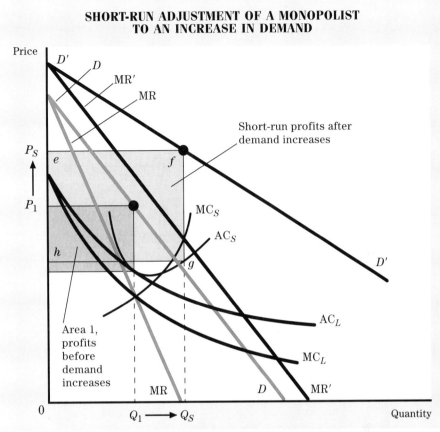

**SHORT-RUN ADJUSTMENT OF A MONOPOLIST
TO AN INCREASE IN DEMAND**

Figure 9-9 Before demand increases, the monopolist produces Q_1 units and sells each one at a price of P_1. Profits are equal to the cross-hatched area. After demand increases to $D'D'$, the monopolist increases output to Q_S where marginal revenue of the new demand function equals short-run marginal cost. The price rises to P_S. Total profits increase and equal rectangle *efgh*.

run marginal cost function MC_S' of the larger plant. Again, the short-run average cost function of the larger plant is just tangent to the long-run average cost function when the monopolist produces Q_2 units. In the long run the monopolist lowers the price from P_S to P_2, and profits equal area *abcd*. The monopolist earns higher profits in the long run since area *abcd* is greater than area *efgh*.

To summarize, a monopolist adjusts to an increase in demand along the same lines that a competitive industry does. In the short run the firm produces an output where marginal revenue equals short-run marginal cost with a given plant. In the long run, when firm size is variable, the monopolist produces a quantity where the new marginal revenue function intersects the long-run marginal cost function.

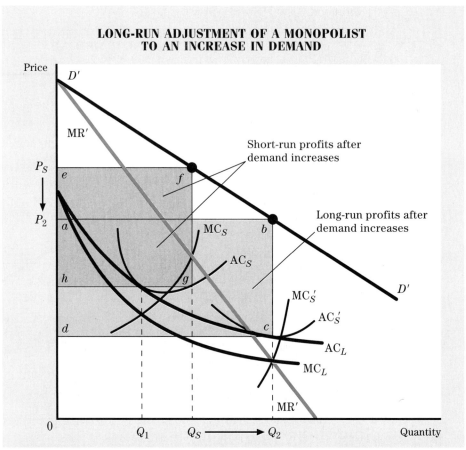

Figure 9-10   After demand increases, the monopolist produces Q_S units in the short run and sells each unit at a price of P_S. After the firm must replace its plant and equipment, it will build a larger plant that produces Q_2 units at the lowest total cost since marginal revenue equals long-run marginal cost when the firm produces Q_2 units. Total profits in the long run are equal to area *abcd*.

*9-5   ADOPTION OF A COST-REDUCING INNOVATION[5]

As in a competitive industry, the cost function of a monopolist can change unexpectedly. This section explores how a monopolist reacts to a cost-reducing innovation. Unlike a competitive firm, a monopolist does not have to worry that it will fall behind if a rival firm adopts a cost-reducing innovation since the monopolist has no rivals. Therefore, it might appear that a monopolist would adopt a cost-reducing innovation less readily than a competitive firm would. However, this reasoning is faulty. A profit-maximizing monopolist has the same incentive to

---

[5] This section borrows from the unpublished writings of R. L. Bishop.

introduce the innovation because it reduces the cost of production and thereby increases profits.

This analysis focuses on the speed with which a monopolist adopts the new technology. A monopolist must decide whether it should scrap the existing plant and equipment immediately or whether it should wait until the old plant wears out.

If this sounds familiar, it is because the monopolist makes the same decision as a competitive firm does. Because this analysis compares a monopolist's response to a cost-reducing innovation to the response of firms in a competitive industry, certain assumptions are adopted that make the two situations analogous. In the previous analysis of a competitive industry, the industry was a constant-cost industry where the long-run industry supply function was horizontal. To compare apples with apples, we assume that the long-run average and marginal cost functions of the monopolist are horizontal. Perhaps the easiest way to think about this is to assume that the monopolist operates a multiplant firm with identical plants. Each plant is comparable to an individual firm in the analysis of a competitive industry. The monopolist's long-run average and marginal cost functions are horizontal because the monopolist simply builds more equally efficient plants in the long run to produce a larger output. With this interpretation we can directly compare the analysis of the adoption of a cost-cutting innovation by a monopolist with the analysis of a competitive industry in Chapter 8.

Figure 9-11a shows the long-run average cost function AC_L of one representative plant that uses the existing technology. The monopolist operates each plant at the minimum point of its long-run cost function so that each plant produces q_0 units at a minimum long-run average cost of AC_0^*. In Figure 9-11c the demand function is DD, and the marginal revenue function is MR. The monopolist sells Q_0 units where the marginal revenue function MR intersects the long-run marginal cost function MC_L and charges P_1. To produce Q_0 at lowest total cost, the monopolist builds m plants so that each one operates at the minimum point of its long-run cost function and $mq_0 = Q_0$. Figure 9-11a shows each plant's short-run average AC_S and marginal cost MC_S functions.

The monopolist has m plants, and each has the short-run marginal cost function MC_S in Figure 9-11a. In the short run the total cost of producing any quantity is minimized by allocating production among its plants so that all m plants have the same short-run marginal cost. (If you need to refresh your memory, re-read Section 6-4 of Chapter 6.) The monopolist's short-run marginal cost function MC_S is the horizontal summation of the short-run marginal cost functions of the m plants. In Figure 9-11c MC_S is the monopolist's marginal cost of increasing output in the short run.

After a cost-reducing innovation becomes available, the long-run average and marginal cost functions of a new plant become $AC_L^{(\text{new})}$ and $MC_L^{(\text{new})}$ in Figure 9-11b. At each quantity the long-run average cost of the new plant lies below the long-run average cost of a plant that uses the older technology. Starting from scratch, the monopolist prefers to use the new technology in all of its plants. However, the monopolist is not starting from scratch because it already has m operating plants. As in the analysis of a competitive industry, assume that the

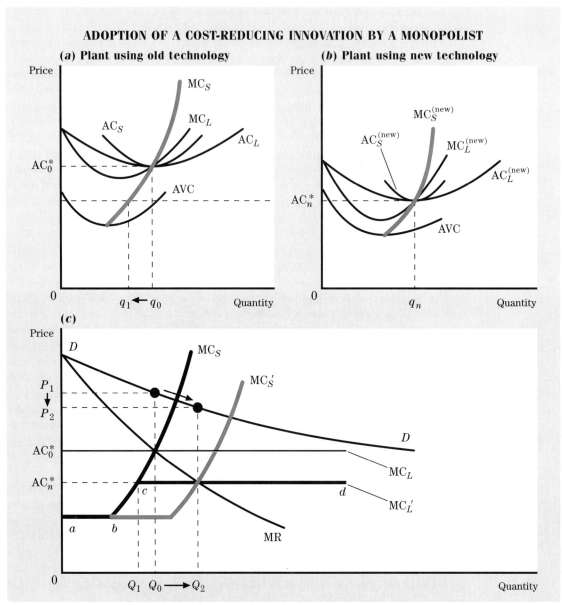

Figure 9-11   A monopolist will expand output and lower price when a cost-reducing innovation becomes available. The price declines from P_1 to P_2, and the quantity produced increases to Q_2 where marginal revenue equals the modified long-run marginal cost function. The monopolist produces $Q_2 - Q_1$ with new plants using the new technology. Q_1 units are produced by plants using the old technology. These plants are later replaced by plants using the new technology.

average variable cost function of the old plant lies below the long-run average cost function of a plant using the new technology. Therefore, it is cheaper for the monopolist to produce q_n units with an old plant than with a new plant, and so it continues to use the m old plants until they wear out.

> A monopolist will continue to use the old technology if the average variable cost function of the plant with the old technology lies below the long-run average cost function of the plant with the new technology.

Although the monopolist continues to use the old plants, this does not mean that it does not build any new plants. Once the new technology becomes available, the marginal cost of expanding output is the new long-run marginal cost function MC'_L. The monopolist's pseudo long-run marginal cost function is the horizontal summation of the short-run marginal cost functions of the m old plants along MC_S up to the minimum long-run average cost function of the new plant, AC^*_n. At AC^*_n the monopolist can expand output along MC'_L by building more new plants and operating each one at q_n. Therefore, the monopolist's new pseudo long-run marginal cost function is *abcd* in Figure 9-11*c*.

All the tools are now in place to analyze the monopolist's response to a cost-reducing innovation. At the initial output Q_0 marginal revenue exceeds the new long-run marginal cost of MC'_L. The monopolist can increase profits by increasing output to Q_2 units where MR equals MC'_L. To produce Q_2 units at minimum total cost, the monopolist must make sure that marginal cost is the same for all the old plants and all the new plants that are built. This is accomplished by reducing the output of each old plant to q_1 (Figure 9-11*a*) so that the short-run marginal cost of each old plant equals the long-run marginal cost of a new plant when the new plant produces q_n units at the minimum long-run average of $AC^*_n = MC^*_n$. Because the old plants reduce their outputs, the monopolist adds more new plants to take up the slack. Therefore, the total output of the m old plants falls to Q_1, and the total output of all new plants is $Q_2 - Q_1$. By assigning Q_1 units to the m old plants and $Q_2 - Q_1$ units to the new plants, the monopolist produces Q_2 units at minimum total cost. After the new plants become operational, the monopolist's new short-run marginal cost function MC'_S is the horizontal sum of the short-run marginal cost functions of the m old plants and of the new plants, so that it intersects MC'_L and MR at $Q = Q_2$.

Because of the new technology, the monopolist's long-run marginal cost of expanding output is lower now than in the past. So it produces more units and reduces price to P_2. This analysis suggests that a monopolist has the same incentive as a competitive industry to adopt a cost-reducing innovation, and it does so as soon as it can. In this regard the incentives that lead new competitive firms to enter the industry with new technology apply equally to the monopolist. Instead of the entry of new firms, entry takes the form of new plants that the monopolist builds. As in the analysis of a competitive industry, the monopolist ultimately replaces the m old plants with new plants once they wear out. During this conversion process the price remains at P_2 since the total quantity produced by the monopolist remains at Q_2 units.

In summary, this analysis suggests that a monopolist will not delay in introducing a cost-reducing innovation because it is not in its interest to do so. In this regard the behavior of a monopolist is qualitatively no different from that of firms in a competitive industry.

9-6 COMPETING TO BE A MONOPOLIST

This chapter has assumed that the firm is a monopolist and has not asked how it came to be one; however, this is a little artificial. If it is profitable to be a monopolist, firms will strive to become one. This rivalry can take many forms. For example, when a government issues a franchise that gives a firm the sole operating authority in a market, firms will go out of their way to secure the franchise. A cable franchise to service a local community can be very profitable. Rivalry among potential hopefuls is usually fierce as each aspirant lobbies, wines and dines officials, contributes to reelection campaigns, and develops market research studies. Another example is a research and development (R&D) race to become a monopolist. Here the rivalry takes the form of competition to be the first firm that introduces a new product in an industry. Firms compete by investing in research, perhaps to find a more effective drug to prevent asthma or a better-tasting, lower-fat soup or dessert.

A simple model of this rivalry to become a monopolist will be developed here. In this model firms compete to become a monopolist by spending more on R&D. In the context of the model, n firms enter a research and development contest. By spending more on R&D, each one improves its chances of introducing a new product before any other competitor. The winner is the firm that introduces the new product first. For example, a drug manufacturer may increase R&D expenditures to gain approval from the U.S. Food and Drug Administration for a new drug that eases the pain from migraine headaches before its rivals can get a competing drug on the market.

The model assumes that the winner of the race will have a monopoly on the product for a single year and charge the monopoly price during that year. The next year the race will begin anew with n firms (not necessarily the same n firms) again competing through new research and development projects to develop another new product. All n firms presumably have the same chance to win the race if they spend the same amount on R&D. If any firm spends less than the others, its probability of winning dwindles to zero. Because n firms are in the race, the probability of any one of them winning is $1/n$ if each spends the same amount. For example, each firm has a probability of winning of $\frac{1}{3}$ if three firms spend the same amount on R&D.

One question of interest concerns how much each firm spends on research and development annually. To answer this question, we must first derive an expression for the expected profits of the firm. The probability that any one firm will win the race is $1/n$ as long as all firms spend the same amount on R&D. The annual net profits of the winning firm are $\pi_m - r$, where π_m is monopoly profits before deducting R&D expenses and r represents the annual R&D expenditures of the firm. In Figure 9-12 DD is the monopolist's demand curve and AC_L and MC_L are the firm's long-run average and marginal cost functions exclusive of R&D expenditures. If a firm wins the race and introduces a new product, it will charge P_m and earn profits of π_m. The probability that a firm will lose the race is $(n - 1)/n$, and the firm's annual losses are r.

Chapter 3 introduced the concept of expected income and considered the decision to purchase insurance. Expected profit of a firm is a similar concept. It is defined as the probability of winning times the net profits earned if a firm wins, plus the probability of losing the race times the loss.

Expected profits = (Probability of winning $\times$ Net profits)
$$+ \text{(Probability of losing} \times \text{Losses)}$$

> Expected profit is the product of the probability of an event occurring and the return from the event summed over all possible events.

The expression for expected profit is

$$E\pi = (\pi_m - r)\frac{1}{n} + (-r)\frac{n-1}{n} \qquad \text{(Expected Profits)} \qquad \textbf{(9-10a)}$$

$$= \frac{\pi_m}{n} - \left(\frac{1}{n} + \frac{n-1}{n}\right)r$$

$$= \frac{\pi_m}{n} - r \qquad\qquad\qquad\qquad\qquad\qquad \textbf{(9-10b)}$$

The first term on the right-hand side of equation 9-10b is π_m/n, expected gross profit. If a firm enters the contest each year, it expects to win $(1/n)$th of the time and will receive π_m. It loses $[(n - 1)/n]$th of the time and receives nothing. This averages out to π_m/n. If the firm earns \$1 million when it wins and there are 100 rivals, it's expected gross profit π_m/n is \$10,000 a year. The second term subtracts r because the firm spends r dollars on R&D per year whether it wins or loses.

There are n firms in this R&D competition, each hoping to finish first. Given the n contestants, what determines how much each firm spends on R&D? Assume that all firms act independently and that competition among firms increases R&D expenditures until expected profits are zero. If expected profits are zero, equation 9-10b requires each firm to spend $r = \pi_m/n$ each year. Then, the firm that finishes first this year will have a net profit of $\pi_m - r = \pi_m - (\pi_m/n) = [(n - 1)/n]\pi_m$.

The winner's profits can be very large. Consider this numerical illustration. Assume the probability of winning is only $\frac{1}{100}$ but that the monopoly profits π_m are \$1 million. If the R&D rivalry continues until the expected profit of each firm is zero, each firm spends $r = \$1 \text{ million}/100 = \$10,000$ a year on R&D. When a firm wins the race, it reports an annual profit of \$990,000 after R&D expenses are subtracted. This happens only 1 in 100 races on average. If the firm loses the race, it loses \$10,000 per year and does not produce the product. If the firm stays in the race year in and year out, it can expect to win 1 percent of the races and in those years reports a huge \$990,000 in profit *net* of R&D expenses. Ninety-nine percent of the time it loses \$10,000 and does not even produce the product. Averaging the infrequent net profits of \$990,000 with the frequent losses of \$10,000 produces an expected profit of zero.

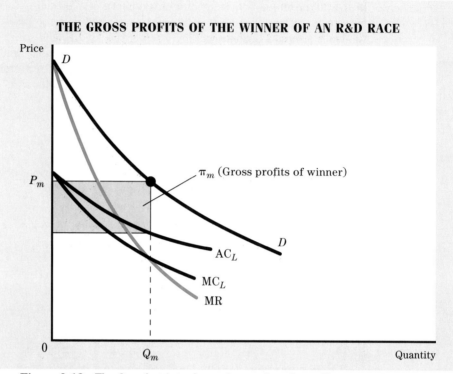

Figure 9-12   The firm that introduces the product first will earn profits equal to π_m before research and development costs are deducted.

This model illustrates the danger of drawing conclusions about the profitability of an industry from the profitability of the actual producers of a product. Each year only the winning firm produces the product and reports net profits of $990,000. The industry appears to be a very profitable one because the losers never produce the product. An outside observer could easily draw the mistaken conclusion that firms in this industry are earning excessive profits: Year after year the winning firm invests only $10,000 in R&D and earns a whopping sum of $990,000 in net profits. The payoff to R&D appears stupendous. Because only the winner of the contest produces the product, this industry looks like a profitable one where competition is nonexistent since profits are huge and are never competed away.

This is an unwarranted conclusion, however, because the outsider observes only the winning firms. Although each winner sells the new product at the monopoly price and earns impressive profits, the expected profit of any firm is zero. Industries like the pharmaceutical industry can look very profitable because we observe the successful survivors. These survivors appear to be profitable when they are only the lucky winners of the race. The proper method of measuring profitability would be to average the profits of the winner and the losses of the losers. Unfortunately, this is difficult to do when the losing firms do not produce the product. The same model applies to the search for oil, gas, gold, and other natural resources.

In this example unrestricted R&D competition for the right to be a monopolist eliminates the expected profits of the monopolist. The rivalry for monopoly uses real resources. Each year total R&D spending is $100 \times \$10,000 = \$1$ million, which is equal to the profits of the winner. Unlike the real world where R&D spending increases the probability of success, R&D spending in this model dissipates profits and constitutes a real cost to society because it does not affect the probability of a successful introduction. In this model, competition is expensive to society. In the elementary model R&D does not shift the demand function for the product. Consequently, the competition to become a monopolist adds to the social cost of monopoly. A later discussion will consider the social cost of monopoly and will include competition to be a monopolist as part of this cost.

Although this model of research and development competition is an elementary one that can be improved upon, it raises two important issues. First, the cost of monopoly can be quite large if the cost of becoming a monopolist is included. Second, the model points out the danger of estimating the profitability of an industry from the profitability of existing firms, especially in industries where there is substantial new product development.

APPLICATION 9-3

Alternative Methods of Selling a Monopoly

A city will award a franchise to a cable company to send television signals by coaxial cable to each home for a monthly fee. There are economies of scale in providing these services. Rather than allow several companies to offer the cable service, each laying a separate underground cable to service a community, the cost of providing the service will be lower with one firm providing a single underground cable.

The city is considering two ways to award the contract:

- *Proposal 1.* Allow competitive bidding for the contract and award it to the company that offers the largest payment to the municipality. The city learns that several established cable firms are opposed to this proposal. They argue that competitive bidding will increase the total costs of the firm that wins the contract and so the monthly fee will be higher.
- *Proposal 2.* Award the contract to the company that offers to charge the lowest monthly fee for the specified service.

Let's use the theory of monopoly pricing to evaluate the likely consequences of the two proposals.

Evaluation of Proposal 1.   In Figure 9-13 the demand function for the cable service is DD. The demand function shows the number of hookups as a function of the monthly fee. The long-run average and marginal cost functions are AC_L and MC_L. Because there are economies of scale in providing cable service, AC_L decreases with the number of hookups.

Which bid will win the contract? To answer this question, you must determine what a firm will charge for the service. After a firm wins the contract, its bid is like a sunk cost, a bygone, and should not affect MR or MC or the monthly fee. The firm maximizes profits by charging a monopoly price P_m and hooks up Q_m homes. The total profits of the firm are equal to area 1 in Figure 9-13. We assume that many firms submit independent bids. If they compete among themselves by offering progressively higher bids, the highest possible bid is equal to area 1, or total profits, in Figure 9-13. Any firm that bids an amount equal to area 1 will win the contract. Therefore, competitive bidding transfers the profits to the municipality.

The firm that wins the contract will find that its long-run average cost function inclusive of its bid shifts upward and becomes AC′, which is just tangent to the demand function at the monopoly price. The marginal cost curve of the firm does not change because the bid is a lump sum amount and is like a fixed cost. While the average cost function shifts upward, the marginal cost of providing the service does not change. Therefore, the firm will continue to produce Q_m because marginal revenue still equals marginal cost at this quantity.

The argument that the high cost of the bidding process will raise the monthly fee is a specious one. The average cost curve of the winner is now higher because of the winning bid. What is more important is that the marginal cost function is

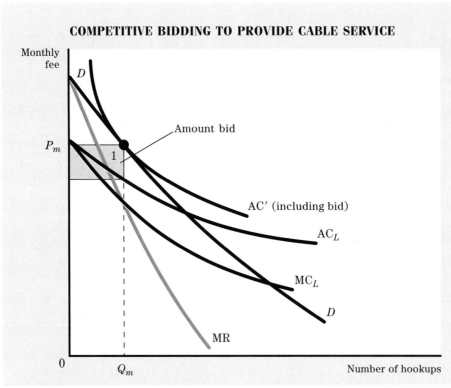

Figure 9-13 Competitive bidding for a monopoly of cable services increases the average cost function from AC_L to AC′. The marginal cost function is unaffected by the amount bid. Area 1 represents the amount bid and received by the municipality. The monthly fee is unaffected by the amount bid for the monopoly.

the same. The additional cost of serving one more customer is the same as it was before the firm submitted a bid. Therefore, the argument made by the cable companies rings hollow, and the claim that competitive bidding will increase the monthly fee is invalid.

Competitive bidding has one desirable feature. It discourages spending resources to win the contract. As long as the size of the bid determines the winner, each contestant has no incentive to use resources to lobby politicians. Profits are transferred to the local government and not eliminated through costly expenditures to win the contract.

Evaluation of Proposal 2.   Proposal 2 requires that the contract be awarded to the firm that offers the lowest monthly fee. In Figure 9-14 the lowest fee that is consistent with zero profits for the winner is the price of P^* where $P^* = \mathrm{AC}_L$. Any higher monthly fee would be undercut by other bidders, and any lower monthly fee would result in losses for the firm. If the firm offers P^* as the monthly fee, the number of subscribers is Q^*. The monthly fee will be lower and the number of

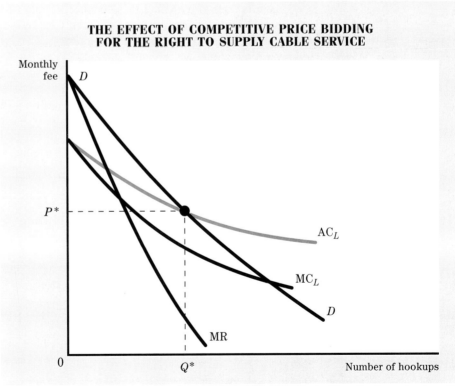

Figure 9-14   If the contract is awarded to the firm that offers the lowest price, the winner will charge a monthly fee of P^* and the total number of hookups equals Q^*. At Q^* the monthly fee still exceeds marginal cost because of internal economies of scale of providing cable services. The winning firm does not earn any profits.

hookups will be larger under proposal 2. Here again, the winning firm earns no profits, but consumer surplus is larger under proposal 2 than under proposal 1. While P^* is not equal to marginal cost, it is closer to marginal cost than the monopoly price in proposal 1. Therefore proposal 2 has more consumer benefits than proposal 1.

This analysis assumes that the city can monitor the firm so that it provides the quality of service specified in the contract. More advanced analyses investigate pricing consequences when it is costly to monitor the quality of service provided by the firm.[6]

9-7   THE TYRANNY OF DURABILITY

The analyses of monopoly implicitly assume that the monopolist produces and sells a nondurable product at the monopoly price in each period. This section makes what at first glance appears to be an unimportant change and investigates how product durability affects the price policy of a monopolist.

This issue was first raised by Nobel Prize winner Ronald Coase who explored the effect of product durability on the price charged by a monopolist.[7] Let's consider the Coase problem in the context of an example. A relative leaves you 80 acres of land on the Oregon coast with a beautiful view of the Pacific Ocean. This is an especially prized possession because the state owns all nearby land. You are the sole owner of this unique parcel of land which is in great demand. Competitors cannot enter and increase the supply of land. You would be a monopoly supplier should you decide to sell the land. The real estate consultant that you hire estimates that this exquisite parcel of land will have maximum value if you develop and sell 50 of the 80 one-acre oceanfront lots. To maximize the value of the parcel, you agree to sell one-acre lots and supervise the types of residential structures that the new owners can place on the lots.

The consultant sketches the likely demand function for the lots and estimates the inverse demand function for the lots as shown in the accompanying table.

QUANTITY OF LOTS DEMANDED	PRICE PER LOT ($)	TOTAL REVENUE ($)
30	700,000	21,000,000
40	600,000	24,000,000
50	500,000	25,000,000
70	300,000	21,000,000
80	200,000	16,000,000

---

[6] For a discussion of this and other issues related to cable television, see W. Kip Viscusi, John M. Vernon, and Joseph E. Harrington, Jr., *Economics of Regulation and Antitrust*, D. C. Heath, Lexington, Mass., 1992, pp. 399–415.

[7] R. H. Coase, "Durability and Monopoly," *Journal of Law and Economics*, vol. XV, no. 1, April 1972, pp. 143–150.

Total revenue is maximized by selling 50 lots, each at the monopoly price of $500,000, and leaving 30 acres unsold.

Equation 9-11 represents the inverse demand function for lots.

$$P = \$1,000,000 - \$10,000Q \tag{9-11}$$

where P is the most consumers will pay per lot for Q lots. The linear demand function DD and the marginal revenue function MR are shown in Figure 9-15. You own 80 one-acre lots. If the cost of selling the lots is negligible, the monopoly price per acre is $500,000, and marginal revenue is zero when you sell 50 acres. However, if you sell all 80 lots, the market-clearing price is $200,000 per lot where the demand function intersects the vertical supply function of 80 lots.

You proceed with the expectation that you will become a multimillionaire by selling 50 acres at a price of $500,000. Although you are a monopolist, Coase claims that no one will buy at a price of $500,000 and you will be able to sell the land only at a competitive price! This claim rests on the following reasoning. After you sell 50 acres, what will you do with the remaining 30 acres? He says you will sell the remaining 30 acres if you want to maximize profits. The marginal cost of selling another acre is zero. If you sell the remaining 30 acres, the price per acre falls to

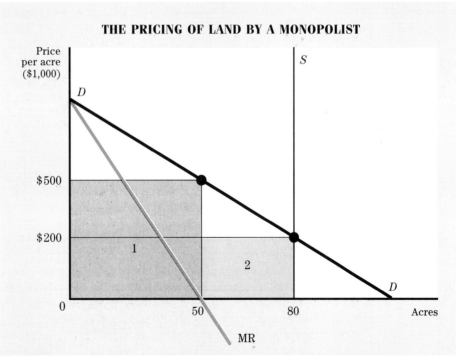

THE PRICING OF LAND BY A MONOPOLIST

Figure 9-15 The sole owner of 80 acres of land will want to sell all 80 acres, not just the 50 acres. After 50 acres are sold, the owner has an incentive to sell the remaining 30 acres. Area 1 represents the revenue from selling the first 50 acres, and area 2 represents the revenue from selling the remaining 30 acres. The key point is that the owner has an incentive to sell all the acres.

$200,000 per lot for all 80 lots. Do you care? Others own that land now and they, not you, will suffer a loss. Based on your own narrow self-interest you are better off. Total profits are now equal to area 1 plus area 2 in Figure 9-15, or $25 million plus 30 more acres at $200,000 per acre for a total of $31 million. Therefore, you have an incentive to sell additional acres as long as you own any acres.

Because you have an incentive to sell more units, potential buyers of the first bundle will be reluctant to purchase at a price of $500,000 because they anticipate that price will fall to $200,000. They recognize that your profits will be higher if you sell all 80 lots. They, not you, will suffer losses when you do. No rational buyer would commit to buying at the monopoly price, fully realizing that the price will be lower in the future. Realizing this, buyers are unwilling to purchase an acre of land unless you sell all 80 acres at a competitive price of $200,000. Then, you will have no more lots to supply to the market and the buyer need not fear a future price reduction. Coase advances the proposition that a monopolist selling a durable good can charge only a competitive price unless it finds a way to protect the interests of buyers.

> With infinitely durable goods the market price is independent of the number of sellers in the market. A monopolist can sell a durable good, but only at a competitive price.

Actions the Monopolist Can Take to Reassure Buyers

There are several policies that the monopolist can adopt which will protect the buyer from subsequent price depreciation. A creative manager may decide to lease rather than sell the land. The monopolist could develop each acre, charge a monopoly rent for each acre, and rent out 50 acres of land. Because the monopolist owns all the land, there is less of an incentive to rent the 50 acres and later rent 30 more acres at a lower rent because of the effect on future rents. If the monopolist increases the number of acres leased above 50 by lowering the rent on the additional units, it will not be able to charge the monopoly rent in future periods. In the next leasing period renters will not trust the monopolist and will not be willing to pay a monopoly rent. If the monopolist tries to obtain larger total rents during the first period by leasing still more acres later at a lower rent, the monopolist acquires a tarnished reputation.

Leasing rather than selling is a preferable option for the monopolist as long as the cost of negotiating the leases is not high and the cost of monitoring the behavior of lessors is not high. Leasing can be costly, however, because a lessor typically exercises less care over the property than an owner would.

The management might try to sell 50 acres but add a number of clauses to reassure buyers of the lots. For example, there could be a clause requiring the owner to give each buyer the best price if the owner sells any acre of land for less than $500,000. The firm commits to give any buyer a discount if the seller reduces the price. Or the owner could place a clause in the contract mandating repurchase of the land at the original price at the buyer's request. In this way any attempt by the monopolist to sell more units will be self-defeating because total profits will decrease. Introducing these provisions into a contract serves a useful purpose, but sometimes they have drawbacks. If demand conditions are highly variable, a buy-back provision could become very costly if demand declines and the value of the land decreases. The monopolist would then suffer a capital loss.

Another solution may be for the monopolist to donate the 30 acres to a non-profit agency or to the government with the provision that land use be noncompetitive. After donating 30 acres to an environmental group or to a government, you can charge a monopoly price of $500,000 per acre.

This theory of the pricing of durable goods explains why a firm might publicly announce a limited production run for a product. For example, a firm may sell a special commemorative lithograph. The producer could promise to destroy the plate after producing a specified quantity. By adopting this policy the firm is posting its reputation as a bond and is signaling that it will not produce more units after selling the original quantity. Limited production runs of automobiles and rare or specialized books are examples where the firm signals the buyer that the quantity sold will not increase. The goal of the sole supplier is to increase the confidence of the buyer that no subsequent price reduction will occur.

APPLICATION 9-4

Disney Limits the Sales of *Fantasia* to 50 Days[8]

In November 1991 Disney sold *Fantasia* on videocassette and laserdisc for only 50 days. To increase its desirability, Disney limited sales to 50 days before Christmas. After December 20, 1991, the original film would never again be sold by Disney in a home video format but would be available at rental stores. Disney priced *Fantasia* from $24.99 to $99.99. The lowest price was for the basic videotape, while the top price was for the movie plus the story of the making of the film, a commemorative lithograph, a large 16-page souvenir book, and a certificate of authenticity signed by Roy Disney, vice president of the Disney board of directors. Disney reported advanced orders of 9.25 million units for the videocassette, and 200,000 units for the laserdisc.

Why did Disney place a 50-day limit on sales of *Fantasia?* One explanation is that it wanted to publicly inform collectors that it would not sell more units at a lower price in the future. Collectors would trust Disney's announcement because the company has other classics that it may one day release and it would not want to spoil its reputation by later selling more units of *Fantasia* at a lower price.

9-8   TAXING A MONOPOLIST

This section investigates the long-run response of a monopolist to a per unit tax. The main purpose here is to demonstrate how a monopolist responds to the tax. After the government levies a per unit tax, the long-run average and marginal cost

---

[8] Based on Richard Christiansen " 'Fantasia' a Hit with Video Audience," *Chicago Tribune*, October 31, 1991.

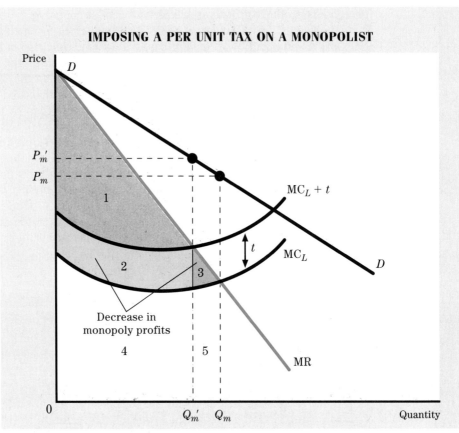

Figure 9-16 The pretax profit of a monopolist is equal to the sum of areas 1, 2, and 3. After the per unit tax of t is imposed, the profits of a monopolist decrease and equal area 1. Total profits decrease by the sum of areas 2 and 3.

functions shift upward by the tax t. In Figure 9-16 the monopolist treats the per unit tax as another cost of doing business. With the per unit tax, the additional cost of producing and selling one more unit equals the original long-run marginal cost plus the per unit tax paid to the government. A profit-maximizing monopolist finds an output where marginal revenue equals the sum of the marginal cost of production and t.[9] Therefore, a monopolist responds to a per unit tax by reducing output and raising price.

$$\text{MR}(Q) = \text{MC}_L(Q) + t \qquad\qquad \textbf{(9-12)}$$

[9] After the per unit tax is imposed, the profit function of the monopolist is

$$\pi(Q) = D(Q)\,Q - C_L(Q) - tQ$$

The monopolist selects Q, so that total profits are maximized, or

$$\frac{d[\pi(Q)]}{dQ} = D(Q) + Q\frac{d[D(Q)]}{dQ} - \frac{d[C_L(Q)]}{dQ} - t = 0$$

This expression can be rearranged to yield $\text{MR}(Q) = \text{MC}_L(Q) + t$.

In Figure 9-16 the new marginal cost function, including the per unit tax, shifts upward by t and intersects the marginal revenue function at the smaller output of Q'_m. The per unit tax reduces the output and increases the price to P'_m. The monopolist's profit decreases after the government imposes a per unit tax. Without a per unit tax total revenue equals the area under the marginal revenue curve up to the quantity Q_m, or the sum of areas 1, 2, 3, 4, and 5, in Figure 9-16. When all factor inputs are continuous, the total cost of producing Q_m units is equal to the area under the marginal cost curve or the sum of areas 4 and 5. Total profits equals the difference between the two areas or the sum of areas 1, 2, and 3. With a per unit tax, total revenue is equal to the sum of areas 1, 2, and 4. The total cost of producing Q'_m equals the sum of areas 2 and 4. Total profits decline and are now equal to area 1. The imposition of a per unit tax decreases the monopolist's profits by the sum of areas 2 and 3.

> A per unit tax increases the monopoly price and reduces the quantity produced and total profits.

9-9   THE SOCIAL OBJECTION TO MONOPOLY

Now that you know how a monopolist determines price and quantity, let's compare prices and quantities under monopoly and competition and consider the social cost of monopoly. In order to compare monopoly with competition, we want to be sure that the monopolized market can function as a competitive market. To make the two situations comparable, assume that the industry can be a constant-cost competitive industry where more firms enter the industry and each produces at the minimum point of their long-run average cost function. To maintain comparability, assume that the long-run supply function of the competitive industry becomes the monopolist's long-run average and marginal cost functions. For example, assume a situation where a monopolist can merge the competitive firms and operates each firm as a plant. Assume that the monopolist can add identical plants so that it can increase total output at constant long-run average and marginal costs.

Figure 9-17a shows the competitive price and output in a competitive industry. Consumer surplus is equal to area 1. Because the long-run supply function is horizontal, producer surplus is zero. In Figure 9-17b the monopoly price P_m is higher and output Q_m is lower. Consumer surplus is smaller and is equal to area 2. Because price is higher, a monopoly transfers part of consumer surplus to the monopolist through the profits earned by the monopolist. Area 3 represents the transfer. Because output is smaller, monopoly creates a deadweight loss of monopoly equal to area 4. Deadweight loss is the loss in value suffered by some group (consumers or producers) that is not offset by a rise in value to some other group.

> There is a social objection to monopoly because it creates a deadweight loss so that the sum of consumer and producer surpluses is not maximized.

The complaint about monopoly is that the monopolist produces too few units and not that it earns profits. If the government expropriated the profits of the

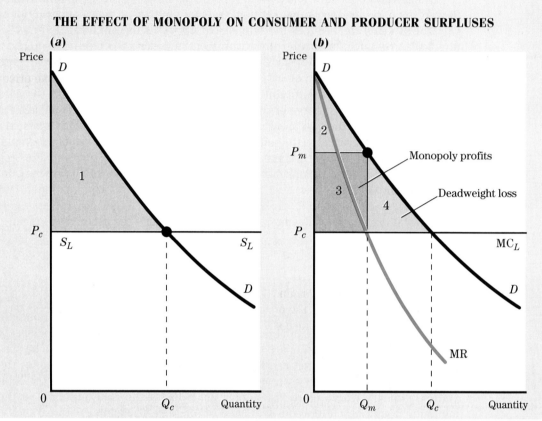

Figure 9-17   In (*a*) the competitive price and output are P_c and Q_c, respectively. Consumer surplus is equal to area 1. In (*b*) price increases to P_m and output contracts to Q_m in a monopolized industry. Consumer surplus decreases to area 2. Producer surplus increases and is equal to area 3. The deadweight loss is area 4.

monopolist through a special levy so that it earned no profit, the objection to monopoly would remain. Because the monopolist produces less than a competitive industry would produce, it employs too few factors of production. The unused factors find employment elsewhere in other industries, with the consequence that too many resources are being employed in other competitive industries scattered throughout the economy. The outputs of the other competitive industries in the economy are larger than they would otherwise be if the monopolist had to set a competitive price. Chapter 18 presents a more general analysis of the consequences of monopoly.

The social cost of monopoly can be larger than area 4 if there is competition to become a monopoly. Area 3, formerly labeled profits, must be added to area 4 in Figure 9-17*b*. Area 3 could represent total R&D spending to win a patent race or spending to persuade government officials to award a franchise to the firm. Whatever the application, these expenditures are part of the social cost of monopoly.

The government uses an antitrust policy and direct regulation of price to eliminate or attenuate deadweight loss caused by monopoly. Ideally, the monopolist should behave as a price taker instead of a price maker. The monopolist can be transformed into a price taker by setting a price ceiling at the competitive price where the demand function intersects the long-run marginal cost function. The regulated monopolist determines output where the competitive price (ceiling) P_c equals long-run marginal cost and quantity demanded equals quantity supplied. With a competitive price ceiling areas 3 and 4 equal consumer surplus and the deadweight loss of monopoly disappears.

Unfortunately, regulation is seldom so perfect. The competitive price is usually unknown. So, there is no guarantee that the price ceiling is set at the competitive price. Furthermore, regulators sometimes identify with the regulated industry and protect it rather than consumers.

SUMMARY

- A pure monopolist determines the price without attracting other firms to the industry or considering the price response of other firms because the products of other firms are not close substitutes.
- The marginal revenue of a monopolist is less than price because the monopolist reduces the price on all units that could be sold at the higher price.
- A profit-maximizing monopolist never produces in the region where demand is price-inelastic.
- A profit-maximizing monopolist determines the quantity where marginal revenue equals marginal cost.
- In the short run an increase in demand causes profits to rise. Profits rise by still more in the long run when plant size can change.
- An innovation that reduces the cost of production lowers the monopoly price, raises output, and increases total profits.
- The sole producer of a durable good can sell a durable good only at the competitive price unless the producer can commit to the monopoly output.
- Levying a per unit tax will reduce the quantity produced by a monopolist.
- The sum of consumer and producer surplus is smaller under monopoly than under competition.

KEY TERMS

Monopolist's demand function
Marginal revenue
Equating marginal revenue to
    marginal cost
Markup over marginal cost
Competing to become a monopolist

Price maker
Monopolist's output decision
Product durability and monopoly
    pricing
Deadweight loss of monopoly
Social cost of monopoly

REVIEW QUESTIONS

1. Under what conditions can a firm behave as a pure monopolist?
2. In the short run a monopolist should expand output until marginal revenue is zero. Explain why you agree or disagree with this statement.
3. The monopoly price and the long-run equilibrium price in a competitive industry always occur in the region of the demand function where demand is price-elastic. Explain why you agree or disagree with this statement.
4. Evaluate the following: I would rather be selling a good where demand is price-inelastic than price-elastic. Then, I can raise price and increase total revenue. If demand is price-elastic, revenue decreases when I raise the price.
5. Why is it correct to say that the price is always on the monopolist's demand function and never on the monopolist's marginal cost function?
6. If there is no competition to be a monopolist, the monopolist earns profits. Explain why you agree or disagree with this statement.
7. In either a monopoly or a competitive industry a cost-reducing innovation reduces the price as soon as the new technology is introduced. However, in a competitive industry price continues to decrease when the new technology completely replaces the old technology, while a monopolist maintains the price when it replaces the old technology with the new technology. Explain why you agree or disagree with these statements.
8. When the government levies a per unit tax against a monopolist, the total revenue of the monopolist may either rise or decline. Explain why you agree or disagree with this statement.
9. Why is the social cost of monopoly smaller when the demand function is more elastic at the monopoly price?

EXERCISES

1. The demand function and the total cost function of a monopolist are:

QUANTITY	PRICE ($)	TOTAL COST ($)
1	40	6
2	38	10
3	34	18
4	28	28
5	24	46
6	18	60
7	12	94

What is the profit-maximizing quantity?

2. At the monopoly price the price elasticity of demand is -2 and the ratio of price to the firm's average cost is 1.3. Can you tell from this information whether the firm is operating in the region where there are economies or diseconomies of scale?

3. Suppose the long-run equilibrium price in a constant-cost competitive industry is P_c. An invention lowers the cost of production for just a new firm so that it can produce each rate of industry output by 20 percent less. The new firm will be the sole producer in the industry as long as it sets the price below the long-run equilibrium competitive price. What is the largest value for the price elasticity of demand at the monopoly price that the new firm can charge and not attract competitive firms to the industry?

4. Instead of assuming that there is only one domestic producer in the industry as in Application 9-2, suppose there are many domestic suppliers. Consider the effect of introducing a quota that allows the current level of imports to continue as in Application 9-2. Predict the effect of the quota when there are many domestic suppliers and compare your results with the situation in Application 9-2 where there is a single domestic supplier. Can you determine whether the domestic industry behaves competitively or not by the response of price to the introduction of the quota? Explain.

5. Suppose the price a monopolist can charge is regulated by the government. Find the regulated price that maximizes the total number of units sold. *Hint:* At the regulated price, the firm's marginal revenue equals price up to the quantity demanded on the demand function.

   Assume the government sets the price ceiling so that the regulated monopolist sells the maximum quantity. Then, a regulator allows competitive bidding for the right to be a monopolist.

   a. With the use of graphs determine how much a firm would pay for the right to be a monopolist under these circumstances.

   b. Does the amount the regulated monopolist pays tell you whether long-run average cost is decreasing or increasing?

6. Countries enter into long-lived tariff agreements with each other. Suppose that country A exports product 1 to country B with a tariff of $50 per unit and country B exports product 2 to country A with a tariff of $100 per unit. Many of these agreements contain a most-favored-nation clause that requires a country to give the lowest tariff to all countries exporting the product to the country. Why would you expect these kinds of agreements to include a most-favorable-nation clause?

7. A monopolist produced 1 million units last year. If a $10 per unit tax is imposed, the profits of the monopolist will decrease by $10 million. Explain why you agree or disagree with this statement.

8. If the government levies a per unit tax on a monopolist, the monopolist increases price and reduces the total quantity sold. Total revenue may either increase or decrease. Explain why you agree or disagree with this statement.

CHAPTER 10

PRICING IN OLIGOPOLY

In some markets where there is neither monopoly nor competition, firms attempt to limit competition by cooperating rather than competing among themselves. By cooperating, they hope to keep the price above the competitive price. Cooperation can occur in markets where there are many sellers and each firm is a price taker or in markets where there are few price-making firms. The firms in markets with few firms are called **oligopolists** and the industry is called an **oligopoly.**

This chapter considers the behavior of firms that attempt to reach cooperative agreements. We begin by covering familiar territory—a competitive industry—and demonstrate how competitive firms benefit when they cooperate. Also discussed is the incentive to cheat when many price-taking firms attempt to cooperate.

Next, we study firm behavior when there are few sellers in the market. The theory of oligopoly describes the way a small number of firms interact with each other to set price and output. Most of the chapter examines the price and output levels of oligopolists who are unable to cooperate perfectly. Two specific models of imperfect cooperative behavior predict what the price will be and how it will change when the number of firms in an industry increases. In addition, the effect of product and industry characteristics on the success of cooperative agreements is investigated. The chapter ends with a brief examination of the contributions of game theory to the study of strategic interactions among oligopolists.

10-1 COOPERATION AMONG PRICE-TAKING FIRMS: CARTEL BEHAVIOR

Competitive firms sometimes seek to escape competition by cooperating rather than competing. A cartel is an arrangement among price-taking firms in an industry whose objective is to reduce output and raise price.

> A **cartel** is an arrangement among price-taking firms whose purpose is to reduce output, raise price, and increase the profits of each member.

Let's demonstrate how a perfectly functioning cartel operates and then consider the special problems it faces. The analysis begins with a constant-cost competitive industry with n firms in long-run equilibrium. Figure 10-1a shows the long-run equilibrium output of a firm, and Figure 10-1b shows the long-run industry equilibrium. The long-run equilibrium price is P_e, and total industry output is Q_e. Each firm produces q_e at minimum cost by building a particular size plant with the corresponding short-run average and marginal cost curves.

Suppose all firms in the industry agree that they must seek relief from price competition because it reduces the profits of each firm. So, they agree to form a cartel whose purpose is to reduce output and raise price. The n firms in the industry take this step only when they believe new firms will not enter the industry immediately after price increases. If new firms can enter the industry immediately, the cartel cannot succeed because the output cutback by the cartel members will be nullified by the output increase of the entrants. A successful cartel must be able to limit the entry of new firms.

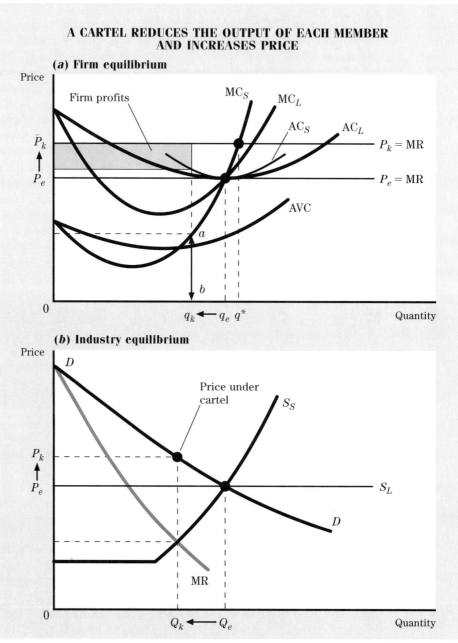

**A CARTEL REDUCES THE OUTPUT OF EACH MEMBER
AND INCREASES PRICE**

(*a*) Firm equilibrium

(*b*) Industry equilibrium

Figure 10-1   (*a*) When firms in an industry form a cartel, each reduces output from q_e to q_k. (*b*) The total quantity supplied decreases from Q_e to Q_k and increases the market price from P_e to P_k. At a price of P_k each member of the cartel would prefer to produce q^*, where P_k is short-run marginal cost in (*a*). The cartel can be successful only if it prevents firms from cheating on the quota of q_k.

The members of a cartel must determine total industry output, market price, and each firm's share of cartel output, usually called its quota. As a collective organization, the cartel can sell more units only by reducing price. To determine total industry output, the cartel equates marginal revenue to its marginal cost. Because the short-run supply function is the horizontal summation of the short-run marginal cost curves of the n firms, it becomes the cartel's short-run marginal cost function. The cartel determines output so that its marginal cost equals marginal revenue. You can see that the cartel would set cartel output equal to monopoly output.

Figure 10-1*b* shows that the intersection of the marginal revenue function and the cartel's marginal cost function occurs at the output Q_k. In the short run the cartel reduces industry output from Q_e to Q_k. How should the cartel allocate the reduced output among the n firms? If it wants to produce Q_k units at minimum total cost, it will equalize the short-run marginal cost of production for all n firms in the industry. If each firm's quota is q_k, the marginal cost of production of each one is equal to the distance ab in Figure 10-1*a* and the cartel minimizes the total cost of producing Q_k. Each member's short-run profits are equal to the shaded area.

Now consider a serious dilemma faced by a cartel of n independent firms. The cartel succeeds if each firm reduces output to q_k units so that the market price increases to P_k. But the difference between the market price P_k and each firm's short-run marginal cost ab when each firm produces q_k units portends trouble. Because a price-taking firm does not affect the price, it maximizes profits by producing q^* units where P_k is equal to the firm's short-run marginal cost. The narrow self-interest of each member dictates an output of q^* units since each price-taking firm maximizes profits by producing more than the assigned quota. This is the fundamental dilemma faced by every cartel. What is in the interest of the cartel organization is not in the interest of each member.

Each price-taking member of the cartel has an incentive to produce more than its assigned quota because price exceeds marginal cost.

A cartel must resolve this conflict between individual self-interest and the collective interest or it will eventually fail. Cartels use several methods to discourage individual firms from increasing sales. For example, it may assign customers to firms because it is easier to detect a cheater by monitoring the customers it attracts from its rivals. In the nineteenth century, German companies used formal legal contracts to form cartels, and some of the agreements specified penalties for cheating. The cartel could sue and collect damages from violators of the agreement. Another favorite enforcement device was joint sales agreements. These agreements stipulated that each firm must sell its output to the cartel which became the sole sales agent for all firms in the cartel. By establishing a joint sales agreement, the cartel discouraged individual firms from increasing output.

The antitrust laws of the United States and of some other countries prohibit firms from forming joint sales agencies, assigning customers to firms, and adopting other means to prevent output expansion. They prohibit cartels from using the more effective devices of maintaining cartel discipline. These laws force cartel members to use less effective methods to police and maintain the cartel and reduce the probability of cartel success.

Cartels are fragile structures. Not only does a cartel have to devise methods for monitoring compliance of members, but in the long run it must cope with the entry of new firms because price is above the competitive price. Without some legal restrictions on entry or without a means of raising the costs of potential entrants, a cartel will have increasing difficulty maintaining the price at the monopoly price in the face of entry. With time, entry will force the price down to the competitive price. Thus, any cartel profits are likely to be short-lived. Still, the persistent efforts to form and then re-form cartels indicate that the short-run benefits of a higher-than-competitive price are large enough in some industries to justify the effort. Firms may form a cartel for the short-run monopoly profits while recognizing beforehand that it will fail in the long run.

APPLICATION 10-1

Trouble in the Orange Cartel[1]

Sunkist Growers Inc. is an association of orange growers and packing houses operating under a federal marketing order that assigns quotas to individual growers to prop up the price of fresh oranges. Marketing orders, which are a product of the depression decade of the 1930s, raise price and the income of growers by placing limits on the output of individual growers. A marketing order is a legal mechanism for restricting output of a product and raising price just as the theory of cartels predicts. In the marketing order for oranges, a committee of members, often the larger growers and packers, determines total output and assigns individual quotas. Membership in the marketing order is compulsory. If a member ignores the quotas, he or she is subject to a federal fine and imprisonment.

Although the committee has assigned quotas for years with the support of the government, it is only lately that charges of cheating by some members of the Sunkist association have surfaced. Many Sunkist directors are affiliated with the larger Sunkist packing houses. The charges indicate that the vexing problem of cheating that faces any cartel exists even in cartels operating under federal jurisdiction. Several dozen citrus packers are accused of exceeding their quotas and reaping profits that exceed $60 million because they were able to sell at the inflated cartel price. The charges allege that some Sunkist directors knew of the violations and that some were affiliated with those who were involved.

10-2 PRICE AND OUTPUT WITH OLIGOPOLY

You have seen how a cartel with price-taking firms attempts to coordinate production and increase its profits by raising the price to the monopoly price. Now let's investigate price and output when the number of firms in the market is relatively

[1] Based on Ralph T. King, Jr., "Navel Battle Poses Threat to Sunkist, Raising Prospect of Lower Retail Prices," *Wall Street Journal*, March 18, 1993.

Table 10-1 COMBINED MARKET SHARE OF THE FOUR LARGEST FIRMS IN SELECTED INDUSTRIES, 1987

INDUSTRY	COMBINED MARKET SHARE OF FOUR LARGEST FIRMS	NUMBER OF COMPANIES
Chewing gum	96	8
Household laundry equipment	93	11
Cigarettes	92	9
Electric light bulbs	91	93
Household refrigerators and freezers	85	40
Primary batteries, dry and wet	88	59

Source: 1987 Census of Manufacturers, "Concentration Ratios in Manufacturing," Subject Series, MC87-S-6.

small and the market shares of the leading firms are large. These firms also can increase their profits by raising price to the monopoly price, and in some ways they should have less difficulty cooperating.

Table 10-1 lists some industries where the concentration ratio, the combined market share of the four leading firms, is over 80 percent. In these industries the leading firms have relatively large market shares. In several cases the number of firms in the industry seems large, but most firms appear to be speciality producers selling relatively low volumes.

The objective here is to find the price and output of firms in oligopolistic markets—those with a small number of firms. Ultimately, the price and output in an oligopoly will be compared with the equilibrium price and output level in a monopoly or in a competitive industry. To make valid comparisons among monopoly, oligopoly, and competition, the demand and cost conditions are specified so that they are the same in all market situations.

Demand and Cost Conditions

This section develops expressions for the cost and demand conditions used throughout the chapter and begins by specifying the long-run total cost function of firms. In this analysis all firms are alike, and each firm's long-run total cost increases proportionately with the quantity produced.

$$C(q_i) = cq_i \qquad \text{(Firm Total Cost Function)} \qquad \textbf{(10-1)}$$

where c is the constant long-run average and marginal costs and q_i is the quantity produced by firm i. If $c = \$10$, the cost of each unit is \$10, and so each firm's long-run average and long-run marginal costs are constant at \$10.

For simplicity, assume the inverse industry demand function is a straight line.

$$P = D(Q) = a - bQ \qquad \text{(Market Demand Function)} \qquad \textbf{(10-2)}$$

where P is the consumers' willingness to pay when the quantity demanded is Q. The vertical intercept is a, and the slope of the straight line demand function is $-b$. A unit increase in the quantity demanded reduces price by b. If $a = \$24$ and $b = \$1$, then the equation becomes

$$P = \$24 - \$1q$$

You may be wondering why we work with linear demand and total cost functions. The main reason for this is that explicit solutions for price and quantity are easily found, and so comparisons between models are that much easier to make.

Total revenue is

$$R = PQ$$
$$= (a - bQ)Q = aQ - bQ^2$$

Marginal revenue is[2]

$$\text{MR} = \frac{\Delta R}{\Delta Q} = a - 2bQ \qquad \text{(Marginal Revenue Function)} \qquad \textbf{(10-3)}$$

When the demand function is linear, the marginal revenue function has the same intercept as the demand function but twice the slope.

Price and Quantity under Monopoly and Competition

These expressions for the industry demand function, marginal revenue, and total cost can be used to develop expressions for price and quantity under monopoly and under competition. The monopoly price and quantity will serve as benchmarks when the time comes to compare oligopoly with monopoly. To derive the monopoly price and quantity, we start with the profit function of a monopolist.

$$\pi(Q) = \text{Revenues} - \text{Costs}$$
$$= (a - bQ)Q - cQ$$
$$= aQ - bQ^2 - cQ$$

The monopolist maximizes total profits by selecting a quantity where marginal revenue equals marginal cost.

$$\text{Marginal revenue} = \text{Marginal cost}$$
$$a - 2bQ = c$$

Marginal revenue is $a - 2bQ$, and marginal cost is c.[3] To rearrange this equation into an expression for monopoly output, subtract c, add $2bQ$ to both sides, and divide both sides by $2b$ to obtain

---

[2] For those readers whose command of calculus has deteriorated with lack of use, the derivative of $y = kq^n$ is

$$\frac{dy}{dq} = knq^{n-1}$$

where k and n are constants. When $n = 1$, the derivative is k. When $n = 2$, the derivative of kq^2 is $2kq$.

[3] From footnote 2 you know that the derivative of aQ is a and the derivative of $-bQ^2$ is $-2bQ$.

$$Q_m = \frac{a - c}{2b} \qquad \text{(Monopoly Output)} \qquad\qquad (10\text{-}4)$$

where Q_m is the profit-maximizing monopoly output.

You can find the monopoly price by substituting $(a - c)/2b$ for Q in the inverse demand function in equation 10-2. The monopoly price P_m is[4]

$$P_m = \frac{a + c}{2} \qquad \text{(Monopoly Price)} \qquad\qquad (10\text{-}5)$$

Equation 10-5 says that the profit-maximizing monopoly price is the simple average of the intercept of the demand function a and marginal cost c. If $a = \$24$, $c = \$10$, and $b = \$1$, the profit-maximizing price is $(\$24 + \$10)/2 = \$17$ and monopoly output is $(\$24 - \$10)/\$2 = 7$ units. Figure 10-2 shows a linear demand function, a constant marginal cost function, and the profit-maximizing monopoly price and

[4] The derivation of this result is

$$P_m = a - b\frac{a - c}{2b} = a - \frac{a - c}{2} = \frac{2a}{2} - \frac{a - c}{2} = \frac{a}{2} + \frac{c}{2} = \frac{a + c}{2}$$

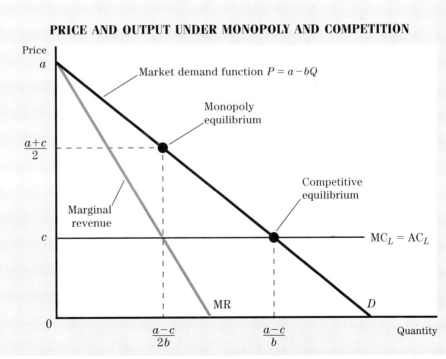

PRICE AND OUTPUT UNDER MONOPOLY AND COMPETITION

Figure 10-2   The profit-maximizing output and price equal $(a - c)/2b$ and $(a + c)/2$, respectively, for a monopolist. Under competition the equilibrium price is lower and is c, and so output is larger at $(a - c)/b$.

Table 10-2   EQUILIBRIUM PRICE AND OUTPUT UNDER MONOPOLY AND UNDER COMPETITION

	PRICE	OUTPUT
Monopoly	$\dfrac{a + c}{2}$	$\dfrac{a - c}{2b}$
Competition	c	$\dfrac{a - c}{b}$

output. Marginal revenue equals marginal cost when the monopolist produces $(a - c)/2b$ units and sells each unit at a price of $(a + c)/2$.

In Chapter 8 you learned that the long-run equilibrium price equals marginal cost in a competitive industry. Therefore, the long-run equilibrium price P_c equals c.

$$P_c = c \quad \text{(Price under Competition)} \tag{10-6}$$

To find total output of a competitive industry in long-run equilibrium, first substitute c for price in the inverse demand function

$$c = P = a - bQ$$

and then solve for Q.[5] Q_c is the total quantity produced by a competitive industry in long-run equilibrium:

$$Q_c = \frac{a - c}{b} \quad \text{(Quantity under Competition)} \tag{10-7}$$

The equilibrium competitive price is $10, and the long-run equilibrium output is 14 units when $a = \$24$, $b = \$1$, and $c = \$10$. In Figure 10-2 a competitive industry produces a larger output of $(a - c)/b$ units and sells at a price of c. When the inverse demand function is a straight line and marginal cost is constant, the monopolist produces half of the competitive industry output.

Table 10-2 shows the equilibrium price and output under monopoly and under competition.

We are able to derive the prices and outputs under monopoly and under competition without referring to the firm's strategic behavior, and there is a reason for this. The manager of a competitive firm does not speculate what another firm will do if he does one thing, or what he will do if the other firm does something else. Strategic behavior is meaningless for a price taker because the firm's output

[5] Solve for Q by adding $bQ - c$ to both sides and then dividing both sides by b.

decision has no effect on price. Strategy comes into play only when action by one firm affects another firm.

The same is true of a pure monopolist by default. The monopolist is insulated from the consequences of the actions of other firms. Because there is only one seller, its decisions have no effect on other firms and the absence of close substitutes makes strategic reasoning extraneous. A monopolist does not need to consider the reactions of other firms in the economy when determining price and output.

Cooperative Behavior

Whether one, a few, or many firms are in an industry, they maximize profits by charging the monopoly price. Unless oligopolists cooperate, they will produce a larger quantity and sell at a lower price, and so total industry profits will be less than maximum profits. This section uses the expressions for the monopoly price and output to find which output each of two firms must produce when they cooperate and share monopoly profits. More importantly, we demonstrate why each member of this duopoly—a market having two firms—has an incentive to deviate from these price and output levels.

Let's investigate how two firms can cooperate and share the market at the monopoly price if each one agrees to produce one-half of the monopoly output so that the price remains at the monopoly price. Figure 10-3 illustrates the cooperative solution. Each firm's demand function is one-half of the total quantity demanded at each price if the firms share the market. Each firm's marginal revenue function (the light color line) is half of the marginal revenue function (the dark color line) of the market demand.[6] Each firm produces $(a - c)/4b$ units, one-half of the monopoly output, and sells each unit at the monopoly price of $(a + c)/2$.

The Incentive to Cheat

Each firm in an oligopoly has an incentive to cheat. A numerical example demonstrates this ubiquitous propensity to cheat. Suppose $c = 0$ so costs can be ignored. Consider the linear industry demand function in Table 10-3 where the intercept of the demand function a is 24 and the slope of the demand function $-b$ is -1, and so the demand function is

$$P = \$24 - \$1Q$$

[6] If the two firms divide the market, the demand function of each firm has a slope that is twice the slope of the market demand function. The demand function of each firm is $P = a - 2bQ$, and the firm's profit function is $\pi = aQ - 2bQ^2 - cQ$.

Each firm maximizes profits if

$$\frac{d\pi}{dQ} = a - 4bQ - c = 0$$

The profit-maximizing quantity is

$$Q = \frac{a - c}{4b}$$

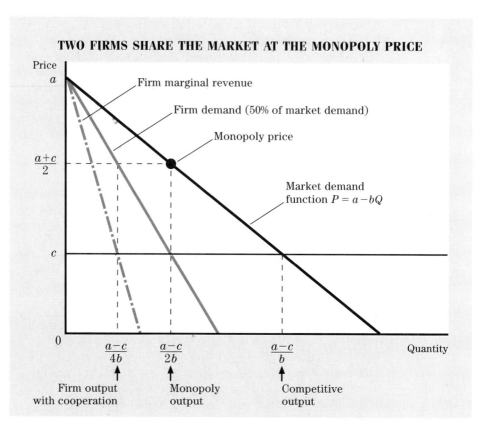

TWO FIRMS SHARE THE MARKET AT THE MONOPOLY PRICE

Figure 10-3   If two firms cooperate and share the market, they will each produce one-half of the monopoly output and charge the monopoly price. Each firm produces $(a - c)/4b$. By cooperating, the two firms share the largest possible profit.

The price, quantity, and total revenue for the industry are in columns 1 through 3 in Table 10-3 for selected prices and quantities. As the equation indicates, when the two firms supply 8 units, the first row of the table indicates the price is $16.

Total revenue equals total profit since each firm can produce the product without cost. A monopolist would maximize profits of $144 by producing 12 units. If there are two firms in the market, they could agree to share the market and sell at the monopoly price of $12. Each would produce 6 units and sell each unit at $12 and receive $72 in profit. Aggregate profits are as large as possible when each produces 6 units. This cooperative solution makes profits as large as possible, and the firms divide the pie equally.

Is it in the self-interest of each firm to honor this agreement? Table 10-4 shows the market price and firm 2's profits for different quantities produced given the output of firm 1. Look at the output decision from firm 2's perspective. If firm 1 produces 6 units, firm 2's profits increase to $81 when it increases output from 6 to 9 units as long as firm 1 stays at 6 units. Firm 2 has an incentive to violate the

Table 10-3   INDUSTRY DEMAND FUNCTION AND TOTAL PROFITS

PRICE ($) (1)	QUANTITY DEMANDED (2)	TOTAL REVENUE OR PROFITS ($) (3)
17	7	119
16	8	128
15	9	135
14	10	140
13	11	143
12	12	144
11	13	143
10	14	140
9	15	135
8	16	128
7	17	119
6	18	108

agreement and produce 9, not 6, units. When an agreement is in the self-interest of both parties, it is called a self-enforcing agreement. In this case the agreement to produce 6 units is not self-enforcing since at least one party will gain by violating it.

A **self-enforcing agreement** exists when both parties maximize profits given the output of the rival.

The same thing can be said about firm 1. If firm 2 produces 6 units, then firm 1's profits are $81 if firm 1 produces 9 units. Herein lies the catch. If both firms produce 9 units, the price falls to $6 and the profits of each are only $54 ($6 × 9). Each firm ends up with profits of only $54, or 25 percent less than the profits of $72 obtained under the cooperative solution. When each rival looks after its own interests, the firms do not maximize industry profits and both are worse off. In summary, what we have shown is that each firm has an incentive to cheat on the cooperative agreement that maximizes industry profits.

This propensity to cheat has general applicability. When the inverse demand function is $P = a - bQ$ in Figure 10-4 and costs are zero ($c = 0$), the monopolist

Table 10-4   PROFITS OF FIRM 2 IF FIRM 1 PRODUCES 6 UNITS

PRICE ($)	OUTPUT OF FIRM 2	TOTAL PROFITS OF FIRM 2
12	6	72
11	7	77
10	8	80
9	9	81
8	10	80

produces $a/2b$ units when marginal revenue is zero since marginal cost is zero. A cooperative arrangement requires each firm to produce $a/4b$ units, one-half of the monopoly output of $a/2b$. Figure 10-4 shows each firm producing one-half of the monopoly output. If a monopolist increases output above $a/2b$ by ΔQ, the price falls by $\Delta P = -b\Delta Q$ and total profits decrease. Area 1 represents the increase in revenue because consumers purchase ΔQ more units. The sum of areas 2 and 3 represents the loss in revenue because $a/2b$ units sell at a lower price. The reason for distinguishing between areas 2 and 3 will soon become self-evident. Because a monopolist maximizes total profits when producing $a/2b$ units, area 1 must be less than the sum of areas 2 and 3, and so total profits decrease. This is why the monopolist only produces $a/2b$ units.

What happens to the incentive to produce more when two sellers share the market at the monopoly price? If firm 2 increases its output by ΔQ, area 1 equals the increase in revenue received by firm 2 when it increases output by ΔQ. What does firm 2 lose? Area 3 represents the loss in firm 2's revenue. The units it previously sold (50 percent of the total) at the higher price now sell at the lower price. Firm 2's loss equals only one-half of the total loss in revenue because firm 1 incurs the other half of the loss. So, a duopolist has an incentive to expand output by ΔQ, while a monopolist does not. Furthermore, the larger the number of firms in the industry, the greater the incentive to cheat. If there are n firms in the industry, a firm that increases output by ΔQ incurs only $1/n$ of the total loss in revenue because the existing quantity sells at a lower price. This explains why the cooperative solution becomes still more difficult to achieve as the number of firms increases. The gains from cheating increase with the number of firms who have signed the agreement.

Because cheating on the cooperative solution is profitable, members must either find ways to prevent others from cheating or recognize the futility of reaching a cooperative solution. Often it is so costly to prevent cheating that firms recognize that the cooperative solution is unattainable and behave noncooperatively.

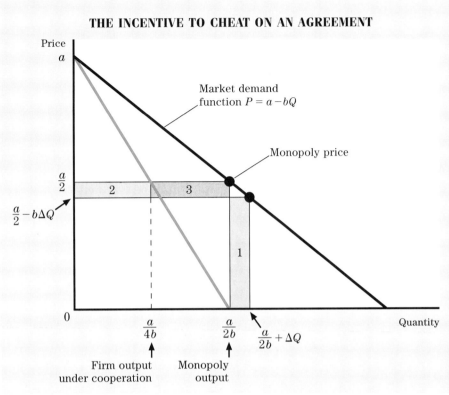

THE INCENTIVE TO CHEAT ON AN AGREEMENT

Figure 10-4   A monopolist maximizes profits by producing $a/2b$ and charging the monopolist price of $a/2$ assuming costs are zero. If the monopolist increases output by ΔQ, the price decreases by $\Delta P = -b\Delta Q$. Area 1 represents the increase in the monopolist's revenue, and the sum of areas 2 and 3 measures the loss in revenue because the price falls. Because profits are maximized at the monopoly output of $a/2b$, area 1 must be less than the sum of areas 2 and 3. If two firms share the market and each produces $a/4b$, the two firms sell each unit at the monopoly price of $a/2$. Suppose firm 2 cheats on the agreement by increasing output by ΔQ and causing price to fall by $b\Delta Q$. Total revenue of firm 2 increases by area 1 less area 3 where area 3 represents the loss in revenue suffered by firm 2 because price falls by ΔP. Area 2 represents the loss in revenue suffered by the other firm because price falls by ΔP. A duopolist has an incentive to cheat and to expand output, while a monopolist does not.

10-3   MODELS OF NONCOOPERATIVE BEHAVIOR

This section presents two well-known models of duopoly. Each one starts with the assumption that cooperative behavior is too costly to achieve. We want to show what price and quantity emerge from each model when firms behave noncooperatively. Then, we show what the two theories say about price and output when the number of rivals increases. Once we know what these theories predict about the relationship between the number of firms and price, we can turn to some evidence and see how accurate the predictions are.

The Cournot Model

The first model of a noncooperative duopoly is the Cournot model, named after the pioneering French mathematical economist.[7] In this model two firms sell identical products and have the same total cost function with a constant marginal cost of c (equation 10-1).

In the Cournot model the two firms decide what quantity to produce independently but simultaneously. The output of firm 1 is q_1, and the output of firm 2 is q_2. Given the combined output of the two firms, the market-clearing price is $P = a - bQ = a - b(q_1 + q_2)$, where $q_1 + q_2$ replaces Q in the demand function so that all units sell at the market-clearing price.

The profit function of firm 1 is

$$\text{Profits} = \text{Revenue} - \text{Cost}$$

$$\pi(q_1) = (a - bq_1 - bq_2)q_1 - cq_1 \qquad \text{(Profit Function of Firm 1)} \qquad \textbf{(10-8)}$$

$$= aq_1 - bq_1^2 - bq_2q_1 - cq_1$$

Total profits of firm 1 depend on how many units it produces and how many units firm 2 produces. Therefore, firm 1's profit-maximizing quantity depends on the quantity that firm 2 produces. The same is true of firm 2's profit-maximizing quantity. Suppose that firm 2 is producing quantity q_2. Then, firm 1 decides that it will produce one quantity if it expects that firm 2 will not change its output, and quite another quantity if it expects that firm 2 will increase or decrease its output when firm 1's output increases. An important assumption of the Cournot model is that firm 1 believes that firm 2 will not change its output when firm 1 changes its output.

$$\frac{\Delta q_2}{\Delta q_1} = 0 \qquad \text{(Cournot Assumption)} \qquad \textbf{(10-9)}$$

Equation 10-9 says that firm 1 expects the output of firm 2 to remain constant when it changes its own output.

> Each Cournot competitor assumes that a change in its output will not change its rival's output.

With the Cournot assumption the demand function facing firm 1 becomes

$$P = (a - bq_2^*) - bq_1$$

where firm 1 considers $a - bq_2^*$ a constant because of the Cournot assumption.

Let's use a graph to illustrate firm 1's demand function given that firm 2 produces q_2^*. DD is the inverse market demand function in Figure 10-5a. If firm 2

[7] Augustin Cournot, *Researches into the Mathematical Principles of the Theory of Wealth*, Nathaniel T. Bacon (trans.), Macmillan, New York, 1897.

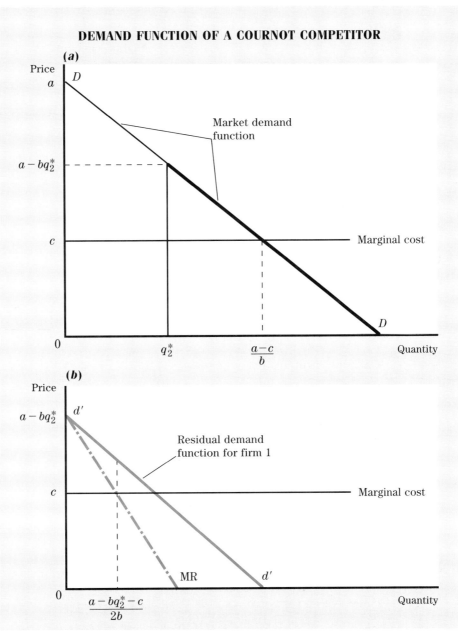

DEMAND FUNCTION OF A COURNOT COMPETITOR

Figure 10-5 If firm 2 produces q_2^*, the residual demand function of firm 1 is the heavy line labeled $d'd'$ in (b). It is the demand function facing firm 1 given that firm 2 produces q_2^*. If firm 1 produces nothing, the price is $a - bq_2^*$. Each unit produced by firm 1 reduces price by $-b$. The marginal revenue function of the residual demand function is MR, the lighter line. Firm 1's marginal revenue equals marginal cost when it produces $(a - c - bq_2^*)/2b$.

produces q_2^* units, the demand function for firm 1 becomes $d'd'$ in Figure 10-5b. If firm 1 produces nothing, the price will be $a - bq_2^*$. Each unit that firm 1 produces reduces price by b, and so the slope of $d'd'$ is the same as the slope of DD. Therefore, $d'd'$ represents the quantity demanded for firm 1 at each price after firm 2 supplies q_2^* units; $d'd'$ is called a residual demand function.

The Reaction or Best Response Function of Each Cournot Rival

Instead of assuming that firm 2 is producing q_2^* units, a specific quantity, let's derive a more general relationship between firm 1's output and firm 2's output. Given q_2, firm 1 selects q_1 to maximize its profits.

$$\frac{\Delta\pi}{\Delta q_1} = 0$$

$$a - 2bq_1 - bq_2 - c = 0$$

We solve this equation for q_1 in terms of q_2.[8]

$$q_1 = \frac{a - c - bq_2}{2b} \qquad \text{(Firm 1's Reaction Function)} \qquad \textbf{(10-10)}$$

Equation 10-10 is firm 1's reaction function. It shows the profit-maximizing quantity of firm 1 for any quantity that firm 2 produces. If the intercept of the demand function $a = \$24$, $b = \$1$, and $c = \$10$, firm 1 maximizes profits if it produces 5 units when firm 2 is producing 4 units.

> The reaction function shows the profit-maximizing quantity for firm 1 for each quantity produced by firm 2.

Because the coefficient of q_2 is $-b$ in firm 1's reaction function, the larger q_2, the smaller the profit-maximizing quantity of firm 1.[9]

Figure 10-6 shows the reaction or best response function of firm 1. The quantity produced by firm 2 is on the vertical axis, and the quantity produced by firm 1 is on the horizontal axis. The intercept on the vertical axis is $(a - c)/b$ because firm 1 produces nothing if firm 2 produces the competitive output. The reason for this is simple. If firm 1 produces any output, it will drive price below long-run average and marginal cost and incurs losses. Therefore, firm 1 produces nothing. The intercept on the horizontal axis shows firm 1 produces $(a - c)/2b$, the monopoly quantity, if firm 2 produces nothing.

Everything said about firm 1 applies to firm 2 as well. Under the Cournot

---

[8] This equation is derived by adding $2bq_1$ to both sides of the equation above and then dividing both sides by $2b$.
[9] The larger the quantity produced by firm 2, the smaller the intercept of the demand function facing firm 1. The residual demand function facing firm 1 shifts to the left as firm 2's output increases. The profit-maximizing output for firm 1 decreases as the demand function shifts to the left.

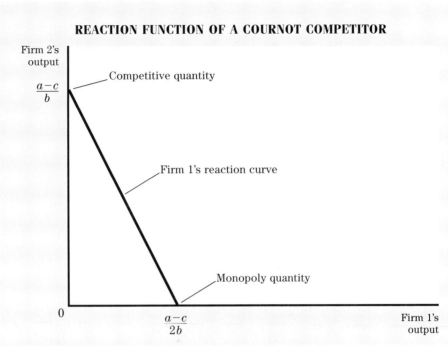

Figure 10-6   The reaction function of firm 1 shows the profit-maximizing quantity of firm 1 for each quantity produced by firm 2.

assumption firm 2 assumes that firm 1's output is constant and will not change when firm 2 changes its quantity. Given q_1, firm 2 selects q_2 to maximize its profits. The reaction or best response function of firm 2 is symmetrical.

$$q_2 = \frac{a - c - bq_1}{2b} \qquad \text{(Firm 2's Reaction Function)} \qquad \textbf{(10-11)}$$

Figure 10-7 shows both reaction functions. Each one indicates the profit-maximizing output of one firm given the output of the other.

The Nash Equilibrium

We have determined the profit-maximizing output of each firm given the output of its rival. However, this information does not indicate what quantity each firm produces. Before finding each firm's quantity, we must define what constitutes an equilibrium. A Nash equilibrium, named after the famous mathematician John Nash, requires each duopolist to maximize its profits given the quantity produced by its rival. Each firm satisfies this condition simultaneously in a Nash equilibrium. So, when neither firm has an incentive to change its behavior, a Nash equilibrium exists. Finding a pair of quantities that satisfies a Nash equilibrium means we have also found a self-enforcing agreement.

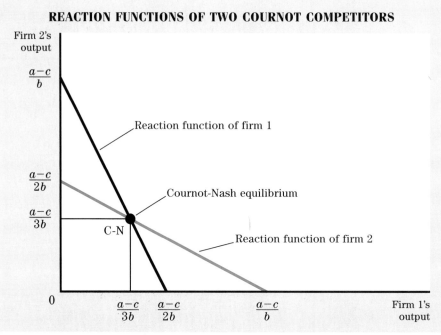

Figure 10-7   The reaction functions of the duopolists show the profit-maximizing output of each firm given the output of the rival. At point C-N each duopolist is maximizing its profits given the rival's output. Each firm produces $(a - c)/3b$. The quantities produced by both firms satisfy the conditions for a Cournot-Nash equilibrium.

> A Nash equilibrium in quantities requires each firm to choose a quantity that maximizes its profits given the quantity produced by a rival.

What pair of quantities satisfies a Nash equilibrium? Each duopolist must be maximizing its profits given the output of a rival in a Nash equilibrium. For this to be true, each must be on its reaction function. There is only one pair of outputs that satisfies this requirement. At point C-N in Figure 10-7 the two reaction functions cross, and each firm produces $(a - c)/3b$.[10] If duopolist 2 produces

[10] This quantity is derived by substituting the expression for q_2 in equation 10-11 into equation 10-10 to obtain

$$q_1 = \frac{a - c - b[(a - c - bq_1)/2b]}{2b}$$

Multiplying both sides by $4b$ yields $4bq_1 = 2a - 2c - a + c + bq_1$. Collecting terms and simplifying leads to

$$q_1 = \frac{a - c}{3b}$$

Then, substitute $(a - c)/3b$ for q_1 in equation 10-11 and derive a similar expression for firm 2.

$(a - c)/3b$, firm 1 expects firm 2 to keep output constant while it produces its profit-maximizing output of $(a - c)/3b$ units. If firm 1 produces $(a - c)/3b$, firm 2's best response is to produce $(a - c)/3b$.

Each firm assumes its rival's output will not change, and this assumption is realized at point C-N and only at point C-N. At this point each firm is producing its profit-maximizing output given the output of its rival, and so a Nash equilibrium exists. Other points on either reaction function do not satisfy the conditions of a Nash equilibrium. Cournot also identified point C-N as an equilibrium as well.[11] For this reason, we refer to point C-N as a Cournot-Nash equilibrium.

In summary, each firm produces $(a - c)/3b$ in a Cournot-Nash equilibrium. The total output of two Cournot firms is $\frac{2}{3}(a - c)/b = \frac{4}{3}(a - c)/2b$. The cooperative (monopoly) output is $(a - c)/2b$, and the competitive output is $(a - c)/b$. So, two Cournot competitors produce one-third more than a monopolist would, or two-thirds of the competitive output.

Because output is higher, price is lower when two firms rather than one are in the market in the Cournot model. The market price is

$$P = a - b\left[2\left(\frac{a - c}{3b}\right)\right] = \frac{a}{3} + \frac{2c}{3} \quad \text{(Price with Two Cournot Rivals)} \quad \textbf{(10-12)}$$

The price in a Cournot-Nash equilibrium is a weighted average of the intercept a and marginal cost c with a weight of $\frac{1}{3}$ placed on a and a weight of $\frac{2}{3}$ placed on c. With a monopoly the price is $(a + c)/2$, and so a and c are weighted equally. Because price is lower with two rather than one firm in the market, the combined profit of the two firms is lower than monopoly profit.

To recapitulate, the Cournot model says that total output is greater and price is lower when the number of sellers increases from one to two. The combined profit of the two Cournot competitors is less than monopoly profit.

APPLICATION 10-2

More Suppliers of Fine Caviar[12]

For many years a Soviet state cartel determined the amount of caviar that Western countries received. In a typical year the catch of Soviet sturgeon, whose eggs are a delicacy, yields about 2,000 tons of caviar, of which the West received only about 150 tons. By controlling the quantity sold abroad, the Soviet government was able to prop up the price of caviar and earn hard currency. The large difference between the price of caviar in Moscow and in New York indicates how effective control has been over shipments of caviar to the West. In Moscow a state-supplied kilogram of top-grade black caviar sells for about $5 on the black market, while the price in New York is more than $500.

The break-up of the former Soviet Union has disrupted the Soviet monopoly,

[11] Cournot justified the equilibrium with an argument that has now been largely discredited. Nevertheless, he also identified point C-N as an equilibrium.
[12] Based on Jane Mayer, "Horrors! Fine Caviar Now Could Become as Cheap as Fish Eggs," *Wall Street Journal*, November 18, 1991.

and the autonomy of the former Soviet states has created more competitors. The two largest Soviet fisheries are now in different republics, one in Russia and one in Kazakhstan. Each republic wants to produce caviar for export. In addition, individual fishermen are entering the business and establishing export channels. The price of fine caviar has dropped with an increase in the number of competitors. The Soviet news agency Interfax has reported a 20 percent drop in the official caviar export price from the previous year. As one official remarked, "All of these small rivals means that the price will fall and the market will be ripped apart. This is a delicacy—we need to keep it elite."

The Cournot Model with *n* Competitors

The results for two Cournot competitors can be extended to n Cournot competitors, where n is any positive integer. This extension indicates how an increase in the number of rivals affects price and quantity. If price falls when the number of sellers increases from 1 to 2, how much lower will it be if there are 100 or 1,000 sellers?

To answer this question, assume that there are n Cournot competitors in the market and each one assumes that the output of all rivals is constant when setting its output. Total quantity demanded equals total quantity supplied by the n Cournot competitors, and so $Q = q_1 + q_2 + \cdots + q_i + \cdots + q_n$. The profit function of the ith Cournot competitor becomes

$$\pi(q_i) = (a - bQ)q_i - cq_i$$

$$= (a - bq_1 - \cdots - bq_i - \cdots - bq_n)q_i - cq_i$$

The appendix at the end of this chapter shows that the quantity that maximizes the profits of firm i is related to the number of rivals in the market by

$$q_i = \frac{1}{n + 1} \frac{a - c}{b} \qquad \text{(Output of a Firm with } n - 1 \text{ Rivals)} \qquad \textbf{(10-13)}$$

Each Cournot competitor produces $1/(n + 1)$ of the competitive output $(a - c)/b$. As the number of Cournot competitors increases, the quantity produced by each seller decreases. For example, if $n = 1$, we have a monopolist and $q_i = (a - c)/2b$, the monopoly solution. If there are 3 Cournot competitors, each firm produces $\frac{1}{4}(a - c)/b$ or one-quarter of the competitive output. The reason this occurs is that the residual demand function facing a firm shifts to the left as the number of rivals increases. The profit-maximizing output of any one firm decreases as the number of rivals increases.

Although each Cournot competitor produces less, the total quantity supplied increases as the number of rivals increases, and so price falls. The price is related to the number of rivals by

$$P = \frac{a}{n + 1} + \frac{nc}{n + 1} \qquad \text{(Price with } n \text{ Cournot Rivals)} \qquad \textbf{(10-14)}$$

As the number of competitors increases, price decreases at a decreasing rate. The first term $a/(n + 1)$ becomes negligible as n increases, and the second term approaches c because $n/(n + 1)$ approaches 1.

> The Cournot model predicts price decreases and approaches marginal cost as the number of rivals becomes large.

Let's review the major features of the Cournot model. With our demand and cost assumptions the Cournot model predicts that price decreases at a decreasing rate as the number of Cournot rivals increases and ultimately approaches the competitive price. It correctly predicts the monopoly price and output when $n = 1$ and the competitive solution when n becomes large. What remains in doubt is whether the Cournot model can accurately predict actual price behavior when n is between these extremes.

The Bertrand Model

The second duopoly model to be considered is the Bertrand model. The structure of the Bertrand model of duopoly is fundamentally different from that of the Cournot model.[13] The sequence of firm and consumer decisions in the Bertrand model is as follows: Firms move first by independently announcing prices. For example, two catalog firms announce prices when they send out their fall catalogs. Then consumers respond to the price quotations by purchasing from the low-price seller. In the Bertrand model, unlike the Cournot model, the low-price supplier supplies the whole market because Bertrand assumes that consumers shift to this seller without cost. If price quotations are identical, the firms divide the market equally.

Let's see what each firm's demand function looks like when firms quote prices. In doing this, it is helpful to express the quantity demanded as a function of price. If the inverse demand function is $P = a - bQ$, the demand function becomes $Q = (a/b) - (1/b)P$. If the price quoted by firm 2 is P_2, firm 1's demand function is shown in the accompanying table.

RELATION BETWEEN P_1 AND P_2	FIRM 1'S QUANTITY DEMANDED
$P_1 > P_2$	0
$P_1 = P_2$	$0.5\left(\dfrac{a}{b} - \dfrac{1}{b}P_1\right)$
$P_1 < P_2$	$\dfrac{a}{b} - \dfrac{1}{b}P_1$

[13] Joseph Bertrand, "Review of 'Theorie mathematique de la richesse social'," *Journal des Savants*, 1883, pp. 499–508. Translated by James W. Friedman.

THE DEMAND FUNCTION OF A BERTRAND COMPETITOR

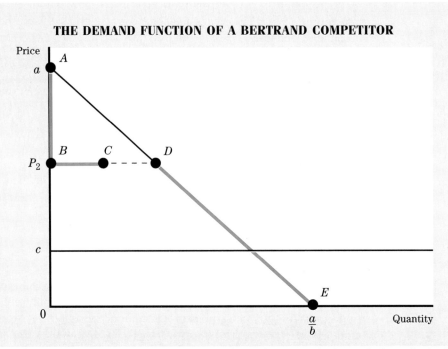

Figure 10-8   In the Bertrand model the demand function facing each duopolist is the discontinuous function *ABCDE*. If firm 2 sets a price of P_2, firm 1 sells nothing if its price exceeds P_2 (segment *AB*). If the two firms charge the same price, they share the market, and so firm 1 produces *BC* and firm 2 produces *CD*. If firm 1 lowers price, it captures the whole market (segment *DE*). What distinguishes the Bertrand model from the Cournot model is that the firm's demand function is horizontal at the price charged by its rival. With a slight price cut a firm can capture the whole market.

Duopolist 1 sells nothing if its price exceeds firm 2's price, shares the market when prices are equal, and attracts all consumers if it quotes the lowest price.

Figure 10-8 shows the demand function facing firm 1 when firm 2's price is P_2. The first part of the discontinuous demand function is the thick segment *AB*. Here, the quantity demanded is zero because $P_1 > P_2$. The two firms share the market when $P_1 = P_2$. Firm 1's demand function is the horizontal segment *BC*. The thick segment *DE* shows that firm 1 satisfies the whole market when $P_1 < P_2$. Therefore, firm 1's demand function runs from *A* to *B*, then from *B* to *C*, and then from *D* to *E*. Along the segment *CD*, demand is perfectly elastic. By offering a tiny price cut, firm 1 can double the quantity it sells.

Now you know what each duopolist's demand function looks like given the price of its rival. Next we determine the pair of prices that will exist in an equilibrium. As in the case of the Cournot model, we need to find an equilibrium and for this purpose we introduce the concept of a Nash equilibrium in prices. A Nash equilibrium is a pair of prices such that each firm's price maximizes its profits given the opponent's price. A Nash equilibrium exists when both prices satisfy this condition.

> A Nash equilibrium in prices requires each firm to choose a price that maximizes its profits given the price of its rival.

What pair of prices satisfies a Nash equilibrium? Let's begin by assuming firm 2 quotes a price above marginal cost: $P_2 > c$. Clearly, firm 1 is not maximizing profits if it charges more than P_2 because it sells nothing. Therefore, firm 1 either matches or undercuts firm 2's price.

If $P_1 = P_2$, the two firms share the market and each firm earns profits since price exceeds c. However, this particular equality of prices cannot represent a Nash equilibrium because firm 1 can increase profits by reducing price by a penny and double its market share. The demand function is perfectly elastic at the price quoted by the rival.

This argument extends to any price greater than c. A tiny price cut by one Bertrand duopolist is profitable. Based on this argument, all price pairs except $P_1 = P_2 = c$ can be eliminated as being inconsistent with a Nash equilibrium in prices. Therefore, the two price quotations must be equal to marginal cost in a Nash equilibrium. The noncooperative solution with two Bertrand sellers in the market is the competitive price and output!

In summary, the Bertrand model predicts that the competitive result emerges just by going from one to two sellers. With the Bertrand model rivalry produces a competitive price. As you can see, this implication is far different from the one in the Cournot model. It is the difference in shape of the firm's demand functions in the two models that is responsible for the different results. In the Cournot model each duopolist faces a downward sloping residual demand function. In the Bertrand model the firm demand function is perfectly elastic at the price quoted by a competitor, and so a price cut is always profitable as long as price exceeds c.

Table 10-5 compares price and output for monopoly, the Cournot and Bertrand models of duopoly, and competition.

APPLICATION 10-3

Encouraging Competition among Suppliers

During the 1980s and early 1990s large firms began to purchase services from specialized firms rather than perform these services internally. Larger firms realized that specialized firms could provide services at a lower price than they could. Examples of some services that large firms disposed of include mail delivery, maintenance, and accounting functions.

Assume that you are a purchasing agent for a large company which has many offices throughout the country that require frequent cleaning. Suppose there are two well-established national cleaning services and you are planning to select one or both of them for this task. You have to decide how many square feet of office space to clean per week and whether one or both firms will provide the services.

Table 10-5   A COMPARISON OF PRICE AND OUTPUT FOR EACH MODEL

MODEL	PRICE	QUANTITY
Monopoly	$\dfrac{a + c}{2}$	$\dfrac{a - c}{2b}$
Cournot ($n = 2$)	$\dfrac{a}{3} + \dfrac{2c}{3}$	$\dfrac{4}{3}\left(\dfrac{a - c}{2b}\right)$
Bertrand ($n = 2$)	c	$\dfrac{a - c}{b}$
Competition	c	$\dfrac{a - c}{b}$

Like all demand functions, your demand function for cleaning offices slopes downward. If the price per 100 square feet cleaned is high, you will reduce the cleaned area. During informal discussions with representatives of the two companies, you provide information about the area to be cleaned at each price, and so each firm knows your demand function.

You must decide how to structure the bidding process and how to award the contract. Should you award it to just a single firm or divide it between the two? One concern of yours is not to be at the mercy of any one firm, and so you are leaning toward dividing the contract between the two firms.

You are considering three methods of assigning the contract.

- *Method 1.* Each supplier offers a bid to clean a certain number of square feet per week. You reveal the two bids at a joint meeting with both parties present. The price per 100 square feet is found by summing the quantities and reading off the price from your demand function. Each firm receives this price per 100 square feet cleaned, and each firm cleans the quantity of space bid. You favor this contract because both firms will supply the services and you will not be at the mercy of a single company.
- *Method 2.* Each firm bids a price per 100 square feet. The firm that bids the lower price wins the whole contract and cleans all units. The total area cleaned is determined by your demand function at the lowest bid price. If the bids are the same, the firms share the market and clean the same number of square feet. You are reluctant to use this method because you fear that you will be at the mercy of one firm.
- *Method 3.* This method is the same as method 2 except that the two firms share the task at the lowest price bid. You are more comfortable with this method because you will not be at the mercy of a single firm.

Given these three alternatives, which method would you select? Would you have the firms bid an area to clean (method 1) or bid a price (method 2 or 3)? What can you say about the idea of dividing the contract between the two bidders at the lowest bid price?

There are two issues to consider: First, the two firms could cooperate and charge a profit-maximizing price. If they get together, they could estimate what it would cost you to perform the service internally and charge a slightly lower price. Because they might get together, you want to adopt the method that puts the greatest strain on any agreement to cooperate. Second, if the firms fail to cooperate with one another, which method will yield the lowest price?

What lessons can you learn from the Cournot and Bertrand models of duopoly? The first assignment method describes the Cournot model. Under method 1 each firm selects a quantity. Method 2 describes the Bertrand model. If the two firms act noncooperatively, price will be lower with method 2 than with method 1. You hope the inducement to win the whole contract will cause the two firms to compete and to bid the competitive price. You want to offer the supplier a carrot—obtaining a large increase in the quantity by offering a lower price. Anything you can do to increase the total area cleaned will encourage a rival to cut price. With a Nash equilibrium in prices, both firms will quote a price equal to marginal cost so that you will not have to rely on a single firm. Therefore, method 2 puts a greater strain on any possible agreement between the two suppliers than method 1 because the gain from offering a lower price is greater. Conversely, you do not want to divide the contract between the firms unless there are compelling reasons to do so. The drawback of method 3 is that it discourages a firm from offering a lower price. No matter what price is bid, the firm receives only 50 percent of the market. By dividing the contract between the two suppliers, you will structure the bidding to discourage independent pricing. If the firms act independently, method 2 has more to recommend it.

10-4   THE EFFECT OF THE NUMBER OF RIVALS ON PRICE

The Cournot and Bertrand models make strikingly different predictions of how the number of rivals affects price. As the appendix at the end of this chapter shows, price declines in the Cournot model at a decreasing rate as the number of rivals grows. In the Bertrand model price falls precipitously to marginal cost when there are two or more competitors. Figure 10-9 compares prices and the number of competitors in the two models. You can see that the price declines at a decreasing rate to marginal cost as the number of Cournot competitors increases. In the Bertrand model the price falls abruptly from the monopoly price to the competitive price as soon as the number of competitors is two.

Now let's turn to some evidence and see whether one or the other theory gives

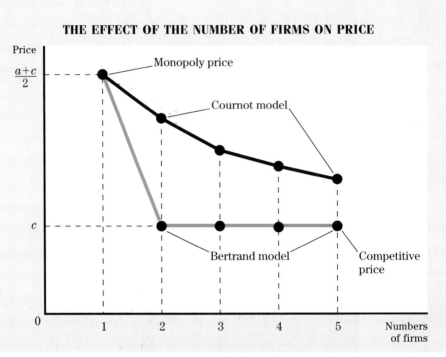

THE EFFECT OF THE NUMBER OF FIRMS ON PRICE

Figure 10-9   Price declines systematically toward marginal cost as more Cournot competitors enter the market. In contrast, the Bertrand model yields the competitive result with two or more Bertrand competitors.

a closer approximation to the real world by surveying some of the empirical studies that explicitly examine this question.

APPLICATION **10-4**

Retail Tire Prices

Timothy Bresnahan and Peter Reiss studied retail tire prices in numerous local markets with different numbers of sellers.[14] They tried to adjust for differences in the cost of operating in small versus large markets, although this was not always easy to do. They found that prices declined with an increase in the number of retail sellers but not in a continuous manner. Median prices for a specific tire are shown in Table 10-6 for towns with one to five sellers and, separately, for large urban markets.

[14] Timothy F. Bresnahan and Peter C. Reiss, "Entry and Competition in Concentrated Markets," *Journal of Political Economy*, vol. 99, October 1991, pp. 977–1009.

Table 10-6   MEDIAN RETAIL TIRE PRICES AND NUMBER OF RETAILERS IN MARKET

	Monopoly	Number of Tire Dealers				→ Competition
	1	2	3	4	5	URBAN
Median price ($)	53.9	55.0	52.9	50.9	49.8	43.2

A statistical analysis of the price data shows that prices fall but not continuously with increases in the number of dealers in the market. The difference between the median price in monopoly and duopoly markets is not statistically significant. Median prices in markets with three to five dealers are significantly lower than in monopoly and duopoly markets. In urban markets where the number of retailers is larger, prices are still lower.[15] If urban markets with more sellers approximate competitive markets, then we can say that the median price exceeds the competitive level in markets with five or fewer sellers. Although these empirical findings do not fit the Cournot model perfectly, the pattern is more consistent with the Cournot model than with the Bertrand model. The similarity of prices in monopoly and duopoly markets is inconsistent with the predictions of both models. The findings suggest that duopolists can and do reach the cooperative solution. The results of this study flatly contradict the prediction of the Bertrand model since the price appears to be above the competitive price when two or more sellers are in the market.

APPLICATION 10-5

Auction Markets[16]

In a comprehensive investigation of the effect of the number of sellers or buyers on price, Leonard Weiss reviewed several studies of auction markets as well as other markets. We report results for auctions of tax-exempt bonds, offshore oil, and timber sales by the National Timber Service. Just as sellers can collude to raise price, buyers can collude to purchase a product at a lower price. Our interest is in

[15] Some of the differences between the median prices in urban markets and in smaller markets may be due to unmeasured cost differences and to differences in the services offered.
[16] Based on Leonard Weiss, ed., *Concentration and Price*, MIT Press, Cambridge, Mass., 1989, Table 4.1. © 1989 Massachusetts Institute of Technology.

Table 10-7 MAXIMUM NUMBER OF BIDS WITH SIGNIFICANT INCREASE IN PRICE

Tax-Exempt Bonds		Offshore Oil Auctions		Timber Sales	
GENERAL OBLIGATION BONDS	REVENUE BONDS	1954–1971	1972–1975	SEALED BID	ORAL BID
8	5	7	7	4	8

determining how many bidders must be in the market before price rises to the competitive price.

Table 10-7 summarizes the findings of these different studies. In all the auction markets the price paid by bidders increased but at a decreasing rate as the number of bidders increased. For each type of auction Table 10-7 shows the maximum number of bidders in the market where there was a statistically significant effect of the number of bidders on price. For example, in offshore oil auctions, the winning bid increased until the number of bidders at the auction exceeded seven. At this auction it is likely that the competitive price was paid when eight or more bidders participated.

This summary indicates that price approximates the competitive price with at most seven or eight bidders in four of six cases and four or five bidders in the other two cases. Therefore, the Cournot model approximates price behavior at these auctions better than the Bertrand model does since price increases with the number of bidders. What these studies suggest is that imperfect cooperation becomes increasingly difficult to achieve when there are more than eight members. Successful collusion with more sellers or buyers appears unlikely.

Comparing the Cournot and the Bertrand models suggests that the Cournot model gives a better, but still imperfect, accounting of itself than the Bertrand model does. Prices appear to rise significantly until the number of buyers reaches eight. From then on, the number of rivals does not have a significant effect on price. So, the predictions of the Cournot model fit the data better than those of the Bertrand model.

10-5 FACILITATING AND PREVENTING COLLUSION

Although cooperation is difficult to achieve, sellers have an incentive to collude and to prevent profits from being competed away. This is particularly true in the Bertrand model where an increase from one to two sellers causes price to drop abruptly to the competitive price. This section considers how sellers or buyers can benefit by changing the rules of the game.

Meeting Competition

Let's modify one assumption of the Bertrand model and assume instead that one firm announces a price policy of "meeting competition." A stereo store or a bookstore is not going to be undercut by a rival and announces that it will compete aggressively by offering to match any price cut.

Let's see if a price policy of meeting competition creates greater rivalry among sellers and lowers price or raises price. If each firm knows that a rival will immediately match its price, the incentive to offer a lower price evaporates. Instead of lowering price, a policy of meeting competition will raise price.

While sellers benefit by adopting a policy of meeting competition, they will not find it a cure-all for the cheating problem. For one thing, the policy is often difficult to administer. There must be an objective, low-cost way of determining quoted prices. How do you know that a competitor is offering the product at a lower price? This policy can be a nuisance and can result in disgruntled consumers and even lawsuits.

APPLICATION 10-6

Detecting the Effects of Facilitating Practices

David Grether and Charles Plott studied the effect of certain facilitating practices on price in an experimental setting.[17] The facilitating practices included (1) meeting the lowest price of a competitor, (2) delivering the product to the buyer at the lowest price received by any other buyer, and (3) providing the buyer with a 30-day notice of any price change. In 1979, the Federal Trade Commission (FTC) challenged these practices in an action against the Ethyl Corporation, E. I. DuPont, Nalco Chemical Company, and PPG Industries. The FTC asked the four producers of lead-based antiknock compounds to cease and desist from using these market practices. The FTC argued that these facilitating practices (1) lowered the incentive of firms to cut price by ensuring that competitors match price decreases, (2) eliminated any incentive for secret price cutting, and (3) ensured simultaneous price changes.

Grether and Plott assessed these claims by creating a market in a laboratory setting. They recruited subjects for participation in several experiments in which each became either a buyer or supplier. Buyers received a different reservation (maximum) value for each unit they purchased. The difference between the reservation value and the actual price paid in the experimental market was their per unit profit. Sellers received a reservation (minimum) value for each unit they supplied. The difference between the price at which they sold each unit and the reservation value was their profit on the unit. Buyers benefited most by buying at the lowest possible price, and suppliers benefited most by selling at the highest possible price. Figure 10-10a shows the demand and supply functions created by

[17] Charles R. Plott, "Laboratory Experiments in Economics: The Implications of Posted-Price Institutions," *Science*, vol. 232, May 9, 1986, pp. 732–738. Copyright 1986 by the AAAS.

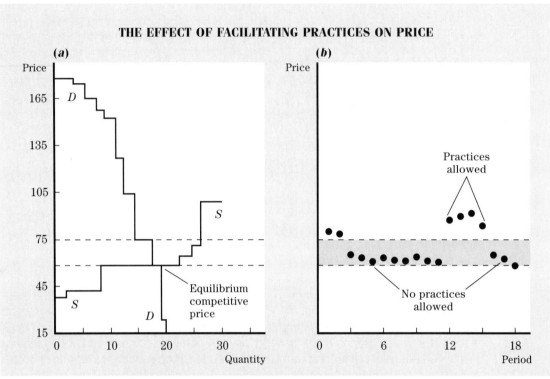

Figure 10-10   Market demand and supply functions are constructed by assigning reservation values to units demanded by buyers and units supplied by sellers. During periods 1 through 11 no facilitating practices are allowed, and the price settles close to the competitive equilibrium price. During periods 12 through 15 suppliers introduce and use facilitating price policies. The price rises and then declines again during periods 16 through 18 when the facilitating practices are prohibited.

Grether and Plott given the reservation values for buyers and sellers and the equilibrium price. The dots in Figure 10-10*b* are the average transaction prices in each period. During periods 1 through 11 the sellers could not communicate or use the facilitating practices. As is true in many experiments of this kind, price settled quickly toward the competitive equilibrium price. The questionable practices were permitted during periods 10 through 15 and then eliminated during periods 16 through 18. Figure 10-10*b* shows that price increased above the competitive equilibrium when the firms adopted questionable practices 1 through 3. Price declined toward the competitive price when the participants discontinued these practices.

The results of these experiments indicate that facilitating practices raised price above the competitive price but not to the monopoly price. They suggest that meeting competitors' prices, preannouncing prices, and guaranteeing a buyer the lowest price raise the price level.

Preventing Collusion

You know that sellers can adopt policies that will increase price. What can a buyer do to prevent a conspiracy among suppliers from functioning successfully? Kenneth Hendricks and Robert Porter have offered several suggestions to make life difficult for conspiring suppliers where contracts are awarded by a bidding system.[18] A buyer benefits by reducing the amount of price information that suppliers have. This can be done by announcing the identity of the winning bidder but not the bid. If suppliers continually submit identical bids, the buyer can refuse to pick randomly among bids when awarding the contract but always award it to the same firm. This will certainly create confusion among the members of a conspiracy. They will suspect price chiseling by the innocent but favored firm that repeatedly lands the contract. The buyer hopes that this will lead to price chiseling by others. If the purchaser finds the bids are different but still suspects a conspiracy, she can periodically select the second lowest bid as the winner but fail to disclose the price. Here again, the buyer's strategy is to sow seeds of distrust among the members of the conspiracy.

When collusion is suspected, the buyer can set a reservation price and announce that no bid above this price will be acceptable. She can also affect the success of any conspiracy by the way she awards the contract. If many short-term contracts are being offered, it may be preferable to combine them all into one large contract rather than offering contracts sequentially. Instead of offering a sequence of five yearly auctions, the buyer can arrange to have one auction covering all five years. When she offers five annual auctions, the cartel can punish a firm that cheats on price in year 1 during subsequent years. The cartel members can lower price in year 2, for example, to punish the price chiseler. However, by offering one 5-year contract, the buyer tempts members of the cartel to offer a price cut to win the whole contract and prevents the cartel from punishing the renegade immediately. An important general message here is that repetitive interaction among sellers tends to reduce cheating.

These suggestions by Hendricks and Porter show that a buyer does not have to stand by idly but can adopt policies to reduce the effectiveness of a supplier conspiracy. Buyers do not have to rely solely on the Antitrust Division of the Justice Department to limit the effectiveness of oligopolists. By structuring the form and type of an auction, the effectiveness of any suspected conspiracy can be reduced.

10-6   A CASE STUDY: THE ELECTRICAL MANUFACTURERS' CONSPIRACY

As noted before, a cooperative agreement among a small number of firms is not easily reached. What is perhaps most surprising is that cooperative agreements are difficult to reach even under the most favorable conditions. The problems that firms have in reaching a cooperative solution can be illustrated in a revealing case

---

[18] Kenneth Hendricks and Robert Porter, "Collusion in Auctions," *Annals D'Economie et de Statistique*, N 15/16, 1989, pp. 217–230.

study of the electrical manufacturers' conspiracy. What becomes clear from this case study is that the number of members in a conspiracy plays a less important role than product and industry characteristics in determining the success of the conspiracy.

In 1960 the principal executive officers of General Electric Company, Westinghouse Electric Company, Allis-Chalmers, and other major electrical manufacturers pleaded guilty to charges of conspiring to fix prices. Seven officers received 30-day sentences—stiff sentences for the time. Numerous lawsuits followed these guilty pleas, and the awards to plaintiffs reached approximately $900 million, or $3.9 billion in 1990 dollars, hardly a trifling sum.[19]

The methods used by the major electrical manufacturers to set prices in several lines of business shocked antitrust authorities and the business community. During the investigation the government learned that representatives of these firms met frequently to discuss prices, to assign contracts to particular suppliers, and to determine the market shares of members of the conspiracy. Meeting and discussing prices with competitors is a violation of U.S. antitrust laws. These practices affected numerous products sold to public and private utilities, ranging from transformers to switchgear to turbines. The orders submitted by utilities are usually large, especially for turbines, and are specific to the particular requirements of each utility.

Collusion and Cheating

Economists learned in considerable detail how the electrical utilities attempted to fix prices and market shares from testimony and court documents. By recounting the events and practices of the conspiracy, we hope to identify the critical factors that caused this conspiracy to break down periodically.

The federal government encouraged communication among electrical manufacturers during the 1930s in the mistaken belief that the Great Depression would end if prices increased. The firms continued to meet periodically and discuss prices and market shares at trade association meetings after World War II. A detailed and elaborate system called the "phase of the moon" evolved which assigned each order to a particular firm. In some lines of business conspirators met to determine which firm would submit the lowest bid on each contract and what bids each loser would submit. The phase-of-the-moon mechanism determined the price each conspirator would submit on each order, with the low price rotating among competitors to create the illusion of competitive bidding. Between December 5, 1958, and April 19, 1959, the position rotated among the competitors every 2 weeks. During one 2-week period ITE, a member of the conspiracy, submitted the low bid and quoted a price of $200 below the book price. Westinghouse offered a $100 discount off the book price, Federal Pacific was $50 below book, General Electric was 0.1 percent off book, and Allis-Chalmers quoted the book price.

The firms adopted a phase-of-the-moon system intermittently from 1953 to

---

[19] This account follows Ralph G. M. Sultan, *Pricing in the Electric Oligopoly*, vol. 1, Harvard University Press, Cambridge, Mass., 1974, chaps. 2 and 3.

1959. In 1954 there were 25 meetings among competitors at various hotels. Although the representatives of the different firms who attended these meetings solemnly agreed to abide by these prices, they often cheated on each other. Frustrated by this cheating, General Electric expressed displeasure at its declining market share as other firms undercut GE's price. The companies ceased meeting after General Electric began pricing independently. The fragile price agreements became especially vulnerable whenever demand decreased. Price cutting became rampant during the 1954 recession and culminated in what became known as the "white sale" in January 1955 when some units sold at 45 percent off book price.

In May 1955 company representatives began to meet again to try to raise prices. Forty-two meetings took place over the next 18 months. Throughout this period the firms circulated detailed memoranda that assigned a bid price for every switchgear order to each firm in hopes of raising prices. Prices increased under this system, but it is unclear how much of the rise was due to the circulation of memoranda or to the rise in backlogs. The next pricing crisis occurred in 1957. A large public utility order was to be split between General Electric and Westinghouse but Westinghouse offered a secret price discount to win a still larger order. The public utility conveniently informed General Electric of the offer, and General Electric matched the secret price cut and won the whole contract. This episode proved fatal to the conspiracy. It triggered another wave of deep price cutting by other firms in the industry. Westinghouse responded by cutting price on the next order. And on the next order Allis-Chalmers offered a still larger price cut. More meetings followed, but the level of suspicion among the firms became so great that the members of the conspiracy were unwilling to trust each other. The meetings became shouting matches with each firm accusing the others of cheating on agreements. The smaller companies claimed the larger companies were pricing to drive them out of the market. The larger companies charged the smaller companies were increasing their market share by aggressive bidding.

By late 1958 the larger firms thought prices of switchgear equipment would increase only if they voluntarily surrendered market share to the smaller firms. Table 10-8 shows the market shares of each company before 1958 and after a

Table 10-8   MARKET SHARES OF FIRMS IN SWITCHGEAR MARKET

COMPANY	BEFORE (%)	AFTER (%)
General Electric	42	39
Westinghouse	38	35
Allis-Chalmers	11	8
ITE	9	11
Federal Pacific	0	7

meeting held to set switchgear prices and market shares. This agreement collapsed when prices began to crumble again in the middle of 1959. The meetings stopped when rumors of an investigation by the Department of Justice began to circulate.

Figure 10-11 shows the time series of book prices, actual prices, new orders, and backlog of orders for switchgears and circuit breakers. The time series indicates that the gap between the book and the actual price level depended on the state of backlogs. It appears that the meetings had a diminishing impact on pricing whenever total backlogs declined as they did in 1954 and in 1957 and 1958. Prices firmed when backlogs grew. It is difficult to distinguish between the effect of the meetings and the effect of backlogs on price. Figure 10-11 suggests that the rather elaborate mechanism of collusion failed to work effectively.

Product and Industry Characteristics and Successful Collusion

This case study reveals the difficulties firms have in reaching a cooperative solution even when the industry has a small number of firms—five firms in the switchgear market—and when firms communicate directly with each other to discuss individual orders. Under conditions that can only be described as favorable to collusion, firms nevertheless cheated on the agreement.

The facts of the case suggest that the number of sellers in the market isn't the only or necessarily the most important determinant of successful collusion. Characteristics of the product and the industry appear to affect the success of an agreement. In the electrical manufacturers' case the Bertrand model seems more applicable than the Cournot model because one firm usually wins the order and firms submit prices. Because each order is large, the desire of a firm to win the order by offering a lower price is difficult to resist. This is especially true when demand declines and the discrepancy between current price and short-run marginal cost increases. Price cutting broke out whenever demand decreased, excess capacity appeared, and backlogs decreased.

Collusion also appears to be less successful when the buyer can suppress or distort price information. In this industry, a utility can conceal a price reduction. Negotiations with private utilities are private, and a private utility can play one firm off against another by revealing or distorting the price information received from other sellers. Given the large size of a typical order, a private utility encourages price chiseling by a conspirator by awarding the whole contract to any firm that will undercut the others. In contrast, public utilities adopt sealed bidding where the prices of all bidders become public knowledge with the announcement of the winning bid. It is easier to determine which firm violated the price agreement when the contract is awarded. Sultan reports the average percentage off-the-book price was 9.5 percent higher for private utilities than for public utilities. By publicly revealing bids, public utilities reduce the incentive to cut prices.

In short, fluctuating demand, secret price negotiations, and the absence of hard information about prices are all responsible for the difficulties experienced by the electrical manufacturers. These are unfavorable conditions for a successful conspiracy. Perhaps these unfavorable circumstances were the reason the conspirators

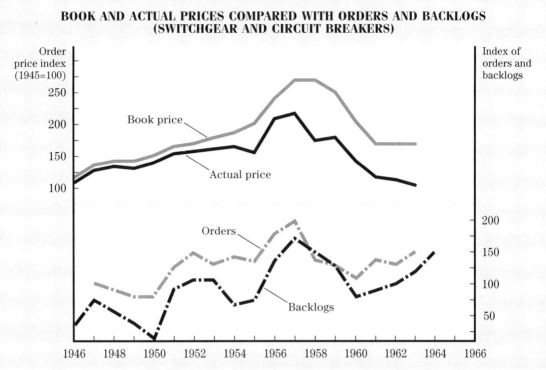

BOOK AND ACTUAL PRICES COMPARED WITH ORDERS AND BACKLOGS (SWITCHGEAR AND CIRCUIT BREAKERS)

Figure 10-11   The difference between book price and actual price increases when backlogs decline. The first large discrepancy between book and transaction price appeared in late 1954 and early 1955 during the "white sale." The second large difference appears in 1957 and 1958 when backlogs decline again. [*After Ralph G. M. Sultan,* Pricing in the Electrical Oligopoly, *vol. 1, Harvard University Press, Cambridge, Mass., 1974, p. 44.*]

had to meet and discuss individual orders if the conspiracy was to achieve even a modicum of success.

The Cost of Detecting Price Chiseling

Although it seems as though conditions favored collusion—a small number of sellers and a large share of industry output—characteristics of the product and the industry favored cheating. The case study of the electrical manufacturers' conspiracy indicates that the success of collusion depends more on the characteristics of the product and industry conditions and less on the number of sellers. Recent developments in the theory of oligopoly have focused more on the conditions that make price cutting easy or difficult to detect. The rationale for this approach is that collusion is more successful when the colluding firms can quickly detect price chiseling and can do so at a low cost. When the cost of detection is low, members of a conspiracy can respond quickly to a price cut by matching the price reduction and limiting the gains of a renegade. When the cost is high, the gain from price cutting is larger and price agreements will either be unsuccessful or firms will not even attempt to collude in the first place.

This line of research has focused on the determinants of the cost of detecting price chiseling. Nobel Laureate George J. Stigler identified the following factors in an important early contribution to these studies.[20] In Stigler's analysis, a firm suspects price chiseling when the quantity that it sells decreases inexplicably. If it can lose only a small quantity to a competitor before inferring that some firm is cutting price, then the gains from price chiseling will be correspondingly small and a price agreement has a better chance of succeeding.

Stigler identifies the following three determinants of the cost of detecting price cutting.

1. *Number of buyers.* When there are many small buyers of a product, keeping a price cut secret is no small achievement. The likelihood of a firm learning of a price cut can be predicted with a simple analysis of the probability that customers will reveal their prices. To see why this is so, consider the likelihood that a rival learns about a price cut that you offer to all n of your customers. Let p be the probability that a rival will hear about your price cut from a buyer. Then $1 - p$ is the probability that the rival will not learn about your price cut to one buyer. If you offer a price cut to n customers, the probability that all n buyers will not inform is $(1 - p)^n$. The probability of detection is therefore $1 - (1 - p)^n$. If $p = .01$, the probability that a buyer will tell is only one chance in a hundred. If you offer a price cut to 100 buyers, then the probability that your rival will learn of the price cut is $1 - (.99)^{100} = .63$. In 63 chances out of 100 your rival will learn of your price cut. The larger the number of buyers, the larger the probability that your rivals will detect the price cut.

2. *Customer turnover.* In some industries there is considerable turnover of customers in the normal course of business, while in others customers tend to always purchase from the same seller. When the probability of a repeat sale to a customer is low, customers move from one seller to another for a host of random reasons. The quantity that a firm sells will fluctuate randomly from period to period from the normal turnover of customers. It will be difficult for a firm to infer whether its sales are down because another firm is chiseling on price or because many customers are purchasing from other sellers for random reasons that have nothing to do with price cutting. A price chiseler can hide behind this smoke screen and take more customers away from rivals by cutting price without being detected. Price agreements are less likely to succeed in this inhospitable environment.

3. *Availability of price information.* If information about prices paid or received is readily available, the gains from price cutting are smaller. Often,

[20] George J. Stigler, "A Theory of Oligopoly," *Journal of Political Economy*, vol. 72, no. 1, February 1964, pp. 44–61.

government agencies must make all submitted prices publicly available. The identity of the renegade and the magnitude of the price reduction become public knowledge. This suggests that collusion will be more successful when suppliers are selling to government agencies than to private firms.

In summary, recent developments in oligopoly theory place greater emphasis on the characteristics of the product, demand stability, and the characteristics of the buyers as determinants of successful collusion.

10-7   GAME THEORY AND NONCOOPERATIVE STRATEGIES

In markets with few firms interdependence among firms is pronounced. What strategy a firm adopts depends on what it thinks the opponent's strategy is. Game theory is the study of the strategic interaction among a small number of players whether they are firms, nations, employers, or employees. A game is a situation of mutual interdependence among agents. Game theory helps economists identify the options available to the firms in an oligopoly and in some cases to deduce what strategy the firm should adopt. This section introduces some of the concepts and methods used in game theory to determine the strategies of two firms. The discussion of game theory concentrates on noncooperative games where each firm maximizes its profits given the strategy of a rival.[21]

As you will see, every game has three components: (1) a set of players, (2) a set of strategies, and (3) a listing of payoffs. In the following examples there are two players and two strategies for each player with the corresponding payoffs.

Dominant Strategies

In some situations a firm can select a profit-maximizing strategy that does not depend on what strategy its rival adopts. A dominant strategy is the firm's best strategy no matter what strategy its rival selects. The idea of dominant strategy can be illustrated by reconsidering the duopoly problem. Let's assume that duopolists each earn $100 if they reach a cooperative agreement. On the other hand, if duopolist 1 cheats on the agreement and produces a larger quantity, it earns $125 while the noncheater earns only $70. If both duopolists cheat by producing a larger quantity, then each earns only $75.

Figure 10-12 is the payoff matrix. Firm 1's payoffs (profits) are in the lower-left-hand corner of each cell, while firm 2's payoffs are in the upper-right-hand corner of each cell. Profits of each duopolist are $100 if they share the market (northwest cell). If either firm cheats while the other does not, the cheater earns $125 and the noncheater earns only $70 (southwest and northeast cells). If both firms cheat, each firm earns $75 (southeast cell).

---

[21] For a thoroughly enjoyable introduction to strategic thinking, the reader should consult Avinash Dixit and Barry Nalebuff, *Thinking Strategically*, W. W. Norton, New York, 1991.

**PAYOFF MATRIX FOR THE STRATEGIES
OF DUOPOLISTS**

Firm 2

		Share the market	Cheat
Firm 1	**Share the market**	$\pi_2 = \$100$ (Cooperative solution) $\pi_1 = \$100$	$\pi_2 = \$125$ $\pi_1 = \$70$
	Cheat	$\pi_2 = \$70$ $\pi_1 = \boxed{\$125}$	$\pi_2 = \$75$ (Noncooperative solution) $\pi_1 = \boxed{\$75}$

Figure 10-12   The dominant strategy of firm 1 is to cheat. No matter which strategy firm 2 selects, firm 1's profits are greater if it cheats. Similarly, firm 2's dominant strategy is to cheat. No matter what strategy firm 1 adopts, firm 2's profits are higher or the same if it cheats.

The special feature of this game is that the strategy that maximizes profits of each firm is independent of the strategy adopted by its rival. When your profit-maximizing strategy is independent of your rival's, you have a dominant strategy.

A dominant strategy is the firm's best strategy no matter what strategy a rival adopts.

To verify this, look at the game from firm 1's viewpoint. If firm 2 shares the market at the monopoly price, firm 1's profits are higher and are $125 if it cheats (southwest cell). If firm 2 cheats, firm 1's profits are higher by cheating too, and so both firms end up in the southeast cell. No matter which strategy firm 2 adopts, firm 1's profits are higher if it follows the cheating strategy. For each strategy adopted by firm 2, there is a square around the maximum profits that firm 1 earns. Notice that the squares around firm 1's profits are in the same row, the southwest and the southeast cells. Firm 1's dominant strategy is to cheat on output no matter what strategy firm 2 selects.

Similar reasoning shows that firm 2's best strategy is to cheat. If firm 1 shares the market, firm 2's profits are at a maximum of $125 if it cheats. If firm 1 cheats, firm 2's profits are $75 if it cheats (southeast cell). So firm 2's dominant strategy is to cheat no matter what firm 1 does. When both firms have a dominant strategy, two circles are in the same column and two squares are in the same row. The cell with a square and a circle identifies the dominant strategy of each rival. In Figure 10-12 the southeast cell identifies the dominant strategy where each firm cheats on the agreement.

If both firms could enforce an agreement to share the market, each would earn $100. Yet both firms cheat on output, and each earns only $75, as happened in the electrical manufacturers' conspiracy. This example illustrates the "Prisoners' Dilemma," which can be described as follows. Two prisoners are interviewed separately. If neither confesses to a crime, each receives a light sentence, say 1 year. If one confesses while the other does not, the prisoner who confesses receives a still lighter sentence of 4 months and the nonconfessor receives a life term. If both confess, each receives a 30-year term. The dominant strategy of each prisoner is to confess. If they could get together and somehow enforce an agreement not to confess, they would both be better off. This is exactly the same problem facing the duopolists. If one firm cheats while the other does not, the firm that cheats earns higher profits of $125. Yet, both cheat and earn only $75. If they could reach and enforce an agreement to share the market, each would earn $100. This is exactly the Prisoners' Dilemma first encountered in Table 10-3, where we observed that each player looking out for his or her own self-interest does not maximize the collective self-interest.

A Dominant Strategy for Only One Firm

In some games only one firm has a dominant strategy. The question becomes: What strategy should the firm without a dominant strategy follow?

Consider the following game. Firm 1 is an auto company with prowess in engineering. It is more adept at introducing technical innovations like sophisticated suspension systems or more responsive engines, while firm 2 has more capable designers and is successful when introducing styling changes. Both firms are planning to introduce a new model automobile. Should each bring out a new model that favors its strength with firm 1 introducing a technically advanced model and firm 2 bringing out an automobile with a new design?

The profits for each combination of strategies are in Figure 10-13. Firm 1 plays to its strength, engineering. Its dominant strategy is to introduce a technical model change. For each strategy adopted by firm 2, firm 1 earns higher profits by introducing a technical model change. Firm 2 does not have a dominant strategy. Firm 2's best strategy depends on what strategy firm 1 follows. If firm 1 introduces a technical model change, firm 2's best strategy is to copy and introduce a technical model change as well. If firm 1 adopts a styling change, firm 2's best strategy is to adopt a styling change.

What strategy should firm 2 adopt given that it does not have a dominant strategy? At this point it should put itself in firm 1's shoes. It knows that firm 1 is a technical colossus. Therefore, it is quite likely that firm 1 will pick a strategy that exploits this strength because its profits will be higher. Therefore, firm 2 expects firm 1 to introduce a technical change. Given this, the best strategy for firm 2 is to adopt a technical change as well, although it cannot match firm 1's strength in this area. If firm 2 adopts a styling change when firm 1 adopts a technical change, it

**PAYOFF MATRIX FOR TWO
AUTOMOBILE COMPANIES**

Firm 2

		Technical model change	Styling model change
Firm 1	**Technical model change**	$\pi_2 = \$20$ $\pi_1 = \$40$	$\pi_2 = \$15$ $\pi_1 = \$60$
	Styling model change	$\pi_2 = \$16$ $\pi_1 = \$8$	$\pi_2 = \$18$ $\pi_1 = \$12$

Figure 10-13 Firm 1 has a dominant strategy. It introduces a model change with numerous technical advances. If it introduces technical innovations, it earns profits of $40 million if firm 2 follows the leader and introduces a new auto with technical changes. Firm 1 earns profits of $60 million if it introduces a technical change and firm 2 introduces a styling change. Consumers place a greater value on technical than on styling changes. On the other hand, firm 2 does not have a dominant strategy. If firm 1 introduces a technical change, then firm 2's best strategy is to introduce a technical change. If firm 1 introduces a styling change, firm 2's best strategy is to introduce a styling change. The profit-maximizing strategy of firm 2 depends on what strategy firm 1 adopts.

earns only $15 million in profits while it can earn $20 million if it introduces a new model with technical innovations. Unfortunately for firm 2, consumers value a technical change more than a styling change.

The lesson to be learned from this example is clear. If you do not have a dominant strategy, see if you can infer your rival's dominant strategy. If your rival has a dominant strategy, assume that your rival is rational and will adopt this strategy. Then select the strategy that maximizes your profits given the favored strategy of your rival.

Let's consider another example. Firms have a choice of when to introduce a new brand. Should a company try to introduce a brand early or late in the evolution of the market? And does this depend on whether the brand name is new or borrowed? Suppose two firms are planning to enter a market. Firm 1 has a well-established, well-recognized brand-name product in another market. Firm 1 wants to take advantage of the recognized name that it has already created and to introduce a product in this new market by using the existing name. Marketing professionals call this a brand extension strategy. For example, Coca Cola introduced

Diet Coke. This is a brand extension in a new market, the diet soft drink market. Firm 2 is a new firm and will introduce the product with a new brand name.

By using a brand extension, the firm hopes that consumers who are familiar with the brand name will try the new product. Firm 1 has to be careful not to damage the reputation of the existing brand if the brand extension fails in the new market. Therefore, having an existing brand can be a help or a hindrance in the new market. One strategy that firm 1 can follow is to wait and learn more about the market before modifying some features of its brand extension to increase its chance of success. Firm 2 does not have an existing brand name. So if its product fails, it does not damage the reputation of an existing brand name. For firm 2 the relative payoff from entering the market early is greater than from entering late. The payoffs of the two firms are shown in Figure 10-14. Firm 2's dominant strategy is to enter the market early. Both circles are in the same column. Firm 1 does not have a dominant strategy because the two squares are in different rows. Firm 2 enters early with a new product and name, and firm 1 enters later with a brand extension.

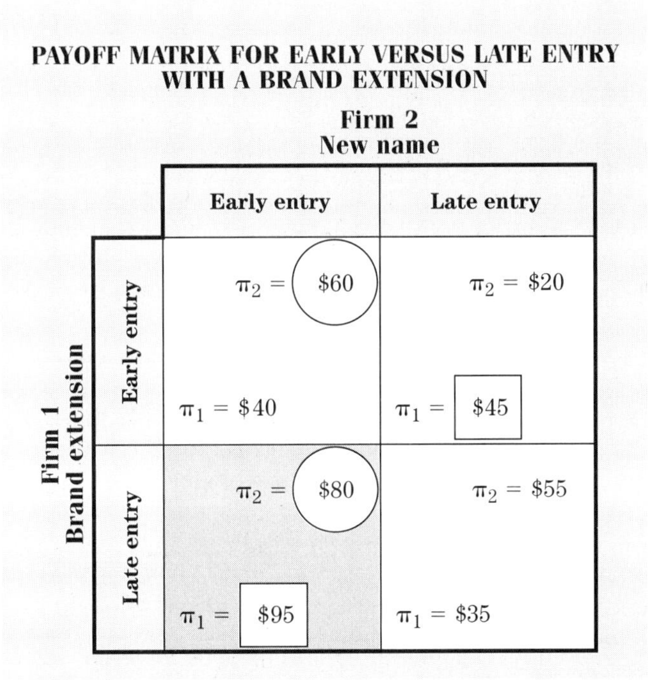

PAYOFF MATRIX FOR EARLY VERSUS LATE ENTRY WITH A BRAND EXTENSION

Firm 2
New name

		Early entry	Late entry
Firm 1 Brand extension	**Early entry**	$\pi_2 = \$60$ $\pi_1 = \$40$	$\pi_2 = \$20$ $\pi_1 = \$45$
	Late entry	$\pi_2 = \$80$ $\pi_1 = \$95$	$\pi_2 = \$55$ $\pi_1 = \$35$

Figure 10-14 Firm 1 has a well-established brand in another market. It decides to adopt a brand extension strategy when entering a new market. It does not have a dominant strategy. If firm 2 enters early, firm 1 enters its brand extension late so that it can judge the market better. It wants to minimize the probability that its brand extension will fail and damage the reputation of its established brand name. If firm 2 enters late, firm 1 will take a chance and enter early since it earns $45 million rather than $35 million when it enters late. Firm 2 has a new brand, and its dominant strategy is to enter early. Therefore, firm 2 enters the market early with its new brand, and firm 1 enters late with its brand extension.

Table 10-9   DISTRIBUTION OF ENTRY TIMES BY TYPE OF BRAND

	EARLY ENTRY	LATE ENTRY
New name	35 (81.4%)	8 (18.6%)
Brand extension	13 (25%)	39 (75%)
Total	48 (50.5%)	47 (49.5%)

APPLICATION **10-7**

Which Brands Enter Late and Which Enter Early?

Are the predictions of the theory consistent with the behavior of firms that introduce brand extensions? Mary Sullivan examined the entry decisions of firms entering the market with new product names and firms entering with brand extensions.[22]

She found that firms introduced brand extensions later than new name brands. The probability of entering either late or early is a function of whether a firm used a brand extension or a new name. Table 10-9 shows the number of products and the percentage of brands that were introduced either early or late for new name and brand extensions. Seventy-five percent of brand extensions entered late, while 81 percent of new names entered early. Sullivan also found that products with brand extensions that entered late had a higher probability of surviving 6 years or more than brand extensions that entered early did.

Frequently, neither party has a dominant strategy. In these types of games each agent cannot use a single or "pure" strategy, for there is no equilibrium. More advanced works show that a "mixed" or a probabilistic strategy is optimal in these types of games.

SUMMARY

▪ A cartel is an arrangement among independent firms whose objective is to raise price by restricting the output of its members. A cartel cannot succeed unless it enforces compliance by members.

▪ The cooperative solution to the duopoly problem is for both firms to share the market and charge the monopoly price. This solution is subject to cheating because it is profitable for a firm to produce more if its rival abides by the agreement.

[22] Mary W. Sullivan, "Brand Extensions: When to Use Them," *Management Science*, vol. 38, June 1992, pp. 793–806.

- In the Cournot model of duopoly each firm selects its profit-maximizing output assuming that the output of its rival is constant.
- A Nash equilibrium requires each firm to choose a quantity strategy that maximizes its profits given the quantity strategy of its rival. As compared to the cooperative solution, in a Nash equilibrium the price is lower and total output is higher with two Cournot competitors.
- In the Bertrand model of duopoly each firm selects a price. In a Nash equilibrium price equals marginal cost and falls abruptly to marginal cost when the number of sellers increases from one to two.
- Observations on prices appear to fit the predictions of the Cournot model more closely than those of the Bertrand model.
- A competitive policy of meeting a rival's price will raise, not lower, price.
- A price conspiracy among sellers will be less successful when the turnover of customers is large, the number of buyers is small, price information is scarce, and the size of the order is large.
- Game theory is the study of strategic interaction between players.

KEY TERMS

Cartel

Concentration ratio

Self-enforcing agreement

Noncooperative behavior

Reaction function

Bertrand model

Meeting competition

Game theory

Dominant strategy

Cooperative behavior

Propensity to cheat

Cournot model

Nash equilibrium in quantities and prices

Effect of number of competitors on price

The cost of detecting price cutting

REVIEW QUESTIONS

1. The larger is the number of members in a cartel, the less stable the cartel. Explain.
2. Why doesn't the cartel immediately shut down some firms so that the remaining ones can produce a quantity where long-run average cost is at a minimum?
3. Why doesn't a competitive firm behave strategically with respect to another competitive firm?
4. What prevents Cournot duopolists from sharing the market at the monopoly price?
5. What is a firm's reaction curve and what does it describe?
6. What prevents Bertrand duopolists from sharing the market at the monopoly price?
7. What are the principal differences between the Cournot and Bertrand models?
8. How do the predictions of the Cournot and Bertrand models differ with respect to the effect of the number of rivals on price?

9. How does the Prisoners' Dilemma capture the essential feature of the oligopoly problem?

10. What factors determine the probability of successful collusion?

11. What policies would you adopt as a buyer if you suspect collusion by sellers?

EXERCISES

1. A cartel includes large and small companies, each with different long-run average and marginal cost curves. A cartel requires each member to reduce output by 15 percent in the short run from the total output produced while behaving competitively so that the cartel can maximize profits. The authority assigns a quota to each firm that is 15 percent less than the output produced by the firm in long-run competitive equilibrium.

   a. Explain why the 15 percent reduction rule will or will not maximize total profits of the cartel.

   b. How would you assign the quota of each firm to maximize total cartel profits?

   c. Can you explain why the cartel would adopt the 15 percent rule?

2. The inverse demand function for a product is $P = \$100 - \$1Q$. There are five identical Cournot competitors in the market, and the marginal cost of each is constant and is \$4. Three of the rivals are foreign firms that import their products into the domestic market. Suppose the government imposes an import quota on foreign suppliers equal to their current imports.

   a. What is the profit-maximizing output for each Cournot competitor and what is the market price?

   b. How will imposing an import quota on three of the foreign Cournot competitors affect the output decision of the two domestic producers?

3. Suppose each Cournot duopolist assumes that its rival will match any change in its output. Show how this assumption will lead to the monopoly output. *Hint:* This assumption implies that $\Delta q_2/\Delta q_1 = 1$. Firm 1's profit-maximizing output is determined by

$$\frac{\Delta \pi}{\Delta q_1} = a - 2bq_1 - bq_2 - bq_1\frac{\Delta q_2}{\Delta q_1} - c = 0$$

$$= a - 2bq_1 - bq_2 - bq_1 - c = 0$$

Use this result to show that each firm will share the market and charge the monopoly price.

4. Can you explain why two Bertrand competitors would build a plant with a fixed production capacity? What size would the plant be?

5. If 50 percent of the firms in an industry produce 50 percent of the output of the industry, the industry cannot be an oligopoly. Explain why you agree or disagree with this statement.

6. Five couples agree to meet for dinner. Before they order, each couple agrees to pay the average of the total bill. After each couple returns home, they complain about how much dinner cost and how much they overate. Can you explain the basis of their complaint? How is this related to the Prisoners' Dilemma?

7. If both firms in a duopoly have a dominant strategy, neither achieves maximum profits. Explain why you agree or disagree with this statement.

8. If a firm has a dominant strategy and its opponent does not, the firm with the dominant strategy maximizes its profits. Explain why you agree or disagree with this statement.

9. Two duopolists may either collude or cheat. The payoffs are summarized in the accompanying matrix. Suppose one duopolist announces a policy of meeting the competitor's price. How will the new entries in the payoff matrix change? Explain how the policy of meeting a competitor's price changes the behavior of duopolists.

Firm 2

		Share the market	Cheat
Firm 1	**Share the market**	$\pi_2 = \$100$ (Cooperative solution) $\pi_1 = \$100$	$\pi_2 = \$125$ $\pi_1 = \$70$
	Cheat	$\pi_2 = \$70$ $\pi_1 = \$125$	$\pi_2 = \$75$ (Noncooperative solution) $\pi_1 = \$75$

CHAPTER 10 APPENDIX

How the Number of Rivals Affects Firm Output and Price in the Cournot Model

The profit function of the ith Cournot competitor is

$$\pi(q_i) = (a - bQ)q_i - cq_i$$

$$= (a - bq_1 - \cdots - bq_i - \cdots - bq_n)q_i - cq_i$$

The profit-maximizing quantity for the ith Cournot competitor satisfies

$$a - bq_1 - \cdots - 2bq_i - \cdots - bq_n - c = 0$$

Solving for q_i by adding $2bq_i$ to both sides of the equation and dividing by $2b$ yields

$$q_i = \frac{a + c}{2b} - \frac{q_1 + \cdots + q_{i-1} + q_{i+1} + \cdots + q_n}{2}$$

Because all firms are alike, all n Cournot competitors must produce the same profit-maximizing quantity that firm i produces, and so $q_1 = \cdots = q_i = \cdots = q_n$. Therefore, we can substitute q_i for the quantity produced by each of the other $n - 1$ firms on the right-hand side of the above equation and rewrite it as

$$q_i = \frac{a - c}{2b} - \frac{(n - 1)q_i}{2}$$

Adding $[(n - 1)q_i]/2$ to both sides of this equation, simplifying, and then multiplying both sides by $2/(n + 1)$ results in equation 10-13.[23]

Although each firm produces less as the number of competitors increases, total output increases. Total output equals $Q = nq_i$

$$Q = nq_i = n\left(\frac{1}{1 + n}\right)\left(\frac{a - c}{b}\right)$$

$$= \frac{n}{1 + n}\frac{a - c}{b}$$

Total output of n Cournot competitors is $n/(n + 1)$ times the competitive output. If $n = 3$, total output equals three-quarters of the competitive output. As n increases, $n/(n + 1)$ increases and approaches 1. Therefore, we can say that the Cournot model predicts that total output approaches the competitive output as the number of competitors becomes large.

The expression for price is[24]

$$P = a - bQ$$

$$= a - b\left(\frac{n}{n + 1}\right)\left(\frac{a - c}{b}\right)$$

Simplifying this equation yields equation 10-14.

---

[23] Adding $[(n - 1)q_i]/2$ to both sides yields

$$q_i\left(1 + \frac{n - 1}{2}\right) = \frac{a - c}{2b}$$

$$q_i\left(\frac{2 + n - 1}{2}\right) = \frac{a - c}{2b}$$

$$q_i\left(\frac{n + 1}{2}\right) = \frac{a - c}{2b}$$

The expression in the text is obtained by multiplying both sides by $2/(n + 1)$.

[24] This expression for price is obtained with the following operations:

$$P = a - b\left(\frac{n}{n + 1}\right)\left(\frac{a - c}{b}\right) = \frac{an + a}{n + 1} - \frac{na - nc}{n + 1} = \frac{a}{n + 1} + \frac{nc}{n + 1}$$

CHAPTER 11

THE GOALS OF
THE FIRM

407

The models developed to predict price and output of a competitive firm, of a monopolist, and of an oligopolist have something in common: they assume that firms maximize profits. Just how valid is this assumption of profit maximization? Can economists simply assume that firms behave this way, or are there circumstances in which other goals might prevail? One reason to question this fundamental assumption is the separation of owners from managers. Although the owners of a firm, the shareholders, want the firm to earn the greatest profit, the individuals responsible for implementing firm strategies—the firm's management—can behave differently. Management is the agent of the owners, but the owners cannot easily monitor and control this agent. When management deviates from the goals of the owners, the owners suffer because profits of the firm are lower than they otherwise could be.

Even though there is a separation of owners from managers, there are economic forces that constrain the behavior of managers. The product and the capital markets are external monitors that compel managers of competitive firms to maximize profits. The capital market operates, whether the product market is competitive or monopolistic, to create the proper incentive for managers to maximize profits. In addition, there are internal monitors of managerial performance. The board of directors has the authority to reward the chief executive with various compensation packages for a good performance or to dismiss managers who do not maximize profits. These external and internal monitors constantly evaluate management performance. Some appear to work more effectively at some times and less effectively at other times. This chapter explains in more detail how external and internal monitors operate and when they are apt to be less effective in inducing managers to act according to the best interests of the owners of the firm.

11-1   EXTERNAL MONITORS: PRODUCT AND CAPITAL MARKETS

For firms in competitive markets, managers maximize profits by minimizing cost and by producing the profit-maximizing quantity. When an industry has many profit-maximizing firms in the market, any firm that does not do the same will not survive because price will be less than long-run average cost. This competition in the product market disciplines those managers who do not pursue the goal of profit maximization. If a manager errs by building too large or too small a firm, the firm's long-run average cost will exceed its minimum long-run average cost and losses will eventually drive it out of the market. Therefore, the survival of the firm creates an incentive for a manager to maximize profits. Competition in the product market is an external monitor of competitive firms.

The capital market also monitors management performance. When a firm is publicly owned, it offers ownership shares called common stock which are traded on organized stock exchanges. Investors who purchase stock become owners of the company, and their investment increases in value when the firm's profits increase and the stock price of the firm increases. Shareholders expect the management to maximize profits so that the stock price reaches a maximum. A manager who does not maximize profits causes the stock price to be lower than it would otherwise be. When a manager does not maximize profits, an outsider or a group of existing shareholders may attempt to buy up enough shares to secure control of the firm and then replace management with new managers who will pursue profit-maximizing strategies.[1] Those who wish to control the firm can accomplish this either by a merger or by buying shares from the shareholders of the firm through a takeover. If outsiders or dissatisfied shareholders acquire control of the firm and increase profits, the rise in the price of the stock is the reward stockholders receive for replacing a management that fails to maximize profits. In this way the capital market penalizes inefficient managers by replacing them. The capital market serves as another external monitor whether the industry has one, a few, or many sellers.

APPLICATION **11-1**

The Effect of a Change in Management on Operations

Do economists have any evidence that firm performance changes after a management or ownership change? In a management buyout some members of the current management group and other investors purchase all the shares from the existing shareholders. The firm becomes privately owned, and shares are no longer traded on organized exchanges. Management buyouts became increasingly important during the 1980s. Buyouts create incentives for the new management team to reduce expenses and increase efficiency. Steven Kaplan analyzed 76 management buyouts of firms to determine their effect on financial performance of the firm.[2] In 19 of the 76 buyouts the chairman of the board or the CEO left the firm and did not join the new firm. The turnover rate for the chairman and the CEO is significantly higher than the turnover rate for all firms and indicates that management buyouts often involve a change in the managers of the firm.

To evaluate the performance of firms before and after a management buyout, Kaplan used different measures of operating performance; only his results for the change in operating income relative to sales are reported here. He examined firms 2 years before and 3 years after a management buyout to determine if operating performance improved.

Table 11-1 summarizes his findings. The results show that increases in operating income relative to sales declined modestly from 2 years to 1 year before the buyout (column 1). From 1 year before to 1 year after the buyout (column 2), operating income relative to sales increased by 7.1 percent, and from 1 year before to 3 years after the buyout (column 3), by 19.3 percent. The results are even more impressive when compared to changes in industry performance. After adjusting for industry changes, operating income relative to sales increased by 12.4 and 34.8 percent, respectively. Kaplan's results show a significant improvement in the op-

---

[1] An early contribution to the study of corporate control is Henry G. Manne, "Mergers and the Market for Corporate Control," *Journal of Political Economy*, vol. LXXIII, April 1965, pp. 110–120.
[2] Steven Kaplan, "The Effects of Management Buyouts on Operating Performance and Value," *Journal of Financial Economics*, vol. 24, 1989, pp. 217–254.

Table 11-1   EFFECT OF MANAGEMENT BUYOUT ON OPERATING PERFORMANCE

OPERATING INCOME RELATIVE TO SALES	Measured from year i before buyout to year j		
	-2 TO -1 **(1)**	-1 TO $+1$ **(2)**	-1 TO $+3$ **(3)**
Percentage change	-1.7	7.1	19.3
Industry-adjusted percentage change	-1.9	12.4	34.8

erating performance of firms after a management buyout. It appears that a change in management and ownership coincides with an improvement in operating performance over a 4-year span.

In another study Frank Lichtenberg and Donald Siegal investigated how employment of production and nonproduction workers changes when there is a change in ownership.[3] Their goal was to assess the contention that CEOs tend to protect their immediate subordinates—administrators and supporting staff at central or regional headquarters. They compared firms that changed ownership from 1977 to 1982 with those that had not and found that employment growth at central and divisional offices declined by 16 percent for firms that changed owners compared to firms that did not, after controlling for industry changes.

Both these studies indicate that a management change leads to an improvement in the operating performance of a firm. The results suggest that the capital market tends to replace managements that are incapable of improving the operating performance of firms.

To sum up, competition in the product and capital markets limits the permissible actions of managers of firms. While the chief executive officer of a large company exercises considerable authority within the firm, these external monitors circumscribe the CEO's authority.[4]

11-2   THE FREE RIDER PROBLEM AND THE TENDER OFFER

Although the capital market penalizes the managements of firms that do not maximize profits, the effectiveness of the capital market can be limited under certain

[3] Frank R. Lichtenberg, *Corporate Takeovers and Productivity*, MIT Press, Cambridge, Mass., 1992, chap. 4.
[4] The terms "CEO" and "manager" are used interchangeably to refer to the individual with executive authority.

conditions. This section describes the lack of incentive an individual shareholder might have to exert control through the capital market over a management team that is not maximizing profits.

Although the shareholders are the owners of a corporation, an individual shareholder has limited power over the management team appointed to represent shareholder interests. Most shareholders do not invest their entire stake in one corporation. Rather, they diversify their resources by investing in several companies or by buying shares in a mutual fund that in turn holds a stake in many corporations. In other words, most shareholders own a very small percentage of a given corporation, and many corporations have thousands of shareholders, with no one shareholder having a large ownership interest. A small shareholder has little incentive to monitor the behavior of the firm's management and determine if the firm maximizes profits.

For firms with many small shareholders, a special problem arises when the capital market attempts to displace a management team that performs poorly. Let's assume that an individual or group of individuals concludes that the current management is not maximizing profits. They believe that a different management could raise the profits of the firm, and so they decide to replace management by soliciting a majority of the firm's shares through a tender offer.[5] The bidder hopes to acquire a majority of the shares and then vote to oust the existing management. In a tender offer, an individual or group offers to pay a price higher than market price for each share provided shareholders tender a specified number of shares.

Does an individual stockholder sell her shares to the bidder or wait to see if the bidder can replace management and install a new management that will maximize profits? To answer this question from the perspective of a stockholder, compare the profit and the stock price before the tender offer, during the tender offer, and after the new managers take control of the firm. Suppose profits are currently π^* under existing management and the current stock price is S^*. An individual or a group believes profits will increase after the existing management is replaced. With new management, this group projects a rise in profits to π' and predicts that the stock price will then rise from S^* to S'. The bidding group then offers a price of S'', where $S^* < S'' < S'$, to existing shareholders if (say) 50 percent of the firm's shares are tendered, so that the group can acquire the majority of the stock and turn out the current management. If the majority does not tender, the takeover fails and no shares change hands. The firm's profit and stock price before, during, and after the tender offer are shown in the accompanying table.

	PROFIT	PRICE
Before tender offer	π^*	S^*
During tender offer	π^*	S'', where $S'' > S^*$
After tender offer	π', where $\pi' > \pi^*$	S', where $S' > S'' > S^*$

[5] This analysis follows Sanford Grossman and Oliver Hart, "Takeover Bids, the Free Rider Problem, and the Theory of the Corporation," *Bell Journal of Economics*, vol. 11, Spring 1980, pp. 42–64.

If you owned shares in the firm, would you sell your shares to the bidder? Economists Sanford Grossman and Oliver Hart, who have studied takeover bids, say no. If the shareholder accepts the tender offer, he or she receives a capital gain of $S'' - S^*$ provided 50 percent of the total shares are tendered. If the tender offer fails, each shareholder's holdings are undisturbed, and the price presumably remains at S^*. A sophisticated shareholder will reason that the bidder will never offer a tender price as high as S' for the shares because the bidder will not gain anything if the tender offer succeeds. The tender price must be less than the price the bidder expects the stock price to reach. The bidder hopes to buy the shares at the tender price of S'' and later sell or retain them when the price reaches S'. By offering a tender offer, the bidder is implicitly announcing that the stock price will ultimately be higher than the tender price. Therefore, a sophisticated shareholder will not tender the shares but will wait until the price increases to S' before selling them. Of course, a sophisticated shareholder hopes that other shareholders tender their shares, the tender offer succeeds, and a new management increases profits so that the stock price increases from S^* to S'. The shareholder experiences greater price appreciation by not tendering.

Shareholders get a free ride because of the tender offer. The bidder has done some research, and this research has yielded valuable private information that profits and the price of the stock will increase with a change in management. There is no simple way for the bidder to charge the existing shareholders for this new information. Shareholders receive the benefits without incurring the cost of obtaining the new information and initiating the tender offer.

> If one shareholder devotes resources to improving management, then all shareholders benefit. Other shareholders free-ride on the efforts of the shareholder.

If most shareholders behave this way, a takeover will fail and the ineffective managers will remain in their jobs. The free rider problem reduces the effectiveness of the capital market as a monitor of managerial performance.

An implication of this argument is that tender offers will fail unless the bidder receives some reward. Grossman and Hart suggest a solution. Corporate charters allow a raider to treat nontendered shares differently from tendered shares. If the raider succeeds and acquires a majority control of the firm, he or she can set the price of the merger or the liquidation of the firm at an unfavorable price for the minority shareholders who did not tender. In the mean time, the raider can change the management of the firm. Sometimes the target is merged with another company owned by the raider. The raider can even offer S' to purchase the majority of the shares. Then he or she can merge the target with the parent company and offer a price less than S' for the minority shares. In this way the bidder earns a capital gain on the remaining shares.

There is another way for a raider to gain from the increase in the stock price. Grossman and Hart assumed that the bidder owns few if any shares to start with. There is nothing to stop him from quietly accumulating stock of the company before announcing a tender offer. With the passage of the Williams Amendment in 1968, an individual or a firm can acquire up to 5 percent of a target's shares before public disclosure of the acquired stake is required. Under this amendment a raider can quietly acquire a 5 percent or larger holding in a firm at S^*. Then, the bidder might even be willing to pay S' for a majority of the stock or, if required by law or a corporate charter, all shares in a tender offer and still earn a gain from the price increase on the 5 percent stake in the firm. Therefore, this is one way to attenuate the free rider problem.

The free rider problem reduces the effectiveness of the capital market in disciplining a grossly inefficient management but does not prevent the capital market from functioning. As you have seen, there are ways around the free rider problem. The rapid growth of tender offers in the 1980s indicates that the capital market still functions to remove inefficient managers from their positions.

11-3 AN INTERNAL MONITOR OF MANAGEMENT

Even if we ignore the free rider problem, the capital market is an expensive and cumbersome mechanism for disciplining management and can perhaps be described as the mechanism of last resort. Individuals attempt to gain control of a firm through the capital market when management performance is so poor that it attracts the attention of outsiders or existing shareholders. When the capital market acts, it indicates that the internal monitors are ineffective. This section explains how an internal monitor can affect management performance.

Internal mechanisms monitor management practices as well. An important function of the board of directors is to monitor, evaluate, and either reward or penalize management performance. The board of directors can be thought of as a first line of defense, protecting shareholders from actions of management that reduce profits and the value of the firm and that cause the capital market to act. In part, the board of directors exists because the individual shareholder has little incentive to incur the cost of monitoring management. The board of directors is an institution which in principle can attenuate the consequences of the free rider problem. How does the board serve this purpose?

Expense Preference

In theory the board of directors is the internal body that monitors and evaluates managerial performance and gives expert advice to management. The board can make the manager pay for decisions that reduce firm profits but increase the manager's utility, but in practice there are limits to what a board can accomplish. It does not have the detailed information or the time to monitor management day by day. Rather, it takes a more distant position by offering advice and periodically evaluating management performance, and, in view of this assessment, rewarding or penalizing the chief executive officer.

In many large corporations the chief executive officer has considerable authority and leeway. He decides what projects the firm will undertake and can indulge his own preferences for some kinds of expenses. The CEO has many opportunities to make decisions that can increase his utility and raise the firm's costs. A CEO may decide to act cautiously and pass up many potentially profitable projects because they would require greater effort by the whole management team. Profitability may be lower than otherwise, but the utility of the manager is higher. If he hires a friend to run the purchasing department when there is a more qualified candidate who would be willing to take the position at the same salary, the utility of the CEO is higher but the costs of the firm are also. For example, a manager with a technical-computer background can become enamored of the latest and most expensive computer system and have it installed for the company when a less expensive system would suffice. This decision lowers company profits but increases the manager's utility. The chief executive officer of RJR-Nabisco had apartments available for the management team, spent lavishly on sports figures to induce them to attend company affairs, and had a fleet of 10 planes and 36 pilots available to fly him and other executives around the United States on official and personal business when the occasion arose.[6]

A CEO can raise expenses above the cost-minimizing amount given the quantity produced. Let's call the excess of expenses above the cost-minimizing amount expense preference.

> **Expense preference** is the excess of expenses over the level that maximizes the firm's profits.

If the firm maximizes profits when it owns two company planes and the manager orders a fleet of four planes, the expense of the extra two planes represents an expense preference.

Ex Post Settling Up

The board of directors has a fiduciary duty to protect the interests of the owners of the firm. Usually, it cannot prevent expense preference of the manager, but it can make the manager pay for the expense preference. The board can adopt a policy of tying the CEO's compensation to expense preference. Periodically, it evaluates and settles up with the manager. For example, the board of directors could pay the manager a base salary and at the end of the year determine a bonus based on the results for the year. It might compare the cost performance of different-sized firms in the industry or in the economy and estimate how the manager's policies inflate costs. If the manager raises costs by indulging his or her tastes, the board reduces total compensation by reducing the bonus. *Ex post settling up* means that the board reduces compensation dollar for dollar for the increase in cost.[7] In this way an active, sophisticated board of directors can adopt a policy that makes the manager pay for any increase in expense preference.

A simple one-period model demonstrates how a manager maximizes utility by selecting a market basket of expense preference and compensation. Let's assume the board of directors sets the manager's compensation at C^* with the expectation

[6] Bryan Burrough and John Helyar, *Barbarians at the Gate*, Harper & Row, New York, 1990, pp. 92–96.
[7] Eugene Fama, "Agency Problems and the Theory of the Firm," *Journal of Political Economy*, vol. 88, April 1980, pp. 288–307.

TRADE-OFF BETWEEN EXPENSE PREFERENCE AND COMPENSATION

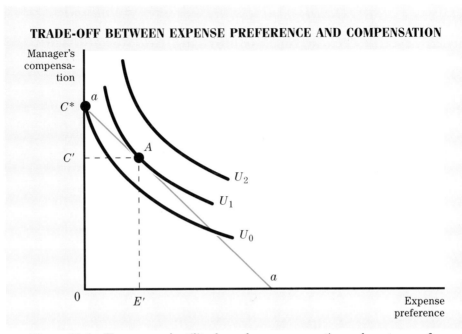

Figure 11-1   The manager's utility depends on compensation and expense preference. The board determines the manager's compensation so that it falls by a dollar for every dollar increase in expense preference. Line *aa* shows the manager's budget constraint and has a slope of -1. The manager maximizes utility when the slope of his indifference curve equals the slope of *aa*. He indulges in expense preference of E' and receives a lower compensation of C'. The manager would receive C^* if he maximized profits, but his utility would be only U_0. The manager pays for indulging his tastes by receiving lower compensation.

that the manager will maximize profits. If the board later finds that the manager increased expense preference and did not maximize profits, it reduces the manager's compensation dollar for dollar with the increase in expense preference. In Figure 11-1 line *aa* is the manager's budget constraint between compensation and expense preference. The slope of *aa* is -1 because the compensation of the manager decreases by \$1 for every \$1 increase in expense preference.

To determine what combination of expense preference and compensation maximizes the manager's utility, you need to consider the manager's utility function. Assume the utility of the manager increases when either compensation or expense preference increases. Expense preference includes the excess expenditure above the expenditure that a profit-maximizing firm incurs for such items as thick carpets for the office, a large supporting staff, a large fleet of company planes, hiring more associates from the manager's fraternity or sorority, etc. Figure 11-1 shows several indifference curves of the manager. The manager maximizes utility at point A where the indifference curve U_1 is tangent to *aa* and expense preference is E' while managerial compensation is C'. The manager prefers the combination of C' and E' to C^* and no expense preference because his utility is only U_0. So, the manager chooses E', and the board matches the increase in expense preference by lowering managerial compensation from C^* to C'. The manager, not the shareholders of the firm, pays for the expense preference.

This analysis assumes that the board of directors is an independent body, has sufficient information, and is capable of an unbiased evaluation of CEO performance, but this is not always the case. The CEO often has a say in the makeup of the board and can subtly influence board members. He can shift business to the companies the members of the board represent. Also, the board may have considerable difficulty observing and verifying whether the costs of the firm are unusually high when it has neither the expertise nor the information to monitor the many activities of the company. Remember, evaluation of a CEO's performance is more of an art than a science. Often it is difficult to distinguish between expenditures that are expense preference and those that aid the firm in maximizing profits. Is a posh office an expense preference or a necessary expense to impress clients? Often, the board of directors lacks the information needed to make the necessary adjustments to the manager's compensation to offset increases in expense preference. It is more likely to act only when there are gross deviations from expected conduct.

11-4 THE PRINCIPAL-AGENT RELATIONSHIP AND OWNERSHIP STRUCTURE

The manager is the agent and the shareholders are the principals in a corporation. When the agent makes decisions that affect the well-being of the principal, there is a principal-agent relationship.

> A principal-agent relationship exists whenever an agent makes decisions that affect the well-being of the principal.

In analyzing managerial behavior, we assumed that the manager did not supply any capital to the firm. In other words, management was separate from the owners of the firm. How does managerial behavior change when the CEO is also an owner of the firm? We can investigate this situation by slightly modifying the analysis of expense preference.

A sole owner of the firm holds the residual rights to the profits or losses of the firm. She receives any residual profit or incurs any residual loss. When the manager is the sole owner, she makes a tradeoff between the profits of the firm and expense preference instead of a tradeoff between compensation and expense preference. Assume the manager-owner would receive compensation of C^* if hired by another firm in the same capacity.

In Figure 11-2 total profits are on the vertical axis and expense preference is on the horizontal axis.[8] Because the manager is the residual owner, any expense preference simply reduces the profits of the manager-owner dollar for dollar. Costs

[8] This section borrows from Michael C. Jensen and William H. Meckling, "Theory of the Firm: Managerial Behavior, Agency Costs and Ownership Structure," *Journal of Financial Economics*, 1976, vol. 3, pp. 305–360.

EXPENSE PREFERENCE WHEN THE MANAGER IS THE SOLE OWNER

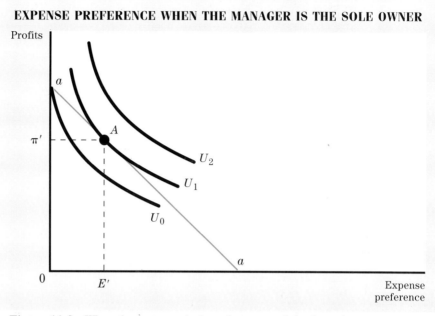

Figure 11-2   When the manager is the sole owner of the firm, she can trade a dollar of firm profits for a dollar of expense preference along the budget line *aa*. The owner-manager maximizes utility at point *A* where the slope of the indifference curve U_1 equals -1. At point *A* expense preference is E' and profits are π'.

of the firm are higher because of expense preference, and the owner's profits are lower if, for example, she hires a college chum as a favor. In Figure 11-2 line *aa* shows the tradeoff between profits and expense preference. The owner's indifference curve U_1 is tangent to *aa* at point *A*, and her utility is at a maximum when profits are π' and expense preference is E'. Here again, the owner that indulges her tastes pays for that indulgence through lower profits. If the firm is in a competitive industry in long-run equilibrium, it earns no profit and line *aa* starts at the origin. When the manager-owner indulges her tastes and raises the cost of the firm, the firm suffers losses. Nevertheless, the owner increases expense preference and suffers losses because her utility is higher.

Figures 11-1 and 11-2 represent two extremes of owner or management types. In both instances it is the owner or the manager who pays for expense preference. The more relevant case is where the manager owns a fraction of the total shares and the board of directors uses ex post settling up to monitor management. In a large company the management team owns only a small fraction of the firm. As the share of ownership of the firm declines, the behavior of the manager changes.

Suppose the sole owner-manager sells $1 - \beta$ of the ownership claims on profits and retains a share β of any profits. β represents the manager's share of the rights to the profits of the firm. For example, she might sell the rights to 30 percent of the profits to outsiders and retain the remaining 70 percent.

If outsiders purchase 30 percent of the rights to profits, how much will they be willing to pay? To answer this question, let's reconsider Figure 11-2. When the manager is the sole owner of the firm, the profits of the firm are π'. It seems reasonable enough to say that outsiders will receive 30 percent of π'. However, this fails to take into account how a change from full to partial ownership affects the behavior of the manager. After selling 30 percent of the rights, she faces a different tradeoff between profits and expense preference than when she was the sole owner. Before outsiders purchase the rights, a \$1 increase in expense preference costs the owner-manager \$1 in profits. Now, she can indulge in expense preference of \$1 and lose profits of only 70 cents since the new owners collectively suffer a loss of the other 30 cents. The partial owner-manager no longer faces a dollar-for-dollar tradeoff between expense preference and profits. This means that the relative cost of increasing expense preference declines for a partial owner. Therefore, a partial owner-manager behaves differently from a full owner by increasing expense preference and decreasing the profits of the firm by more than a sole owner would.

> A manager consumes more expense preference as the share of ownership declines.

If the new owners correctly anticipate the increase in expense preference, they will pay only 30 percent of π'', where π'' is the profit of the firm after expense

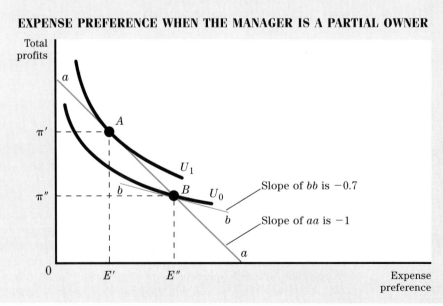

EXPENSE PREFERENCE WHEN THE MANAGER IS A PARTIAL OWNER

Figure 11-3 When the manager retains 70 percent of the profits of a firm, the slope of her budget constraint bb is -0.7. The manager maximizes utility by selecting E'' for expense preference and receives π'' in profits at point B. She increases expense preference as her ownership share decreases.

preference increases to E''. As a result, a reduction in the share of ownership moves the owner along the budget constraint aa from point A to a point like B in Figure 11-3. A consequence of dispersed ownership is that the owner's total profit declines. Two conditions must be satisfied if the manager maximizes utility. First, she must be on aa, which describes the firm's tradeoff between profit and expense preference, and second, she must maximize utility so that the slope of her budget constraint equals the slope of her utility function.

Both conditions are satisfied at point B. The manager's budget line bb has a slope of -0.7 and is tangent to indifference curve U_0. At point B the slope of her indifference curve is -0.7, and her budget constraint bb is tangent to this indifference curve. The manager's utility at point B is U_0, expense preference is E'', and her profits from the sale of the shares and from the remaining shares are π''. Since bb intersects aa at point B, the manager is simultaneously on aa, which describes the firm's tradeoff between profits and expense preference. Therefore, we conclude that expense preference increases as the ownership share of the manager decreases.

Partial ownership increases expense preference and reduces firm profits by $\pi' - \pi''$. How much should outsiders pay for 30 percent of the rights to profits? They should anticipate that the partial owner-manager will increase expense preference and therefore should pay only 0.3 of π'', not 0.3 of π'.

Let's pause here and state the main conclusion. Greater separation of management from ownership increases expense preference and lowers the profits of the firm. The smaller the fraction of profits owned by the manager, the greater the incentive for the manager to indulge in expense preference.[9] Therefore, the distribution of ownership shares between managers and shareholders should affect the behavior of a firm.

11-5   EXPENSE PREFERENCE UNDER A PROFIT CONSTRAINT

The analysis used so far applies to an unregulated firm whether it is a competitive firm, an oligopolistic firm, or a monopolistic firm. We have assumed that the board of directors can enforce a dollar-for-dollar tradeoff between expense preference and either compensation or profits. Therefore, a manager pays for an increase in expense preference by a reduction in profits (or compensation).

Now let's turn to regulated firms to determine how a profit constraint changes the behavior of managers. You will see how profit regulation can allow a manager to escape paying for an increase in expense preference.[10] Examples of firms that operate under a profit constraint are public utilities, regulated commercial banks, and regulated insurance companies. This analysis can also apply to a private firm

---

[9] An extended discussion of these ownership issues is in Michael C. Jensen and William H. Meckling, "Theory of the Firm: Managerial Behavior, Agency Costs and Ownership Structure," *Journal of Financial Economics*, 1976, vol. 3, pp. 305–360.

[10] This section is based on Armen A. Alchian and Ruben A. Kessel, "Competition, Monopoly and the Pursuit of Money," *Aspects of Labor Economics*, Princeton University Press, Princeton, N.J., 1962, pp. 157–183.

that might come under regulatory scrutiny if the firm's profits become too large. A critical assumption of this analysis is that these firms are scrutinized by regulatory agencies if they become too profitable.

How does the behavior of the manager change when the firm operates under a profit constraint? The following discussion assumes that the manager of a regulated monopoly is not an owner but receives a compensation package equal to C^*, the compensation package she qualifies for.

First, look at the behavior of the manager when the monopolist is unregulated. As a convenient starting point, assume that the manager's utility is maximized when total compensation is C^* and she does not indulge in any expense preference. This is merely a starting point and is not essential to the subsequent argument. Figure 11-4a shows the profit-maximizing price is P_m and the profit-maximizing quantity is Q_m. The profits of the unregulated monopolist are π^* or are equal to the area *abcd*. Line *aa* in Figure 11-4b is the budget constraint of the manager between compensation and expense preference. In this example, maximum utility of the manager occurs when compensation is C^*, expense preference is zero, and the firm's profits are π^*. The manager is on the indifference curve U_1. The profit function of the unregulated monopolist is *cc* in Figure 11-4c, and the firm maximizes profits by producing Q_m units.

The Profit Constraint

What happens when the firm becomes regulated and the regulator places a profit constraint of π' on the monopolist? Assume that the regulator has enough information to impose an effective profit constraint but does not have enough information to know whether the firm is producing any quantity at minimum total cost. The firm expects the regulator will reduce price if profits exceed the profit constraint π' where π' is less than π^*. In effect, the regulator imposes a profit cap of π'. How does a profit constraint change the behavior of a manager?

The manager can satisfy the profit constraint in two ways.

- *Option 1.* The manager can lower the price from P_m to P_r and sell more units. Figure 11-4a shows that the price falls to P_r and profits fall to the mandated π', and Figure 11-4c shows that profits decrease to π' when price falls to P_r and output increases to Q_r. The firm is still a cost-efficient producer because it is producing Q_r units at the lowest total cost so that it remains on *cc* in Figure 11-4c. The manager receives C^* in compensation before and after the firm operates under a profit constraint.
- *Option 2.* The manager can indulge her tastes and allow costs to increase until profits fall to π' while still producing the profit-maximizing quantity Q_m. In Figure 11-4a the firm's average cost function shifts upward and becomes AC_r under a profit constraint. Area *efcd* measures the increase in expense preference. Figure 11-4b shows that the tradeoff between profits and expense preference becomes *bb* and expense preference increases to E^*. Figure 11-4c shows that the profit function of the monopolist shifts downward and becomes *ee* because expense preference increases by E^*. At each quantity the difference between *cc* and *ee* is E^*. The increase in expense preference

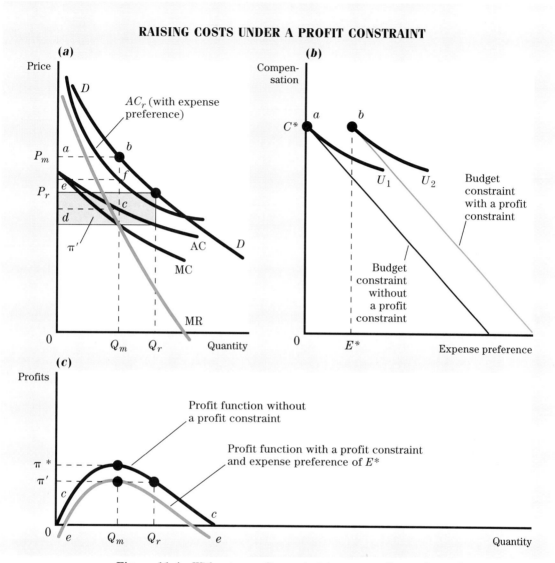

RAISING COSTS UNDER A PROFIT CONSTRAINT

Figure 11-4   Without a profit constraint a monopolist produces Q_m units and earns π^* in (*c*). The manager receives C^* in compensation and utility of U_1 in (*b*). With a profit constraint of π' the utility of the manager increases to U_2 when he or she receives the combined package of C^* and E^*. The regulated firm continues to produce Q_m, but the total cost of producing Q_m increases by E^*.

is like an increase in lump sum cost and can take different forms depending on the monitoring ability of the regulator. If the regulator can detect excessive compensation of the manager or the management team more easily than an increase in other types of expenses, the manager's compensation may not rise much, but staff size may increase, offices may be better equipped and furnished, etc.

When a firm operates under a profit constraint, the manager can increase expense preference without paying for the increase by a reduction in compensation. Therefore, the manager's utility increases when expense preference increases to E^*. Figure 11-4b shows that the budget constraint of the manager becomes bb under a profit constraint. Given C^*, expense preference increases to E^* and firm profit falls to π'. The manager moves from indifference curve U_1 to the higher indifference curve U_2. Clearly, the manager prefers option 2 to option 1.

A profit constraint increases expense preference and the utility of the manager.

With a profit constraint the cost of being inefficient decreases. The management of the firm has less incentive to operate the firm efficiently, and stockholders have less incentive to monitor the performance of the management team. Just what will shareholders gain if they replace the existing management? With the current management, the profits of the firm equal the profit constraint of π'. If a new management team operates the firm more efficiently, the firm will have to produce Q_r and sell the larger quantity at a lower price so that total profit is still π'. Shareholders cannot benefit from a change in management. Therefore, a profit constraint reduces the incentive of shareholders or raiders to monitor the practices of management. The fundamental problem with a profit constraint is that current shareholders or outsiders can no longer benefit by penalizing wasteful management practices. Therefore, these practices will receive less scrutiny, and the firm will no longer minimize costs. A common criticism of regulated firms is that they are run inefficiently, have inflated cost structures, and are less demanding companies to work for.

A profit constraint raises the total compensation package of the current management group. Without a profit constraint the manager receives C^* and no expense preference. With a profit constraint she still receives C^* in compensation and increased utility because expense preference increases from zero to E^*. The utility of the manager is now higher than it would be if she managed a company in an unregulated industry. The manager of the regulated firm now holds a more desirable position.[11] Managers with the same qualifications in other industries receive only C^* in compensation and no expense preference. Yet, shareholders of the regulated firm have no incentive to reduce the manager's compensation or to replace the manager even if they could.

---

[11] Because others would like to hold the position, the existing management team will have to put obstacles in the path of would-be managers. The existing management can protect its position by making it more difficult for would-be managers to obtain control of the firm by owning enough stock so that a hostile takeover will not succeed.

Deregulation and Import Competition

This model of a profit constraint explains why a regulated firm does not minimize costs. A profit constraint reduces the price of indulging the manager's tastes. While costs are inflated, these firms are not subject to takeover threats. Indeed, a profit constraint dulls the incentive to take over a regulated firm and to increase its efficiency. The theory predicts that firms operating under a profit constraint are less likely to be targeted for a merger or takeover. Not only will it be difficult to increase profits, but any takeover of a regulated firm must submit to regulatory scrutiny and receive regulatory approval.

However, the story changes when the government deregulates the firm. Even if deregulation is not accompanied by the entry of domestic and foreign competitors, the firm is subject to attack by raiders because its costs are not minimized. The problems of a deregulated firm are magnified when the entry of competitors forces price to fall and the market share of the deregulated firm to decline. In either case the profit function of the firm shifts downward because the entry of competitors reduces prices and the market share of the recently deregulated firm. Before deregulation, the profit function of the firm is ee in Figure 11-5 where the effective profit constraint is π'. As noted above, the regulated firm satisifes the profit constraint by increasing expense preference to E^*.

With deregulation, new firms enter the industry, prices fall, and the profit function of the formerly regulated firm shifts downward. Suppose the profit func-

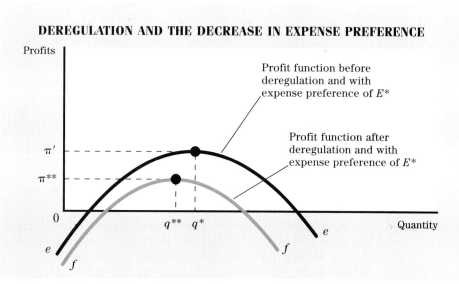

DEREGULATION AND THE DECREASE IN EXPENSE PREFERENCE

Figure 11-5   With deregulation new firms enter the industry and price falls. The profit function of the deregulated firm shifts downward, and becomes ff. Maximum profits decline and are π^{**} when the firm produces q^{**} units. The profit constraint of π' is no longer binding. A capital gain can be realized if the existing or a new management reduces expense preference below E^*.

tion shifts downward and becomes *ff* in Figure 11-5. Maximum profits are now only π^{**} and are less than π'. The profit constraint is no longer binding. Now, management practices come under scrutiny and attack. Total profits have declined, and dissident shareholders complain that the firm is being run inefficiently. If management responds by eliminating expense preference, profits will increase and the stock price of the company will increase.

What kind of reaction can be expected from the management? It might recognize the changed circumstances, accept the inevitable, and adjust to deregulation. Yet, evidence suggests that the existing management frequently does not adapt to these changes. Just why it often fails to respond is not fully understood by researchers. One explanation is that it has developed specialized skills over the years in negotiating with regulators and in providing service to customers, not in developing and introducing new products and in keeping costs down. The existing management has skills and abilities that are more suitable for a protected regulatory environment. It appears that some managements find the transition difficult to make and are incapable of restructuring their companies. The same puzzling behavior can occur when a successful unregulated firm suddenly faces import competition and must reduce the scale of operations. Some managements that are successful in an expanding market appear incapable of changing gears and making the difficult decision to reduce the size of the firm and to lower costs. These are the companies that are most subject to hostile takeovers.

11-6 THE UNREGULATED FIRM AND EXPENSE PREFERENCE

In a regulated environment a firm that operates under a profit constraint has less incentive to minimize costs. When an unregulated firm does not minimize costs, it must mean that the internal monitor is ineffective and product competition is relatively weak. A takeover attempt indicates that internal monitors are not functioning and outsiders believe that lower costs and higher profits are possible. A failed takeover attempt indicates that management has strong allies and cannot be displaced at low cost.

Often management policies receive less scrutiny when the firm manages to perform on par with other firms in the industry although it may not be maximizing profits. These policies are examined more closely when a major change occurs, such as a reduction in demand or the entry of new firms, that reduces the profitability of the firm. In recent years several American industries have faced increased competition from foreign suppliers. Price competition has been sufficiently intense that firms with enviable records unexpectedly incur losses. These losses focus greater shareholder attention on management policies. Shareholders raise pointed questions at stockholder meetings about the size of the research and development program, the compensation packages of management, new product decisions, the deployment of assets, etc.

The case of Cummins Engine Company aptly illustrates these issues.

APPLICATION **11-2**

Cummins Engine Company

Cummins Engine Company,[12] founded in 1919, is a major American manufacturer of high-quality diesel engines for heavy-duty trucks. Historically, the company has supported an extensive research and development program. In 1979 it could report 43 consecutive years of profits, a proud achievement.

Cummins Engine has a history of remarkable public service. The company has sponsored or subsidized many public activities in Columbus, Indiana, the home of its headquarters. For many years it has paid recognized architects to design all public buildings in Columbus. It has built homeless shelters, financed drug counseling programs in local schools, and sent engines and generators to flood victims in South Carolina in 1989. It helped build a school in Brazil near its new factory. Henry Schacht, Cummins's chairman, says the company's goal is "being fair and honest and doing what is right even when it is not to our immediate benefit."

Most companies do not participate in these types of activities, but such activities can be consistent with profit maximization if the company creates goodwill with local and state governments. So, we cannot decisively conclude that the firm is not engaging in profit-maximizing activities just because it performs a public service.

After years of relative prosperity, the decade of the 1980s was not kind to Cummins Engine Company. Besides a deep recession, competition from foreign suppliers heated up when Nissan Motor Company entered the U.S. market and offered engines at a substantial price discount. Prices fell. Cummins cut prices to maintain its market share and sustained losses. Still, the firm had to announce layoffs in 1983. The company continues to spend lavishly for R&D, about 5 percent of sales, and for its charity programs even at the expense of short-run profits. Among the Fortune 500 firms only 95 spend more on charity than Cummins does. Mr. Schacht notes that no one stopped to say, "Hey, we aren't making money."

Cummins became a takeover target when Hanson PLC, a British conglomerate, acquired 8.8 percent of the stock in the fall of 1988. The takeover attempt suggests that the internal monitor was not functioning in this case. Fortunately for Cummins, it had a friend. The J. Irwin Miller family of Columbus, which had helped found Cummins, bought Hanson's stock for $72 million and returned it to the company in exchange for a package of high-yield securities.

Shortly afterward, Industrial Equity purchased 14.9 percent of the stock but in May 1990 agreed to end its battle with Cummins. It abandoned its efforts to obtain a seat on the board and agreed not to purchase anymore shares for 10 years. Some analysts speculated that Industrial Equity decided to become a passive shareholder

---

[12] Based on Robert Johnson, "With Its Spirit Shaken But Unbent, Cummins Shows Decade's Scars," *Wall Street Journal*, December 13, 1989; Alison Leigh Cowan, "Cummins Thwarts Latest Threat," *New York Times*, May 11, 1990.

because of the hostile attitude toward takeovers at the federal and state levels. Commenting on the management at Cummins Engine, Robert G. Sutherland, president of Industrial Equity, said, "We got tired of it. They're deeply entrenched. Shareholders should be concerned."

Before the 1980s the management was involved in many charitable activities without fear of a takeover because of the support of the Miller family and a demonstrated record of profitability. Before the 1980s, takeovers of firms the size of Cummins rarely occurred. Management support for charitable activities in the pre-1980 period could mean either that this support was consistent with profit maximization or that the external and internal monitors were ineffective.

Several changes occurred during the 1980s. First, import competition reduced prices and created losses. Second, the increase in the number of takeovers and the growth of the junk bond market to finance takeovers enabled corporate raiders to seek out larger firms that were underperforming. Third, the support of the Miller family began to wane. Even so, the management has maintained its charitable activities and has warded off two challenges. The takeover attempts indicate that the internal monitor was not performing. In this instance, the external monitor did not succeed in displacing management.

In part Cummins management retained control because of its efforts to cut costs by introducing robots and reducing its labor force to combat foreign competition. Nevertheless, it continues to spend considerable sums on R&D and on charity. Cummins was also protected by the growing hostility of state governments toward takeovers. The future of the management at Cummins Engine Company depends on its ability to return the company to profitability and the increased difficulty of mounting a successful takeover.

11-7 HOW THE MARKET FOR CORPORATE CONTROL FUNCTIONS

Although all monitors exert control over management performance, they are not all equally cost-effective. As noted earlier, the capital market is a cumbersome disciplinary mechanism. Therefore, we might expect it to be a last-resort monitor. If internal monitoring is less costly to apply, that is, more effective, then external monitors should play a minor role. Yet, evidence from the 1970s and 1980s indicates that external monitors played an important role in forcing managements to maximize profits and in replacing managements that did not. The role of external monitors increased throughout the 1970s and especially in the 1980s with the acquisition of firms through friendly and hostile takeovers. Therefore, we may infer that internal monitoring was not the cheapest method for monitoring management practices in recent decades. With the growing opposition of states to hostile takeovers that began in the late 1980s, the cost-effectiveness of external monitors has decreased and internal monitors appear to be playing a more active role. The number of tender offers has declined since 1988, and there are some faint signs of greater reliance on internal monitors. Some boards of directors are showing more independence and intervening directly in management practices, and mutual fund managers are now voting less frequently to support management positions. Dissident shareholders are bringing more proxy contests to obtain representation on the board.

The Effectiveness of Internal Monitors

This section documents changes in the performance of internal and external monitors and determines which monitors have functioned to limit deviations from profit maximization. As you read this discussion, recall that studies have already been cited showing that the operating performance of firms improves when ownership changes.

Let's look at the effectiveness of internal monitors over the years. Is there any evidence that they have changed over long periods of time? Researchers have begun to examine the role of internal monitoring only recently, and so we can give only a tentative answer to this question. However, evidence indicates that the effectiveness of internal monitors has declined over time.

Michael Jensen and Kevin Murphy examined this question in an interesting study of the compensation of the chief executive officer in large corporations.[13] They wanted to determine by how much CEO compensation increases when the performance of the firm improves. What reward does the CEO receive for improving firm performance? If the CEO's compensation is very sensitive to the performance of the stock, then he or she has a greater incentive to increase profits and the stock price. These researchers used the annual change in the market value of a company's stock as a measure of firm performance. Total CEO compensation includes salary, bonus, and, when available, the value of stock options. They compared the annual change in total CEO compensation to the change in the market value of the firm. What makes this study particularly interesting is how the pay-performance relationship has changed over time. Jensen and Murphy estimated the sensitivity of managerial compensation to changes in the firm's market value over several decades. Their study indicates whether managerial compensation has become more closely tied to the stock price of the firm over time.

Over the 1974–1986 period, the lifetime wealth of an average chief executive increased on average by just $1.85 for each $1,000 increase in the market value of a large firm and $8.05 for each $1,000 of market value of a small firm. Pay and performance appear to be more closely related in smaller corporations. Although these sums appear to be small, we cannot really tell whether they are large or small without a standard of reference. What is more interesting is the change over time in the pay-performance relationship. First, the researchers looked at the pay-performance of CEOs in the 1930s and then in the 1970s and 1980s. They found that executives in the top quartile of firms on the New York Stock Exchange received a 17.5 cent increase in salary and bonus for each $1,000 increase in market value in the 1930s, but only 1.9 cents in the 1974–1986 period. In other words, the reward for performance has declined over time.

---

[13] Michael Jensen and Kevin J. Murphy, "Performance Pay and Top-Management Incentives," *Journal of Political Economy*, vol. 98, April 1990, pp. 225–264.

Table 11-2 CHANGE IN REAL COMPENSATION OF CEO IN LARGE CORPORATIONS BETWEEN 1934–1938 AND 1974–1986 (1986 DOLLARS)

	1934–1938	1974–1986
Mean of CEO salary plus bonus	813,000	645,000
Mean market value of firm (billions)	1.6	3.4
Mean annual change in salary and bonus	31,900	27,800
Average standard deviation of annual change in salary and bonus	205,000	127,000

Source: Michael Jensen and Kevin J. Murphy, "Performance Pay and Top-Management Incentives," *Journal of Political Economy*, vol. 98, April 1990, p. 256.

Table 11-2 shows mean CEO compensation (adjusted for inflation), size of firm, mean and standard deviation of the annual change in salary, and bonus for the two periods. It indicates that CEO total salary and bonus have declined after adjusting for inflation, although firm size as measured by market value has more than doubled. This surprising finding contradicts the often heard complaint that CEO compensation has gone through the roof in recent years. Row 4 shows that the change in compensation from year to year is more stable now than in the past. The standard deviation of the annual change in compensation is a measure of dispersion and has been smaller in recent years. These data suggest that the tie between compensation and firm performance in large corporations is weaker now than it was in the past.

Table 11-3 shows that the share of total shares of the firm owned by the chief executive has decreased in the largest 120 firms in the sample. The median share

Table 11-3 VALUE OF STOCK AND PERCENTAGE OF FIRM OWNED BY CHIEF EXECUTIVE IN 120 LARGEST FIRMS BY MARKET VALUE, 1938–1984

YEAR	MEDIAN VALUE OF STOCK OWNED (1986 DOLLARS)	Percentage of Firm Owned by Chief Executive	
		MEDIAN	MEAN
1938	2,250,000	0.30	1.7
1974	2,061,000	0.05	1.5
1984	1,801,000	0.03	1.0

Source: Michael Jensen and Kevin J. Murphy, "Performance Pay and Top-Management Incentives," *Journal of Political Economy*, vol. 98, April 1990, p. 258.

of the firm owned by the chief executive declined from 0.3 percent in 1938 to 0.03 percent in 1984. The total compensation of the chief executive is less dependent on the performance of the firm.

The Jensen-Murphy study suggests that the interests of the chief executive have been less closely aligned with those of shareholders in recent times. It appears that managerial compensation is less closely tied to firm performance.[14] Performance-based compensation appears to have declined over time.

The board of directors monitors management performance directly. It determines CEO compensation and can dismiss the chief executive. Yet, the board of directors does not appear to be an effective monitoring institution. Board members are often insiders who favor management or outsiders with little information, little time, and sometimes financial reasons to side with existing management. This does not mean that the board of directors plays no role. A higher turnover of CEOs follows poor stock performance. And so the board does dismiss those CEOs who do not produce results.

The Effectiveness of External Monitors

If internal monitors have become less effective over time, we can expect to find greater reliance on external monitors of management performance. A sign of this is the increase in acquisition activity. Acquisitions through friendly or hostile takeovers expanded throughout the 1970s and most of the 1980s. However, takeovers have declined in the 1990s when state laws have made them more difficult to achieve and the growth of the economy has slowed.

Throughout the 1970s and 1980s mergers and takeovers occurred more frequently than in earlier decades. This reliance on acquisitions perhaps indicates that internal mechanisms were not as effective in monitoring non-profit-maximizing behavior by managers. The increasing number of acquisitions, whether friendly or hostile, suggests that they were a lower-cost method of preventing non-profit-maximizing behavior. The growth of creative financing such as junk bonds enabled corporate raiders to target larger firms. The primary function of such raiders is to transfer managerial control from the existing management to a new management. External monitors became a more cost-effective method of penalizing non-profit-maximizing practices of management. Today the pendulum appears to be swinging back toward internal monitors as the takeover market has cooled and greater opposition to takeovers is evident at the state level.

Evidence about Takeovers

Let's summarize some of the better known findings about takeovers. The scale of the takeover wave is impressive. Takeovers drastically altered the U.S. economy throughout the 1980s. Economists Andrei Shleifer and Robert W. Vishny report that 143 of the Fortune 500 in 1980 were acquired by another company by 1989 in

---

[14]Why this has occurred is not completely known and requires more study. Jensen and Murphy offer several possible explanations for the change.

either a friendly or a hostile takeover. The total value of assets changing hands amounted to \$1.3 trillion.[15]

It appears that a disproportionate share of takeovers took place in deregulated industries. Transportation and broadcasting accounted for 20 percent of all mergers and acquisitions from 1981 to 1984, and oil and gas accounted for 26.3 percent.[16] Also, the takeover wave appears to have concentrated on conglomerate firms— firms that produce a variety of products. The birth of many conglomerates occurred in the late 1960s through mergers of specialized independent firms.

Often, the breakup of a conglomerate follows a successful takeover. Parts of the conglomerate are sold off, and the remaining firm is focused on one or a few lines of business. Some researchers consider the takeover wave an antidote for the unsuccessful diversification wave of the late 1960s.

Another finding is that takeovers occur disproportionately in industries that are in decline or where some major change has occurred. The value of the firm has declined because the industry is in decline. It may be that management has failed to reduce the scale of the firm considering the decrease in product prices. Firms in these kinds of industries are subject to takeovers by corporate raiders that specialize in reducing the size of the firm by selling off parts of it.[17]

The Effect of Takeovers on the Stock Performance of Targets and Acquirers

An important question is whether a takeover increases or decreases the value of the combined firm by transferring managerial control from existing management to a new management group. Why should the combination be worth more? Among the reasons are (1) more efficient use of management resources, (2) redeployment of assets for more profitable uses, (3) greater earnings resulting from increases in monopoly power, and (4) greater responsiveness to changing demand and supply conditions. "Synergy" is the all-purpose term used to describe these effects. If there are synergistic effects, the value of the stock of the two firms combined is greater than the sum of the values of the stock of the separate parts.

Several research studies have focused on the magnitude of synergistic gains, and most have reached the same conclusion. The stock price of a target firm increases appreciably with the announcement of a planned takeover, and the stock price of the acquiring firm increases proportionately by much less at the same time. Indeed, in recent years the stock price of the acquirer has not increased significantly and may even have declined modestly. Increasingly, a takeover begins to resemble an auction with many firms entering the bidding for the target. Nevertheless, the total value of the target and the acquiring firms increases. On average, takeovers create wealth.

[15] Andrei Shleifer and Robert W. Vishny, "The Takeover Wave of the 1980's," *Science*, vol. 249, pp. 745–749.

[16] Gregg A. Jarrell, James Brickley, and Jeffrey M. Netter, "The Market for Corporate Control: The Empirical Evidence Since 1980," *Journal of Economic Perspectives*, vol. 2, no. 1, pp. 49–68.

[17] Andrei Shleifer and Robert W. Vishny, "Value Maximization and the Acquisition Process," *Journal of Economic Literature*, vol. 2, Winter 1988, pp. 7–20.

Table 11-4   MEAN PERCENTAGE CHANGE IN STOCK PRICE IN 236 SUCCESSFUL TENDER OFFERS, 1963–1984

	Period			All Contests
	7/63–6/68	7/68–12/80	1/81–12/84	7/63–12/84
Target	18.9	35.3	35.3	31.8
Acquirer	4.1	1.3	− 2.9	1.0
Combination	7.8	7.1	8.0	7.4
Number of contests	51	133	52	236

Source: Michael Bradley, Anand Desai, and E. Han Kim, "Synergistic Gains from Corporate Acquisitions and Their Division Between the Stockholders of Target and Acquiring Firms," *Journal of Financial Economics*, May 1988, p. 11.

Table 11-4 shows the mean percentage change in the stock price of the target, the acquiring firm, and the combination following the announcement of 236 successful tender offers between 1963 and 1984. The last column shows that the stock price of a target firm increases on average by 31.8 percent on announcement of a tender offer after controlling for other factors. The stock price of a typical acquirer increases by only 1.0 percent, and the combined revaluation increases by an average of 7.4 percent. The reason the combined percentage revaluation is closer to 1 percent and not 31.8 percent is that the acquirer was typically larger than the target.

The results for the subperiods are also of interest. From 1963 to 1968, there was little government regulation of tender offers. In 1968 Congress passed the Williams Amendment that brought tender offers under the purview of the Securities and Exchange Commission. Also, state antitakeover acts had been passed in 36 states by 1978, which had the effect of lengthening the takeover process. It appears that the effect of greater government scrutiny was to lower the return to the acquirer. The last period was affected by the Reagan administration's more relaxed attitude toward takeovers and the development of management defenses against them. The mean return to acquirers has decreased over time, while the mean return to targets has increased.

The principal conclusion is that there are synergistic gains from takeovers. The market value of the two firms is higher after the proposed takeover is announced than before. The owners of acquired firms appear to benefit more than the owners of the acquiring firms. Shleifer and Vishny interpret this evidence as transferring resources from less able managers to more able managers.

In summary, the market for corporate control is an intricate one with many monitors at work. Economists do not have to assume that the endowment of management includes a natural drive to maximize profits. Rather, incentive to maximize profits varies with the relative cost of using different imperfect internal and external monitors. No one monitor appears appropriate in all cases, and their relative importance has changed over time. External monitors were more important during the 1970s and 1980s. A public policy that muzzles the capital market gives managements a greater opportunity to deviate from maximizing profits.

Economists often simply assume that firms maximize profits without stopping to justify this assumption. There are external and internal monitors that discipline managements who depart from maximizing profits. Boards of directors have cashiered managers that do not perform, and the external capital market was very active in the 1980s in disciplining managers by replacing CEOs. This does not mean that firms always maximize profits. However, the discipline of external and internal monitors places limits on these deviations from profit-maximizing behavior.

SUMMARY

- Competition in the product and capital market disciplines managers who stray from maximizing profit.
- If one shareholder devotes resources to improving management, then all shareholders benefit. The free rider problem lessens the effectiveness of the capital market.
- Expense preference is the excess of expenses over the level that maximizes the profits of the firm.
- Ex post settling up reduces the compensation of the manager by the amount of expense preference.
- A manager consumes more expense preference when ownership is separate from management.
- A profit constraint on a firm increases expense preference and the utility of the manager.
- The compensation of executives appears to be less closely related to firm performance over time.
- One reason for the increase in takeovers is the declining effectiveness of internal monitors.
- The total value of a target and an acquirer increases with the announcement of a takeover.

KEY TERMS

External and internal monitors

Capital market

Free rider problem and
   the tender offer

Ex post settling up

Market for corporate control

Takeovers

Product market

Tender offer

Expense preference

Profit constraint and expense preference

Compensation and firm performance

Stock performance of targets and
   acquirers

REVIEW QUESTIONS

1. Explain the difference between an external and an internal monitor of a firm.
2. Does the diversification of stock holding through the purchase of mutual funds mean that an individual shareholder has little incentive to monitor management practices?
3. Pension funds have grown enormously over time. Would you expect pension fund managers to be effective monitors of firms? Explain why or why not.
4. What is meant by the free rider problem facing a typical shareholder who wants to unseat management?
5. What evidence indicates that the internal monitor is ineffective?
6. Explain why expense preference increases as the manager's share of ownership declines.
7. A profit constraint exists in every competitive market. Therefore, competitive firms do not minimize the cost of producing any rate of output. Explain why you agree or disagree with this statement.

EXERCISES

1. In a noncompetitive market managers can lead a quieter life by earning profits but not necessarily maximizing profits. What conditions must exist for this statement to be true?
2. During a recession a firm operating under a profit constraint becomes a more efficient producer. Use graphs to show why a demand reduction during a recession affects the behavior of a firm operating under a profit constraint.
3. Assume a private firm is not regulated. However, the firm believes its profits will be regulated if they become too high. Would you expect this firm to produce each rate of output at the lowest total cost?
4. How will a regulated monopolist behave if a regulator imposes a profit constraint and knows the minimum cost of producing each rate of output? How will the behavior of the firm change when the regulator does not know the minimum cost of producing output?
5. Suppose a regulator suspects a firm is not producing output at minimum cost. What benefits would accrue to the firm and the regulator if the regulator commits to a fixed regulated price over a certain number of years?
6. What changes would you expect in managerial behavior if an industry is deregulated and no longer operates under a profit constraint?
7. If a CEO engages in expense preference, he or she must pay for it. Explain what this statement means. Under what conditions is it true and when is it not true?

PRICING: PRACTICES AND POLICIES

CHAPTER 12

PRICE DISCRIMINATION

The analyses of firms with market power in Chapters 9 and 10 assumed that a firm sells all units at one price, either the monopoly price or some oligopolistic price. This chapter deals with a price-making firm that can engage in price discrimination—charging different prices for the same product—whether it involves different prices for different units to a single consumer or different prices to different groups. What you will learn in this chapter is something about the motivation for, the conditions under which, and the means by which firms engage in price discrimination.

A common goal of price discrimination is to raise revenue and profits by reducing consumer surplus. Firms can achieve this goal by using different pricing techniques. In some cases they charge different prices to a single consumer; in other cases they charge uniform but different prices to different groups of consumers; and in still other cases they apply a two-part tariff, charging for the right to purchase a product as well as a uniform price for each unit. No matter which of these pricing techniques is adopted, the goal is the same—to raise a firm's profits by reducing consumer surplus. Lest one think that two-part tariffs always harm consumers, the appendix to this chapter considers a case where firms use a two-part tariff in an easy-entry industry as a competitive weapon that increases consumer surplus.

12-1   REVENUE ENHANCEMENT: THE GOAL OF PRICE DISCRIMINATION

There are some markets where identical items sell for different prices.[1] For example, a new car dealership may sell 75 new automobiles a week of the same make. Some consumers pay lower prices than others for the same automobile, depending on their knowledge of market prices and on their bargaining skills.[2] Each student in your class listens to the same lectures, reads the same textbook, and pays the same tuition. However, some receive fellowships and other aid and others do not, and so the net tuition paid by students differs. These are just some of the types of pricing policies considered in this chapter.

This investigation assumes that the firm is a price maker. Just what does a price-making firm achieve by charging different prices? Chapter 3 showed that a

---

[1] For a comprehensive and more advanced treatment of price discrimination the interested reader may consult Louis Phlips, *The Economics of Price Discrimination*, Cambridge University Press, Cambridge, 1983; and Dennis Carlton and Jeffrey M. Perloff, *Modern Industrial Organization*, Scott, Foresman/Little, Brown, Glenview, Ill., 1990, chaps. 14 and 15.

[2] Not all price differences are due to price discrimination. Many differences are a result of differences in costs. When a firm charges a higher price for delivering nails to a distant customer, the nails are the same but the product is not. The nails sold to nearby consumers are a different product than the nails sold at a distant location. In a competitive industry a firm will charge a higher price to a consumer located at a distance than to one nearby because of the cost of transportation. The difference in price equals the cost of transportation between the distant and the nearby consumers. Another caveat is worth emphasizing: There is a danger of equating the absence of price differences with an absence of price discrimination. If a supplier sells lumber at the same delivered price throughout the United States when there are significant transportation costs, the seller is engaging in price discrimination. In this case the firm discriminates in favor of the more distant buyers.

buyer receives a surplus when he or she purchases a product at a given price. Because the customer's utility is higher when consuming the product than when doing without it, each unit consumed is viewed as a bargain because the buyer is willing to pay more than the market price. **Consumer surplus** is the difference between the maximum amount the consumer would pay to obtain a given quantity of a good and the actual amount paid.

Firms recognize that consumers receive a surplus by purchasing a product and that they are often willing to pay more than the market price. Let's consider a simple example that shows by just how much more a firm's revenues and profits can be increased when the consumer receives a surplus.

A monopolist sells a product with inverse market demand function D in Figure 12-1. The long-run marginal cost of production, MC_L, is constant, and the monopolist sells all units at a single price. The marginal revenue function, MR, intersects the marginal cost function when the firm produces Q^* units and sells each unit at P^*. Total profits are equal to the area labeled M, and consumer surplus is equal to the area labeled M^*.

Notice that even a monopolist does not collect all the consumer surplus by

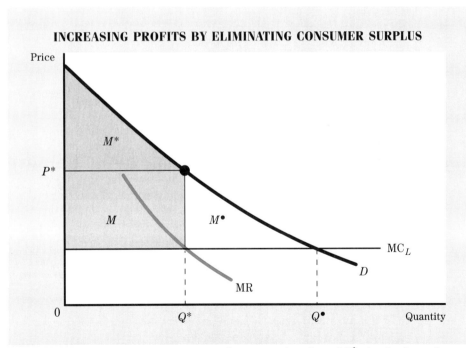

Figure 12-1   When consumers pay the monopoly price of P^*, the firm's profits are equal to area M and consumer surplus is equal to M^*. If the monopolist charges a price equal to the consumer's willingness to pay for each successive unit, it will increase the quantity sold to $Q^\bullet$. The profits of the monopolist equal the sum of areas M, M^*, and $M^\bullet$. By charging different prices for each unit, the monopolist maximizes total profits and completely eliminates consumer surplus.

charging the monopoly price, P^*, because the consumer is still left with a surplus of M^*. While the monopolist's profits would increase if it received area M^* in additional revenue, it has greater profit aspirations. The monopolist would like to receive not only area M^* but also area $M^\bullet$ in higher revenue, so that it can collect all the consumer surplus by increasing the quantity sold from Q^* to $Q^\bullet$ units.

For example, suppose the firm can charge a price equal to the most that consumers will pay for each successive unit. Then, it collects all the consumer surplus by charging a high demand price for the first unit, a somewhat lower demand price for the second unit, and so on. Thus, marginal revenue equals the demand price. The firm will set price equal to marginal cost, which is MC_L and sell $Q^\bullet$ units, so total profit is equal to the sum of areas M, M^*, and $M^\bullet$. When a monopolist collects all the consumer surplus, its profits are maximized by producing $Q^\bullet$ units, the same output that a competitive industry produces. Therefore, a monopolist collects all the consumer surplus, or $M^* + M + M^\bullet$, when it produces $Q^\bullet$ units.

Since a firm's revenue and profit can be increased by charging different prices to a consumer or to different consumers, let's look at the different ways revenue can be increased by reducing consumer surplus. How much of an increase in revenue a monopolist can obtain depends on the information it has about the consumer. As a result, there are three types of price discrimination—first-, second-, and third-degree—which are discussed in the following three sections.

12-2 FIRST-DEGREE (PERFECT) PRICE DISCRIMINATION

With first-degree price discrimination a firm captures all of a consumer's surplus because it has detailed information about how much the consumer is willing to pay for each unit. In Figure 12-2 the buyer is willing to pay P_1 for the first unit, P_2 for the second unit, and so on, and these are the prices the firm charges for successive units. With perfect price discrimination the firm captures all the consumer surplus and achieves maximum revenue enhancement.

As you might suspect, first-degree price discrimination requires detailed information about consumers and, for this reason, is seldom achieved. You can appreciate why few firms have enough information about each consumer's demand function to use this pricing strategy. To capture all the consumer surplus, the company must know the demand curve of each buyer. Each consumer has an incentive to feign disinterest in the firm's product or to camouflage information about his or her true demand function in hopes of retaining some consumer surplus. An example that approximates but does not replicate perfect price discrimination is the haggling between a consumer and a new car dealer. The salesperson sizes up the customer and attempts to find out what price he or she is willing to pay before deciding whether to quote the sticker price or to cut below the list price and eat into the dealer's profit margin. Acquiring detailed information about consumer demand is so costly that it prevents firms from practicing perfect price discrimination. Just imagine the insurmountable problems that would face Disney

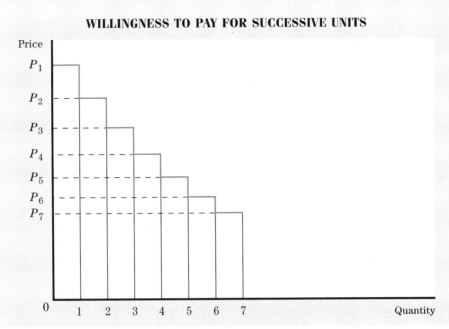

Figure 12-2   Under first-degree price discrimination, the price equals the willingness to pay for successive units. The consumer is willing to pay at most P_1 for the first unit, P_2 for the second unit, and so on. The firm captures all the consumer surplus in the form of higher revenues. Firms seldom have the necessary information to implement first-degree price discrimination and to capture all the consumer surplus.

World if it had to identify the individual demand functions of the diverse group of visitors attending its entertainment parks.

12-3 SECOND-DEGREE PRICE DISCRIMINATION

Second-degree price discrimination, or declining block pricing, is a more limited version of perfect price discrimination. Instead of charging the consumer a separate price for each unit purchased, the firm offers a limited number of prices. With second-degree price discrimination it offers a price schedule to the consumer where a different price is paid for different blocks of units. Assume that DD in Figure 12-3 is the inverse demand function of a consumer and the profit-maximizing price is P_2, and so the monopolist's total revenue is P_2Q_2. With declining block pricing the consumer pays P_1 for each unit up to Q_1 units, P_2 for each unit between Q_1 and Q_2 units, and P_3 for each unit between Q_2 and Q_3 units. Figure 12-3 shows that second-degree price discrimination generates more revenue than a uniform price of, say, P_2 would but less revenue than perfect price discrimination.

We can interpret block pricing in another way. The firm announces a block

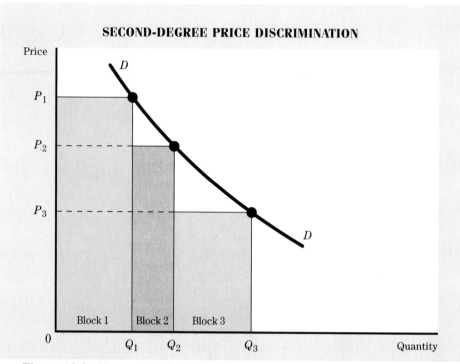

Figure 12-3 With second-degree price discrimination a firm offers a block price function. The first Q_1 units are purchased at a per unit price of P_1, the second block from Q_1 to Q_2 is purchased at a per unit price of P_2, and quantities between Q_2 and Q_3 are purchased at a per unit price of P_3. Second-degree price discrimination yields greater revenue and consumer surplus is smaller than under a uniform price policy.

price schedule where the price depends on the quantity consumed. Each consumer then sorts into one of the blocks depending upon how many units he or she purchases. With second-degree discrimination the firm does not have enough information to sort each consumer into a particular block. In setting the block prices the company must take into account some very complicated substitutions made by consumers who might shift into another block if the price of a nearby block is decreased.

Under block pricing a firm might charge a lower price to a large-volume user if consumer surplus is inversely related to total volume purchased. As an example, large consumers sometimes have less consumer surplus than small ones. To illustrate, suppose the demand function of each small consumer limits the quantity consumed to less than Q_1. These small consumers pay a high price of P_1 for each unit. Larger users purchase quantities between Q_2 and Q_3 and pay a lower average price. Block pricing allows the firm to charge a lower average price to large buyers than to small buyers.

Regulated public utilities frequently use declining block pricing. The price paid for electricity depends on the quantity consumed per month. There are other examples where the price depends on the quantity purchased. Buying a monthly public transit pass costs less per ride than buying individual tickets. Quantity discounts offer consumers a lower per unit price for a larger quantity and may allow a firm to extract a greater surplus from smaller consumers than from larger ones. However, quantity discounts have other explanations and may be related to the cost savings of serving a consumer who buys larger quantities.

12-4   THIRD-DEGREE PRICE DISCRIMINATION

A price-making firm that practices first-degree and, to a lesser exent, second-degree price discrimination knows something about the buyer's demand function and benefits from this information by charging the consumer different prices. In a third type of price discrimination, the firm has no information on individual demand functions but knows from experience that different groups of consumers have different demand functions. With third-degree price discrimination the price-making firm uses a certain characteristic to divide consumers into groups. Then it picks different prices for the different groups that maximize its profit. With third-degree price discrimination the firm can sort consumers into groups so that most of those who pay a higher price cannot purchase in the lower-priced market.

With third-degree price discrimination, firms use some characteristic of consumers to segment consumers into groups. The following list of characteristics is meant to be informative but not exhaustive.

Methods of Grouping Consumers: Examples

To illustrate some of the characterisics that a price-making firm uses to group consumers, we examine some situations where consumers pay different prices. As you read through the examples, try to identify the differences between consumer groups to determine how a price-making firm can take advantage of the groupings.

1. The price of a professional journal is lower for an individual subscriber than for a library.

2. If a traveler returns home from a trip on Sunday instead of Saturday, the airfare is lower. Table 12-1 shows coach fares for a round-trip flight with a Wednesday departure and a Saturday or a Sunday return for March 1991. The fare for a round-trip from New York to Los Angeles is in column 2, the fare for a round-trip from Atlanta to Denver is in column 3, and the fare for a round-trip from Chicago to San Francisco is in column 4. If you left New York for Los Angeles on Wednesday and returned on Saturday, the round-trip fare was $932, or 2.76 times higher than if you returned on Sunday when the round-trip fare was $338. The fare for a round-trip from Chicago to San Francisco with a Saturday return is 3.74 times that with a Sunday return. Why are coach fares so much higher for a Saturday return than for a Sunday return?

Table 12-1 SELECTED ROUND-TRIP AIRFARES, MARCH 1991

DAYS OF THE WEEK (1)	NEW YORK–LOS ANGELES ($) (2)	ATLANTA-DENVER ($) (3)	CHICAGO–SAN FRANCISCO ($) (4)
Leave Wednesday and return on Saturday	932	816	1,114
Leave Wednesday and return on Sunday	338	258	298
Ratio of fare with a Saturday return to fare with a Sunday return	2.76	3.16	3.74

3. Doctors, lawyers, and tax consultants charge different fees to different customers. A doctor may charge me substantially more for an appendix operation than she charges you for the same operation.[3] Yet, we can both walk into a grocery store or dry cleaner and pay the same prices for the same merchandise or for the same cleaning service.

4. A child's haircut is less than an adult's haircut.

5. Some movie houses offer student discounts.

6. In many cities senior citizens receive discounts if they show a card when using public transit facilities.

7. Apparel prices are higher at the beginning of the season than at the end. Figure 12-4 shows the percentage of men's dress shirts that are sold on sale and the average percentage markdown of these shirts by month. The percentage of dress shirts that are sold on sale and the percentage reduction in price are lower at the beginning of the spring and summer season (April to June), and at the beginning of the fall and winter season (September through December). Markdowns increase during January and February and in July and August, the traditional sale months. The seasonal pattern for women's apparel is similar and even more pronounced.

8. Tourists usually pay higher prices for jewelry or souvenirs than do long-term residents of a city or town.

---

[3] For a classic, if dated, analysis of price discrimination in medicine, the reader is encouraged to read Reuben Kessel, "Price Discrimination in Medicine," *Journal of Law and Economics*, vol. I, October 1958, pp. 20–53.

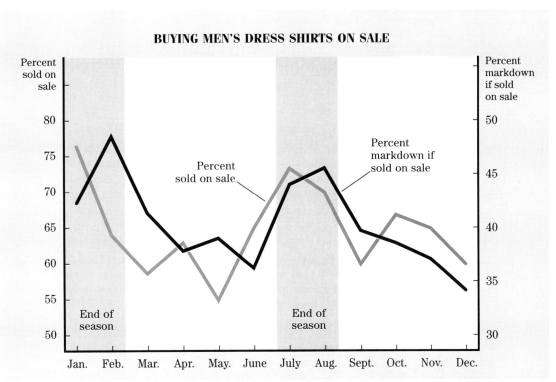

BUYING MEN'S DRESS SHIRTS ON SALE

Figure 12-4   The percentage of men's dress shirts put on sale and the percentage markdown if the shirt is put on sale are larger at the end of seasons. [*After B. Peter Pashigian and Brian Bowen, "Why Are Products Sold on Sale?: Explanations of Pricing Regularities,"* Quarterly Journal of Economics, *November 1991, p. 1026.*]

These examples illustrate four characteristics that firms use to separate consumers into groups:

- *Time.* Airlines and department stores use time of use or time of purchase to segment consumers. The supersaver rate applies only to flyers who stay over on Saturday. End-of-season shoppers receive discounted prices.
- *Age.* A discount for a child's haircut or a senior citizen's use of public transit depends on the age of the individual.
- *Income.* The income of the individual is the basis for lower medical fees for lower-income patients or for lower movie prices for students.
- *Information.* The amount of information possessed by the consumer is another basis for discrimination. Long-term residents of an area have more information about alternative sellers than tourists do.

Whatever means a price maker uses to segment the market, the underlying goal is to increase profits by lowering consumer surplus. To show how a monopolist discriminates among groups of consumers, we divide the analysis into two parts—one in which the total quantity to be sold is fixed and the monopolist has to determine how much to sell to each group, and another in which the monopolist determines the quantity as well as the allocation of the quantity to each group.

Finding the Optimal Pricing Policy for a Given Total Quantity

In the first part of the analysis the monopolist sorts consumers into two groups using some characteristic of consumers. For example, either an individual or a library subscription is being offered. Consumers in market 1 have a different group demand function than consumers in market 2. To start with the simplest case, assume that the monopolist has already produced Q^* units that it expects to sell in markets 1 and 2. Because the goods have already been produced, we can ignore the cost of production since it is a sunk cost. The monopolist wants to sell the total quantity in the two markets so as to maximize total revenue, and by maximizing revenue the firm also maximizes profits since all costs are sunk.

Consumers in the two markets have different inverse group demand functions. The demand functions in markets 1 and 2 are

$$P_1 = D_1(Q_1) \quad \text{and} \quad P_2 = D_2(Q_2) \quad \begin{array}{l}\text{(Inverse Demand Function}\\ \text{in Markets 1 and 2)}\end{array} \quad \text{(12-1)}$$

Given each demand function, the marginal revenue functions in markets 1 and 2 are $MR_1(Q_1)$ and $MR_2(Q_2)$, respectively, where marginal revenue in each market is related to the price and the point price elasticity of demand in that market.

$$MR_1 = P_1\left(1 + \frac{1}{E_1}\right) \quad \text{and} \quad MR_2 = P_2\left(1 + \frac{1}{E_2}\right) \quad \begin{array}{l}\text{(Marginal Revenue}\\ \text{Functions in}\\ \text{Markets 1 and 2)}\end{array} \quad \text{(12-2)}$$

Total revenue of the firm is

Total revenue = Revenue from market 1 + Revenue from market 2

$$R = Q_1 D_1(Q_1) + Q_2 D_2(Q_2) \quad \text{(Total Revenue)} \quad \text{(12-3)}$$

In addition, the total number of units sold in markets 1 and 2 must equal Q^*. The monopolist wants to allocate Q^* units to each market to maximize total revenue. Once the quantity to sell in each market is known, the prices are determined from the market demand functions in equation 12-1. To find the number of units to sell in each market so that total revenue is maximized, the monopolist must decide:

1. Whether to charge a common price or a different price in each market

2. Which group should get the lower price if the firm charges different prices

Let's take up the first issue. Should the monopolist charge the same or different prices? If it charges a uniform price of P^*, it sells Q_1^* in market 1 and Q_2^* in market

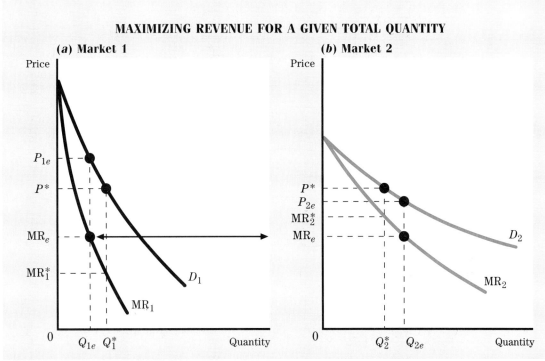

MAXIMIZING REVENUE FOR A GIVEN TOTAL QUANTITY

Figure 12-5   At a common price of P^* the marginal revenue in market 1, MR_1^*, is less than the marginal revenue in market 2, MR_2^*. The monopolist can increase total revenue by raising the price in market 1 to P_{1e} and raise marginal revenue to MR_e while lowering the price in market 2 to P_{2e} and lower marginal revenue to MR_e. Of the Q^* units available for sale, Q_{1e} are sold in market 1 and Q_{2e} are sold in market 2. The firm maximizes total revenue when marginal revenue is the same in both markets.

2, so that $Q^* = Q_1^* + Q_2^*$ (Figure 12-5). Because the demand functions of the two groups differ, marginal revenue from selling the last unit in market 1, MR_1^*, is less than marginal revenue from selling the last unit in market 2, MR_2^*. Because MR_2^* is greater than MR_1^*, total revenue will increase if the firm sells fewer units in market 1 and more units in market 2. You can probably see a resemblance between this problem and the one of allocating total production between two plants to minimize cost discussed in Chapter 6.

    To illustrate why the firm should sell fewer units in market 1 and more units in market 2, consider this numerical example. Suppose all units are currently sold at a uniform price of \$100. At this price the price elasticity of demand in market 1 is -2 and the price elasticity of demand in market 2 is -4. Demand is therefore more elastic in market 2 than in market 1 ($E_2 = -4$ is less than $E_1 = -2$). Marginal revenue from the last unit sold in market 1 is $P_1[1 + (1/E_1)] = \$100[1 + (1/(-2)]$

= \$50. In market 2 marginal revenue from the last unit sold is $P_2[1 + (1/E_2)]$ = \$100[1 + (1/(-4))] = \$75. Transferring the last unit from market 1 to market 2 increases total revenue by \$25 because revenue in market 1 decreases by \$50 but revenue in market 2 increases by \$75. The firm sells more units in market 2 and fewer units in market 1 by lowering the price in market 2 and raising the price in market 1. Revenue is higher when the monopolist charges different prices rather than a uniform price.

As long as marginal revenues in the two markets differ, total revenue will continue to increase if the firm sells more units by lowering the price in the market with the more elastic demand function and raising the price in the market with the less elastic demand function. Although the prices in the two markets are moving in opposite directions, the difference between marginal revenues is narrowing and the firm always sells Q^* units. At some point the marginal revenues will be equal. Marginal revenues equal MR_e in both markets when the firm sells Q_{1e} at a price of P_{1e} in market 1 and Q_{2e} at a price of P_{2e} in market 2. While marginal revenues are now equal, prices are different in the two markets.

Total revenue reaches a maximum when the marginal revenues in the two markets are equal.[4]

$$MR_1(Q_1) = MR_2(Q_2) \quad \text{(Equality of Marginal Revenue in the Two Markets)} \quad \textbf{(12-4)}$$

> A firm maximizes total revenue by selling a fixed number of units so that marginal revenue is the same in each market.

Price Elasticity and Pricing Strategy

If a monopolist allocates Q^* so that marginal revenue is the same in both markets, how does the price in market 1 compare to the price in market 2? Substitute the expression for marginal revenue in each market in equation 12-2 into equation 12-4 to obtain

---

[4] Let $P_1 = D_1(Q_1)$ and $P_2 = D_2(Q_2)$ be the demand functions in the two markets. Suppose the firm has Q^* units to sell, so that $Q_1 + Q_2 = Q^*$. The firm wants to maximize $R = Q_1 D_1(Q_1) + Q_2 D_2(Q_2)$ subject to the condition that $Q_1 + Q_2 = Q^*$. Solve this constraint for Q_2 and substitute the result into the equation for total revenue: $R = Q_1 D_1(Q_1) + (Q^* - Q_1)D_2(Q^* - Q_1)$. The equation is now simply a function of Q_1. Using calculus, we find the first-order condition for a revenue maximum requires

$$\frac{dR}{dQ_1} = Q_1 \frac{dD_1}{dQ_1} + D_1(Q_1) + (Q^* - Q_1)\frac{dD_2}{dQ_2}\frac{dQ_2}{dQ_1} + D_2(Q_2) = 0$$

Because $dQ_2/dQ_1 = -1$, a unit increase in Q_1 must decrease Q_2 by a unit if the total output is Q^*. Therefore,

$$Q_1 \frac{dD_1}{dQ_2} + D_1(Q_1) = Q_2 \frac{dD_2}{dQ_1} + D_2(Q_2)$$

The first two terms on the left-hand side represent marginal revenue in market 1, and the two terms on the right-hand side represent marginal revenue in market 2. A firm maximizes the total revenue from selling a given quantity by making marginal revenue the same in the two markets.

$$P_1\left(1 + \frac{1}{E_1}\right) = P_2\left(1 + \frac{1}{E_2}\right)$$

After dividing both sides of the equation by P_2 and then by $1 + (1/E_1)$ and simplifying, the equation becomes

$$\frac{P_1}{P_2} = \frac{E_1(E_2 + 1)}{E_2(E_1 + 1)}$$

$$= \frac{E_1E_2 + E_1}{E_1E_2 + E_2} \qquad \text{(Ratio of Prices that Maximize Profits)} \qquad \textbf{(12-5)}$$

Equation 12-5 shows that the ratio of the prices that maximize the firm's profits depends on the values of the two price elasticities. The numerator and the denominator on the right-hand side of equation 12-5 have a common term, E_1E_2. The product of the two price elasticities is positive since each price elasticity is negative. From E_1E_2 we add a negative number E_1 in the numerator and E_2 in the denominator.

The price elasticity of demand is more elastic in market 2 than in market 1 if $E_1 > E_2$. Because the numerator is greater than the denominator, the right-hand side of equation 12-5 is greater than 1 and P_1 is larger than P_2. If $E_1 = -3$ while $E_2 = -5$, then the right-hand side of equation 12-5 is $(15 - 3)/(15 - 5) = 1.2$. P_1 is 20 percent higher than P_2. In which market segment will the price be lower? Equation 12-5 indicates that the price is lower in the market with the more elastic demand function. A profit-maximizing monopolist charges a lower price to the segment of the market where demand is more elastic. Collectively, the group of consumers that pays a lower price has a more elastic demand function at the profit-maximizing price. A monopolist charges a lower price to the group for which the quantity demanded will decline by proportionally more for a given percentage increase in price. The demand of this group is more sensitive to a price increase than the demand of the other group, and so the price paid by its members is lower.

> The profit-maximizing price is lower in the market with the more elastic demand function.

It is clear that a monopolist receives greater revenue by charging different prices if the price elasticities of demand differ. We can also determine when a monopolist that can engage in price discrimination will not do so. If $E_1 = E_2$ at a common price, the price elasticities in the two markets are the same and equation 12-2 says that marginal revenues in the two markets are equal at the common price; $P_1/P_2 = 1$. Total revenue will fall if the firm charges different prices to the two groups of consumers. So, a monopolist will forsake price discrimination if the price elasticities of demand are the same for the two groups at the uniform profit-maximizing price.

Reconsideration of the Examples

Now that you know that the group with the more elastic demand function pays a lower price, can it be plausibly argued that the group paying the lower price in each of the previous examples has the more elastic demand function? Would you expect the demand function for individual journal subscriptions to be more elastic than the demand function for library journal subscriptions? Because faculty members and students expect a university library to subscribe to the important journals in each field, many but not all libraries will continue to subscribe if a journal raises the subscription price. On the other hand, proportionally more individual faculty members and graduate students will cancel subscriptions and rely on library holdings if the individual subscription price increases. It appears plausible that the demand function for individual subscriptions is more elastic than the demand function for library subscriptions.

Why is the round-trip fare substantially lower if a traveler returns on Sunday rather than on Saturday? Here the goal is to distinguish between the business traveler and the tourist. The tourist has flexibility in scheduling a flight, whereas the business traveler is eager to report back to the home office, catch up on office work, and rest over the weekend. The business traveler has a less elastic demand function for a Friday return trip than a tourist and finds it more costly to stay over until Sunday. On the other hand, the inconvenience of returning on Sunday or later is less for tourists, who have a more elastic demand function for travel on a particular day of the week. Why do airlines require a Sunday departure rather than a Saturday departure? A plausible answer to this question is that they can more effectively separate the business market from the tourist market by doing so.

At a higher price, lower-income patients are more likely to delay or to put off seeing a physician than higher-income consumers are. And so, the price elasticity of demand appears more elastic for lower- than for higher-income patients.

The demand for children's haircuts is likely to be more elastic than the demand for adults' haircuts. If the price of a child's haircut increases, parents are more likely to cut the child's hair themselves or to visit the barbershop less frequently.

The demand for films by students may be more elastic than the demand by the general public. The lower average income of students or the availability of substitute films at reduced rates on campus could explain why the students' demand function is more elastic.

It is less clear that price discrimination is the motivation for senior citizen discounts. Unlike the general public, senior citizens often do not have access to an automobile, an important substitute for public transit. This suggests that the demand function for senior citizens is less elastic. On the other hand, a fare increase might cause a larger decrease in the quantity demanded because senior citizens do not use public transit to journey to work but for more discretionary functions. Overall, we cannot conclude that senior citizens have a more elastic demand function for public transit rides. Other hypotheses may better explain senior citizen discounts for public transit.

The prices for men's and women's apparel are higher in October and November, at the beginning of the fall-winter apparel seasons, than in January and February, the end of the fall-winter season. Early in the season buyers demand the latest creations, while late in the season they are less exacting in their demands. It is possible that early buyers have less elastic demands and late buyers have more elastic demands. Price discrimination could be the underlying reason for these long-standing pricing practices but is only one of several hypotheses that could explain this type of pricing pattern. One problem in applying the price discrimination theory is that merchandise sold at the beginning of the season is different from that sold at the end of the season. At the end of the season only the remnants that did not sell earlier remain on the shelves and only a limited selection is available. The second problem is that there are many sellers in most retail markets. Later in this chapter, we will discuss the difficulty of engaging in price discrimination when there are many sellers in the market. Chapter 15 considers a demand uncertainty explanation for these pricing practices.

When shopping in a foreign country, tourists have less information about alternative suppliers than the local population does. Because they know of fewer substitute suppliers and have less information about prices, they may have a less elastic demand function. The seller can usually determine if customers are tourists from the questions they ask and how they dress. Firms can then set prices based on the information possessed by the buyer.

Finding the Optimum Output to Produce and Prices to Charge

The first part of the analysis of third-degree price discrimination demonstrated how a firm with a fixed quantity divides its product between two markets and sets prices in each market that maximize total revenue. A more typical situation facing a price-discriminating firm is to determine what quantity to produce and how to distribute that quantity between markets. This section investigates how a monopolist determines the total quantity to produce and the distribution of that quantity. Before beginning the analysis, you should understand why this section focuses on profits while the last section focused only on revenue. In the last section all costs were sunk. By maximizing revenue, a firm automatically maximized profits. In contrast, production costs are variable in this section because the monopolist determines what quantity to produce.

First, we derive an expression for the profits of the firm:

Profits = Revenue in market 1 and market 2 − Cost of production

$$\pi = D_1(Q_1)Q_1 + D_2(Q_2)Q_2 - C_L(Q) \qquad \text{(Total Profits of a Price-} \qquad \text{(12-6)} \\ \text{Discriminating Monopolist)}$$

In this case, total revenue depends on the units sold in the two markets, and total cost depends on the total number of units produced. The sum of the quantities sold in the two markets must equal total production Q.

$$Q = Q_1 + Q_2 \qquad \text{(Total Output)} \qquad \text{(12-7)}$$

You already know from the previous analysis that no matter what output the monopolist produces, that quantity will be allocated so that the marginal revenue is the same in both markets. To decide how much to produce, the monopolist increases output until the marginal cost of production is equal to the marginal revenue from selling another unit in either market. To maximize profits, a price-discriminating monopolist equates marginal cost to marginal revenue in *both* markets.[5] The necessary conditions for profit maximization by a price-discriminating monopolist are

$$MR_1(Q_1) = MC(Q_1 + Q_2)$$

$$MR_2(Q_2) = MC(Q_1 + Q_2)$$

(Necessary Conditions for a Price-Discriminating Monopolist)   **(12-8)**

Therefore,

$$MR_1(Q_1) = MR_2(Q_2)$$

> **The firm expands output until marginal revenue in each market equals marginal cost of production.**

The following graphical method can be used to find the total quantity produced and the profit-maximizing prices. After you become familiar with this technique, you can apply it in finding solutions to many price discrimination problems.

The first requirement is to find a way to equate marginal revenue across markets. To do this, pick a value for marginal revenue and then find the quantity that must be sold in each market so that marginal revenue in each market equals this prespecified value. Sum the two quantities and determine a point on a new graph that relates the prespecified marginal revenue to this total quantity.

Figure 12-6 shows how this is done when the specified marginal revenue is MR^*. When selling Q_1^* in market 1 (Figure 12-6*a*) and Q_2^* in market 2 (Figure

---

[5] For the calculus-trained reader, we show the derivation of these profit maximization conditions. The firm maximizes $\pi = D_1(Q_1)Q_1 + D_2(Q_2)Q_2 - C_L(Q)$ subject to the condition $Q_1 + Q_2 = Q$. After substituting this constraint and eliminating Q, the profits of the firm depend on Q_1 and Q_2. The two first-order conditions for a maximum are

$$\frac{\partial \pi}{\partial Q_1} = D_1(Q_1) + Q_1 \frac{dD_1}{dQ_1} - \frac{dC_L(Q)}{dQ} \frac{dQ}{dQ_1} = 0$$

$$\frac{\partial \pi}{\partial Q_2} = D_2(Q_2) + Q_2 \frac{dD_2}{dQ_2} - \frac{dC_L(Q)}{dQ} \frac{dQ}{dQ_2} = 0$$

where ∂ denotes partial differentiation. Because a unit increase in Q_1 or Q_2 increases Q by a unit, $dQ/dQ_1 = dQ/dQ_2 = 1$. The two first-order conditions become

$$MR_1(Q_1) = D_1(Q_1) + Q_1 \frac{dD_1}{dQ_1} = \frac{dC_L(Q)}{dQ}$$

$$MR_2(Q_2) = D_2(Q_2) + Q_2 \frac{dD_2}{dQ_2} = \frac{dC_L(Q)}{dQ}$$

Marginal revenue (the first two terms on the left-hand side) in market 1 or market 2 must equal the marginal cost of production. Because marginal cost is the same, it follows that marginal revenue across markets will be equal.

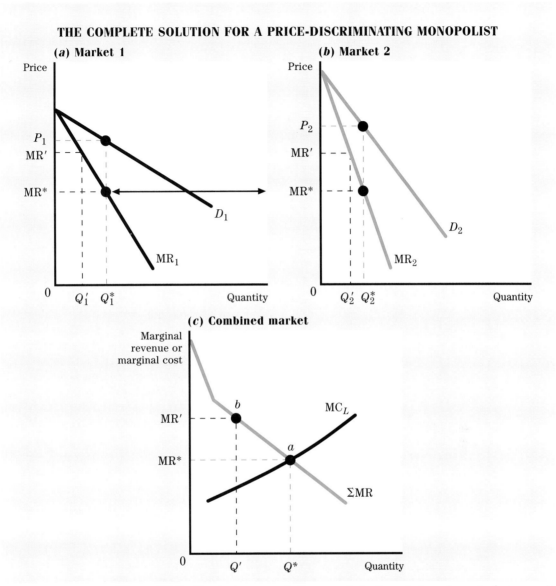

THE COMPLETE SOLUTION FOR A PRICE-DISCRIMINATING MONOPOLIST

Figure 12-6   Marginal revenue is the same in both markets and marginal revenue in each market is equal to marginal production cost. The ΣMR function is the horizontal summation of the individual marginal revenue functions. It intersects the marginal cost function at point a. If the firm produces Q^* units, the ΣMR function indicates that the firm can obtain MR^* in each market. Of the Q^* units produced, Q_1^* are sold in market 1 at P_1 and Q_2^* are sold in market 2 at P_2. Marginal revenue is the same in both markets, and marginal revenue in each market equals marginal cost of production.

12-6*b*), the marginal revenue in each market is MR*. The total quantity sold when MR* is the marginal revenue in each market is $Q_1^* + Q_2^* = Q^*$ (point *a* on the ΣMR function) in Figure 12-6*c*, where marginal revenue is on the vertical axis and total quantity is on the horizontal axis.

We derive the ΣMR function by repeating this procedure for all possible values of marginal revenue. To demonstrate this point, consider a second value of marginal revenue, MR′, and determine how many units the firm can sell while achieving MR′ in each market. If it sells Q_1' in market 1 (Figure 12-6*a*) and Q_2' in market 2 (Figure 12-6*b*), marginal revenue in each market is equal to MR′. In Figure 12-6*c* the total quantity Q' ($= Q_1' + Q_2'$) and MR′ determine point *b* on the ΣMR function. The firm can sell a total of Q' units so that marginal revenue in each market is equal to MR′. Geometrically, ΣMR is constructed by summing the individual marginal revenue functions horizontally. Each point on the ΣMR function indicates what marginal revenue will be in each market when the firm produces a given total quantity.

The second requirement is to equate marginal cost to marginal revenue in each market. The long-run marginal cost function of the monopolist in Figure 12-6*c* intersects the ΣMR function at point *a* and determines the total quantity produced. If the firm produces Q^*, it knows that it can sell Q^* units so that marginal revenue is MR* in each market. It sells Q_1^* units in market 1 at P_1^*, and Q_2^* in market 2 at P_2^*. Because MR* in each market equals marginal cost of production, the firm selects a total quantity where marginal revenue in each market equals marginal cost of production. Therefore, the equalities in equation 12-8 are satisfied.

To review the two-part technique: The horizontal sum of the marginal revenue functions is the ΣMR function. The intersection of the ΣMR function with the marginal cost function determines the total quantity produced and the marginal revenue, MR*. The firm determines the quantity to sell and the price in each market so that marginal revenue is MR*. This graphical method can be used to find solutions to the exercises at the end of this chapter.

APPLICATION 12-1

Should a Firm Expand into the European Market?

The following situation is an opportunity for you to apply the graphical method and to test your understanding of price discrimination.

A company is the sole supplier of a product and sells it in the domestic market at a price of P_0. Because the firm has been successful in the domestic market, several members of the firm have resisted recent suggestions to expand into the foreign market. They feel that they know much more about domestic demand conditions than those in the European market. For example, their best guess is that the price elasticity of demand in the domestic market is -5 at the current price of P_0. They know much less about the level of demand and the price elasticity of demand overseas.

Other officials of the company think that they are missing an exciting profit opportunity by failing to expand into foreign markets. The CEO believes the firm should develop more information before making a decision, and so he appoints a committee of three to study the problem, develop the facts, and present a recommendation.

The committee decides to obtain more information about the size of the European market by hiring a consulting firm. The consulting firm reports that European demand will not exist at a price of P_0, estimating that there will be no demand for the product unless the price is 15 percent lower than P_0. If the price is $0.75P_0$, the consulting firm estimates that European demand will be about 25 percent of current domestic demand. It appears that the firm can break into the European market but only if it is willing to offer the product at a price considerably lower than the domestic price.

After a lengthy discussion, it becomes clear that the committee cannot reach a consensus recommendation. The arguments of the committee members are as follows.

- *Group 1.* One member raises three objections to expansion into the European market. First, to obtain a foreign volume equal to 25 percent of domestic volume, the company will have to offer a price that is 25 percent lower. She asks, "Why sell the product at a 25 percent discount when we can sell it in the domestic market at a full price of P_0?" Second, she worries about a potential arbitrage problem. Some of the foreign sales could leak back into the domestic market. Third, she fears that an output expansion of 25 percent would cause the long-run marginal cost of production to increase even if a new plant is constructed in Europe. There is a reasonable chance that diseconomies of scale will set in if the firm expands by 25 percent. This will inevitably lead to a reduction of sales in the profitable domestic market. She recommends a cost study be conducted to determine if diseconomies of scale are likely to set in before the firm expands into the European market. She might support the expansion proposal if the study shows that marginal cost of production will not rise and if the firm can prevent arbitrage.
- *Group 2.* The other two members strongly favor the expansion proposal. They argue that expansion into foreign markets should not interfere with domestic output at all. They recommend a prudent expansion by the company into foreign markets where sales can be made at a price higher than $0.8P_0$. They argue that the arbitrage problem can be minimized by requiring that the warranty on the product be valid only in the country of initial purchase. They recognize that the marginal cost of production may rise; however, they say that this should not prevent the firm from expanding prudently. They believe that the profits of the firm will increase with expansion.

Which of the two positions would you support? Using the theory of price discrimination, evaluate the different points raised by the two groups. The member who objects to the expansion has made three points. First, she claims the price discount is too large to justify the expansion. Second, the potential arbitrage problem concerns her. Third, she says the decision to expand into the European market depends critically on the absence of diseconomies of scale.

How valid are these points? The first point fails to distinguish between price and marginal revenue. If the firm is a price maker, marginal revenue is less than price in both the export and the domestic markets. The 25 percent difference between the domestic and the export prices does not mean that the difference between the marginal revenues in the two markets is 25 percent. Marginal revenue from the *first* unit sold in the European market could be greater than marginal revenue from the *last* unit sold in the domestic market although the European price is less than the domestic price. If marginal revenue from selling the first unit in the foreign market exceeds marginal revenue from selling the last unit in the domestic market, total revenue will increase by increasing sales in the European market and reducing sales in the domestic market. Notice that the decision to enter the European market does not depend on knowing whether there are or are not diseconomies of scale. The expansion decision depends solely on whether marginal revenue from the first unit sold in the foreign market is greater than marginal revenue from the last unit sold in the domestic market. How much is produced will depend on whether there are or are not diseconomies of scale.

Is marginal revenue from the first unit sold in the foreign market greater than marginal revenue from the last unit sold in the domestic market? At the current rate of domestic output the latter can be estimated from the expression for marginal revenue:

$$\text{MR} = P_0\left(1 + \frac{1}{E}\right) = P_0\left(1 + \frac{1}{-5}\right) = 0.8P_0$$

Marginal revenue from the last unit sold in the domestic market is 80 percent of the current price. For example, it is \$64 if $P_0 = \$80$ and $E = -5$. If marginal revenue from the first unit sold in the foreign market is greater than \$64, then entry into the foreign market will increase total revenue.

The consultant study estimated that the quantity demanded becomes positive in the foreign market if the European price is 15 percent less than the domestic price or when the European price is $0.85P_0$, or \$68. This means that the first unit will sell at $0.85P_0$. Although the foreign price is less than the domestic price, marginal revenue from the first unit sold abroad is greater than marginal revenue from the last unit sold at home. By reducing the number of units sold in the domestic market and increasing the number sold in the European market, total revenue can be increased for a given total quantity. Therefore, expansion must *increase* total profits.

Figure 12-7*a* shows the domestic demand function, *DD*, the domestic marginal revenue function, MR, and the marginal cost function, MC. The original equilibrium price and output are P_0 and Q_0, respectively. The foreign demand and marginal revenue functions in Figure 12-7*b* are *dd* and mr, respectively. Note that the intercepts of *dd* and mr are $0.85P_0$.

How many units should the firm sell in the domestic and in the foreign markets? Is it true that entry into the European market should not affect the quantity sold in the domestic market? We can answer these questions by finding the optimum quantities and prices that maximize firm profits. The first step is to sum the marginal

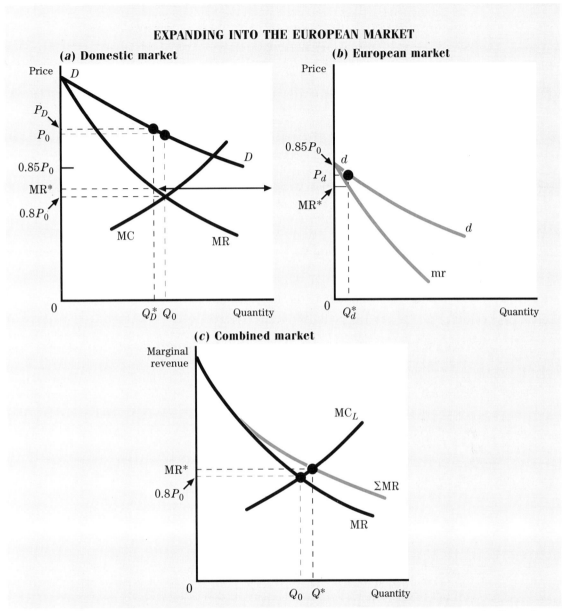

EXPANDING INTO THE EUROPEAN MARKET

Figure 12-7   The firm produces Q_0 units in the domestic market and sells each at a price of P_0. Marginal revenue in the domestic market is $.8P_0$ because the price elasticity is -5. The first unit can be sold only at a price of $0.85P_0$ in the European market, or 15 percent less than in the domestic market. Nevertheless, the firm should expand into the European market. The marginal revenue from the first unit sold in the European market is greater than the marginal revenue from the last unit sold in the domestic market. The firm should produce Q^* units and sell Q_d^* units at a price of P_d in the European market. The quantity sold in the domestic market decreases to Q_D^* units.

revenue functions horizontally to obtain the function labeled ΣMR in Figure 12-7c. This function intersects the marginal cost function when total output is equal to Q^*. Expansion into the European market increases marginal revenue from $0.8P_0$ to MR*. The firm allocates Q^* between the domestic and the European markets so that marginal revenue in each market equals MR*. Therefore, the total number of units sold in the domestic market decreases to Q_D^*. Penetration into the domestic market does decline (as one member predicted), and the domestic price rises to P_D. The firm sells Q_d^* units at a price of P_d in the European market, and total profits increase. If entry into the foreign market increases marginal cost of production, marginal revenue in the domestic market must increase. Entry into the European market increases the domestic price and reduces the quantity sold in the domestic market. What this analysis shows is that operations in the domestic market cannot and should not be isolated from those in the European market. Compartmentalizing operations will not maximize firm profits. Entry into the European market affects the price in the domestic market if the firm's marginal cost function is not flat.

A question about arbitrage is also raised. It is a serious problem and must be prevented for profits to increase. The proposal to use a warranty deserves a more thorough investigation to determine if it would be effective.

How would you evaluate the suggestion by the two members who recommend that the firm enter any foreign market as long as the first sale is at $0.8P_0$? The overall conclusion of the two members of group 2 is correct, but the suggested criterion is faulty. There may be several foreign markets the company could enter. As it enters each market, total production increases and marginal cost of production rises. For example, suppose the company enters the European market and marginal cost of production increases to $0.83P_0 = $ MR$_d = $ MR$_f$. Then it would not pay to enter another foreign market where the first unit sells at a price of $0.8P_0$. If marginal cost is increasing, the firm should not adopt a general policy of entering any market where at least one sale can be made at $0.8P_0$.

Preventing Arbitrage

This analysis of third-degree price discrimination assumes that the firm can separate markets. If it tries to practice price discrimination when the markets are not separated, it will find that it is selling units only in the low-priced market. Middlemen will appear who will purchase in the low-priced market, resell in the high-priced market, and earn a profit. This process is called *arbitrage*. When arbitrage occurs, price differences disappear and price discrimination cannot persist. Therefore, a firm must always be on guard to prevent arbitrage. It is less costly to prevent arbitrage for some products than for others. For example, services are more costly to arbitrage than are goods. It would be very expensive for you to resell an appendix operation or the specific advice you receive from a tax consultant. Tariff barriers and import controls also limit arbitrage. Firms can charge a different price abroad than in the home market if there are barriers preventing low-priced items sold abroad from being imported back into the domestic market. Companies also dump products abroad at lower prices than in the home market. For example, American drug companies sometimes sell drugs at lower prices abroad than in the United States. Likewise, Japanese companies sell consumer electronic products abroad at lower prices than in Japan.

APPLICATION **12-2**

Pricing a Renault in Belgium and in England

New car prices are lower in Belgium than in England. An account in *The Economist* reveals that the price of a Clio RT hatchback was equivalent to $5,750 if purchased in Belgium, but $7,519 in England, or 30 percent more in England.[6] How can this difference persist? A correspondent for *The Economist* wished to purchase a Clio before returning to England, and so he ordered a right-hand-drive car in Belgium. Renault said that the only right-hand-drive model it could supply in Belgium was one destined for the British market and at the British price. The correspondent referred Renault to a ruling by the European Court of Justice in 1985 requiring Ford to supply its German dealers with right-hand-drive cars at prices close to those charged for left-hand-drive cars. Renault argued that the right-hand-drive Clio RT included fuel ejection, tinted windows, a sun roof, and so on, and that these features were optional on the left-hand-drive versions sold in Belgium. The account in *The Economist* noted that the options could not explain the 30 percent price differential.

An auto manufacturer can therefore separate automobile markets by shipping cars with different features to the two markets. In this way, it prevents arbitrage and is able to practice price discrimination.

If arbitrage is prevented on the demand side of the market, third-degree price discrimination may still be impossible when there are many sellers in the market. The reason is that arbitrage can occur on the supply side as well. If there are enough other firms in the market that act as price takers, a discriminatory price structure will crumble because arbitrage on the supply side is difficult to prevent. Entry into the high-price segment of the market will eliminate any price differences between markets that cannot be explained by cost differences. Price-taking suppliers will respond to a higher price on the West Coast by shipping the product to the West Coast rather than to the East Coast, causing price to fall on the West Coast and to rise on the East Coast until any price difference disappears. This is why price discrimination is less likely to be observed in competitive markets where firms are price takers. Price discrimination can occur only if arbitrage on both sides of the market is prevented.

> A firm will engage in price discrimination if (1) it is a price maker, (2) it can separate markets and prevent arbitrage, and (3) the price elasticities of demand differ between groups.

---

[6] Based on "Price Sensitive," *The Economist*, February 22, 1992, p. 66.

The Difference between Second- and Third-Degree Price Discrimination

Now that we have reviewed the different types of price discrimination, let's reconsider the difference between second- and third-degree price discrimination. With third-degree price discrimination the company can identify and assign consumers to groups based on some characteristic, for example, their age, student status, or mailing address. If the firm sets one price for a student, it is assumed that only students can purchase at this price. The assumption is that there is a low-cost way of identifying and sorting consumers. With second-degree price discrimination the firm cannot identify at low cost what type of customer each is beforehand. Therefore, consumers can shift into one group from another. The firm cannot sort consumers directly; however, it can quote prices that indirectly sort buyers into groups. Given the firm's prices, consumers self-select into different groups in a way that maximizes the firm's profits. For example, a utility offers a block price schedule and customers self-select into one block or another.

To illustrate the difference between second- and third-degree price discrimination, let's return to the example of airline travelers who must decide on their day of return. Until now, we have assumed that business travelers must return before Sunday and that tourists could return on Sunday or later. Now let's entertain the possibility that business travelers will shift and delay their return to Sunday if the price inducement is attractive compared to that for a pre-Sunday return. Several considerations go into calculating the prices the airline charges as a function of the day of return. To be specific, an airline must determine what prices to charge for Friday, Saturday, and Sunday returns. We already know that airlines charge substantially higher fares for travelers who do not stay over Saturday night, and we want to consider a numerical example that captures the essence of the pricing problem.

Assume the airline has only two classes of consumers, business and tourist. Table 12-2 shows the willingness to pay for each type of customer for a return on each of the three days. The business traveler will pay up to $1,200 to return on Friday, $600 to return on Saturday, and only $400 for a coach ticket with a Sunday return. We assume that the tourist is indifferent about the return date and is willing to pay $350 for any of the three days.

If you could identify a customer as business or tourist when he or she makes a reservation, you would charge the business traveler $1,200 no matter what day

Table 12-2   WILLINGNESS TO PAY FOR BUSINESS AND TOURIST CONSUMERS

	FRIDAY RETURN ($)	SATURDAY RETURN ($)	SUNDAY RETURN ($)
Business	1,200	600	400
Tourist	350	350	350

she returns, charge the tourist $350 no matter what day he returns, and receive a total revenue of $1,550, the maximum revenue because it leaves no consumer surplus for either traveler. In this simple example perfect price discrimination and third-degree price discrimination are identical since there is only one type of customer in each class, and the firm maximizes profits by charging the willingness to pay for each class of customer.

Suppose you cannot identify the type of customer when the reservation is made. What prices should the airline charge for a return on each day? To answer this question assume that the traveler selects the return day that maximizes his or her consumer surplus, the difference between willingness to pay and the price charged by the airline.

$$\text{Consumer surplus of traveler} = \text{Willingness to pay} - \text{Price paid}$$

This analysis of the problem ignores costs. However, it is assumed that the airline cannot identify consumers who are willing to pay more and therefore cannot practice third-degree price discrimination. Faced with this situation, it sets prices for each return day that sort the business traveler from the tourist.

For the moment, let's ignore Sunday and just consider what will happen if the price is $350 for a Saturday return and $1,200 for a Friday return. Clearly, the tourist will return on Saturday because his consumer surplus is negative, $350 - $1,200 = -$850, when returning on Friday. Unfortunately, from the airline's perspective, the business traveler will also return on Saturday. We reach this conclusion because each traveler selects a return day that maximizes consumer surplus. The business traveler's consumer surplus with a Friday return is zero since price equals willingness to pay. She prefers to return on Saturday because consumer surplus is $600 - $350 = $250. Because both travelers return on Saturday, the prices charged by the airline produce a total profit of only $350 + $350 = $700.

To induce the business traveler to return on Friday, the price of a Friday return must be no higher than $949 so that consumer surplus is greater than $250. Then, consumer surplus with a Friday return is $1,200 - $949 = $251, and the business traveler selects a Friday return because consumer surplus is larger on Friday than on Saturday. The airline's profits increase to $949 + $350 = $1,299. The price for a Friday return is $949, and for a Saturday return, $350. With these prices both the business traveler and the tourist self-select into groups.

Because the difference in willingness to pay for a Saturday return between the business traveler and the tourist is large, the airline can entice the business traveler to return on Friday only by reducing the price of a Friday return. This suggests that it can do still better by getting the tourist to return on Sunday since the difference between the willingness to pay of the tourist and of the business traveler is smaller. Suppose the airline announces a price of $350 for a Sunday return, a price above $549 for a Saturday return, say $550, and a price of $1149 for a Friday return. For these prices the consumer surplus of the business traveler with a Friday return is $1,200 - $1,149 = $51. Consumer surplus is $50 with a Saturday return and $400 - $350 = $50 with a Sunday return. Therefore, the business traveler will return on Friday. The tourist will return on Sunday since his consumer surplus is negative for any return day other than Sunday. The airline's profit is

$1,149 + $350 = $1,499. Therefore, airfares are $1,149 for a Friday return, any price greater than $549 for a Saturday return, and $350 for a Sunday return. With these prices the business traveler and the tourist self-select into different return days so that the airline maximizes profits.

In summary, with second-degree price discrimination a company cannot identify which group customers belong to and therefore cannot sort them into groups at a low cost, while with third-degree price discrimination it can. Because the firm cannot sort consumers directly, its profits are lower than they would be if it could. Recall that airline profits would be $1,550 if the airline could identify business travelers, but are only $1,499 because it cannot.

Geographical (Spatial) Price Discrimination

There is a close analogy between the separation of consumers over time and the separation of consumers over space. Just as the demand function of customers who buy early in the season can differ from that of those buying later in the season, so too can the demand functions at different points in space. A firm can discriminate between consumers at different locations when a product is costly to transport over space. It can charge different prices over space to maximize its profits and discriminate between consumers located close to the production source and those located some distance away. This section shows how a monopolist determines prices over space to maximize profits.

Suppose a plant is in town a (see the accompanying diagram). Consumers are in towns a and b. The inverse demand function of consumers located in town a is $P_a = D(Q_a)$. Assume that town b is the same size as town a but is located k miles away from the plant, and so the inverse demand function is the same in both towns; that is, $P_b = D(Q_b)$. Each demand function shows what consumers will pay for a product at their doorstep. For simplicity, assume that marginal cost of production c equals average cost of production and is constant. Transportation costs are zero for sales in town a, but the firm incurs transportation costs of t for each unit sold in town b.

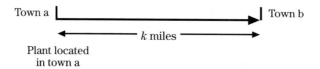

Town a |_____| Town b

←——————— k miles ———————→

Plant located
in town a

The total profits of the firm selling to consumers at two locations can be expressed as

$$\pi = \text{Revenue from town a} + \text{Net revenue from town b} - \text{Total cost}$$

$$= D(Q_a)Q_a + [D(Q_b) - t]Q_b - c(Q_a + Q_b) \qquad \text{(12-9)}$$

The first term in equation 12-9 is the delivered price in town a multiplied by the total units sold in town a. The second term is the delivered price in town b less t, the transportation costs to town b, multiplied by the total units sold in town b.

And the third term represents total production cost, where marginal cost is c and is constant.

NP_b is the net price received by the firm for each unit sold in town b and is equal to the delivered price paid by the consumer in town b less the transportation costs.

$$NP_b(Q_b) = D(Q_b) - t \qquad \text{(Net Price)}$$

The inverse *net* demand function shows the highest price that the firm can charge for each quantity after deducting t. The net demand function is derived by subtracting t from the delivered price in town b for each quantity.

Figure 12-8 shows the common demand function of consumers located in either town a or town b as well as the net demand function of consumers located in town b. The firm must decide how many units to sell in town a, Q_a, and in town b, Q_b,

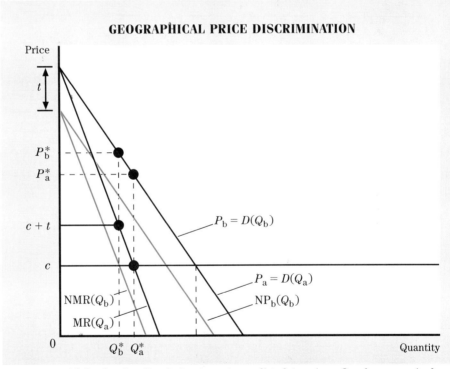

GEOGRAPHICAL PRICE DISCRIMINATION

Figure 12-8   A price-discriminating monopolist determines Q_a where marginal revenue in market a equals marginal cost. Q_b is determined where net marginal revenue in market b equals marginal cost. The profit-maximizing quantities are Q_a^* and Q_b^*. The delivered price in town a is P_a^*, and P_b^* in town b. Marginal revenue in town b exceeds marginal revenue in town a by t. The difference between the delivered price in town b and the delivered price in town a is less than t, $P_b^* - P_a^* < t$. Therefore, the net price for units sold in town b is less than the net price for units sold in town a. The firm absorbs freight on sales to more distant consumers. When the net price differs from one location to another, the firm is engaging in geographic price discrimination.

so that it maximizes total profits. Once these quantities are found, the delivered prices can be determined directly from the inverse demand functions. If the delivered price in town b is less than the delivered price in town a plus t, arbitrageurs will suffer losses if they buy in town a at a price of P_a and then sell in town b at a price of P_b. When this is true, the delivered prices maximize the firm's profits.

First, let's find the quantities sold in both markets that maximize the firm's profits.[7] The company determines the number of units to sell in town a where marginal revenue from the last unit sold, $MR(Q_a)$, equals c. If $MR(Q_a)$ was greater than c, the firm can sell more units in town a and increase profits. Therefore, the quantity sold in town a is determined where

$$MR(Q_a) = c \qquad \text{(Determining the Quantity Sold in Town a)} \qquad \textbf{(12-10)}$$

Now consider how the firm selects the quantity to sell in town b. By selling one more unit in town b, it obtains marginal revenue but incurs a transportation cost of t. Net marginal revenue is equal to marginal revenue from the last unit sold in town b less t.

$$NMR(Q_b) = MR(Q_b) - t$$

Figure 12-8 shows the net marginal revenue function in town b, $NMR(Q_b)$, and the marginal revenue function in town a, $MR(Q_a)$. The firm determines the number of units to sell in town b where the $NMR(Q_b) = c$. If $NMR(Q_b)$ was greater than c, the firm's profits can be increased by selling another unit in town b after paying t to ship the last unit.

$$NMR(Q_b) = MR(Q_b) - t = c \qquad \text{(Determining the Quantity Sold in Town b)} \qquad \textbf{(12-11)}$$

The firm determines the quantity Q_b^* to sell in town b where net marginal revenue equals c. Therefore, the profit-maximizing conditions for price discrimination over space are the familiar ones.

$$NMR_b = MR(Q_b) - t = MR(Q_a) = c \qquad \begin{array}{l}\text{(Profit-Maximizing Condition for} \\ \text{Geographical Price Discrimination)}\end{array} \qquad \textbf{(12-12)}$$

Net marginal revenue in town b must equal marginal revenue in town a, and both must equal marginal cost. Equations 12-10 and 12-11 determine the profit-maximizing quantities Q_a^* and Q_b^*.

Condition 12-12 requires Q_a^* and Q_b^* to be determined so that $MR(Q_b^*) - t = MR(Q_a^*)$. Marginal revenue in town b is greater than marginal revenue in town a by exactly t. An example will demonstrate why this condition is true. Suppose the

---

[7] The firm selects Q_a and Q_b to maximize

$$\pi = D(Q_a)Q_a + [D(Q_b) - t]Q_b - c(Q_a + Q_b)$$

The two first-order conditions are

$$\frac{\partial \pi}{\partial Q_a} = Q_a \frac{dP_a}{dQ_a} + D(Q_a) - c = 0 \qquad \frac{\partial \pi}{\partial Q_b} = Q_b \frac{dP_b}{dQ_b} + D(Q_b) - c - t = 0$$

where ∂ denotes partial differentiation. These conditions imply that

$$MR(Q_a) = c \qquad MR(Q_b) - t = c$$

last unit sold in town a increases revenue by \$25. If the last unit sold in town b increases revenue by \$45 but it costs \$10 to transport the unit to town b, then the firm's profits can be increased by transferring the last unit sold in town a to town b. Net revenue is decreased by \$25 by selling one less unit in town a, but increased by \$45 − \$10 = \$35 by selling one more unit in town b. The firm's profits increase by \$10 after paying transportation cost.

Figure 12-8 shows the quantities sold in towns a and b that maximize profits, and the corresponding prices for each town.[8] The linear demand and marginal revenue functions are also shown at each location. The profit-maximizing quantity sold in town a is Q_a^* where marginal revenue in town a equals c, and the delivered price is P_a^*. The quantity sold in town b is Q_b^* where net marginal revenue equals c, and the delivered price is P_b^*. Marginal revenue in town b equals marginal revenue in town a plus t. Q_b^* must be smaller than Q_a^* because marginal revenue in town b exceeds marginal revenue in town a.

In Figure 12-8 the net marginal revenues in the two markets differ by t when the firm produces Q_a^* and Q_b^*. Before we can confidently say that these quantities will be consumed in the two towns, we must be certain that an arbitrageur cannot earn profits by buying a unit at P_a in town a and selling it at the higher price of P_b in town b after paying t. Because the inverse demand functions are the same and consumers buy fewer units in town b than in town a, the delivered price in town b is higher than the delivered price in town a, $P_b > P_a$. When the demand function is linear, the slope of the marginal revenue function is twice as steep as the slope of the demand function.[9] When the quantity decreases from Q_a^* to Q_b^*, marginal revenue increases by t. Because the demand curve is flatter than the marginal revenue function, the difference between P_b and P_a is less than t. Therefore, no one can make profits by buying in the low-priced market, incurring transportation costs, and selling in the high-priced market. Arbitrage does not occur because it is unprofitable.

$$P_b^* < P_a^* + t$$

The firm maximizes profits by discriminating against nearby consumers. The delivered price in town b is not \$$t$ higher than the delivered price in town a. Remember that the net price was defined as the delivered price less transportation

[8] M. L. Greenhut and H. Ohta, "Monopoly Output under Alternative Spatial Pricing Technics," *American Economic Review*, vol. LXII, no. 4, 1972, pp. 705–713. Greenhut and Ohta present the solution to a more general problem where there are demands at three or more locations. They prove that the difference between the delivered prices for adjacent locations will be less than t even if the demand functions are not linear.

[9] Let the demand function be $P = a − bQ$. The slope of the demand function is $dP/dQ = −b$. The total revenue function is $R = PQ = aQ − bQ^2$. Marginal revenue equals the slope of the revenue function:

$$\mathrm{MR} = \frac{dR}{dQ} = a − 2bQ$$

The slope of the marginal revenue function is

$$\frac{d(\mathrm{MR})}{dQ} = −2b$$

The slope of the demand function is $\frac{1}{2}$, the slope of the marginal revenue function.

costs. The net price received by the monopolist is lower for units sold in town b than in town a because the firm absorbs freight. Absorbing freight simply means that the difference between delivered prices does not equal transportation costs. When the firm engages in geographical price discrimination, the net price is lower for units sold in a distant market.

A price-discriminating monopolist charges a lower net price at the distant location.

The price policy of a price-discriminating monopolist differs from that of a competitive firm in several ways. Of course, the monopolist's prices are higher. Another less obvious difference is that competitive prices are set so that the net price is the same at both locations, and this is not true when prices are set by a price-discriminating monopolist. Let's see why net prices are equal across locations if the firm sets price in each market equal to marginal cost. Figure 12-9 shows the delivered price equals c in town a when the firm sells Q_a^c units at a price of P_a^c. The delivered price in town b must equal $c + t$ since this is the marginal cost of

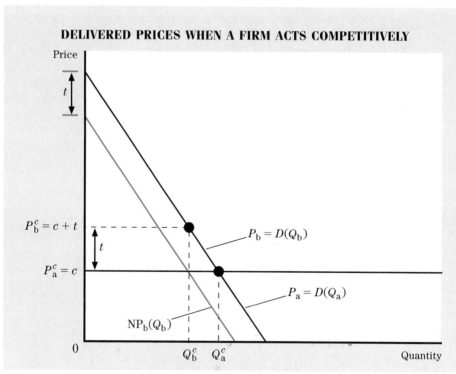

DELIVERED PRICES WHEN A FIRM ACTS COMPETITIVELY

Figure 12-9 A competitive firm sets price at marginal cost. A competitive firm will produce Q_a^c where the delivered price equals marginal cost. The firm will sell Q_b^c units in town b, where the delivered price is $c + t$. The net price in town b is the delivered price less t and equals marginal cost. The net price is the same at both locations.

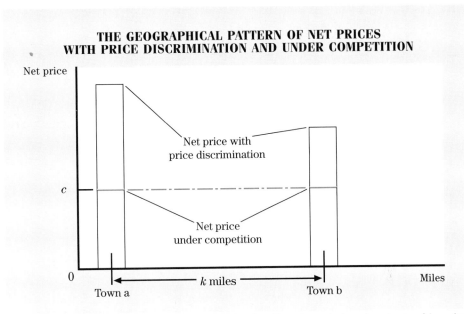

Figure 12-10 The net price is lower in the distant market under geographic price discrimination. A price-discriminating monopolist absorbs freight on sales in town b. Under competition net prices are equal at both locations and equal to marginal cost.

producing and transporting the last unit. The firm sells Q_b^c units in town b, and so $P_b^c = c + t$. The net price in town a also equals c since $t = 0$. The net price in town b equals $P_b^c - t = c$. If the firm behaves like a competitive firm, the net price is the same at both locations and equal to marginal production cost. A competitive firm does not absorb freight.

> The net price will be the same at all locations when the firm behaves like a competitive firm.

Figure 12-10 shows the geographical pattern of net prices for (1) a price-discriminating monopolist and (2) a competitive firm. A price-discriminating monopolist will charge a lower net price in town b than in town a. Under competition the net price is independent of distance and equals marginal cost. If a firm absorbs freight when selling the same product at two locations, it is engaging in geographical price discrimination.

12-5   TWO-PART TARIFFS

A two-part tariff is a pricing technique that firms often use to reduce consumer surplus. It requires consumers to pay a fixed fee that gives them the right to purchase units of a good at a specified price. After paying the fixed fee, consumers can purchase as many units as desired at a specified per unit price. The consumer's total expenditure on the good is the fixed fee plus the per unit price times the quantity purchased.

Two-part tariffs are used at amusement parks, at health and golf clubs, and by firms renting specialized durable goods. In each case consumers pay a fixed fee and then an additional amount that depends on the number of units purchased. For many years Disneyland charged an entrance fee as well as a per ride cost when visitors purchased a book of tickets. Health and golf clubs charge an annual membership fee to join the club and sometimes an additional charge that depends on the use of the facility or the course. If a firm rents a copying machine, the renter pays a monthly rental fee and an additional amount that depends on the number of pages copied.

This section examines how a monopolist sets the fixed fee and the per unit price to maximize the firm's profits and to extract some or all consumer surplus.

Setting the Fixed Fee and Per Unit Price for Identical Consumers

As always, we start with the simplest case where all consumers are alike. Let's see how a firm that rents a copying machine to a user determines the two-part tariff. The supplier of the machine needs to determine the monthly rental fee and the per copy price to charge. Assume that the number of copies made per month can be metered through a counting device on the copying machine.

The demand function for copies by the renter, DD, is shown in Figure 12-11. The price per copy is on the vertical axis, and the number of copies per month is on the horizontal axis. The marginal cost of producing each copy, mc, includes wear and tear on the machine and the cost of service. Suppose the firm charges a per unit price equal to mc. At this price the consumer demands q_1 units, and consumer surplus is $s_1 + s_2 + s_3$. Why consumer surplus is divided into three areas is explained below. If the supplier sets the monthly fee at $s_1 + s_2 + s_3$, or consumer surplus, total profits of the firm become $s_1 + s_2 + s_3$. Since each copy costs mc, the price of the copy, the firm does not earn any profits from the copies made by the user. The firm's profit comes from the monthly fee.

You may wonder whether total profits can be increased still more by charging a higher price per copy. At first glance this seems to be an attractive proposal. The firm would earn profits not only from the fixed fee but from copying as well. What this suggestion neglects is the inverse relationship between the per unit copying price and the monthly fee. The monthly fee must decrease if the copying price increases, or the consumer will not rent the machine.

To see why this is so, let's suppose the per unit copy price P^* is greater than mc. Because of the higher price, the number of copies demanded decreases to q^* units and consumer surplus to s_1. The user will not rent the copying machine unless the monthly fee decreases to s_1. Has the increase in the per unit price from mc to P^* increased profits? Total profits consist of the monthly fee, or s_1, plus the profits from making q^* copies. The per unit price is P^*, and the cost of each copy is mc. The profits from the copies made by the firm are $(P^* - \text{mc})q^*$, or s_2. The total

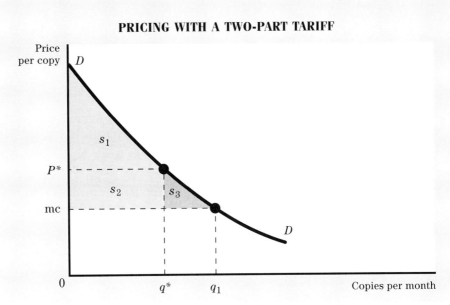

Figure 12-11   Total profits are maximized when the per unit price equals marginal cost and the fixed fee equals consumer surplus. The fixed fee is $s_1 + s_2 + s_3$ and represents the profits of the firm. If the per unit charge is P^*, the firm can charge a fixed fee of only s_1. The profits of the firm are equal to $s_1 + s_2$, and so total profits decrease by s_3.

profits of the firm are now $s_1 + s_2$ and are lower by s_3. If all consumers are identical, maximum profits are obtained by setting the per unit price equal to marginal cost and the monthly fee equal to consumer surplus. This pricing policy eliminates all consumer surplus and is similar to first-degree price discrimination.

> When there is a single consumer or many consumers of the same type, total profits are maximized by setting the per unit price at marginal cost and the monthly fee equal to consumer surplus.

Setting the Fixed Fee and Per Unit Price for Different Types of Consumers

Now let's examine a somewhat more typical case where there are different types of consumers. Suppose the firm rents a copying machine to two types of consumers, light and heavy users. In Figure 12-12*a, dd* is the demand function of a typical light user, and in Figure 12-12*b, DD* is the demand function of a heavy user. The demand function of the light user is also superimposed on Figure 12-12*b*. If the firm can charge different monthly fees for the same copying machine, maximum profits

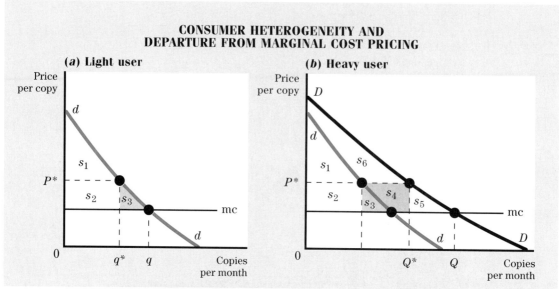

Figure 12-12   When the demand functions of consumers differ, the firm will not set the per unit price equal to marginal cost (mc) when the firm charges a uniform monthly fee. If the per unit price equals marginal cost, the heavy user retains a substantial portion of consumer surplus. When the price is raised to P^*, the increase in profit from the copies made by the heavy user more than offsets the reduced profit from the fewer copies made by the light user. When the price is increased from mc to P^*, the profit from the copies made by the light user decreases by s_3. The profit from the copies made by the heavy user increases by s_4. When s_4 exceeds s_3, the firm sets the per unit price equal to P^*.

occur when the per unit price equals marginal cost and the monthly fee equals the consumer surplus of each user. The light user pays a monthly fee of $s_1 + s_2 + s_3$, and the heavy user pays a monthly fee of $s_1 + s_2 + s_3 + s_4 + s_5 + s_6$.

Assume that the supplier of the copying machine cannot charge a different monthly fee to the two types of users. The firm wants to maximize profits while charging a uniform two-part tariff and therefore faces a dilemma. If the monthly fee is set too high, the small user will drop out of the market. On the other hand, a low monthly fee will allow the heavy user to retain a substantial portion of consumer surplus. By experimenting with the pricing of the monthly fee, the supplier will learn that $s_1 + s_2 + s_3$ is the maximum monthly fee the light user will pay.[10] Any higher monthly fee will cause this user to discontinue renting. Figure 12-12b shows that the heavy user retains $s_4 + s_5 + s_6$ as consumer surplus because each user pays a monthly fee of only $s_1 + s_2 + s_3$. The firm would like to obtain

[10] For a pioneering and extended discussion of two-part tariffs, see Walter Oi, "A Disneyland Dilemma: Two-Part Tariffs for a Mickey-Mouse Monopoly," *Quarterly Journal of Economics*, vol. LXXXV, February 1971, pp. 77–96.

more of the consumer surplus of the heavy user even if the small consumer contributes less consumer surplus.

One way to do this is to raise the per unit price. Suppose the company raises the per unit price from mc to P^*. Will total profits increase? The light user will rent the machine only if the monthly fee falls to s_1. Therefore, the firm reduces the monthly fee paid by both users to s_1. The number of copies made by the light user is q^*, and the profit from these copies is s_2. The total profit from the light user is equal to $s_1 + s_2$. When the per unit price is raised from marginal cost to P^*, the profit on sales to the light user declines by s_3.

However, the profit earned on sales to the heavy user increases. The monthly fee paid by the heavy user also equals s_1 in Figure 12-12b. This user makes Q^* copies, and the profit from these copies is $s_2 + s_3 + s_4$. Total profit from the copies made by the heavy user is $s_1 + s_2 + s_3 + s_4$, and total profit from renting to the heavy user increases by s_4 when the copy price increases to P^*. Total firm profits increase if s_4 exceeds s_3. In Figure 12-12b, s_4 is larger than s_3, and so profit increases.

If the two demand functions are far apart, the firm will ignore the light user, setting the monthly fee equal to the consumer surplus of the heavy user and the price of each copy equal to marginal cost. When the demand functions are close together, the per unit price will depart from marginal cost. When there are many different groups of customers with different demand functions, the firm raises the per unit price above marginal cost.

> When consumers differ, a firm that charges a uniform fixed fee to two different buyers will not set the per unit price at marginal cost.

Using Two-Part Tariffs to Price Consumer Capital Goods

Often a consumer buys a capital good from a firm and then purchases another good to obtain the services from the capital good. For example, a firm may sell a camcorder and a special tape. Another example is a manufacturer that sells a razor and razor blades. The model of a two-part tariff can be used to determine the price of the consumer capital good as well as the price of the other product.

Assume that a firm develops a new camcorder that takes excellent pictures at a lower cost than any camcorder on the market. This camcorder requires a special tape that your firm alone produces at a marginal cost of mc per roll. The consumer receives utility directly from the home videos he or she shoots but not from the camcorder.

There are two sources of demand, light and heavy camcorder users. (Figure 12-13 shows the two demand curves for tapes.) Your firm must determine what price to charge for the tape and what price to charge for the camcorder. In this discussion we assume that it is more profitable to sell to both consumers than just to the heavy user. Because the demands of the two consumers are different, the firm sets the price per tape above marginal cost, mc. In Figure 12-13 P^* is the price of a tape that maximizes the total profits of the company. Consumer surplus for

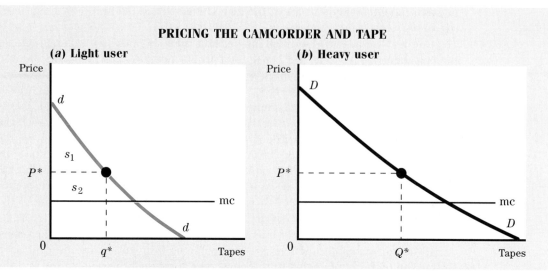

Figure 12-13   The firm must determine a separate price for the camcorder and for tapes. If the profit-maximizing price of a tape is P^*, the firm will charge a price of s_1 for the camcorder. As long as it is profitable to sell to both types of consumers, the firm cannot set the price of the camcorder above s_1.

consumer 1 (the light user) is s_1. What is the maximum amount the firm can charge for the camcorder? Clearly, it can charge at most s_1 and consumer 1 will still purchase the camcorder. If the fixed fee for the camcorder exceeds s_1 when the price of a tape is P^*, consumer 1 will not purchase the camcorder or any tapes.

Assuming the firm must charge both consumers the same price for the camcorder, the price of the camcorder is s_1. If the marginal cost of producing the camcorder is C, the profits of the firm from the sale of the camcorder and tapes to consumer 1 are

$$\pi_1 = (s_1 - C) + (P^* - mc)q_1 \qquad \text{(Profits from Sales to Consumer 1)} \quad \textbf{(12-13)}$$

where P^* is the price of a tape, mc is the marginal cost of producing tapes, and q_1 is the number of tapes purchased. The profits from the sale of the camcorder and tapes to consumer 2 (the heavy user) are

$$\pi_2 = (s_1 - C) + (P^* - mc)q_2 \qquad \text{(Profits from Sales to Consumer 2)} \quad \textbf{(12-14)}$$

You can see from this analysis that the marginal cost of producing tapes affects the price of the camcorder. If the marginal cost of producing a tape falls, it will not only lower the price of a tape but will also increase the price of the camcorder. A decrease in the marginal cost of producing a tape increases the profits of the firm. It is less clear how the firm will fare if competitors can produce the tapes at a lower marginal cost. Exercise 9 at the end of this chapter raises the interesting question of whether the firm's profits increase or decrease when competitive producers of tapes introduce a lower-priced substitute for the company's tapes.

APPLICATION 12-3

Why Did IBM and Xerox Lease Rather Than Sell Their Machines?

In several instances firms with monopoly power are willing to rent a machine to a customer but refuse to sell the machine. Two well-known examples are IBM and Xerox. In the 1930s IBM manufactured tabulating equipment—punch card machines and sorters—but refused to sell it to customers. Similarly, in the 1960s Xerox refused to sell copying machines. Both companies were willing to rent tabulating or copying machines, and each charged a monthly fee and a per unit price based on usage of the equipment.

IBM had a near-monopoly on tabulating machines but did not have a monopoly on the perforated punch cards used with the sorting machines. Still, it sold approximately 81 percent of the cards used since it required each lessee to purchase tabulating cards only from IBM. It charged the same monthly lease to all users and set the per card price above marginal cost for renters who used more than a minimum number of cards per month. Charging a premium price for punch cards was a device whereby IBM reduced the consumer surplus of large users.

The pricing policy of Xerox in the early 1960s was similar. It leased its copying machines at $25 per month, charged the user 3.5 cents per copy, and required a minimum of 2,000 copies per month.[11] A renter who made 2,000 copies per month paid $25 + $70 per month, or $1,140 per year, or $5,700 over the 5-year lifetime of the machine. On the other hand, a renter who made 20,000 copies a month paid $43,500 over the 5-year lifetime of the machine. The same machine produced different levels of profit depending on who rented it. Table 12-3 shows the revenue Xerox received from two different customers.

These two examples raise the question of why these companies preferred to rent and would not sell the machines. Why was leasing more advantageous than selling? Chapter 9 explained why a monopolist prefers leasing rather than selling in order to dispel the fears of consumers that it will act opportunistically. This is a possible explanation for the leasing preference of these companies.

Another explanation is that the firm can better control arbitrage by leasing. If Xerox sold the machines and arbitrage prevented it from selling them at different prices to different users, total profits would be lower. It would either sell a machine at $43,500 to only the large user (ignoring any cost of maintenance) or to both users but at a drastically lower price of $5,700 per machine. By leasing, it collected a combined total of $49,200 from both users.

---

[11] E. A. Blackstone, "Restrictive Practices in the Marketing of Electrofax Copying Machines and Supplies: The SCM Corporation Case," *Journal of Industrial Economics*, vol. 23, 1975, pp. 189–202.

Table 12-3   REVENUE FROM LEASING

COPIES PER MONTH	MONTHLY FEE ($)	MONTHLY REVENUE FROM COPYING ($)	TOTAL REVENUE PER YEAR ($)	TOTAL REVENUE OVER FIVE YEARS ($)
2,000	25	70	1,140	5,700
20,000	25	700	8,700	43,500

Moreover, there is another more subtle point here. Xerox did not know which customers were intensive users. Therefore, it did not know who was willing to pay a higher price for the machine. By leasing, the company relied on the actual use patterns of its clients to identify low- and high-intensity users and collected more from the intensive users. If more-intensive machine users had greater consumer surplus, Xerox could collect some of it by setting the copy price above marginal cost. So, leasing dominates selling for two reasons: First, it avoids the arbitrage problem on the demand side of the market. Second, it allows the firm to discover who is an intensive user and to collect more of the consumer surplus from these users.

In summary, leasing is a more profitable strategy when arbitrage in the sale market is costly to prevent and when the intensity of use differs across consumers and is unknown. Even if a firm can prevent arbitrage, it prefers leasing because leasing identifies the intensity of demand of users.

SUMMARY

- A firm charges different prices for the same good to reduce consumer surplus and increase its revenues and profits.
- First- second-, and third-degree price discrimination are different methods of decreasing consumer surplus and raising the profits of a firm.
- Under third-degree price discrimination maximum profits of a firm occur when marginal revenue is the same in all markets and marginal revenue equals marginal cost.
- A firm charges a lower price in the market with a more elastic demand function.
- Third-degree price discrimination requires (1) a price maker, (2) a separation of markets, and (3) different price elasticities between markets.
- Under geographic price discrimination the net price of a monopolist is lower for units sold in the distant market than in the nearby market. The firm absorbs freight for units sold in the distant market, and so the net price decreases with distance. In a competitive market the net price is the same in all markets.

■   Under a two-part tariff a consumer pays a fixed fee and a variable amount that depends on the number of units consumed. When all consumers are alike, the firm sets the fixed fee equal to consumer surplus and the per unit price equal to marginal cost. If the demand functions of consumers differ, the per unit price that maximizes profits will not equal marginal cost.

■   Leasing is preferable to selling when arbitrage cannot be prevented or where the intensity of consumer demands is unknown.

KEY TERMS

Consumer surplus and revenue
  enhancement
Grouping consumers
Setting prices based on elasticity of
  demand
Geographic price discrimination
Two-part tariff
Leasing versus selling

Three types of price discrimination
Equating marginal revenue across
  markets
Preventing arbitrage
Distance and net price
Setting the per unit price and the
  fixed fee

REVIEW QUESTIONS

1. Define first-degree price discrimination. Describe two price policies that will achieve the goal of first-degree price discrimination.
2. List the conditions under which a firm will charge different prices to different groups of customers, that is, engage in third-degree price discrimination. How can a firm divide customers into groups? Give three illustrations.
3. Price discrimination by physicians occurs because higher-income patients have inelastic demands and arbitrage on the demand side is costly. Are these two conditions sufficient when there are many suppliers in the market?
4. A monopolist that practices perfect price discrimination captures all the consumer surplus in the form of higher profits. Explain why you agree or disagree with this statement.
5. Why does third-degree price discrimination lower consumer surplus?
6. How does second-degree price discrimination differ from third-degree price discrimination?
7. If arbitrageurs were punished by the death penalty, a spatial monopolist would change the prices it charges over space. Explain why you agree or disagree with this statement.
8. Could a monopolist who does not find it profitable to expand abroad before demand decreases in the domestic market find it profitable to expand abroad after domestic demand decreases?
9. If the price elasticity is -2 in market A and -6 in market B, the price in market B is one-third the price in market A. Explain why you agree or disagree with this statement.

EXERCISES

1. The theory of third-degree price discrimination predicts that a monopolist will charge a lower price in the market where demand is price-elastic and a higher price in the market where demand is price-inelastic. Explain what is wrong with this statement.

2. The following questions refer to the decision to expand into the European market.

   a. Show the optimal quantities and prices in the domestic and European markets if marginal cost of production is declining. Will the price in the domestic market stay the same if the firm enters the European market?

   b. Assume the price elasticity of demand in the domestic market is -10 instead of -5 and marginal cost is increasing. Explain why it would or would not be profitable to expand into the European market.

3. A firm is the sole producer of a good in a country where imports of the good are banned. When the firm exports the product, it is a price taker in the international market and can sell each unit at a world price of P_w. Assume that marginal cost of production increases with output and ignore transportation costs.

   a. What determines whether the firm exports some of its output?

   b. Assume that the firm sells in both the domestic and the international markets. What is the effect of a decline in the world price on the domestic price, on the units sold in the domestic market, and on the total units sold?

   c. If the marginal cost function shifts downward, reflecting a decline in the marginal cost of production, what is the effect on the domestic price, total units sold in the domestic market, and total number of units sold?

4. A firm produces a product and sells it to two types of customers, C_1 and C_2. Normally, it offers a 25 percent discount to group C_2. Periodically, the company upgrades the quality of the product, and after a lag of a year, competitors copy the improvements. In those years when the firm has an advantage over competitors, the demand for the product by both groups increases. The company raises the price by 10 percent and eliminates the 25 percent discount to group C_2. Frequently, the firm has difficulty meeting orders, and does not feel that it should offer a discount when it can sell all that it can produce at a higher price. The price policy of the firm is summarized in the accompanying table.

	PRICE TO GROUP C_1	PRICE TO GROUP C_2
Year when no product upgrade is offered	P_1	$0.75P_1$
Year when product upgrade is introduced	$1.1P_1$	$1.1P_1$

   Assuming the firm is a price-making firm, critically evaluate this pricing policy. Is it wise not to offer a price discount in those years when demand increases?

5. The willingness to pay of a business traveler and a tourist for a return on Friday, Saturday, or Sunday are shown in the next table. What price policy should the airline adopt to maximize profits?

	FRIDAY RETURN ($)	SATURDAY RETURN ($)	SUNDAY RETURN ($)
Business	1,200	1,000	850
Tourist	600	600	350

6. A book publisher thinks it would be a good idea to publish all 20 chapters of a book in a conventional textbook format suitable for a semester course in microeconomics. In addition it would like to offer a version that includes only the first 10 chapters for use in quarter courses and plans to publish chapters 11 through 14 separately for use in specialized courses in business schools. The publisher's estimates of the size of the market for each version, the willingness to pay for each market segment, and marginal cost of production for each version are shown in the accompanying table.

TYPE OF MARKET	SIZE OF MARKET (THOUSANDS)	VERSION 1 (MARGINAL COST = $10)	VERSION 2 (MARGINAL COST = $5)	VERSION 3 (MARGINAL COST = $2)
Semester course	30	60	45	2
Quarter course	20	50	30	5
Specialized courses	5	10	5	30

    a. Explain what price the publisher should charge for version 1, version 2, and version 3 when only one version is sold.

    b. If the publisher decides to produce multiple versions of the book, which versions should be introduced and what prices should be charged? Explain how the publisher should determine the prices.

7. Your plant is located in town a. You are the sole seller of a product in towns a and b. The demand function is the same in both towns: $P_a = D(Q_a)$ and $P_b = D(Q_b)$. The cost of shipping the product to town b is t per unit. No transportation costs are incurred for units sold in town a. Marginal cost of production is c and is constant and independent of output.

    a. Explain how you will determine the price in towns a and b. Will the quantity sold in town a be larger or smaller than that sold in town b?

    b. Define what is meant by the net price. How will the net price vary with distance from your plant?

8. A monopolist supplies rides at an amusement park. The demand function for rides of a typical consumer is shown in the figure on the next page. The per unit cost of supplying the rides has two components: c, the cost of supplying the equipment, and d, the cost of printing and collecting the tickets at each ride. Each per unit cost is independent of the number of rides offered at the park. The capital letters in the figure represent areas. The monopolist is considering two pricing policies:

    ■ *Policy 1.* An entrance fee and a per unit charge for each ride.

    ■ *Policy 2.* Just an entrance fee. (The advantage of this policy is that the firm can save on printing and collecting tickets.)

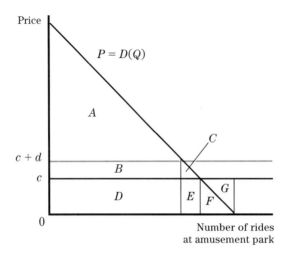

a. On the graph, show the entrance fee, per unit charge, total number of rides supplied, and total profits under each policy.

b. Under what conditions will the profits under policy 2 exceed the profits under policy 1?

c. What is the disadvantage of policy 2? Can you think of another pricing policy that allows the firm to earn higher profits?

9. This question extends the analysis of pricing consumer capital discussed in Section 12-5. You have developed a new camcorder that takes excellent pictures at a lower cost than any camcorder on the market and requires the use of a special tape that you alone produce at a marginal cost of c per tape. Your market research department predicts that the demand for tapes will come from small- and large-demand buyers. The demand curves for tapes of each type of customer are shown in the figure below. Assume that you have priced the tape and camcorder to maximize total profits of the firm. Now suppose that competitors develop a lower-cost substitute for your tapes and sell the substitute at f per tape that is less than c per tape.

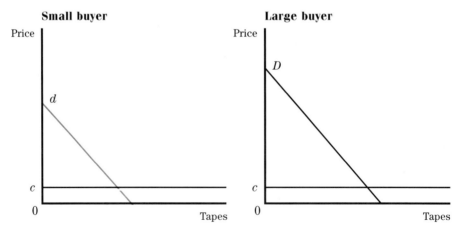

a. How will the availability of the competitive supply of tapes affect the price of the camcorder? Explain.

b. With the aid of graphs show how the supply of lower-cost tape affects the profits obtained from the small buyer and the profits gained from sales of the camcorder and tapes to the large buyer. Will total profits decrease?

10. In the accompanying figure, DD is the daily demand function of a customer for a good. A monopolist charges P_1 for each unit of the good and sells q_1 units; d denotes marginal cost, and MR represents marginal revenue. The letters A, B, and C denote areas. A consumer can store the product for a day, but the product spoils from then on. A market research firm reviews the pricing policy and recommends that the firm charge an entrance fee for each day if the consumer purchases the product, along with a per unit charge. It recommends a daily entrance fee equal to $A + B + C$ and a per unit fee of d. After this pricing policy is introduced, the purchases of the consumer follow a 2-day cycle. The consumer purchases q_2 units on the first day and nothing on the second day.

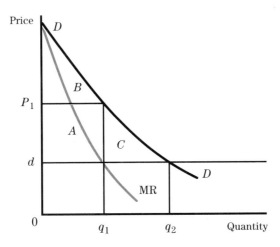

a. Will the profits with the new pricing policy be greater than the profits with the old policy over a 2-day period?

b. Suppose your answer to part a is that the profits with the old pricing policy are higher over a 2-day period. Would you then eliminate the two-part tariff and simply charge P_1 in each period? Can you suggest a different two-part pricing policy that will yield greater profits?

▨ CHAPTER 12 APPENDIX

Can Consumer Surplus Be Higher with a Two-Part Tariff?

This appendix assumes that firms can enter an industry freely. The intent is to show how a two-part tariff can raise consumer surplus. Until now, we have assumed the firm is a price maker and earns monopoly profits. It would be a mistake to conclude that the presence of two-part pricing always means consumer surplus is lower and profits are higher. For example, health clubs use two-part tariffs. They require a monthly or yearly membership fee, and some charge a fee for each workout. Many health clubs are located in major metropolitan areas. Entry into the market appears relatively easy, and many clubs enter and leave the market each year. These facts are difficult to reconcile with the presence of long-run profits.

What purpose can two-part pricing serve in the health club market? Why don't health clubs charge a uniform price each time a member uses the facilities? One possible explanation is that a two-part pricing policy allows them to adopt marginal cost pricing and *raise* consumer surplus—something they cannot achieve by just charging a uniform price per workout.

This situation can be modeled as follows. Let's assume that each health club incurs a fixed cost of L dollars per period. For example, L might be the overhead costs. Marginal cost of supplying workouts is mc and is constant. Because of the fixed cost L, there are economies of scale for each health club. The marginal cost of providing another workout is less than the average cost of supplying the workout.

Suppose the health club has N identical members, each with a demand function of dd in Figure 12-14. Price per workout is on the vertical axis, and number of workouts per month is on the horizontal axis. Because all customers are alike, each one's share of the overhead cost is L/N. In Figure 12-14 the marginal cost to the health club of supplying each workout is mc. This covers the cost of towels, labor, and so on. Adding the overhead cost per member per workout to the marginal cost of a workout yields the average cost per workout for this member (aa in Figure 12-14). Because total overhead cost per member is a fixed amount, the average cost function declines as the number of workouts per month by the member increases.

As noted above, entry into the health club industry is relatively easy. This implies that no firm in the industry can earn profits in the long run. It is this threat of entry by other firms that prevents each club from raising the price and earning profits.

What pricing policies are consistent with this zero profit constraint? One possibility would have the health club charge P^* per workout. If the price per workout is P^*, the consumer will demand w^* workouts per month, and so P^* is the average cost of providing w^* workouts per month. The health club has adopted average not marginal cost pricing and does not earn any profits. Total overhead cost per consumer is equal to $(P^* - \text{mc})w^*$, or areas 1 and 2 in Figure 12-14.

Suppose you purchase a health club and are trying to decide what price policy to introduce. Should you copy the policy of other clubs and set the price of a workout at P^*? Is there another pricing policy that would make consumers better off and give your health club a temporary competitive advantage until other clubs begin to copy your strategy? Remember, your pricing policy must satisfy the long-run zero profit constraint. If you set

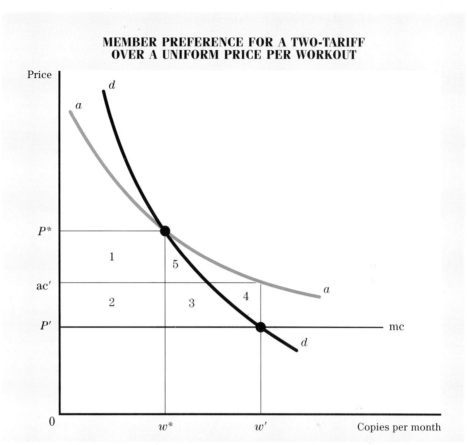

MEMBER PREFERENCE FOR A TWO-TARIFF OVER A UNIFORM PRICE PER WORKOUT

Figure 12-14   If the health club charges a uniform price, it will charge P^* for each workout. A member uses the club w^* times per month. Because P^* is average cost per workout, the club earns a competitive rate of return. The sum of areas 1 and 2 equals the total overhead cost per member. If the health club sets the price of a workout at marginal cost and charges a membership fee equal to the sum of areas 2, 3, and 4, it will not earn profits. The membership fee covers the total overhead cost per member. The member works out w' times a month. However, consumer surplus of the member is larger under the two-part tariff than under a uniform price policy.

your price P' at marginal cost, each consumer will increase quantity demanded from w^* to w' workouts. However, the average cost of providing w' workouts is ac′, which is greater than P'. The difference between ac′ and mc is the members' share of overhead cost per workout. Total overhead cost per member is equal to (ac′ − mc)w', or the sum of areas 2, 3, and 4. To recover your overhead costs, you require each member to pay a monthly membership fee equal to the sum of areas 2, 3, and 4. In essence, your pricing policy is a two-part tariff. The consumer pays a monthly membership fee equal to the sum of areas 2, 3, and 4 and pays a per workout charge of P' that is equal to marginal cost. Because of competition, the monthly fee covers only overhead cost and P' equals marginal cost.

If you adopt this two-part tariff, will your health club have a competitive advantage over a club that simply charges P^* per workout? Because *total* overhead cost per member is L/N and is the same whether the club charges a uniform price of P^* or a two-part tariff, area 1 plus area 2 must equal the sum of areas 2, 3, and 4. Suppose you set the price of a workout at P'. For the moment, assume that a member uses the facilities just w^* times per month. Then, consumer surplus will be exactly the same as if she paid P^* per workout and used the facilities w^* times per month. Of course, she will demand w' workouts per month if the price per workout is w'.

How does consumer surplus change when the number of workouts increases from w^* to w'? The club member is willing to pay just slightly less than P^* for one more workout beyond w^*. Yet the marginal cost of another workout is only mc. Therefore, consumer surplus will increase. As long as willingness to pay exceeds marginal cost, consumer surplus increases when the number of workouts is greater than w^*. The increase in consumer surplus is equal to the sum of areas 3 and 5. Because consumer surplus is higher, consumers prefer to join a club with a membership fee and a per unit charge of P' rather than one that just charges P^* for a workout. In this instance a two-part tariff is used and yet the profits are zero and consumer surplus is higher. In the long run, competition among health clubs will force other clubs to adopt a two-part tariff. Those that do not will lose customers and be forced to exit from the industry.

In this example a two-part tariff creates a competitive result where price is equal to marginal cost. The number of workouts, w', is determined where the demand function intersects the marginal cost function. When the market demand is small relative to the extent of economies of scale, so average cost exceeds marginal cost, consumer surplus is higher under a two-part tariff than under a uniform price for each workout. The club does not earn profits because of the ease of entry into the industry. We conclude that the use of a two-part tariff does not imply that consumer surplus would be higher if firms charged a uniform per unit price, nor does its use imply that a firm earns long-run profits.

C H A P T E R 13

THE FREE RIDER PROBLEM AND PRICING

A free rider problem can arise whenever valuable information or goods that one agent creates can be appropriated by other agents without compensating the owner of the information or goods. The free rider problem was first encountered in Chapter 11 when we considered a situation where other shareholders benefit from the efforts of one or several shareholders to improve management performance. However, free rider problems can appear in numerous market situations. This chapter examines how private markets cope with free rider problems.

We present a portfolio of free rider problems that may arise in different market situations and then study two free rider problems that occur in retailing industries. We show how firms develop policies to cope with these problems and in this way prevent them from surfacing. Firm behavior that would otherwise appear puzzling and inexplicable becomes comprehensible as rational adaptations to free rider problems.

13-1 FREE RIDER PROBLEMS IN DIFFERENT MARKETS

Free rider problems crop up in different markets. This section describes four such problems, demonstrating the wide range and scope of this issue.

Free rider problems can appear in labor markets. Companies often establish research and development (R&D) teams to work secretly on new projects. To benefit from an R&D problem, the sponsoring firm must keep research results under wraps so that its competitors cannot appropriate this information. As the research project evolves, the members of the project team accumulate valuable information. For example, they know which approaches were unsuccessful and which succeeded. A rival firm working on a similar research project, or any competitor, may go to extraordinary lengths to acquire this knowledge. One way that competitors do this is by hiring the personnel on the research team. A free rider problem emerges because one firm has invested considerable resources to create valuable information that other firms can acquire typically at a nominal cost.

How can firms prevent employees from leaving with trade secrets? Often they attempt to solve the problem by using contracts that require them to remain with the company for a given number of years and not to sell or transmit information to competitors. However, the legal status of these contracts remains unclear. Another way that firms can protect themselves is to parcel out parts of a project to different teams so that only the manager and a few other employees are fully aware of all the results. However, there are limits to these restrictions since the success of a project depends on the interchange of information and ideas. Still another way that firms protect themselves is by assigning experienced members of the firm to the project. These individuals have been with the company for many years and are more valuable to their current employer than they would be to another firm. However, this may not be a successful deterrent to members of a large, successful research team who may leave the firm and take trade secrets with them.

APPLICATION 13-1

IBM Sues a Former Employee

In 1991 Seagate Technology, Inc., hired away Peter Bonyhard, one of IBM's star engineers.[1] Bonyhard's speciality at IBM was developing disk-drive heads, and Seagate promptly told him to develop the next generation of disk-drive heads.

IBM sued Seagate to prevent its employee from skipping from one company to another with trade secrets and in December 1991 won an injunction preventing Bonyhard from working on the Seagate project. IBM said the case was unique because Bonyhard took a similar job with a competitor. It claimed that Bonyhard could not help revealing its secrets in his new job and wanted him to avoid working on heads. Seagate's countersuit charged that IBM expected its top technical people "to remain in lifetime servitude" to the company. Bonyhard argued that a knowledge of heads was his speciality and that other work would not be suitable for him. In April 1992 an appeals court lifted the injunction, and Bonyhard is currently working on the Seagate project. The suit has not been resolved as of this writing.

The second illustration comes from the retailing industry. In 1992 Barneys New York, an up-scale specialty store, entered the Chicago market by opening a store in a fashionable shopping area.[2] Barneys carries expensive domestic and international designer clothing for men and women, with prices for men's suits starting at about $595 and reaching the four-digit level.

As Barneys was opening its new store, Urban American Club, a less well-known firm, set up shop just around the corner from Barneys New York. Moving in close to Barneys was not an accident. Jerry Kamhi, owner of the store, wanted to open a retail shop in a high-density area for consumers looking for international fashions.[3] Urban American Club's prices are below Barneys, ranging from $395 to $595 for men's suits. Urban American appears to be free-riding on Barneys' reputation for attracting consumers who prefer international fashions. In such situations it is difficult for firms like Barneys to prevent free riding unless they locate in a mall and negotiate with the mall owner to prevent competitors from opening stores nearby.

Free rider problems turn up when firms create intellectual property. Trademarks or brand names like Sanka reduce the cost of search for consumers, who associate some property of the product with the name.[4] Sanka, for example, denotes decaffeinated coffee made by General Foods. Manufacturers have an incen-

---

[1] Based on Michael W. Miller, "IBM Sues to Silence Former Employee," *Wall Street Journal*, July 15, 1992.

[2] Karen E. Klages, "The Brothers Pressman," *Chicago Tribune*, Section 7, August 19, 1992.

[3] T. J. Howard, "Trickle-down Retailing," *Chicago Tribune*, Section 7, August 19, 1992.

[4] This discussion is based on William M. Landes and Richard A. Posner, "Trademark Law: An Economic Perspective," *Journal of Law and Economics*, vol. XXX, October 1987, pp. 265–310.

tive to develop trademarks when they can produce a consistent quality over time. Then, consumers receive one or several desirable benefits with each use of the product. A manufacturer that maintains a trademark through advertising has an incentive to produce a product of consistent quality, and the producer of a consistent-quality product has an incentive to advertise the name.

The cost of creating a valuable trademark is high. A company spends considerable sums of money on quality control, quality of service, and advertising. On the other hand, the cost of duplicating a trademark—a label or a name—is small. Without legal restrictions, once a firm has developed a valuable trademark, competitive firms could easily copy it and earn profits temporarily. The competitors could produce the good and the label at a lower cost than the original producers, and unless the owner of the trademark could prevent this, there would be little incentive to develop a trademark or a brand name. In such cases, however, trademarks receive protection from the courts. The law prohibits them from being copied, although fraudulent use of trademarks remains a problem for many firms, especially in countries that do not enforce the copyright laws of other countries.

A final example comes from the software industry. The unauthorized copying of software is a serious problem for many companies. The cost of copying software is relatively low, and each program sold can be copied many times. Software companies have become increasingly ingenious in overcoming the free rider problems: Large firms pay software companies considerable sums of money for site licenses giving them the right to use a program on multiple computers throughout the company to avoid suits involving unauthorized copying. Some software companies deliberately redesign software programs to reduce unauthorized copying. In an interesting application of copy protection one company sells a game whose level of difficulty increases with each copy made. The game becomes virtually impossible to play if the owner makes several copies. Another technique that raises the cost of copying requires the user to type a word picked at random from a page in the user manual. Finally, sophisticated programs require the user to consult a manual. Someone who has the program but lacks the manual is at a considerable disadvantage in learning and working with the program. Each of these techniques reduces copying but increases the cost to the user by making the game or program more cumbersome to use.

While these are only four possible cases, they demonstrate the diversity of situations where free rider problems appear. Although these four illustrations come from different industries, they have two points in common. First, in each instance a firm creates valuable *general* information. The information is valuable not only to its creator but to other firms as well. It is not firm-specific. The more basic the research, the more general the information created. The second point is that other firms can appropriate the information without fully compensating its creator. Therefore, the owner cannot completely control the use of the information.

> Free rider problems occur when information is general and the creator of the information cannot establish property rights to it.

In these illustrations the firm can use an incentive to prevent the free rider problem from emerging such as compensating the worker at the end of the project, or the firm can rely on the courts to establish its property rights to a brand name or to certain information (as in the case of a trademark), or the firm can redesign the product to eliminate or reduce the severity of the free rider problem. This chapter concentrates on the first case, where firms develop policies that prevent the free rider problem from arising.

This analysis of the free rider problem focuses on the retailing industry because it is a fertile source of free rider problems and because firms in the industry have developed pricing policies to prevent free rider problems from occurring.

13-2 THE INFLUENCE OF MANUFACTURERS ON THE RETAIL PRICE

We begin our investigation of the free rider problem somewhat indirectly by examining three cases where manufacturers in different industries limit the quantities that retailers can sell and prevent retail price competition.

Case 1: GM's Restriction on Dealer Sales

General Motors and other automobile manufacturers require their dealers to carry an adequate inventory, to employ a sales and service staff appropriate for the size of the market, and to provide aftersale service. However, a General Motors dealer on the outskirts of a large metropolitan area became dissatisfied with the traditional method of retailing autos and came up with an idea to reduce costs.[5] He cut the sales staff and inventories to the bone and advertised a price of "$49 over invoice." The dealer was willing to take orders from customers who knew what kind of car and what options they wanted, and he promised delivery to each customer after the customary time required to obtain delivery. His advertising campaign was a success, and orders increased when consumers jumped at the opportunity to purchase GM autos at lower prices.

You might think that GM's management would eagerly embrace a more efficient way of operating a dealership since a lower retail price would not only increase the dealer's volume but GM's volume as well. But GM's reaction was decidedly cool, and the new strategy failed when the dealer could no longer obtain deliveries. The dealer claimed that GM forced him out of business when it conspired to slow delivery of orders to him because it disapproved of his new advertising and pricing policies.

What explains GM's hostility toward a policy that would lower the retail price of autos and increase the number sold?

---

[5] D. Levin, "FTC Probes Charges GM Forced Dealer Out of Business over Discount Pricing," *Wall Street Journal*, February 15, 1985.

Case 2: IBM and Apple Restrictions on Dealers

IBM and Apple Computer police and, if necessary, terminate dealers who regularly sell out of their marketing areas to gray marketers. Gray marketers are retail outlets that systematically sell outside their customary local market and include mail-order suppliers, some local computer stores, and other electronics stores.[6] Authorized IBM and Apple dealers that sell primarily in their own local markets have complained to their respective manufacturers that discounters drive prices down and take customers away. These dealers claim that customers who buy in the gray market are "tire kickers," individuals who frequent authorized IBM or Apple retail outlets but buy elsewhere.

Why do IBM and Apple discourage competition among dealers by preventing authorized retailers from selling outside their immediate local markets?

Case 3: Discounting Prince Tennis Rackets

Racket Doctor, a retail outlet selling Prince tennis rackets in Los Angeles, lowered the price of certain Prince rackets to just a few dollars below the lower bound of retail prices suggested by Prince Manufacturing, Inc.[7] Prince Manufacturing had sent each of its dealers a memorandum with suggested price ranges for six of its top lines. For example, the suggested range for Thunderstick, its best racket, was between $229.95 and $250. The memo included a warning that dealers who set prices below the guidelines would no longer receive Prince rackets. After other retailers complained, Prince Manufacturing terminated Racket Doctor. Why did the company prevent Racket Doctor from selling its tennis rackets at lower prices?

In each case the manufacturer's policy attenuates retail price competition and encourages retailers to raise rather than lower prices. This behavior may strike you as odd since it seems logical for a manufacturer to encourage dealers to sell as many units as they can. Yet, in each instance, the manufacturer limits competition by preventing retailers from lowering prices. Why do these companies discourage competition among their dealers?

13-3   BENEFITING FROM RETAIL PRICE COMPETITION

What makes these cases puzzling is that the manufacturer's behavior appears to be inconsistent with profit maximization. Why does a manufacturer maximize profits with a higher, not a lower, retail price? To answer this question we develop a model where a monopoly manufacturer charges a wholesale price when selling a product to many competitive retailers. In the model the manufacturer maximizes

---

[6] "Blue vs. Gray: IBM Tries to Stop the Discounters," Time Inc., 1985, as seen in *Fortune*, May 27, 1985, p. 79.
[7] Paul Barrett, "Anti-Discount Policies of Manufacturers Are Penalizing Certain Cut-Price Stores," *Wall Street Journal*, February 27, 1991.

profits by deciding the quantity produced, the wholesale price and, indirectly, the number of retailers that sell the product.

Initially, assume that the retailer's primary role is to supply retail inventory. He or she provides inventory of an established product to consumers who are familiar with the product. For example, virtually all supermarkets and drugstores carry Crest toothpaste. Most consumers are familiar with the Crest name and know about the benefits of brushing with it.

Allowing Free Entry of Retailers

Let's begin the analysis by assuming a manufacturer has Q^* units to sell. Given the retail demand function for the product, Q^* units sell at the market-clearing retail price of R^*. Since the cost of producing Q^* units is sunk, the manufacturer maximizes its total revenue by charging W^*, the highest possible wholesale price that allows it to sell Q^* units. Since the retail price is R^*, the manufacturer sets the wholesale price to minimize the difference between retail and wholesale prices while still selling Q^* units. The manufacturer can accomplish this by permitting the free entry of retailers so that each one's long-run average cost of retailing is minimized. Let's see why a policy of allowing free entry of retailers maximizes the manufacturer's revenue from selling Q^* units.

Figure 13-1 shows a retailer's long-run average cost function, $\text{AC}_L(q)$, and long-run marginal cost function, $\text{MC}_L(q)$. The long-run average cost function has two components, the wholesale price, W^*, and the long-run average operating cost $\text{AOC}_L(q)$. The retailer pays W^* for each unit shipped by the manufacturer to the retailer. It also incurs operating costs that include labor, depreciation of the retail plant, and supplies, but excludes the wholesale price of the product. The long-run average cost function of the firm, $\text{AC}_L(q)$, is U-shaped in Figure 13-1. It is equal to the long-run average operating cost function of the retail firm, $\text{AOC}_L(q)$, plus the wholesale price, W^*. The retailer achieves economies of scale as volume increases, but then diseconomies of scale set in. When the retailer sells q^* units, long-run average operating cost reaches a minimum of AOC_0 and long-run average cost reaches a minimum value of $W^* + \text{AOC}_0$.

The long-run average cost function of the retail establishment is $W^* + \text{AOC}_L(q)$ and is U-shaped because $\text{AOC}_L(q)$ is U-shaped.

$$\text{AC}_L(q) = W^* + \text{AOC}_L(q) \qquad \text{(Long-Run Average Cost Function of Retailer)} \qquad \textbf{(13-1)}$$

If the retail price is R^*, each price-taking retailer maximizes profits by selling q^* units where R^* is equal to minimum long-run average and long-run marginal cost. Each retailer operates at the minimum point of the long-run average cost function.

We assume that the retailing industry is a constant-cost industry. Given the wholesale price, it can supply an indefinite quantity at a price of R^* because equally efficient retailers enter the industry and each entrant sells only q^* units in the long run. In Figure 13-2, *SaS* is the horizontal long-run supply function of the retailing industry, and its height is determined by the minimum long-run average cost, $W^* + \text{AOC}_0$. In Figure 13-2 the inverse retail market demand function, *DD*, inter-

THE LONG-RUN AVERAGE COST CURVE OF A RETAILER

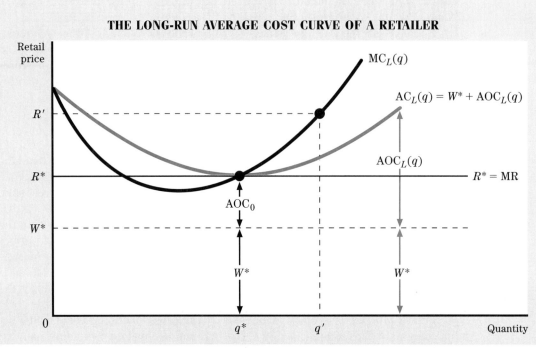

Figure 13-1   The long-run average cost function of a retailer is $AC_L(q)$ and is equal to the sum of wholesale price and the long-run average operating cost function. If the number of retailers is n^* and the wholesale price is W^*, the retail price is R^* and each retailer sells q^* units. The minimum long-run average cost of the retailer is $W^* + AOC_0$. Because the retail price, R^*, is equal to minimum long-run average cost, the retailer earns no profit. The revenue received by the manufacturer from the sale of q^* units is W^*q^*. By limiting the number of retailers to less than n^*, the manufacturer causes the retail price to rise to R', and each of a smaller number of retailers supplies q' units.

sects the long-run supply function, *SaS*, when consumers purchase Q^* units. Given the wholesale price W^*, each retailer sells q^* units at a price of R^*. Because the total quantity supplied is Q^* and each retailer sells q^*, the number of retailers is $n^* = Q^*/q^*$.

A numerical example may help clarify these points. Suppose the manufacturer sells 1 million units per year at a wholesale price, W^*, of \$18. Given the retail demand function, the million units are sold at a retail price of \$25. Assuming the long-run average operating cost of a retailer reaches a minimum of \$7 when 10,000 units per year are sold, the minimum long-run average cost of the retailer is \$18 + \$7 = \$25. The number of retailers in the market is $n^* = Q^*/q^*$, or 100. In the retail market the long-run equilibrium retail price is \$25, and each of the 100 retailers sells 10,000 units and earns no profits.

Since the manufacturer sells Q^* units at a wholesale price of W^*, total revenue of the manufacturer is W^*Q^*. In this model the manufacturer does not limit the

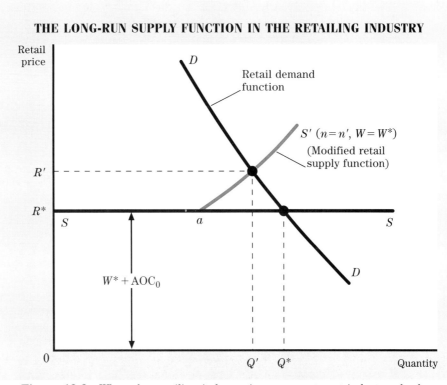

THE LONG-RUN SUPPLY FUNCTION IN THE RETAILING INDUSTRY

Figure 13-2   When the retailing industry is a constant-cost industry, the long-run supply function is SaS and the industry supplies indefinite quantities at R^* which equals the retailer's minimum long-run average cost. The height of SaS is determined by $W^* + \text{AOC}_0$, the minimum point on the retailer's long-run average cost curve. The market demand function intersects the long-run supply curve when the retailing industry supplies Q^* units at a price of R^*. Each retailer sells q^* units and operates at the minimum point of the long-run average cost curve. The total number of retailers is $n^* = Q^*/q^*$. If the manufacturer limits the number of retailers to n', the long-run supply curve becomes SaS'. The retail price rises to R' and the retailing industry sells only Q' units but each retailer earns profits.

number of retailers. Given W^*, it allows retailers to enter the market until the retail price falls to R^*. At that point profits disappear and no more retailers desire to enter the industry. Once the manufacturer selects the wholesale price, W^*, free entry of retailers determines how many are in the industry.

What will happen to the manufacturer's profits if the monopolist tries to sell Q^* units with only n' retailers, where $n' < n^*$? If the manufacturer limits the number of retailers to only n', the long-run retail supply function changes from SaS to SaS' as in Figure 13-2. It is horizontal at a retail price of R^* until all n' retailers enter the industry. Over the horizontal segment Sa, each retailer that enters supplies q^* units (Figure 13-1) in the long run at a price of R^*. At point a in

Figure 13-2 all n' retailers are in the industry. No more can enter because the manufacturer restricts the number to n'.

Because there are internal diseconomies of scale, each retailer will supply more than q^* units if the retail price rises above R^*. The long-run marginal cost function for prices above R^* becomes the retailer's long-run supply function. For example, at a price of R', each retailer maximizes profits by selling q' units (Figure 13-1), and the n' retailers collectively supply Q' units. In Figure 13-2, the segment aS' of the modified supply function is a horizontal summation of the long-run marginal cost functions of the n' retailers.

In Figure 13-2 the inverse market demand function intersects the modified long-run supply function when the equilibrium retail price is R' and the n' retailers supply Q' units. When the manufacturer limits entry into the industry, each retailer sells q' units and earns profits because R' is equal to long-run marginal cost which is greater than long-run average cost in Figure 13-1.

By limiting the number of retailers to n', the manufacturer causes the retail price to rise to R', and the quantity falls to Q' units. To sell Q^* units with only n' retailers, the manufacturer must reduce the wholesale price. When the wholesale price is lowered, each of the n' retailers is willing to sell more than q' units. As the monopolist lowers the wholesale price, the modified long-run retail supply function shifts downward and to the right, and the intersection of the demand and supply functions occurs at progressively lower retail prices and larger quantities. At some lower wholesale price the demand function intersects the retail supply function where the n' retailers sell Q^* units at a retail price of R^*. Figure 13-3 shows that the modified supply function, sas', intersects the demand function where the total quantity sold is Q^* units after the wholesale price declines to W'.

Figure 13-4 shows that the retailer sells q'' units after the manufacturer reduces the wholesale price to W'. R^* equals the retailer's new long-run marginal cost. When q'' units are sold, each of the n' retailers expands the quantity sold from q' to q'', and the manufacturer is selling Q^* units again. The wholesale price must decrease by enough so that $n'q'' = n^*q^* = Q^*$, where q'' is the new profit-maximizing quantity of each retailer after the wholesale price declines to W'.

We have demonstrated that a monopolist can sell Q^* units with either n^* or n' retailers. However, revenue is lower when the number of retailers is limited to n' because the manufacturer receives only W' for each unit. Therefore, total revenue, $W'Q^*$, is less than W^*Q^*. The main conclusion is that the manufacturer maximizes total revenue from selling Q^* units by allowing free entry into retailing and not by limiting the number of retailers or price competition among them.

> When selling a product whose features are familiar to consumers, a manufacturer maximizes profits by selecting a wholesale price and allowing free entry of bona fide retailers into the industry.

The basic point of the analysis applies not only to Q^* units but to any quantity. To sell any total quantity, the manufacturer maximizes total revenue by setting the wholesale price where the difference between the retail and wholesale prices is minimized. After the wholesale price is specified, any bona fide retailer is allowed

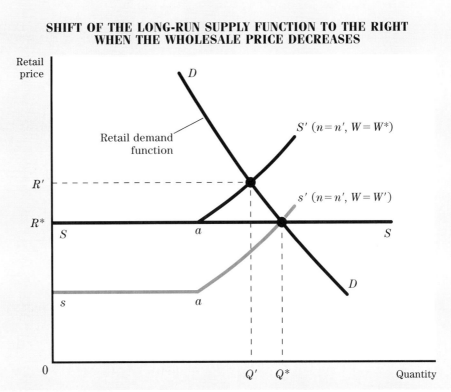

**SHIFT OF THE LONG-RUN SUPPLY FUNCTION TO THE RIGHT
WHEN THE WHOLESALE PRICE DECREASES**

Figure 13-3   When the wholesale price is W^* and the manufacturer limits the number of retailers to n', the retail price increases to R' and the manufacturer sells only Q' units. To sell Q^* units, the manufacturer reduces the wholesale price to W' and each retailer's long-run average and marginal cost functions shift downward. The long-run retail supply function of the n' retailers shifts downward and becomes sas'. The market demand function intersects sas' when Q^* units are sold at a retail price of R^*. When a manufacturer restricts the number of retailers, it must reduce the wholesale price to sell Q^* units. Therefore, the manufacturer's total revenue from selling Q^* units will be lower if it restricts the number of retailers.

to sell the product. When the manufacturer allows free entry of retailers into the industry, each one operates at the minimum point of the long-run average cost function and incurs a long-run average operating cost of AOC_0.

Maximizing the Profits of the Manufacturer

This analysis has explained how a manufacturer determines the wholesale price and indirectly the number of retailers selling any given quantity. To determine the quantity that maximizes the manufacturer's profits, we must first derive the inverse wholesale demand function since revenue equals wholesale price times quantity sold. The manufacturer's inverse wholesale demand function shows the highest wholesale price that can be charged for each quantity demanded by retailers.

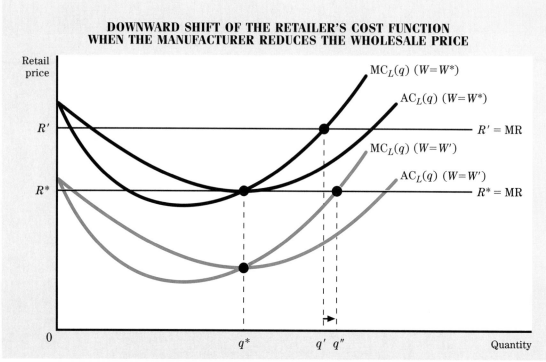

Figure 13-4   When the manufacturer lowers the wholesale price to W', the average and marginal cost functions of the retailer shift downward. The manufacturer must reduce the wholesale price to W' if it hopes to sell Q^* units with n' retailers. Each retailer increases the quantity sold from q' to q'' units because the wholesale price decreases from W^* to W'. When each of the n' retailers sells q'' units, the retail price, R^*, equals the retailer's marginal cost. Each retailer earns profits because long-run marginal cost is greater than long-run average cost.

If there is free entry of retailers, the long-run average operating cost of each one is AOC_0. The wholesale demand function, NN, is derived by subtracting AOC_0 from the inverse retail demand function $D(Q)$ in Figure 13-5 at each quantity demanded. The wholesale demand function is

$$\text{Wholesale price} = \text{Retail price} - AOC_0$$

$$W = D(Q) - AOC_0 = N(Q)$$

$W = N(Q)$ is the inverse wholesale demand function and is the highest wholesale price the firm can charge for each Q. For each quantity, the vertical difference between the retail market demand function, DD, and the wholesale demand function, NN, is AOC_0.

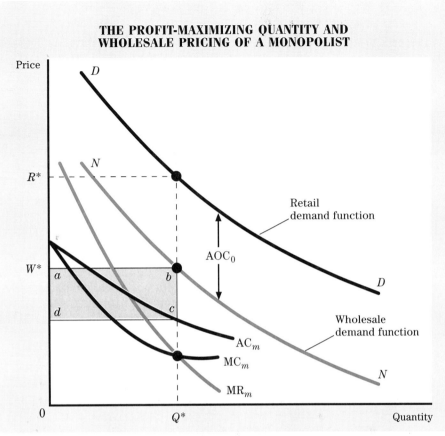

**THE PROFIT-MAXIMIZING QUANTITY AND
WHOLESALE PRICING OF A MONOPOLIST**

Figure 13-5   When the monopolist allows the free entry of retailers, the difference between the retail price and the wholesale price is equal to AOC_0. NN is the wholesale demand function. The monopolist determines the profit-maximizing quantity Q^* and wholesale price W^* where the manufacturer's marginal revenue equals marginal cost. The retail price is R^*, and the manufacturer's profits are equal to area $abcd$.

> The inverse wholesale demand function of the manufacturer equals the inverse retail demand function less the retailer's minimum long-run average operating cost.

The profit function of the manufacturer is equal to total revenue from units sold to dealers less manufacturing costs.

$$\pi_m = WQ - M(Q)$$

$$= N(Q)Q - M(Q) \qquad \text{(Manufacturer's Profits)} \qquad \textbf{(13-2)}$$

where $M(Q)$ represents the manufacturer's production costs.

The monopolist selects the profit-maximizing output where marginal revenue from the last unit sold (derived from the wholesale demand function) equals marginal cost of production.[8]

$$MR_m(Q) = MC_m(Q) \qquad \text{(Equilibrium Condition for Manufacturer)} \qquad \text{(13-3)}$$

$MR_m(Q)$ is the manufacturer's marginal revenue from selling another unit to retailers and is derived from the wholesale demand function. MC_m denotes the marginal cost of producing another unit. In Figure 13-5 the manufacturer produces Q^* units where marginal revenue equals marginal cost. W^* is the profit-maximizing wholesale price, and equilibrium retail price is R^*. Total profits of the manufacturer are equal to the area *abcd*.

The difference between R^* and W^* is AOC_0.

$$R^* - W^* = AOC_0$$

$$R^* = AOC_0 + W^* \qquad \text{(Equilibrium Condition for Retailer)} \qquad \text{(13-4)}$$

Equation 13-4 says the retailer operates on a scale where long-run average cost is at a minimum and is equal to retail price. The left-hand side of equation 13-4 represents the marginal revenue of a price-taking retailer, and the right-hand side represents the sum of minimum per unit operating cost and wholesale price. Because the retailer operates at the minimum point on the average cost function, long-run marginal cost equals long-run average cost.

In summary, the manufacturer receives the highest wholesale price for any quantity the manufacturer sells by allowing free entry of retailers so that each one operates at the minimum point of the long-run average operating cost function. It is in the self-interest of the manufacturer to have the most cost-effective retailers so that the total operating cost of selling Q^* units is minimized. The manufacturer then determines the profit-maximizing quantity and the wholesale price by equating its marginal revenue, derived from the wholesale demand function, to its marginal cost of production. Because retailers are free to enter, they do not earn profits.

---

[8] The wholesale demand function is derived by subtracting AOC_0 from the market demand function.

$$W = N(Q) = D(Q) - AOC_0$$

Substituting this expression for W into the manufacturer's profit equation gives

$$\pi_m = [D(Q) - AOC_0]Q - M(Q)$$

Using calculus, we find that profits are maximized when

$$\frac{d(\pi_m)}{dQ} = D(Q) + Q\frac{d[D(Q)]}{dQ} - AOC_0 - \frac{d[M(Q)]}{dQ} = 0$$

The first two terms on the right-hand side represent marginal revenue of the retail demand function. The third term represents minimum long-run average operating cost, and the last term represents marginal production cost. Marginal revenue of the wholesale demand function is equal to the sum of the first three terms, or marginal revenue of the retail demand function less AOC_0. Therefore, the profit-maximizing quantity occurs where marginal revenue of the wholesale demand function equals marginal production cost.

13-4   THE SPECIAL SERVICE THEORY AND THE FREE RIDER PROBLEM IN RETAILING

The analysis says that manufacturer's profits are higher when retailers are free to enter and compete among themselves and each operates at its minimum point on the long-run average cost function. However, in each of the cases we observed that manufacturers limited competition by preventing retailers from *lowering* price. Why is their behavior so different from what economic theory predicts? This section offers an alternative explanation for this behavior.

The Special Service Theory

Lester Telser has advanced an interesting theory that features the free rider problem to explain why and when a manufacturer resists retail price competition.[9] According to the special service theory retailers not only provide inventory but also supply educational services to consumers that shift the manufacturer's demand function outward. Therefore, the manufacturer develops policies that encourage retailers to provide these educational services.

> A **special service** is a service that the consumer receives without charge and shifts the retail and wholesale demand functions to the right.

The theory has four assumptions.

1. The retail and wholesale demand functions shift to the right if retailers provide special (educational) services to consumers.

2. The retailer supplies the special service at the point of sale more cheaply than the manufacturer can through general promotion messages.

3. The information supplied by the retailer is brand-specific.

4. It is too costly for the retailer to charge separately for the special service.

Given these assumptions, how does the special service theory explain why manufacturers limit retail price competition and favor a minimum suggested retail price? To explain this theory, we examine events in the retailing of personal computers when the industry was just evolving.

Step back in time and consider the problem faced by computer manufacturers when PCs were first introduced in the early 1980s. They were a new and unknown product to most people and to many businesses, and customers required information about their possible uses. They wanted to know about the special characteristics of computers and how the manufacturer's computer would help solve

[9] Lester Telser, "Why Should Manufacturers Want Fair Trade?" *Journal of Law and Economics*, vol. 3, October 1960, pp. 86–105.

their particular problems. To sell their products, manufacturers arranged to have retail distribution of these special (educational) services. Local dealers can better supply information to diverse consumers by providing detailed answers at the point of purchase.

Initially, each manufacturer adopts a general policy that guarantees retailers will supply the information. The manufacturer might insist that each dealer have a well-trained sales staff that understands the special requirements of each customer and conducts hands-on demonstrations. These services are costly to provide, and so the retail margin, the difference between the retail and wholesale prices, had to be large enough to cover the costs incurred by these service-rich retailers.

Let's suppose a computer manufacturer initially appoints a large number of service-rich retailers. Assume that several years later you decide to enter the retail computer market but wonder how you can succeed in such a competitive business. The difference between the retail and wholesale prices is large because dealers provide support services to potential customers. How will you be able to price aggressively when the existing dealers are already competing vigorously among themselves?

You wonder if the high retail markup could be the key to your success. Instead of operating a retail outlet with a large sales staff and an extensive and expensive inventory, your retail operation will be "lean and mean." If the customer knows what type of computer he or she wants, your sales staff will supply it promptly and at a lower price. You will focus your retail operation on customers who know what they want in a computer. You did not design your business for the less informed customer who needs more prepurchase support, advice, and handholding. By managing a bare bones operation, you expect to pass on significant cost savings.

Figure 13-6*a* shows the long-run average and marginal cost functions of a retailer that supplies special services, and Figure 13-6*b* shows the long-run average and marginal cost functions of one that does not. In both cases the wholesale price is W^*. The minimum long-run average operating cost of the retailer that provides special services is AOC_0, and the long-run average operating cost of the retailer that does not is AOC_1. Figure 13-6*b* shows that the volume where long-run average cost reaches a minimum is larger for a discount type of operation than for a retailer that provides special services.

How do consumers react when this different type of retailer enters the market? More customers become "tire kickers." They visit service-rich computer stores and receive useful and valuable prepurchase educational services. But when the salesperson tries to close the transaction, they mutter something to the effect that they want to think more about the purchase before making a final decision. Then they purchase at a lower price from a service-lean dealership.

These consumers receive and benefit from a free ride. They obtained valuable services from the service-rich dealer without having to pay for them. Because customers purchase from service-lean dealers, service-rich dealers suffer losses. They have incurred the cost of making these services available but do not recover this cost when customers purchase elsewhere. The market is no longer in equilib-

RETAILER COST FUNCTIONS WITH AND WITHOUT SPECIAL SERVICES

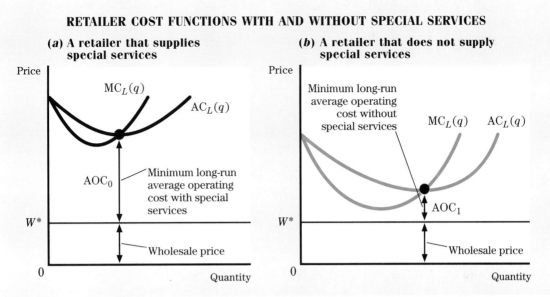

Figure 13-6   (*a*) Long-run average and marginal cost functions of a retailer who supplies special services. (*b*) Long-run average and marginal cost functions of a retailer who operates a bare bones operation and does not supply special services.

rium. Either the service-rich dealers will have to go out of business or they will have to convert their operations to service-lean dealerships. Either way, the manufacturer loses. When retailers do not supply special services, the market demand function facing the manufacturer shifts to the left and profits decline.

Resale Price Maintenance and the Special Service Theory

Under resale price maintenance (RPM) or a more informal system where the manufacturer suggests a range of retail prices, a manufacturer sets the minimum price at which a retailer can sell the product.

> Under **resale price maintenance** a manufacturer prohibits its retailers from selling the product below a minimum suggested price.

How does a manufacturer benefit from the use of a minimum retail price? Suppose a computer manufacturer sets a minimum retail price and enforces it. A service-lean store can no longer sell computers at prices below those charged by the service-rich retailer. Now the shoe is on the other foot. The service-lean dealer is at a disadvantage because customers have less incentive to visit his dealership. By shopping at the service-rich dealership, customers pay the same price as at the service-lean dealership *and* receive the valuable educational services. Now it is the

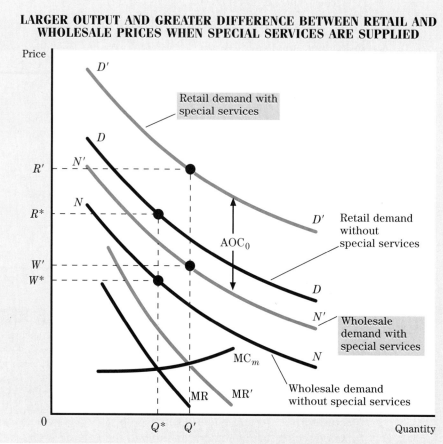

LARGER OUTPUT AND GREATER DIFFERENCE BETWEEN RETAIL AND WHOLESALE PRICES WHEN SPECIAL SERVICES ARE SUPPLIED

Figure 13-7   If no special services are provided by retailers, the retail and wholesale demand functions are DD and NN. The monopolist sells Q^* units at a wholesale price of W^*, and the retail price is R^*. When special services are provided, the retail and wholesale demand functions shift outward and become $D'D'$ and $N'N'$. The manufacturer increases output from Q^* to Q' and raises the wholesale price from W^* to W'. The retail price rises to R', and the retail margin increases to $R' - W'$.

service-lean dealer who must decide whether to leave the market or to revamp store operations and become a service-rich dealer.

When the manufacturer sets a minimum retail price, retailers supply special services and the demand function for the product shifts outward, as shown in Figure 13-7. DD is the inverse retail market demand function and NN is the manufacturer's wholesale demand function if retailers do not supply special services. $D'D'$ is the retail demand function, and $N'N'$ is the wholesale demand function when retailers supply special services. MR and MR′ are the marginal revenue functions of the two wholesale demand functions, and MC_m is the marginal cost function of the manufacturer.

The manufacturer's profits are higher if retailers supply special services. Then, the retail and wholesale prices that maximize these profits are R' and W', respectively. If retailers do not provide special services, the retail and wholesale prices that maximize profits are R^* and W^*. Under RPM the manufacturer sets the retail price at R'.[10] When retailers supply special services, the difference between the retail and wholesale prices must be large enough to cover the higher long-run average operating cost, AOC_0, of providing the special services.

When the manufacturer enforces a minimum retail price, retailers have a greater incentive to provide special services.

Applying the Theory to Explain Behavior

Let's consider how the special service theory might explain why the manufacturers discouraged retail price competition in the three cases discussed in Section 13-2.

In the GM case the offending dealer was free-riding on the services supplied by other franchised dealers. These dealers offered customers a broad inventory of autos and a trained sales staff. The sales staff was available to answer questions about the automobile, option packages, and color choice and to take customers out for a test drive. Buyers obtain prepurchase information from these dealers about the automobile they want to purchase as well as the options they find useful. Once they have this information, they purchase at a dealership that essentially takes orders like a catalog operation. This type of dealership clearly has lower costs than those that provide a full range of informational services. GM's assessment is that catalog operations affect the position of the demand function. If it feels that the long-run demand for GM autos increases when dealers provide these informational services, it will disapprove of dealers who do not provide them.

IBM and Apple include clauses in their contracts that prevent dealers from becoming wholesalers selling to mass distributors or to mail-order houses. Initially, both manufacturers discouraged sales through mass distributors and mail-order firms and encouraged their dealers to provide prepurchase educational information to consumers. A mail-order operation that offers IBM or Apple computers has the potential for creating a free rider problem. Customers can obtain information from service-rich IBM and Apple dealers and then order computers at a lower price from the mail-order firm. The attempts by IBM and Apple to restrict price competition represent possible solutions to the free rider problem that these companies faced at the time.

Prince Manufacturing discouraged price competition for its upper-priced tennis rackets. When selling expensive tennis rackets, it may want the retailer to spend time with the consumer describing the different features of the racket and determining which type of racket is the most suitable. Prince has made a judgment that

---

[10] The model considers only a monopoly manufacturer. However, studies show that firms in industries with many firms also use RPM, and it can be inferred that RPM is a feasible business arrangement even in industries with many firms. The existence of RPM in industries with many firms implies that special services for their products are brand-specific, even when the products are close substitutes.

consumers who purchase expensive tennis rackets value this information, and it wants to discourage other stores from free-riding by selling rackets below the minimum suggested price.

The Role of Each Assumption

Let's review each assumption of the special service theory to see how the conclusions would change if the assumption were relaxed.

1. If the wholesale demand function does not shift to the right when retailers supply special services, the manufacturer's profits are lowered when retailers are required to supply services that consumers do not value. The average operating cost function of the retailer shifts upward, and the wholesale demand function shifts to the left because the retail demand function does not change. Under these circumstances the manufacturer has no incentive to impose a minimum retail price.

2. The special service theory assumes that retailers can supply special services more cheaply than the manufacturer can. If the manufacturer could supply the special services at a lower cost, it would provide them directly to consumers and the free rider problem would disappear. Dealers could not free-ride on other dealers because the manufacturer would provide the education function. However, information received through advertisements in the mass media is usually less effective than information obtained from retailers because retailers can tailor information to the individual requirements of each customer.

3. Special services are brand-specific. If the information provided by retailers is general, customers can obtain it from the retailers of one manufacturer and purchase from a retailer selling a different brand. If the information is applicable to several brands, the dealers of one manufacturer can free-ride on the information supplied by the dealers of another manufacturer and consequently can underprice the dealers of a competitor. In recent years clones, PCs that use the same operating system as IBM computers, have become popular. Purchasers of IBM clones may be able to free-ride on some but not necessarily all of the educational services offered by IBM retailers. When the information supplied by retailers is brand-specific, this is impossible.

4. If transaction costs are small, the retailer can charge separately for the time the consumer spends with a salesperson. The buyer pays for the educational services separately and is then free to purchase the computer at the same store or elsewhere. The customer cannot free-ride on a service that must be paid for. The free rider problem exists because there is no cheap way to charge for special services. Charging each customer for time spent with the salesperson is usually costly and can lead to endless disputes between customers and salespeople.

This analysis explains why and when a manufacturer responds to a free rider problem by supporting minimum retail prices. When the assumptions of the model are applicable and when a free rider problem would otherwise appear, a manufacturer can introduce policies that prevent this problem from surfacing rather than trying to deal with it after it appears. Now let's consider those situations where a free rider problem is more likely to surface.

When Do Free Rider Problems Appear?

A free rider problem can appear wherever there is a demand for prepurchase information by consumers. By recognizing these conditions in advance, a firm can prevent the problem from emerging by taking the appropriate steps. We list some of the conditions that cause free rider problems to develop.

1. Free rider problems are more severe for new products than for established products because consumers are less knowledgeable about new items than about established goods. If a manufacturer wants retailers to provide special services, it must anticipate the possibility of a free rider problem and protect retailers that provide these services. A manufacturer is more likely to discourage retail price competition by setting a minimum suggested price early in the product life cycle. Later, as the product ages and consumers gain more experience with it, the company can terminate the suggested minimum price.

2. A free rider problem is more likely to develop when a firm is selling a complex durable or technical good. In these cases consumers often lack information and need advice. For example, when buying nonprescription drugs, a person is likely to ask the druggist for advice when confronted with 20 alternative cold remedies. Drugs and small consumer durable goods were frequently sold under RPM when this practice was legal.

3. The free rider problem is more severe when the cost of time of the consumer is low relative to the cost of the product. A busy executive has a high cost of time. He or she is less likely to comparison-shop and more likely to purchase from a high-service store. Consumers are more likely to shop for a lower price when buying an expensive consumer durable good or appliance when the price of the good is high relative to the cost of the consumer's time.

Dealing with the Free Rider Problem without Using a Minimum Suggested Retail Price

The Supreme Court's attitude toward resale price maintenance has fluctuated over the years. Recently, antitrust authorities and the courts have softened their treatment of a minimum suggested retail price when evidence of a price conspiracy is absent. Firms like Prince Manufacturing suggest a range of prices at which retailers may sell a product rather than specifying a minimum suggested price. Retailers receive a warning that selling below this range will be grounds for termination. As long as the courts do not view this as price collusion between retailers or between manufacturers, this practice appears acceptable. While manufacturers have become more venturesome as they sense a more relaxed attitude toward a minimum suggested retail price by the courts and antitrust authorities, RPM remains a gray area in which some antitrust vulnerability exists.

Some firms have adopted other distribution policies to control the free rider problem. Some alternatives are the following.

1. Provide information at company-owned demonstration stores that do not sell products. Some examples are IBM in personal computers and, many years ago, Zenith in radio and television. Demonstration stores are expensive to operate, and so manufacturers limit their number and usually establish them in large metropolitan areas. They can help but do not fully solve the free rider problem. Major cosmetic companies purchase space in department stores and have their own personnel demonstrate products. In this way the manufacturer's role expands to include providing consumer information.

2. Offer a subsidy to stores that provide special services.

3. Lower the wholesale price to stores that provide special services.

4. Limit the number of dealers and implicitly grant each dealer an exclusive territory to discourage customers from shopping around among competing dealers.

5. Select retailers who have a history of providing a service-rich environment. A high-quality department store is more likely to merchandise your product in a similar style than to adopt a completely different method of retailing just for your product. Prescreening applicants prevents or at least reduces the probability that a free rider problem will arise. Given the high cost of terminating dealers, a prescreening policy is essential.

6. Design products with unique features or operating systems that make it more costly for other manufacturers to clone products and therefore to free-ride off your dealers. The first section of this chapter mentioned how software companies design their programs to raise the cost of copying software. This is an example of how companies can redesign products.

These alternatives are partial and often imperfect substitutes for direct limits on retail price competition. Administration of alternatives 2 and 3 is both expensive and time-consuming. In most cases the cost of monitoring dealers to determine whether special services are being provided is very high. A manufacturer must take extreme care in offering differential subsidies or differential wholesale prices to dealers. Such policies may violate the Robinson-Patman Act that prohibits firms from charging retailers different prices unless they can justify the prices by showing differences in their costs. Companies have had considerable difficulty sustaining a cost justification defense before the Federal Trade Commission for differential pricing. Limiting the number of dealers raises the cost of comparison shopping for consumers. This attenuates the free rider problem but reduces dealer density and encourages monopoly pricing by the dealer. There is much to be said for a policy of carefully screening potential dealers. The history of the retailer can provide clues about what type of retailer an applicant is likely to be. Is the candidate currently operating or has the candidate ever operated a service-rich retail establishment? Of course, an applicant with promise but little history is more difficult to assess. Clearly, the firm should seek expert legal advice so that contracts clearly specify which business practices will and will not be acceptable. Appointing dealers without an appreciation of the consequences of the free rider problem will lead to problems. Trying to rectify the problem by later changes in the terms of the contract leads to a quagmire of legal problems.

Implications of the Special Service Theory

The special service argument implies that the total units sold by a monopolist are higher under RPM or a suggested minimum price. A second implication is that the retail margin, the difference between the retail and wholesale prices, is higher with RPM than without it. Figure 13-7 showed the optimal retail and wholesale prices and total output when retailers do and do not provide special services. The retail demand function is DD when retailers do not provide special services, and $D'D'$ when they do. The corresponding wholesale demand functions are NN and $N'N'$. Note that quantity demanded is greater at each wholesale price on $N'N'$ than on NN. The wholesale demand function shifts to the right when retailers provide special services. Otherwise, the manufacturer would not want these services supplied since consumers value them at less than the cost of providing them. The profit-maximizing quantity is Q^* and the wholesale price is W^* when retailers do not supply special services, and Q' and W' when they do. Profits of the manufacturer are higher when retailers supply special services. The retail margin, the difference between the retail and wholesale prices, is $R^* - W^*$ when retailers do not supply special services and $R' - W'$ when they do.

> A manufacturer that voluntarily adopts a suggested minimum retail price policy expects the quantity sold to increase and the retail margin to increase.

Voluntary Termination of a Suggested Retail Price

For some products the requirements of consumers change over time as they gain more experience with the item. The policies of a manufacturer should change as consumers change. As mentioned earlier, a manufacturer might favor a minimum retail price when a product is new and consumers are unfamiliar with it. Later, as they become more familiar with it, their demand for information declines. At this point the manufacturer's profits will increase when the use of a minimum suggested retail price is voluntarily discontinued.

By dropping a minimum suggested retail price, the manufacturer is signaling that it no longer considers it essential to provide special services since consumers are now better informed. Retailers respond by changing their operations and providing fewer services. The long-run average operating cost function of each dealer shifts downward, and the minimum long-run operating cost decreases. The cost

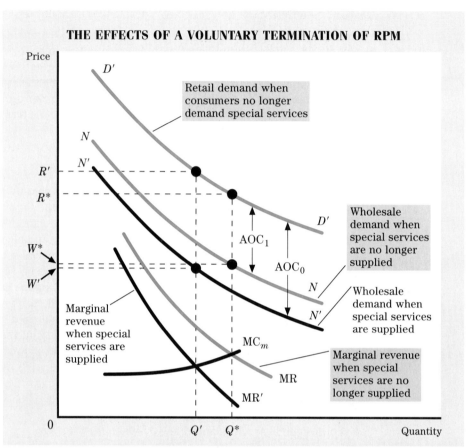

Figure 13-8 As consumers become familiar with a product, they demand fewer special services and the manufacturer terminates RPM voluntarily. If the manufacturer no longer requires retailers to provide special services, the long-run average and marginal operating cost functions shift downward. When the special services are terminated, the retail demand curve does not shift. The wholesale demand function shifts upward because the minimum long-run average operating cost decreases. The monopolist produces Q^* and raises the wholesale price to W^*. The retail margin and the retail price both decrease.

functions of retailers shift from the long-run average cost function in Figure 13-6*a* to that in Figure 13-6*b* as the retailer provides fewer special services. The minimum long-run average operating cost falls from AOC_0 to AOC_1.

In Figure 13-8 the retail demand function is $D'D'$ because retailers have provided special services. It does not shift to the left when retailers no longer supply special services because consumers have become informed about the product. On the other hand, the difference between the retail demand function and the wholesale demand function at each quantity decreases because the minimum long-run average operating cost of the dealer shifts downward. Consequently, the wholesale demand function shifts upward to *NN*, and the equilibrium retail margin declines. The retail price decreases from R' to R^*, and the wholesale price increases from W' to W^*. In this situation the retail margin decreases, output increases to Q^*, and the manufacturer's profits increase.

The consequence of voluntary elimination of a minimum suggested retail price when special services are no longer demanded is an increase in the output and profits of the manufacturer.

APPLICATION 13-2

Apple Decides to Sell Computers through Superstores

In the computer industry the informational requirements of consumers have changed over time as customers have become better informed about products, and manufacturers have responded by modifying their price and distribution policies. In a major change in distribution policy Apple Computer authorized Comp USA, one of the faster-growing chains of computer stores, to sell lower-priced Macintosh computers in its superstores.[11] Apple's policy had formerly relied on specialty stores to sell its computers. This change in policy follows IBM's decision to sell more computers through mass distributors like Sears Roebuck. Apple and IBM are hoping to reduce operating costs by relying more on large computer stores. One reason for the change appears to be the changing requirements and the computer sophistication of consumers. An article in *MacWeek*, a weekly magazine covering the Macintosh scene, notes that a smaller dealer still has an advantage over superstores in the area of technical support but that consumers do not require that kind of support and will not pay for it. In addition, computers have changed. One of the imposing tasks in the past was to initialize the hard drive or assemble the components or load the applications. The machines now available have eliminated these tasks.

The Objection to RPM: Facilitating a Cartel

You may be wondering why the courts take a hostile attitude toward RPM if consumers benefit when retailers provide special services. Part of the objection is political, and part is intellectual. Most discounters oppose RPM. They argue that it raises retail prices and does not permit stores with fewer services to compete with full-service stores. This complaint is partly correct but is not a justification for a ban on RPM. Discount stores offer fewer services and lower prices and face a competitive disadvantage if all stores must charge the same price. On the other hand, a manufacturer seeks a more efficient method to distribute its product at the retail level. If the position of the inverse demand function is unaffected, the manufacturer always prefers the lowest-cost method of retailing the product and would rather rely on low-margin discount stores. The manufacturer has no reason to

---

[11] Based on Andrew Gore, "Apple to Authorize Comp USA Superstores," *MacWeek*, June 4, 1991.

discriminate against a store offering the product with fewer services at a lower retail margin than a high-margin store. Indeed, many manufacturers currently sell their products to discounters and would continue to do so even if RPM were permitted.

The case against RPM is that it can be a facilitating device to increase the effectiveness of a cartel. RPM can be used along with other devices to shore up an imperfect cartel. As noted in Chapter 10, a cartel is a fragile instrument subject to member cheating. To be effective, it must limit the increase in the quantity sold by a price cheater. With a fixed retail price a manufacturer who gives a secret wholesale price cut to its dealers will not experience an increase in sales because the retailer cannot lower the retail price. The gains from price cutting are smaller with than without RPM. RPM can be employed with other mechanisms that limit the increase in the quantity sold by a manufacturer who is a price chiseler. For example, the members of the cartel may agree to have exclusive retail dealers, not to raid the retailers of another cartel member, and to prevent secret price cheating at the retail level. All these arrangements reduce the increase in the quantity sold by a secret price cutter and therefore discourage price cutting. Therefore, opponents of RPM claim that manufacturers can use RPM to shore up a weak cartel and to make collusion more effective.

13-5   QUALITY CERTIFICATION AND THE FREE RIDER PROBLEM

Howard Marvel and Stephen McCafferty examined a different type of free rider problem where one type of retailer free-rides off another type of retailer.[12] They present the **quality certification** theory to explain why a manufacturer uses RPM and why it limits the number and kinds of dealers selling the product.

The three assumptions of the quality certification theory are:

1. Retailers incur costs to certify the quality or fashion characteristics of a product. Any up-front investment qualifies.

2. Retailers cannot charge separately for the certification function. If the certifying retailer could sell the information about quality to consumers separately, the free rider problem would disappear.

3. The decision to certify a brand by stocking it is general information. Consumers will purchase the brand elsewhere if it is available at a lower price.

The decision of a store to carry a brand is valuable information for consumers. If a store carries a certain brand, consumers infer it must meet the store's minimum specifications. When Marshall Field's, Neiman Marcus, or Macy's stocks a less well-known brand, that decision reveals valuable information to consumers about

[12] H. Marvel and S. McCafferty, "Resale Price Maintenance and Quality Certification," *Rand Journal of Economics*, vol. 15, Autumn 1984, pp. 346–359.

either its quality or its fashion characteristics. The information is *general* in the sense that the value of the information does not depend on where the consumer ultimately purchases the product. However, this information is useful whether the consumer purchases the brand at Marshall Field's or at a discount or specialty store.

As mentioned in the first section of this chapter, free rider problems surface when information is general and not specific to the firm. Let's examine the free rider problem that appears when a store decides to carry a lesser-known brand following an investigation of the product and the reputation of the manufacturer. The retailer invests resources to identify brands that meet or surpass its minimum quality or fashion standards. That's the rub. The firm incurs the costs of certifying quality but cannot establish ownership over the information that it creates.

Suppose the manufacturer of the brand does not exercise care but ships the brand to any retail store that orders it. Some of these stores simply copy the decision of the certifying retailer to carry the brand and can underprice the certifying store because they do not incur the costs of certification. They are free-riding on the decision of the certifying store to carry the brand. The certifying store incurred the cost but cannot appropriate the value of the information from the copying stores. If a majority of consumers are indifferent as to where they buy, they will purchase the brand at a lower price from stores that do not perform the certification function.

Clearly, a store will be reluctant to perform the certifying function if other firms can quickly free-ride on the decision. Suppose the demand for the manufacturer's brand decreases if a higher-quality store does not perform the certification role. The manufacturer must anticipate the consequences of allowing other stores to copy the adoption decision of the certifying store. It must guarantee that copying competitors will not receive the same merchandise as the certifying store does by limiting the distribution of the brand to only those stores that perform the certification function. The manufacturer can refuse to deal with lower-quality retailers and might agree to sell the product under RPM to prevent stores from underpricing the certifying store.

The quality certification theory can explain why manufacturers are reluctant to allow any retailer to sell their products but prefer to select similar types of stores to carry a brand. Just as the manufacturer selects retailers who will not free-ride on other retailers when it wants retailers to provide special services, so too does the manufacturer discourage retailers from free-riding on the information created by the certifying store.

APPLICATION 13-3

Testing New Toys at Small Toy Stores

With the growth of large discount stores such as Wal-Mart and Toys "R" Us, it is more difficult to introduce toys that require special handling, demonstrations, and instruction to succeed. Some manufacturers introduce new toys or reestablish older toys by relying exclusively on small toy shops for displays and demonstrations.[13] Many small stores associate with manufacturers that sell only to small toy stores because they cannot compete on price with the larger impersonal discount stores.

Small stores can claim partial credit for the success of such toys as Thomas the Tank Engine, Koosh balls, Erector sets, and Playmobile building sets. Massive advertising campaigns do not succeed with all types of toys. To be successful, some must be sold with demonstrations and displays that allow children to touch and play with them in the store. An example of this type of toy is Playmobile's playpens. Retailers are encouraged to set up playpens to give children a hands-on opportunity to play with them. No small toy store is likely to set aside space and encourage demonstrations if customers can then run down the street to a nearby discount store and purchase the toy in a box. Therefore, Playmobile limits its distribution to small specialty toy stores.

Small toy stores recognize that their exclusivity with a toy may end if the toy becomes popular, because some toy manufacturers will then sell it in discount stores. Still, manufacturers give the smaller stores an opportunity to recoup their higher costs by preventing discount stores from immediately cashing in on toys that prove to be successful because of the efforts of small stores.

APPLICATION 13-4

Was RPM Used to Overcome a Free Rider Problem or to Facilitate a Cartel?

We have considered two free rider problems in retailing and suggested how the special service and the quality certification theories may explain why manufacturers prefer a minimum price and limit the types of stores that sell their products. You have also seen how a minimum price policy can be used to shore up a weak cartel. The study discussed below tried to determine which of these two explanations appears to be more important.

Until recently, RPM had been considered a per se violation under the antitrust laws since the repeal of state fair trade laws in 1975. Pauline Ippolito reviewed public and private cases since 1975 with the goal of finding out what motivated companies to use RPM.[14] She began by investigating cases where RPM involved a minimum price. These are the cases where the special service or the product certification theory might apply. To test for the relevance of these theories, she classified products, on an admittedly subjective basis, as to complexity. She found 72 (47.1 percent) out of 133 cases involved a complex product. In addition, 2 of the simple product cases were against new entrants and 22 involved clothing and cosmetics where fashion and quality certification could be important. Consumers purchased 6 of the simple products infrequently. By combining these simple prod-

[13] Based on Joseph Pereira, "Toys 'R' Them: Mom-and-Pop Stores Put Playthings Like Thomas on Fast Track," *Wall Street Journal*, January 14, 1993.
[14] Pauline M. Ippolito, *Resale Price Maintenance*, Federal Trade Commission, April 1988.

uct cases with the complex cases, she concluded that 102 (66.7 percent) of the 153 cases could involve some form of special service or product certification. Her study suggests that the underlying motivation for the use of RPM is often to overcome a free rider problem.

13-6   FREE RIDER PROBLEMS BETWEEN MANUFACTURERS

Free rider problems can occur among manufacturers as well as among retailers. This section describes a free rider problem involving manufacturers.

In the following application, a manufacturer of premium ice cream requires a distributor to sell only the manufacturer's product and prevents the distributor from wholesaling the product of a new entrant into the industry. By restricting the distributor to only one brand, the manufacturer raises its cost of distribution. Why would a manufacturer adopt a policy that raises the per unit cost of distribution?

APPLICATION 13-5

Ben and Jerry versus Goliath

Originally, Ben and Jerry's Homemade, Inc., was a small maker of premium (and very rich) natural ice cream located in Vermont.[15] The company experienced considerable success first in Vermont and then throughout the Northeast and has become a nationwide supplier. However, Ben and Jerry's did not pioneer gourmet ice cream. Haagen-Dazs was one of the early entrants and is the industry leader. When Ben and Jerry's began to expand into other New England states, they signed on with some New England distributors who also distributed Haagen-Dazs ice cream. Haagen-Dazs did not take kindly to this turn of events and soon made it clear that the distributors had to make a choice—either Haagen-Dazs or Ben and Jerry's. Since Haagen-Dazs outsold Ben and Jerry's at the time by 10 to 1, it was an easy though distasteful decision for the distributors. Ben and Jerry's decided to fight back in its own imaginative way. Jerry went to Minneapolis, the home office of Pillsbury, the owner of Haagen-Dazs, where he was the lone picket carrying a placard reading "What's the Doughboy Afraid Of?"

At first glance this appears to be a straightforward case of Haagen-Dazs, the industry leader, placing an entry barrier before a young upstart, Ben and Jerry's. However, there is more here than meets the eye. Why was Haagen-Dazs willing to forgo the economies of scale in distribution by restricting a distributor to just its brand? If there are economies of scale from joint distribution, as there appear to be, exclusive dealing restrictions lower the profits of Haagen-Dazs by raising the costs of distribution. In more typical cases manufacturers do not insist on exclusive distribution because they realize the cost of distribution will be higher.

---

[15] Based on Sanford L. Jacobs, "Gourmet Ice Cream Company Fights for Store Freezer Space," *Wall Street Journal*, December 17, 1984.

Perhaps Haagen-Dazs was trying to establish a monopoly in premium ice cream. While possible, this does not appear plausible because other producers have entered the gourmet ice cream market. Could there be another reason for the behavior of Haagen-Dazs? Reuben Mattus, creator of Haagen-Dazs, raised an interesting point in a *Wall Street Journal* article. He recalled the problems he faced when he first tried to establish Haagen-Dazs in the marketplace: "I had to go and break into the market myself. Ben and Jerry's can put out their own trucks like I did in California in 1971."

In a sense Haagen-Dazs certified the gourmet ice cream market. It entered the industry when the market was small and when few believed there was a demand for the product. It conducted formal and informal market studies, identified neighborhoods where there might be a demand, and persuaded store managers to stock premium ice cream. Haagen-Dazs invested considerable resources to identify and develop the market. The information produced was *general*, not firm-specific. Other competitors could free-ride on this information by copying some of the location decisions of Haagen-Dazs. The routes of the Haagen-Dazs distributors and the stores served by the distributors have provided valuable information to competitors about the locations of markets for gourmet ice cream.

This interpretation puts the exclusive distribution policy of Haagen-Dazs in a different light. One of several possible interpretations is that the company hoped to circumvent the free rider problem and to establish ownership of the valuable information it had created. When firms cannot establish ownership of the information they produce, they allocate fewer resources to produce this information. Some markets will not develop or expand because of a free rider problem. Society recognizes the serious nature of the free rider problem by granting trademarks and issuing patents to protect the use of brand names and technical discoveries. This case illustrates the difficult dilemma that society faces. Should other firms be prevented from appropriating the general information that a firm creates if one consequence is either a short- or long-term monopoly?

SUMMARY

- If the position of the demand function does not depend on the number of retailers or the type of retailer, the manufacturer's profits will be higher if retailers are free to enter the industry.
- A free rider problem exists if consumers obtain valuable services without paying for them.
- A special service is a service that consumers obtain without charge and shifts the retail and wholesale demand functions to the right.
- Resale price maintenance establishes a minimum retail price and prevents retailers from free-riding on the special services provided by other retailers.
- A firm that creates general information by investing resources to certify product quality or the fashion features of a product is subject to a form of free-

riding. The quality certification theory explains why a manufacturer might use a minimum retail price and might refuse to deal with some retailers who would like to carry its product.

KEY TERMS

Free entry of retailers   **Free rider problem**
Special services   **General information**
Resale price maintenance   **Quality certification**

REVIEW QUESTIONS

1. A manufacturer that limits the number of retailers reduces the cost of distributing the product to consumers. Explain why you agree or disagree with this statement.
2. Evaluate the meaning and logic of the following statements: A major objective of our firm is to have a profitable dealer group. A dealer who signs up with us rather than a competitor will over the years earn higher profits than with another manufacturer. What's good for our dealers is good for our firm.
3. A manufacturer wants higher retail prices so that it can increase profits by raising the wholesale price. Evaluate this statement if the manufacturer is (*a*) a competitive firm and (*b*) a monopolist.
4. State the four assumptions of the special service theory.
5. A special service is one that can be obtained free of charge. This definition is clear, but it is not always obvious whether a service is or is not special or whether a special service will cause a large shift in the demand function. Indicate which of the following are special services and explain why.

   ▪ A store provides free delivery for all purchases.
   ▪ A store stocks different sizes, colors, and styles of merchandise.
   ▪ A store provides fitting rooms for customers to try on merchandise.
   ▪ A store provides a pleasant shopping environment and an informed retail sales staff.
   ▪ A store provides credit for customers who finance their purchases.

6. How would you test the special service theory? List two implications of this theory.
7. Would you expect automobile manufacturers to sell automobiles under resale price maintenance if it were legal? Explain.
8. State the three assumptions of the quality certification theory.

EXERCISES

1. Suppose some firms in an industry use RPM while others do not. For example, firms selling higher-quality products use RPM, while firms selling lower-quality products do not. Would you expect some firms to use RPM while others do not under the special services or under the cartel argument?

2. A manufacturer that has sold its product under RPM for many years discontinues the use of RPM. There are rumors that the firm stopped the practice to forestall a possible legal challenge. In an interview a company vice president says, "RPM has outlived its usefulness." How would you determine whether the firm voluntarily or involuntarily terminated RPM?

3. Your company has developed a new microcomputer and is focusing on sales to the home market. You plan to sell your computer through a network of authorized dealers. The capital requirements for establishing a dealership are relatively modest, and so a plentiful supply of qualified applicants seems assured. Field tests reveal that you will have to rely on your dealers to perform two distinct and important educational functions. First, most buyers are unfamiliar with what your computer can do, and so potential customers must learn about its special properties as well as the general role of a personal computer. Second, customers will need help in learning the mechanics of using the microcomputer to perform such functions as data base management, playing CD disks, and other new features.

   Members of your marketing staff think the problem of educating the consumer will disappear if the dealer sells the computer with a promise to supply 10 hours of free instruction time at the dealership after the consumer has purchased the machine. However, your staff is struggling with the problem of how the company can ensure that all dealers will offer the computer instruction package to customers. Some dealers might promise to and then not supply the prepurchase information, and some might promise to provide postsale instruction but then decide to save on costs by not delivering the lessons or by delivering fewer services. Everyone agrees that it will be prohibitively expensive for the company to monitor dealers individually. Moreover, they all believe that it would be beneficial in the long run to have a stable group of dealers and less dealer turnover.

   Two proposals are being considered:

   - *Proposal 1.* Select the wholesale price so that the difference between the retail and wholesale prices is large enough to cover the costs of providing educational and other dealer functions.
   - *Proposal 2.* Let the company sell under resale price maintenance (assuming that it is legal).

   Evaluate the two proposals in terms of ensuring that dealers supply pre- and postpurchase educational information.

4. Suppose there are both experienced and first-time buyers in an industry. The first-time buyers are willing to pay for dealer information services, but the experienced buyers demand fewer special services. A monopolist manufacturer sells to dealers at a uniform wholesale price and is considering two distribution policies:

   - *Policy 1.* Adopt resale price maintenance.
   - *Policy 2.* Sign up selected dealers who will sell under resale price maintenance to first-time buyers. A different group of dealers will sell to experienced buyers at a market-determined price.

a. Will first-time buyers receive the information under each policy. Explain.

b. Will the two types of dealers earn the same rate of return under each policy? Explain.

5. A cooperative association of newspaper publishers is formed to engage in the collection, assembly, and distribution of news to its members. Members of the association develop stories and quickly place them on the association's wire so that other members have access to news originating in other cities and can use the stories in their newspapers. Charter members are to be selected from newspapers in one- and multiple-newspaper cities and towns. The association faces two problems: Which newspapers should be members of the association, and what bylaws should the association adopt? A consulting firm recommends that only one newspaper from each market be included in the association. It also proposes the following bylaws:

- Members cannot supply news to nonmembers. Violators will be suspended from the association for not less than 3 months.
- Members will have veto power to block another newspaper in the same market from joining the association.

After the membership adopts the bylaws, the government sues the association for monopolizing the market for information and orders it to allow any newspaper to join.

a. What is the purpose of these bylaws?

b. Predict the economic effects of allowing all newspapers who desire to join the association.

PROBLEM SET

A Young Designer and the Free Rider Problem

A young aspiring designer of women's dresses has had little success persuading larger stores to feature her collection. She has gained recognition in the fashion industry because she has recently won several design contests. Her artistic successes attract the attention of Fashion Originators (called Fashion hereafter), a trade association whose members design, manufacture, and distribute women's fashion dresses to retail stores. The association invites her to join. She is eager to join because she knows her collection will appear in better stores.

Fashion was formed in 1987 by designers who wanted to improve their access to the retail market. Its members do market research and have earned a reputation for anticipating fashion trends. Fashion was very successful from 1989 to 1992, and there are high hopes for even greater success. Fashion has everything going for it—talented designers, rapid sales growth, and good relations with stores.

The designer becomes a member of Fashion at the end of 1992. The next two years prove disappointing to all members of the association. Sales growth slows down, and the market share of Fashion in the stores selling their products declines.

The turnaround is baffling. Some members think that their present difficulties are transitory and just due to bad forecasting of fashion trends. Others are not so sure.

Fashion commissions you to do a study and to present some recommendations. You select a random sample of retail stores that have sold Fashion dresses since 1987 and obtain the data in the accompanying table.

	1989–1992	1993–1994
Average price of Fashion dresses sold in stores that sell Fashion and the dresses of other manufacturers ($)	250	260
Average price of non-Fashion dresses sold in stores selling Fashion and other manufacturers' dresses ($)	225	210
Average dress volume per store ($1,000)	320	420
Advertising budget of Fashion ($1,000)	30	44
Fashion's market share of all dresses sold in stores selling Fashion dresses (%)	60	33
Number of fashion awards received by members of Fashion	4	12
Number of fashion awards received by other manufacturers selling dresses in stores featuring Fashion dresses	2	1
Per capita income (1982 dollars)	11,750	12,120

Use the information in the table to identify the reasons why Fashion did so poorly in 1993 and 1994. How can you explain why its market share dropped although real income, advertising, and size of market increased?

■ C H A P T E R 14

MARKET BEHAVIOR WITH ASYMMETRIC INFORMATION

In each market studied in earlier chapters, buyers and sellers had complete information about each other. Buyers knew the quality of the product before purchase, and sellers knew what types of buyers they were dealing with. Yet, as you know from your own experience as a consumer, this is not always true. Some products are complex and difficult to assess before purchase. How can you judge the ease of use of a VCR or the difficulty of learning a computer program before you've bought the product and tried it? How do you know a car mechanic or a roofer will provide the quality of service that you need? They will assure you that they do high-quality work and will charge you accordingly, but you cannot determine the quality of the job before they begin and, in some cases, even after the job is complete. Only time will tell whether your roof is watertight.

Sellers have problems in evaluating the behavior of buyers. Should a salesclerk believe a woman who buys a formal dress on Friday and returns it on Monday when she says it doesn't fit? Or has the woman worn the dress over the weekend and simply wants to avoid paying for a garment she no longer needs? If the woman has worn the dress, she has used it rent-free. Some buyers pay their bills on time, while others do not, and firms must spend extra time calling delinquent buyers to receive payment. Some buyers constantly find fault with a product, and their satisfaction requires frequent and extra service.

Asymmetric information exists when one side in a potential transaction has more information than the other side. This chapter examines the consequences of asymmetric information. Buyers and sellers behave differently than they do when both sides have complete information. Products that trade under complete information may not trade when asymmetric information exists. After describing some of the problems that result from asymmetric information, we look at the output and pricing decisions of price-taking firms in markets where sellers have more information than buyers to determine why and when firms acquire a reputation for reliability.

14-1   CONSEQUENCES OF ASYMMETRIC INFORMATION

Asymmetric information is more likely to exist in a new situation. A firm may be dealing with a customer for the first time, or an inexperienced consumer may be purchasing a complex product for the first time. Some examples of asymmetric information are the following.

Example: Health Insurance

Empire Blue Cross and Blue Shield is a nonprofit organization that provides health insurance to many New Yorkers.[1] In 1991 it dropped group coverage health insurance for several professional and trade groups, among them 700 lawyers who are members of the state bar association. By law Blue Cross must accept all members

---

[1] Milt Freudenheim, "Associations' Coverage Cut by Blue Cross," *New York Times*, June 13, 1991, C1.

of the association without requiring a health checkup when it agrees to offer the association group health insurance. Blue Cross discontinued the policies after finding that the healthy younger members of the group purchased lower-priced insurance elsewhere. Empire Blue Cross was insuring older and sicker members who did not have alternatives.

In this instance asymmetric information exists because consumers know more about their health than Blue Cross does. The fees set for the insurance contract depend on the health status of the average member of the group. However, members of the New York bar self-select into the bar association and are more likely to join the association because group rates are lower than the rates for individuals. However, individuals in poor health are more likely to join because they find the premium to be a bargain since the health of the average member of the association determines the premium and members can join without an examination. This creates a problem of adverse selection because those with fewer health problems leave the group and find lower-cost alternatives when they find their rates increasing as less healthy members join.

From the company's perspective, adverse selection occurs because the sample of individuals who sign up for health insurance does not represent a random sample of all members of the New York State bar. In this case the market presumably collapsed because rates are regulated and Blue Cross could not raise rates sufficiently to cover the cost of the insurance program.

> **Adverse selection** exists when members of a group are not a random selection of the group.

Example: Automobile Insurance

I have purchased my automobile insurance from the same company for many years but decided to change companies when the insurer replaced agents who provided service and advice with impersonal representatives. When I contacted a new company, the agent immediately asked me if I had a renewal form from my present company. I said that my renewal was not yet due. He replied that without a renewal form he would have to charge me a substantially higher rate. He suggested that I wait until a renewal notice arrived, at which time he would offer me a policy at a considerably lower rate.

How was the insurance company's pricing policy affected by asymmetric information? The company knows less about the driving ability of an individual than the individual does. It suspects that walk-ins are not a random sample of drivers but an adverse selection of the general driving public with poor driving and accident records. Every insurance company wants to avoid signing up the rejects from other insurance companies. Because the company does not have information about each candidate, it assumes the worst. The company prices insurance higher to compensate for the adverse selection of walk-in candidates that results from asymmetric information. After I provided the renewal notice from my old company, the new company had more information about me, and so the asymmetric information problem became less serious and the insurance company lowered the premium.

Example: Buying a Used Car

If you are in the market for a used car, you know that there is a huge difference between the price of a new car and its value 1 year later. An automobile may depreciate more than 30 percent in its first year, depending on the make and price class. One explanation of the large percentage decline in value is the presence of asymmetric information.

Why does asymmetric information cause a large price difference between a new and a recently new car? The automobiles entering the used market within a year of sale are not a random selection of all 1-year-old cars with the same name-plate. Buyers of used cars fear that the owners have had trouble with them and are ridding themselves of lemons. Because lemons appear on the market more quickly, buyers are wary of paying high prices for problem cars. The autos that reappear in the used market are an adverse selection of all autos of the same age. Therefore, the prices of recent-model autos are lower to reflect the presumed lower quality.

14-2 ASYMMETRIC INFORMATION AND ADVERSE SELECTION: THE LEMONS PROBLEM

To explain why markets with asymmetric information experience adverse selection, we examine one of the markets described in Section 14-1—the market for used cars.[2] Owners are willing to supply both high- and low-quality used automobiles to the market. Asymmetric information comes into play because owners know more about the quality of the cars they offer for sale than buyers do. By determining the equilibrium price and quantity in such a market, we can observe how asymmetric information causes adverse selection.

The model assumes that N individuals own automobiles of a given vintage and of a particular brand. Some of the cars have never given their owners any trouble. The engine, the transmission, the suspension system, and the brakes operate flawlessly. Let's call these cars gems and assume that gems represent a fraction, f, of all N autos. On the other hand, the owners of the remaining cars have had one problem after another. These autos are lemons.[3] Therefore, $1 - f$ is the fraction of the N autos that are lemons.

Owners of gems and of lemons each have minimum prices at which they are willing to sell their autos in the used car market. The lowest price at which owners of gems will sell their autos is S_g, while owners of lemons will sell their autos at a minimum price of S_l, where $S_l < S_g$. On the demand side of the market buyers are willing to pay B_g for a known gem and B_l for a known lemon, where $B_l < B_g$. Assume that $B_g > S_g$ and $B_l > S_l$ so that both markets can exist.

---

[2] The material in this section draws on the excellent chapter on asymmetric information in David M. Kreps, *A Course in Microeconomic Theory*, Princeton University Press, 1990, chap. 17. An interested reader who wants to delve deeper into the problems raised by asymmetric information should consult this source.

[3] Ackerlof, "The Market for 'Lemons': Quality Uncertainty and the Market Mechanism," *Quarterly Journal of Economics*, vol. LXXXIV, August 1970, pp. 488–500.

Equilibrium Prices and Quantities with Complete Information

The first step in the analysis is to find the equilibrium price and quantity that prevail when the participants in the market have complete information. This will permit a comparison of the effects of asymmetric information later when we find the equilibrium prices and quantities when sellers know more than buyers.

To simplify the analysis, assume that the demand functions for gems and for lemons are perfectly elastic. This means that the demand function for gems is horizontal at a price of B_g for gems and B_l for lemons. These are prices that consumers are willing to pay for each type of car if they know the quality.

Figure 14-1*a* and *b* shows the separate demand and supply functions when buyers have complete information about the quality of an automobile. Because a supplier of a lemon cannot pass it off as a gem, separate markets exist for lemons and for gems. The demand function is horizontal at the buyer's bid price of B_l for lemons in Figure 14-1*a* and is horizontal at the buyer's bid price of B_g for gems in Figure 14-1*b*. The quantity of lemons supplied is $(1 - f)N$ as long as the price of

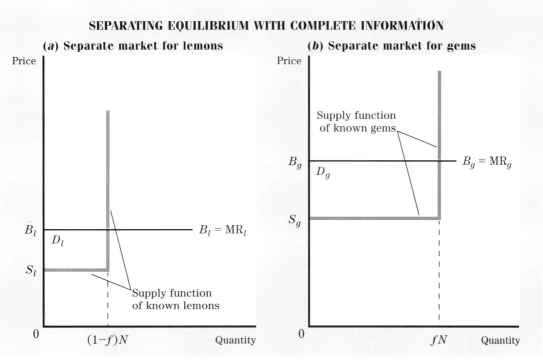

SEPARATING EQUILIBRIUM WITH COMPLETE INFORMATION

(a) Separate market for lemons

(b) Separate market for gems

Figure 14-1   When the quality of a used automobile can be assessed prior to purchase, two markets emerge, one market for high-quality automobiles (gems) and a second market for low-quality automobiles (lemons). Some buyers purchase lemons and pay B_l for the lower-quality automobile. Other buyers purchase gems at a higher price of B_g. With complete information the used car market separates into two markets.

a lemon equals or exceeds S_l. In the market for gems the quantity supplied is fN if the price equals or exceeds S_g. The equilibrium prices are B_g for gems and B_l for lemons, and the market for gems is separate from the market for lemons.

Equilibrium Price and Quantity with Asymmetric Information

Now let's see how the behavior of buyers and sellers changes when buyers cannot distinguish gems from lemons. Because they cannot tell the difference at the time of purchase, they treat all cars alike and all cars sell for a single price.

No consumer is willing to pay B_g for an auto selected at random because the probability that it will turn out to be a lemon is $1 - f$. This analysis assumes that consumers are willing to pay a weighted average price for a car picked at random from those offered by owners. The bid price, P_b, that a consumer is willing to pay for a car picked at random is

$$P_b = \frac{fB_gN + (1 - f)B_lN}{N} \qquad \text{(Bid Price)} \qquad \text{(14-1)}$$

Canceling the N's yields

$$P_b = fB_g + (1 - f)B_l$$

P_b is a weighted average price, and it depends on the prices that consumers are willing to pay for a known gem and a known lemon and the fraction f of gems in the population of autos. For example, if consumers estimate that gems make up 90 percent of the autos so $f = 0.9$, $B_g = \$12{,}000$ for a known gem, and $B_l = \$6{,}000$ for a known lemon, they will bid only $\$11{,}400$ for an auto picked at random, and this will be the equilibrium price when there is asymmetric information. Figure 14-2 shows the horizontal demand function at P_b for two cases—when $f = 0.9$ and when $f = 0.1$. When $f = 0.9$, P_b is closer to B_g, and when $f = 0.1$, P_b is closer to B_l.

What does the supply function of autos look like when asymmetric information exists? If the market price is less than S_l, no owner is willing to supply a used automobile to the market. Lemon owners are willing to supply $(1 - f)N$ autos if the price is less than S_g but equal to or greater than S_l. If the price equals or exceeds S_g, owners of gems also supply autos to the market. Figure 14-3 shows that the "hybrid" supply function of autos is S_labcS'. This is a hybrid supply function because the average quality of the autos supplied increases when the price equals or exceeds S_g since gems are supplied. To find the equilibrium price, assume that consumers can estimate from experience the fraction of gems that are usually in the market. They estimate the fraction, f, of all autos that are gems, although they cannot tell whether any particular automobile is a gem or a lemon.

To describe the industry equilibrium completely, we must distinguish between two cases: (1) where both lemons and gems trade and (2) where just lemons trade. The fraction of gems in the population of autos determines which equilibrium exists. If this fraction is relatively high, P_b will exceed S_g, and so owners of gems are willing to supply gems to the market, as of course are owners of lemons. On

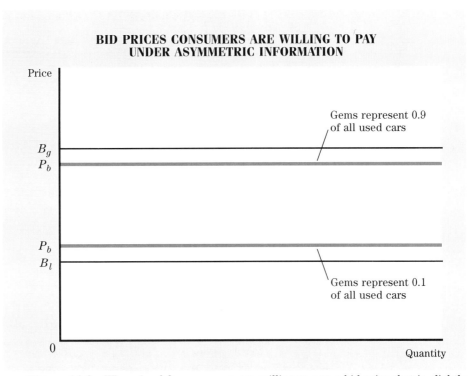

**BID PRICES CONSUMERS ARE WILLING TO PAY
UNDER ASYMMETRIC INFORMATION**

Figure 14-2   When $f = 0.9$, consumers are willing to pay a bid price that is slightly less than B_g, the price that they are willing to pay for a known gem. When $f = 0.1$, consumers are willing to pay slightly more than B_l, the price they would pay for a known lemon.

the other hand, if the fraction of gems is lower, then the P_b that consumers are willing to pay will be less than S_g and owners of gems will not supply any cars to the market. Only lemons will appear in the used car market.

In between these extremes, there is a critical value of f, say f^*, at which owners of gems are just willing to supply gems to the market. If the actual fraction of gems equals or is greater than f^*, then owners will supply both types of autos. If f is less than f^*, owners will supply lemons to the market, but the owners of gems will not trade their autos and the used car market will be partially curtailed. We want to find f^* in order to determine when owners will supply both types of cars to the market and when only owners of lemons will supply autos.

Owners are just willing to supply gems to the market if

$$S_g = P_b$$

Substituting the expression for P_b from equation 14-1 gives

$$S_g = f(B_g) + (1 - f)B_l$$

or $$\quad\quad = f(B_g - B_l) + B_l \quad\quad \text{(Condition for Gems to Be Supplied)} \quad\quad \textbf{(14-2)}$$

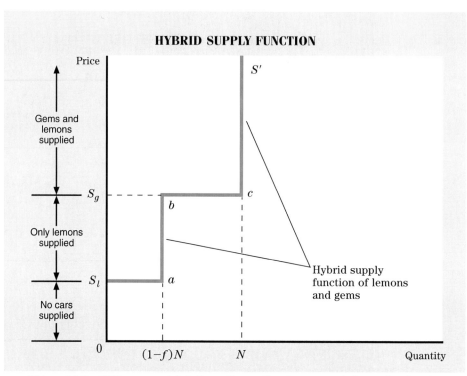

HYBRID SUPPLY FUNCTION

Figure 14-3   With asymmetric information, sellers have more information than buyers. Buyers cannot distinguish between high- and low-quality automobiles. If the price is less than S_g but equal to or greater than S_l, the quantity supplied equals $(1 - f)N$, the supply of lemons. If the price equals or exceeds S_g, all N automobiles are supplied. The total quantity supplied is a mixture of lemons and gems. The supply function is $S_l abcS'$.

To determine f^*, solve equation 14-2 for f by subtracting B_l from both sides of the equation and then dividing both sides of the equality by $B_g - B_l$ to obtain[4]

$$f^* = \frac{S_g - B_l}{B_g - B_l} \tag{14-3}$$

Equation 14-3 says that f^* depends on the maximum buying prices for gems and lemons and the minimum price at which owners are willing to supply gems. A numerical example will show you how to calculate f^*. If the offer price for a gem is \$10,000 (S_g), the bid price for a gem is \$12,000 (B_g), and the bid price for a lemon is \$6,000 (B_l), gems must equal 66.7 percent of used automobiles. So the price that consumers are willing to pay for a randomly selected car is then \$10,000, the price that owners of gems must receive to part with them. If gems make up *less* than

---

[4] Starting with $S_g = f(B_g - B_l) + B_l$, subtract B_l from both sides of the equation to obtain $S_g - B_l = f(B_g - B_l)$. Then, divide both sides by $B_g - B_l$ to get equation 14-3.

MARKET EQUILIBRIA WITH ASYMMETRIC INFORMATION

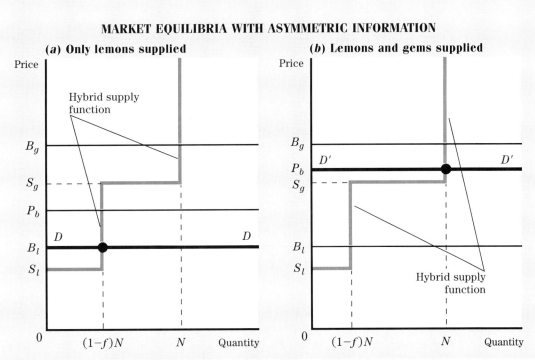

Figure 14-4   The demand function is *DD* in (*a*) where P_b is less than S_g. Only owners of lemons supply used cars to the market. When the share of gems is sufficiently high so that P_b is greater than S_g, the demand function is $D'D'$ in (*b*) and owners of gems and lemons supply autos to the market. Both types of autos sell at the higher value for P_b. One equilibrium has only lemons selling in the market, and the second equilibrium has lemons pooled with gems. The owners of lemons benefit, while the owners of gems are harmed.

two-thirds of the market, they will not appear in the used car market because consumers are unwilling to pay $10,000 for a used car. The used car market is therefore full of lemons. Because of asymmetric information, there is adverse selection because autos that trade in the market do not represent a random selection of all used cars but are only lemons.

> Adverse selection of used cars occurs when the price that consumers are willing to pay is less than the price at which owners are willing to supply gems. The traded autos are not a random selection of all used cars.

Figure 14-4 shows two possible equilibria in the market. In Figure 14-4*a* the fraction of gems is less than the critical fraction, and so $f < f^*$ and $P_b < S_g$. Consumers realize that only owners of lemons are willing to supply used cars to the market and are only willing to pay B_l. The horizontal demand function at the price B_l intersects the hybrid supply function at the quantity $(1-f)N$. The equilib-

Table 14-1 PRICE AND QUANTITY TRADED FOR TWO EQUILIBRIA

FRACTION OF GEMS	BID PRICE RELATIVE TO S_g	MARKET PRICE	QUANTITY SOLD	TYPE OF AUTOS TRADED
$f \geq f^*$	$P_b \geq S_g$	P_b	N	Gems and lemons
$f < f^*$	$P_b < S_g$	B_l	$(1 - f)N$	Lemons

rium price for a used car is B_l, and there is adverse selection because only lemons trade. However, notice that no one is fooled in this equilibrium. Buyers expect and find only lemons, and so they are only willing to pay the price of a lemon. This equilibrium occurs when there are too many lemons in the population of autos.

In Figure 14-4b f is greater than f^*, and so $P_b \geq S_g$. The share of gems in the population of used cars is high enough so that the price that consumers are willing to pay is above the price that owners of gems must receive to supply them. The demand function is horizontal at a price of P_b. Both types of autos trade in the used car market. Of those traded, fN have satisfied new owners, but disappointment is the rule for the unlucky buyers of the remaining cars. Consumers know the probability of buying a lemon is $1 - f$, and that is why they are only willing to pay P_b, not B_g, for a used auto. In this equilibrium both gems and lemons trade in the market, and so there is no adverse selection in the autos offered. Yet, this equilibrium is different from the equilibrium with complete information, where both gems and lemons trade at different prices, because both gems and lemons sell at the same price and there is a pooling equilibrium. Because of the asymmetric information in the market, differentiation of lemons from gems proves impossible. Table 14-1 summarizes the two equilibria.

In summary, we find that markets function more imperfectly when information is asymmetric. Sometimes the problem is so severe that gems do not appear and the supply of used autos does not represent a random selection of all used autos. Some transactions that would occur when both sides have complete information do not take place under asymmetric information. Even when both qualities trade, they trade at one equilibrium price with asymmetric information and at two when information is complete. More advanced analyses show situations where a market for used automobiles does not exist.

Measuring the Loss to Gem Owners

When $f < f^*$, owners do not supply gems to the market although the price that buyers would gladly pay for a known gem, B_g, is greater than the offering price of S_g. Asymmetric information prevents a potentially profitable transaction from occurring. If $f \geq f^*$, the owner of a gem can sell the auto, but only for P_b, not B_g.

Because consumers cannot distinguish a gem from a lemon, the owner of a gem loses $B_g - P_b$, or

$$\text{Loss} = B_g - P_b$$
$$= B_g - [fB_g + (1 - f)B_l]$$
$$= (1 - f)B_g - (1 - f)B_l$$
$$= (1 - f)(B_g - B_l) \qquad \text{(Loss Due to Asymmetric Information)} \qquad \textbf{(14-4)}$$

where $f \geq f^*$. Returning to our numerical example, an owner of a gem loses $0.333 \times \$6,000 = \$2,000$ if $f = 0.667$, and $\$1,200$ if $f = 0.80$. The greater the difference between the buyer's valuation of a gem and a lemon, and the smaller the number of gems in the population of autos, the larger the loss suffered by an owner of a gem.

Overcoming Asymmetric Information

There is an incentive for owners of gems to separate their autos from lemons, and several market institutions have developed to convey product information to potential customers. Three such mechanisms are warranties, testing, and reputation. These market institutions arise to deal with the consequences of asymmetric information, but they are expensive to create and do not always eliminate the problem completely.

    1. Warranties The owner of a gem can distinguish her gem from a lemon by offering a warranty. Suppose she offers to pay the buyer for repair expenses during the first year and the agreement can be enforced. The owner of a gem has a greater incentive to do this than the owner of a lemon does. Suppose the repair cost of a true gem is zero, while the buyer of a lemon has repair costs of $2,500 in the first year. If an expenditure of $2,500 transforms a lemon into a gem, buyers would be indifferent between purchasing a gem or a lemon if the difference between B_g and B_l is $2,500. Now an owner of a gem is perfectly willing to offer a warranty to the buyer and sells the auto for B_g. The owner of a lemon is in a bind. He must either sell his auto for B_g and issue a warranty or sell it for $B_g - \$2,500$ with no warranty. If he refuses to do either, the buyer infers that the auto is a lemon. In either event, the market separates lemons from gems. Owners of gems sell them for B_g, and owners of lemons sell them for B_l.

    A limitation of warranties is the cost of enforcement. What guarantees that the seller will comply with the terms of the warranty? Also, the coverage of the warranty must be clear because sometimes it is difficult to verify the cause of the defect. Is it due to the initial condition of the automobile or is it due to poor maintenance by the new owner? Warranties may solve one problem but create others. The buyer has less incentive to exercise care and to maintain the automobile if the warranty is all-inclusive. Economists call the reduced incentive to exercise care the moral hazard problem. Moral hazard deals with behavior after a contract has been entered into.

2. Testing   In some markets it is possible to pretest the product. A repair facility can pretest an auto and, perhaps, issue a guarantee. Usually, the cost of checking a car does not increase proportionally with its value. The testing cost is more like a lump sum. Tests of more expensive cars are therefore more likely, and so the lemon problem is likely to be more serious for cheaper than for expensive used automobiles.

3. Reputation   The lemons problem is usually more severe when it involves a one-shot transaction between a buyer and a seller with no possibility of a repeat sale. With repeated transactions, the seller has less incentive to take advantage of the buyer because the buyer is less likely to return. In these situations you would expect a market institution to evolve that alleviates the problem, and one such institution is the reputation of the seller. An automobile dealer has greater expertise in evaluating automobiles than an individual buyer and wants to establish a reputation for fair dealing to attract repeat business.

Identifying Markets for Lemons

You might expect asymmetric information to be a more serious problem in a new market where buyers have little information to go on. We now investigate two situations where asymmetric information could be a potential problem.

APPLICATION 14-1

The Free Agency Market in Professional Baseball

The first example of a new market is the development of the free agency market in professional baseball which Ken Lehn studied.[5] With the arrival of free agency in 1976 a baseball player with 6 years of service could sign a new contract (usually a multiple-year contract) with his current team or become a free agent and sign with another team. Before free agency, the player could only negotiate with his current team. Free agency was a revolutionary change and presented a new challenge to team owners.

The management of a professional baseball team presumbly knows more about the players on its team than about players on other teams. It has more information about the players' motivation, desire to win, conditioning, willingness to play with injuries, and so on. The existing management may also know more about how a particular player will respond to a lucrative long-term contract. If current owners know more about their own players, management is less likely to err when assessing the value of a player to the team.

Lehn assumed that after free agency arrived, current owners knew more about their players than other owners did, and so there was asymmetric information in the market for players. He reasoned that existing management would pay higher

[5] Kenneth Lehn, "Information Asymmetries in Baseball's Free Agent Market," *Economic Inquiry*, vol. XXII, January 1984, pp. 37–44.

Table 14-2   NUMBER OF DAYS ON DISABLED LIST

PLAYER STATUS	BEFORE FREE AGENCY	AFTER FREE AGENCY	PERCENTAGE CHANGE
Pitchers (58 in sample):			
Remained with team	3.66	9.57	167
Became free agent	5.12	28.07	448
Nonpitchers (97 in sample):			
Remained with team	5.30	9.74	84
Became free agent	4.31	9.83	128

compensation to retain players who would be less likely to shirk after signing a long-term contract. Lehn used the number of days a player was on the disabled list per season before and after the arrival of free agency as a measure of player tendency to shirk—a higher number indicates a player is more likely to complain about injuries and not play.

Table 14-2 shows the number of days on the disabled list for players who did not become free agents and remained with their original team and those who became free agents and signed with other teams. Lehn considered pitchers separately from nonpitchers.

Lehn found that pitchers who remained with their teams, although eligible for free agency, had been on the disabled list for 3.66 days per season before the arrival of free agency. Pitchers who became free agents subsequently had missed 5.12 days per season before free agency. On the other hand, after free agency, pitchers who remained with their teams were on the disabled list 9.57 days per season, a 167 percent increase. However, pitchers who became free agents and signed with other teams were on the disabled list an average of 28.07 days per season, a 448 percent increase! These results suggest that current owners were better able to filter out those players who would take it easy after signing a longer-term contract. Those players signed with other less informed teams and subsequently complained about sore arms and other ailments so that they were on the disabled list for relatively more days under free agency.

Table 14-2 shows that pitchers are primarily responsible for the difference between players who remained with their teams and players who became free agents. The difference is smaller for nonpitchers. This suggests that asymmetric information is a more serious problem for a new owner when evaluating pitchers than when evaluating players of other positions.

This example provides evidence of asymmetric information in the free agency market.

Table 14-3   PROPORTION OF TRUCKS REQUIRING MAJOR ENGINE MAINTENANCE

YEAR	PURCHASED NEW	PURCHASED USED
1976	0.08	0.05
1975	0.10	0.11
1974	0.11	0.13
1973	0.15	0.15
1972	0.13	0.15

APPLICATION 14-2

The Used Pickup Truck Market

The second application focuses on the used pickup truck market. Eric Bond tried to determine whether asymmetric information is a serious problem in the market for used pickup trucks by examining the repair history of these vehicles.[6] Bond reasoned that if there is asymmetric information in the market, pickup trucks with higher maintenance expenditures would be overrepresented in the used truck market. Used trucks purchased from their original owners should have higher average maintenance expenditures per truck before being sold in the used market than a random sample of trucks of the same age, mileage, and so on, that were kept by their original owners. Bond looked at major maintenance expenditures for the engine, transmission, brakes, and rear axle during the 12 months before the sale of the truck.

Table 14-3 shows the proportion of pickup trucks that required major engine maintenance in the past 12 months classified by whether they were purchased new or used by the current owner.

Bond assumed that adverse selection occurs because of asymmetric information in the market. Therefore, only lemons trade, and buyers of used pickup trucks incur maintenance expenditures after purchases. If so, trucks purchased used should have higher annual maintenance expenditures than trucks kept by their original owners. However, Bond did not find significant differences in repair expenditures between the two groups of trucks. The results of this study suggest that adverse selection is not a serious problem in this market, perhaps because so few lemons are produced.

[6] Eric Bond, "A Direct Test of the 'Lemons' Model: The Market for Used Pickup Trucks," *American Economic Review*, vol. 72, September 1982, pp. 836–840.

14-3 ASYMMETRIC INFORMATION AND POTENTIAL CHEATING BY COMPETITIVE FIRMS

When sellers know more about their products than buyers, what prevents them from misrepresenting the product's quality? That is, can an owner of a lemon unload it as a gem? Under what conditions can a seller get away with this practice? The answer depends on what information the consumer has and what the seller can do to assure the buyer that she sells only gems. This section extends the analysis of the lemons problem and determines when honesty is the most profitable policy for a competitive firm.

An Overview of the Model

What prevents a competitive firm from deliberately misrepresenting the product that it is selling? Your immediate response might be that the seller is honest if he expects the buyer to return, that is, when the probability of a repeat sale is high. An attorney would probably agree with this answer but would be quick to point out that a buyer's right to obtain legal redress is what forces a supplier to act honestly. She would say that the threat of legal penalties is what ultimately guarantees honest behavior by profit-motivated competitive firms.

Is it the loss of future sales or the threat of legal penalties that prevents cheating by the seller? Ben Klein and Keith Leffler have developed a model of potential cheating by firms in a competitive industry and claim that neither answer is completely correct.[7] Surprisingly, they believe that neither the opportunity for repeat sales nor the presence of legal penalties is necessary to guarantee that a competitive firm will be a reputable seller. Klein and Leffler go on to argue that competitive firms can have the proper incentive to develop a reputation for living up to their obligations even in the absence of legal penalties.

Before proceeding to the details of their model, let's look at an overview of the cheating problem in a competitive industry and the authors' proposed resolution. Their analysis involves a product whose quality cannot be assessed by consumers prior to purchase. If the product is supplied by firms in a competitive industry, no firm earns profits in the long run. When faced with the choice between not earning profits in the long run by promising and delivering a high-quality product year in and year out and earning profits for a single year by promising a high-quality product but delivering a low-quality product, a profit-maximizing firm prefers to earn the one-time profits even if it must exit the industry after a year because it acquires such a bad reputation. Nonetheless, profits will be higher if it promises a high-quality product and does not deliver than if it supplies a high-quality product and earns no profits.

However, consumers are not stupid, and they will recognize that they cannot rely on the promises of sellers when asymmetric information exists. They will refuse to purchase products from competitive firms when they cannot assess qual-

---

[7] Ben Klein and Keith Leffler, "The Role of Market Forces in Assuring Contractual Performance," *Journal of Political Economy*, vol. 89, August 1981, pp. 615–641.

ity before purchase. If competitive firms are to produce high-quality products, they must have an incentive to pass up one-time profits in favor of future profits. A competitive firm is less likely to cheat consumers today if it can earn profits in the future. It is the possible loss of future profits that discourages firms from cheating consumers today.

To earn profits, a firm must receive a price premium. Since this is a competitive industry with free entry, profits cannot persist in the long run. The interesting twist of the Klein-Leffler model involves how profits are competed away. Firms compete for consumers by making specific investments in ways that not only eliminate profits but also make them hostages to the industry. Companies that make these investments are signaling to consumers that it is not profitable for them to cheat consumers and take a one-time profit because the firm will suffer losses on investments that are specific to the company. By making itself a hostage to the industry, a competitive firm assures uninformed consumers that cheating is not the most profitable policy.

Now that you are familiar with a general outline of the Klein-Leffler model, let's consider its assumptions.

1. The total cost of production, C, depends on the quantity produced, X, and the quality, q, of the output; $C = C(X, q)$. We omit the subscript L since all the cost functions in this chapter are the firm's long-run cost functions. Keep in mind that X stands for units of output and q measures the quality of the product. For a given X, the cost of production rises with increases in the quality of the product. Initially, we assume that there is a ready market for the assets of the firm, and so the company does not suffer losses if it sells these assets.

2. Each competitive seller supplies a product whose quality cannot be assessed before purchase (except for the minimum-quality product described below) and promises to supply a high-quality product at a price of $P(q_h)$, where P is the price and q_h is the promised high-quality product. (An example of product quality is durability.) The seller charges a higher price for a higher-quality product.

3. Courts do not penalize firms that supply a lower-than-promised quality.

4. A seller can deceive existing customers for only one period before being detected. The tarnished reputation of such a seller precludes future sales to all current and future customers.

5. There is a low-quality product, q_{min}, that consumers can assess accurately before purchase.

6. Consumers know the minimum per unit cost of producing each level of quality. For example, they know that an electric saw with a lifetime of 2 years with normal use costs $140 to produce, whereas one that lasts 4 years costs $300. Although all consumers have this information, they cannot tell whether the product purchased is a low- or a high-quality item.

Given these assumptions, will each competitive firm deliver the promised high-quality product to customers or promise to deliver a high-quality product, receive payment for a high-quality product, but deliver a minimum-quality product that costs less to produce?

Promising and Delivering a High- or a Minimum-Quality Product

How will a competitive firm fare when it promises and delivers a high-quality product. Figure 14-5 shows the firm's long-run average cost function, $AC(X, q_h)$, and marginal cost function, $MC(X, q_h)$ if it produces the high-quality product. If the firm decides to produce the minimum-quality product, then the long-run average and marginal cost functions are $AC(X, q_{min})$ and $MC(X, q_{min})$, respectively. Figure

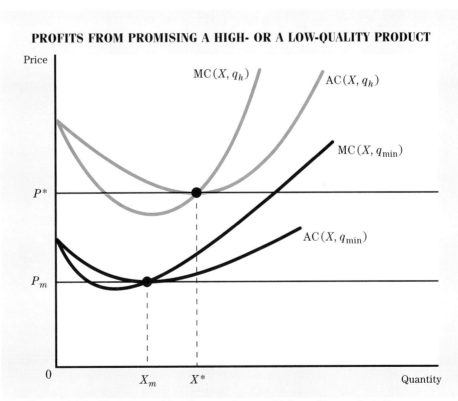

PROFITS FROM PROMISING A HIGH- OR A LOW-QUALITY PRODUCT

Figure 14-5 If a competitive firm produces a high-quality product, its average and marginal cost functions are $AC(X,q_h)$ and $MC(X,q_h)$, respectively. If the firm produces a minimum-quality product, the average and marginal cost functions are $AC(X, q_{min})$ and $MC(X, q_{min})$, respectively. At each quantity the average cost of producing the higher quality is higher.

14-5 shows that the average cost of producing the high-quality product exceeds the average cost of producing the low-quality product at each quantity.

If there is free entry into the industry and the firm delivers q_h, the long-run equilibrium price is P^* and the firm produces X^* units. Because of free entry, the firm does not earn profits in long-run industry equilibrium. Since it delivers the promised quality, however, satisfied customers give it their repeat business.

> A competitive firm that promises and delivers a high-quality product receives repeat business but does not earn profits.

If the firm promises and delivers q_{min}, the long-run equilibrium price is P_m with free entry and the firm produces X_m units. Again, consumers expect and receive the minimum-quality product. A competitive firm that supplies the minimum-quality product receives the repeat business of consumers but does not earn profits in long-run industry equilibrium.

Promising High Quality but Delivering Low Quality

Suppose a competitive firm promises a high-quality product but delivers a minimum-quality product. The cheating firm receives a per unit price of P^* because customers expect it will deliver a high-quality product. Figure 14-6 shows that the firm maximizes profits by producing X^{**} units where P^* equals the marginal cost of producing a minimum-quality product.

If the firm delivers a minimum-quality product, it will earn profits but they will last for only 1 year because consumers know the firm has taken advantage of them and they will no longer patronize it. The company's annual profit is equal to the sum of areas C and D in Figure 14-6. Area C represents the profits from the first X_m units produced and is $(P^* - P_m)X_m$. And P_m is equal to the minimum long-run average cost of producing X_m units of a minimum-quality product. So, the difference between P^* and P_m equals the profit per unit from X_m units. In other words, area C represents the profit per unit times X_m units. Area D is the area between the P^* price line and the marginal cost function between X_m and X^{**} units and represents the additional profit the firm earns by increasing production from $X = X_m$ to $X = X^{**}$. The area under the price line of P^* between X_m and X^{**} is equal to the increase in total revenue resulting from the increase in the quantity sold, and the area under the marginal cost function measures the additional cost of increasing production from X_m to X^{**}.

> A competitive firm that promises a high-quality product but delivers a low-quality product does not receive repeat customers but earns profits for one period.

To illustrate the relationships in Figure 14-6, suppose $P^* = \$10$, $P_m = \$5$, $X_m = 10$, and $X^{**} = 13$. The profits on the first 10 units produced is $(\$10 - \$5)$ times 10 units, or \$50. If the marginal cost of producing the eleventh unit is \$8, the additional profit earned by producing and selling this unit is $\$10 - \$8 = \$2$. If the

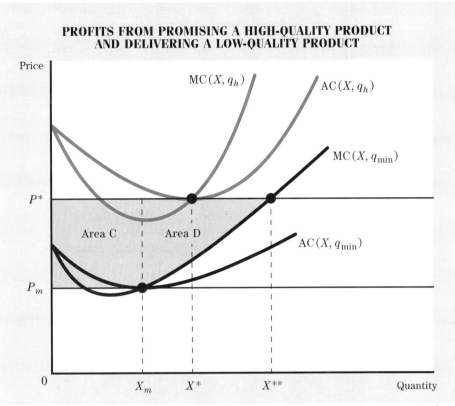

**PROFITS FROM PROMISING A HIGH-QUALITY PRODUCT
AND DELIVERING A LOW-QUALITY PRODUCT**

Figure 14-6   By promising to supply high quality, the firm receives a price of P^* for each unit. If the firm delivers low quality, the firm produces X^{**} units. The total profits from promising high quality while delivering low quality is equal to the sum of areas C and D.

marginal cost of producing the twelfth unit is $9, the additional profit from selling this unit is $1. By proceeding in this manner and adding the difference between price and marginal cost for all units between the tenth and thirteenth, the increase in total profit from increasing production from 10 to 13 units can be measured.

To summarize, a competitive firm that promises to deliver a high-quality product but delivers a low-quality product will earn annual profits equal to the sum of areas C and D before being detected.

The profits last for only 1 year because consumers refuse to purchase the firm's product again. What are these profits worth today? To answer this question, we must find the present value of this profit stream. The present value of *any* profit stream is an amount which if received immediately would leave the firm indifferent between receiving this amount or receiving the profit stream. The appendix at the end of this chapter shows how to derive the present value of the sum of areas C and D. The present value PV_1 of the profits earned at the end of 1 year (followed by a stream of zero profits) is equal to total profits divided by $1 + i$, where i is the discount rate (the rate the firm can earn on its investment). If the discount rate is 10 percent and annual profits are \$5,000, then the present value of next year's profits is \$5,000/1.10 = \$4,545.45. This means that a firm that receives \$4,545.45 immediately could invest it for a year at 10 percent interest and would have \$5,000 at the end of the year. Therefore, the firm would be indifferent between receiving \$4,545.45, the present value of \$5,000, immediately or receiving \$5,000 a year later.

Therefore, the present value of annual profits that result from promising a high-quality product but delivering a low-quality product is

$$PV_1 = \frac{1}{1 + i} \, (C + D)$$

$$= \frac{1}{1 + i} \left\{ (P^* - P_m)X_m + \sum_{X=X_m}^{X=X^{**}} [P^* - MC(X, q_{min})] \right\} \qquad \text{(14-5)}$$

The first term in brackets, $(P^* - P_m)X_m$, is the profits earned by the firm from the first X_m units produced since P_m is equal to the long-run average cost of producing X_m units of a minimum-quality product. The second term in the brackets represents the additional profits the firm earns from increasing output from X_m to X^{**} units. Dividing the one-period profit by $1/(1 + i)$ brings those profits to the present.

The key point of this analysis is that the present value of profits based on a cheating strategy is higher than the present value of profits based on a strategy of delivering the promised quality. Assuming firms make decisions to maximize present value, a competitive firm will promise but not deliver a minimum-quality product. However, consumers will either anticipate this behavior or will learn from experience that these firms take advantage of them when they are unable to assess quality before purchase. They will refuse to purchase from vendors promising to deliver a high-quality product and purchase only the minimum-quality version of the product so they can evaluate the quality before purchase. The theory suggests that higher-quality products will not appear in the market. In the presence of asymmetric information the range of qualities that will be produced by competitive firms shrinks drastically to only the minimum quality.

Actual Quality Produced in Competitive Markets

If the analysis is correct, how do we reconcile the prediction of the model—that competitive firms supply only minimum-quality goods to the market—with observations that firms do produce a range of goods? The model can be extended to show what it takes to induce a competitive firm to supply a high-quality good.

You might think that the extension merely requires the introduction of warranties or other types of guarantees. Would warranties solve the quality problem? Not really. Here again, the same question arises: Why should the buyer believe that the seller will fulfill the terms of the warranty? If I receive a guarantee from my roofer that my roof will be watertight for 5 years, what assurance do I have that the roofer will still be in business in 5 years? Moreover, the roofer may claim that someone tampered with the roof or that a leak is due to a structural defect. As noted earlier in this chapter, warranties will not always solve the problem of deception in situations where legal sanctions are too expensive.

14-4 HOW DOES A COMPETITIVE INDUSTRY SUPPLY A HIGH-QUALITY PRODUCT?

For a competitive firm to supply a high-quality product, it must expect to earn profits in the future, and so it does not have an incentive to grab short-run profits and then leave the industry. The firms in a competitive industry must receive a price premium so that there are long-run profits. Let's determine what the price premium must be if the firm acts honestly.

Delivering a High-Quality Product with a Price Premium

If a competitive firm receives a price $P' > P^*$, it earns profits, and these profits are an incentive for it to supply a high-quality product. If high-quality products are delivered, consumers become repeat customers and the firm continues to earn profits. If the price is P' in Figure 14-7, a competitive firm that delivers high quality maximizes profits by producing X' units where P' is equal to the marginal cost of supplying a high-quality product. The firm earns profits equal to area A when it receives a price premium of $P' - P^*$. Area A is the sum of two areas, just as the sum of areas C and D represents the total profits of a cheating firm. One part of area A is $(P' - P^*)X^*$ (not shown separately), the profits from sales when the firm produces X^* units. P' is price and P^* is equal to the minimum long-run average cost of producing X^* units. The second part of area A is between the price line, P', and the marginal cost function, $\text{MC}(X, q_h)$, from X^* units to X' units and is equal to the increase in profits gained from raising output from X^* units to X' units. Area A is the sum of these two areas and measures the firm's annual profits when a competitive firm delivers a high-quality product. Because the firm lives up to its promises, satisfied customers become repeat customers.

> A price premium gives a firm a greater incentive to forgo short-term profits in favor of future profits.

Therefore, we conclude that a competitive firm receives annual profits equal to area A indefinitely. What is this profit stream worth today? To answer this question, we determine the present value of a profit stream of A dollars per year. The appendix at the end of this chapter shows that the present value of an indefinite profit stream equal to area A is area A/i, where i is the discount rate. If the discount rate is 10 percent and annual profits are \$5,000, then the present value of future profits is \$5,000/0.10 = \$50,000. This means that a firm is indifferent between receiving \$50,000 immediately or \$5,000 annually for the indefinite future.

Given demand and cost conditions, PV_2 is the present value of this infinite annual stream of profits when the price is P':

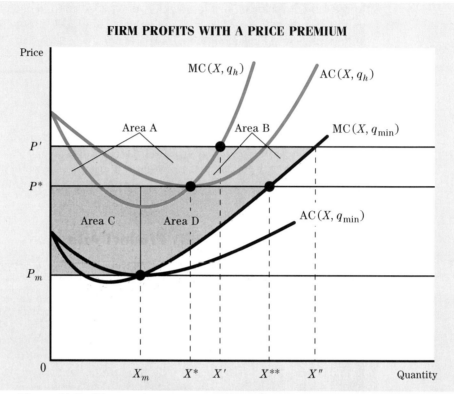

Figure 14-7   When a price premium of $P' - P^*$ exists, a firm that delivers high quality earns profits equal to area A indefinitely. A firm that promises high quality but delivers low quality earns profits equal to the sum of areas A, B, C, and D but only for a single period.

$$\text{PV}_2 = \frac{1}{i}\,A$$

$$= \frac{1}{i}\left\{(P' - P^*)X^* + \sum_{X=X^*}^{X=X'}[P' - \text{MC}(X, q_h)]\right\} \tag{14-6}$$

It is this prospect of future profits that creates the incentive for the firm to deliver the higher-quality product so that consumers return. If the company delivers a low-quality item after promising a high-quality product, customers do not return and the firm loses future sales and the future stream of annual profits.

The Incentive to Cheat

However, a premium price of P' also increases the profits gained using the cheating strategy. The annual profit obtained by cheating looks more inviting as well. When the price is P', a cheating firm maximizes profits by producing X'' units, as shown in Figure 14-7 where P' is equal to the marginal cost of supplying a minimum-quality model. The total profits of the cheater now equal the sum of areas A, B, C, and D. Since the sum of areas C and D are equal to the cheater's profits when the price is P^*, profits increase by the sum of areas A and B when the price rises from P^* to P'. A premium price raises the present value of a cheater's profits as well.

Because the firm earns these profits for only 1 year, their present value is the sum of areas A, B, C, and D multiplied by $1/(1 + i)$. The present value of profits when high quality is promised and low quality is delivered is

$$\text{PV}_3 = \frac{A + B + C + D}{1 + i}$$

$$= \frac{1}{1 + i} \left\{ (P' - P_m)X_m + \sum_{X = X_m}^{X = X''} [P' - \text{MC}(X, q_{\min})] \right\} \qquad \textbf{(14-7)}$$

Cheating versus Honesty

The firm must choose between these two strategies. With the first option it delivers a high-quality product and earns profits equal to area A as long as it does not violate the trust of consumers. The second option is the "grab-and-run" strategy. The company promises a high-quality product but supplies a low-quality product and receives a 1-year profit equal to the sum of areas A, B, C, and D. The annual profit obtained by cheating is larger than the annual profit gained from acting honestly, but it lasts only 1 year.

When will a competitive firm adopt a strategy of delivering a high-quality product? Assuming the firm selects the policy that maximizes the present value of profits, it will supply a high-quality product when the price is P' if $\text{PV}_2 \geq \text{PV}_3$. Substituting the two expressions for the present values into this inequality yields

$$\text{PV}_2 \geq \text{PV}_3$$

$$\frac{A}{i} \geq \frac{A + B + C + D}{1 + i} \qquad \text{(Condition for Providing High Quality)} \qquad \textbf{(14-8)}$$

where the letters represent the areas in Figure 14-7. Multiplying both sides of the inequality by $1 + i$ gives[8]

$$\frac{A}{i} + A \geq A + B + C + D$$

$$\frac{A}{i} \geq B + C + D \qquad \textbf{(14-9)}$$

If 14-9 is satisfied as an equality, a competitive firm maximizes the present value of profits by delivering a high-quality product at a price of P'.

---

[8] The firm earns profits equal to area A in the first year whether it cheats or delivers the high-quality product. Therefore, profits equal to area A in the first year have no bearing on the decision to supply a high-quality product. Equation 14-9 says that the firm will act honestly if the present value of future profits in years 2 and later from acting honestly exceeds the sum of areas B, C, and D received at the end of year 1.

Will there always be a premium price P' greater than P^* that satisfies 14-9 as an equality? Not necessarily. If P' is just slightly higher than P^*, then area A will be very small relative to the sum of areas C and D and 14-9 cannot be satisfied as an equality. As P' increases, area A, the profits from the production of a high-quality product, increase, and areas C and D do not change. Therefore, the ratio $(C + D)/A$ decreases as P' increases. As P' rises, B/A also changes, but the direction of change in B/A depends on the shapes of the marginal cost functions for producing high- and minimum-quality products. There is no guarantee that B/A will decrease.

In some situations no price will satisfy the inequality 14-9, and so there is no price premium that makes honesty the policy with the highest present value. Under these circumstances a competitive industry will not supply the higher-quality product, and it is in these instances that the strongest case for government regulation exists. Otherwise, firms will produce only the lowest quality and consumers will be willing to purchase only the minimum quality for fear of being taken advantage of. By imposing sanctions for misrepresenting a product, government regulation may introduce the proper incentive for firms to supply high-quality products.

There are other cases where the smallest premium price P' satisfies 14-9 as an equality. Let's assume that P' is the smallest price above P^* that satisfies 14-9. $P' - P^*$ is therefore the smallest price premium that will induce a competitive firm to deliver the promised quality. By paying a premium price P', consumers are willingly paying protection money to bribe the firm to behave honestly. With a price premium the seller owns the stream of future profits as long as it delivers the promised quality. If it takes advantage of consumers, it loses this profit stream. Consequently, the opportunity cost of cheating is loss of this attractive profit stream.

APPLICATION 14-3

The Price Premium at McDonald's

It is possible that a price premium can prevent a firm from cheating. This application looks at the operating performance at McDonald's franchisees to determine if McDonald's provides them with a price premium. McDonald's wants all of its stores to provide fast service, meals of a uniform quality, and a clean and cheerful atmosphere. We want to determine if McDonald's entices franchisees to meet these responsibilities with a price premium.

McDonald's determines the number of franchises and can limit this number so that each one receives P' and earns profits. If there is a price premium for McDonald's franchisees, it should be profitable to own and operate a franchise. Economists Patrick Kaufmann and Francine Lafontaine examined the profitability of McDonald's franchises in 1982 and 1989.[9] Their results for 1982 are summarized here and are comparable to those for 1989. They present publicly available infor-

[9] Patrick J. Kaufmann and Francine Lafontaine, "Costs of Control: The Source of Economic Rents for McDonald's Franchisees," July 1992 (unpublished paper).

Table 14-4   ESTIMATED PROFITABILITY OF MCDONALD'S FRANCHISES IN 1982

	Yearly Sales (in Thousands)		
	900	1100	1300
Yearly profits	3.4	62.8	107.7
Present discounted profits	44.5	821.7	1409.3
Up-front costs	371.5	404.5	535.5
Present value after subtracting up-front costs (before taxes)	(327.0)	417.2	873.8

mation about the profitability of 1,283 McDonald's-owned restaurants that have been in operation for 13 months or longer. In 1982 73 percent of these restaurants had annual revenues of $1.1 million or more. They then adjust the operating profits of company-owned stores for royalty payments of 11.5 percent of sales that a franchisee must pay to McDonald's, the security deposit, inventory, maintenance, and the opportunity cost of labor of the franchisee. Row 1 of Table 14-4 shows the estimated annual profits for franchises of three different sizes (as measured by annual sales) after making these adjustments.

For example, a restaurant with annual revenues of $1.3 million expects to earn $107,700 in annual profits in 1982. Row 2 shows the present value of the profit stream when the inflation-adjusted discount rate is 5 percent. For a franchise with annual revenues of $1.3 million, the present value of profits is $1.4 million. Row 3 subtracts the up-front costs that each franchisee incurs when starting a franchise—for equipment, for time spent in training, and the franchise fee. The net before-tax present value is $873,800 for such a restaurant. These calculations suggest that all but the smallest McDonald's franchises are very profitable. Because they are, McDonald's must be giving its franchisees a price premium.

Kaufmann and Lafontaine supplement their conclusions with other information about the average price paid for 11 existing McDonald's franchises that owners have sold and the corresponding average value of their tangible assets. They find that the average price paid for a franchise was $570,000 and that the average value of the tangible assets was $100,000. Therefore, the average value of these 11 franchises was $470,000 in 1982 dollars.

The reason that potential owners are willing to pay so much more than the value of the tangible assets is that they expect to earn profits. The evidence from these market prices for McDonald's franchises also indicates that the parent company limits the number of franchises so that a price premium exists and the franchises earn profits. The question of why McDonald's allows its franchises to earn profits will be considered later.

Table 14-5 AVERAGE HOURLY WAGE RATE

TYPE OF WORKER	FRANCHISEE-OWNED ($)	COMPANY-OWNED ($)	PERCENTAGE DIFFERENCE
Assistant and shift manager	4.35	4.75	9.2
Crew worker	3.57	3.61	1.1

APPLICATION 14-4

A Price Premium in Labor Markets

Paying a premium to ensure honest behavior has applications in markets other than product markets. The same question arises in the labor market where a firm cannot monitor a worker and pays a premium wage to discourage him or her from shirking on the job. By paying a premium wage the employer makes the job a lucrative one that the worker wants to keep. The employee is then less likely to shirk on the job whether this involves the way the worker treats customers or the effort exerted by the worker. The employer is willing to pay a premium wage if it reduces the firm's cost of monitoring workers.

In an interesting case study Alan Kreuger[10] investigated the pay of managers and workers in company-owned and in operator-owned fast food outlets. He claims that an owner-manager has a greater incentive to exert effort in supervising workers because the owner's total reward is directly tied to the profits of the outlet. On the other hand, at company-owned outlets a manager receives a salary but does not share in the profits of the outlet. Therefore, he or she has less incentive to monitor employees closely since there are no direct benefits.

Because of the different incentives for monitoring workers, company-owned outlets can substitute higher pay for less direct monitoring. Is there any evidence that this occurs? Kreuger examined the average hourly wage of assistant and shift managers and crew workers in franchisee-owned and in company-owned fast food outlets. Table 14-5 shows his results.

Kreuger found that companies pay a premium wage to assistant and shift managers but not to ordinary workers in fast food outlets. Thus, it appears that in the fast food industry company-owned firms rely on a premium wage to discourage managers from cheating.

---

[10] Based on Alan B. Kreuger, "Ownership, Agency, and Wages: An Examination of Franchising in the Fast Food Industry, *Quarterly Journal of Economics*, vol. CVI, February 1991, pp. 75–102.

McDonald's may be able to control the number of outlets, but this is not possible in a competitive industry. If entry into a competitive industry is unrestricted, how can a price premium exist in the long run?

Since new firms enter the industry because profits exist, this ordinarily causes price to fall. However, consumers will be reluctant to purchase the product at a lower price than P'. Because of assumption 6 of the Klein-Leffler model, consumers can estimate the minimum necessary price premium that discourages cheating on quality by the firms in the industry. No rational consumer will purchase from a seller promising to supply a high-quality product at a price less than P' because he or she knows it is more profitable for the firm to deliver the minimum-quality product. The demand for the high-quality model simply disappears at any price less than P'. What this means is that new entrants cannot enter the market by offering a lower price and realistically expect customers to switch sellers. There is no demand for a high-quality product at a price less than P'. Entry through price competition will not succeed.

Nonsalvageable Investments

Since price competition is not feasible, the only way firms can enter the industry is by competing through nonprice means. They can do this by making investments that not only increase their costs and eliminate profits but also convince consumers that they will be around in the future. Their capital improvements must be firm-specific and, if possible, produce services on which customers place some value. By making nonsalvageable investments, firms send a signal to consumers that they will suffer a large capital loss if they cheat on quality and must exit the industry.

Firm-specific investments are less valuable in alternative uses. Competing by investing in nonsalvageable capital raises the firm's cost, eliminates profits, and discourages cheating because the company becomes a hostage to the industry.[11] Each firm in the industry must participate in this type of competition if it expects to retain consumers since consumers receive some utility from the nonsalvageable investments made by the firm. If a company raises its costs by simply giving money to charity, it will lose customers to other firms that increase the utility of the consumer by investing in nonsalvageable assets. It is this type of nonprice competition among firms that eliminates profits and establishes a long-run industry equilibrium.

> Nonsalvageable investments eliminate profits and make a firm a hostage to the industry.

Perhaps the best example of a nonsalvageable asset is the development of a brand name through the firm's advertisements. By advertising, the company establishes goodwill or brand name capital. The brand name represents certain characteristics of the product that consumers are willing to purchase, and the goodwill

---

[11] Deliberately creating a hostage to induce exchange is treated in Oliver E. Williamson, "Credible Commitments: Using Hostages to Support Exchange," *American Economic Review*, vol. 83, September 1983, pp. 519–540.

is an asset, just as the firm's plant is an asset. Brand name capital helps the company make sales in the present and in the future. If the firm stops advertising, demand does not immediately fall precipitously but continues because the company has established brand name capital. Therefore, advertising has a short- and a long-term effect on the demand for the firm's product. The value of the brand name depreciates and may become worthless if the firm cheats and must exit the industry.

Another example of a nonsalvageable investment is the purchase of distinctive fixtures for a store. The fixtures are firm-specific and elaborate and therefore are less valuable to other companies. For example, you might place a special logo on a rug or on the fixtures of your store. If your firm goes out of business, it suffers a capital loss when it sells the fixtures because the investment in fixtures is firm-specific.[12]

In each example the firm suffers a capital loss if it cheats and is forced to leave the industry. It is for this reason that a grab-and-run policy is no longer attractive. We can determine the size of the capital loss that the firm would suffer in equilibrium if it did cheat. Let's consider the special case where firm-specific investments are like a fixed cost, and so they do not affect the position of the long-run marginal cost function of the firm. These investments shift the long-run average cost function upward until profits disappear where the firm produces X' units when the price is P' in Figure 14-7. If the firm invests in firm-specific projects and then cheats on quality, it gains the present value of the one-period profit, or $(A + B + C + D)/(1 + i)$. The opportunity cost of the cheating strategy is the capital loss on the firm-specific investment that it has made. The capital loss, β, must equal the present value of the profits gained from delivering the promised quality. In long-run industry equilibrium β is

$$\beta = \frac{A}{i} \qquad \text{(Capital Loss Incurred by Firm)} \qquad \textbf{(14-10)}$$

The capital loss just equals the present value of the one-period profit obtained by delivering the promised quality since the price premium is determined where

$$\frac{A}{i} = \frac{A + B + C + D}{1 + i}$$

The value of the capital loss that the firm suffers if it cheats is on the left-hand side of this equality, while the present value of the gain from cheating is on the right-hand side. Therefore, the capital loss on the nonsalvageable assets is equal to the present value of the one-period profit gained from cheating.

For example, assume that a firm's total investment is $100,000. If the one-period profit obtained from cheating is $4,200 and the discount rate is 5 percent, then the capital loss that the firm suffers if it cheats must be $4,000. Therefore, the

---

[12] A firm can make specific investments that tie it to the industry but do not increase the utility of the consumer. The design of the factory building is specific to the production of a product. If you have to leave the industry and sell the building to a competitor, you will take a capital loss because your competitor will have to modify the layout of the building to suit its special requirements.

firm's total investment must be worth only $96,000 if the firm cheats and has to exit the industry. This implies that area A is equal to $4,000(.05) = \$200$.

Of all the nonsalvageable investments that the firm can make, it will select those that yield greater service value to customers. In any case, the salvage value per unit of output must be less than the per unit service value of the service to the consumer. This explains why a firm does not simply raise costs by raising the salary of all its workers. Customers prefer to shop at a store where they obtain the product along with services from the nonsalvageable investments rather than at a store that offers just the product at the same price.

APPLICATION 14-5

Why Does McDonald's Allow Franchises to Earn Profits?

The study by economists Kaufmann and Lafontaine documents the profitability of McDonald's franchises.[13] The question is: Why does McDonald's allow its franchises to earn profits? McDonald's could raise the franchise fee or the required security deposit, which it does not pay interest on and returns at the end of 20 years if performance is satisfactory, and in this way could obtain the profits from a price premium. It could appropriate the profits by requiring franchisees to put up a large bond in the form of a security deposit that they lose if terminated. The bond is like β. It represents the loss in capital value if the franchisee cheats the consumer and is terminated by McDonald's.

Kaufmann and Lafontaine argue that McDonald's does not use the bonding mechanism because of the wealth constraints of franchisees. A large initial bond would eliminate many otherwise qualified individuals. McDonald's requires franchisees to be owner-operators and to put up 40 percent of the initial capital requirements for new franchises and 20 percent for established franchises. It does not want doctors and lawyers who merely provide the capital and hire others to run the restaurants. Few lenders would be willing to lend a large sum to a potential franchisee with the risk of losing their money because a franchisee shirks. Because of the liquidity problem, McDonald's has developed a business facility lease that allows promising franchisees to purchase restaurants. The authors argue that McDonald's does not require potential owners to post large bonds because that would shrink the pool of capable applicants.

When the Required Price Premium Is Unknown

The Klein-Leffler model assumes that consumers know the required price premium that discourages cheating. If we relax assumption 6 and suppose that buyers do not know the exact quality–average cost relationship, firms must adopt policies that allow consumers to infer that a price premium exists. Consumers do this by

[13] Based on Patrick J. Kaufmann and Francine Lafontaine, "Costs of Control: The Source of Economic Rents for McDonald's Franchisees," July 1992 (unpublished paper).

observing signals that a firm has made specific investments. For example, they deduce that a company that advertises heavily and develops a brand name has made nonsalvageable investments. Firm- or brand-specific investments indicate the existence of a price premium. By observing what they believe to be brand-specific investments, they infer that the firm is selling the product at a premium price and that it will suffer a loss if it leaves the industry.

Obviously, uncertainty about the necessary price premium that ensures quality places an additional burden on consumers. They are even less capable of determining whether firms have made adequate brand-specific investments than of assessing the quality of the product. Moreover, the firm will have more difficulty convincing them that its brand-specific investments are large enough to prevent cheating. When there is uncertainty, there are more opportunities for firms to pretend that they have made the required nonsalvageable investments when they have not, and this presents more possibilities for cheating.

Conclusions about the Klein-Leffler Model

In summary, the Klein-Leffler model offers an explanation of why firms in competitive industries do not deceive consumers even in the absence of legal sanctions. The model stresses the role of the price premium in ensuring honest behavior. In this model managers of firms can be either saints or sinners depending on the incentives. If they are potential sinners because the wrong incentives exist, consumers purchase only the minimum-quality product. If they are saints because a price premium exists, consumers purchase higher-quality products and honesty is the most profitable policy. Therefore, the theory explains the absence of misrepresentation. In either case the firm cannot or will not cheat on quality. Here again, as in the lemons model, consumers get what they pay for. The Klein-Leffler model solves the asymmetric information problem by requiring competitive firms to receive a price premium and to invest in nonsalvageable costs.

The model also demonstrates that the prospect of repeat sales is not by itself an adequate explanation of honest behavior. A competitive firm will cheat to obtain short-term profits if the alternative is repeat sales and no profits. The model also shows that firms can act honestly without the threat of legal sanctions.

The price premium is one device that companies use to discourage opportunistic behavior by those selling the firm's product. However, the firm also has other options at its disposal. For example, it can monitor the retailers selling its product. This is what McDonald's does when it combines a price premium with monitoring to control the behavior of its franchisees. Firms can use the two instruments as substitutes. A larger price premium requires less direct monitoring. A more advanced model incorporates the use of both instruments.

SUMMARY

■   Asymmetric information exists when one side of a potential transaction has more information than the other side.

- When there is asymmetric information, the owners of high-quality products suffer losses. They offer high-quality products and sell them in a pool that includes low-quality products and therefore at a lower price.
- With adverse selection the products that appear in the market are different from the products that firms sell when both sides have complete information.
- When asymmetric information exists, market institutions such as warranties and testing arise, and there is greater reliance on the seller's reputation.
- In long-run equilibrium competitive firms have a profit incentive to promise a high-quality product but supply a low-quality product. If there is nothing to tie the firm to the industry, it will supply only those qualities that consumers can assess before purchase. There will be an adverse selection of all product qualities in long-run industry equilibrium.
- A competitive firm may overcome the adverse selection problem if it receives a price premium and makes nonsalvageable investments. These nonsalvageable investments make the firm a hostage in the industry.

KEY TERMS

Asymmetric information	**Adverse selection**
Separating versus pooling equilibrium	**Warranty**
Reputation	**Promising and delivering high quality**
Promising high quality and delivering minimum quality	**Present value of profits**
Price premium	**Nonsalvageable investments**
Capital loss	**Brand name**

REVIEW QUESTIONS

1. If S_g = \$20,000, B_g = \$24,000, and B_l = \$12,000, what is the P_b and what percentage of used autos must be gems before gems appear in the market?
2. When there is asymmetric information in the market, all used cars sell at the P_b. Explain why you agree or disagree with this statement.
3. In a pooling equilibrium owners of lemons are able to sell their autos as gems, and the only individuals harmed are the unfortunate purchasers. Explain why you agree or disagree with this statement.
4. Would you expect the lemons problem to be more serious for insurance firms offering insurance plans to employers with a minimum group size than for companies offering plans to trade associations? Explain. How would the incidence of AIDS affect adverse selection?
5. If there is asymmetric information, would you expect the prices paid for free agents to be lower than those paid for players who remained with their teams, with all other factors held constant? Explain why or why not.

6. Would you expect cheating by one department in a department store to be less likely because of the potential loss of sales in other departments? Does the Klein-Leffler theory address this issue?

7. Would you expect a tourist to be more vulnerable to cheating? Why would you expect this to be true? What market institutions have emerged to lessen the cheating problem?

8. How does the price premium change when the discount rate increases? How does the price premium change if a firm can get away with cheating for 2 years instead of for 1 year?

9. If a manufacturer's total investment is $50,000, what information do you need to determine what the value of the investment will be if the firm goes out of business?

10. Suppose a competitive firm sells a product whose qualities consumers cannot assess before purchase. The firm tries to enter the industry by charging the market price and also offers free delivery after investing in a fleet of delivery trucks. Explain why consumers will or will not purchase the product from the firm.

EXERCISES

1. Suppose you are trying to determine whether a lemons problem exists in the market for used pickup trucks. Explain why each of the following tests would or would not reveal a lemons problem.
   a. The percentage of pickup trucks that trade in the first year.
   b. The percentage of trucks sold to dealers by the original owners is increasing over time.
   c. The maintenance cost of trucks after they are sold by the original owners is greater than the maintenance costs of trucks that original owners retain.

2. If the consumer knows the total quantity produced by the firm before purchasing the product, he or she can tell if the firm will deliver a minimum-quality product or a high-quality product, and so the cheating problem disappears. Explain why you agree or disagree with this statement.

3. You have invented a new home burglar alarm system. You plan to franchise the system to independent retail outlets. Customers purchase alarm systems infrequently, and so they have little information. You are fearful your franchisees will strive for short-run profits by saving on installation costs and thereby ruin the reputation of the alarm system. While you could try to monitor the installations of individual franchisees, it would be very expensive. Assume that the retailers are price-taking firms and use the Klein-Leffler theory to explain how many franchises you would issue to prevent cheating.

4. Suppose you are planning to open a health club. Customers have been burned in the past because a few of these clubs have closed abruptly without refunding unused memberships. You know that consumers are wary of joining a new health club. Evaluate whether the following policies will overcome the problem of consumer wariness.

a. Raising the price of a membership to obtain a premium price.
b. Prohibiting the sale of lifetime memberships.
c. Starting a trade group with local and nationwide clubs and extending reciprocal privileges to individual members. If a club goes out of business, the members may use the facilities of another club. What kinds of problems would you face if you joined such a club? Would you place any restrictions on reciprocity?
d. Investing in health equipment with your own distinctive label on the equipment.

5. A monopolist can either produce a high-quality (q_h) product at an average (=marginal) cost of MC or a low-quality product (q_{min}) at an average (=marginal) cost of MC', where MC' < MC. If the monopolist produces the high-quality product, it will produce X^* units and charge a price of P^*. The letters in the accompanying figure represent areas. Assume that the assumptions of the Klein-Leffler theory apply when answering the following questions.

DEMAND AND COST FUNCTIONS OF A MONOPOLIST

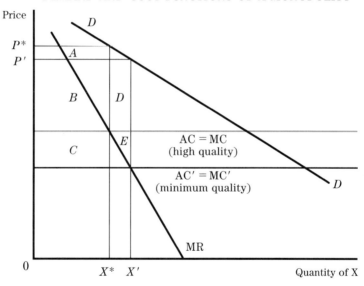

a. Use the areas in the figure to derive an expression for the present value of profits if the monopolist promises and supplies a high-quality product.
b. What output will the monopolist produce if it promises a high-quality product but delivers a minimum-quality product?
c. Under what conditions will the monopolist promise and deliver a high-quality product?

6. Your company produces an advanced model of a PC every year. Assume that you are a monopolist. A market research study reveals that two types of consumers use the computer. Type 1 buyers are sophisticated and use all the new

features that the new model offers. Type 2 users are computer-phobic, are intimidated by the latest technology, and are content to use older, familiar models. Your company wants to sell the new computer to the sophisticated users, but they complain about the cost of finding and selling their old computers in the used computer market. As the CEO, you know that more consumers will purchase the new model if they can sell their used computers at the end of the year to a type 2 user. Any arrangement facilitating the transfer will increase the demand for the new model. (Assume that firms cannot lease the equipment.) Two possible policies are being considered:

- *Policy 1.* Rent a large facility once a year where these two types of consumers can meet and a type 2 consumer can purchase a used computer from a type 1 user.
- *Policy 2.* Give exclusive rights to a limited number of dealers who act as intermediaries between the two types of consumers.

a. Present a brief discussion of the advantages and disadvantages of these two policies.
b. Which policy would you select? Defend your decision against the alternative policy.

PROBLEM SET

Integration and Opportunistic Behavior

There are times when a buyer or a supplier is vulnerable when fulfilling the terms of a contract. One party to a transaction must make an up-front investment that is specific to the transaction. Once made, that party is in a vulnerable position because the other party can threaten to pull out unless the terms of the contract are made more favorable retroactively. If these situations can reoccur, it may be more efficient for one of the firms to integrate (make rather than buy the product) and eliminate the market transaction.

Firm X has supplied a part to firm Y for many years. At the beginning of each year the two firms sign a contract whereby X agrees to supply its total production to Y at a competitive price negotiated by the two parties before production begins. Because X signs a contract before production begins, it insisted long ago that a safety margin be built in just in case X's costs rise after it signs the contract. Y agreed to include a clause in the very first contract that X would always have the right to increase prices by at most P percent above the cost-based competitive price without giving Y any special explanation. The two firms have been doing business for many years, and X has only infrequently increased price and then only when it appeared justified.

Relations between the two firms had always been amicable. X was a reliable supplier, delivered goods on time, and supplied uniform quality. Two years ago, however, there was a change in the management at X, and since then X has increased the price retroactively by P percent each year. Y begins to suspect that X is taking advantage of the relaxed and amicable long-term relationship between the two firms and is acting opportunistically by raising the price even though the increase is not cost-justified.

Y forms a committee to reevaluate the arrangement and to suggest alternative courses of action. The committee estimates X's per unit cost of production at capacity output, q^*, is A in the accompanying figure.

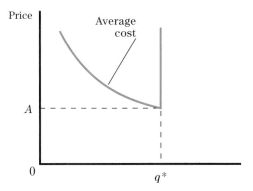

The committee also investigates whether Y should consider producing the part. There isn't much information to go on; but a recent research study of Y's operations in other areas, where it produces other parts, concluded that Y is not a particularly efficient producer of parts. The report concluded that Y's average cost of production averaged I percent above the market prices for a sample of eight parts.

Given this unimpressive experience with producing parts internally compared to buying in the open market, the committee is not too optimistic and is reluctant to recommend that Y produce this particular part internally. It decides to make use of the price system and recommends that Y offer X a premium price of more than A dollars, the cost-based competitive price. It recommends that X be told clearly that if it raises the price above this premium price in the future without justification, Y will terminate purchases from X in all future years.

Questions

1. Use the Klein-Leffler analysis to develop an expression for the present value of X's profits if it raises price by P percent above A dollars in the coming year without justification.
2. What price should Y offer X to discourage X from raising price by P percent above A dollars (assuming no unforeseen contingency)? Let that price be $(1 + k)A$ (where $k > 0$). Derive an expression for k and show how it depends on the discount rate i and the maximum price increase P.
3. What determines how high the discount rate can rise before it pays Y to make the part rather than buy it?

CHAPTER 14 APPENDIX

Present-Value Calculations

A dollar received at the end of the year is worth less than a dollar received today because a dollar in hand earns interest. At the end of 1 year a dollar has increased in value to $1 + i$ if the interest rate is i percent per year. A dollar becomes $1.05 if the interest rate is 5 percent. The 5 percent is a real return if it is assumed that the general price level neither increases nor decreases. This appendix evaluates two profit streams by calculating the present value of each one. Present value of profits in a future year is an amount, if received today, that is equivalent to the profits received in some future year. The procedure for determining the present value of a future dollar is called **discounting.**

> The **present value** of future profits is an amount received immediately that is equivalent to the profit received in some future year.

One strategy a firm can pursue is to cheat and receive profits at the end of the first year. Let's consider the present value of the profit stream consisting of earning profits of π_1 at the end of the year 1. What is the present value of π_1? What amount received at the beginning of the year is equivalent to receiving π_1 at the end of year 1? You should be indifferent between receiving π_1 at the end of the year or $\pi_1/(1 + i)$ at the beginning of year 1. For example, receiving $1,000 at the end of year 1 is equivalent to receiving $1000/(1 + 0.05) = \$952.38$ immediately if the interest rate is 5 percent. Why are these two equivalent alternatives? If you receive $\pi_1/(1 + i)$ at the beginning of year 1 and earn an annual interest rate of i on this amount, you will have $[\pi_1/(1 + i)] (1 + i) = \pi_1$ at the end of year 1. There is an exact equivalence between receiving $\pi_1/(1 + i)$ at the beginning of year 1 and receiving π_1 at the end of the year. We say that the present value of π_1 is $\pi_1/(1 + i)$. Therefore, to calculate the present value of the one-time profits at the end of the year from cheating, the firm divides these profits by $1 + i$.

If the firm does not cheat but delivers the promised quality, it receives profits equal to area A at the end of each year when the price is P' in Figure 14-7. The present value of this steady stream of profits is equal to the sum of the present value of the profits in each year. If the profits in year 1 are A, we already know that the present value of the profits in year 1 are $A/(1 + i)$. What is the present value of profits of A received at the end of year 2? What sum received immediately is equivalent to receiving A 2 years from now? If you receive an amount equal to $A/(1 + i)^2$ immediately and invest it in year 1 and again in year 2 along with the interest earned in year 1, at the end of year 2 you will have $[A/(1 + i)^2](1 + i)$ $(1 + i) = A$. At the end of year 1, you will receive $[A/(1 + i)^2](1 + i)$, or $A/(1 + i)$. Then, if you earn interest on this amount in year 2, you will have $A/(1 + i)(1 + i) = A$ at the end of year 2. The present value of A received at the end of year 2 is $A/(1 + i)^2$.

The algorithm for calculating the present value of profits received at the end of some future year should be clear by now. Say you want to determine the present value of A received at the end of year n. Divide A by $(1 + i)$ raised to the power n, or $A/(1 + i)^n$.

The last column of Table 14A-1 shows the present value of future profits in each year when the firm receives profits at the end of the year.

The present value of the steady profit stream is equal to the sum of the present value of each year's profits. The present value of an indefinite profit stream is

Table 14A-1   PRESENT VALUE OF A STREAM OF PROFITS

YEAR	PROFITS	PRESENT VALUE OF PROFITS RECEIVED AT END OF YEAR
1	A	$\dfrac{A}{1+i}$
2	A	$\dfrac{A}{(1+i)^2}$
3	A	$\dfrac{A}{(1+i)^3}$
.	.	.
.	.	.
.	.	.
n	A	$\dfrac{A}{(1+i)^n}$

$$\text{Present value} = \frac{A}{1+i} + \frac{A}{(1+i)^2} + \cdots + \frac{A}{(1+i)^n} + \cdots \qquad \textbf{(14A-1)}$$

The present value, PV, of an indefinite stream of A is

$$\text{PV} = (D + D^2 + \cdots + D^n + \cdots)A$$

where $D = 1/(1+i)$. Multiply and divide the right-hand side of the expression by $1 - D$ to obtain

$$\text{PV} = (1 - D)(D + D^2 + \cdots + D^n + \cdots)\frac{A}{1-D}$$

Multiplying through by $1 - D$ yields

$$\text{PV} = (D - D^2 + D^2 - D^3 + D^3 + \cdots)\frac{A}{1-D}$$

$$= \left(\frac{D}{1-D}\right)A$$

Since $D = 1/(1+i)$ and $1 - D = i/(1+i)$, $D/(1-D) = 1/i$. Therefore, the present value of an indefinite profit stream A is

$$\text{PV} = \frac{A}{i} \qquad \begin{array}{l}\text{(Present Value of a Perpetual Constant-Profit Stream} \\ \text{Received at the End of Each Year)}\end{array} \qquad \textbf{(14A-2)}$$

PRICING UNDER UNCERTAINTY

In some industries uncertainty has a major influence on a firm's pricing policies—policies that would not exist were it not for uncertainty. This chapter views uncertainty and its effect on pricing policy through the eyes of a clothing retailer. Specifically, it examines the reasons clothing stores hold end-of-season clearance sales—sales that take place at the end of each selling season and promise 20 to 50 percent off list prices. To explain why these stores offer one price at the start of the season and a lower one later on, we present a theory of pricing under uncertainty. When consumer tastes are uncertain, a store benefits by not charging a single price throughout the season but by first charging a higher price and then holding a clearance sale. The theory is applied to explain why women pay relatively higher prices for apparel than men at the start of the season but relatively lower prices at the end.

15-1   TYPES OF SALES

Many retailers change the prices of their goods during the selling season by offering sales to customers. Sales fall into three categories: preseason sales, within-season sales, and end-of-season clearance sales. Why firms offer different types of sales is an interesting question that has only recently attracted the attention of researchers. Consequently, economists and market researchers have an uneven understanding of the different types of sales. More is known about the reasons for clearance sales, and so this chapter concentrates on these types of sales.

Preseason Sales

Although the focus is on clearance sales in this chapter, the two other types of sales deserve mention. In a few industries, stores offer preseason sales. The introductory price is less than the within-season price for a week or two just before the arrival of the main selling season. A typical preseason sale is the sale of men's fall and winter suits and overcoats in late August or early September.

Economists have no definitive explanation for preseason sales. One hypothesis is that these sales are held to determine what styles will be popular during the season. Another is that some consumers have lower storage costs for goods than the seller. A lower price induces the consumer to purchase earlier than otherwise and to assume storage costs. For the time being, these are merely hypotheses that need further elaboration to explain why stores offer preseason sales for some types of clothing and not for others. In many markets retailers of middle-priced men's clothing sell new fall-winter overcoats and suits for X percent off in late August or early September. However, you will seldom find preseason sales for more expensive clothing sold, for example, under the Giorgio Armani label.

Within-Season Sales

With increasing frequency, retailers are holding short-term sales throughout the season. Hal Varian has developed a model that explains episodic short-term sales.

His explanation is an extension of the price discrimination hypothesis. He assumes that *some* consumers are knowledgeable about prices. They search all N stores that sell the product and always purchase from the store with the lowest price. Other consumers are uninformed about prices, and they purchase from the first store they visit. If a store always offered a high price, it would sell *only* to a fraction of the uninformed customers who happened to patronize the store. If the store always charged the lowest price, it would sell to all the informed consumers and to those uninformed consumers who happened to walk in. However, the store wants to have the best of both worlds by pricing to discriminate between the two types of buyers. According to Varian, stores adopt a mixed strategy and select prices randomly from a range of prices for a given item. Each store sells to informed shoppers at random intervals when its price is the lowest among the N stores that follow the same policy. At other times it just sells to some of the uninformed customers who patronize the store. Varian's model helps to explain why a retailer might offer sales at random intervals throughout the season.[1]

Clearance Sales and Uncertainty

The more common, well-known sale is the clearance sale that occurs at the end of a season. During a clearance sale the store reduces prices of merchandise that did not sell at higher prices.

Uncertainty is the root cause of price reductions during clearance sales.[2] When a store buyer places an order for a line of dresses about 8 to 12 months before the selling season, she is uncertain which dresses will be popular when the merchandise arrives at the store. The source of this uncertainty is in the unpredictable changes in consumer tastes concerning the color, length, silhouette, and style of a dress. Predicting which style, length, and color will be popular is difficult even for those who have spent a lifetime in the fashion business.

APPLICATION 15-1

Entering the Fashion Market

Although the women's apparel market gets most of the attention when clothing manufacturers introduce new fashions, changes in styles are occurring more frequently than in the past in the men's apparel market. More shirt and suit manufacturers are producing fashion apparel.

Some unexpected problems surfaced when Arrow Shirt introduced more stylish sport shirts.[3] In the spring of 1988 Cluett Peabody, the manufacturer of Arrow shirts, presented a new line of sport shirts with bolder colors, busier patterns, and higher prices. Arrow hoped to attract younger, more affluent customers to Arrow

---

[1] Hal R. Varian, "A Model of Sales," *American Economic Review*, vol. 70, September 1980, pp. 651–659.
[2] The section on clearance sales is based on Edward P. Lazear, "Retail Pricing and Clearance Sales," *American Economic Review*, vol. 76, March 1986, pp. 14–32; B. Peter Pashigian, "Demand Uncertainty and Sales: A Study of Fashion and Markdown Pricing," *American Economic Review*, vol. 78, December 1988, pp. 939–953.
[3] James R. Schiffman, "Cluett Peabody & Co. Loses Shirt Trying to Jazz Up the Arrow Man," © 1988 by Dow Jones Company, as seen in *Wall Street Journal*, July 28, 1988.

shirts with new vibrant colors and stripes rather than safe solid colors like blue, beige, and gray.

Arrow created the new line in the spring and summer of 1987 and introduced it in the spring of 1988. A year had elapsed between the time the shirts were designed and introduced, and consumer tastes had changed in the meantime. The shirts were overpriced, misstriped, and miscolored. Since they were overpriced, they did not sell. Arrow compounded the problem by trying to sell polyester sport shirts at $40. Critics said that the $40 sport shirt customer is looking for a cotton or a cotton blend shirt. Recognizing its errors, Arrow unloaded the shirts at distressed prices.

This episode illustrates the crucial role that uncertainty plays in the marketing of a fashion product.

15-2   SEASONAL VARIATION IN MEN'S AND WOMEN'S APPAREL PRICES

Figure 15-1 illustrates the price behavior observed during the fall-winter season for both men's and women's clothes—higher initial prices followed by a sharp decline in January and February. The fall-winter season starts sometime in September and continues through February, after which the spring-summer season begins. The horizontal line in the figure represents the average price for the year set equal to 1.00. Notice the different price behavior for women's and men's clothing. Women's apparel prices are higher initially but drop more than the prices for men's clothes by the end of the season.[4] For example, in October 1988 the price index for women's clothing was about 5.5 percent higher than the yearly average price and slightly less than 4 percentage points lower than the yearly average in January 1989. Between October and January there is a seasonal swing in prices of about 9.5 percentage points.

In contrast, the seasonal swing in men's apparel prices is more modest, about 3.5 percentage points. Women's apparel prices are higher relative to the average compared to men's apparel prices at the beginning of the season and fall by a larger percentage during January and February when clearance sales are held.

Women's apparel prices fluctuate seasonally more than men's apparel prices.

Another example of this seasonal price change was discussed in Chapter 12. In Figure 12-4 the percentage markdown for men's dress shirts followed a seasonal pattern, with larger markdowns offered at the end of the fall-winter and spring-summer seasons. What causes these seasonal swings in apparel prices and why are they greater for women's than for men's apparel? We develop a pricing model that will answer these questions.

---

[4] The rise in prices from September to October may partially reflect early season sales. However, the price increases are more likely to reflect the sales offered on remaining summer clothing and the lighter-weight clothing sold in early fall.

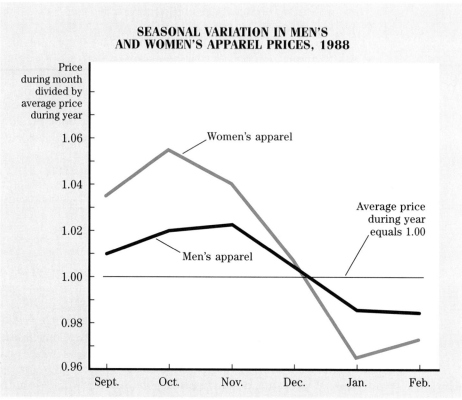

**SEASONAL VARIATION IN MEN'S
AND WOMEN'S APPAREL PRICES, 1988**

Figure 15-1   The seasonal variation in price is greater for women's clothes than for men's clothes.

15-3   UNCERTAINTY ABOUT CONSUMER TASTES

The first step in building the model is to identify the uncertainty that causes a retailer to offer clearance sales. To see what this environment is, let's examine the problems a retail clothing store manager or department manager faces.

We must go back 8 to 12 months to explain why the retail manager is offering clearance sales. A year ago, the buyer for the store ordered a line of fashion dresses in 10 bright, bold colors. Once the dresses are in the store, the store manager or department manager must decide what price to charge for them. Uncertainty is present when the buyer places the order because she cannot predict what consumer tastes for colors will be 10 months later. Similarly, the store manager faces uncertainty because he doesn't know what value consumers will place on each color. Are consumers willing to pay $300 for a coral dress this season? The manager cannot answer this question with certainty because he doesn't know which of the 10 colors will prove to be more popular. His crystal ball is no clearer than that of the buyer.

Of course the manager is not a babe in the woods and has some experience to fall back on. Experience tells him that dresses of this quality in the most popular

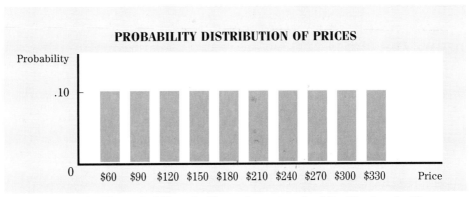

Figure 15-2   The probability of selling a dress at each of the 10 prices is .10.

color of the season could sell as high as $330. On the other hand, a dress in the color disaster of the season will not sell for anything more than a distress price of $60.

Figure 15-2 shows the probability distribution of prices that consumers are willing to pay. Table 15-1 shows the manager anticipates that the most popular color of the season will sell for $330, the second most popular color for $300, the third most popular for $270, and so on. The probability that any one of the 10

Table 15-1   PROBABILITY DISTRIBUTION OF PRICES

PRICE ($) (1)	NUMBER OF COLORS SOLD AT EACH PRICE (2)	PROBABILITY THAT A COLOR PICKED AT RANDOM WILL NOT SELL AT THIS PRICE (3)
360	0	1.00
330	1	.90
300	2	.80
270	3	.70
240	4	.60
210	5	.50
180	6	.40
150	7	.30
120	8	.20
90	9	.10
60	10	.00

colors will be the most popular is $\frac{1}{10}$ = .10. At the other extreme there is a probability of $\frac{1}{10}$ that one of the colors will sell for only $60. If you think of the store
selling a coral dress season after season, the probability distribution of prices says
coral will be the most popular color 10 percent of the time and sell for $330.
Another 10 percent of the time consumers will value a coral dress at $300, and so
on. Another interpretation of the probability distribution is that consumers will
value one of the 10 colors at $330, another at $300, and so on.

   According to Table 15-1, 6 of the 10 colors will sell if the price is $180 per
dress. Some consumers are willing to pay up to $330 for 1 of the 10 colors. Similarly,
one other color will prove to be slightly less popular, and so consumers are willing
to pay $300 for a dress of that color. Consumers will gladly purchase a dress in
either of these colors if the price is $180. Table 15-1 indicates that they value 4
of the colors at less than $180, and therefore these colors will not sell if the price
of each dress is $180.

   The values in Table 15-1 can be used to derive the inverse demand function
for colors.

$$P = \$360 - \$30C \qquad \text{(15-1)}$$

where C is the number of colors demanded. This function is shown in Figure
15-3. Solving equation 15-1 for C gives the number of colors that consumers demand
at each price.

$$C = \frac{\$360 - P}{\$30} \qquad \text{(15-2)}$$

P varies from a low of $60 to a high of $330, and C can equal 1, 2, 3, . . . , 10.[5]
According to equation 15-2, when P = $210, C = ($360 − $210)/$30 = 5, and so 5
of the 10 colors will sell. The store manager does not know which 5 colors will
sell, only that 5 colors will sell when the price is $210.

   Given these probabilities, we can calculate the expected or average price that
consumers are willing to pay for the 10 colors. Let a_1, a_2, a_3, . . . , a_{10} be the
probabilities that each color will sell at each of the 10 prices. In other words, the
manager believes the probability that a dress will sell for P_1 (the lowest price) is
a_1, for P_2 (the second lowest price) is a_2, and so on, and in this illustration the
probabilities are equal. Therefore, $a_1 = a_2 = a_3 = \cdots = a_{10} = \frac{1}{10}$.

   Since the 10 values exhaust all price possibilities, the sum of the probabilities
must equal 1.

$$\sum_{i=1}^{i=10} a_i = 1 \qquad \text{(15-3)}$$

The expected or average price consumers are willing to pay for the 10 colors is

$$EP = \sum_{i=1}^{i=10} a_i P_i \qquad \text{(15-4)}$$

---

[5] There could be more than 10 colors in the line. No matter how many colors are ordered, 10 percent
of them will sell at $330, 10 percent at $300, and so on.

DEMAND FUNCTION FOR COLORS

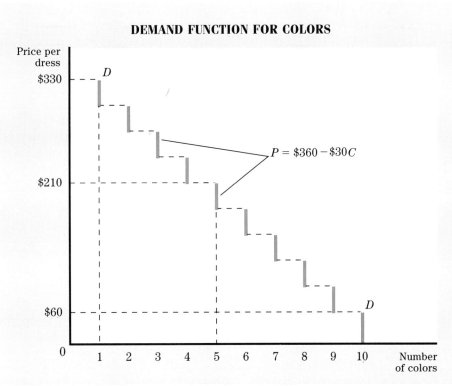

Figure 15-3   *DD* is the inverse demand function for dresses of different colors. If the price is $210, consumers demand 5 colors. If the price is $60, consumers demand all 10 colors.

The expected price is a weighted average of the 10 prices where the weights are the probabilities. The expected price is calculated by multiplying each price by its probability and summing the product over all possible prices. Since the probabilities are equal, the expected price in this illustration is $195, or the simple average of the 10 prices.

> The **expected price** is a probability-weighted average price. It represents the mean price that consumers are willing to pay for the 10 colors.

Since the demand function for colors indicates how many colors will sell at each price, we can use that information to derive an expression for the probability that a color picked at random will not sell at each price. See column 3 of Table 15-1. For example, the probability that the color will not sell at a price of $150 is (1) the probability that the color will sell only at $60 ($=\frac{1}{10}$) plus (2) the probability that the color will sell only at $90 ($=\frac{1}{10}$) plus (3) the probability that consumers will value the color at $120 ($=\frac{1}{10}$). Therefore, the probability that a color will not sell when the price is $150 is the sum of these probabilities, or .30.

More generally, the cumulative distribution of prices shows the probability that a color picked at random will not sell at each price and is equal to the sum of the probabilities that consumers will value a color at less than the price charged.

> The **cumulative distribution of prices** gives the probability that a color picked at random will not sell at each price.

The cumulative distribution of prices can be derived by subtracting the number of colors that sell from the total number of colors in the line and then expressing this difference as a fraction of the total. Let $F(P)$ be the probability that a dress picked at random will not sell at each price. $F(P)$ is defined by

$$F(P) = \frac{10 - C}{10} \qquad \text{(15-5)}$$

The number of colors that sell, C, depends on the price. The number of colors that do not sell is $10 - C$. By dividing $10 - C$ by 10, we express the probability that a color will not sell as a function of C, which in turn depends on P.

Substituting the demand function for colors in equation 15-1 for C in equation 15-5 yields[6]

$$F(P) = \frac{P - \$60}{\$300} \qquad \text{(15-6)}$$

where $P = \$60, \$90, \$120, \ldots, \$360$. $F(P)$ is the probability that a color picked at random will not sell if the price is P. For example, equation 15-6 says the probability that a color will not sell is .4 if the price is $180. Figure 15-4 shows a graph of $F(P)$, the probability that a color will not sell at each of the 10 prices.

Let's pause here and restate just what the store manager does and does not know when he sets the price. He knows the probability distribution of prices and therefore equation 15-6, the probability that a color will not sell. However, he does not know what retail price consumers are willing to pay for each color. Although he knows the probability distribution and therefore knows one color will sell for $330 and another for $300, and so on, he does not know which color will sell at $330, which at $300, and so on. The fickleness of consumer tastes is the fundamental cause of the uncertainty.

15-4   SELECTING A PRICE POLICY

How does the manager set a price when facing this uncertainty, and what goal does he have in mind when setting the price? This section compares two possible pricing policies that could be adopted. First, you will look at a single-price policy

---

[6] Substituting equation 15-1 into equation 15-5 gives
$$F(P) = \frac{10 - [(\$360 - P)/\$30]}{10} = \frac{\$300 - \$360 + P}{\$300}$$
from which equation 15-6 is obtained.

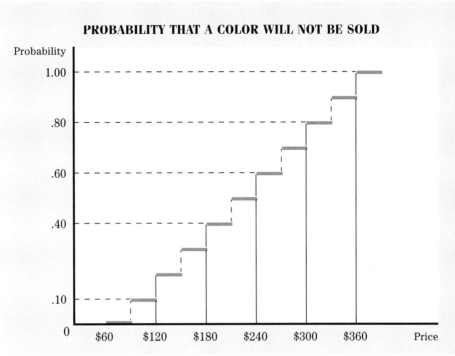

Figure 15-4   The probability that a color will not sell increases with the price. When the price of a dress is $180, the probability that a color will not sell is .40. If the price is $300, the probability that a color will not sell is .80.

where the store charges a single price throughout the season. Then, you will see how the store can earn higher revenues by charging two prices during a season, an initial price and a markdown price.

When the manager determines the price under either pricing policy, the cost of purchasing the dresses is a sunk cost. It is also assumed that the other costs of the store are fixed at this point. Therefore, the store manager can ignore these costs when determining the price.

A Single-Price Policy

Under a single-price policy, the store charges a single price throughout the season. Assume that a manager selects a price that maximizes expected revenue per dress, ER.

Expected revenue = Price × Probability of selling a color picked at random

$$\text{ER} = P[1 - F(P)] \tag{15-7}$$

Expected revenue per dress is equal to the price times the probability of selling a color picked at random. Since $F(P)$ is the probability that a dress will not sell if the price is P, $1 - F(P)$ is the probability that a color will sell if the price is P. When setting the price, the manager considers two effects of price on expected revenue. If he selects a high price, the probability of selling a dress picked at random falls because consumers are willing to pay for only a few colors at this price. On the other hand, at a lower price the probability of selling a dress picked at random increases because more colors will sell. The manager selects a price that strikes a balance between a lower price and a higher probability that a color will sell.

Substituting the expression for $F(P)$ in equation 15-6 into equation 15-7 yields

$$\text{ER} = P\left[1 - \left(\frac{P - \$60}{\$300}\right)\right] = P\frac{\$300 - P + \$60}{\$300}$$

$$= P\frac{\$360 - P}{\$300}$$

$$= \frac{1}{\$300}(\$360P - P^2) \tag{15-8}$$

Equation 15-8 shows how expected revenue changes as price changes, and Figure 15-5 graphs the relationship. Expected revenue is $60 if the price charged by the store is $60 because all colors sell and the firm receives $60 per dress. If the store sets higher prices, expected revenue increases at first, reaches a maximum, and then declines. The store manager maximizes expected revenue[7] by selecting a price where

$$\$360 - 2P = 0$$

Solving this equation for P yields

$$P = \$180$$

Figure 15-5 shows that the store maximizes expected revenue by setting a price of $180 per dress where expected revenue per dress ordered is $108. In Table 15-2 price is in column 1, the probability of not selling a given color is in column 2, the probability of selling a color is in column 3, and expected revenue is in column 4.

The maximum value for expected revenue is $108, and the probability that a color will sell is .6 when the price is $180. Table 15-2 shows that expected revenue per dress is less than price when the selling price is $180. The reason for this difference is that 40 percent of the colors do not sell. Only 6 of the 10 colors sell at $180, and we assume that the store donates the remaining 4 colors to charity. The store's total revenue is $180 \times 6 = \$1,080$. The average revenue received per ordered dress is only $1,080/10 = \$108$. On average the store receives only $108

---

[7] The quadratic equation for expected revenue includes two terms, $\$360P$ and $-P^2$. This is an equation of the form $aP + bP^2$, where $a = \$360$ and $b = -1$. Using calculus, we find the derivative of $aP + bP^2$ is $a + 2bP$. After substituting the expressions for a and b, the slope of the expected revenue function is $\$360 - 2P$. Therefore, the firm maximizes expected revenue by selecting the price so that

$$\frac{d(\text{ER})}{dP} = \frac{1}{\$300}(\$360 - 2P) = 0$$

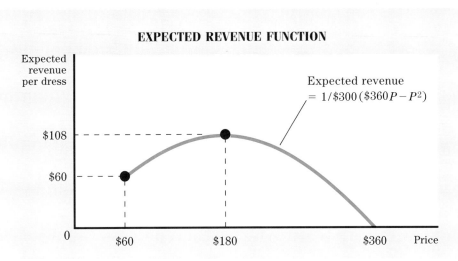

Figure 15-5   Expected revenue depends on the price charged. Expected revenue is maximized when the firm charges $180 for each of the dresses.

per dress when the price is $180 because it does not sell 4 of the 10 colors it ordered.

A Two-Price Policy

The main shortcoming of this single-price policy is that the manager learns little about willingness to pay for the different colors. When the price of a dress is $180 throughout the season, 6 of the 10 colors sell. What troubles the manager is knowing that 5 of these 6 colors could be sold for more than $180 if he only knew the values consumers placed on each color.

> A fundamental defect of a single-price policy is that it does not allow the manager to sort consumers into those who are willing to pay still more for certain colors and those who are not.

A single-price policy does not isolate the more popular colors for which consumers are willing to pay much more than $180 from colors for which they are willing to pay $180 or slightly more. The manager never finds out which of the colors that sell are the more highly valued colors.

A more informative pricing policy would allow the manager to learn more about what consumers are willing to pay for the different colors. Instead of charging a single price over the season, the store could charge two prices—a higher initial price and a markdown price. At the higher initial price, only those colors that consumers value highly will sell. The remaining colors will simply sit on the racks throughout the first period. However, customers will reveal to the manager what the more popular colors are by the colors they purchase at the higher price. For example, if the initial price is $270, only 3 of the 10 colors will sell. The manager learns that these 3 colors are the more popular colors this season and that con-

TABLE 15-2   FINDING THE PRICE THAT MAXIMIZES EXPECTED REVENUE

PRICE (\$) (1)	PROBABILITY THAT A COLOR PICKED AT RANDOM WILL NOT SELL AT THIS PRICE, $F(P)$ (2)	PROBABILITY THAT A COLOR PICKED AT RANDOM WILL SELL AT THIS PRICE, $[1 - F(P)]$ (3)	EXPECTED REVENUE, $P[1 - F(P)]$ (\$) (4)
360	1.00	.00	.00
330	.90	.10	33
300	.80	.20	60
270	.70	.30	81
240	.60	.40	98
210	.50	.50	105
180	.40	.60	108
150	.30	.70	105
120	.20	.80	96
90	.10	.90	81
60	.00	1.00	60

sumers are unwilling to pay \$270 for the remaining 7 colors. Later, the store will sell some or all of the remaining colors at a lower markdown price.

Selecting the Initial and Markdown Prices to Maximize Expected Revenue

Before developing a formal expression for expected revenue, it is useful to consider the following thought experiment. Let's pick a color at random and ask what expected revenue is from selling dresses of this color under a two-price policy. Let the initial price be P_i and the markdown price be P_m. For a color picked at random, three outcomes are possible. First, it may be one of the more popular colors of the season and all dresses of that color sell at the initial price of P_i. The probability that this will occur is $1 - F(P_i)$. Recall that $1 - F(P_i)$ is the probability that consumers will value a color at P_i or higher. A second possible outcome is that consumers may not value the color that highly, and so dresses of that color do not sell at the price P_i but do sell at a markdown price of P_m. In other words, consumers value the color less than P_i but equal to or greater than P_m. The probability that this will occur is $F(P_i) - F(P_m)$.[8] The third possible outcome is that consumers will value the color at less than P_m and dresses of this color do not sell even during

---

[8] The probability that a color will sell in the markdown period is the probability that it will not sell in the initial period, $F(P_i)$, times the conditional probability that it will sell in the markdown period, $[F(P_i) - F(P_m)]/F(P_i)$, or $F(P_i) - F(P_m)$.

the markdown period. The color is the color disaster of the season, and dresses of this color just remain on the racks. The probability of this outcome is $F(P_m)$. The three outcomes are summarized in the accompanying table.

VALUE PLACED ON COLOR	COLOR VALUED AT A PRICE GREATER THAN P_i	COLOR VALUED AT A PRICE LESS THAN P_i BUT EQUAL TO OR GREATER THAN P_m	COLOR VALUED AT A PRICE LESS THAN P_m
Probability color will sell at price	$1 - F(P_i)$	$F(P_i) - F(P_m)$	$F(P_m)$
When dress sells	In regular season	On sale in markdown season	Does not sell

Let's see what a two-price policy looks like on a graph of the inverse demand function for colors. The store has 10 dresses, each of a different color. In Figure 15-6 price is on the vertical axis and number of colors is on the horizontal axis. If the firm sets the initial price at $300, only 2 of the 10 colors will sell. Area 1 represents the revenue received in the first period. If the markdown price is $150, 5 of the remaining 8 colors sell and the total revenue from selling these colors is equal to area 2. Throughout the season 7 of the 10 colors sell. The total revenue is 2($300) + 5($150) = $1,350. Revenue per dress ordered is only $1,350/10 = $135, although the initial price is $300, and the markdown price is $150 because 3 colors do not sell.

To find the optimal initial and markdown prices, we must first develop a general expression for expected revenue. As described above, expected revenue is P_i times the probability of selling a color when the initial price is P_i plus P_m times the probability of selling a color at the markdown price of P_m. The expression for expected revenue is

$$\text{ER} = P_i \,(\text{probability of selling color at } P_i)$$
$$+ \, P_m \,(\text{probability that color will be valued between } P_i \text{ and } P_m)$$
$$= P_i[1 - F(P_i)] + P_m[F(P_i) - F(P_m)] \tag{15-9}$$

Substituting the corresponding expressions for $F(P_i)$ and $F(P_m)$ from equation 15-6 into equation 15-9 yields

$$\text{ER} = P_i\left[1 - \left(\frac{P_i - \$60)}{\$300}\right)\right] + P_m\left[\left(\frac{P_i - \$60}{\$300}\right) - \left(\frac{P_m - \$60}{\$300}\right)\right]$$

$$= P_i\frac{\$360 - P_i}{\$300} + P_m\frac{P_i - P_m}{\$300}$$

$$= \frac{1}{300}(\$360P_i - P_i^2 + P_iP_m - P_m^2) \tag{15-10}$$

Equation 15-10 shows that expected revenue depends on the initial and markdown prices. The manager selects P_i and P_m to maximize expected revenue of selling a color picked at random.

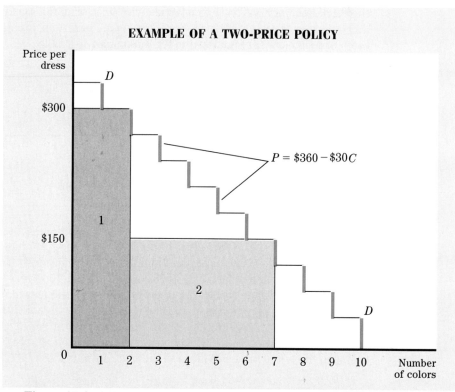

EXAMPLE OF A TWO-PRICE POLICY

Figure 15-6 *DD* is the demand function for dresses of different colors. When the initial price is $300, 2 of the 10 colors sell. In the second period the markdown price is $150 and 5 of the remaining 8 colors sell. Area 1 is the revenue received in the first period, and area 2 is the revenue received in the second period.

Care must be exercised when using the expression for expected revenue to find the optimal prices. The first point to note is that the optimal markdown price depends on what initial price the store charges. The lower the initial price, the lower the markdown price. Because of this, how the markdown price changes when the initial price changes must be taken into account when determining the optimal initial price.

To find the optimal initial and markdown prices, we work backward by first considering the second period. When a retail store sets the markdown price, it has already set the initial price. We want to derive a relationship that shows the store's optimal markdown price for each initial price. Once this relationship is known, we can return to the first period and find the optimal initial price, taking into account how the initial price affects the optimal markdown price.

With this suggested procedure in mind, the first step is to derive a relationship between the firm's markdown price and its initial price. The manager has already selected the initial price in the first period and now wants to select the markdown price to maximize expected revenue given the initial price.

The markdown price that maximizes expected profit in equation 15-10 satisfies[9]

$$P_i - 2P_m = 0 \qquad\qquad\qquad\qquad (15\text{-}11)$$

Solving this equation for P_m, we derive a relationship between the markdown price and the initial price,

$$P_m = \frac{P_i}{2} \qquad \text{(Optimal Markdown Price Policy)} \qquad (15\text{-}12)$$

Equation 15-12 describes the relationship between the markdown price and the initial price. It is a decision rule for the manager to follow and says the optimal price policy is to set the markdown price at 50 percent of the initial price. For the time being, assume that the optimal markdown price is either equal to or greater than $60, the lowest price that consumers are willing to pay.

Now that the optimal markdown *price policy* is known, we can go back to the initial period and find the initial price that maximizes expected revenue while explicitly taking account of the optimal markdown pricing policy. Substitute $P_m = P_i/2$ into equation 15-10 to obtain

$$\text{ER} = \frac{1}{\$300}\left[\$360P_i - P_i^2 + P_i\frac{P_i}{2} - \left(\frac{P_i}{2}\right)^2 \right]$$

$$= \frac{1}{\$300}(\$360P_i - \tfrac{3}{4}P_i^2)$$

Now, expected revenue depends only on P_i, and the firm maximizes expected revenue[10] when P_i satisfies

$$\$360 - \tfrac{3}{2}P_i = 0 \qquad\qquad\qquad\qquad (15\text{-}13)$$

Solving equation 15-13 for P_i yields the initial price that maximizes expected revenue.

$$P_i = \tfrac{2}{3}(\$360) = \$240 \qquad \text{(Optimal Initial Price)} \qquad (15\text{-}14)$$

Notice that the initial price is two-thirds of the vertical intercept of the inverse demand function for colors in equation 15-1. Since the optimal markdown price is one-half of the initial price, it is one-third of the vertical intercept of the inverse demand function for colors, or $120.

$$P_m = \$120 \qquad \text{(Optimal Markdown Price)} \qquad (15\text{-}15)$$

When the store charges these two prices, 80 percent of the dresses sell by the end of the markdown period. Forty percent of the colors sell at a price of $240 per

---

[9] The firm maximizes expected revenue by selecting the markdown price so that

$$\frac{d(\text{ER})}{dP_m} = \frac{1}{\$300}(P_i - 2P_m) = 0$$

[10] To maximize expected revenue, the firm selects P_i so that

$$\frac{d\text{ER}}{dP_i} = \frac{1}{\$300}(\$360 - \tfrac{3}{2}P_i) = 0$$

dress, another 40 percent sell at the markdown price of $120, and only 20 percent are given to charity. The expected revenue from a dress picked at random is $240(.4) + $120(.4) = $96 + $48 = $144. The expected revenue from a two-price policy is 33 percent higher than $108, the expected revenue from a single-price policy. The two-price policy is far superior to the single-price policy.

> Expected revenue for the two-price policy exceeds expected revenue for the one-price policy.

With a two-price policy, consumers purchase dresses at the higher initial price and reveal which colors will be the fashion hits of the season. The store manager learns more about what consumers are willing to pay for selected colors by implementing this more sophisticated pricing policy. This kind of learning does not occur with a single-price policy.

Changing the Probability Distribution of Prices

The preceding example shows why a two-price policy is superior to a single-price policy. However, it is also somewhat misleading. It appears to say that stores will always mark down goods by 50 percent when the inverse demand function for colors is a straight line (equation 15-1). Now, you know from observation that this is not always true. As an example, the different patterns of men's and women's apparel prices indicate that the percentage markdown is larger for women's than for men's clothing.

Can the uncertainty theory be extended to include markdown policies different from 50 percent? The optimal percentage markdown depends on the range of the probability distribution of prices. Uncertainty is greater for clothing where consumer preferences change rapidly, especially for fashion clothing sold to younger customers. For other types of clothing, there is less price uncertainty.

When there is less dispersion in the probability distribution of prices that consumers are willing to pay, the store maximizes expected revenue by reducing price by less than 50 percent. To demonstrate this, two examples are considered. In these examples the probability distribution of prices has the same expected price ($195) as that observed for dresses in fashion colors but has a smaller range of prices that consumers are willing to pay. Therefore, we keep the expected price constant while changing the range of prices that consumers will pay.

The simplest case is where there are only two prices that consumers are willing to pay. Let's assume that the store sells a very conservative line of solid black and blue dresses that the store manager knows from experience will sell for either $210 or $180. Consequently, the expected price is still $195, as in the example involving fashion colors. Table 15-3 shows the price, the probability that a color will not sell at each price, and the probability that a color will sell at each price.

Here the store's optimal two-price policy is to charge $210 in the first period and sell 50 percent of the dresses, and then to charge $180 in the markdown period, the minimum price that consumers are willing to pay for the least preferred color. Expected revenue is ER = .5($210) + .5($180) = $195.

Table 15-3   PROBABILITY DISTRIBUTION OF PRICES

PRICE ($)	PROBABILITY THAT A COLOR PICKED AT RANDOM WILL NOT SELL AT THIS PRICE, $F(P)$	PROBABILITY THAT A COLOR PICKED AT RANDOM WILL SELL AT THIS PRICE, $1 - F(P)$
210	.50	.50
180	0	1.00

All dresses sell, and the expected revenue from the sale of a color picked at random equals the expected price. In this case the percentage markdown is only ($30/$210)100% = 14.3%. When the dispersion in the prices of the probability distribution is sufficiently small, the store will mark down price by less than 50 percent and the optimal markdown price will equal the minimum price that consumers are willing to pay for the least desirable color.

To reinforce this point, let's consider another example where the store is selling a moderately conservative line of dresses. The manager estimates that the six colors in the line will sell from a high of $270 to a low of $120, and so the expected price is still $195, as with the fashion line and the very conservative line of dresses. But the range from the highest to the lowest price is only $150, in contrast to $30 for the very conservative line of colors and $270 for the fashion line of colors. The probability distribution of colors is shown in Table 15-4 and in Figure 15-7.

Table 15-4   PROBABILITY DISTRIBUTION OF PRICES

PRICE ($) (1)	PROBABILITY THAT A COLOR WILL NOT SELL AT THIS PRICE (2)	PROBABILITY THAT A COLOR WILL SELL AT THIS PRICE (3)
300	1.00	.00
270	.833	.167
240	.667	.333
210	.500	.500
180	.333	.667
150	.167	.833
120	.00	1.00

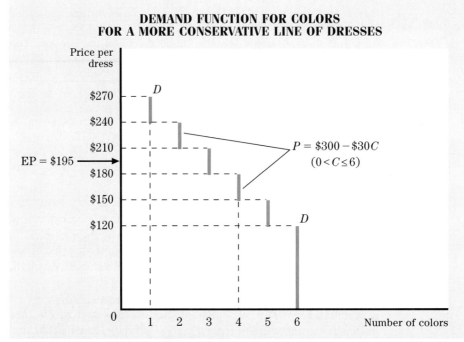

Figure 15-7 *DD* is the demand function for colors for a more conservative line of dresses. The expected price is $195, but the dispersion of prices that consumers will pay is smaller because there is less uncertainty.

The equation for the inverse demand function for colors becomes

$$P = \$300 - \$30C$$

where C represents the number of different colors and is 1, 2, 3, 4, 5, or 6. For example, when only one color sells, the price is $270, and so on.

We must be especially careful when applying the previous method of solution to this example. A problem arises if the store's initial price is less than $240. One-half of any initial price that is less than $240 will be less than $120, the price that consumers will pay for the least preferred color. If the optimal initial price is $210, for example, there is no rhyme or reason for the store to charge $105, half the initial price, in the markdown period because it can still sell the remaining three colors at a markdown price of $120. Therefore, expected revenue is higher when the store sets the markdown price at $120 whenever the optimal initial price is less than $240.

The increase in expected revenue can be calculated when the store charges $210 rather than $240 in the initial period and $120 in the markdown period. In the first case expected revenue is .333($240) + .667($120) = $80 + $80 = $160. With the second price policy expected revenue is .5($210) + .5($120) = $105 + $60 = $165. Therefore, expected revenue is higher when the store charges $210 in the initial period and departs from the 50 percent markdown rule by charging $120 in the markdown period. Consequently, the retailer will reduce price by less than 50 percent when the dispersion of prices that consumers are willing to pay becomes small. When the dispersion is sufficiently small, the manager sets the markdown price at the price of the least preferred color.

In this example the expression for expected revenue becomes[11]

$$\text{ER} = P_i \frac{\$300 - P_i}{\$180} + P_m \frac{P_i - P_m}{\$180}$$

The store sets the markdown price at $120, the lowest price that consumers will pay, and so the expression for expected revenue becomes

$$\text{ER} = P_i \frac{\$300 - P_i}{\$180} + \$120 \frac{P_i - \$120}{\$180}$$

$$= \frac{1}{\$180} [\$300 P_i - P_i^2 + \$120 P_i - (\$120)^2] \qquad \textbf{(15-16)}$$

Equation 15-16 depends on only P_i. The store maximizes expected revenue by selecting a P_i that satisfies[12]

$$\$300 - 2P_i + \$120 = 0$$

or
$$P_i = \$210$$

The optimal initial price is $210 with a markdown price of $120.

As with the very conservative line of dresses, when the dispersion of prices becomes sufficiently small, the store sets the initial price at the expected price or at the next higher price if the expected price is not an eligible candidate. The markdown price is equal to the lowest price that consumers will pay.[13]

---

[11] Substituting $C = (\$300 - P)/\$30$ into $F = (6 - C)/6$ gives the expression $F(P) = (P - \$120)/\$180$. Therefore, $1 - F(P) = (\$300 - P)/\$180$.

[12] Expected revenue is maximized when

$$\frac{d(\text{ER})}{dP_i} = \frac{1}{\$180} (\$300 - 2P_i + \$120) = 0$$

[13] The equation for the demand for colors is $P = P_a - \$30C$, where P_a is the intercept of the inverse demand function and is to be determined. The firm follows the 50 percent rule when the markdown price is one-third of the demand function's intercept. Therefore, the markdown price is equal to $P_m = \frac{1}{3} P_a = P_a - \$30 C^*$, where C^* represents the number of colors sold if the markdown price equals the price of the least desirable color.

The expected price is $195 and equals the average of the highest price that a color can command $(P_a - 30)$ and the lowest price that a color can command $(P_a - 30C^*)$:

$$\frac{(P_a - \$30) + (P_a - \$30C^*)}{2} = \$195 \quad \text{or} \quad 2P_a - \$30 - \$30C^* = \$390$$

Solving this equation for $-\$30C^*$ and substituting the resulting expression into the expression for the markdown price yields $\frac{1}{3} P_a = P_a + \$390 - 2P_a + \$30$. Solving for P_a yields $P_a = \$315$. Substituting $P_a = 315$ into the equation $2P_a - \$30 - \$30C^* = \$390$ shows that C^*, the number of separate prices, equals 7. When the inverse demand function is $P = \$315 - \$30C$, where $C = 1, 2, \ldots, 7$, the optimal initial price is $210 and the optimal markdown price is $105, the lowest price that the least desirable color can command. The store reduces price by 50 percent as long as the intercept of the inverse demand function equals or exceeds $315.

Table 15-5   EXPECTED REVENUE AT DIFFERENT INITIAL AND MARKDOWN
PRICES

INITIAL PRICE ($) (1)	MARKDOWN PRICE (2)	EXPECTED REVENUE ($) (3)
240	120	160
210	120	165
210	150	155
210	105	157.50

In this example, 50 percent of the dresses sell at $210 and 50 percent at $120. In contrast to the example with the high-fashion dresses, the store sells all the moderately conservative dresses. Expected revenue is 0.5($210) + 0.5($120) = $105 + $60 = $165. Table 15-5 shows that expected revenue is lower for other selected price pairs. In the first row the initial price is $240, higher than $210, while the markdown price remains at $120. Only one-third of the dresses sell at $240, two-thirds sell at $120, and expected revenue falls from $165 to $160. The optimal price policy is in the second row. In the third row the initial price is $210, but the markdown price is set at $150 and so one color does not sell. Expected revenue decreases from $165 to $155. The fourth row shows that expected revenue would decrease to $157.50 [0.5($210) + 0.5($105)] if the store blindly followed the 50 percent rule and reduced the initial price of $210 to $105.

In this example the percentage markdown is

$$\frac{P_i - P_m}{P_i}100\% = \frac{\$210 - \$120}{\$210}100\% = 42.9\%$$

which lies between the 50 percent markdown for the fashion colors and 14.3 percent for the very conservative colors. Extrapolating from these results, we can conclude that the percentage markdown decreases as the dispersion in the prices that consumers will pay for the different colors decreases.

In this analysis of markdown pricing the store charges just two prices and sorts colored dresses by identifying those colors for which consumers are willing to pay at least P_i from those for which they are willing to pay less than P_i but P_m or more. If the firm could charge as many prices as there are colors, it could start with the highest price and sell the color that consumers prefer the most, then charge the price of the second most preferred color, and so on down to the price of the least preferred color. In this way the store learns the price that consumers are willing to pay for each color. Expected revenue equals expected price since all colors sell at the price at which consumers value each color. By moving down the demand function in this way the store learns the value that consumers place on every color. Stores seldom price in this way because a certain amount of time must pass for them to determine if a color is not selling because not enough serious customers have come into the store or because consumers do not value the color so highly. However, some stores do have a systematic policy of reducing the price every Y days until a garment is sold.

15-5 COMPETITIVE INDUSTRY EQUILIBRIUM

The preceding analysis of store pricing behavior considered the store in isolation. Now we place the store in a competitive industry to learn more about the percentage markup and markdown when the industry is in competitive long-run equilibrium.

Let's start with the assumptions that the retail market is competitive and that there is free entry. To simplify the analysis of the uncertainty case, we assume that the firm's long-run average and marginal cost are constant, so that the firm's long-run average and marginal cost functions are horizontal. As Chapter 8 demonstrates, profits must be zero in long-run industry equilibrium in the certainty case. When there is uncertainty, the equivalent zero profit condition requires that expected revenue per dress equal the marginal cost of purchasing and selling the dress. Since expected revenue is the revenue received per dress ordered, expected profits can be zero only if the long-run marginal and average cost of a dress equal expected revenue per dress.

> In the long run expected revenue must equal the marginal cost of a dress.

In the examples of high-fashion and moderately conservative dresses, we considered those price distributions where the expected price equaled $195 and found that expected revenue equaled $144 per dress when consumers were willing to pay from $60 to $330 for fashion colors, and $165 per dress when consumers were willing to pay from $120 to $270 for a moderately conservative line of colors. Given the same expected price, the greater the uncertainty, the lower the expected revenue. If one store sells a fashion line of clothing and another sells a more conservative line, a competitive market equilibrium in the market for high fashion and in the market for moderately conservative clothes requires long-run average and marginal costs equal to $165 for the conservative line and $144 for the fashion line. Then, the expected profits are zero for both stores and both markets are in long-run equilibrium.

The **percentage markup** is defined as the initial price less the marginal cost of the dress divided by the marginal cost, with the result multiplied by 100 percent.

$$\text{Percentage markup} = \frac{P_i - \text{MC}}{\text{MC}}100\%$$

For the fashion colors, the percentage markup of the initial price over marginal cost is $[(\$240 - \$144)/\$144]100\% = 66.7\%$ for the fashion colors, and the percentage markup of the initial price over marginal cost is $[(\$210 - \$165)/\$165]100\% = 33.3\%$ for the moderately conservative colors. The percentage markup is higher when uncertainty is greater. So, the uncertainty theory predicts that the equilibrium percentage markup over marginal cost will be higher for the fashion line than for the moderately conservative line and that fashion clothes will have larger percentage markups and percentage markdowns.

This chapter began by noting that women's apparel prices start higher at the beginning of the season and end lower than men's apparel prices do. The uncertainty theory explains this pattern of price movements. We can think of men's clothing as being more akin to the moderately conservative clothing and having a smaller dispersion in prices. The average price of dresses sold during the season is $180, and is $165 for the moderately conservative dresses. For the fashion colors, the initial price of $240 is 1.33 of the average price for the season, and the markdown price of $120 is .667 of the average price. For the moderately conservative line the initial price of $210 is 1.27 of the average price, and the markdown price of $120 is .73 of the average price. Relative to the average price, women's apparel prices start higher and end lower than men's apparel prices do. Figure 15-1 does indeed show larger seasonal price movements for women's than for men's clothes, and this evidence is consistent with the predictions of the uncertainty theory.

Differences in Market Equilibrium Prices under Certainty and Uncertainty

Let's contrast the market equilibrium under uncertainty and certainty. Instead of assuming the store does not know what prices consumers will pay for each color, assume that every store manager in a competitive industry is clairvoyant and knows what price customers are willing to pay for each color. As long as there is free entry into the industry, competition among stores lowers the price to the marginal cost of the dress. All dresses sell at the same price and at marginal cost. For example, if the store faces the price distribution for the fashion line and the long-run average and marginal cost of producing a dress is $180, the store manager orders only the six colors for which consumers are willing to pay $180 or more. He never orders dresses that consumers value at less than their marginal cost because they will not sell. Free entry of stores and competition among stores guarantee that all ordered dresses sell at a price equal to marginal cost. There is a single price of $180 and no clearance sales. Prices are stable throughout the season. Consequently, uncertainty plays a critical role in explaining the seasonal behavior of prices and the incidence of clearance sales.

Another explanation for the seasonal variation in prices is that each store practices third-degree price discrimination. It discriminates between consumers who buy early in the season and who have less elastic demand functions and those who buy late in the season and have more elastic demand functions. The price discrimination theory can also explain why prices fall throughout the season. However, this hypothesis does not explain why product selection is different in the two periods. If a store practices price discrimination under certainty, the demand functions for colors will differ in the two periods, but the store will order enough merchandise to sell at least some of the same colors in both periods but at different prices. The price discrimination–certainty hypothesis does not adequately explain why the merchandise selection is different in the initial and in the markdown periods.

When to Apply the Uncertainty Theory

The uncertainty theory developed in Sections 15-3 and 15-4 should be applied only in certain market situations. First, the firm must be uncertain about consumer tastes—the prices that consumers will pay for different colors or styles. Therefore, the theory applies to products subject to periodic changes in tastes such as fashion clothing. Another market in constant change with frequent new product introductions is the toy industry. In this industry manufacturers develop many new toys each year under uncertainty and have considerable difficulty predicting which will be successful.

The uncertainty theory does not explain the pricing of most hardware and canned grocery products. The designs of hammers, for instance, are very stable from season to season or from year to year. If hardware dealers increased prices at the beginning of the year and lowered them later, most consumers would refuse to buy at the beginning of the year. They know that the same product will be available later in the year at a lower price. Indeed, a season has little meaning. This is what distinguishes some but not all clothing from hardware. Automobile manufacturers face the same problem when they discontinue offering rebates in the middle of a model year. Consumers stop purchasing until the rebates are restored because they know that they will be able to purchase the same auto if they wait.

In the fashion market consumers buy early rather than late because they will not be able to purchase the same merchandise later at a lower price. The successful styles sell early. By waiting, consumers risk not being able to purchase a particular color or style later during the markdown period. If they were assured of purchasing a favorite color in the markdown period, some would indeed delay their purchases. The uncertainty model applies when the merchandise sold during the initial period is different from the merchandise sold during the markdown period.

In contrast, consider a classic blue blazer or a cashmere topcoat. Since the style does not change from year to year, some consumers will wait and purchase these items during the markdown period. Therefore, the theory applies less to a blazer or to more conservative or basic clothing. If this were true, we would expect less seasonal variation in the prices of blue blazers.

15-6   CHANGES IN THE PERCENTAGE MARKUP AND MARKDOWN OVER TIME

The uncertainty theory predicts that the percentage markup and markdown will be larger during times when uncertainty is greater and for products where there is more uncertainty about the values that consumers place on different colors, styles, fabrics, and silhouettes. Some evidence is consistent with these predictions.

APPLICATION 15-2

Growth of Markups and Markdowns for Department Stores

Figure 15-8 shows the percentage markup and markdown given by department stores on merchandise sold since 1925. This graph reveals that a distinct change occurred in the late 1960s. After about 40 years with no trend in either series, both began to increase in the late 1960s. One explanation for the growth of markups and markdowns is that uncertainty began to increase as consumers demanded more fashionable clothing. For example, a greater use of prints and colors would mirror a shift toward more fashionable attire. Some data on color use are available, and they indicate a shift throughout the 1960s away from whites to greater use of solid colors and to prints. Also, consumers shifted away from more formal and tailored clothing to greater reliance on sportswear and casual wear where there are fewer accepted guidelines. Each of these changes increases uncertainty and

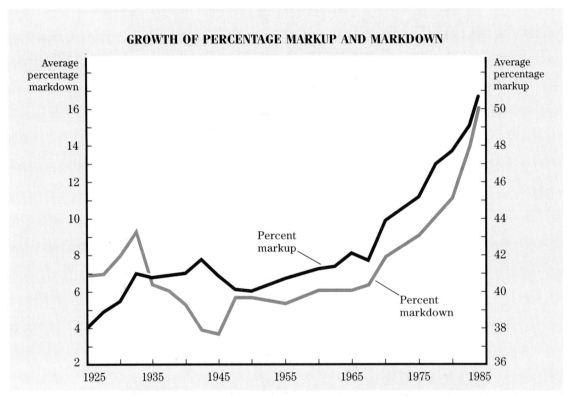

Figure 15-8   The percentage markup and the percentage markdown have increased since the late 1960s after remaining stable for about 40 years. [*Adapted from B. Peter Pashigian, "Demand Uncertainty and Sales: A Study of Fashion and Markdown Pricing,"* American Economic Review, *December 1988, fig. 1, p. 941.*]

makes it more difficult to predict the demand for colors and styles and could explain the increase in the percentage markup and markdown.

APPLICATION 15-3

Markdowns by Merchandise Group

There are other differences in price behavior based on merchandise group that for the most part are consistent with the uncertainty hypothesis. Department stores report the dollar value of all markdowns as a percentage of the total value of goods sold by merchandise group. For example, in the first example involving fashion colors the price of four of eight colored dresses decreases by $120 from an initial price of $240 to $120. Total dollar markdowns are 4($120) = $480. The store's total sales volume equals four colors sold at $240 each and four colors sold at $120 each, for a total of $960 + $480 = $1,440. The ratio of dollar markdowns to total dollar sales is $480/$1440 = 0.333.

Table 15-6 shows dollar markdowns as a percentage of total sales volume of department stores by merchandise groups in 1966, 1977, and 1984. Columns 2 and 3 list dollar markdowns relative to sales volume for women's fashion merchandise (shoes, dresses, coats, and so on) and for women's standard merchandise (undergarments) where fashion changes have been less important. Column 4 shows the percentage for men's apparel, and column 5, the percentage for junior and teens' clothing and accessories.

Style and fashion changes are more frequent in some merchandise lines than in others. In 1965 markdowns relative to dollar sales were higher for women's fashion apparel than for women's standard apparel where uncertainty is lower. Markdowns were also higher in the teens' and junior clothing group.

Table 15-6   DOLLAR MARKDOWNS AS A PERCENTAGE OF TOTAL DOLLAR VOLUME

YEAR (1)	WOMEN'S FASHION APPAREL AND ACCESSORIES (2)	WOMEN'S STANDARD APPAREL (3)	MEN'S APPAREL AND ACCESSORIES (4)	TEENS' AND JUNIOR APPAREL (5)
1965	10.2	4.5	6.6	10.8
1977	11.8	8.2	10.8	18.2
1984	19.8	13.8	19.3	27.0

Source: Adapted from B. Peter Pashigian, "Demand Uncertainty and Sales: A Study of Fashion and Markdown Pricing," *American Economic Review,* vol. 78, December 1988, table 3, p. 947.

These long-standing historical differences began to change slowly after 1965. By 1984 markdowns had exploded in the teens' and junior merchandise group, where fashion has become so much more important and where fashion successes are very transient. One surprising change was the rapid growth of markdowns for men's apparel. By 1984 markdowns relative to sales volume were slightly less than the markdowns for women's apparel, although well below the relative markdowns for teens' and junior clothing. While fashion has become more important over time in the selling of men's apparel, the size of the change is puzzling. More research is required before all these changes can be fully explained.

A reasonable interpretation of these broad trends is that department stores are selling more fashion merchandise in recent years than they did in 1965, and so greater uncertainty is present now than before. Now it is more difficult to predict which styles, colors, and silhouettes will sell than before, and this rise in uncertainty has caused an increase in percentage markdown.

SUMMARY

- Sales can be classified as preseason, within-season, and end-of-season clearance sales.
- Uncertainty about consumer tastes is the primary cause of clearance sales.
- Uncertainty about consumer tastes is described by a probability distribution of prices that consumers are willing to pay for different colors.
- Expected revenue per dress is higher if a firm charges an initial and a markdown price rather than a single price throughout the season.
- The uncertainty theory predicts that the percentage markdown and percentage markup will be larger and the fraction of goods sold will be lower for fashion-type goods as uncertainty increases.
- The uncertainty theory applies to products subject to frequent new product introductions such as fashion clothing.

KEY TERMS

Preseason, within-season, and   Seasonal variation
    clearance sales   Expected price
Uncertainty and the demand   Expected revenue
    function for colors   Two-price policy
Cumulative distribution of prices   Percentage markup
Single-price policy

REVIEW QUESTIONS

1. What is expected price?
2. What is expected revenue?

3. Why does expected price differ from expected revenue?
4. Describe in your own words what the expected revenue of a store is when it charges a single price thoughout the season.
5. Describe in your own words what the expected revenue of a store is when it charges two prices throughout the season.
6. Explain why expected revenue can be less than the price at which dresses are sold.
7. Predict how the seasonal variation in prices of made-to-order men's suits would differ from prices for ready-made suits.

EXERCISES

1. Explain why you would expect the percentage markdown to be lower for men's white shirts than for striped shirts.
2. The demand function for colors is

$$P = \$390 - \$30C$$

where $C = 1, 2, \ldots , 12$. If a firm charges only a single price, what price maximizes expected revenue. What is expected revenue? Do all the colors sell?
3. The demand function for colors is

$$P = \$390 - \$30C$$

where $C = 1, 2, \ldots , 12$. What are the optimal initial and markdown prices? What is the expected revenue per dress? Do all colors sell?
4. Suppose the demand function for colors is

$$P = \$270 - \$30C$$

where $C = 1, 2, 3,$ or 4. Derive an expression for $F(P)$ and show that the initial price is \$210 and the optimal markdown price is \$150. Do all colors sell?
5. Suppose a department store decides to compensate the firm's buyers of merchandise by the formula

$C = a + b$ (total retail sales of the line) $+ c$ (percentage of units not sold)

where C is annual compensation and a, b, and c are constants; a and b are positive, and c is negative. What effect will this compensation formula have on the behavior of employees whose responsibility is to purchase merchandise a year in advance?
6. A few years ago Sears announced and adopted an "everyday low price" policy. The goal was to charge a stable price for each item and to eliminate sales. The company also announced a new policy of selling brand name women's clothing. Comment on the wisdom of this policy. Under what conditions will an "everyday low price" policy be justified and when will it fail?
7. Explain why you would expect to find a higher percentage markdown for imported goods than for domestically produced goods, other factors being constant.

8. A recent study found that men's dress shirts, men's sweaters, women's blouses, and women's sweaters that had a higher initial price sold at a higher average percentage markdown than the clothing in each category that had a lower initial price. Use the theory of pricing under uncertainty to explain these pricing patterns.

9. A study of men's dress shirts found that the average initial price for shirts not sold on sale was $19.24, and for those subsequently sold on sale, $24.89. Present an explanation for these findings.

CONSUMER AND SUPPLIER BEHAVIOR OVER TIME

Most of this book has dealt with the choices of consumers and producers who maximize utility or profits over a single period. The time horizon of these agents, be they consumers or producers, was a single period. In the models the consumer maximized utility as if there were no tomorrow, and so too did the profit-maximizing producer. We deliberately avoided some difficult but interesting questions about behavior over time, for the greater simplicity of the single-period analysis.

Economists can justify this apparent tunnel vision when the consequences of ignoring the future are not serious. If the determinants of the demand for a perishable good are of interest, the one-period model presented in Chapters 2 through 4 describes the consumer's actual consumption decisions. But the future cannot always be ignored. In any explanation of savings and borrowing behavior, there must be a tomorrow, otherwise the motivation for savings would evaporate. To describe consumer behavior over time, we formulate a theory that, among other things, explains why a consumer chooses to save and therefore consumes less today in order to have more tomorrow. The intertemporal theory of consumer behavior explains how the consumer decides how much to spend and save over time and creates a link between current and future spending.

There is a link between the present and the future on the supply side of the market as well as on the demand side. The number of bushels of tomatoes that a competitive producer supplies this year depends primarily on this year's price because tomatoes are costly to store from one season to another. The quantity supplied this year does not depend on what the price will be next year. In contrast, an owner of a gold mine thinks differently. He or she needs to know the future as well as the current price to decide how much gold to sell this year. Knowing what to do today requires knowledge of current *and* future prices. In the second half of this chapter prices are linked over time in an intertemporal market equilibrium as consumers and suppliers determine the depletion of a nonrenewable resource.

This chapter expands the theory of consumer and producer behavior under perfect foresight and shows how foreseen changes in future demand and supply conditions affect the present behavior of consumers and suppliers.

16-1 TELESCOPING THE FUTURE INTO THE PRESENT

Most individuals would prefer to receive a dollar today than a dollar in some future year because a dollar in hand earns interest if invested. (See the appendix to Chapter 14 for a discussion of present value and its calculation.) At the end of one year a dollar increases in value to $1 + i$ if the real interest rate is i percent per year. A dollar today becomes $1.05 if the annual interest rate is 5 percent. The 5 percent is a real return because it is assumed throughout the chapter that there is neither inflation nor deflation.

This chapter considers a series of two-period problems where an individual receives income I_1 at the beginning of period 1 and I_2 at the beginning of period 2. To find the amount you would accept today instead of receiving I_2 at the beginning of year 2, you must calculate the present value of this truncated stream of income. Present value is an amount received today that is equivalent to an amount received in some future year. The procedure for determining the present value of a future dollar is called **discounting.**

> The **present value** of future income is an amount received immediately that is equivalent to the income received in a future year.

The present value of I_1 is simply I_1, because income is received at the beginning of year 1 and no lesser amount can be equivalent to I_1. What is the present value of I_2? In other words, what amount received at the beginning of year 1 is equivalent to receiving I_2 at the beginning of year 2? You are indifferent between receiving I_2 in year 2 or receiving $I_2/(1 + i)$ in year 1. For example, receiving $1,000 at the beginning of year 2 is equivalent to receiving $1,000/(1 + 0.05) = $952.38 at the beginning of year 1 if the interest rate is 5 percent. If you receive $I_2/(1 + i)$ at the beginning of year 1 and earn an annual interest rate of i on this amount, you will have $[I_2/(1 + i)](1 + i) = I_2$ at the beginning of year 2. There is an exact equivalence between receiving $I_2/(1 + i)$ in year 1 and receiving I_2 in year 2. We can say that the present value of I_2 is $I_2/(1 + i)$. To determine the present value of income received at the beginning of year n, divide income in year n by $1 + i$ raised to the power $n - 1$, or $I_n/(1 + i)^{n-1}$.

Column 3 of Table 16-1 shows the present value of income in each future year when an individual receives income at the beginning of the year.

The present value of an income stream is equal to the sum of the present value of each year's income. The present value of an income stream of $I_1, I_2, I_3, \ldots, I_n$ is

Table 16-1   PRESENT VALUE OF INCOME

YEAR (1)	INCOME (2)	PRESENT VALUE OF INCOME RECEIVED AT BEGINNING OF YEAR (3)
1	I_1	I_1
2	I_2	$\dfrac{I_2}{1 + i}$
3	I_3	$\dfrac{I_3}{(1 + i)^2}$
.	.	.
.	.	.
.	.	.
n	I_n	$\dfrac{I_n}{(1 + i)^{n-1}}$

Table 16-2   **PRESENT VALUE BASED ON NUMBER OF PAYMENTS AND INTEREST RATE**

INTEREST RATE (%)	5 PAYMENTS RECEIVED ($)	10 PAYMENTS RECEIVED ($)
3	94,342	175,722
4	92,598	168,707
5	90,919	162,156
6	89,302	156,034

$$\text{Present value} = I_1 + \frac{I_2}{1+i} + \frac{I_3}{(1+i)^2} + \cdots + \frac{I_n}{(1+i)^{n-1}} \qquad \textbf{(16-1)}$$

Equation 16-1 assumes that the interest rate is constant. If it changed from year to year, a time subscript would be attached to each interest rate. The formula for the present value of an income stream reduces to a concise and useful expression when the income stream is constant. In the special case where $I_1 = I_2 = I_3 = \cdots = I_n = I^\bullet$, the present value of the income stream[1] at the beginning of the year is

$$\text{PV} = \frac{1 - [1/(1+i)^n]}{1 - [1/(1+i)]} I^\bullet \qquad \begin{array}{l} \text{(Present Value of} \\ \text{a Finite Constant Income Stream)} \end{array} \qquad \textbf{(16-2)}$$

Table 16-2 shows the present value at different interest rates if you receive $20,000 at the beginning of each year for 5 years or if you receive $20,000 each year for 10 years. If the interest rate is 5 percent, the present value of income is $90,919 when there are 5 installments, and $162,156 if there are 10 installments. Notice that doubling the number of years comes nowhere near doubling the present value. The contribution to present value of income received far into the future is progressively lower because of the discounting effect. The larger the interest rate, the lower the present value, since any sum received immediately will increase more rapidly with a higher rate of interest. Here again, the higher the interest rate, the smaller the contribution of a more distant payment to present value.

---

[1] The present value of n equal annual payments of $I^\bullet$ is

$$\text{PV} = \text{Present value} = (1 + D + D^2 + \cdots + D^{n-1})I^\bullet$$

where $D = 1/(1+i)$. Multiplying and dividing the expression for present value by $1 - D$ yields

$$\text{PV} = \text{Present value} = (1 - D)(1 + D + D^2 + \cdots + D^{n-1})\frac{I^\bullet}{1 - D}$$

$$= (1 - D + D - D^2 + D^2 + \cdots - D^n)\frac{I^\bullet}{1 - D}$$

Canceling successive terms results in

$$\text{PV} = \frac{1 - D^n}{1 - D}I^\bullet = \frac{1 - [1/(1+i)^n]}{1 - [1/(1+i)]}I^\bullet$$

APPLICATION 16-1

Mustering Out of the Military

With the decline of the Soviet Union and the diminished intensity of the Cold War, the United States reduced the size of the armed forces drastically. The army planned for a 25 percent reduction in personnel starting in 1992 and recognized that it would have to offer financial incentives to reach this target.[2] For example, a staff sergeant leaving the Army with 13.5 years of service can choose between a lump sum payment of $34,000 (plus the standard involuntary separation pay of $25,000) or time payments of 27 annual checks of $5,600 each for a total of $151,200 (as well as the involuntary termination pay of $25,000). If you ignore discounting, the 27 annual checks of $5,600 each far exceed the one-time payment of $34,000. However, this is not the right comparison to make because a dollar received in the future is worth less than a dollar received in the current year.

Assume that a staff sergeant decides to separate from the Army and must select one of the two options. He or she must calculate the present value of the income stream and determine if it is greater than $34,000. To get a sense of the magnitudes involved, let's find an interest rate that equates $34,000 to the present value of 27 annual checks of $5,600 each. Then the sergeant can decide if the interest rate that he or she can hope to earn is greater or less than this interest rate. If it is less, then the sergeant should select the 27 annual payments of $5,600 each because the present value of the series of payments exceeds $34,000.

Equation 16-2 can be used to calculate present values. The present value of 27 annual checks at a 19 percent interest rate is $34,753, and for a 20 percent interest rate, $33,355. It appears that the sergeant would have to earn an interest rate of slightly more than 19 percent on savings before the lump sum payment would be the superior choice. This seems an unlikely eventuality for most individuals. In most cases the present value of 27 annual checks of $5,600 each is larger than $34,000. On the other hand, some individuals may have a severe liquidity constraint, and so they will accept the lump sum payment. (Incidentally, we have ignored any reductions in income because of taxes.) It appears that the Army hopes those leaving the service will select the option with 27 annual payments.

16-2 CONSUMPTION SPENDING OVER TIME

The present-value concept comes in handy in studying a consumer's intertemporal consumption decisions. In Chapters 2 through 4 the consumer maximized utility given the income and prices in a one-period model. The savings decision was ignored because there is no reason to save in a one-period model.

The limitations of the static model become apparent when we ask what deter-

---

[2] Based on David Evans, "Army Lures Volunteers to Retire," *Chicago Tribune*, January 10, 1992.

mines how much a consumer saves or borrows. Answering this question requires a more sophisticated model of consumer behavior that explains savings and borrowing decisions over time.

Consider the following scenario that you will hopefully experience sometime during your career. Your annual salary in year 1 is I_1. In January of year 1 you receive some great news during your annual job performance review. Your manager tells you that the company is very pleased with your job performance. She announces your promotion to her position in January of year 2 when she retires, at which time you will receive a 50 percent raise and I_2 will be $1.5I_1$.

You can look forward to a hefty salary increase. How will your salary increase in year 2 affect your consumption spending in year 1 and in year 2? If you mechanically applied the theory in Chapter 2 to this situation, you would predict that your consumption spending in year 1 will remain relatively low because your annual income remains low, but will soar in year 2 when your income increases by 50 percent. You will go from a relative pauper in year 1 to a prince or princess in year 2.

This prediction assumes that you are unable to borrow, an unlikely event in an economy awash in credit cards and personal loans. If you can borrow by promising to repay the loan when you earn the higher income, you can moderate the sharp swing in consumption spending and, depending on your preferences, may be able to increase your utility. Somehow, your future income should affect your current consumption spending.

To analyze consumption spending over time, we introduce a theory of intertemporal consumption behavior. We develop a two-period model in which the income of the consumer differs in each period and then we demonstrate how a consumer determines how much to save or borrow.

The Intertemporal Budget Constraint

A building block of the revised theory of consumer behavior is the intertemporal budget constraint. This concept shows how future consumption spending is related to current consumption spending. Let's demonstrate how to derive the intertemporal budget constraint. I_1 is the income of the consumer in the first year, and I_2 is the income in year 2. Given the income earned in the two years and an annual interest rate i, we can derive a relationship between consumption spending in year 2 and in year 1. Savings in year 1 equal income less spending on consumption, or $S_1 = I_1 - C_1$, where S_1 represents savings in year 1 and C_1 is spending on a composite good in year 1. The consumer saves if income is greater than consumption spending in year 1 and borrows if income is less than consumption spending in year 1.

Consumption spending in year 2 (C_2) is related to consumption spending in year 1 (C_1) through the equation

$$\text{Consumption in year 2} = \text{Income in year 2} + \text{Savings in year 1} + \text{Interest on savings in year 1}$$

$$C_2 = I_2 + (I_1 - C_1) + i(I_1 - C_1)$$

Rewriting this equation to show how C_2 is related to C_1 results in

$$C_2 = I_2 + (1 + i)(I_1 - C_1)$$

$$= [I_2 + (1 + i)I_1] - (1 + i)C_1 \qquad \text{(Intertemporal Budget Constraint)} \quad \textbf{(16-3)}$$

Equation 16-3 is the intertemporal budget constraint of the consumer. It shows how spending in year 2 relates to spending in year 1. If borrowing is not permitted, the budget constraint in equation 16-3 is valid only for $I_1 \geq C_1$. If the consumer does not save in year 1, so $I_1 = C_1$, consumption in year 2 must be I_2. Suppose the consumer saves $I_1 - C_1 > 0$ in year 1. Then, total consumption in year 2 exceeds I_2 by $(1 + i)(I_1 - C_1)$, or the savings in year 1 plus the interest earned on the savings in year 1.

> The intertemporal budget constraint shows how consumption spending in year 2 is related to consumption spending in year 1.

By borrowing in year 1, spending on consumption will exceed income in year 1, and so $I_1 - C_1 < 0$. Equation 16-3 says that consumption spending in year 2 decreases by $1 + i$ for every dollar borrowed in year 1 to increase C_1. Throughout this analysis we assume that the lending and borrowing rates are the same.

Equation 16-3 shows the tradeoff between future consumption, C_2, and current consumption, C_1. The intertemporal budget constraint is graphed in Figure 16-1. The vertical axis measures consumption spending, C_2, on a composite good in year 2, and the horizontal axis measures consumption spending, C_1, on a composite good in year 1. Given an income of I_1' in year 1 and I_2' in year 2 and the interest rate on savings, the intertemporal budget constraint is a straight line. The intercept on the vertical axis is $I_2' + (1 + i)I_1'$, or the consumer's maximum consumption spending in year 2 if nothing is spent on consumption in year 1. The slope of the intertemporal budget constraint is $-(1 + i)$. For every dollar increase in consumption in year 1, consumption in year 2 decreases by a dollar plus the forgone annual interest of i percent. Therefore, the opportunity cost of increasing consumption in year 1 by a dollar is a fall in consumption in year 2 by $1 + i$.

$$\frac{\Delta C_2}{\Delta C_1} = -(1 + i) \qquad \text{(Slope of Intertemporal Budget Constraint)} \qquad \textbf{(16-4)}$$

The intertemporal budget constraint is line $a'a$ in Figure 16-1a if the consumer cannot borrow and represents all affordable market baskets. Point a is the endowment point of the consumer. It shows that the income of this individual is I_1' in year 1 and I_2' in year 2. In Figure 16-1a income is lower in year 1 than in year 2 at point a. Consumption spending in year 1 cannot exceed I_1' because the individual cannot borrow. Although the future looks rosy, it is not possible to convert future prosperity into greater immediate consumption because the consumer cannot borrow.

Figure 16-1b shows that the affordable market baskets of the consumer expand to include the dashed segment ab when the consumer can borrow at an annual interest rate of i. The intertemporal budget constraint now becomes the extended

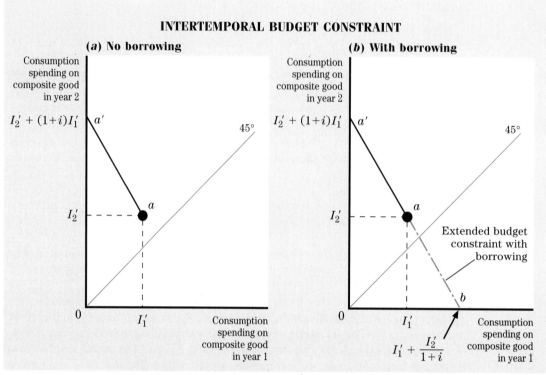

Figure 16-1 (*a*) The intertemporal budget constraint is line $a'a$ when the consumer cannot borrow. Consumption in year 1 cannot exceed I_1', income in year 1. Consumption in year 2 can increase to $I_2' + (1 + i)I_1'$. (*b*) The individual can borrow at an annual interest rate of i percent per year. Although income is lower in year 1 than in year 2, consumption in year 1 can exceed income in year 1 because the consumer can borrow. The intertemporal budget constraint is extended to include the segment ab.

line $a'ab$. By borrowing against future income, the individual can spend more than I_1' on consumption in the first year.

By how much can consumption be increased in year 1 by borrowing against income in year 2? Hypothetically, let's assume the consumer is willing to use all the income in year 2 to pay off a loan assumed in year 1 to support consumption spending in year 1. In this case consumption in year 2 is zero. The maximum value of C_1 can be determined by setting C_2 equal to zero in the consumer's intertemporal budget constraint and solving equation 16-3 for C_1.

$$0 = [I_2' + (1 + i)I_1'] - (1 + i)C_1$$

$$C_1 = I_1' + \frac{I_2'}{1 + i} \qquad \text{(Maximum Spending on Consumption in Year 1)} \qquad \textbf{(16-5)}$$

The expression on the right-hand side of equation 16-5 is the present value of income. The consumer can spend $I_1' + I_2'/(1 + i)$ in year 1 by borrowing $I_2'/(1 + i)$ from the lender in year 1 and paying I_2' to the lender in year 2.

Intertemporal Preferences

The intertemporal budget constraint shows all affordable market baskets for the two years. To determine which one the consumer selects in each year, we must describe the consumer's preferences between present and future consumption.

The intertemporal preference map of the consumer describes his or her intertemporal tradeoffs. Utility depends on consumption spending on a composite good in each year.

$$U = U(C_1, C_2) \qquad \text{(Intertemporal Utility Function)} \qquad \textbf{(16-6)}$$

The indifference curves of the utility function show the rate at which the consumer is willing to substitute future consumption for current consumption, keeping utility constant.

> The slope at a point on an indifference curve is defined as the marginal rate of time preference (MRTP).

$$\text{MRTP} = \left. \frac{\Delta C_1}{\Delta C_2} \right|_{U = U_0} \qquad \text{(Marginal Rate of Time Preference)} \qquad \textbf{(16-7)}$$

Consumers' relative valuations between future and current consumption differ just as their indifference curves between goods differ. Some individuals are willing to sacrifice more than a dollar of future consumption for a dollar of current consumption, and others are willing to sacrifice less than a dollar of future consumption. The intertemporal utility functions of consumers differ because their time preferences between present and future consumption differ.

Figure 16-2 shows indifference curves for three consumers. Figure 16-2a illustrates an indifference curve of an impatient consumer. At any point on the thin 45-degree line spending on current consumption is equal to spending on future consumption. When future and current consumption spending are equal, this consumer remains indifferent by substituting more than a dollar of future consumption for a dollar less of current consumption. He values current consumption so much that he must receive more than a dollar of future consumption for a dollar less of current consumption to remain indifferent. For example, he might be indifferent between sacrificing a dollar of current consumption for $1.25 more in future consumption when current and future consumption are equal. The line aa has a slope of -1 and cuts through the indifference curve as it crosses the 45-degree line. The line bb is tangent to the indifference curve U_0 at the point where the indifference curve passes through the 45-degree line, and its slope is less than -1. The marginal rate of time preference of an impatient consumer is therefore numerically less than -1. In other words, the indifference curve is steeper than aa when C_1 and C_2 are the same.

In contrast, Figure 16-2b shows the indifference curve of a consumer who is neutral between current and future consumption spending. She has a marginal rate of time preference equal to -1 when current spending and future spending are equal and is indifferent between forgoing a dollar of current consumption for one more dollar of future consumption.

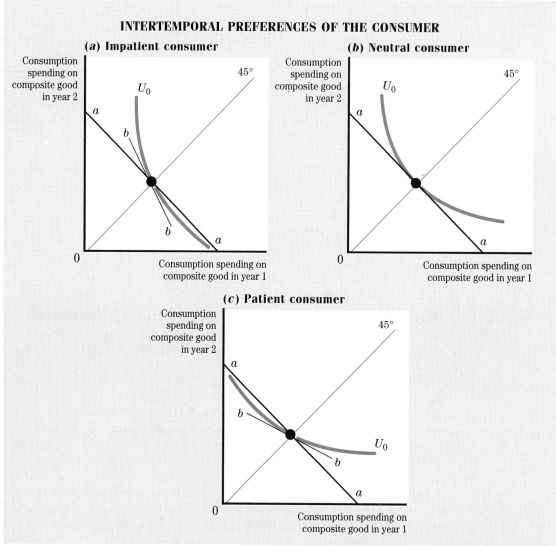

Figure 16-2 (*a*) Indifference curve of an impatient consumer. The slope of line *aa* equals −1. Line *bb* is tangent to the indifference curve when consumption in the 2 years is the same and has a slope that is less than −1. Therefore, the slope of the indifference curve is less than −1. This consumer will be indifferent by giving up a dollar of current consumption only if future consumption spending increases by more than a dollar. The indifference curve of the consumer in (*b*) has a slope equal to −1 when spending is the same in both years. The consumer in (*c*) remains indifferent by giving up a dollar in current spending if future consumption spending increases by less than a dollar.

Finally, Figure 16-2c shows an indifference curve of a patient consumer who remains indifferent when sacrificing a dollar of current consumption for less than a dollar increase in future consumption. The marginal time preference is numerically greater than -1 when current and future consumption are the same.

Intertemporal Utility Maximization of the Consumer

The goal of a consumer is to maximize utility while satisfying the intertemporal budget constraint. To achieve this goal she must decide how much to spend on current and future consumption. To find a market basket of current and future consumption spending that maximizes utility, we superimpose the intertemporal budget constraint cc' on the intertemporal preference map in Figure 16-3. Consumers reach the highest indifference curve and maximize utility by equating the marginal rate of time preference to the slope of the intertemporal budget constraint.

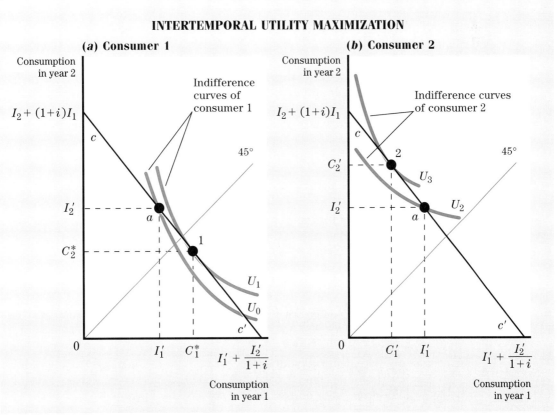

INTERTEMPORAL UTILITY MAXIMIZATION

Figure 16-3   Point a in (a) and (b) shows that two consumers have the same income endowment. (a) Consumer 1 reaches indifference curve U_1 at point 1 by borrowing $C_1^* - I_1$ in year 1, spending C_1^* in year 1, and spending C_2^* in year 2. The marginal rate of time preference equals the slope of the intertemporal budget constraint at point 1. (b) Consumer 2 is more patient and saves $I_1' - C_1'$ in year 1 and reaches indifference curve U_3 at point 2.

$$\text{MRTP} = -(1 + i) \qquad \text{(Condition for Maximizing Utility)} \qquad \textbf{(16-8)}$$

Figure 16-3 shows the indifference curves of two consumers. The endowment point of both is at point a on cc'. For each consumer income is I_1' in year 1 and I_2' in year 2. While the two individuals have the same income endowment, they have different time preferences and their saving or borrowing behavior differs. The indifference curves U_0 and U_1 in Figure 16-3a are the indifference curves of consumer 1, an impatient consumer. When current and future consumption are equal, he remains indifferent by substituting more than a dollar of future consumption for one less dollar of current consumption. At point a his indifference curve is steeper than the intertemporal budget constraint. He is willing to give up more dollars of future consumption for one more dollar of current consumption than is required by the market. The indifference curves U_2 and U_3 in Figure 16-3b are those of consumer 2, a patient consumer. At point a the slope of the indifference curve is less steep than the slope of the intertemporal budget constraint.

In Figure 16-3a consumer 1 maximizes utility by moving from point a to point 1 where the slope of the intertemporal budget constraint equals the marginal rate of time preference. At point 1 the rate at which the consumer can trade future consumption for current consumption equals the rate at which he is willing to do so. In contrast, at point a he is willing to give up more future consumption for one more dollar of current consumption than is required by the intertemporal budget constraint. Therefore, his utility increases by increasing current consumption. Consumer 1 borrows $C_1^* - I_1'$ in year 1 and spends C_1^* in year 1 and C_2^* in year 2 on a composite good. He reaches the indifference curve U_1 by borrowing to increase consumption spending in year 1 and to reduce consumption spending in year 2. If he were prohibited from borrowing, he would remain at point a on indifference curve U_0, a lower indifference curve.

In Figure 16-3b consumer 2 maximizes utility at point 2. By saving $I_1' - C_1'$ in year 1, she is willing to forgo current consumption to increase future consumption to C_2'. Consumer 1, unlike consumer 2, does not want to postpone consumption. As you can see, consumer 1 is demanding loanable funds at the interest rate i, while consumer 2 is supplying loanable funds at the interest rate i. A consumer who maximizes utility at some point along the line segment ca saves in year 1, whereas a consumer who maximizes utility at some point along the line segment ac' borrows in year 1.

This comparison of the behavior of impatient and patient consumers shows that two consumers with the same income endowment make different consumption choices because they have different time preferences between current and future consumption. Impatient consumers tend to borrow and demand loanable funds, while patient consumers tend to save and indirectly lend funds. Both are better off by being allowed to either borrow or save as the case might be.

The Importance of Present Value of Income

The theory of intertemporal utility maximization contains a key implication that is easy to miss if you are not careful. Given the interest rate, spending on a composite good in year 1 and in year 2 is determined not by current income but by the present value of income. Consumer spending in either year does not depend on the particular values of I_1 and I_2 but on the present value of income, $I_1' + I_2'/(1 + i)$.

The theory of maximizing utility over time predicts that a change in the distribution of income between the first and second years that does not affect present value of income has no effect on consumption spending. To demonstrate this, consider an example where you receive two job offers, one from a firm in industry A and another from a firm in industry B. The position in industry A pays a higher income than the position in industry B in year 1, but a lower income in year 2. Although the two jobs involve different salaries over time, the present value of income is the same for both. To illustrate, let's assume the interest rate on savings is 8 percent per year and the position in industry A pays $35,000 in year 1 and $38,000 in year 2. The present value of future income is $35,000 + $38,000/ (1 + 0.08) = $35,000 + $35,185 = $70,185. The position in industry B pays $29,444 in year 1 and $44,000 in year 2. The present value of future income is $29,444 + $44,000/(1 + 0.08) = $29,444 + $40,741 = $70,185, and so the present values of the incomes for the two positions are equal.

Will your consumption spending differ if you select one job instead of the other? The theory of intertemporal utility maximization says it should not. In the perfect foresight model point *a* in Figure 16-4 shows your income in the two years if you accept job A. Point *b* represents your income in the two years if you accept job B. Income in year 1 is lower in industry B but higher in year 2. The horizontal intercept of the intertemporal budget constraint equals the present value of income, or $70,185 at an 8 percent interest rate, whether you take job A or job B. The vertical intercept of the intertemporal budget constraint is $I_1 + (1 + i)I_2 =$ $76,964. Because the present value of future income is the same, the intertemporal budget constraint is the same no matter which of the two positions you accept, assuming that you can borrow at the interest rate i. Even if you select job B and earn only $29,444 in year 1, you will go into debt and spend C_1^* on consumption in year 1 and C_2^* in year 2. Although you have less income in year 1, you maximize utility by spending C_1^* on consumption in year 1. You borrow more in year 1 when you accept job B, but your borrowing power is greater because you will have a higher income in year 2. You maximize utility by consuming C_1^* in year 1 whether you accept the position in industry A or industry B. In the perfect foresight model, no matter what the starting point on the intertemporal budget constraint is, the consumer will spend C_1^* in the first year.

> When a consumer can borrow, the intertemporal theory of utility maximization says that the present value of income and not the income in any one year determines consumption spending in each year.

The theory of intertemporal utility maximization changes our predictions of consumer behavior. The intertemporal theory of consumption predicts that an individual with a short-term or transitory increase in earnings in the current year will increase consumption spending in year 1 by less than another individual who receives the same increase in the current year but whose income increase is permanent. The permanent increase raises the present value of income by more

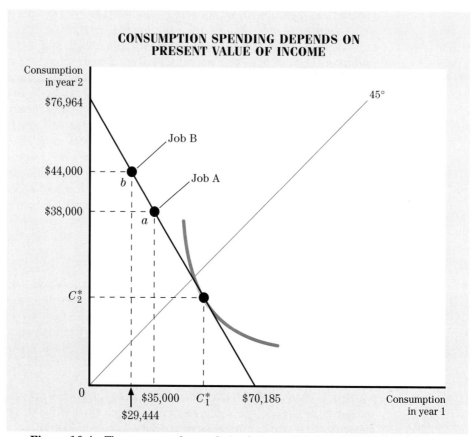

**CONSUMPTION SPENDING DEPENDS ON
PRESENT VALUE OF INCOME**

Figure 16-4   The consumer has a choice between job A and job B. Job A pays more in the first year than job B but less in the second year. The present values of the two jobs are the same since they are on the same intertemporal budget constraint. The theory of intertemporal consumption behavior says that the consumer will spend C_1^* in year 1 and C_2^* in year 2 no matter which job is selected.

than the short-term increase. We can contrast the implications of the simpler one-period theory of consumer behavior with those of the intertemporal theory. The simpler theory of consumer behavior presented in Chapter 2 says that the two workers would increase their spending by the same amount in year 1 since both receive the same increase in income in year 1.

Another example comes from a situation facing newly elected President Clinton in 1993. When the President took office, he faced the short-run problem of reviving the economy and the long-run problem of reducing the deficit. There was talk of passing a short-run tax cut to boost the economy and later raising taxes to prevent the deficit from increasing. Let's look at an individual consumer and determine how lowering and then raising taxes will affect his or her intertemporal consumption decisions. Given total spending, a reduction in taxes in year 1 requires the government to borrow an additional amount just equal to the decrease in taxes.

Because taxes are lowered in year 1, the individual's after-tax income increases. In year 2 the increase in taxes lowers after-tax income. Assume that the increased taxes in year 2 equal government borrowing in year 1 plus the interest paid on the amount borrowed. After-tax income in year 1 increases from I_1 to $I_1 + \Delta I$ because taxes fall and borrowing increases. However, taxes increase in year 2, and so the consumer's income in year 2 decreases from I_2 to $I_2 - \Delta I(1 + i)$ to repay the amount borrowed in year 1 with interest. Therefore, the present value of income is unchanged because

$$I_1 + \Delta I + \frac{I_2 - \Delta I(1 + i)}{1 + i} = I_1 + \frac{I_2}{i + i}$$

Consequently, the intertemporal theory of utility maximization predicts that consumption spending will be unaffected. In contrast, the simpler theory of consumer behavior developed in Chapter 2 incorrectly predicts that a fall in taxes in year 1 will increase after-tax income and consumer spending in year 1 and that just the opposite would happen in year 2 when taxes increase.

The intertemporal theory of utility maximization predicts that an increase in current income will affect current consumption differently depending on whether the increase is or is not permanent. For an example of this situation consider two individuals who experience a salary increase in year 1. The first individual is a fire fighter who extinguishes oil fires. After the 1991 Gulf War, he experienced a large short-term blip in earnings. Let's say for the sake of argument that his earnings doubled. The second individual is an executive whose salary doubles when she is promoted. Income doubles in year 1 for both, but the increased earnings of the executive continue into the second year as well, whereas the fire fighter's income in year 2 drops back to what it would have been had the Gulf War not taken place. Assume that the earnings of the fire fighter would have been $_f I_1$ in year 1 and $_f I_2$ in year 2 if the Gulf War had not occurred, and that the earnings of the executive would have been $_e I_1$ in year 1 and $_e I_2$ in year 2 if she had not been promoted. Because of the Gulf War and because of the executive's promotion the present value of the earnings of the two individuals at the beginning of year 1 are $2_f I_1 + {}_f I_2/(1 + i)$ for the fire fighter and $2_e I_1 + 2[_e I_2/(1 + i)]$ for the executive.

The present value of earnings of the executive doubles, while the present value of the earnings of the fire fighter increases but does not double, and so the consumption behavior of these two individuals will differ. A simple one-period model predicts that both individuals will increase consumption in year 1 by approximately the same percentage because the current income of both doubles. The intertemporal theory predicts that the consumption spending of the executive will rise by a larger percentage in year 1 because her present value of future earnings increases by a larger percentage.

The Effect on Saving of an Increase in Current or Future Income

Given current income, a rise in an individual's future income shifts the intertemporal budget constraint outward. In Figure 16-5 a consumer with an income en-

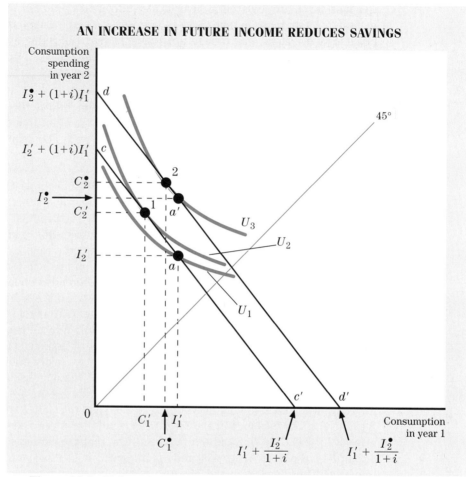

Figure 16-5 If C_1 and C_2 are normal goods, a higher income in year 2 causes the consumer to reduce savings and increase consumption spending in year 1 from C_1' to $C_1^{\bullet}$.

dowment of I_1' and I_2' would maximize utility by consuming C_1' in year 1, saving $I_1' - C_1'$ in year 1, and consuming C_2' in year 2. Suppose this individual learns at the beginning of year 1 that income in year 2 will be $I_2^{\bullet}$ rather than I_2', and so the endowment point shifts up vertically from point a to a' because income in year 2 is higher. How will this consumer's intertemporal behavior change because the intertemporal budget constraint becomes dd' and the present value of income is now $I_1' + I_2^{\bullet}/(1 + i)$? The consumer maximizes utility at point 2 by increasing consumption spending from C_1' to $C_1^{\bullet}$ and by saving less in year 1. Assume that consumption is a normal good, so that an increase in the present value of income increases consumption in both years. Because future income is higher, this individual does not have to save as much in year 1 as before to increase consumption in year 2. Therefore, we conclude that an increase in future income prospects will reduce the share of current income saved. For example, an individual on a fast track may rationally save less and spend more lavishly in the current year compared to others who have the same current income but who do not have future prospects that are as bright.

Instead of examining the effect of an increase in future income on savings, let's consider the effect of an increase in current income on current consumption spending. When income in year 1 increases from I_1' to I_1'', so that the present value of income is the same as in the previous example where income in year 2 increased to $I_2^\bullet$, the consumer maximizes utility by moving to point 2 in Figure 16-6. While the intertemporal consumption behavior is the same because the present value of

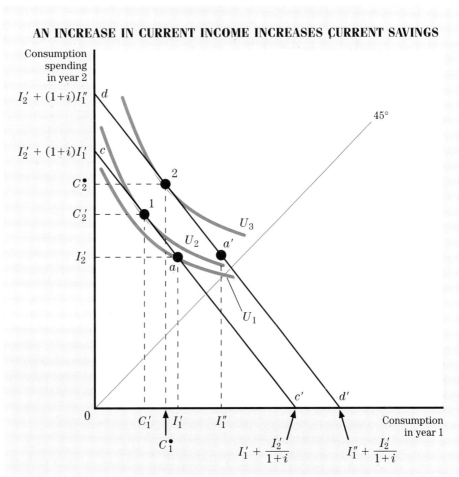

AN INCREASE IN CURRENT INCOME INCREASES CURRENT SAVINGS

Figure 16-6 If C_1 and C_2 are normal goods, a higher income in year 1 increases savings and increases consumption spending in year 1 from C_1' to $C_1^\bullet$ and from C_2' to $C_2^\bullet$ in year 2.

income is the same in the two circumstances, the consumer saves more in year 1 because of the increase in current income. A rise in current income raises savings, while a rise in future income reduces savings.

The Equilibrium Interest Rate

As we've seen, the interest rate affects how much a consumer saves or borrows—and a change in the interest rate affects the amount he or she saves or borrows in year 1. However, just what determines the interest rate that prevails in any year? This section answers this question by deriving the equilibrium interest rate from the demand for and supply of loanable funds.

Our first task is to derive the individual's demand function for loanable funds. Consumers who borrow in the first period are demanding loanable funds in year 1. The amount they demand depends on the interest rate. Let's consider a demander of loanable funds and derive the individual's demand function for these funds.

In Figure 16-7a income is I_1' in year 1 and I_2' in year 2 as represented by point e, and the intertemporal budget constraint is cc when the interest rate is i'. The consumer maximizes utility by borrowing $C_1' - I_1'$ and spends C_1' on consumption in year 1. In Figure 16-7b loanable funds demanded is $DL' = C_1' - I_1'$ when the interest rate is i'. As the interest rate increases, the intertemporal budget constraint rotates around the endowment point e in Figure 16-7a and becomes line aa when the interest rate is i'' and then line bb when the interest rate increases to $i^\bullet$. Point e is on each of the intertemporal budget constraints as the interest rate changes because the individual can choose to consume all income in each year. Consumption spending on a composite good decreases to C_1'' when the interest rate is i'', and the amount borrowed decreases to $C_1'' - I_1'$. At an interest rate of i'', loanable funds demanded by the consumer decreases to $DL'' = C_1'' - I_1'$. When the interest rate increases to $i^\bullet$, this individual reduces consumption spending on the composite good in year 1 to $C_1^\bullet$ and the amount borrowed decreases to $C_1^\bullet - I_1'$. Figure 16-7b shows that loanable funds demanded is $DL^\bullet = C_1^\bullet - I_1'$ if the interest rate is $i^\bullet$. Connecting all the points on the demand function for loanable funds produces the consumer's demand function dd for loanable funds. As the interest rate increases, the demand for loanable funds decreases because the opportunity cost of borrowing increases. Other consumers will have different endowment points and tastes, and their demand functions for loanable funds will differ. It is a short step from an individual's demand function to the aggregate demand function for loanable funds derived by adding the individual demand functions horizontally. One caution should be mentioned. Although the impatient consumer is a demander of loanable funds over the interest rates investigated, even this individual can become a supplier of loanable funds if the interest rate becomes high enough and induces him to lend rather than borrow.

A consumer's supply of loanable funds can be derived similarly. In Figure 16-8a the intertemporal budget constraint of a more patient consumer is cc when the interest rate is i', and the endowment point is point e. The consumer saves $I_1' - C_1'$ and spends C_1' on a composite good in year 1. Figure 16-8b shows that the amount of loanable funds supplied by this consumer is $SL' = I_1' - C_1'$ when the

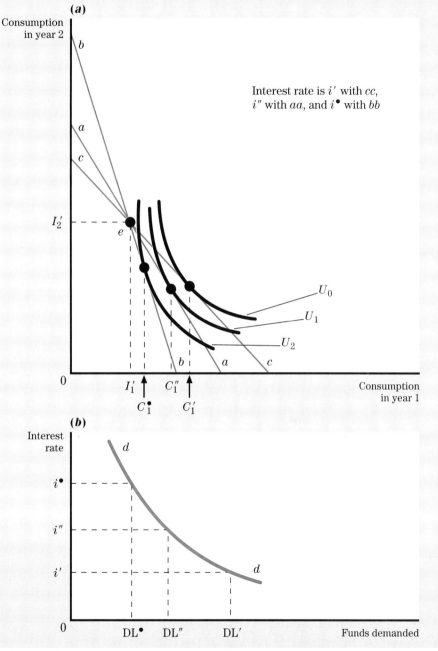

THE INTEREST RATE AND THE DEMAND FOR LOANABLE FUNDS

(a)

Consumption in year 2

Interest rate is i' with cc,
i'' with aa, and $i^{\bullet}$ with bb

Consumption in year 1

(b)

Interest rate

Funds demanded

Figure 16-7 (*a*) Point e is the consumer's income endowment. The intertemporal budget constraint is cc when the interest rate is i'. The impatient consumer borrows $C_1' - I_1'$ in year 1. The interest rate increases to i''; the intertemporal budget rotates around endowment point e, becoming aa. The consumer reduces the loan to $C_1'' - I_1'$. When the interest rate increases to $i^{\bullet}$, the budget constraint is bb and the demand for loanable funds is $C_1^{\bullet} - I_1'$. (*b*) The individual's demand function for loanable funds.

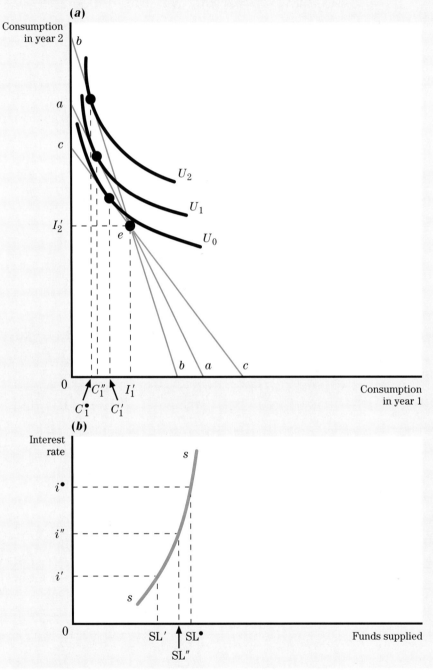

THE INTEREST RATE AND THE SUPPLY OF LOANABLE FUNDS

Figure 16-8 (a) Point e is the consumer's income endowment. The intertemporal budget constraint is cc when the interest rate is i'. This patient consumer saves $C_1' - I_1'$ in year 1. The interest rate increases to i'', and the intertemporal budget rotates around the endowment point e and becomes aa. The consumer increases savings to $C_1'' - I_1'$. When the interest rate increases to $i^\bullet$, the supply of loanable funds is $C_1^\bullet - I_1'$. (b) The supply function of loanable funds.

DETERMINATION OF EQUILIBRIUM INTEREST RATE

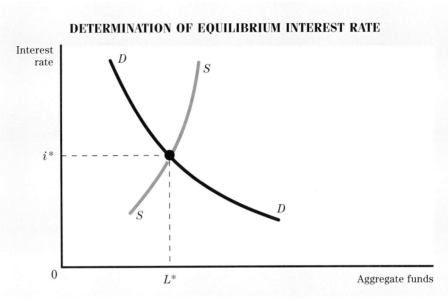

Figure 16-9 *DD* represents the aggregate demand for loanable funds and is derived by summing the individual demand functions horizontally. *SS* is the aggregate supply of loanable funds and is derived by summing the individual supply functions horizontally. The equilibrium interest rate i^* determines the equilibrium quantity of funds where funds demanded is equal to funds supplied.

interest rate is i'. As the interest rate increases, the intertemporal budget constraint rotates around point e in Figure 16-8a. At an interest rate of i'', the consumer saves $I_1' - C_1''$. The supply of loanable funds increases to $\mathrm{SL}'' = I_1' - C_1''$. When the interest rate increases to $i^\bullet$, the supply of loanable funds increases to $\mathrm{SL}^\bullet = I_1' - C_1^\bullet$. Connecting all the points on the supply function produces the supply function of loanable funds of this more patient consumer.[3] Other consumers with different endowment points and tastes will have supply functions as well. Summing these supply functions horizontally produces the aggregate supply function of loanable funds.

The market equilibrium interest rate is the interest rate that equates the market demand to the market supply of loanable funds. In Figure 16-9 the equilibrium interest rate is i^* and the equilibrium volume of loans is L^*. This analysis has assumed that there is only one interest rate. In fact, there are many markets for

---

[3] The supply function can have a negative slope if an increase in the interest rate reduces the quantity supplied. We can decompose the effect of a change in the interest rate on the funds supplied into a substitution effect and an income effect. As in the discussion in Chapter 3, the substitution effect always increases the quantity of loanable funds supplied when the interest rate increases and contributes to a positively sloped supply function. The income effect can either increase or decrease the quantity of funds supplied. The slope of the supply function depends on the sign and size of the income effect. If it is positive, the supply function has a positive slope since both the substitution and income effects increase the supply of loanable funds. If the income effect is negative and overwhelms the substitution effect, the supply function will have a negative slope.

loanable funds that depend on the duration of the loan and the risk characteristics of the borrower.

> The market equilibrium interest rate equates the quantity demanded to the quantity supplied of loanable funds.

The equilibrium interest rate and the total amount saved and borrowed will depend on the distribution of income among consumers in the economy and on differences in the preferences between current and future consumption.

The distribution of income frequently depends on the age distribution of individuals in an economy and is one determinant of the interest rate. The interest rate is higher in an economy with more relatively young individuals who have lower current earnings but higher future earnings. Because current income is low, these consumers borrow to finance spending on such items as durable goods and housing. The aggregate demand function for loanable funds shifts to the right when there are more relatively young individuals in a population, and this causes the equilibrium interest rate to rise.

The supply of loanable funds is greater when there are more relatively old individuals in the economy who have higher current earnings but face lower future earnings prospects as they age. These individuals prefer to save for the future when their earnings will be lower. When there are relatively more individuals of this type in the population, the aggregate supply function for loanable funds shifts to the right and causes the equilibrium interest rate to fall.

Let's pause here and recap the main points of the intertemporal theory of consumer behavior. This theory states that consumer spending depends on the present value of income. Changes in the distribution of income between years that leave the present value of income constant do not affect consumption behavior. The shape of the indifference curves of the intertemporal utility function indicates whether an individual is an impatient or a patient consumer. The amount saved or borrowed depends on the interest rate, the income endowment, and the rate of time preference. The market equilibrium interest rate is determined where the demand and the supply of loanable funds are equal.

16-3 DEPLETION OF A NATURAL RESOURCE

The future affects current decisions on the supply side of the market also. Suppliers have to decide how much to supply in each period. If an automobile parts retailer has an inventory of parts, he or she must decide whether to sell them in the current month or in the next month or in both months. Similarly, Saudi Arabia has huge oil reserves and must decide when to sell. Interest rates affect supplier decisions just as they influence decisions of consumers over time. To explain intertemporal decisions of suppliers, let's first examine the market for a nonrenewable resource— a resource that cannot be augmented, for example, a known stock of some mineral or energy source. Later, we investigate the case of a renewable resource.

> A **nonrenewable resource** is a stock of units that cannot be augmented.

This section develops a theory that explains how the price of a nonrenewable resource changes as the stock of this resource is depleted. To develop the analysis, let's first look at the decisions of a single owner of a nonrenewable resource and derive the decision rules for such an individual. Then, we will turn to the market for a nonrenewable resource where there are many individual owners and demanders and determine the market equilibrium prices over time as owners sell units of this resource.

When to Sell a Nonrenewable Resource

When is the best time for a single supplier of a nonrenewable resource—say, an oil producer—to sell the resource? This question can be answered by employing our favorite two-period model. Let's clearly specify the situation to be analyzed. An owner has a stock of b^* units of a nonrenewable resource at the beginning of year 1. The owner is a price taker and can sell each unit costlessly at a price of P_1 at the beginning of year 1 or at a price of P_2 at the beginning of year 2. The objective is to determine how many units to sell in year 1 and in year 2 so that the present value of the stock, b^*, is maximized.

The amount sold in year 1 is b_1, and the amount sold in year 2 is b_2. Therefore,

$$b_1 + b_2 = b^* \qquad \text{(Quantity Constraint)} \qquad \text{(16-9)}$$

Equation 16-9 simply says that the quantity sold in years 1 and 2 must equal the total initial stock.

You already know that a dollar next year is worth less than a dollar this year. The price of a unit sold at the beginning of year 2 is worth only $P_2/(1 + i)$ at the beginning of year 1 because of discounting. To determine when to sell the nonrenewable stock, the owner has to compare the per unit price, P_1, received at the beginning of year 1 with the discounted price, $P_2/(1 + i)$, if a unit is sold in year 2.

To maximize the present value of selling b^* units, the owner follows these decision rules:[4]

---

[4] To derive the decision rules, we determine how many units the owner should sell in year 1 so that the present value of selling b^* units is maximized.

$$\text{PV} = \text{Present value} = P_1 b_1 + \frac{P_2}{1 + i} b_2$$

Substituting $b_2 = b^* - b_1$ for b_2, the expression for present value becomes

$$\text{PV} = \text{Present value} = P_1 b_1 + \frac{P_2}{1 + i}(b^* - b_1)$$

In this equation present value depends only on b_1. If we change b_1 by Δb_1, the change in present value is

$$\frac{d\text{PV}}{db_1} = P_1 - \frac{P_2}{1 + i}$$

If $P_1 > P_2/(1 + i)$, the present value increases as owners sell more of the stock in the first year, $d\text{PV}/db_1 > 0$. For each unit sold, the owner receives P_1 that can be invested. The owner will have $P_1(1 + i)$ at the beginning of year 2, which is greater than P_2. Therefore, the owner maximizes present value by selling all the stock in year 1. If $P_1 < P_2/(1 + i)$, then the owner maximizes present value by holding all the stock in year 1 and selling all of it in year 2 since $d\text{PV}/db_1 < 0$.

1. Sell all units in year 1 if the price in year 1 is greater than the present value of the price at the beginning of year 2, $P_1 > P_2/(1 + i)$.

2. Sell units in either year or in both years if the price in year 1 equals the present value of the price at the beginning of year 2, $P_1 = P_2/(1 + i)$.

3. Sell all units in year 2 if the price in year 1 is less than the present value of the price at the beginning of year 2, $P_1 < P_2/(1 + i)$.

There is a more intuitive explanation of these conditions in terms of the price appreciation of the resource and the appreciation of a dollar. In essence, the owner of the resource decides when to sell by comparing P_2/P_1, the price appreciation of the resource, with $(1 + i)/1$, the appreciation because a dollar earns interest, before deciding when to sell. If the price appreciation of the resource is greater than $1 + i$, then the optimal policy is to hold the stock for a year and sell it in year 2. If the price appreciation is less than $1 + i$, then the present value is maximized by selling the resource in year 1 and investing the proceeds to obtain the greater appreciation of a dollar. Therefore, the selling decision depends on the price appreciation of the resource versus the appreciation of a dollar.

For example, suppose that the price in year 1 is $5.00 per unit and $5.50 in year 2 and the interest rate is 6 percent. The price appreciation ratio is $5.50/$5.00 = 1.10, while the appreciation of a dollar is only 1.06. So the owner should hold the stock for a year and then sell all of it at $5.50 in year 2.

A single owner of a resource will sell a resource in year 2 if the price appreciation ratio of the resource is greater than $1 + i$.

APPLICATION 16-2

Freeing Prices in Russia

On January 1, 1992, Russia entered a brave and uncertain world by freeing prices. In 1992 stores could sell at whatever price they desired except for certain exempt foods, medicines, and gasoline. For years, the former Soviet Union had kept prices artificially low and nowhere near the marginal cost of production for many goods. Some government economists predicted prices would double or triple for many consumer goods. Freeing prices was the first courageous step toward privatization and a market economy.

Suppose it is November 1991 and you own a small herd of cattle. Say you expect prices will be free to rise at the beginning of the new year and you think they will double. What should you do? If you are a present-value maximizer, you compare the current low controlled price with the present value of the future higher free price. If you expect prices to double, the choice will be an easy one for you to make. You will hold the cattle off the market until prices are higher. What are the consequences of announcing that prices will be free in the future? The immediate consequences have to be disastrous. The plan to free prices will drastically reduce the total supply of goods until prices rise, and before the freeing of prices the shortage of goods will become still more severe.

While the rationale for allowing prices to rise is to increase supplies in the long run, the announcement to raise them in the future discourages suppliers from offering goods in the short run. This example also illustrates one of the many difficulties of gradual reform versus a rapid transition to a market economy.

Market Equilibrium Prices

Let's move from the optimal actions of a single price-taking owner of a nonrenewable resource to the behavior of the market as a whole in years 1 and 2. When examining the market as a whole, we cannot take the prices as given, as in analyzing the behavior of a single seller, but must determine the equilibrium prices in each year. To determine these prices, assume that a downward sloping inverse demand function exists for the good in each year. Furthermore, assume that there are many owners of the nonrenewable resource, so that each is a price taker who maximizes the present value of the stock held.

Assuming each owner follows these decision rules, what will be the market-clearing equilibrium prices in years 1 and 2? How P_1 relates to P_2 in a market equilibrium can be determined through a process of elimination. Can there by a market equilibrium if $P_1 < P_2/(1 + i)$? The answer is clearly no. The present value of the price in year 2 exceeds the price in year 1. Every owner would sell in year 2. As more of the stock is supplied in year 2 and less in year 1, the price declines in year 2 and increases in year 1. Therefore, an equilibrium cannot exist if $P_1 < P_2/(1 + i)$. The same reasoning says that an equilibrium does not exist if $P_1 > P_2/(1 + i)$. Now all owners want to sell in year 1. If they all sell the stock in year 1, the price will fall in year 1 and rise in year 2. This pair cannot represent an equilibrium pair of prices either. Therefore, only one other alternative remains. An equilibrium pair of prices exists if

$$P_1 = \frac{P_2}{1 + i}$$

or $(1 + i)P_1 = P_2$ (Market Equilibrium Prices)   **(16-10)**

An intertemporal market equilibrium exists if the current price equals the present value of the future price.

This condition was first stated by Harold Hotelling, who predicted price increases by i percent a year for a nonrenewable resource as equation 16-10 indicates.[5] If the interest rate is 3 percent per year, the price of the nonrenewable resource will increase by 3 percent a year. The price must rise by just 3 percent to induce enough owners to hold their stock for another year and then sell it in year 2.

We know the relationship between the prices in the two years if the market is

[5] Hotelling analyzed the problem of allocating a nonrenewable resource over n periods and reached the conclusion that the discounted price must be equal for all periods: Harold Hotelling, "The Economics of Exhaustible Resources," *Journal of Political Economy*, vol. 39, April 1931, pp. 137–175.

in equilibrium. However, we still do not know what the price will be in year 1 or how much of the total aggregate stock consumers will purchase in year 1 and in year 2. To find these values, assume that the total quantity of the nonrenewable resource held by all others is B^*. B_1 represents the total units sold in the market in year 1, and B_2 is the total quantity sold in the market in year 2, with $B_1 + B_2 = B^*$. To determine the price in each year, we must know the market demand functions in each year. Our investigation assumes that the demand function for the nonrenewable resource is the same in each year. However, the analysis is more general than that and applies when the demand functions differ in the two years.

Let the demand functions be

$$P_1 = D(B_1) \qquad P_2 = D(B_2) \qquad \text{(Market Demand Functions)} \qquad \text{(16-11)}$$

The same symbol, $D(\ )$, for both periods signifies that the market demand functions are the same in each year.

Given this information, let's find the quantity sold in each year and the equilibrium price in each year. In Figure 16-10 the length of the horizontal axis is equal to B^*, the total stock of the nonrenewable resource. The vertical axis on the left side measures the price in year 1. Starting at the left-hand origin 0 and reading from left to right, we find the market demand function, $P_1 = D(B_1)$, in year 1. Now consider the vertical axis on the right-hand side. This axis shows the price in year 2. Starting at the origin $0'$ and moving from right to left, we find the market demand function $P_2 = D(B_2)$ in year 2. Because demand functions are the same, they are mirror images of each other.

Any point on the horizontal axis identifies an allocation of the total stock to the two periods. For example, if owners sell B_1' units in year 1 and B_2' units in year 2, the prices in the 2 years will be the same and will equal P'. You can immediately see why this allocation does not describe a market equilibrium. By selling in the first year, owners receive P' that they can invest and have $(1 + i)P'$ in year 2 which is greater than P', the price that they would receive by selling in year 2. Equation 16-10 says that the price in year 1 must equal the discounted price in year 2 in a market equilibrium. This condition is not satisfied when owners sell the same quantity in both years and the prices are equal in the 2 years.

An allocation of the total stock of B^* where the price in year 1 equals the discounted price in year 2 can be found by constructing a discounted price demand function for year 2.[6] This function shows the present value of P_2 for each B_2. The discounted price, DP, is defined as $[1/(1 + i)]P_2$. Therefore, the discounted price demand function is

$$\text{DP} = \frac{1}{1 + i}P_2 = \frac{1}{1 + i}D(B_2) \qquad \begin{array}{l}\text{(Discounted Price} \\ \text{Demand Function)}\end{array} \qquad \text{(16-12)}$$

---

[6] For an extended analysis of intertemporal equilibrium, the reader should consult Paul A. Samuelson, "Intertemporal Price Equilibrium: A Prologue to the Theory of Speculation," *The Collected Papers of Paul A. Samuelson*, vol. II, J.E. Stiglitz, ed. MIT Press, Cambridge, MA, 1966, pp. 946–984.

MARKET PRICES IN AN INTERTEMPORAL EQUILIBRIUM

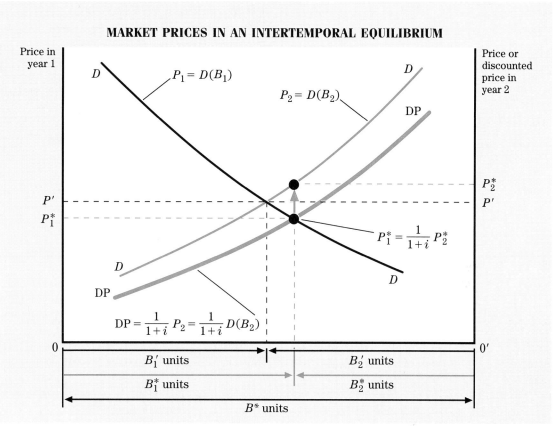

Figure 16-10   The stock of a nonrenewable resource is allocated to the two years so that B_1^* is sold in year 1 and B_2^* is sold in year 2. The equilibrium market-clearing prices are P_1^* and P_2^*. $P_2^* = (1 + i)P_1^*$.

For each value of B_2, calculate $D(B_2)/(1 + i)$. Since $1/(1 + i)$ is less than 1, the discounted price demand function is below $P = D(B_2)$ for year 2. For example, if the interest rate is 10 percent, the discount factor is $1/1.10 = 0.9094$. For each B_2, find the discounted price by reducing P_2 to $0.9094P_2$. The discounted price demand function for year 2 is DP-DP in Figure 16-10 and lies below DD for year 2. The vertical distance between the DD and DP-DP demand functions increases as P_2 increases. This occurs because the discounted price is a constant fraction of P_2. In this illustration the discounted price is \$90.94 if $P_2 = $ \$100, and \$9.094 when $P_2 = $ \$10.

It is easy to find the equilibrium prices once you have the discounted demand function for year 2. You know that P_1^* must equal the discounted price in year 2. This condition is satisfied at the point where the demand function in year 1 intersects the discounted demand function in year 2. At the intersection point

$P_1^* = P_2^*/(1 + i)$. In Figure 16-10 the market-clearing equilibrium price in year 1 is P_1^*, and the quantity sold in year 1 must be B_1^*. Therefore, the quantity of the nonrenewable stock sold in year 2 is B_2^*, and $B_1^* + B_2^* = B^*$. The equilibrium price in year 2 is P_2^* which can be found by extending the point where DD and DP-DP cross vertically to the demand function $P_2 = D(B_2^*)$. When owners sell B_1^* units in year 1 and B_2^* units in year 2, $P_2^* = (1 + i)P_1^*$. An intertemporal equilibrium exists at prices P_1^* and P_2^*, and consumers purchase B_1^* and B_2^* units in years 1 and 2, respectively.

One implication of the two-period model of a nonrenewable resource is that consumption of the resource decreases over time when the demand functions are the same in the 2 years. Because the price in the second year is higher than in the first year, the quantity consumed is lower in year 2 than in year 1. Because price increases, consumption of the resource decreases and its depletion rate slows down over time. If the model were expanded to include n years, we could prove that price increases from year to year by a factor of $1 + i$ and consumption declines over time when the demand functions are the same in all years. Therefore, the depletion rate of the nonrenewable resource decreases over time.

This basic model of the depletion of a nonrenewable resource points up a common fallacy that marks public policy discussions of natural resources. Many natural resources are often treated as nonrenewable resources. There is a nagging suspicion if not a fear that the world will run out of these resources. What better way of estimating the time when a resource will be depleted than by dividing total known reserves by current consumption? The ratio of total reserve to annual consumption is the number of years before the resource will be depleted. If the known total reserve of a natural resource is 100,000 units and current annual consumption is 10,000, this logic predicts that the resource will be depleted in 10 years.

The ratio of total reserve to annual consumption predicts the number of years before the resource runs out, and in terms of the two-year model, this ratio is B^*/B_1^*. What is wrong with this estimate? The glaring defect of this procedure is that it assumes that the demand for the resource is completely inelastic, so that consumption does not change when price rises. It fails to recognize the effect of a rising price on consumption. In Hotelling's analysis of intertemporal equilibrium, price rises over time and consumption of the resource decreases. Therefore, B^*/B_1^* underestimates the time when the nonrenewable resource will be depleted. Failure to recognize the effect of price on quantity demanded often leads to erroneous and pessimistic forecasts.

The Effect of the Interest Rate on Equilibrium Prices

In the analysis of equilibrium prices in an intertemporal equilibrium the interest rate was taken as given. Let's consider how a change in the interest rate changes the behavior of owners of a nonrenewable resource. At higher interest rates, the opportunity cost of holding a resource increases, and so consumption in year 1 will increase because suppliers want to convert the stock into dollars so they can

EQUILIBRIUM MARKET-CLEARING PRICES

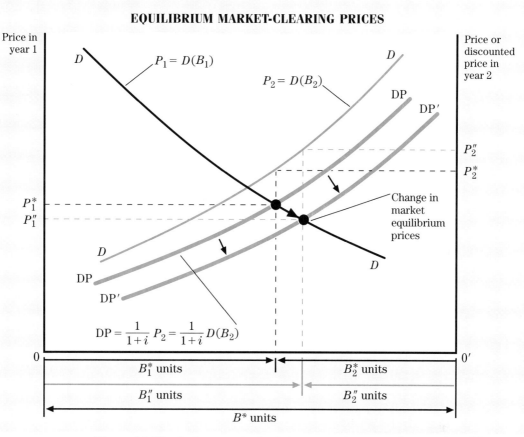

Figure 16-11   An increase in the interest rate increases the quantity sold in year 1 from B_1^* to B_1'' and decreases the quantity sold in year 2 from B_2^* to B_2''. The price in year 1 decreases to P_1'', and the price in year 2 increases to P_2''. A rise in the interest rate increases current consumption and decreases future consumption.

earn the higher interest. To use the model to find the effect of a higher interest rate on prices and quantities consumed, we have to determine how the market-clearing prices change when the interest rate changes. Figure 16-11 shows that the discounted price demand function for year 2 shifts downward by still more than it did in Figure 16-10 and becomes DP'-DP' because of the higher interest rate. The intersection of the new discounted price demand function and the demand function in year 1 occurs farther to the right. Therefore, owners sell more units of the nonrenewable resource in year 1 when the interest rate increases ($B_1'' > B_1^*$). A rise in the interest rate decreases the price in year 1 and increases the price in year 2, thereby increasing the percentage difference between the prices in years 1 and 2. Because an increase in the interest rate raises the opportunity cost of holding the resource, owners sell more of the total stock in the first year and invest the proceeds to earn a higher interest rate. The percentage difference between prices in years 1 and 2 increases by enough to induce some owners to hold their stocks and sell in year 2. This analysis shows that changes in the interest rate affect the level and the rate of price increase.

> An increase in the interest rate causes the percentage difference between prices in years 1 and 2 to increase.

From this analysis, we can derive the strongest prediction of the model—the price of a nonrenewable resource will increase by i percent a year. In the two-period model the price of a nonrenewable resource increases from P_1^* in year 1 to $P_2^* = (1 + i)P_1^*$ in year 2. If this model is expanded to cover three or more periods, the generalization will yield the same prediction. In an intertemporal equilibrium the equilibrium price in the next year equals $(1 + i)$ times the equilibrium price in the current year. In an intertemporal equilibrium price increases over time as the nonrenewable stock is slowly depleted.

How well does the Hotelling model describe the price behavior of natural resources? Is the assumption of a nonrenewable resource applicable to such minerals as nickel, lead, copper, and iron ore or such fuels as coal, natural gas, and crude oil? Strictly speaking, no. In virtually all of these cases there are discoveries that create random additions to the existing stock of reserves. So, few natural resources would qualify under this strict definition. Nevertheless, the Hotelling model may yet produce reasonably accurate predictions if the additions to reserves are small in comparison with the total initial stock. For those natural resources where this is the case, the assumption of a nonrenewable stock is not far from the truth.

The Hotelling model serves as a useful benchmark for determining whether a natural resource is nonrenewable. If the price behavior of the resource is consistent with the predictions of the theory, the resource can be considered a nonrenewable resource. If the price predictions of the model are wrong, then we must conclude that the theory of a nonrenewable resource is not applicable and try to understand what went wrong.

APPLICATION 16-3

The Historical Trend in Crude Oil Prices

While we could look at the price behavior of any number of natural resources—from aluminum to lead to nickel to coal or to petroleum—we examine the price behavior in the petroleum market. The crude oil price is often in the news, and claims that there is only so much crude oil in the earth and that it will run out sometime in the future are commonplace. If this view is correct, the stock of crude oil is a nonrenewable resource, at least as a first approximation. The validity of this claim can be examined by determining if inflation-adjusted crude oil prices increase over time. Robert Manthly has studied the long-term price trends for many

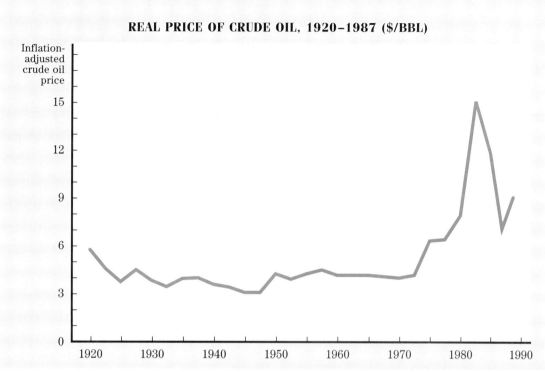

Figure 16-12   Real crude oil prices were steady from 1920 to 1973. [*After Robert S. Manthly*, Natural Resource Commodities—A Century of Statistics, Resources for the Future, *Johns Hopkins University Press, 1978; and U.S. Bureau of the Census*, Statistical Abstract of the United States, *Washington, D.C.*]

minerals and fuels up to 1973.[7] Figure 16-12 extends his series and shows the inflation-adjusted price of crude oil from 1920 to 1987. What is striking about this graph is the absence of a rising price trend from 1920 to 1973. The per barrel price did rise after 1973 when OPEC increased prices, but the inflation-adjusted price declined throughout the 1980s. While there are short intervals of price increases and decreases, no long-term trend is discernible over the 53-year period from 1920 to 1973. Certainly, price has either declined or remained steady over long periods of time rather than increased. Manthly's study shows that the long-term real price for many minerals and fuels does not exhibit an upward trend.

The nonrenewable resource theory predicts that real prices increase over time. In the case of petroleum the theory's predictions seem to go haywire. We must recognize and accept what history tells us. Price behavior from 1920 to 1973 indicates that the assumption of a fixed initial stock of crude oil is untenable.

[7] Robert S. Manthly, *Natural Resource Commodities—A Century of Statistics*, Resources for the Future, Johns Hopkins Press, 1978.

A Renewable Resource

The behavior of crude oil prices appears to differ from the predictions of Hotelling's model of intertemporal equilibrium. What modification of the model might help explain why prices do not increase annually by $1 + i$? By modifying the model we might be able to explain the price movements and still retain some of its essential features.

The assumption of a fixed initial stock appears to be the most questionable. Fortunately, additions to the stock of crude oil have been forthcoming in the past. Let's modify this assumption and see how it helps to explain why price in year 2 can be equal to or less than $(1 + i)$ times price in year 1. Instead of assuming that B^* units are available at the beginning of year 1, let's assume that only some fraction of B^* is available at the beginning of period 1 and that the remaining fraction becomes available only in the second period because of new discoveries in year 2. The information about new discoveries is public knowledge at the beginning of the first year. For example, at the beginning of year 1, discoveries of a known size are announced, but it takes a year before owners can sell any units from these new discoveries.

Admittedly, this scenario is rather extreme. The size of a discovery is often uncertain, and the actual size becomes known over time. Discoveries are similar to random events with considerable luck involved. We will not model discovery as a random variable because such an analysis requires a more extensive set of analytical tools. A simpler certainty formulation can be adopted that can still explain why prices are stable or fall over time.

Assume that the total quantity consumed during the 2 years is B^*. Owners of the initial stock must still decide whether to sell their stocks in year 1 or in year 2, but owners of new discoveries cannot sell units from their discoveries in year 1. The new discoveries cannot increase consumption in year 1. This way of formulating the problem places more constraints on the solution. The original model assumed that the total stock, B^*, was available at the very beginning and that owners could sell all units in the first period if they decided to. In the renewable version of the theory the most that owners can sell in the first year is the stock available in year 1.

How large must the discoveries be in year 2 before the equilibrium price in period 2 will be less than $(1 + i)P_1$? Figure 16-13 reproduces the demand functions in Figure 16-10. In Figure 16-10 $P_2^* = (1 + i)P_1^*$ when owners sell B_1^* units in year 1 and B_2^* units in year 2. If the discoveries are therefore greater than B_2^*, so that the initial stock in year 1 is less than B_1^*, P_2 will be less than $(1 + i)P_1$. In Figure 16-13, when the initial stock in year 1 is B_1' and discoveries are equal to B_2' units, the equilibrium price is P_1' in year 1 and P_2' in year 2. The owners of B_1' have no incentive to hold the stock and sell it in year 2 since the price in year 2 is less than the price in year 1. While it is true that the price in year 1 exceeds the present value of the price in year 2, there is no way to sell more units in year 1 since only B_1' units are available. For a renewable resource, P_2 can be less than $(1 + i)P_1$.

$$P_2 \leq (1 + i)P_1 \qquad \text{(Intertemporal Price Condition with a Renewable Resource)} \qquad \textbf{(16-13)}$$

EQUILIBRIUM PRICES FOR A RENEWABLE RESOURCE

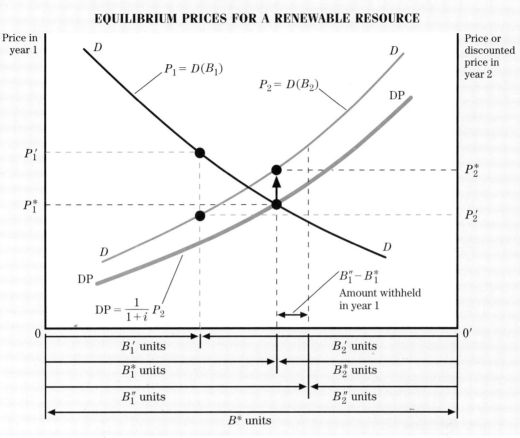

Figure 16-13 The initial stock of a renewable resource available in year 1 is B_1'. Discoveries in year 2 make B_2' units available. The equilibrium market price in year 1 is P_1'. The equilibrium market-clearing price in year 2 is P_2'. The price in year 2 is less than $(1 + i)P_1'$. A long-term decline in real prices indicates that the assumption of a nonrenewable resource is untenable since additions to the stock cause the price to fall. If the initial stock is B_1'', the equilibrium prices in an intertemporal equilibrium equal $P_2^* = (1 + i)P_1^*$. $B_1'' - B_1^*$ of the initial stock is sold in year 2.

If, on the other hand, the new discoveries in year 2 are less than B_2^* and therefore the initial stock is greater than B_1^*, then the discounted price in year 2 would be greater than P_1 if owners sell all the initial stock in year 1. Consequently, owners will hold some of the initial stock off the market and sell the remainder in year 2. This raises the price in year 1 and lowers the price in year 2 until $P_2^* = (1 + i)P_1^*$. When the initial stock is B_1'', the quantity that owners carry over to year 2 is $B_1'' - B_1^*$ in an intertemporal equilibrium. Therefore, if future discoveries of a renewable resource are relatively small, prices will again increase by

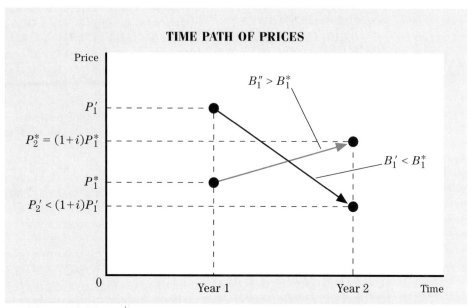

TIME PATH OF PRICES

Figure 16-14   If the initial stock of a renewable resource is greater than B_1^*, then the equilibrium price in year 2 is $(1 + i)P_1^*$. If the initial stock is B_1', the price in year 2 is less than $(1 + i)P_1'$.

$1 + i$. Figure 16-14 shows two possible price paths. The arrows indicate the direction of prices. When the initial stock B_1'' in Figure 16-13 is greater than B_1^*, the colored arrow slopes upward because price increases by $1 + i$ from year 1 to year 2 in an intertemporal equilibrium. When the initial stock is B_1' and is less than B_1^*, the black arrow slopes downward because P_2' is less than $(1 + i)P_1'$.[8]

The long-run stability in inflation-adjusted crude oil prices from 1920 to the early 1970s suggests that Hotelling's model of a nonrenewable resource does not explain the price behavior of crude oil. Crude oil prices have been stable, although the demand function has shifted to the right over time. The stability of crude oil prices over this period suggests that the fundamental assumption of a fixed initial reserve of crude oil is not valid. Rather, the long-run behavior of prices indicates that the available stock increases over time through a combination of new discoveries and because of technological changes in extracting more oil from known formations.

Since the formation of OPEC and throughout the 1970s and 1980s, resource economists have vigorously debated whether Hotelling's nonrenewable model might have greater current applicability than in the past. Some economists, policy makers, and conservationists claimed that there was a break in the data after the

---

[8] If the stock in year 1 is slightly less than B_1^*, price will increase, but by less than iP_1.

1970s and that generous additions to reserves would no longer be forthcoming. They believed the future was more likely to be one of fixed supply and increasing real prices. In other words, the Hotelling model would be more applicable in the future than it had been in the past. The debate continues. However, the behavior of mineral and fuel prices in the 1980s indicates that inflation-adjusted prices have eased. It appears that more pessimistic predictions made during the dark days of the early 1970s have not been borne out.

SUMMARY

- The present value of future income is an amount received immediately that is equivalent to the income received in a future year.
- The intertemporal budget constraint shows how consumption spending in year 2 relates to consumption spending in year 1.
- The intertemporal utility function shows that the utility of a consumer depends on current and future spending on a composite good.
- A consumer maximizes utility when the marginal rate of time preference is equal to $-(1 + i)$, the decline in future consumption because of a dollar increase in current consumption.
- The intertemporal theory of consumption predicts that consumption spending in each year depends on the present value of income.
- If C_1 and C_2 are normal goods, a rise in future income with current income fixed reduces the amount saved by a consumer.
- If C_1 and C_2 are normal goods, a rise in current income with future income constant increases the amount saved by a consumer.
- The amount saved or borrowed in an economy depends on the interest rate.
- The equilibrium interest rate equates the quantity demanded to the quantity supplied of loanable funds.
- In a two-period model of a nonrenewable resource equilibrium the current price is equal to the present value of the future price. Equilibrium prices of a nonrenewable resource increase by i percent per year.
- The depletion of a nonrenewable resource occurs more rapidly at a higher interest rate.
- Equilibrium prices do not necessarily increase by i percent per year for a renewable resource.

KEY TERMS

Present value of income

Intertemporal preferences

Impatient consumer

Maximizing intertemporal utility

Demand function for loanable funds

Intertemporal budget constraint

Marginal rate of time preference

Patient consumer

Saving and borrowing

Supply function for loanable funds

Equilibrium interest rate
When to sell a nonrenewable
   resource
Equilibrium prices over time
Prices rise by *i* percent per year

Nonrenewable resource
Price appreciation ratio
Discounted demand function
Renewable resource

REVIEW QUESTIONS

1. If the interest rate is 6 percent, would you be indifferent between receiving $20,000 per year at the beginning of the year or $25,000 per year at the end of the year?
2. What distinguishes a patient from an impatient consumer?
3. A neutral consumer has a marginal rate of time preference equal to -1 when spending on a composite good is the same in each of 2 years. Will a neutral consumer spend more on a composite good in year 2 than in year 1 if the interest rate is positive?
4. Why does a higher interest rate cause a consumer to borrow less?
5. If an individual receives the same income in years 1 and 2, he will spend the same amount on consumption in both periods if he cannot borrow. Explain why you agree or disagree with this statement.
6. If the price of a resource increases by 6 percent and you can borrow at 4 percent, would you sell the resource in year 1 or in year 2? Explain.
7. If demand is stable, the theory of a nonrenewable resource predicts that consumption in year 2 will be less than consumption in year 1. Explain why you agree or disagree with this statement.
8. Suppose the market demand function for a nonrenewable resource decreases over time. Explain why a decrease in demand can or cannot explain why the price is lower in year 2 than in year 1?
9. For a nonrenewable resource the equilibrium price in year 2 is $(1 + i)$ times the equilibrium price in year 1. For a renewable resource, the price in year 2 can equal or be less than $(1 + i)$ times the equilibrium price in year 1. Explain why you agree or disagree with this statement.

EXERCISES

1. In the past the government placed no restrictions on borrowing by individuals. A new government sweeps into power on a platform of prohibiting the payment of interest. If consumers are no longer able to borrow, explain why you would or would not expect them to respond in the following ways.
   a. Decrease savings in year 1.
   b. Decrease consumption spending in year 1.
   c. Decrease consumption spending in year 2.
   d. Increase savings in year 1.

2. Suppose the government announces a tax of 33 percent on income in year 2. Show how this tax policy changes a consumer's saving decision if there is no tax in year 1.

3. The larger the increase in the demand function for a nonrenewable resource over time, the larger the rate of increase in the price of the resource over time. Explain why you agree or disagree with this statement.

4. How do the equilibrium prices of a nonrenewable resource in years 1 and 2 change if the initial stock of the resource is larger?

5. Suppose the quantity demanded in year 1 is twice the quantity demanded at each price in year 2. Show that the equilibrium price in year 2 is $(1 + i)P_1^*$ for a nonrenewable resource.

6. If the equilibrium price in year 1 is greater than $(1 + i)$ times the equilibrium price in year 2, an increase in the interest rate will have no effect on the equilibrium prices for a renewable resource. Explain why you agree or disagree with this statement.

7. If the government announces in year 1 that it will sell all of its reserves of crude oil in year 2, what effect will this have on prices in year 1 and in year 2?

WAGE DETERMINATION IN LABOR MARKETS

Chapter 5 showed how a firm combines workers and machines to minimize the total cost of producing each quantity. In that analysis the prices of the factors of production were given to the firm and there was no discussion of what determines the factor prices. This chapter answers this question by considering how the wage is determined in the labor market from the derived demand and supply functions of labor.

Firms are demanders and individuals are suppliers of labor. The first part of the chapter considers the demand function for labor by a firm that is a price taker in both the output and labor markets. Then the supply function of labor is derived from the utility-maximizing behavior of each worker. After discussing the equilibrium wage in this price-taking setting, we then consider what changes are required when the firm has market power in the product market.

The remainder of the chapter extends the analysis in several directions by considering a variety of interesting questions about the labor market: What are the benefits and costs of education, and how are earnings related to educational attainment? Who pays for on-the-job worker training—the firm or the worker? How can firms structure their wage policies to sort workers into firms and to reduce or eliminate shirking?

17-1   THE DERIVED DEMAND FUNCTION FOR LABOR

To find a company's demand function for labor, assume initially that the firm is a price taker in both the product and the factor markets. Therefore, it can sell each unit at a given price and employ workers at a given wage. Later we will consider a firm that is a monopolist in the product market but is still a price taker in the labor market, for example, a cable TV firm that has a local monopoly but competes with many other firms for technicians and executives in factor markets.

In this section we determine the short- and long-run demand functions for labor. Economists describe the demand functions for factors of production as derived demand functions. The demand function for each factor of production exists because there is a demand function for the product. Consequently, the demand function for every factor is derived from the market demand function for the product.

The analysis begins with the production function of a firm which, you will recall, shows how it combines factors of production to produce output. In Chapter 5 the production function of the firm was defined as

$$q = f(L, K) \qquad \text{(Production Function)} \qquad \textbf{(17-1)}$$

where q is total quantity produced per period, L is labor input, and K is capital input. For example, in a clerical office, the output might be the number of pages per month of word processing. The factors of production are the number of operators skilled at word processing (L) and the number of personal computers (K). The price of labor is w, and the price of capital is the rental value of capital, r.

A Competitive Firm's Short-Run Demand Function for Labor

In the short run the firm has a fixed quantity of capital, K_0, and the cost of the K_0 units of capital is a sunk cost. So, rK_0 is a sunk cost. Given K_0, the marginal product of labor is defined as

$$\text{MP}_L = \left.\frac{\Delta q}{\Delta L}\right|_{K=K_0} \qquad \text{(Marginal Product of Labor)} \qquad \text{(17-2)}$$

The marginal product of labor function shows the increase in output, Δq, when the number of workers increases by ΔL with the number of machines held constant. Figure 17-1 displays the marginal product of labor function with capital held constant. The increment in output relative to the increment in labor, $\Delta q/\Delta L$, is on the vertical axis, and the units of labor, L, are on the horizontal axis. In the figure the marginal product of labor increases initially, but adding still more labor to a fixed number of machines causes it to decline eventually so that the marginal product function slopes downward and to the right when the firm hires more than L' units.

The incremental revenue due to an increase in labor of ΔL is the marginal revenue product of labor (MRP_L):

$$\text{MRP}_L = \frac{\Delta R}{\Delta L} \qquad \text{(Marginal Revenue Product)} \qquad \text{(17-3)}$$

$$= \left.\frac{\Delta R}{\Delta q}\frac{\Delta q}{\Delta L}\right|_{K=K_0}$$

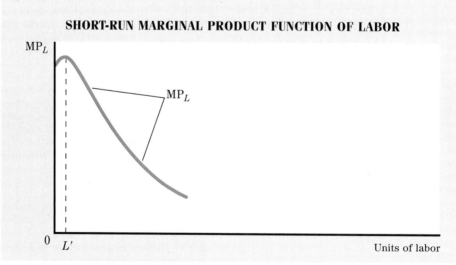

SHORT-RUN MARGINAL PRODUCT FUNCTION OF LABOR

Figure 17-1   The marginal product of labor eventually declines as more workers are added to a fixed number of machines.

Table 17-1   DERIVING THE MARGINAL REVENUE PRODUCT OF LABOR FOR A PRICE-TAKING FIRM

NUMBER OF WORKERS, L (1)	TOTAL OUTPUT, q (2)	MARGINAL PRODUCT, $\Delta q/\Delta L$ (3)	PRICE, P ($) (4)	TOTAL REVENUE, R ($) (5)	MARGINAL REVENUE, $\Delta R/\Delta q$ ($) (6)	MARGINAL REVENUE PRODUCT, $MRP_L = (\Delta R/\Delta q)(\Delta q/\Delta L)$ ($) (7)
1	5	5	20	100	20	100
2	9	4	20	180	20	80
3	12	3	20	240	20	60
4	14	2	20	280	20	40

The marginal revenue product of labor equals the marginal revenue from selling the additional output times the marginal product from employing ΔL more units of labor.

The marginal revenue product measures the additional revenue the firm receives when it sells the additional output produced with ΔL more workers.

Table 17-1 shows how the marginal revenue product is derived in a numerical example when the price is $20. For example, when the firm increases the number of workers from 1 to 2, total output in column 2 increases from 5 units to 9 units. The marginal product from adding the second worker is 4 units of output (column 3). Because the firm is a price taker, the price remains at $20 (column 4) although the firm is now selling 9 rather than 5 units and is receiving $180 rather than $100 in total revenue (column 5). The marginal revenue, $\Delta R/\Delta q$, from the sale of 4 additional units is $80/4 = $20 per unit (column 6). The marginal revenue product from adding the second worker is 4($20) = $80 (column 7).

When the firm is a competitor in the product market, marginal revenue equals price. When price is substituted for MR into equation 17-3, we have the marginal revenue product of a price-taking firm, which is called by convention the value of the marginal product.

$$\text{VMP}_L = P\frac{\Delta q}{\Delta L} \qquad \text{(Value of the Marginal Product)} \qquad \text{(17-4)}$$

The value of the marginal product measures the increase in revenue due to an increase in the number of workers, or $\Delta R/\Delta L$, for a price-taking firm and equals price times the marginal product of labor.

For a price-taking firm the value of the marginal product equals the price times the marginal product of labor.

To determine how many workers it should employ, the firm must compare the incremental revenue from employing another worker with the incremental cost of hiring another worker. Let's demonstrate this important proposition and show how the firm determines the number of workers.

The short-run profits of the firm are

$$\text{Profits} = \text{Revenue} - \text{Labor cost} - \text{Capital cost}$$

$$\pi = Pq - wL - rK_0 \qquad \text{(Short-Run Profits of Firm)} \qquad \textbf{(17-5)}$$

where r is the rental value of capital and rK_0 is a sunk cost. Substituting $f(L,K_0)$ for q yields an equation showing how the firm's short-run profit depends on the number of workers.

$$\pi = Pf(L, K_0) - wL - rK_0$$

Assume that the firm selects the number of workers, L, to maximize short-run profits. The value of the marginal product measures the increase in revenue a competitive firm receives by employing another worker. Equation 17-5 shows that the additional cost of another worker is w since the firm pays each worker w per period. Therefore, the firm increases the number of workers until the value of the marginal product equals the marginal cost of hiring another worker.[1]

$$\text{VMP}_L = w \qquad \begin{array}{l}\text{(Profit-Maximizing Employment Condition} \\ \text{for a Price-Taking Firm)}\end{array} \qquad \textbf{(17-6)}$$

Substituting $P\,(\Delta q/\Delta L)$ for VMP_L,

$$P\frac{\Delta q}{\Delta L} = w$$

A price-taking firm increases the number of workers until the value of the marginal product equals the wage of the additional worker.

To repeat, the value of the marginal product is on the left-hand side of equation 17-6 and measures the incremental revenue the firm receives from employing another worker. The marginal cost of hiring another worker, w, is on the right-hand side of equation 17-6. In Figure 17-2 the wage is w_0 and the firm demands L_0 units of labor in the short run, where $\text{VMP}_L = w_0$. This is one point on the firm's short-run demand function for labor. The firm maximizes profits if it employs L_0

---

[1] In the short run the fixed factor is capital. The short-run profits of the firm are

$$\pi = Pf(L,K_0) - wL - rK_0$$

where rK_0 is a sunk cost. The company maximizes profits by increasing L until

$$\frac{d\pi}{dL} = P\frac{\partial q}{\partial L} - w = 0$$

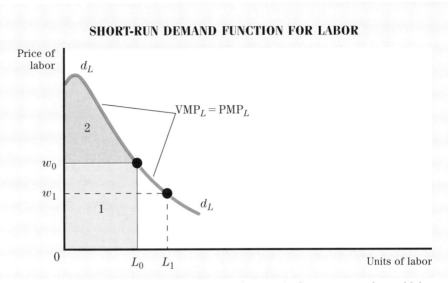

SHORT-RUN DEMAND FUNCTION FOR LABOR

Figure 17-2   The vertical axis measures the marginal revenue product of labor, or price of labor. The firm's short-run demand function is the value of the marginal product function and represents the firm's short-run demand function for labor. If the wage is w_0, the firm will demand L_0 units of labor to produce the profit-maximizing quantity in the short run. The value of the marginal product function represents the firm's demand for labor as long as revenues at least equal total labor cost.

workers when the wage is w_0, given the price of the product, the rental value of capital, and K_0. Area 1 shows the total labor cost of the firm, or $w_0 L_0$. The total revenue received by the firm when it employs L_0 workers is equal to the area under the value of the marginal product function up to L_0. Since area 1 is equal to total payments to labor, area 2 represents the total amount paid to all other factors of production plus any profits or losses. If the wage decreases to w_1, Figure 17-2 shows that quantity demanded increases to L_1 units of labor. This is another point where $VMP_L = w_1$ but where the wage is lower. Other points on the value of marginal product function are also points on the firm's short-run demand for labor function.

> The value of the marginal product function is a competitive firm's short-run demand function for labor.

Because the value of the marginal product of labor slopes downward, the number of workers hired by the firm increases in the short run when the wage decreases.

A Competitive Firm's Long-Run Demand Function for Labor

The long-run effect of a change in wage on the employment of a factor differs from the short-run effect. In the long run the firm is able to substitute labor for capital

THE EFFECT OF A LOWER WAGE ON THE LONG-RUN DEMAND FOR LABOR

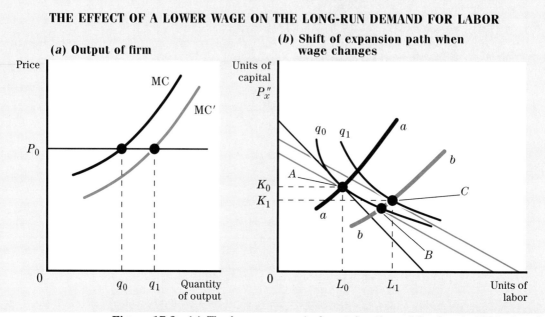

Figure 17-3 (*a*) The long-run marginal cost function of the firm is MC before the wage rate decreases from w_0 to w_1. The expansion path of the firm is aa in (*b*). At a price of P_0 the company produces q_0 at minimum total cost by combining L_0 units of labor with K_0 units of capital. When the wage is w_0, the firm demands L_0 units of labor. A fall in the wage rate shifts the marginal cost function to MC′, and the company expands output to q_1. (*b*) A fall in the wage rate makes labor less expensive relative to capital, and the isocost lines become flatter. Because of the lower wage, the firm's new expansion path becomes bb. It produces q_1 units by increasing the number of workers to L_1.

when the wage declines and change its scale of output. The long-run effect of a change in the price of a factor must take account of the substitution effect and the scale effect.

To observe how these changes influence the firm's long-run demand function, consider how a single firm responds to a wage reduction assuming the price of the product is constant. Recall from Chapter 5 that when a firm produces a given quantity at minimum total cost, it is at some point on its expansion path. The expansion path identifies that combination of factors that produces each quantity at lowest cost. At each point on this path the slope of the firm's isocost line equals the slope of the isoquant as the firm uses the least-cost combination of factors to produce each rate of output.

When the firm is on its expansion path,

$$\text{MRTS}_{\text{KL}} = -\frac{w}{r} \qquad \text{(Condition for Minimum Cost)} \qquad \textbf{(17-7)}$$

$MRTS_{KL}$ is the marginal rate of technical substitution between capital and labor—the slope of an isoquant—and the slope of the isocost line is $-w/r$. You may want to review Chapter 5 to see why a firm must satisfy equation 17-7 if it is going to produce a given output at minimum total cost. Given the price of the product, there is one point on the firm's expansion path that coincides with its profit-maximizing quantity. In Figure 17-3a the firm maximizes profits by producing q_0 units where P_0 equals the long-run marginal cost. This profit-maximizing quantity can be used in Figure 17-3b to find the corresponding isoquant q_0 at point A. Point A shows that the lowest cost of producing q_0 units combines L_0 workers with K_0 machines. Given P_0 and r_0, we can say that this company's long-run demand for workers is L_0 when the wage is w_0. This is one point on the firm's long-run demand function for labor.

To produce q_0 at long-run minimum cost, the firm combines K_0 machines with L_0 workers. The value of the marginal product of labor given that the firm has K_0 machines is VMP_0 in Figure 17-4. Notice that the short-run demand function for labor, VMP_0, intersects the long-run demand for labor when the wage is w_0 and employment is L_0. Given that the firm has K_0 machines and the wage is w_0, the firm maximizes short-run profits by employing L_0 workers. In the long run, when the numbers of machines and workers are variable, the company maximizes profits

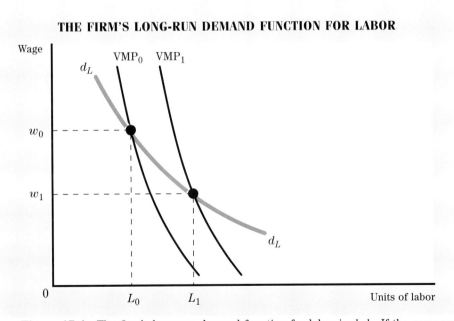

THE FIRM'S LONG-RUN DEMAND FUNCTION FOR LABOR

Figure 17-4   The firm's long-run demand function for labor is $d_L d_L$. If the company has K_0 machines, the value of the marginal product is VMP_0. If the firm has K_1 machines, the value of the marginal product is VMP_1. The long-run demand function for labor is more elastic than the short-run demand function.

by producing q_0 units with L_0 workers and K_0 machines. Therefore, we can say that the firm demands L_0 workers when the wage is w_0, given r_0 and P_0.

To grasp how a change in the wage changes the number of workers demanded by the firm in the long run, consider what happens to quantity demanded when the wage rate decreases from w_0 to w_1. First, the isocost lines in Figure 17-3b pivot and become flatter because w decreases relative to r. Labor becomes cheaper relative to capital, and so the firm substitutes labor for capital to produce any given output at minimum cost.

In Figure 17-3b the firm's expansion path becomes bb because the wage falls. The long-run total and average cost functions of the firm shift downward. The quantity where long-run average cost reaches a minimum may either increase or decrease when the wage falls. In the more common case the new long-run marginal cost function shifts to the right. This can be seen in Figure 17-3a, where the MC function shifts to the right and becomes the MC' function and the firm's new profit-maximizing output becomes q_1. In the long run the firm produces q_1 units at lowest total cost at point C in Figure 17-3b, where the slope of the new isocost line equals the slope of the isoquant for q_1. Therefore, the firm incurs the minimum cost of producing q_1 units by combining K_1 machines with L_1 workers when the wage rate falls to w_1. This is another point on the firm's long-run demand function for labor. Given P_0 and r_0, the company demands L_1 workers when the wage is w_1.

Figure 17-4 highlights two points on the firm's long-run demand function for labor when the wage is either w_0 or w_1. When the company has K_1 machines, the value of the marginal product function is VMP$_1$ and it intersects the long-run demand for labor where the firm hires L_1 workers when the wage is w_1. The firm maximizes short-run profits by employing L_1 workers when the wage is w_1. So, the quantity of labor demanded by the firm is L_1 in the short run when the wage is w_1, a point on the short-run demand function for labor. This point is also on the firm's long-run demand function for labor because the company maximizes profits by producing q_1 units with L_1 workers and K_1 machines given the price of the product and factor prices.

The firm's long-run demand function for labor is the net result of two effects caused by the decline in the wage. The first is the substitution effect. For a given output, the firm substitutes more labor for less capital when the wage falls. In Figure 17-3b the substitution effect is the move from point A to point B along the isoquant representing q_0 (holding output constant). The second effect is the scale effect. A fall in the wage rate can (but need not) lower the long-run marginal cost of producing the product near q_0. When it does shift the long-run marginal cost function to the right in the vicinity of q_0, a wage cut increases the firm's profit-maximizing quantity. This is shown in Figure 17-3a where the profit-maximizing output increases to q_1 units. Since output increases, the scale effect is the move from point B to point C in Figure 17-3b. The scale effect also increases the firm's long-run demand for labor.[2]

[2] A more advanced analysis would show that the firm demands more units of labor at a lower wage even when the scale effect causes the firm to produce less output.

SHIFTS IN THE FIRM'S LONG-RUN DEMAND FUNCTION FOR LABOR

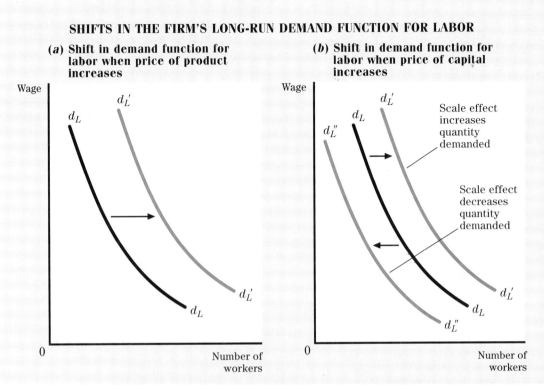

Figure 17-5   (*a*) An increase in the price of the product causes the firm's demand function for labor to shift to the right. (*b*) The firm's demand function for labor can shift to the right or to the left when the price of capital increases.

> The change in the quantity of labor demanded by a firm due to a wage change is equal to the sum of a substitution effect and a scale effect.

Until now, the analysis has focused exclusively on deriving the short- and long-run demand function for labor. Now we want to consider several factors that cause the demand function for labor to shift. The firm's long-run demand function shifts when the price of the product changes. An increase in the price of the product shifts the value of the marginal product to the right. In Figure 17-5*a* the company's demand function for labor shifts from $d_L d_L$ to $d_L' d_L'$ when the price of the product increases and the firm produces more units. Another factor that causes the demand function for labor to shift is the price of capital. The firm substitutes labor for capital when the price of capital increases. The substitution effect measures the increase in the number of workers employed when the price of capital changes, holding output constant. When the price of capital increases, the firm may produce a smaller or a larger output, and so the scale effect can either increase or decrease its long-run output and the number of workers employed. Figure 17-5*b* shows that the demand function shifts to the right and becomes $d'_L d'_L$ because the scale effect increases output and, consequently, the quantity of labor demanded. The figure also shows the case where the demand function shifts to the left and becomes $d''_L d''_L$ because the scale effect decreases output and the demand for labor by more than the substitution effect increases the quantity of labor demanded. Therefore, a rise in the price of capital can either shift the firm's long-run demand function for labor to the right or to the left depending on the size and sign of the scale effect.

The Short- and Long-Run Market Demand Functions for Labor

Now let's move from the firm's demand function for labor to the industry's demand for labor. In the model, workers are employed in many industries, and so the aggregate demand for labor (of a given quality) is made up of the demand by companies operating in many industries.

Since the firm is a price taker, the price of the product does not change when the firm's output changes because of a wage change. While the firm has no effect on the price, the price of the product does change whenever a wage change causes the total industry output to change. Therefore, the long-run market demand function for labor by all firms in a competitive industry must take account of the effect of an increase in industry output on price when the wage rate falls.

Therefore, we cannot simply add up each firm's long-run demand function to get the industry's long-run demand function for labor because the firm's demand function was derived by assuming the price is constant. While a change in the output of one firm does not affect price, the market price will change when all firms in the industry respond to the wage change. When the wage falls, the long-run average cost function of all existing firms and for potential entrants into an industry shifts downward. When the long-run industry supply function of the product shifts to the right, the equilibrium price decreases and industry output increases. The industry scale effect increases the quantity of labor demanded by all firms in the industry in the long run. Therefore, each industry's long-run demand function for labor slopes downward—a wage decrease increases the total quantity of labor demanded.[3]

Similar logic applies to the short-run industry demand function for labor. A fall in the wage rate shifts the industry short-run supply function of the product to the right and causes the price to fall. The fixed number of firms in the industry will supply more units in the short run, and so the industry scale effect is positive and the short-run industry demand function for labor also slopes downward.

> The market demand function for labor slopes downward in both the short and long runs.

---

[3] If other firms in the economy used this type of labor, the demand functions of these firms would have to be included in deriving the long-run demand for labor.

The analysis of the demand side of the market for labor is now complete. We have derived the short- and the long-run market demand functions for labor for each industry. Now let's turn to the supply function of labor.

17-2   THE SUPPLY FUNCTION OF LABOR

The objective in this section is to derive the supply function of an individual worker. Then, the supply functions of all individuals combine to produce the aggregate supply function of labor.

The Work-Leisure Choice

Our starting point is the individual's utility function. Consider a one-period model and assume that each consumer has a utility function that depends on C, total spending on a composite good, and h, hours or days of leisure. The consumer's utility increases with an increase in either C or h, and the utility function is

$$U = U(C, h) \qquad \text{(Utility Function)} \qquad \textbf{(17-8)}$$

The individual's indifference curves in Figure 17-6 slope downward to the right because an increase in either C or h must coincide with a decrease in the other good for utility to remain constant.

The budget constraint of the individual requires total spending on goods to equal income. The wage per unit of time is w, and so total income of the individual is $w(H - h)$, where H is total time available and can represent 24 hours per day or 365 days per year depending on what the model is to explain.

Total income = Total spending (C)

Total spending (C) = Wage rate [Total hours (H) − Hours of leisure (h)]

$$C = w(H - h) \qquad \text{(Budget Constraint)} \qquad \textbf{(17-9)}$$

Because this is a one-period model, the consumer spends all income on consumption. To keep within the confines of the two-good model, assume that H represents the total time for work and leisure activities. The budget constraint of the consumer is line bc in Figure 17-6. The cost to the consumer of an additional hour of leisure is a reduction of w in spending on goods, and so the slope of the budget line is $-w$. The consumer maximizes utility when the marginal rate of substitution between goods and leisure is $-w$, so that the individual consumes h_0 hours of leisure and spends C_0 on a composite good.

If the wage rate increases to w_1, the budget constraint rotates around point c on the horizontal axis and becomes cc. Hours of leisure decrease to h_1 because the worker has the incentive to devote more time to work and less time to leisure, and so spending increases to C_1. If the wage rate increases to w_2, the budget constraint becomes cd and hours of leisure increase to h_2. At the higher wage, the consumer's income is sufficiently high that he or she wants to consume more leisure.

The curve ABC connects all points of tangency between the different isocost lines and the corresponding indifference curves. From point A to point B along the

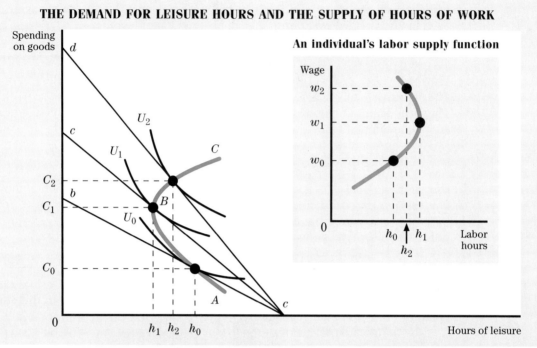

Figure 17-6   When the wage is w_0, the budget line is bc and the consumer demands h_0 hours of leisure. When the wage increases to w_1, the budget line becomes cc and the demand for leisure decreases to h_1 hours. At a still higher wage the demand for leisure increases to h_2. The wage-leisure curve is ABC and shows how the wage affects leisure hours. The supply function of work hours is $24 - h$ and is shown in the inset.

curve the wage increase decreases leisure and increases work. From point B to point C an increase in the wage increases leisure and reduces hours of work. The graph in the inset shows that the individual works more hours when the wage increases from w_0 to w_1 and then works fewer hours when the wage increases to w_2.

The curve ABC shows how much leisure the individual demands at each wage. Since the number of hours of work per day is simply $24 - h$, we also know the hours of work supplied at each wage and have derived an individual's labor supply function.

The Income and Substitution Effects of a Wage Change

We can better understand the different responses of the individual to a wage increase by developing the income and substitution effects of a wage change. In Figure 17-7a an increase in wage decreases hours of leisure from h_0 to h_1. The total change in leisure caused by the change in wage is the sum of a substitution effect

INCOME AND SUBSTITUTION EFFECTS OF A WAGE CHANGE

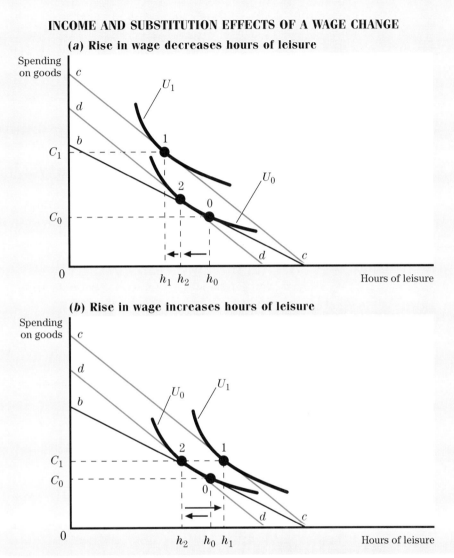

(a) Rise in wage decreases hours of leisure

(b) Rise in wage increases hours of leisure

Figure 17-7   (*a*) The wage increases and the demand for leisure falls from h_0 to h_1. The substitution effect is the move from point 0 to point 2 where the demand for leisure decreases from h_0 to h_2. The utility of the individual remains U_0 when the wage rate increases because income of the individual is reduced. As a result, the new budget line *dd* is tangent to U_0 at point 2. The income effect is the move from point 2 to point 1. An increase in income also decreases the demand for leisure from h_2 to h_1. The substitution and income effects work in the same direction to reduce the demand for leisure. (*b*) The income effect increases the demand for leisure from point 2 to point 1, and so hours of leisure increase from h_2 to h_1. In this case the income effect increases the demand for leisure and is greater than the substitution effect, which always decreases the demand for leisure.

and an income effect. Recall from Chapter 3 that the substitution effect of a price change with utility held constant measured the change in the quantity demanded when the price of one good fell relative to that of another. In the same way the substitution effect of a wage change measures the change in hours of leisure when wage changes, holding utility constant. The substitution effect is the move from point 0 to point 2 in Figure 17-7a. Utility is constant, and we measure the change in hours of leisure from h_0 to h_2 because of the increase in wage. The substitution effect measures the change in the demand for leisure when wage changes with utility held constant. The income effect measures the change in hours of leisure due to a parallel shift in the budget line, in this case from dd to cc. As income increases, this individual's demand for leisure decreases from h_2 to h_1. In this instance, the income effect is negative since a rise in income decreases the demand for leisure and increases the demand for work. Leisure is an inferior good. The income effect works in the same direction as the substitution effect. In summary, a rise in wage decreases the demand for leisure and increases the demand for work hours.

Figure 17-7b differs from Figure 17-7a because the income effect increases the demand for leisure and is larger than the substitution effect. Again, the substitution effect is the move from point 0 to point 2 where the demand for leisure decreases from h_0 to h_2 when wage increases. The income effect is the move from point 2 to point 1 and in this case increases the demand for leisure from h_2 to h_1. In this case leisure is a normal good. The income effect is opposite in sign and is larger than the substitution effect. Consequently, a rise in wage rate increases the demand for leisure and decreases the demand for hours of work. It can be concluded that a backward-bending supply function of labor will occur when the income effect for leisure is positive and is larger than the substitution effect.

A worker supplies less labor at a higher wage if leisure is a normal good and the income effect is larger than the substitution effect.

APPLICATION 17-1

A General Assistance Program and the Work-Leisure Choice

The model of individual labor supply can be used to evaluate the impact of public policies on labor supply. In many countries governments administer general assistance programs that establish a safety net for individuals with low incomes. The voting public is unwilling to allow the income of those with low earning power to fall below a minimum income. A general assistance program establishes a safety net by guaranteeing each person a minimum income.

Let's look at the effect of a general assistance program on the work-leisure choice. In Figure 17-8a the individual's budget constraint is aa'. Given the wage rate of this individual, he chooses to consume h^* days of leisure a year and to spend C^* on a composite good. Now suppose that society deems this outcome

EFFECTS OF A GENERAL ASSISTANCE PROGRAM

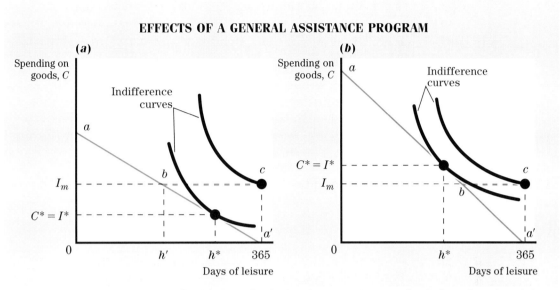

Figure 17-8 (*a*) An individual with private income that is less than the minimum income of I_m increases days of leisure from h^* to 365 and income from I^* to I_m. (*b*) An individual has a private income of I^* and h^* days of leisure before a general assistance program becomes available. When the general assistance program becomes available, this individual increases leisure from h^* to 365 days, preferring 365 days of leisure and an income of I_m to h^* days of leisure and I^* income.

unacceptable and introduces a general assistance program which guarantees an individual a minimum income of I_m per period. The first step in analyzing the economic effects of a general assistance program is to determine how it changes the budget constraint. The new budget constraint of the individual becomes *abc* since income cannot fall below I_m. If private income is less than I_m, he receives general assistance, and so the sum of private earnings plus public assistance equals I_m.

If the individual does not work at all, general assistance guarantees an annual income of I_m. If he earns a daily wage of w, each day of work results in a decrease in general assistance. Along the flat segment *bc*, there is a dollar-for-dollar tradeoff between an increase in private income and a decrease in public assistance. In essence there is 100 percent taxation of private income. For every dollar increase in private income, general assistance falls by a dollar. You can imagine the disincentive effects of a general assistance program. At any point on the flat segment the individual is still receiving some general assistance. If he consumes less than h' days of leisure, his market income exceeds I_m and he is no longer eligible for general assistance.

What are some of the consequences of general assistance programs? First, there is a redistribution of income. However, the redistribution of income creates a disincentive effect because of the 100 percent tax on private earnings. Figure

17-8*a* shows an individual moving to a higher indifference curve at point *c* by opting for general assistance and performing no work at all. The reward for not working is an increase in income *and* an increase in days of leisure from h^* to 365 days.

You might think that this analysis of the economic effects of a general assistance program is complete. However, it has wrongly assumed that only those with incomes below I_m are affected. In the long run a general assistance program can affect individuals with private incomes greater than I_m. Figure 17-8*b* shows an individual with higher earning power and a budget constraint of *aa'*. Without a general assistance program, she selects h^* days of leisure and earns income of I^* that is greater than I_m. With the introduction of a general assistance program she reaches a higher indifference curve by opting for the combination of I_m and 365 days of leisure. So, this type of assistance also encourages some individuals with earnings greater than I_m to reduce their hours of work in order to qualify for the program.

The disincentive effects that the theory points out have become a matter of controversy in political debates over the years. A growing recognition of the disincentive effects of general assistance programs has led to calls to modify these programs in ways that will reduce these effects.

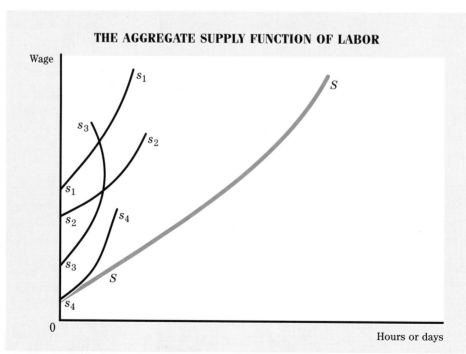

Figure 17-9   The aggregate supply function of labor is *SS*. It is formed by summing horizontally the individual supply functions of workers in many firms and industries. The supply functions of only four workers are shown here.

The Aggregate Supply Function of Labor and the Equilibrium Wage

Individual supply functions are summed horizontally to derive the aggregate supply function of labor. Each point on the aggregate supply function is obtained by simply summing the labor supplied by all individuals at that wage. Figure 17-9 shows the different supply functions of hours worked for selected workers and a positively sloped aggregate supply function *SS*. The long-run supply of labor has a positive slope even though some but not all workers have backward-bending supply curves.

In a competitive labor market, the equilibrium wage occurs where the demand and the supply functions intersect. In Figure 17-10 quantity demanded equals quantity supplied when the wage is w^* (for a given quality of worker) and the total units of labor employed in the industry is L^* units. Total labor earnings are w^*L^*, and area 1 represents "worker surplus." The supply function shows how much of a wage increase is required to increase the quantity of workers supplied. While every worker except the last one employed is willing to work at a lower wage, all workers receive w^*. For example, the first worker is willing to supply labor if the wage is only w_0. The difference between w^* and w_0 is the surplus the first worker receives. By adding up all these surplus areas, we arrive at area 1 which is worker surplus. Area 2 is equal to total payments to other factors of production.

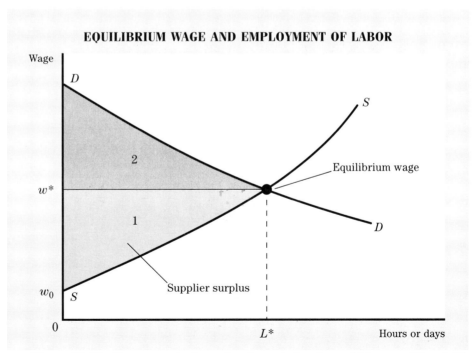

EQUILIBRIUM WAGE AND EMPLOYMENT OF LABOR

Figure 17-10   The aggregate demand and supply functions of labor are *DD* and *SS*. The aggregate demand function is formed by summing each industry's demand function horizontally. Equilibrium wage is w^*, and total employment is L^*.

To retrace our steps, we began with the production function of the firm and derived the firm's and the market demand functions for labor in the short and long runs. By relying on utility maximization, we determined the individual's labor supply function and the aggregate supply function. Finally, we noted that the intersection of the aggregate demand and supply functions determines the equilibrium wage.

17-3 DEMAND FOR LABOR BY A PRICE-MAKING FIRM

While the firm's demand function for labor was derived assuming that the firm is a price taker, the analysis can be extended to include a price-making firm where marginal revenue is less than price. We can substitute marginal revenue for price and calculate the marginal revenue product which is equal to the firm's marginal revenue times the marginal product of labor. Therefore, MRP_L is less than VMP_L for a price-making firm. For this type of firm the MRP_L automatically takes account of how the increased output produced by another worker affects price.

Table 17-2 displays a numerical example where the price decreases as the firm sells more units. It differs from Table 17-1 in two ways. First, the price decreases as the firm sells more units (column 4). Second, column 8 shows that the marginal cost of hiring another worker is $30 per day. The marginal revenue product can be determined by calculating the marginal revenue per unit increase in quantity. For example, when the firm hires the second worker, total output increases by four units (column 3). This causes the price to fall to $18, and so total revenue increases to $162. Therefore, the marginal revenue product of labor $\Delta R/\Delta L = \$62/1 = \$62$.

Table 17-2 DERIVING THE MARGINAL REVENUE PRODUCT OF LABOR FOR A PRICE-MAKING FIRM

NUMBER OF WORKERS q (1)	TOTAL OUTPUT, q (2)	MARGINAL PRODUCT, $\Delta q/\Delta L$ (3)	PRICE, P ($) (4)	TOTAL REVENUE, R ($) (5)	MARGINAL REVENUE, $\Delta R/\Delta q$ ($) (6)	MARGINAL REVENUE PRODUCT, $MRP_L =$ ($\Delta R/\Delta q$) ($\Delta q/\Delta L$) ($) (7)	MARGINAL COST OF FACTOR ($) (8)
1	5	5	20	100	20.00	100	30
2	9	4	18	162	15.50	62	30
3	12	3	16	192	10.00	30	30
4	14	2	14	196	2.00	4	30

Since the marginal cost of hiring another worker is $30 per worker, the marginal revenue product of labor exceeds w, and so the firm's profits increase. The company maximizes profits when it hires three workers where the marginal revenue product of labor is equal to the marginal cost of hiring another worker.

With a price-taking firm the marginal revenue product of the company becomes its demand function for labor whether it is operating in the short or in the long run. The only difference between the short- and long-run analysis is that the marginal product is calculated with units of capital that are fixed in the short run and variable in the long run. In either case the firm increases profits by expanding employment until the marginal revenue product of labor equals the marginal cost of labor.

17-4   INVESTMENT IN HUMAN CAPITAL

Until now, it has been assumed that each unit of labor is of a uniform quality and so all workers receive the same wage. Yet, we know that there are many wage rates and that workers are not all alike. Two important determinants of a worker's earnings are educational attainment and experience. Some workers enter the work force with considerable schooling—some with professional degrees—whereas others have only a high school degree or less.

What are the added benefits and costs that a worker receives from the additional schooling? Consider a high school graduate who must decide whether to enter the work force or to attend college. If she enters the work force immediately, annual earnings per year average I_h. If she attends college, she forgoes earning income for four years. This choice is reasonable if she expects to earn sufficiently more on average as a college graduate than as a high school graduate.

Figure 17-11 shows what the typical income streams will be if the individual has a high school degree or a college degree. The earning stream will be hh if she has a high school degree. If she attends college and enters the labor force after graduating from college, the income stream will be cc. In both instances earnings rise with experience and then level off and subsequently decline. If the average earnings of a high school graduate would equal $20,000 per year over the first four years of work, the college student's opportunity cost, or the income forgone, is $80,000 if we ignore discounting and other amounts such as tuition and summer earnings while in college.

The Present Value of Earnings

Because an individual forgoes income while attending college, a college education can be worthwhile only if the average annual earnings of the college graduate not only exceed those of the high school graduate but exceed them by enough to make college an optimal choice. To compare the two earning streams, you must calculate the present value of each stream. Let the annual earnings of the high school graduate in year i be H_i and the annual earnings of a college graduate in year i be C_i. The present value of the earnings of the high school graduate is

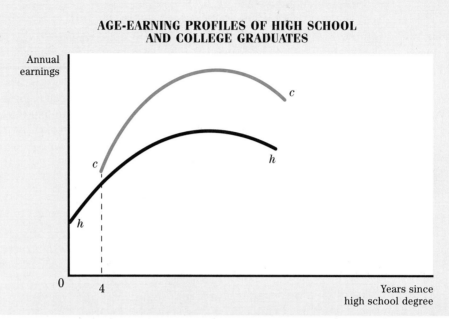

Figure 17-11 Typical age-earnings profiles of high school and college graduates. High school graduates earn income while college graduates are taking college courses. College graduates begin work four years later.

$$PV_h = \frac{H_1}{(1 + i)^1} + \frac{H_2}{(1 + i)^2} + \frac{H_3}{(1 + i)^3} + \frac{H_4}{(1 + i)^4} + \frac{H_5}{(1 + i)^5}$$

$$+ \frac{H_6}{(1 + i)^6} + \frac{H_7}{(1 + i)^7} + \cdots + \frac{H_i}{(1 + i)^i}$$

The present value of the college graduate's income stream is

$$PV_c = \frac{C_5}{(1 + i)^5} + \frac{C_6}{(1 + i)^6} + \frac{C_7}{(1 + i)^7} + \cdots + \frac{C_i}{(1 + i)^i}$$

The college graduate forgoes income in years 1 to 4. Going to college is an investment, and in this case it is an investment in human capital. By forgoing income the college student hopes to increase future earning power by increasing her human capital.

A high school graduate is more likely to go to college if

$$PV_c > PV_h$$

This means that an individual is more likely to earn a college degree when there is a large difference between the earnings of college graduates and high school graduates. The attractiveness of attending college depends on the present values of the two degrees. When the difference between the present value of a college degree and that of a high school degree becomes larger, attending college becomes more appealing. As more students opt for college degrees or some post-high school education (associate degrees, certification for different jobs, and so on), then the difference between the earnings of a college graduate and a high school graduate might narrow.

By comparing the two earning streams, we can identify the main factors that encourage individuals to postpone earning income and to continue schooling. One factor is the interest rate. Given the two income streams, a higher interest rate makes a college education a less attractive choice because the higher future income earned by a college graduate contributes still less to the present value of a college degree.

Why are college campuses populated with younger members of society? The later one begins a college education, the lower the present value of a college or postgraduate degree. The horizon over which income is earned shrinks as the age of the individual increases. A second reason an older individual is less likely to attend college is that the opportunity cost of an education is usually higher. Earnings increase with age as an individual gains experience. Therefore, the opportunity cost of attending college—the forgone earnings—is higher because the individual is more productive in the labor force. It is no accident that most people make investments in schooling when they are young and not at the end of their lifetime.

The Equilibrium Earnings of a College Graduate

This section compares the benefits of a college degree with those of a high school diploma and determines how much more valuable a college degree has been and is now. The decision to go to college depends on how much higher an income an individual will earn with a college degree than with a high school diploma. Given the salary earned with a high school diploma, let's find out what a college graduate's minimum earnings must be before an individual would consider going to college. To develop this analysis, we make a few assumptions.

1. The average annual earnings of high school graduates are I_h in each year, and the average annual earnings of college graduates are I_c in each year. We are simplifying the analysis by assuming that the annual income of each type of graduate is constant over time. Furthermore, we assume that each individual is paid at the end of the period.

2. Both types of graduates have infinite lives.

3. Tuition and part-time earnings are ignored.

4. The decision to attend college is based on present values.[4]

---

[4] For some individuals who value learning for learning's sake, our analysis would not be appropriate. Some students attend college to obtain a liberal education or to broaden their understanding. Others attend to have a broader set of job opportunities. They might be willing to attend college even if the present value of a college education is less than the present value of a high school education.

These assumptions simplify the analysis. In any real-world application they would be modified to take account of finite lifetimes or for different age-earning profiles of the two groups or for nonpecuniary benefits of a college education.

Given these assumptions, the present value of the stream of income of the high school graduates is $PV_h = I_h/i$. The high school graduate receives an annual income of I_h at the end of the first year. The college graduate receives an annual income of I_c at the end of the fifth year. The present value of the stream of income for the college graduate is $PV_c = I_c/i(1 + i)^4$.

Assuming the decision to pursue a college degree depends strictly on present-value considerations, the minimum annual earnings of the college graduate can be determined, given the earnings of the high school graduate, for the two present values to be equal. In other words, we can find the minimum earnings of a college graduate that will just compensate the individual for postponing income for the four years it takes to earn a degree—and it will provide a measure of the value of a college degree when we look at actual earnings data. If the earnings of a college graduate exceed the minimum required earnings, then the present value of a college

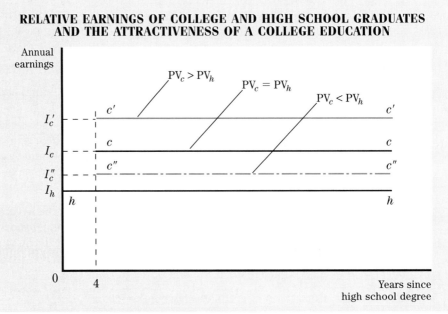

RELATIVE EARNINGS OF COLLEGE AND HIGH SCHOOL GRADUATES AND THE ATTRACTIVENESS OF A COLLEGE EDUCATION

Figure 17-12   If the earnings of college graduates are I_c', the present value of a college graduate's earnings is greater than the present value of a high school graduate's earnings and more high school graduates enroll in college. If the earnings of college graduates are only I_c, fewer high school graduates enroll in college since the present value of a college graduate's earnings is the same as the present value of a high school graduate's earnings. If the annual earnings of a college graduate are *only I_c''*, still fewer high school graduates enroll in college.

degree exceeds the present value of a high school degree, and so the benefits of a college education are greater and more individuals will attend college.

Given these assumptions, we can describe a long-run equilibrium in the market for a college education when the present values are equal. The present values of the two income flows are equal when

$$\frac{I_c}{i(1 + i)^4} = \frac{I_h}{i}$$

This equation can be solved for I_c/I_h by dividing both sides by I_h and then multiplying both sides by $i(1 + i)^4$. The ratio of a college graduate's earnings to the earnings of a high school graduate is

$$\frac{I_c}{I_h} = (1 + i)^4 \qquad \text{(Equilibrium in the Market for College Graduates)} \qquad \textbf{(17-10)}$$

Figure 17-12 shows three possible values for the earnings of a college graduate while the earnings of a high school graduate are I_h. The present value of a college graduate's earnings exceeds the present value of a high school graduate's earnings, and so more high school graduates enroll in college if the earnings of college graduates are I'_c. If the earnings of a college graduate are I_c, the present value of a college graduate's earnings is equal to that of a high school graduate, and so fewer high school graduates enroll in college. If the earnings of a college graduate are only I''_c, the present value of a college graduate's earnings is less than that of a high school graduate, and so still fewer high school graduates will enter college.

Table 17-3 shows the equilibrium ratio of earnings for selected interest rates. If the interest rate is 5 percent, then a college graduate must earn 22 percent more than a high school graduate to make the college education worth it, whereas if the interest rate is 10 percent, then the individual must earn 46 percent more annually. The higher i, the higher the annual earnings of college graduates must be relative to the annual earnings of high school graduates so that the present values of earnings are equal. These estimated ratios of annual earnings are suggestive. The

Table 17-3   EFFECT OF THE INTEREST RATE ON THE EQUILIBRIUM RATIO OF EARNINGS

ANNUAL INTEREST RATE (%)	EQUILIBRIUM RATIO OF EARNINGS OF COLLEGE GRADUATE TO EARNINGS OF HIGH SCHOOL GRADUATE
5.0	1.22
7.5	1.34
10.0	1.46

Table 17-4   RELATIVE EARNINGS OF FULL-TIME WORKERS WITH HIGH SCHOOL AND COLLEGE DEGREES (1984 DOLLARS)

YEAR (1)	AVERAGE EARNINGS OF MALES WITH 4 YEARS OF HIGH SCHOOL ($) (2)	AVERAGE EARNINGS OF MALES WITH 4 YEARS OF COLLEGE ($) (3)	RATIO OF EARNINGS, (2)/(3) (4)	IMPLIED VALUE OF i (5)
1967	23,779	35,586	1.50	10.6
1970	25,562	37,062	1.45	9.7
1975	23,636	34,970	1.47	10.3
1980	25,247	32,483	1.29	6.5
1985	23,064	34,454	1.49	10.6
1989	21,937	34,445	1.57	11.9

Source: Current Population Reports, Series P-60, annual issues.

particular numerical values will change some when tuition costs, earnings from part-time work, and different age-earnings profiles are introduced.

Let's look at how actual annual earnings of college graduates compare to earnings of high school graduates. Table 17-4 compares the average earnings of full-time male workers with four years of college with the average earnings of full-time male workers who completed four years of high school from 1967 to 1989.

Columns 2 and 3 of Table 17-4 list the earnings of the two groups in 1984 dollars. Column 4 shows the ratio of the average earnings of college graduates and high school graduates. Using equation 17-10 and the actual ratio of earnings, we can derive an estimate of what value of i equates the present values. For each year we substitute the ratio in column 4 into equation 17-10 and solve for i. The derived estimate of i tells us what the interest rate must be in that year—given the ratio of earnings—that equates the present values. Column 5 shows the estimates of i.[5] The estimated interest rates vary from a low of only 6.5 percent in 1980 to a high of 11.9 percent in 1989. Therefore, if an individual could borrow and invest at an interest rate of more than 6.5 percent in 1980, a college education would not be as attractive an investment.

As Table 17-4 demonstrates, the actual ratio of earnings has fluctuated over

[5] Since $I_c/I_h = (1 + i)^4$, both sides can be raised to the power $\frac{1}{4}$ to obtain

$$\left(\frac{I_c}{I_h}\right)^{1/4} = 1 + i$$

Therefore

$$i = \left(\frac{I_c}{I_h}\right)^{1/4} - 1$$

time, and so the benefits of a college education have changed from decade to decade. The ratio of incomes was relatively high in the late 1960s, and college enrollments soared. By the late 1970s and early 1980s the ratio of incomes had fallen dramatically. The 1980s witnessed a complete reversal as the ratio increased. However, the rise in the ratio was due to a decline in the real income of high school graduates and not to an increase in the real income of college graduates. Researchers have attempted to understand the reasons for these fluctuations in the benefits of a college education. Currently, they are investigating the possible causes of the decline in the real earnings of high school graduates throughout the 1980s and are focusing on the effects of import competition in such industries such as steel and autos and the introduction of computers in the workplace on the earnings of workers with different educational attainments.[6]

APPLICATION 17-2

The Rate of Return of a Medical Education

Monica Noether compared the actual earnings of physicians to her estimates of what physicians' incomes would have to be to compensate them for the extra years spent in medical school and in residence programs after completing college.[7] She used a more complicated version of equation 17-10 to estimate what the average earnings of a doctor would be if the present values of a physician's earnings and a college graduate's earnings were equal. Then she calculated the ratio of actual physicians' earnings to estimated earnings for each year from 1946 to 1981. The time series of this ratio from 1946 to 1981 appears in Figure 17-13. Actual physicians' incomes average about 15 percent higher from 1946 to 1964 than what would be predicted by loss of income because of the length of medical training and other costs. Introduction of the Medicaid and Medicare programs in 1965 significantly increased the demand for doctors' services, and actual earnings exploded. After 1964, the average physician's income increased dramatically and remained above the amount required for the present value of the earnings of college graduates to equal the present value of the earnings of physicians. This trend continued until the early 1970s. Since the early 1970s this ratio has declined as the number of U.S. medical schools and the number of foreign-trained physicians have increased rapidly. In subsequent work Noether found that the ratio continued to decline into the mid-1980s.

---

[6] For an informative study, see Lawrence F. Katz and Kevin M. Murphy, "Changes in Relative Wages, 1963–1987: Supply and Demand Factors," Working Paper No. 3927, National Bureau of Economic Research, December 1991; John Bound and George Johnson, "Changes in the Structure of Wages in the 1980's: An Evaluation of Alternative Explanations," *American Economic Review*, vol. 82, June 1992, pp. 371–392.
[7] Monica Noether, "The Effect of Government Policy Changes on the Supply of Physicians: Expansion of a Competitive Fringe," *Journal of Law and Economics*, vol. XXXIX, no. 2, October 1986, pp. 231–262; "How Profitable Is a Medical Career?" *Journal of Medical Practice Management*, vol. 4, no. 1, Summer 1986, pp. 21–30.

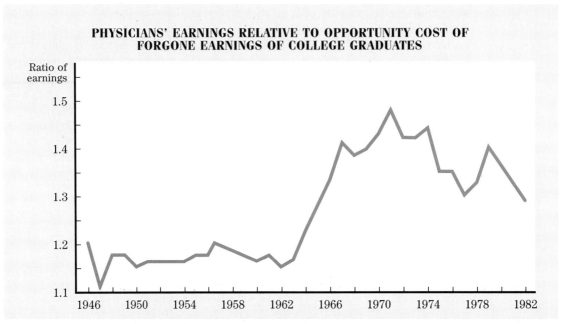

**PHYSICIANS' EARNINGS RELATIVE TO OPPORTUNITY COST OF
FORGONE EARNINGS OF COLLEGE GRADUATES**

Figure 17-13 Physicians' earnings increased dramatically in the 1960s when Medicare increased the demand for medical care.

17-5   TRAINING EMPLOYEES

Contrary to common opinion, education does not stop the moment the graduate clutches the diploma.[8] In many occupations worker skills improve with on-the-job training. Some firms may offer training to employees to improve their skills, such as teaching a worker how to repair a scanner or to operate a computer program. Other companies provide orientation programs for new workers to introduce them to company rules and practices. Often firms encourage employees to take courses such as accounting or business writing to improve their business skills. A company trains workers because it expects their marginal product to increase. From the workers' perspective, the training makes them more productive and increases their future wages. If both workers and employers benefit from training, you would think that no special problems arise when firms offer training programs. Unfortunately, this isn't always true. There are some special and interesting problems that occur when firms offer on-the-job training.

A two-period analysis can be used to examine these special problems where a firm offers training in the first period and the worker qualifies as a trained worker in the second period. If the worker does not receive on-the-job training, he or she

[8] The material in this section is based on Gary S. Becker, *Human Capital*, National Bureau of Economic Research, New York, 1964; Ronald G. Ehrenberg and Robert S. Smith, *Modern Labor Economics*, Scott, Foresman, Glenview Ill., 1982.

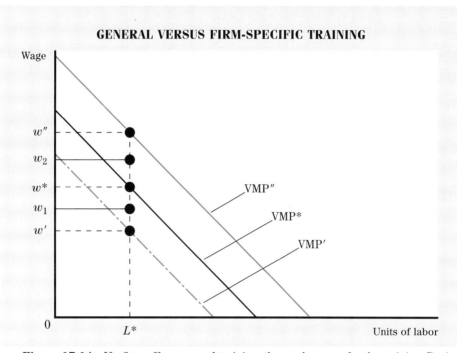

GENERAL VERSUS FIRM-SPECIFIC TRAINING

Figure 17-14   If a firm offers general training, the worker pays for the training. During the training period the worker receives w' because the marginal product of the employee is reduced. After completing the training, the worker receives w'' because the value of the marginal product increases no matter where the individual is employed. If the training is specific, the worker and the firm share the training cost. The pay of the employee during the training period is w_1. After the training period is completed, the firm pays w_2, a wage that is less than the value of the marginal product of the trained worker.

receives a wage of w^* in both periods. In Figure 17-14 the firm hires L^* workers if the wage is w^*, and the value of the marginal product is VMP^* in each period for workers without training.

General Training

First, let's consider a case where the training offered by the firm is general. When training increases the marginal product of workers in this *and* in other firms, we say the training is general. If a worker enrolls in an introductory accounting course or learns welding techniques, the training is general. The marginal product of the worker increases whether he is employed by the firm that supplies the training or by another firm. What the worker learns is applicable in many companies.

General training increases the worker's marginal product in many firms.

Let's consider what happens to the value of the marginal product of the worker during and after training. While he is receiving training, he is less productive because some time and effort are devoted to training and not to production. Consequently, the value of his marginal product during the first period declines to VMP′ in Figure 17-14. After the worker completes the training program, his marginal product shifts up to VMP″ in the second period.

Who pays for the training? If the firm continues to pay the worker w^* during the training period, it is paying for the training. The company is making an investment in the worker of $w^* - w'$ which is equal to the decrease in the worker's marginal product during the training period. The firm will incur this loss in the training period only if it expects to earn a surplus in the second period by paying the trained worker less than w'', the increased value of the marginal product of the trained worker in period 2, to recoup its loss in the first period. However, there is a hidden defect in this wage policy. If the firm pays less than w'' in period 2, the worker will resign and seek employment at some other firm because other firms in the labor market will pay w'' for a trained worker. The implication of this is that the firm will not pay for general training. Consequently, we conclude that the wage of the worker falls to w' during the training period because his marginal product is smaller. Then, the company will pay w'' for the services of the trained worker in the second period.

A worker pays for general training that raises the value of his or her marginal product in other firms.

The experience of the armed forces is an example of an employer offering general training. For many years young recruits received training in the military and acquired skills that the private market valued highly. For example, before the voluntary army, the armed forces trained many pilots who subsequently were bid away by commercial airlines. Because military wages were below those in the private market, the military could not retain individuals with these valuable skills when the recruitment period expired. The training provided by the military performed a valuable educational service for certain industries and occupations. Because a recruit could receive w'' by leaving the military, the turnover of military personnel was relatively high.

The same issue arises when firms pay for courses that their employees take at universities and vocational schools. Many companies pay for some or all of the tuition of workers who earn MBA degrees. Since an MBA degree is a form of general training, you would expect that the worker and not the firm would pay for the training. Is this a contradiction of the theory? Most firms protect themselves with contracts requiring employees to remain with the firm for x years or to compensate the company for tuition if they leave prematurely. There are some firms that do not impose this restriction, and this behavior is puzzling. In another situation some companies pay tuition for employees to attend executive programs. Usually, the firm selects employees for such programs who have been with the company for many years and are likely to remain even after completing the program.

Firm-Specific Training

Let's go to the opposite extreme and assume that the training is firm-specific. This means that the value of the marginal product increases in the second period only if the employee remains with the firm. Because the training is firm-specific, the worker would not be as productive if employed by another firm. Learning how to operate a firm-specific machine is an example of firm-specific training.

> Specific training increases the value of the marginal product of the worker to the firm offering the training.

Who pays for firm-specific training? If the firm pays for the training by paying workers w^* during the training period and a worker leaves in period 2, the company suffers a loss. For example, suppose the firm pays w^* in the first period. Since the value of the marginal product of the worker decreases during the training period, the firm loses money by providing the training in the first period if she leaves in the second period.

Suppose the worker pays for the training. Then, she suffers a loss if the firm does not pay her the higher value of the marginal product in the second period. She has made the investment by taking a wage of w' during the training period since she would have received a higher wage of w^* without training. She wants a guarantee of being paid more than w^* in the second period. However, the firm can pay her just w^* although her marginal product increases to w''; because the training is firm-specific, she cannot earn more than w^* elsewhere.

When the firm offers specific training, both the worker and the employer must make a commitment to the employment relationship by sharing the cost of training. Suppose the firm pays w_1 in Figure 17-14 in the first period, which is greater than the value of the marginal product when $L = L^*$. The worker also loses because she receives less than w^*, but the firm pays for some of the training. In the second period the firm pays w_2, less than w'', and recoups its losses (after taking account of discounting which we ignore here) in the first period. The worker also recoups her first-period loss because the company pays more than w^* in the second period.

> The worker and the firm share the cost of firm-specific training.

Because the firm pays more than w^* in the second period—what the worker could earn if employed by another firm—she has no incentive to leave the firm in the second period. Because w_2 is less than the value of her marginal product in the second period, the firm would be foolish to lay off the worker. In this solution both sides make an investment in the employment relationship. Neither has an incentive to terminate the relationship unless there is a significant unforeseen event. Therefore, the theory of firm-specific training predicts that the turnover of employees will be lower in firms that provide firm-specific training. In some large American and Japanese firms the turnover of employees is very low. In these cases it is likely that the training of workers is firm-specific. In contrast, the turnover of university professors is relatively high because little university-specific training occurs.

Table 17-5   PERCENT OF WORKERS STAYING WITH SAME FIRM BY AGE AND TENURE OF WORKER IN JAPAN AND IN THE UNITED STATES

AGE OF MALE WORKER IN JAPAN (1962) AND IN THE UNITED STATES (1963) (YR)	TENURE CLASS WITH FIRM IN JAPAN (1962) AND IN THE UNITED STATES (1963) (YR)	PERCENT STAYING WITH SAME FIRM AFTER 15 YEARS (1962–1977) IN JAPAN	PERCENT STAYING WITH SAME FIRM AFTER 15 YEARS (1963–1978) IN THE UNITED STATES
20–24	0–5	45.1	13.0
	5+	65.3	30.0
25–34	0–5	42.7	22.2
	5+	73.0	47.3
35–39	0–5	37.7	24.4
(35–44 for Japan)	5+	75.9	54.5

Source: This table is a condensed version of Table 1 in the original article.

APPLICATION **17-3**

Turnover and Tenure in the United States and in Japan

Japanese firms appear to invest more in training their workers than U.S. firms do. Moreover, available evidence suggests that the training is firm-specific. Researchers Masanori Hashimoto and John Raisian studied turnover rates in Japan and in the United States.[9] Table 17-5 shows the percentage of workers in different age-tenure classes that remain with the same employer over 15 years in Japan and in the United States.

The results in Table 17-5 show considerably more stability in the employment relationship in Japan than in the United States. For example, 45 percent of Japanese workers who were between 20 and 24 years old and had anywhere from 0 to 5 years of tenure with their employer in 1962 remained with the same company after 15 years, while only 13 percent of American workers with the same initial characteristics did so. Long-term employment relationships are clearly more common in Japan than in the United States. These findings suggest that more firm-specific investment and training occur in Japan than the United States.

A different explanation for the different employment practices in the two countries emphasizes cultural differences between Japan and the United States. Could it be that large Japanese employers are more paternalistic than large U.S.

[9] Masanori Hashimoto and John Raisian, "Employment Tenure and Earnings Profiles in Japan and the United States, *American Economic Review*, vol. 75, September 1985, pp. 721–735.

employers are and could this explain the differences? Hashimoto and Raisian think not; they note that Japan had higher turnover rates before World War II and so it is unlikely that cultural factors are the primary reason for the lower turnover rate of Japanese workers.

17-6   COMPENSATION BASED ON INPUT OR OUTPUT

A firm can make compensation of an employee depend on some measure of worker effort or on worker output. If an employee receives a straight salary or is paid by the hour, compensation depends on some measure of worker effort. The firm agrees to pay the employee a salary as long as he makes an effort to show up for work a certain number of days per month or hours per day.

Compensation based on output is piece work because the output of the worker determines his compensation. For example, firms often pay salespeople by commission and so compensation is a function of the dollar volume of sales each generates, or a farm worker's pay depends on the number of bushels harvested.

Whether compensation depends on output or effort is determined partly by which is less costly to measure. When the output of the worker is easier to measure, compensation will depend on worker output. When an employee shirks by not working conscientiously, he bears the cost because compensation depends on output.

The theory of wage determination presented at the beginning of the chapter assumed that measurement problems are unimportant. If the cost of measuring output is negligible, the wage equals the value of the marginal product of labor. In practice, it is easier to measure output when a worker's marginal product is independent of the marginal product of other workers. In many job situations it is costly to base pay on output. Paying on the basis of piece work means that the firm must measure output, and measurement uses up resources. Defining just what a unit of output is is not always straightforward. If the pay of an agricultural worker depends on pounds of fruit harvested, the worker will pay little attention to the quality of the fruit or pick only the larger fruit.

More often than not, the output of the individual worker is so costly to measure that compensation does not depend on worker output. This is especially true when output depends on team production or committee deliberations. Measuring the contribution of each member to a team is often difficult and costly. The number of yards gained by a running back in professional football depends on the performance of other members of the team, for example, the blocking ability of his teammates. In other situations output depends on a random factor like weather. A risk-averse worker may prefer compensation that depends on effort rather than output because compensation based on output is too variable. A drawback of compensation based on effort is that it encourages shirking by employees. Workers show up for the job and go through the motions but find ways of shirking from work.

APPLICATION 17-4

Problems with the Use of Incentive Pay

Incentive pay for officers of large firms is common. Incentive pay for employees is less common but appears to be slowly increasing over time. The slow pace of acceptance of pay for performance indicates that it is more difficult to implement than it first appears.[10]

Firms are making greater efforts to introduce pay for performance, but this deceptively simple idea is often difficult to put into practice. In the early 1990s DuPont's attempt to introduce incentive pay was a resounding failure. The company introduced performance pay in its fiber business group and required employees to risk some of their pay for a higher return if fiber business profits increased. If profits increased, employees would earn more than they earned under the old compensation policy. If profits fell, they would earn less. Management was trying to encourage workers to find ways to reduce costs but unfortunately, the profit incentives created some unintended effects. One employee noted that her secretary would route her well out of her way if it reduced the cost of a business trip. Mailroom employees began to question her mailings, suggesting she should lower costs. The new compensation plan faced an acid test at DuPont when the profits of the business fell because of a slow-down in the industry. The employees revolted and wanted out of the new plan, which DuPont eliminated. Many employees appear to be risk-averse and prefer steady pay to variable pay.

At Corning, Inc., a pay-for-performance plan was adopted and enabled workers to earn bonuses of from 4 to 6 percent of pay for special performances. One manager implemented the new awards policy hoping to keep the awards confidential but was unable to do so. He noted the good news–bad news effect of giving a bonus. Employees are happy because they receive a bonus but are upset when they don't receive the bonus they believe they deserve. Managers are often a major stumbling block to introducing pay-for-performance plans.

Pay for performance can create unintended incentives if firms using it fail to anticipate all the consequences of an incentive plan. One company introduced a bonus plan hoping it would encourage its buyers to reduce the cost of the raw materials they purchased. The firm expected the bonus plan would induce the buyers to search more intensively for lower prices in the market and to negotiate lower prices. It failed to recognize that the plan would create a perverse incentive for buyers to purchase a lower-quality raw material and thereby lower costs. Later, the company incurred higher costs to repair the defective product that the firm sold to customers long after the firm had paid bonuses to the buyers.

---

[10] Based on Amanda Bennett, "Paying Workers to Meet Goals Spreads, But Gauging Performance Proves Tough," *Wall Street Journal*, September 10, 1991.

17-7   USING WAGE POLICY AS A SORTING OR INCENTIVE MECHANISM

Firms shape their wage policies over the years to solve the particular problems that they face. This section highlights two different labor problems and describes how a firm can structure its wage policy to solve each one. The first problem is how to devise a wage policy that sorts workers so that the firm attracts only a certain type of worker. The second problem is how to structure a wage policy that discourages shirking by workers.

Creating a Wage Policy That Sorts Workers

Suppose there is an advantage in attracting employees who are willing to work long hours or many days per year or both. For example, a young analyst employed by a top-drawer investment banking firm might work 6 or 7 days a week and average 12 to 14 hours a day. Investment banking firms want to attract individuals who work intensively and are intelligent, motivated, adaptable, and capable of moving on short notice from one project to another.

Suppose the output of each worker depends in some part on the output of coworkers. If some workers are unwilling to work intensively for long hours, the productivity of the other workers suffers. In this situation there is an advantage to sorting workers into firms so that those who work long hours (more intensively) join one type of firm and receive appropriate compensation. Workers who prefer more leisure, shorter work hours, and a less hectic pace can then find employment in firms in other industries.

This would be easy to do if a company could distinguish workers who will be successful in an intense work environment from those who will not. But suppose a firm cannot distinguish between different types of workers. To attract employees who prefer to work intensively, it must compensate these individuals handsomely. The problem arises because high pay attracts both types of workers, a situation the firm wants to avoid. The company wants to pay individuals who work intensively without attracting those who lower the productivity of the more conscientious workers.

To keep matters as simple as possible, let's assume that there are just two types of workers. In Figure 17-15 consumption spending on a composite good is on the vertical axis, and hours of leisure are on the horizontal axis. A type 1 employee works intensively and has a reservation wage of w_1. A reservation wage is the wage the worker could earn in the next best job. The budget constraint of the type 1 worker is $C = w_1(24 - h)$, or the line ACD. The firm must pay a type 1 worker so that he or she can at least reach indifference curve $_1U_1$. If the firm pays w_1 per hour, the worker's reservation wage, the indifference curve is tangent to the budget line ACD where the type 1 worker consumes h_1 hours of leisure per day, works $24 - h_1$ hours, and spends $w_1(24 - h_1)$ on the composite good. The reservation wage of the type 2 worker is w_2, which is less than w_1. The budget

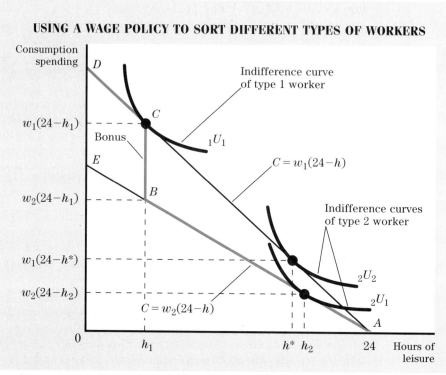

USING A WAGE POLICY TO SORT DIFFERENT TYPES OF WORKERS

Figure 17-15   By setting *ABCD* as the wage policy, a firm discourages workers of type 2 from joining the firm and reducing the marginal product of workers of type 1. Workers of type 2 are worse off joining the firm and therefore join other firms and receive their reservation wage, w_2. The compensation of the type 1 worker is $w_1(24 - h_1)$.

constraint of this worker is $C = w_2(24 - h)$, or line *ABE*. This budget constraint is tangent to indifference curve $_2U_1$ when the type 2 worker has h_2 hours of leisure per day, works $24 - h_2$ hours, and spends $w_2(24 - h_2)$ on consumption.

The firm must pay w_1 if it is to attract workers of type 1. Because it cannot distinguish between workers of types 1 and 2 beforehand, it will attract both types of individuals if it pays the higher wage, w_1. Type 2 workers are attracted to the firm because they can reach indifference curve $_2U_2$ by working only $24 - h^*$ hours while type 1 workers are working $24 - h_1$ hours per day. The firm wants to avoid hiring both types of workers.

Can the firm devise a wage policy that discourages type 2 workers from voluntarily joining the firm? It could adopt a wage scale that pays a low wage to workers who spend less than $24 - h_1$ hours on the job and then gives a bonus to workers who devote more than $24 - h_1$ hours per day to their work. The wage that it pays is less than w_2 by, say, a penny for all hours worked up to $24 - h_1$. If a type 1 worker joins the firm, he or she earns slightly less than $w_2(24 - h_1)$. The firm ups the ante by paying a bonus equal to BC for employees who work $24 - h_1$ hours per day. Total compensation for these workers is $w_2(24 - h_1)$ *plus* a bonus of BC. Therefore, a type 1 worker reaches indifference curve $_1U_1$. With this wage policy the budget constraint of a worker is $ABCD$. The firm's wage policy pays a low hourly wage but augments it with a large bonus of BC for employees who work $24 - h_1$ hours per day.

The firm's wage policy effectively sorts workers by basing pay on work effort and by paying a bonus at the end of the year. This practice of paying a bonus at the end of the period is sometimes called backloading pay since the worker receives the bonus at the end of the period. Employees who prefer to work long hours join firms with this type of wage policy. Type 2 workers, who prefer shorter hours and less intensity, sort into other firms and receive $w_2(24 - h_2)$ in compensation.

This wage policy has the effect of sorting employees into companies and prevents those who for one reason or another cannot work long hours from joining the firm. It might prevent some individuals with families from joining this type of firm since the firm requires a tremendous time commitment from the employee. Of course, this wage policy also has the effect of imposing a glass ceiling on some workers since they are effectively precluded from joining firms with this type of backloading pay. Yet, the firm adopts the wage policy because it believes that mixing the two different types of workers reduces the productivity of workers who work long hours.

We have interpreted work effort in terms of hours per day; however, this was only for illustrative purposes. Work effort can be interpreted in terms of the years spent in some junior capacity at a firm. During the first few years with the firm, workers pay their dues. They work for low wages initially, but the company rewards them with a promotion and a bonus, for example, promotion to partner in a law or consulting firm. Initially, the hard-working associate receives only $w_2(24 - h_1)$, the low pay that an associate earns in a law or consulting firm before promotion to partner.

Incentive Compensation and Mandatory Retirement

Compensating a worker at the end of the period or at the end of a job can be an effective mechanism for reducing shirking by workers. If workers are likely to remain with a firm for most of their lifetime, an age-pay profile where compensation is backloaded discourages shirking and malfeasance.

Backloading pay can help explain the wage policies of some firms. It is a central idea in one explanation of why firms insist on mandatory retirement. In many large firms all employees must retire at a specific age, usually by their seventieth birthday. For many years, the firm would send you on your way with a retirement party or a wristwatch when your seventieth birthday arrived no matter how effectively you were performing. Why does a firm force all employees to retire at seventy no matter how productive a worker is? If the marginal product of the worker declines after a certain age, why doesn't the firm simply lower the wage of the employee instead of arbitrarily terminating the employment relationship? On the face of it, mandatory retirement appears to be a short-sighted, capricious policy.

Edward Lazear has advanced an interesting explanation for the use of mandatory retirement.[11] In his model the firm pays a wage w^* to an employee when the worker reaches seventy years of age, but once the worker reaches seventy, the firm is no longer willing to offer him a contract. What this implies is that the worker's wage w^* exceeds his marginal product at age seventy, the year of mandatory retirement.

Why does the firm pay the employee more than his marginal product when he reaches seventy years of age? To explain this, Lazear introduces the notion of worker shirking. Shirking can take many forms. Perhaps, the worker slacks off or "borrows" tools from the factory or uses the fax machine for his private business. The firm would like to discourage such conduct.

It can reduce shirking by altering its wage policy. Workers are more productive and shirk less if the firm pays them less than their marginal product in the early stages of the employment relationship and more than their marginal product later in the employment relationship. This type of wage policy penalizes malfeasance and shirking. The firm fires a worker who steals from the company or does not put forth the expected effort if the violation is gross enough. Since the wage is initially less than the value of the marginal product, the worker suffers a loss if the firm discharges her for shirking because her wage is less than the wage she could earn in the next best job. The worker makes an investment in the firm in the early years of the employment relationship when the wage is less than the value of the marginal product and therefore is less likely to shirk.

We can present the argument in more detail with the aid of a graph. In Figure 17-16 the wage is on the vertical axis and time with the firm is on the horizontal axis. The value of the marginal product of the worker is line bb. If there is no shirking problem, the worker's wage is equal to the value of the marginal product in each period. The line rr is the worker's reservation wage and measures the opportunity cost of working at the firm. It is shown rising over time, perhaps because the worker desires to spend more time in nonwork activities as she grows older. When the wage of the worker is less than the reservation wage, she retires voluntarily. Assuming the worker's wage equals the value of the marginal product, the worker will retire voluntarily at date T_m where rr intersects VMP. Before T_m, the wage of the worker exceeds her reservation wage, and so she continues to work. After T_m, the reservation wage is greater than the worker's wage ($=$VMP), and so she voluntarily retires. If the firm pays the value of the marginal product, it does not have to introduce a mandatory retirement policy. Each worker will retire voluntarily at T_m.

Now suppose shirking is a problem and the firm adopts the wage policy ww in Figure 17-16. To discourage shirking by workers, it pays less than the marginal product up to date T' and then pays more than the value of the marginal product. The firm selects ww so that the present value of the wage payments along ww equals the present value of the wage payments along bb when the wage equals the value of the marginal product. Therefore, a risk-neutral employee is indifferent between the two wage streams. With the pay scale ww the worker's wage is more

[11] Edward P. Lazear, "Why Is There Mandatory Retirement?" *Journal of Political Economy*, vol. 87, 1979, pp. 1261–1284.

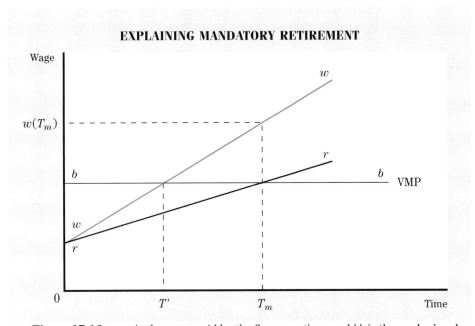

Figure 17-16 ww is the wage paid by the firm over time, and bb is the worker's value of the marginal product, VMP. The wage is less than the value of the marginal product until T', after which the worker is paid more than the VMP. If she were paid the value of the marginal product, she would retire at time T_m when the opportunity cost rr equals her wage. With the wage function ww the wage of the worker is $w(T_m)$ at T_m and exceeds the opportunity cost. She will not retire voluntarily, and the firm forces her to retire through a mandatory retirement policy.

than VMP at time T_m. This explains why the employee does not retire voluntarily at T_m.

Lazear assumes that wage policy ww induces more worker effort than the constant wage policy along bb does. If so, the wage policy ww solves or at least reduces the incidence of shirking, but it creates another problem. Because the wage exceeds the opportunity cost of the worker at T_m, she will not retire voluntarily. Without a mandatory retirement program, she is eager to continue working. The firm must prevent this. Otherwise, the present value of the wage payments ww will exceed the present value of the marginal product of the worker over the whole work experience. Therefore, the firm adopts a mandatory retirement program and requires the worker to retire at age T_m to prevent this from happening.

In this model mandatory retirement is a derivative policy that springs from a wage policy designed to reduce shirking by employees. The wage policy ww is another illustration of backloading pay to foster the desired behavior by employees.

Soon federal law will make it illegal for firms and nonprofit institutions to adopt mandatory retirement. A firm that has a wage policy such as ww will not be able to impose mandatory retirement. It will be interesting to see what changes in compensation policies emerge because of this change in federal law.

This chapter has investigated how the wage is determined in many different labor market situations. Our examination of the labor market has touched on explanations for differences in the earnings of workers with different educational attainment, on-the-job training of workers by firms and how the wage policy of a firm depends on the type of training, and using wage policy to select certain types of workers and to create incentives that discourage employee shirking.

SUMMARY

- A competitive firm determines the quantity of labor to employ where the value of the marginal product equals the worker's wage.
- In the long-run the market demand function for labor slopes downward to the right. Firms demand more units of labor at a lower wage.
- The supply function of labor of an individual is derived from utility maximization. An individual's supply of work function may have either a positive or a negative slope.
- The major cost of attending college is the forgone income. The decision to enter college depends on the difference between the earnings of a college graduate and a high school graduate and on the interest rate.
- The worker pays for general training, while the worker and the firm share the cost of firm-specific training.
- A firm attracts a preferred group of workers by paying a wage that is less than the reservation wage of the less preferred group and by paying each worker a bonus at the end of the period.
- By paying a worker less than his or her value of marginal product initially, a firm can structure its wage policy to reduce shirking by workers.

KEY TERMS

Marginal product	**Paying less than the value of the**
Value of the marginal	**marginal product**
product	**Marginal revenue product**
Firm scale effect	**Substitution effect**
Work-leisure choice	**Industry scale effect**
Schooling and earnings	**Substitution and income effects**
Firm-specific training	**General training**
Sorting workers	**Measurement of output and input**
Mandatory retirement	**Shirking**

REVIEW QUESTIONS

1. Why do economists describe the demand for labor as a derived demand?
2. How does the value of the marginal product differ from the marginal revenue product?
3. What are the substitution and the scale effects for a single competitive firm?

4. If the price of capital increases, a firm will increase the demand for labor. Explain why you agree or disagree with this statement.
5. If the price of capital increases, each firm will demand fewer units of capital, and so the firms in the industry will demand more units of labor. Explain why you agree or disagree with this statement.
6. Why is a firm's long-run demand function for labor more elastic than its short-run demand function for labor?
7. What is the industry scale effect?
8. Predict the effect of a decline in military spending on the wage of aeronautical engineers? Show the effect on a graph.
9. If an increase in income increases hours of leisure, a worker will supply less work when the wage increases. Explain why you agree or disagree with this statement.

EXERCISES

1. If a price-taking firm receives a higher price for a product, this will increase the firm's demand for labor and increase the wage rate of its workers. Explain why you agree or disagree with this statement.
2. Explain why an individual is either not affected or stops working completely after the introduction of a general assistance program.
3. If a general assistance program establishes a minimum income of $7,500, it will affect the work-leisure choice of only those individuals with incomes less than $7,500. Explain why you agree or disagree with this statement.
4. The current distribution of income in a country is shown in column 2 below:

PER CAPITA INCOME ($) (1)	ACTUAL DISTRIBUTION OF INCOME (%) (2)	PREDICTED DISTRIBUTION BY EXPERT 1 (%) (3)	PREDICTED DISTRIBUTION BY EXPERT 2 (%) (4)
0–4,999	15	0	0
5,000–9,999	30	50	50
10,000–14,999	25	20	26
15,000–19,999	15	15	11
20,000–29,999	10	10	8
30,000–39,999	3	3	3
40,000+	2	2	2

Suppose a general assistance program is being considered with a maximum payment of $5,000. The predictions of two experts concerning the effect of the program on the size distribution of income are in columns 3 and 4. Select one of the two predicted distributions and explain why it better describes the program's effect. Explain why you did not select the alternative prediction.

5. With the aid of graphs show how days of leisure are affected if the current income tax of 28 percent of income increases to 40 percent on income above $120,000.

6. How would you explain why most students enter college immediately after graduating from high school?

7. The average age of MBA students has increased over time. These students begin their studies after four to five years of work experience, whereas in the past MBA students entered school with fewer years of experience. Why do you think this change has occurred? Does your answer explain why the same change has not occurred to the same degree in law and medicine?

8. A firm pays a low daily wage but a large bonus at the end of the year. Why does a company adopt this policy?

9. Assume a worker is risk-averse and prefers certain earnings of E. The company wants to introduce a pay-for-performance plan that ties the compensation of the employee to the profits of the company in hopes of reducing costs. Given the market that the firm operates in, a worker will either receive $0.8E$ with probability .5 or $1.2E$ with probability .5 under the new compensation plan. With the aid of graphs show what E the firm must pay the worker to accept the pay-for-performance plan if the employee maximizes expected utility. Use the expected utility hypothesis (see Chapter 3) to explain your answer.

10. If there are two types of workers and a firm wants to attract type 1, what conditions must be placed on the shape of the indifference functions of type 2 workers for the wage-bonus policy of the firm to successfully sort the workers into firms?

11. One firm pays a worker based on output, and another pays a worker on the basis of input. Which firm is more likely to have a mandatory retirement policy? Explain why.

18

ECONOMIC EFFICIENCY AND GENERAL EQUILIBRIUM

Our investigation of markets has largely focused on how individual markets work. The scope of this investigation has ranged from how a competitive price is determined by the interplay of demand and supply, to how a monopolist sets the price of a product, to how a small number of sellers affects price, to how a firm sets discriminatory prices. In each discussion, the impact of changes in one market on other markets was on the whole ignored. The analysis was clearly a partial equilibrium analysis. We assumed implicitly that the theoretical predictions of the partial equilibrium analysis are reasonably accurate even if a change in one market causes several rounds of repercussions in other markets in the economy. In earlier chapters we resisted any inclination to examine how a change in one market affects other markets. When we conclude that a monopolist sets marginal revenue equal to marginal cost and thereby raises the price of a good and produces less than a competitive industry would, we did not stop to ask what happens to the resources that leave the monopolized market and go to other markets because a monopolist produces less than does a competitive industry.

This chapter abandons the partial equilibrium approach for another which looks at several markets simultaneously. The reason for this change in emphasis is that we are interested in exploring the elusive but important topic of the economic efficiency of a whole economy, not of just a single market. This requires an investigation of more than one market at a time, indeed all markets in an economy, and is such an imposing task that a more measured investigation seems appropriate. The investigation will be less venturesome by considering the simultaneous equilibrium in a simple economy with just two goods and two factors of production. Still, our investigation of multimarkets is more general than a partial equilibrium approach, and economists describe this type of analysis as general equilibrium analysis to contrast it with the partial equilibrium analysis discussed in earlier chapters.

The goals of this chapter are to define what economists mean by economic efficiency and to explain how competitively organized markets for goods and for factors of production can achieve economic efficiency. Chapter 19 extends the analysis to cover more complicated but realistic situations when a monopoly exists in one product market, where the behavior of one or several parties affects other parties, or where there are demands for public goods.

18-1 GENERAL EQUILIBRIUM ANALYSIS

A general equilibrium analysis examines the repercussions of a change that occurs in one market on prices and outputs in other markets. Because general equilibrium analysis is more difficult, we make the transition from partial equilibrium to general equilibrium analysis somewhat easier by employing the familiar demand and supply model to study how several markets simultaneously adjust to equilibrium. Chapter 2 noted that the price of chicken declined by 75 percent from 1950 to 1990 and suggested this decline was due to the adoption of new methods of raising chickens. Chapter 2 also showed how technological change shifted the supply function for chickens to the right and lowered the equilibrium price. A general equilibrium analysis expands this approach and investigates the effect of this technological change not only on the market for chickens but on other markets as well. Figure

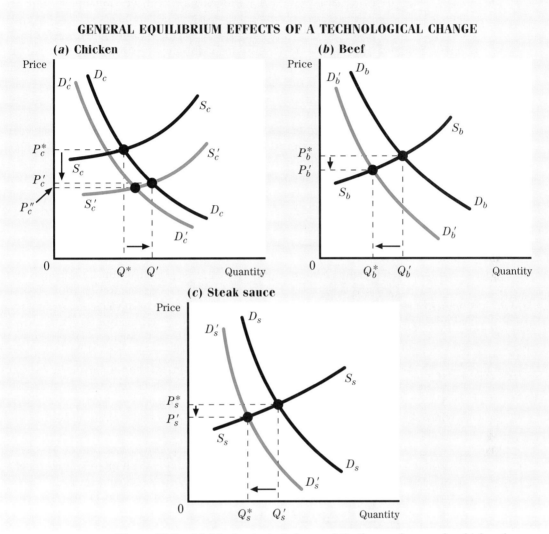

GENERAL EQUILIBRIUM EFFECTS OF A TECHNOLOGICAL CHANGE

Figure 18-1   (*a*) A technological change shifts the supply curve for chicken downward and causes the price of chicken to fall. (*b*) The fall in the price of chicken causes the demand function for beef to shift to the left and the price of beef declines to P_b' since beef and chicken are gross substitutes. (*c*) The demand for steak sauce shifts to the left and the price of steak sauce falls to P_s' because beef and steak sauce are gross complements. Secondary repercussions cause the demand for chicken to shift from $D_c D_c$ to $D_c' D_c'$.

18-1*a* shows that the supply function for chicken shifts to the right and the equilibrium price falls from P_c^* to P_c'. The fall in the price of chicken creates repercussions in other markets. Figure 18-1*b* shows that because chicken and beef are gross substitutes the demand function for beef shifts to the left from $D_b D_b$ to $D_b' D_b'$ when the price of chicken falls to P_c' since $D_b D_b$ was derived assuming the price of chicken was P_c^*, The equilibrium price of beef falls from P_b^* to P_b' because of the shift in the demand function for beef. Figure 18-1c shows how the technological change in the chicken industry affects the demand and supply functions for steak sauce. The demand function for steak sauce shifts to the left from $D_s D_s$ to $D_s' D_s'$ because chicken and steak sauce are also gross substitutes. Because the demand function for steak sauce shifts to the left, the price of steak sauce falls to P_s'. This more general analysis has traced some of the effects of the technological change in the chicken industry. Not only is the chicken industry affected by the change, but repercussions are felt in the beef and the steak sauce industries as well.

You might think the analysis is complete by now. However, there are secondary repercussions. The fall in the price of beef causes the demand function for chicken to shift to the left since the demand function for chicken assumes the price of beef is P_b^*. So the demand function for chicken in turn shifts to $D_c' D_c'$, and the price falls to P_c''. The fall in the price of chicken in turn shifts the position of the demand function for beef. There may be several rounds of adjustments before the demand and supply functions in these markets stabilize and all three reach a new equilibrium.

As you can imagine, general equilibrium analysis can become complicated with so many markets to keep track of. To simplify the analysis and yet retain a semblance of reality, we will look at a simpler economy with two goods and two factors of production throughout this chapter.

18-2   COMMAND AND CONTROL POLICIES OF THE WIZARD

We introduce the topic of economic efficiency in a general equilibrium setting with a parable about the Wizard of Zeoz.

Your spacecraft touches down on a newly discovered planet called Zeoz, and strange-looking inhabitants surround the ship. You become a prisoner and receive notice that you will be interviewed by the Wizard, the stern ruler of Zeoz. On the way to the Wizard's castle you learn that the Wizard rules with an iron but paternalistic hand; he has a reputation for being capricious, but he can be swayed by a logical argument.

You enter a magnificent room in the castle for your encounter with the Wizard. The Wizard strides in and says he will ask you one question. If you answer the question satisfactorily, you will become his life-long adviser. If you answer it incorrectly, your life will end.

The Wizard begins by noting that there are two types of beings on Zeoz, an A type and a B type. Each year a large bureaucracy distributes stocks of nutrients X and Y to each inhabitant. Somehow, the A types know how to manipulate the bureaucracy and manage to get more of the nutrients than the B types. Upset by this, the B types petition the Wizard to redistribute the nutrient stocks so that they receive more. Each year the Wizard spends valuable time redistributing the stocks, only to receive an earful of complaints from the A types.

Since the Wizard has to spend considerable time and effort redistributing the nutrients, he expects each B inhabitant to consume all the nutrients received. Executive decree 1074 imposes the death sentence on any inhabitant caught selling or buying nutrients.

In public the Wizard proclaims that his redistribution policy is the fairest, but in private he expresses some reservations. He does not know whether Zeoz is better off with or without the redistribution and hopes you will supply a scientific justification for the policy. This leads to the fateful question. The Wizards asks, "Is Zeoz better off after my redistribution of the nutrient stocks?" With your life hanging in the balance, you stall for time and ask for an hour to prepare an answer. Fortunately, you have brought along your copy of *Price Theory and Applications* and you quickly read the relevant sections of this chapter. After an hour you rejoin the Wizard who is awaiting your response.

You come directly to the point: "After consulting a state-of-the-art textbook from planet Earth, I cannot say whether you should or should not redistribute the nutrients." The Wizard jumps up from his chair and shouts, "What kind of adviser will you be if all you can say is that you cannot say?" The Wizard becomes extremely angry and is about to call the guards to lead you away. Anticipating this reaction, you quickly add, "But I do know how you can redistribute the nutrient stocks and increase the welfare of all inhabitants of Zeoz." Upon hearing this, the Wizard grows interested and asks you to expound your views. At this point you weave the following argument.

18-3   ECONOMIC EFFICIENCY

The Wizard wants to know whether his kingdom is better off with his redistribution policy. A similar question has baffled scholars and policy analysts for centuries because the Wizard's redistribution policy increases the utility of each B inhabitant but decreases the utility of each A inhabitant. As an economic adviser, you cannot say whether the redistribution makes Zeoz better or worse off because the modern theory of consumer behavior makes no allowance for interpersonal comparisons of utility. You have no objective way of determining if the kingdom is better off because you have no scientific basis for comparing the utilities of the different inhabitants. As an economic advisor, you do not want to take sides in the tradeoff between the A's and the B's and thus simply plan to present the conclusions that can be drawn without showing partiality toward either side.

To demonstrate your point in the simplest way, you argue as follows. Suppose a small economy consists of just one A and one B inhabitant. Each starts with a market basket of the two nutrients or, more generally, goods. Let's call them good X and good Y. Between them, the two inhabitants have a total of X' units of good X and Y' units of good Y. An *endowment* is an assigned market basket of goods that each inhabitant starts with. The Wizard assigns an initial endowment of $_0X_A$ units of X and $_0Y_A$ units of Y to consumer A and an initial endowment of $_0X_B$ units of X and $_0Y_B$ units of Y to consumer B. The sum of the endowments of each good adds up to the total units of the good available.

$$_0X_A + {}_0X_B = X' \qquad {}_0Y_A + {}_0Y_B = Y' \qquad \text{(Endowment Constraint)} \quad \textbf{(18-1)}$$

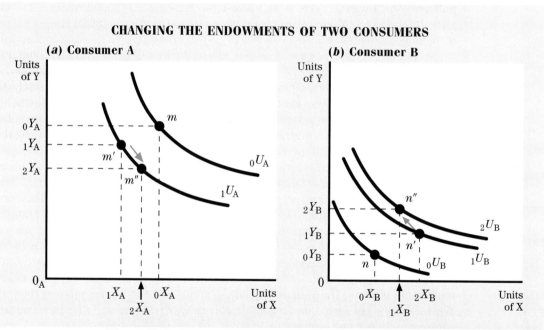

Figure 18-2   The initial endowment is at point m in (a) for inhabitant A and at point n in (b) for inhabitant B. After a redistribution of each consumer's endowment, consumer A moves from m to m', making A worse off, and consumer B moves from n to n', making B better off. Because interpersonal comparisons of utility cannot be made scientifically, you are unable to say whether the Wizard's redistribution increases welfare of the inhabitants of Zeoz. On the other hand, the move from m' to m'' leaves A indifferent, and the reciprocal move from n' to n'' increases B's utility. Although the total endowment is still X' and Y', B would be better off given the utility of A if the trade were allowed.

Figure 18-2a shows the indifference curves of consumer A, and the endowment of A is at point m. The indifference curves of consumer B are shown in Figure 18-2b where the endowment of B is at point n. Consumer A is more adept at manipulating the bureaucracy and has more of both goods than consumer B. Since the Wizard's redistribution policy moves consumer A from point m to point m', consumer A is now on $_1U_A$, a lower indifference curve, and is worse off. However, consumer B moves to point n' on $_1U_B$, a higher indifference curve, because of the redistribution policy and is better off. As an economic analyst, you have no objective way of comparing A's discomfort from a loss of both goods with B's satisfaction from receiving more of both goods. Therefore, you cannot determine whether the welfare of all the inhabitants (A and B) of Zeoz is higher or lower under the redistribution policy.

The Wizard mistakenly thinks all redistribution policies either make B better off and A worse off, or vice versa, and inevitably require interpersonal comparisons of utility. The first point that you hope to impress upon the Wizard is that some policies can improve the welfare of at least one inhabitant without harming the other inhabitants. Only a capricious ruler would *not* implement such policies.

There is a second but more delicate point that you think the Wizard should consider. It is clear to you that the Wizard's demonstrated penchant for command and control policies is an expensive luxury. Commands determine what goods the economy of Zeoz produces and how they are distributed to each consumer. Although the Wizard has more information about the economy than any other being on Zeoz, he does not have complete information. It is likely that there exists some redistribution that could increase the utility of one consumer without reducing the utility of the other. You hope to persuade the Wizard to rely more on competitive markets and less on command and control policies to achieve his goals.

Let's consider the first point. Is there a redistribution policy, other than the one selected by the Wizard, that allocates X' units and Y' units so that at least one consumer's utility increases while the other's remains unchanged? The Wizard's command and control policy requires A to consume the market basket at point m' in Figure 18-2*a*, and B to consume the market basket at point n' in Figure 18-2*b*. How does the Wizard know that the mandated allocation is optimal? If the Wizard's allocation is in the best interest of the inhabitants, why must he issue a decree that requires A and B to consume the redistributed market baskets under a threat of death? By mandating consumption, the Wizard is coercing consumption and implicitly admitting that another allocation of goods could make one consumer better off without making the other one worse off.

By mandating consumption and preventing trade between A and B, the Wizard is preventing other voluntary redistributions that are superior to his redistribution. For example, suppose that consumer A is indifferent if she receives one more unit of X and one less unit of Y. Consumer B gives up one unit of X but receives one more unit of Y as compensation. Consumer A moves from point m' to point m'' on the same indifference curve, but consumer B moves from point n' to point n'' on a higher indifference curve and his utility increases. The inhabitants of Zeoz are clearly better off if they could make this trade. This is what you had in mind when you told the Wizard that you knew how to increase the welfare of his subjects.

Pareto Efficiency in Exchange

The proposed deviation from the Wizard's mandated market baskets shows that not all redistributions inevitably make one consumer better off at the expense of another. There are some redistributions of X and Y that can increase B's utility while holding A's utility constant. How can we find an allocation of goods X and Y to the two consumers that maximizes B's utility given A's utility?

> An allocation of goods among consumers is **Pareto-efficient**[1] if any reassignment of the goods that holds the utility of one consumer constant reduces the utility of the other consumer.

---

[1] Vilfredo Pareto derived the Pareto efficiency conditions at the beginning of the twentieth century.

AN INITIAL ALLOCATION BETWEEN A AND B

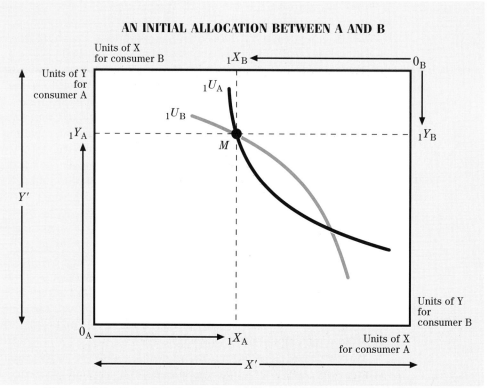

Figure 18-3 The initial distribution of X' units of X and Y' units of Y is at point M. Consumer A has $_1X_A$ units of X and $_1Y_A$ units of Y. With these market baskets the utility of A is $_1U_A$ and the utility of B is $_1U_B$.

How can the Wizard determine whether an allocation satisfies the criterion of Pareto efficiency? Figure 18-3 is an Edgeworth box diagram.[2] The dimensions of the box are X' by Y', the total endowment of the two goods. The horizontal axis measures X' units, and the vertical axis measures Y' units. The point 0_A is the origin for consumer A's indifference curves. Starting from 0_A, a movement from the southwest to the northeast increases A's utility since A has more of both goods. Point 0_B in the northeast corner is the origin for B's indifference curves. Starting from 0_B, a movement from the northeast to the southwest represents an increase in B's utility.

Any point in the box represents an allocation of the total endowment between the two consumers. For example, point M represents an allocation of X' and Y' units between A and B. Consumer A has an initial market basket consisting of $_1X_A$ units of X and $_1Y_A$ units of Y, and consumer B's market basket includes $_1X_B$ units of X and $_1Y_B$ units of Y. The sum of the endowments of X is X', and the sum of the

[2] Named for Francis Edgeworth who appears to have been the first to introduce it.

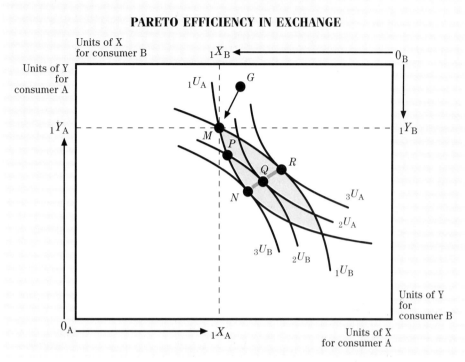

PARETO EFFICIENCY IN EXCHANGE

Figure 18-4   The initial distribution of resources is at point *M*. Any point in the shaded area increases the utility of A and B. Points along *NR* are Pareto-efficient allocations. Starting at any point on *NR*, a redistribution of resources will lower the utility of at least one inhabitant, holding the utility of the other constant.

endowments of Y is Y'. Given $_1X_A$ and $_1Y_A$, A is on indifference curve $_1U_A$ and, given $_1X_B$ and $_1Y_B$, B is on indifference curve $_1U_B$.

Is point *M* Pareto-efficient? Compare point *M* with the allocation at point *P* in Figure 18-4. Consumer A has more of X and less of Y at point *P* but is still on $_1U_A$, and so A's utility is the same. Consumer B has less X but more Y but is now on $_2U_B$, a higher indifference curve, and is therefore better off. The redistribution of the goods between points *M* and *P* increases B's utility, while A's utility is unchanged. Therefore, the allocation at point *M* is not Pareto-efficient. Now let's compare *P* with *N*, where A has still less Y but more X. Again, consumer A's utility is constant since A remains on $_1U_A$, but B's utility increases by moving to indifference curve $_3U_B$ and so the allocation at point *P* is not Pareto-efficient. On the other hand, any reallocation of the total stocks of goods that moves A and B away from point *N* along the indifference curve $_1U_A$ in either direction reduces B's utility. Therefore, point *N* is Pareto-efficient in exchange.

What distinguishes point *N* from points *M* and *P* is that the indifference curves of A and B are tangent to each other at point *N* and intersect at points like *M* and

P. Therefore, a Pareto-efficient allocation requires that the marginal rates of substitution between Y and X be equal for the two consumers.

$$^AMRS_{YX} = \ ^BMRS_{YX} \quad \text{(Condition for Pareto Efficiency in Exchange)} \quad \textbf{(18-2)}$$

> Pareto efficiency in exchange requires that the marginal rates of substitution between the two goods be equal for all consumers.

Consumers A and B prefer any point in the shaded area of Figure 18-4 to point *M* because a redistribution of the total endowment that places both consumers at some point in the shaded area increases the utility of both. Among all the points in the shaded area, only those where the indifference curves are tangent to one another are Pareto-efficient in exchange. For example, point *Q* is Pareto-efficient because the indifference curves $_2U_A$ and $_2U_B$ are tangent to each other, and so point *Q* represents another Pareto-efficient allocation. The indifference curves are also tangent at point *R*, and so point *R* is still another Pareto-efficient allocation. Indeed, all points on the curve running from *N* to *R* represent Pareto-efficient allocations where the slopes of the indifference curves of A and B are equal.

The Wizard's redistribution policy moves A and B from point *G* to point *M* in Figure 18-4. Consumer A has less of both goods at point *M* and is worse off, while consumer B has more of both goods at point *M* than at point *G*. You cannot prove to the Wizard that the inhabitants of the kingdom are better off after he redistributes the goods. However, you can conclude that the Wizard's policy of mandating consumption at point *M* is not Pareto-efficient in exchange. Only those points along the curve from point *N* to point *R* are Pareto-efficient allocations, starting from point *M*. But the inhabitants of Zeoz cannot reach any of these points because of the Wizard's policy of prohibiting trade.

The Contract Curve

While the Wizard's redistribution policy at point *M* serves to demonstrate that other allocations of X and Y improve the welfare of the inhabitants of Zeoz, your argument has broader applicability. Whatever the initial distribution of the total endowments of *X'* and *Y'* between the two consumers, both can benefit by reaching a Pareto-efficient allocation. As long as the indifference curves are not tangent at the initial allocation, there is another allocation that can make one consumer better off given the utility of the other consumer.

For example, suppose the initial allocation is at point *S* in Figure 18-5. The curve running from *T* to *W* connects all points of tangency of the indifference curves. Therefore, all points along the curve from point *T* to point *W* are preferable to point *S* and are also Pareto-efficient points because the indifference curves of A and B are tangent all along this curve. The curve running from 0_A to 0_B is the contract curve and connects all points of tangency of the indifference curves of A and B. All points on the contract curve are Pareto-efficient in exchange.

> The contract curve connects all points of tangency for the indifference curves of the two consumers.

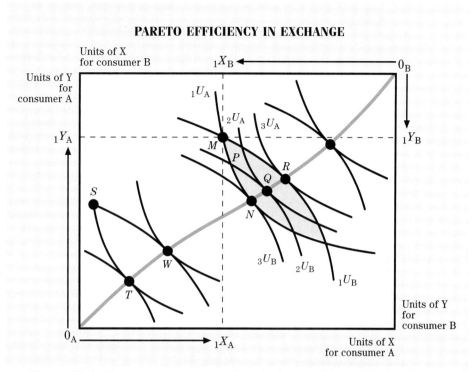

PARETO EFFICIENCY IN EXCHANGE

Figure 18-5   The curve running from 0_A to 0_B is formed by connecting all points of tangency between indifference curves and is called the contract curve. Any movement along the contract curve increases the utility of one consumer at the expense of the utility of the other consumer.

You cannot say that a redistribution from one point to another on the contract curve is preferable since movements along this curve increase the utility of one consumer at the expense of the other.

A Competitive Market and Pareto Efficiency in Exchange

The Wizard recognizes the logic of your argument but raises a serious objection. He admits he knows little about the shapes of the indifference curves of either type of consumer. How can he ever know whether his redistribution makes the inhabitants' indifference curves tangent? He says the theory is elegant but irrelevant because he cannot see how to apply it, and his impatience shows again.

You expected the Wizard to ask this question and have prepared an answer. You agree that the Wizard cannot possibly know what the inhabitants' indifference curves look like. Fortunately, you tell the Wizard, he does not have to know the shapes of the indifference curves to reach the contract curve if only he is willing to lift the ban on trading and allow markets to function. In other words, he must relinquish his command and control policies. You bluntly tell the Wizard that a competitive market will produce Pareto efficiency in exchange, while his command

and control policies will not. The Wizard finds your claim intriguing but remains dubious. He has more information than anyone else about the economy, and even he does not know whether the economy is Pareto-efficient in exchange. How can trading by imperfectly informed but self-interested consumers magically produce a Pareto-efficient allocation?

You present this argument: When a market exists, inhabitants can trade so many units of Y for a unit of X. The relative price of Y and X indicates how many units of Y a consumer can exchange for a unit of X. For example, A and B can trade two units of Y for one unit of X if the price of X is $10 and the price of Y is $5, so that $-P_X/P_Y = -2$. Because there are many A consumers and many B consumers in Zeoz, not just two, each A or B is a price taker and can trade as much of each good as desired if the exchange rate is two units of Y for one unit of X.

Starting with the allocation at point M in Figure 18-6, A and B determine independently how many units of each good they will trade at each $-P_X/P_Y$. Each consumer maximizes utility subject to a budget constraint by trading Y for X or X for Y until the slope of the indifference curve equals the slope of the budget constraint.

Consumer A maximizes utility when

$$^A\mathrm{MRS}_{YX} = -\frac{P_X}{P_Y} \qquad \text{(Equilibrium for Consumer A)} \qquad \text{(18-3)}$$

where $^A\mathrm{MRS}_{YX}$ is the marginal rate of substitution between Y and X for consumer A. The slope of the budget constraint is $-P_X/P_Y$, and so each consumer receives $\Delta Y = (-P_X/P_Y)\Delta X$ units of Y in exchange for ΔX units of X. For example, if $-P_X/P_Y = -2$, then $\Delta Y = -2\,\Delta X$, and so consumer A can exchange two units of Y for one unit of X. Similarly, consumer B maximizes utility when

$$^B\mathrm{MRS}_{YX} = -\frac{P_X}{P_Y} \qquad \text{(Equilibrium for Consumer B)} \qquad \text{(18-4)}$$

Therefore, in a competitive equilibrium we have

$$^A\mathrm{MRS}_{YX} = -\frac{P_X}{P_Y} = {}^B\mathrm{MRS}_{YX} \qquad \begin{array}{l}\text{(Condition for Pareto Efficiency}\\ \text{in Exchange)}\end{array} \qquad \text{(18-5)}$$

Equation 18-5 says that the marginal rates of substitution are equal for the two consumers when each trades as many units as desired at the equilibrium price ratio.

The Wizard claims that he understands what the symbols mean, but you suspect that he does not grasp the significance of your proof. So, you decide to use a geometrical proof. In Figure 18-6 the initial allocation is at point M. The slope of budget line bb equals $-P_X/P_Y = -\$10/\$5 = -2$. So, A and B can trade two units of Y for one unit of X. Consumer A is willing to trade two units of Y for one unit of X along budget line bb until it is tangent to the indifference curve $_1U_A$ at point E. To reach point E, A is demanding $_2X_A - {}_1X_A$ more units of X and is supplying $_1Y_A - {}_2Y_A$ units of Y to the market when $-P_X/P_Y = -2$.

Consumer B is willing to supply $_1X_B - {}_2X_B$ more units of X for $_2Y_B - {}_1Y_B$ more units of Y when the exchange rate is -2. Because point E is on the contract curve,

COMPETITIVE EQUILIBRIUM AND PARETO EFFICIENCY IN EXCHANGE

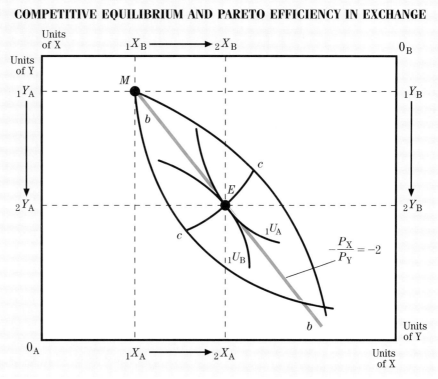

Figure 18-6 Budget line bb shows that each consumer can trade two units of Y for a unit of X. Consumer A is willing to supply $_1Y_A - _2Y_A$ units to the market and demands $_2X_A - _1X_A$ units of X. Consumer Y demands $_2Y_B - _1Y_B$ units and is willing to supply $_1X_B - _2X_B$ units of X when two units of Y can be traded for a unit of X. The quantity supplied of Y equals the quantity demanded of Y, and the same is true of good X. Trade between competitive demanders and suppliers places consumers A and B on the contract curve at point E.

cc, the slope of consumer B's indifference curve is tangent not only to budget line bb but to A's indifference curve as well. The markets for X and for Y are in equilibrium because the quantity demanded of X by A equals the increased quantity supplied of X by B when the price of X is twice that of Y. Both A and B are better off by trading because there are gains from trade.

This is a remarkable result even for a relatively simple two-person exchange economy. Each participant knows only his or her own utility function. Yet, trading by price-taking participants yields a result where the quantity demanded equals the quantity supplied and both participants reach the contract curve by exchanging goods. Adam Smith's invisible hand guides demanders and suppliers to a point on the contract curve although each participant in the market has only a tiny piece of private information about the market—what quantity the individual will demand or supply at each price ratio. Neither A nor B knows anything about the utility of the other market participants or the quantities of X and Y held by them. Each takes the price ratio as given and trades with the sole objective of maximizing his or her own utility. Yet, in this atmosphere of complete self-interest, a competitive market guides all inhabitants to the contract curve so that the marginal rates of substitution of all consumers in the economy are equal and the economy achieves Pareto efficiency in exchange.

APPLICATION 18-1

Minimizing Information Requirements in Experimental Competitive Markets

Researchers have constructed markets in a laboratory setting to determine just how much information market participants must have before the market reaches a competitive equilibrium price. These experiments shed light on a proposition advanced by Friedrich Hayek that competitive markets economize on the acquisition of information by market participants.

In these experiments the researcher designates an individual as a demander or a supplier and assigns an individual demand function to each demander and a firm supply function to each supplier. For example, the researcher instructs a demander that the highest (reservation) price the demander will pay for the first unit of a hypothetical good is $15, for the second unit is $10, and so on. Each demander receives a monetary reward equal to the difference between the reservation price of the unit and the price the demander pays for the good. A demander maximizes her winnings from participating in the experiment by buying each unit at as low a price as possible.

If a participant is a supplier, the researcher gives each firm a supply function. For example, the supplier offers one unit at $3, a second unit at $6, and so on. The monetary reward for a supplier is equal to the difference between the actual price received for the unit and the lower (reservation) price. Each supplier maximizes his winnings from participating in the experiment by selling each unit at as high a price as possible.

In a typical experiment, there are several demanders and several suppliers, with demanders trying to purchase the good at the lowest price possible and suppliers trying to sell it at the highest price possible. Market demand and supply functions are simply the horizontal sum of the individual demand and supply functions. Only the researcher knows what the aggregate demand and supply functions look like and the equilibrium competitive price. The individual demand and supply functions of the market participants are private information that only each participant knows.

The experiments create a double-auction trading process similar to that seen on the New York Stock Exchange. Each demander and supplier sits at a computer terminal. Each demander enters a bid price, the price that the consumer is willing to pay for a unit, and the bid price flashes on all the terminals. All participants can see if it is higher than an outstanding bid price. A supplier may enter an ask price, the price at which the individual is willing to supply a unit. If the ask price is less than an outstanding ask price, it replaces the existing ask price and appears on the screen. What each market participant knows is the highest bid and the lowest ask. A bid or an ask is binding until another bid or ask displaces it or a sale occurs. When that happens, the auction for that unit ends and the computer waits for a new pair of bid and ask prices.

Vernon Smith has summarized the results of about 200 experiments performed by different researchers and reports that they invariably indicate that the double-auction trading mechanism converges quickly to the competitive equilibrium price where quantity demanded equals quantity supplied, whether experienced or inexperienced subjects participate in the experiment.[3] This uniformity of results is especially true when individual demand and firm supply functions are stable. The experimental results indicate that convergence to the competitive price does occur, although each participant has only a tiny bit of information about the market and no information about other demanders and suppliers. The demanders or suppliers do not have to know what the market demand and supply functions look like for the market to reach the competitive equilibrium price. Not only does price settle to the equilibrium price, but it appears in a way that economizes on the amount of market information that each participant must possess.

Impediments to Pareto Efficiency

To reach the contract curve, traders must be free to trade in competitive markets. If hurdles are placed in the way, consumers will not reach the contract curve. There are instances where legal restrictions prevent a competitive market from developing, and so voluntary trade is prevented. For example, during the recent drought in California many communities adopted water rationing. There was no provision for a household to sell part of its water allotment for money in a market. Another example concerns an owner of a historical building who cannot sell it to a developer who plans to tear it down and replace it. In the Graduate School of Business at the University of Chicago each MBA student is endowed with points that he or she uses to bid for courses. Students cannot sell their points to other students. In some of these cases the prohibition of voluntary transactions can be justified because the transaction might adversely affect other parties. In other cases the prohibition is an indirect way of redistributing income from one group to another group. In still others, trade is prohibited because the principle of consumer sovereignty is rejected.

APPLICATION 18-2

Impediments to Trading Water Rights in California

Water is often treated differently from other goods.[4] In many states legal codes establish a hierarchical set of priorities for uses of water. Certain "higher" uses

---

[3] Based on Vernon L. Smith, "Markets as Economizers of Information: Experimental Examination of the 'Hayek Hypothesis'," *Economic Inquiry*, vol. XX, April 1982, pp. 165–179.
[4] Based on Jack Hirschleifer, James C. De Haven, and Jerome W. Milliman, *Water Supply*, University of Chicago Press, 1960, chap. 3.

receive a priority status over "lower" uses. This makes it costly to transfer water designed for higher uses to lower uses. These restrictions make the sale of water rights more costly and prevent the sale of water to the *higher-valued* user. By limiting transfers of water from one use to another, differential prices for water exist. For example, water is cheap in California when used for farming but is very expensive when used by urban dwellers. Why should water be priced differently for different uses? If there were a competitive market for water in California, the price of water would be the same for all uses unless costs are different. Yet the purchase price paid can be over 100 times higher for urban use than for farm use.

Let's illustrate the water situation with an Edgeworth box diagram. Consider two individuals, one of whom is a farmer endowed with W_f acre-feet of water. The farmer's endowment is W_f and I_f, where $S_f = I_f$ is spending on a composite good and is equal to the farmer's income. The other individual is an urban dweller who has little water, W_u, but spends more on a composite good $S_u = I_u$. The endowment of the urban resident is W_u and S_u. Figure 18-7 shows the Edgeworth box diagram for the two consumers. The dimensions of the box are $W_f + W_u$ by $S_f + S_u$.

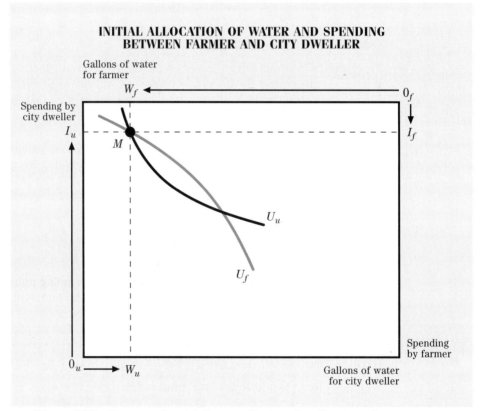

INITIAL ALLOCATION OF WATER AND SPENDING BETWEEN FARMER AND CITY DWELLER

Figure 18-7   Because of restrictions on the transfer of water, urban consumers are unable to trade water for income. Therefore, Pareto efficiency in exchange is not reached.

Both consumers are at point M in Figure 18-7. Given the existing endowments, their utility functions intersect at point M. Therefore, there is room for trade. The city dweller is willing to trade income for water, and the rural inhabitant is willing to trade water for income. Both will be better off. Yet, this trade will not occur. Why? Because, the property rights to the land limit the transfer of water. The trading of water depends on the water laws of each state, and in California state laws have made it very difficult to sell water for other uses. There may be justification at times for this prohibition, but often the restrictions reduce economic efficiency. Except where the sale of water causes parties apart from those involved in the transaction to suffer losses, economic efficiency would improve if the property rights to water were clear and owners of water were able to trade water just as they are able to enter into trades for workers, fertilizer, and tractors.

Another impediment that prevents traders from reaching the contract curve is price control. Pareto efficiency in exchange is attained when the price ratio between X and Y equals the competitive equilibrium price ratio where the quantity demanded of X and the quantity supplied of X are equal. Let's consider the consequences when the government regulates the price ratio and sets it below the equilibrium price ratio. For example, in Figure 18-8 a regulatory commission sets the price ratio so that one unit of X trades for one unit of Y. In the previous analysis consumer A's endowment at point M contained relatively more Y than X, and consumer A had to trade two units of Y to get one unit of X. When the price is regulated, A is made better off because she has to give up only one unit of Y to get one unit of X. Consumer A's budget line starts at M and is the dashed line aa that has a slope of $-P_X/P_Y = -1$. Consumer A is willing to exchange more units of Y for more units of X at this lower price ratio and maximizes utility by moving along budget line aa to point d where aa is tangent to a higher indifference curve $_3U_A$. Consumer A is demanding $_2X_A - {_1X_A}$ more units of X and is supplying $_1Y_A - {_2Y_A}$ units of Y when she can trade one unit of Y for one unit of X and the budget line is aa.

Consumer B has relatively more units of X than of Y and responds to a lower relative price for X by supplying only $_1X_B - {_2X_B}$ of X at point e on $_2U_B$. With the regulated one-for-one price ratio, the quantity demanded of X by A is greater than the quantity supplied of X by B. Consumer A is demanding more units of X than consumer B is willing to supply when the slope of the budget line is -1, and so there is an excess demand for X. In this two-person competitive economy B is the sole supplier of X, and so A can purchase only the number of units that B is willing to supply. When the relative price of X is below the equilibrium price, A and B end up at point e, which is not on the contract curve. Therefore, the indifference curves of A and B intersect at point e. When the price ratio is other than the competitive equilibrium price ratio, this two person exchange economy fails to reach the contract curve cc, and so Pareto efficiency in exchange is not attained. Most economists oppose price controls because they recognize that they prevent the economy from achieving Pareto efficiency in exchange.

By now, the Wizard's understanding of and fascination with the role of com-

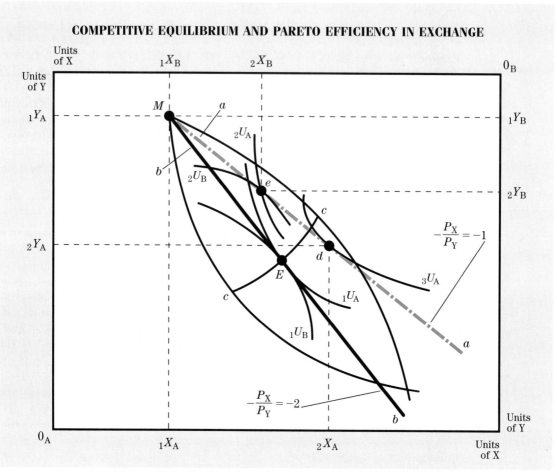

COMPETITIVE EQUILIBRIUM AND PARETO EFFICIENCY IN EXCHANGE

Figure 18-8   Because the price ratio is regulated, the budget constraint has a slope of -1. Consumer A demands $_2X_A - {}_1X_A$ more units of X, but consumer B is willing to supply only $_1X_B - {}_2X_B$ units of X. There is an excess demand for X. The two consumers end up at point e where the slopes of the indifference curves are not equal. This allocation is not Pareto-efficient since it is not on the contract curve cc.

petitive markets have grown immensely. With a functioning competitive market, the marginal rates of substitution are equal for all market participants at the equilibrium competitive price ratio, and so exchange is Pareto-efficient. Moreover, this equilibrium appears to minimize information requirements since it does not require every participant to know everything about all the other market participants.

Pareto Efficiency in Production

Our Wizard of Zeoz fable does not end here. The Wizard correctly notes that the economy in Zeoz produces as well as exchanges goods. While he admits shortcomings in his command and control policies, he wants to know how markets can function to produce goods more efficiently than with the use of these policies.

You begin your explanation by specifying what resources are available in Zeoz to produce goods X and Y. The economy has factors of production of L' units of labor and K' units of capital. To produce the goods that the Wizard assigns to inhabitants, he must assign these factors of production to industry X and industry Y so that the required quantities of X and Y are produced. The production function of each good shows the quantity produced for any combination of labor and capital that the Wizard assigns to produce the good.

Suppose the Wizard assigns $_1L_X$ units of labor and $_1K_X$ units of capital to produce X and $_1L_Y$ and $_1K_Y$ units of labor and capital to produce Y. The total number of units of labor assigned to produce X and Y must equal L' and K'.

$$_1L_X + {}_1L_Y = L' \qquad _1K_X + {}_1K_Y = K' \qquad \text{(Endowment of Factors)} \qquad \textbf{(18-6)}$$

The Wizard's assignment of factors to products determines the quantities of X and Y that the economy produces. We illustrate the amounts of X and Y produced with this assignment of factors in a production version of the Edgeworth box diagram. In Figure 18-9 the dimensions of the Edgeworth production box are L' by K'. 0_X is the origin for the production function of good X. By proceeding from southwest to northeast, more units of labor and capital produce more units of X. The production function of Y starts with point 0_Y at the origin in the northeast corner. Proceeding from northeast to southwest represents an increase in the production of Y. Figure 18-9 shows several isoquants of the production function for X and of the production function for Y. The Wizard's initial allocation of factors is at point a, and so the economy of Zeoz produces X_0 units of X and Y_0 units of Y.

How should the Wizard assign factors to the two industries so that production is efficient? The natural procedure is to adopt a standard similar to the one for efficiency in exchange. Production is Pareto-efficient if any reallocation of factors of production reduces the output of one good given the output of the other good.

> An allocation of factors is Pareto-efficient if any reallocation of factors reduces the output of one good given the output of the other good.

Which points in Figure 18-9 satisfy this definition? Starting at point a, suppose the Wizard reassigns the factors so that the output of X remains constant and the movement is along the isoquant X_0 to point b and then to point c. The output of Y increases from Y_0 to Y_1 and then to Y_2, while the output of X is constant. Therefore, neither point a nor point b is Pareto-efficient in production because the output of Y is increasing for a given output of X. However, point c is Pareto-efficient. Given X_0, a movement away from point c in either direction lowers the output of Y.

The slopes of the isoquants X_0 and Y_2 are equal at point c.

$$^X\text{MRTS}_{KL} = {}^Y\text{MRTS}_{KL} \qquad \text{(Condition for Pareto Efficiency in Production)} \qquad \textbf{(18-7)}$$

where $^X\text{MRTS}_{KL}$ is the marginal rate of technical substitution between capital and labor in the production of X and $^Y\text{MRTS}_{KL}$ has the corresponding interpretation in the production of Y. Therefore, Pareto efficiency requires the slopes of the iso-

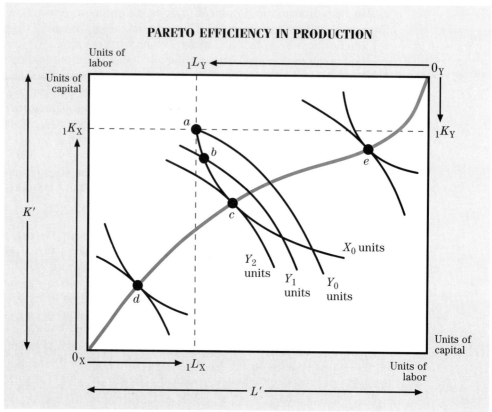

Figure 18-9   The initial allocation of factors is at point *a*. An allocation is Pareto-efficient if any reallocation of factors reduces the output of one good while holding the output of the other good constant. At point *c*, the slopes of the isoquants are equal and the allocation of factors is Pareto-efficient. The curve running from 0_X to 0_Y connects all points of tangency and is called the contract curve.

quants to be equal. In Figure 18-9 all points of tangency between the isoquants are connected to derive the contract curve $0_X 0_Y$. For example, the slopes of the two isoquants are equal at points *d* and *e*.

Pareto efficiency in production requires the marginal rate of technical substitution between labor and capital to be equal for the two products.

Competitive Factor Markets and Pareto Efficiency

If factor markets are competitive, each firm in the economy is a price taker in all factor markets and employs as many units of each factor as it desires at given factor prices. When prices of factors are determined so that quantity demanded equals quantity supplied for each factor, production is Pareto-efficient.

The proof of this proposition is similar to the proof that exchange is Pareto-efficient with competitive product markets. The slope of the isocost line facing each firm producing either X or Y equals $-w/r$, the factor price ratio. From Chapter 5 you know that a firm maximizes output given a total cost by equating the slope of the isoquant with the slope of the isocost line. Let's consider a single competitive firm supplying X. A firm produces X at minimum cost when the marginal rate of technical substitution between capital and labor equals the factor price ratio.

$$^{\mathrm{X}}\mathrm{MRTS}_{KL} = -\frac{w}{r} \qquad \text{(Minimum Cost Condition for X)} \qquad \textbf{(18-8)}$$

Similarly, a firm produces product Y at minimum cost when the marginal rate of technical substitution equals the factor price ratio.

$$^{\mathrm{Y}}\mathrm{MRTS}_{KL} = -\frac{w}{r} \qquad \text{(Minimum Cost Condition for Y)} \qquad \textbf{(18-9)}$$

Because all firms in the economy pay the same prices for the factors of production and each firm minimizes total costs, the slope of the isoquant of a firm producing X equals the slope of a firm producing Y.

$$^{\mathrm{X}}\mathrm{MRTS}_{KL} = -\frac{w}{r} = \,^{\mathrm{Y}}\mathrm{MRTS}_{KL} \quad \begin{array}{l}\text{(Condition for Pareto Efficiency}\\\text{on Production)}\end{array} \qquad \textbf{(18-10)}$$

In Figure 18-10 aa' is the isocost line faced by both firms. It shows the exchange rate of factors so that total production cost is constant. If the price of labor is \$36 per worker per period and the price of capital is \$12 per machine per period, the slope of the isocost line is -3 and each firm can purchase three units of capital by releasing one unit of labor and keep total cost constant. At point a the firm produces X_0 units at a total cost of \$36 times $_0L_{\mathrm{X}}$ units of labor plus \$12 times $_0K_{\mathrm{X}}$ units of capital. The isocost line aa' shows the rate of exchange between labor and capital. A firm producing good X can increase the output of X to X_1 by substituting labor for capital until it reaches point e. The firm wants to expand employment by $_1L_{\mathrm{X}} - _0L_{\mathrm{X}}$ more workers and reduce the number of machines by $_0K_{\mathrm{X}} - _1K_{\mathrm{X}}$ units of capital if the exchange rate between factors is -3. The firm producing Y increases the output of Y from Y_0 to Y_1 by substituting capital for labor. It is demanding $_1K_{\mathrm{Y}} - _0K_{\mathrm{Y}}$ more units of capital and employing $_0L_{\mathrm{Y}} - _1L_{\mathrm{Y}}$ fewer workers. The quantity demanded of labor by the firm producing X equals the quantity supplied of labor by the firm producing Y when the price of labor is three times the price of capital. In moving from point a to point e, each firm produces more units at the same total cost as at point a.

The curve $0_{\mathrm{X}}0_{\mathrm{Y}}$ is the contract curve for production and connects all points of tangency. The contract curve shows the maximum quantity of Y for each quantity of X. The *production possibility curve* in Figure 18-11 is another way of showing this. It indicates the maximum quantity of Y for each quantity of X and is derived from the contract curve in Figure 18-9. For example, point c in Figure 18-11 corresponds to point c in Figure 18-9. Given an output of X_0, the maximum output of Y is Y_2 units. Production is Pareto-efficient at any point on the production possibility curve. Any point inside the production possibility curve implies that produc-

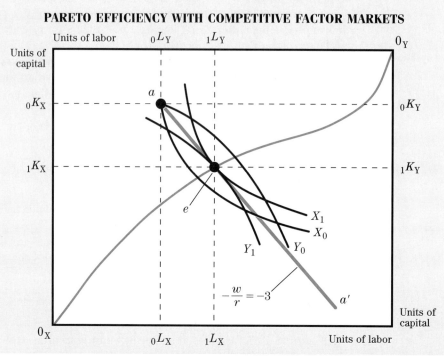

PARETO EFFICIENCY WITH COMPETITIVE FACTOR MARKETS

Figure 18-10   The initial allocation of factors is at point a. When a firm can hire three units of capital for one unit of labor, the firm producing X increases the output of X while holding total costs constant by moving to point e. The output of X increases from X_0 to X_1. The firm producing Y increases the output to Y_1 when moving to point e.

tion is not Pareto-efficient, and so the economy does not maximize the output of Y given the output of X. Note that point a is inside the production possibility curve in Figure 18-11. This point corresponds to point a in Figure 18-9 which is off the contract curve so that the economy produces only Y_0 units and X_0 units because of inefficient allocation of the factors of production.

The production possibility curve shows the opportunity cost of increasing the output of one good in terms of the other good. Starting at point e we can increase the output of Y by ΔY but only by decreasing the output of X by ΔX as we move along the contract curve in Figure 18-9 from the northeast to the southwest. The opportunity cost of increasing Y by ΔY is ΔX. Factors released from producing X enter industry Y to produce more Y in such a way that production is always Pareto-efficient.

The slope of the production possibility curve is defined as the marginal rate of transformation between Y and X, or

$$\mathrm{MRT_{YX}} = \frac{\Delta Y}{\Delta X} \qquad \text{(Marginal Rate of Transformation)} \qquad \textbf{(18-11)}$$

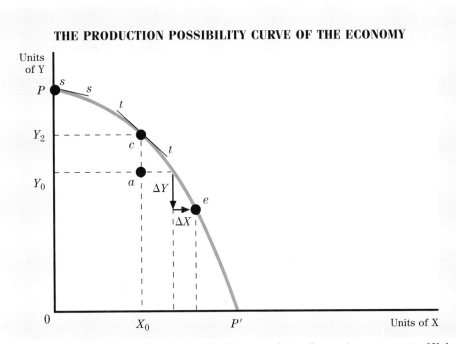

Figure 18-11   The production possibility curve shows the maximum amount of Y that can be produced for a given output of X. The production possibility curve is derived from the contract curve.

You may have noticed that the production possibility curve in Figure 18-11 bows outward. When the economy is producing only Y at point P, a unit decrease in the output of Y causes a relatively large increase in the production of X. Geometrically, this means that the production possibility curve is relatively flat at this point. The reason for this is that the marginal cost of producing the last unit of Y is relatively high when virtually all the factors in the economy are employed in industry Y. In contrast, the marginal cost of producing the first unit of X is relatively low. For example, at point P the marginal cost of producing the last unit of Y might be \$20, whereas the marginal cost of producing the first unit of X is only \$2. By producing one less unit of Y and transferring the costs saving of \$20 to increase the output of X, the economy produces 10 more units of X. Therefore, the marginal rate of transformation is $\Delta Y/\Delta X = -MC_X/MC_Y = -\$2/\$20 = -1/10$. Line ss is tangent to the production possibility curve at point P and is virtually flat because a reduction of 1 unit of Y increases the output of X by 10 units.

$$\text{MRT}_{YX} = \frac{\Delta Y}{\Delta X} = -\frac{MC_X}{MC_Y} \qquad \begin{array}{l}\text{(Marginal Rate of Transformation Equals}\\ \text{Minus the Ratio of Marginal Costs)}\end{array} \qquad \textbf{(18-12)}$$

As the economy produces fewer units of Y and more units of X, the marginal cost of producing Y decreases and the marginal cost of producing X increases. At point c in Figure 18-11 the marginal cost of Y falls to \$10, while the marginal cost of producing X increases to \$10. When the economy produces one less unit of Y, it can produce only one more unit of X, and so the marginal rate of transformation is $-MC_X/MC_Y = -\$10/\$10 = -1$. The line tt has a slope of -1 and is tangent to the production possibility curve at point c. To summarize, the slope of the production possibility curve equals the negative of the relative marginal costs of producing X and Y.

APPLICATION 18-3

Reducing the Price of Capital by Subsidizing Small Businesses

Suppose that industry C has many small firms and industry D only has large firms. The many small firms in industry C successfully lobby Congress to give them a capital subsidy. Congress writes the law so that firms below a certain size receive a subsidized interest rate on purchases of machines. The firms in industry D are too large to qualify for the subsidy. What is the effect of this subsidy on one factor of production on Pareto efficiency in production?

Figure 18-12a shows an isoquant Q_C of a representative small firm in industry C. The isocost line is cc and reflects the subsidy in the purchase of capital. Figure 18-12b shows an isoquant Q_D of a representative large firm in industry D. The isocost function of the large firm is dd and is less steep than that of the small firm because the subsidy allows the small firm to purchase capital at a lower net price than the large firm can.

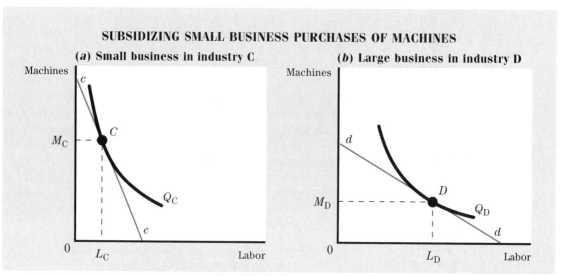

SUBSIDIZING SMALL BUSINESS PURCHASES OF MACHINES

(a) Small business in industry C

(b) Large business in industry D

Figure 18-12   By giving small firms a subsidy for the purchase of machines, the economy is no longer Pareto-efficient in production.

Both firms minimize the cost of producing any rate of output by equating the slope of the isoquant to the slope of the isocost line. The small firm minimizes cost of producing Q_C by employing M_C machines and L_C workers at point C. The large firm produces Q_D by employing M_D machines and L_D workers at point D. Because the slopes of the isocost lines of the large and small firms differ, the slopes of the isoquants of these firms differ as well. Therefore, the marginal rates of technical substitution differ and production is no longer Pareto-efficient. Subsidizing the use of a factor of production for one firm and not another creates a production distortion. For a given output of the small firm, the subsidy prevents the economy from maximizing the output of the large firm.

Pareto Efficiency in Product Mix

You have patiently described the requirements for Pareto efficiency in exchange and in production to the Wizard. He is already thinking ahead and wonders how the quantities of X and Y produced are related to the quantities of X and Y demanded by consumers A and B. He asks, "It is all well and good that competitive markets can produce any combination of X and Y efficiently and that competitive markets will distribute what is produced so that exchange is Pareto-efficient, but what assurance do I have that competitive markets will produce the combination of X and Y that consumers demand?" To answer this important question, you need to demonstrate that competitive markets can align the production side of the market with the consumer demand side of the market by producing the product mix that maximizes the efficiency of the economy.

Pareto efficiency in product mix requires the marginal rates of substitution between Y and X in exchange to equal the marginal rate of transformation of the economy.

> Pareto efficiency in product mix requires the marginal rates of substitution of consumers to equal the marginal rate of transformation.

$$^A\mathrm{MRS}_{YX} = {}^B\mathrm{MRS}_{YX} = \mathrm{MRT}_{YX} \qquad \text{(Condition for Pareto Efficiency in Product Mix)} \qquad \textbf{(18-13)}$$

Equation 18-13 requires that the slope of the production possibility curve equal the slope of each consumer's indifference curve.

To show this, you ask the Wizard to consider a point on the production possibility curve where a small movement along the curve reduces the output of Y by one unit and increases the output of X by four units so that $\Delta Y/\Delta X = -\frac{1}{4}$. Suppose the economy's product mix is distributed to consumers so that exchange among consumers is Pareto-efficient and that each consumer is indifferent between substituting one less unit of Y for one unit of X. By producing four more units of X and one less unit of Y, the economy can make at least one consumer better off while holding the utility of the other constant. In other words, one consumer is left undisturbed so that this consumer's utility is constant. Yet the economy produces four more units of X for one less unit of Y. The utility of the other consumer will increase if she receives four more units of X for one less unit of Y since she is indifferent with a one-to-one tradeoff. By changing the product mix, the utility of one consumer can be increased holding the utility of the other consumer constant. Therefore, the product mix of the economy is not Pareto-efficient because the marginal rates of substitution of consumers are *not* equal to the marginal rate of transformation of the economy. The economy is producing too little X and too much Y for it to be Pareto-efficient in product mix.

You ask the Wizard to consider the production possibility curve in Figure 18-13. At point a the economy is producing X' and Y' units efficiently. Given the production of X' and Y' units, let's say that consumer A has $_1Y_A$ of Y and $_1X_A$ units of X at point g, where point g is on the contract curve (not shown). Consumer B has the remaining units of goods X and Y. Because nn is tangent to the indifference curves of A and B at point g, there is Pareto efficiency in exchange.

Although there is Pareto efficiency in exchange (because the marginal rates of substitution are equal) and Pareto efficiency in production (because we are on and not inside the production possibility curve), we still do not have product mix efficiency. The slopes of the indifference curves at point g equal the slope of nn, but the slope of nn is not equal to the slope of dd on the production possibility curve at point a. If this economy produced more X and less Y, at least one consumer could be made better off given the utility of the other consumer.

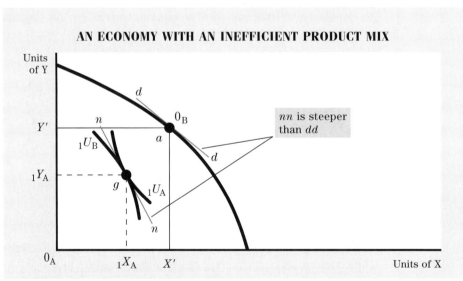

AN ECONOMY WITH AN INEFFICIENT PRODUCT MIX

Figure 18-13   The product mix at point a is inefficient. The economy produces X' and Y' units efficiently at point a on the production possibility curve. If consumer A consumes $_1Y_A$ and $_1X_A$ units, then consumer B consumes the remainder of both goods. At point g the marginal rates of substitution for consumers A and B are equal. However, the marginal rates of substitution of consumers A and B do not equal the marginal rate of transformation at point a. The economy is producing too many units of Y and not enough units of X. An increase in the production of X and less of Y will increase the utility of one consumer while the utility of the other remains constant.

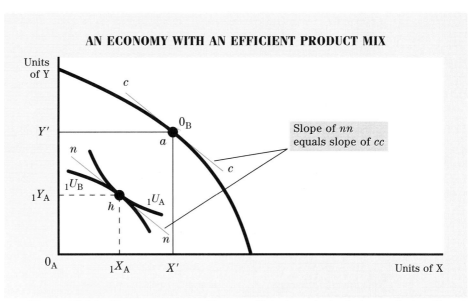

AN ECONOMY WITH AN EFFICIENT PRODUCT MIX

Figure 18-14   The economy provides an efficient product mix by producing X' and Y' units at point a on the production possibility curve. If A consumes $_1Y_A$ and $_1X_A$ units, then B consumes the remainder of both goods. At point h, the marginal rates of substitution of the two consumers are equal and equal the slope of nn. The marginal rates of substitution of each consumer equal the marginal rate of transformation at point a (the slope of cc) on the production possibility curve.

If the economy is producing a Pareto-efficient product mix, the slopes of the indifference curves of consumers must equal the slope of the production possibility curve. Figure 18-14 shows an economy that is producing a Pareto-efficient product mix. In this figure line nn is tangent to the indifference curve $_1U_B$ and to $_1U_A$ at point h and has the same slope as line cc. The slope of cc equals the marginal rate of transformation of the production possibility curve at point a. Therefore, the marginal rates of substitution of A and B are equal, and both are equal to the marginal rate of transformation on the production possibility curve at point a.

Competitive Markets and Product Mix Efficiency

If all participants in each market act competitively and all markets are competitive, the economy will produce a Pareto-efficient product mix. If both product markets are competitive, then price equals marginal cost in each market, a hallmark condition for a competitive industry. If price equals marginal cost in each market, then the ratio of prices equals the ratio of marginal costs.

$$\frac{P_X}{P_Y} = \frac{MC_X}{MC_Y}$$

With competitive markets the ratio of prices conveys accurate information to consumers about the relative marginal costs of producing X and Y. We already know that each consumer maximizes utility by equating marginal rate of substitution to $-P_X/P_Y$. Furthermore, we already know that $-MC_X/MC_Y$ equals marginal rate of transformation.

If all product and factor markets are competitive, then we know that price equals marginal cost in the market for A and for B. Therefore,

$$^AMRS_{YX} = {^B}MRS_{YX}$$

$$= -\frac{P_X}{P_Y} = -\frac{MC_X}{MC_Y} = MRT_{YX} \qquad \text{(Condition for Pareto} \atop \text{Efficiency in Product Mix)} \qquad \textbf{(18-14)}$$

When all markets are competitive, the marginal rate of substitution of each consumer in the economy is equal to the marginal rate of transformation, a requirement for Pareto efficiency in product mix.

The Wizard leans back in his chair, impressed by your arguments, and he decides to appoint you as his lifelong adviser. You are impressed by the Wizard's ability to absorb so many new ideas in a short time. The most important point that you hope the Wizard appreciates is that Pareto efficiency conditions can be achieved by relying on competitive product and factor markets. The Wizard can rely on the self-interest of consumers, producers, and factor suppliers, all of whom are price takers in competitive markets, to satisfy all Pareto efficiency conditions although individual agents, be they consumers, producers, or factor suppliers, have only tiny bits of information about the economy. The Wizard does not have to rely on command and control policies. The next chapter considers some qualifications to these general conclusions.

SUMMARY

- Pareto efficiency in exchange requires the marginal rates of substitution of all consumers to be equal.
- If consumers trade goods in competitive markets, they reach the contract curve and achieve Pareto efficiency in exchange.
- Pareto efficiency in production requires all marginal rates of technical substitution to be equal for all firms.
- If all firms face the same factor price ratio, they reach the contract curve and achieve Pareto efficiency in production.
- Pareto efficiency in product mix requires the marginal rates of substitution of all consumers to equal the marginal rate of transformation.
- When all product and factor markets are competitive, an economy satisfies the Pareto efficiency conditions.

KEY TERMS

Consumer endowment   Exchange of goods
Pareto efficiency in exchange   Equating marginal rates of
The contract curve   substitution

Pareto efficiency in production
Competitive factor markets and Pareto efficiency in production
Competitive product and factor markets and Pareto efficiency in product mix
Competitive markets and Pareto efficiency in exchange
Equating marginal rates of technical substitution
Pareto efficiency in product mix

REVIEW QUESTIONS

1. What is a consumer's endowment?
2. Consumer A has all units of good X, and consumer B has all units of good Y. Show this position in an Edgeworth box diagram.
3. What is the required condition for Pareto efficiency in exchange?
4. When will two price-taking traders end up on the contract curve?
5. What is the required Pareto efficiency condition if firms are to reach the contract curve in production?
6. What is the production possibility curve and how is it derived?
7. What does Pareto efficiency in product mix mean?
8. Does an economy produce a Pareto-efficient product mix when all markets are competitive?

EXERCISES

1. Consumer A has an endowment of 20 units of good Y and 6 units of good X, while consumer B has an endowment of 12 units of Y and 30 units of X. Draw an Edgeworth box diagram and show the endowment point. Given this information, will A trade Y for X or X for Y if a competitive market opens? Explain.
2. Consumer A's endowment includes 6 units of Y and 1 unit of X. Consumer B's endowment includes 3 units of Y and 1 unit of X. If A and B trade, the equilibrium price ratio will be between -6 and -3. Explain why you do or do not agree with this statement.
3. If the government regulates the relative price of X, what determines whether the price ratio between good X and good Y equals the marginal rate of substitution of the demander or the supplier of good X? Does it make a difference whether the relative price is above or below the equilibrium price? Explain.
4. Is there some justification for calling the contract curve in exchange a "conflict curve"?
5. If you were the Dean of the Graduate School of Business at the University of Chicago and students asked you why they cannot sell points they receive to bid for courses, what explanation would you give?
6. Use the Edgeworth box diagram in Figure 18-6 to show how the utility of consumers A and B changes when the government regulates the price of Y. Suppose the price of Y falls to $2 while the price of X is $10.

7. Suppose the assignment of labor and capital to the production of good X and good Y is not Pareto-efficient. Show what the wage-rental factor price ratio must be if the firm that produces X is minimizing cost and if the firm that produces Y is minimizing cost. Will the wage-rental factor price ratio be different for the two firms?

8. Suppose a technological change allows firms in industry X to produce more units of X for each combination of L and K. Show how this technological change shifts the production possibility function of the economy.

9. If more immigrants enter the United States, how will this affect the production possibility curve?

10. What are the consequences of imposing a quota on U.S. wheat production on the relative price of wheat and the quantity of wheat produced? Use the production possibility curve to illustrate the consequences. Show how the price ratio facing consumers is related to the relative marginal costs of producing wheat and another good.

CHAPTER 19

IMPEDIMENTS TO ECONOMIC EFFICIENCY

Chapter 18 demonstrated that Pareto efficiency conditions are satisfied when all markets are organized competitively. However, this conclusion is far less sweeping than it first appears. Chapter 18 not only assumed that all markets are competitive but that information is distributed symmetrically, external effects are nonexistent, and no public goods exist in the kingdom of Zeoz. This chapter investigates each of these topics with the exception of asymmetric information which was discussed in Chapter 14.

19-1 DEPARTURES FROM PARETO EFFICIENCY BECAUSE OF MONOPOLY

Monopoly power is one impediment to achieving Pareto efficiency. This section shows how the presence of monopoly in a product market prevents the economy from achieving all the Pareto efficiency conditions.

In an economy with two goods, X and Y, we assume that the production of X is monopolized and that Y is produced competitively. Price exceeds marginal cost in the monopolized market, while price equals marginal cost in industry Y. When a monopolist produces X,

$$\text{Price} > \text{Marginal revenue} = \text{Marginal cost}$$

$$\text{Price} > \text{Marginal cost}$$

Because the monopoly price exceeds the marginal cost in industry X, the price of X relative to the price of Y is greater than the marginal cost of producing X relative to the marginal cost of producing Y. The relative price of X is no longer an accurate measure of the relative marginal cost of producing X.

$$\frac{P_X}{P_Y} > \frac{MC_X}{MC_Y} \tag{19-1}$$

In this situation consumers will sensibly substitute away from X and purchase relatively more units of Y because the monopoly price of X is higher relative to the price of Y than it would be if X were supplied by competitive firms. Because every consumer faces the same higher price ratio, each purchases a market basket where the higher price ratio equals the consumer's marginal rate of substitution. Consequently, the marginal rates of substitution are still equal for all consumers in the economy. So, the economy is Pareto-efficient in exchange even when a monopolist produces product X.

Although the producer of X is a monopolist in the product market, the firm is still a price taker in factor markets. Consequently, all producers in the economy, whether they are producing Y or X, are price takers in factor markets and face the same factor price ratio. Therefore, the marginal rates of technical substitution will still be equal in the two industries, and so production is Pareto-efficient.

Nevertheless, the economy is not hitting on all cylinders. The problem is that the product mix is no longer Pareto-efficient. Because price is higher under monopoly than under competition, the economy produces too little of X and too much of Y. We have

$$^A\text{MRS}_{YX} = {}^B\text{MRS}_{YX} = -\frac{P_X}{P_Y} < -\frac{MC_X}{MC_Y} = \text{MRT}_{YX} \qquad \begin{array}{l}\text{(Product Mix Is Not} \\ \text{Pareto-Efficient)}\end{array} \qquad \textbf{(19-2)}$$

where $^A\text{MRS}_{YX}$ is the marginal rate of substitution of consumer A and $^B\text{MRS}_{YX}$ is the marginal substitution of consumer B. Therefore, the marginal rate of substitution of each consumer is less than the marginal rate of transformation.

$$^A\text{MRS}_{YX} = {}^B\text{MRS}_{YX} < \text{MRT}_{YX}$$

When a firm monopolizes the market for X, the marginal rates of substitution of consumers no longer equal the economy's marginal rate of transformation. For example, consumers might be indifferent when giving up one unit of Y for two units of X given P_X/P_Y, but the economy can produce four more units of X by producing one less unit of Y. The economy is producing too few units of X, the monopolized good, and too many units of Y, the competitive good. This means that the slope of each consumer's indifference curve is steeper than the slope of the production possibility curve when there is a monopoly in X given the mix of goods produced in the economy.

Figure 19-1 shows a situation where P_X/P_Y is greater than MC_X/MC_Y when a monopolist produces X. At point e, mm is tangent to the indifference curves of consumers A and B but is steeper than bb, the slope of the production possibility curve at point a. The marginal rates of substitution of the two consumers are equal,

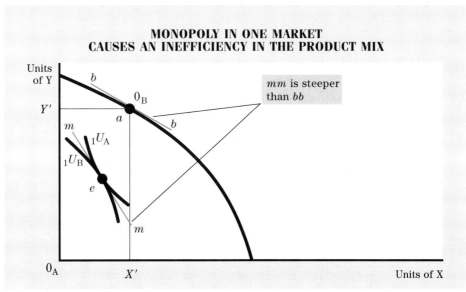

Figure 19-1   When a firm monopolizes the production of X, the economy produces Y' and X' units. Less of X is produced and more of Y because a monopolist produces X. At point e the slope of mm equals the marginal rate of substitution of consumers A and B. Line bb is tangent to the production possibility curve at point a. Line mm is steeper than line bb. Therefore, the product mix is not Pareto-efficient because the ratio of prices does not equal the ratio of marginal cost.

but they do not equal the marginal rate of transformation. A monopoly producer of X creates a distortion by causing resources that would produce more X to shift to the production of Y. Because the price ratio no longer mimics the relative marginal costs, there is a wedge between each consumer's marginal rate of substitution and the marginal rate of transformation of the economy, and so the product mix is no longer Pareto-efficient.

The intellectual case against monopoly relies on the fact that a monopoly creates a wedge between marginal rates of substitution of consumers and the marginal rate of transformation and not on the idea that a monopolist earns profits. The objection to monopoly is still valid even if the profits of a monopolist are negligible, as they would be when the monopoly price equals the monopolist's average cost of production. The rationale for the Sherman Antitrust Act and other laws that foster greater competition is to reduce if not eliminate the gap between price and marginal cost and to reduce or eliminate any discrepancy between marginal rates of substitution of consumers and the marginal rate of transformation.

Just as monopoly creates a wedge between price and marginal cost, so too will a per unit tax or subsidy. These too create distortions by introducing a wedge between price and marginal cost of production. A per unit tax on X raises the price of X above the marginal cost of producing it (excluding the per unit tax). Here again, relative price is no longer an accurate signal of relative marginal cost of production. Imposing a per unit tax on the production of X raises the price of X, reduces the amount of X produced, shifts the demand function for Y outward, and increases the quantity of Y produced. A per unit tax changes the product mix so that the economy cannot achieve Pareto efficiency in product mix.

19-2 EXTERNAL EFFECTS AND PARETO EFFICIENCY

Until now, we have assumed that a decision by a consumer or by a firm has no external effects on other consumers or other firms. However, there are many situations where external or third-party effects are important. If I have asthma and the maître d' seats someone who smokes at a nearby table, I begin to cough and have difficulty breathing. The transaction between the smoker and the restaurant imposes a cost on me, the offended party. If a steel factory's emissions pollute the air, it adversely affects nearby residences or could raise the cost of production of a firm located nearby. If airplanes fly over my residence periodically, noise interrupts all conversation until the planes pass. If you get a flu vaccination, others benefit because you (hopefully) are less likely to be a carrier of the flu. If my wonderful view of San Francisco Bay is blocked because my neighbor allows his trees to grow, I suffer a loss in utility. If my neighbor allows his trees to grow and extend over my fence so that my yard receives little sun and I am unable to plant a beautiful garden with attractive flowers and foliage, my utility decreases. If my neighbor keeps her dog inside the house at night, my utility increases because I do not hear her barking dog.

In all these cases a consumer or a firm receives an external benefit or suffers a loss because of the behavior of another consumer or firm. We say there is a

Table 19-1   MARGINAL PRODUCTION COST, MARGINAL DAMAGE COST, AND SOCIAL COST

QUANTITY PRODUCED BY BRIGHT PAINT (UNITS)	MARGINAL PRODUCTION COST OF BRIGHT PAINT, MC ($) (1)	MARGINAL DAMAGE (EXTERNAL) COST INCURRED BY PURE WATER PER UNIT INCREASE IN OUTPUT, MDC ($) (2)	MARGINAL SOCIAL COST PER UNIT INCREASE IN OUTPUT, MSC = MC + MDC ($) (3)
1	5	2	7
2	6	4	10
3	7	7	14
4	10	11	21
5	14	18	32

negative externality if third parties are worse off, or a positive externality if third parties benefit. In each case a consumer or a firm incurs costs and receives no compensation for the costs incurred or receives benefits and pays nothing for the benefits enjoyed. For example, no feasible mechanism may exist for airlines to pay the owners of the homes for the discomfort caused by noise pollution or for the owners of the steel factories to pay the nearby residents for their discomfort. We want to examine the consequences of externalities on Pareto efficiency when markets for compensation do not exist and, later, when they do.

> An **externality** exists when a firm or individual benefits from or is harmed by the behavior of other firms or individuals.

The externality problem can be introduced by way of a numerical example. The Bright Paint Company produces paint and discharges wastewater into a river. Bright Paint sells its paint at the equilibrium competitive price of $14 a unit. Pure Water Company sells bottled water and is downstream from Bright Paint. Because of the lower water quality, Pure Water must incur additional costs to purify the water before bottling it.

Table 19-1 shows the marginal production cost of Bright Paint (column 1) and the marginal external (damage) cost incurred by Pure Water (column 2) for different quantities of paint produced by Bright Paint.

Since Bright Paint is a competitive firm, it sells each unit of paint for $14 and maximizes its profits by producing five units of paint where the price equals Bright Paint's marginal cost of production. Yet, the fifth unit imposes a marginal cost on society that is far greater than $14 because Pure Water Co. incurs a marginal damage (external) cost of $18. Marginal social cost is in column 3 and equals marginal production cost (MC) plus marginal damage cost (MDC). The marginal social cost incurred by society when Bright Paint produces the fifth unit is not $14 but $32. From a societal perspective, Bright Paint is producing too much output because it takes only its marginal production cost into account when it maximizes its profits by producing five units.

An environmentally concerned individual might demand that the polluting facility shut down to eliminate the external effect completely. Note that the optimal solution does not require Bright Paint to shut down completely but rather to determine production where price equals marginal social cost. Marginal social cost equals $14 when Bright Paint produces three, not five, units of paint. Completely eliminating Bright Paint's output would leave price above the marginal social cost of producing the first unit. The sum of consumer and producer surplus is maximized when Bright Paint produces three units, not zero units. Just because there are negative externalities, this does not mean Bright Paint should not produce any paint.

Now let's consider the externality problem somewhat more generally. In Figure 19-2 Bright Paint is a price taker and can sell each unit at P'. The firm's marginal cost function is MC. The marginal damage cost incurred by Pure Water is MDC. MSC is marginal social cost and equals the sum of the private marginal production cost of Bright Paint and the marginal damage cost incurred by Pure Water.

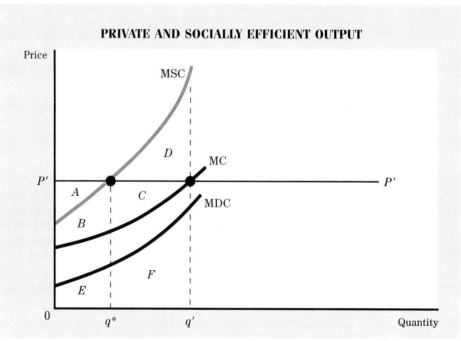

PRIVATE AND SOCIALLY EFFICIENT OUTPUT

Figure 19-2 A competitive firm maximizes profits by producing q' units where $P' = $ MC. MSC is the marginal social cost caused by the discharges of Bright Paint and MDC is the marginal damage cost incurred by Pure Water. If Bright Paint had to pay marginal damage cost, it would produce only q^* units. Because the firm incurs only its marginal cost, the output of Bright Paint is too large when there is a negative externality.

Bright Paint maximizes its profits when it produces q' units where $P' =$ MC. Producer surplus is equal to the sum of areas A, B, and C in Figure 19-2. However, from a social point of view, producer surplus is smaller because Pure Water incurs marginal external costs. We can measure total damage costs incurred by Pure Water in either of two ways. It is equal to the area under the marginal damage cost function, $E + F$, or the area between MSC and MC, $B + C + D$.

Social surplus, S, is defined as the producer surplus of Bright Paint less the total external (damage) costs incurred by Pure Water.

$$S = \text{Producer surplus} - \text{Total external cost}$$

When Bright Paint produces q' units, producer surplus equals $A + B + C$. The total damage costs incurred by Pure Water are equal to $B + C + D$. Therefore, social surplus is

$$S = (A + B + C) - (B + C + D) = A - D$$

An all-knowing omniscient central planner would maximize social surplus by setting Bright Paint's output at q^* so that social surplus equals area A. In the absence of an all-knowing central planner, how can a market system, where agents are maximizing either utility or profit, induce Bright Paint to produce q^* and not q' units? Until a path-breaking article by Nobel Prize winner Ronald Coase appeared, most economists argued that a decentralized competitive price system could reach the social optimum by either costlessly internalizing the externality or by government assessing taxes on the firm creating the negative externality.[1] Let's consider the two possibilities in order.

Internalizing the Externality

In some but not all cases the externality problem can be dealt with by internalizing the externality. Paint manufacturing and the bottling of water are figuratively placed under one roof. Instead of assuming that Bright Paint and Pure Water are two separate companies, let's assume that they are simply two divisions of a diversified firm and that the cost functions for producing paint and bottled water are unchanged. The manager of the diversified firm must decide paint output of the Bright Paint division and number of bottles of water supplied by the Pure Water division so that the firm earns maximum profits. In this situation the manager knows that a unit increase in the output of the Bright Paint division costs the firm the marginal cost of paint plus the marginal damage cost incurred by the Pure Water division. The manager will take account of the marginal damage cost inflicted by the Bright Paint division on the Pure Water division when determining the output of the paint division.

> An externality is internalized when the decision maker bears the full cost or receives the full benefit of a decision.

---

[1] R. H. Coase, "The Problem of Social Cost," *Journal of Law and Economics*, vol. 3, 1960, pp. 1–44.

The significance of this point is that the manager of a profit-maximizing firm will want the paint division to produce an output where $P' =$ MSC. By internalizing the externality, the decision maker takes account of the external cost when determining the profit-maximizing output of paint and selects the socially correct output.

This is the desired solution if the manager of the firm can perform both functions without a loss in efficiency. Clearly, there are limits to this. Otherwise, one giant firm in the economy could internalize all externalities. A single firm does not produce all the goods where there are external effects because at some point the firm experiences diseconomies of scale or incurs higher costs because it produces diverse goods.

APPLICATION 19-1

Internalizing an Externality in a Shopping Mall

An interesting example of internalizing an externality is the modern shopping mall. Typically, a shopping mall has one or more anchor stores—well-known department stores—and a group of specialty and other types of stores. Historically, the recognized name of a department store is the magnet that attracts customers to the shopping mall. The other stores want to be in the mall because they can take a free ride on the name of the department store and receive a positive externality since the department store name attracts shoppers to the mall. Therefore, they save on promotion expenses. A standard contractual arrangement is for the developer of a shopping plaza to give the anchor store a lower rental fee per square foot or to offer some other subsidy. In this case the marginal social cost is less than the marginal cost of operating a specialty store because of the presence of a well-known department store. Without a shopping mall, discount stores might locate near a stand-alone department store and free-ride on the location of the department store. Therefore, the shopping mall is a market institution that allows an externality to be internalized.

Maximizing Social Surplus with a Per Unit Tax

The government could use its taxing power to maximize social surplus. By imposing a per unit tax on Bright Paint, it raises the marginal cost inclusive of the per unit tax and reduces Bright Paint's output. Bright Paint's marginal cost inclusive of the tax becomes MC $+ t$, where t is the per unit tax. If Bright Paint is to produce the socially optimal output of q^*, the government would set the per unit tax so that the MC $+ t$ function intersects P' at q^*. Figure 19-3 shows the required per unit tax. The function MC $+ t$ goes through point a. Therefore, the optimum per unit tax equals the marginal damage cost caused by producing the q^*th unit.

In Table 19-1, the socially optimal output is three units, at which the marginal damage cost is \$7. If the per unit tax is \$7, Bright Paint will produce only three units, the socially optimal quantity.

Economists thought that the invisible hand of Adam Smith became truly invisible when there were externalities. In these situations some form of governmental

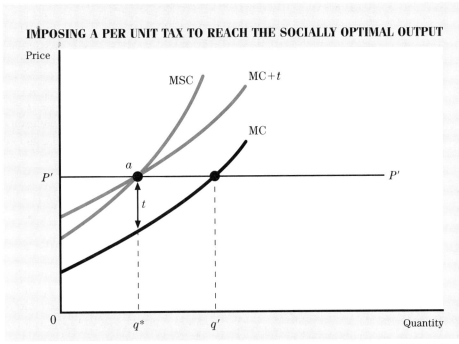

IMPOSING A PER UNIT TAX TO REACH THE SOCIALLY OPTIMAL OUTPUT

Figure 19-3   When a per unit tax of t is imposed, the marginal cost of Bright Paint shifts upward and becomes MC + t. The optimum per unit tax equals the marginal damage cost when Bright Paint produces q^* units. The tax induces Bright Paint to produce the socially optimal output of q^* units.

intervention was required because the self-interest of Bright Paint would prevent the economy from reaching the social optimum. By judiciously using taxes, many economists believed the government could guide a decentralized competitive price system to the socially optimum output when there are external effects. Later, we will see that a per unit tax is not always the ideal solution to the externality problem and, in some cases, can lead to an inferior solution.

The Coase Theorem

In 1960 Nobel Prize-winner Ronald Coase published an influential article that suggested the traditional analysis was incomplete. In terms of our example, Coase would say that the fundamental difficulty is not that Bright Paint creates an externality but that no one owns the quality of water. Coase argued that Bright Paint will produce the socially correct output if (1) transaction costs are negligible and (2) one or the other party has clearly defined property rights in water quality. Transaction costs refer to the cost of negotiating, verifying, and enforcing contracts. What was truly remarkable at the time was Coase's claim that the output produced by Bright Paint did not depend on which party possesses the property right. Coase claimed that Bright Paint would produce the socially optimum output even though the law gave it the unrestricted right to pollute the river. He argued that private markets would solve the externality problem without the need for direct government intervention if transaction costs were negligible. This was a startling claim because economists believed that government intervention was absolutely essential to solve the externality problem. Equally astonishing was his second claim that the socially optimal output would emerge no matter which party owned the property rights.

To expound on Coase's reasoning, we compare the solutions when Pure Water possesses the property rights in the river's water quality and then when Bright Paint has the right to pollute the river. Suppose the law gives Pure Water property rights in the water quality of the river. What does this mean? Pure Water can costlessly collect damages from Bright Paint if Bright Paint degrades the pristine water quality of the river by producing paint.

With the property rights assigned in this way, Bright Paint pays for the damages it causes. What options does Bright Paint have? It can:

- *Option 1.* Continue to produce paint *and* pay damages.
- *Option 2.* Clean the water before it is released so that the quality of water is not degraded.
- *Option 3.* Pay to have Pure Water invest in expensive filtering equipment to clean the discharges of Bright Paint or pay to have Pure Water relocate.

For the time being, let's set aside options 2 and 3 for later consideration and investigate only option 1. If Bright Paint pays the marginal damage cost to Pure Water for each unit produced, it will produce only q^* units where $P' = \text{MSC}$ because MSC is Bright Paint's marginal cost when the law assigns the property rights to Pure Water. For your convenience, Figure 19-4 reproduces the graph in Figure 19-2. The area between MSC and MC up to q^*, or area B in Figure 19-4, is equal to the total damage costs that Bright Paint pays to Pure Water.

Now assume Bright Paint possesses the unencumbered right to degrade water quality, although this does appear to be a bizarre institutional arrangement. Bright Paint is creating the externality by producing paint, and yet Coase says society does not have to fear the consequences even if Bright Paint possesses the right to pollute the river. Coase argues that the apparent mistake in delegating property rights to Bright Paint is inconsequential and will have no effect on water quality as long as transaction costs are negligible. To see this, put yourself in Pure Water's shoes. True, Pure Water can no longer collect damages. Even so, is it in the self-interest of Pure Water to allow Bright Paint to pollute the river? The answer is no. The management of Pure Water has an incentive to make the production of paint more expensive for Bright Paint, although Pure Water does not "own" the water quality.

If Pure Water could somehow persuade Bright Paint to reduce paint output from q' *to* q^*, by how much would Bright Paint be worse off and by how much would Pure Water be better off? Bright Paint is worse off because its producer surplus decreases by area C in Figure 19-4. Pure Water is better off because marginal damage costs incurred by it decrease by area C *plus* area D. Therefore, the loss by Bright Paint is less than the gain by Pure Water. Clearly, a mutually

REACHING A MUTUALLY BENEFICIAL AGREEMENT

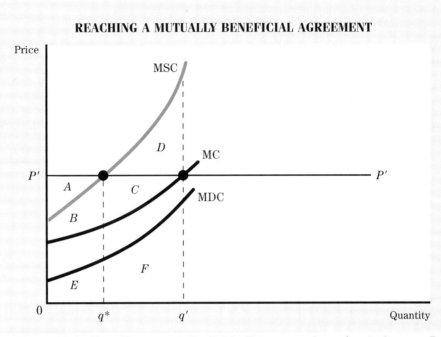

Figure 19-4   Pure Water can bribe Bright Paint to produce q^* units because Pure Water gains more (area C plus area D) than Bright Paint loses (area C) by reducing output from q' to q^* units.

beneficial deal is possible. Suppose Pure Water offers to pay Bright Paint area C plus some fraction of area D if Bright Paint reduces output to q^*. Bright Paint and Pure Water will both be better off by striking a deal whereby they share the proceeds of area D. Of course, it is assumed that both parties will not be so stubborn while bargaining over area D that no deal is possible. This is what we mean when we say there is no transaction cost.

In the extreme case, Pure Water could pay Bright Paint all of area D and would not be worse off when Bright Paint produces q^* and not q' units. How might Pure Water structure the deal? Suppose Pure Water agrees to pay Bright Paint the marginal damage cost for each unit not produced by Bright Paint. How does this offer affect the marginal incentives of Bright Paint? For each unit produced, the marginal costs of Bright Paint are equal to MC *plus* the opportunity cost of not receiving a check from Pure Water for marginal damage cost of that unit. Therefore, MSC becomes Bright Paint's relevant marginal cost of producing another unit of paint. Bright Paint will produce only q^* units where $P' =$ MSC. In this extreme case Pure Water pays $C + D$ to Bright Paint. For example, consider Bright Paint's alternatives as it decides whether to reduce output from five units to four units and then from four units to three units. When it reduces output from five units to four units, Bright Paint loses $14 from the lost sale but receives a check for $18 from Pure Water and does not incur the marginal production cost of $14. On

Table 19-2   THE EFFECTS OF THE ASSIGNMENT OF PROPERTY RIGHTS

VARIABLE	Assignment of Property Rights to:		
	NO ONE (1)	BRIGHT PAINT (2)	PURE WATER (3)
Output	q'	q^*	q^*
Value of damages	$B + C + D$	B	B
Payment by Pure Water	0	Between C and $C + D$	—
Payment by Bright Paint	0	—	B

balance it pays Bright Paint not to produce the fifth unit. Similarly, when Bright Paint reduces output from four units to three units, it loses $14 in revenue but receives a check worth $11 from Pure Water and it does not incur a marginal cost of $10. Bright Paint is clearly worse off by producing the fourth unit.

The central point of Coase's argument is that the quantity produced by Bright Paint is independent of the assignment of property rights when transaction costs are negligible. The output produced by Bright Paint will be the same. This does not mean that the assignment of property rights is an idle issue. The assignment of property rights does have distributional consequences. Clearly, Bright Paint is better off when it rather than Pure Water owns the property rights because Bright Paint receives checks from Pure Water. When Pure Water owns the property rights, Bright Paint sends a check to Pure Water. Either way, Bright Paint produces q^* units of paint.

Table 19-2 summarizes the solutions under different property right assignments. In column 1 no one owns property rights, and so Bright Paint produces q' units and total damages are equal to $B + C + D$. In column 2 Bright Paint owns the property rights and produces only q^*. Payments by Pure Water are somewhere between C and $C + D$ depending on the bargaining strengths or negotiating capabilities of the two parties. The monetary value of the damages is area B. In column 3 Pure Water owns the property right to clean water. Bright Paint produces q^* and pays Pure Water area B for the damages sustained.

Transaction Costs

This discussion of the externality problem is somewhat artificial because it sweeps aside the cost of negotiating and enforcing agreements among the parties. The magnitude of transaction costs will vary from one situation to another and presumably will increase as the number of parties who must agree increases. Anyone who has worked in small and large groups recognizes that the cost of negotiating an agreement increases with the number of members in the group.

Negotiation costs can be considerable even when there are only a few parties involved. Let's consider a firm that would like to renew an area by buying out several dilapidated properties on a city block and building a large apartment complex. The developer must negotiate with a small number of independent owners. The total value of the city block will be higher with the development than without it. The question is: What price can each property in the development command? If you owned one of the properties in the middle of the block, you may be in a particularly envious position. The development cannot proceed unless you agree. You are willing to be bought out but at the highest feasible price. Your best strategy might be to wait until the developer acquires the other properties. Then, you can hold out for a higher price. Without your property it will be difficult but not impossible for the development to proceed. The cost of negotiating the deal can be considerable for the developer, and the hold-up problem is a potential stumbling block in the deal.

Let's see how the assignment of property rights makes a difference when transaction costs are large. Instead of assuming Pure Water is the only downstream firm, let's assume there are other downstream firms. Perhaps, there is a soft drink manufacturer, a beer manufacturer, and several food processors located downstream. Now, the production of paint harms all users but in varying degrees. If Bright Paint owns property rights in water quality, the other firms must get together and haggle over how much to pay Bright Paint Co. and determine the contribution of each downstream firm. The negotiations among the downstream firms can be lengthy and frustrating because of legitimate differences of opinion about the size of the damage costs and strategic bargaining among the parties. There is apt to be a free rider problem. Each downstream firm wants the others to incur the negotiating costs.

We assume the transaction costs of getting together and agreeing are higher for the downstream firms. Now let's reconsider options 2 and 3, repeated here:

- *Option 2.* Clean the water before it is released so the quality of water is not degraded.
- *Option 3.* Pay to have Pure Water and others invest in expensive filtering equipment to clean the discharges of Bright Paint or pay to have Pure Water and other firms relocate.

Which of the two options will the parties adopt? Let's assume that it is cheaper for Bright Paint to clean the water before discharging it into the river than for each of the downstream firms to clean the water separately. In Figure 19-5 MSC is the marginal social cost function described earlier when options 2 and 3 did not exist and where q^* is the initial optimal quantity. MSC_1 is the marginal clean-up cost of Bright Paint (option 2) and is less than MSC_2, the marginal cost of a clean-up by all the downstream firms at each rate of output (option 3). Therefore, the lower-cost solution is for Bright Paint to clean the water before discharging it into the river.

If transaction costs are higher for the downstream firms, then the assignment of property rights does affect the quantity of paint produced by Bright Paint.

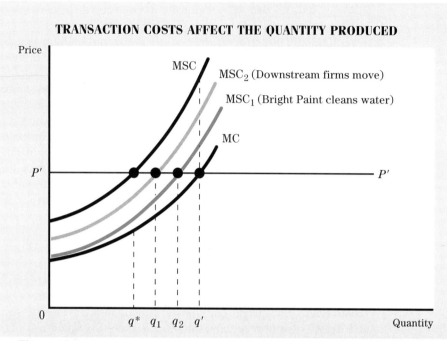

Figure 19-5   The marginal social cost is MSC_1 if Bright Paint cleans the water before discharge into the river. The marginal social cost is MSC_2 if the downstream firms move farther downstream or elsewhere. The lower-cost solution is for Bright Paint to clean the water and to produce q_2 units of paint. If the property rights are given to Bright Paint and transaction costs are higher for the downstream firms, then Bright Paint will produce q' units. Transaction costs affect the quantity of paint produced.

Suppose Bright Paint has the property rights. Consider the extreme case where the potential transaction costs for the downstream firms are so large that they do not even attempt to meet. Then, Bright Paint produces q' units because it owns the rights to water quality.

On the other hand, Bright Paint will produce q_2 units, the socially efficient output given the different clean up costs, if the downstream plants have property rights to clean water. The low-cost solution has Bright Paint cleaning the waste-water before discharge into the river rather than paying damages to each down-stream firm.

This example shows why the initial assignment of property rights is critical when transaction costs are significant. When Bright Paint owns the property rights, the high transaction costs prevent the downstream firms from meeting and bribing Bright Paint to clean the water, the efficient solution. If the downstream firms own the property right, then Bright Paint produces the socially optimal output. An improper assignment of property rights leads to a higher cost and to a socially inferior solution.

Neighborhoods for Sale

Living next to a refinery can be a trying experience. The odors are hardly pleasant, and the health consequences are unknown. Refineries and nearby residences are becoming increasingly strange bedfellows.

In Port Arthur, Texas, one oil company, Fina Inc., has agreed to buy out a neighborhood so that the residents can leave.[2] Fina's Port Arthur refinery is at the forefront of technology, and so it is not as if the refinery is emitting sulfur dioxide on a daily basis. Nevertheless, the patience of nearby residents is wearing thin with each confrontation between their representatives and the refinery. Residents are demanding plant inspections whenever they detect real or imagined odors, confronting company executives, petitioning the city council, and persuading state regulators to threaten to close the refinery after neighbors reported leaks of sulfur dioxide and hydrogen sulfide, two dangerous gases.

What Fina decided to do, after publicly stating it would not, is to create a buffer zone, a greenbelt. Fina plans on purchasing the 211 residences. It could cost over $10 million, but after the purchase no one will be left to protest pollution.

In this case the property rights are somewhat fuzzy. However, the residents appear to have effectively organized so that regulators listen to them with sympathetic ears. In this uncomfortable situation Fina Inc. has the option of closing down, introducing still more expensive controls to prevent additional leaks, or buying out the neighborhood. It appears that Fina Inc. is convinced that the low-cost solution is to buy out the neighborhood.

If Fina Inc. possesses the property right to pollute, it is unlikely that the residents will be capable of organizing and bargaining at low cost to buy out the refinery. Although some of them have demonstrated remarkable skill in organizing and bringing considerable political pressure on Fina, it is likely that the transaction costs of negotiating an agreement among 211 independent parties would be extremely high. Therefore, the efficient solution may well be for the property rights to be assigned to the residences in the neighborhood and for Fina to buy out the neighborhood rather than close the refinery or to reduce the probability of a leak by introducing more costly equipment.

Situations similar to this one exist in other industries. Airport noise is another typical illustration of external effects. Airports purchase nearby residences to minimize the consequence of external noise or airlines pay the costs of soundproofing. Here again, this appears to be a lower-cost solution than closing the airport or modifying or replacing airplane engines. The residents own certain but not all property rights. The airlines are liable for the reduced market value of nearby houses. If the cost of noise abatement is cheaper than the cost of the noise to the nearby residents, then the airlines will voluntarily reduce airplane noise by install-

---

[2] Based on Caleb Solomon, "How a Neighborhood Talked Fina Refinery into Buying It Out," *Wall Street Journal*, December 10, 1991.

ing quieter engines. If the cost of abatement is relatively high, then the airline will pay to soundproof the nearby residences. Here again, there could be a significant holdout problem since the airline must get the approval of all nearby residents to continue with its flight pattern.

APPLICATION 19-3

View Wars and Defining Property Rights

Along the Pacific coast, neighbors are going to war over who owns the property rights to a view.[3] Some neighbors have even taken the law into their own hands and have damaged or poisoned their neighbor's trees.

Here are some illustrations of view wars. A neighbor asked Catherine Armstrong if he could cut her tree so that he would have a better view of the Olympic Mountains. She ignored him. A few months later Armstrong heard a chain saw and when she rushed out of the house she saw a tree trimmer in her fifty-year-old fir cutting away. When she asked the trimmer what he was doing, he said the owner of the property had given permission to cut down the tree. Armstrong made it abundantly clear that she was the owner and that she had given no such permission. She ordered the trimmer off the property immediately.

In another case the Arnolds had a beautiful view of the cliffs, ocean, and Catalina Island. Over time two eucalyptus trees on the McNabb property grew taller and taller until they interfered with the Arnolds' view. The Arnolds asked the McNabbs to trim the trees, but the McNabbs refused to do so. The Arnolds then tried unsuccessfully to cut the trees. The McNabbs then obtained an injunction prohibiting the Arnolds from cutting the trees. Later the town of Rolling Hills passed a view law and the McNabbs reluctantly trimmed their trees.

Some towns and cities are passing view laws, which can reduce negotiation costs. In such cases, the cost of negotiating agreements is likely to be high so that the assignment of property rights is likely to make a difference.

Take the McNabb case. Before passage of the view law, the McNabbs valued their trees more than the Arnolds did. We infer this because the Arnolds did not pay the McNabbs enough to have the McNabbs trim the trees voluntarily. The view law passed the property rights from the McNabbs to the Arnolds. If transaction costs were low, the Coasian solution would have the McNabbs agree to pay the Arnolds to waive their right to the view. Both would be better off after the payment. Yet, this did not happen. The McNabbs reluctantly trimmed their trees. Here, we can infer that the transaction costs of negotiating between hostile neighbors were great and so the solution changed from no tree trimming to tree trimming when the view law reassigned the property rights.

[3] Based on Kathleen A. Hughes, "Neighbors Seeking to Better Their Lot Are Often up a Tree," *Wall Street Journal*, April 15, 1992.

The externality problem becomes increasingly intractable when the ownership of the rights is unclear. When property rights are fuzzy, the cost of negotiating a bargain increases substantially because no one knows what is to be transacted. If no one owns the rights, everyone owns the rights. So, a transaction with one party does not transfer the rights since others can claim that they own the rights. Without clearly defined property rights it is next to impossible to reach the low-cost solution.

APPLICATION **19-4**

Saving the African Elephant

The tusks and hide of an elephant are very valuable. In recent years an average tusk has been valued at $2,000 and the hide could be worth this much or more. Because they are so valuable, profit-maximizing poachers have been killing African elephants at an alarming rate. The elephant population in Central and East Africa dropped from 1,044,050 to 429,520 between 1979 and 1989. Because of this slaughter, some have called for a total worldwide ban on the ivory trade.

What are the possible causes of the predicament of the African elephant? We can learn much from a study by researchers Randy Simmons and Urs Kreuter of the different policies of African governments.[4] In Kenya the government is dedicated to ending the trading of ivory and for more than a decade has banned the hunting of elephant. Yet, Kenya's elephant population has fallen from 65,000 in 1979 to 19,000 in 1989. Clearly, declaring a ban on hunting has produced disastrous results, and poaching is common.

On the other hand, in Zimbabwe the selling of ivory is legal but controlled and ivory is readily available in shops. Zimbabwe's elephant population increased from 30,000 to 43,000 between 1979 to 1989. Why are the trends in elephant population so different in the two countries? In Zimbabwe elephants are culled from the herds and the proceeds from the sale of tusks and hides are returned to the game parks and used in part to prevent poaching. Even more important, native villages earn more than $5 million by selling elephant hunting rights on their common lands to safari operators. The government of Zimbabwe discovered the best way to protect the elephant was to give the villagers property rights to the elephants.

When the peasants do not own the property rights to the animals, they have an incentive to kill elephants and other wild animals because wild animals compete for the use of the land. Elephants and other wild animals destroy crops, kill domestic animals, and drink valuable water. In Zimbabwe poachers are shot on sight. The government spends over $500 per square mile protecting the wildlife on state-owned land and sells the rights to hunting and photographing for handsome prices. On communal lands peasants have the right to hunt a certain number of elephants

---

[4] Based on Randy T. Simmons and Urs P. Kreuter, "Herd Mentality, Banning Ivory Sales Is No Way to Save the Elephant," *Policy Review*, Fall 1989, pp. 46–49.

per year and they often sell these rights to safari operators. The villagers have a property right to the elephants and therefore they protect them. In one situation villagers near a national park gave up some land in return for hunting permits that the village sells to safari operators. The village used the proceeds to improve community facilities and distributed some of the proceeds to the villagers.

The different policies of African governments illustrate the consequences of establishing property rights to a common resource that would otherwise not be owned by anyone. Where property rights did not exist, the size of the elephant herds decreased; because the government did not create any property rights, poachers had every incentive to kill elephants since they did not own the future property rights to the resource. In Zimbabwe the government established a property rights system that created funds to protect the elephants and provided incentives for villagers to protect the elephants.

Taxation and Pareto Efficiency

Now that you know that the assignment of property rights can affect the equilibrium outcome when transaction costs are large, let's examine a potential pitfall from using per unit taxes to solve the externality problem. Suppose that society adopts the principle that a per unit tax is assessed on the party causing the externality. What are the possible repercussions of this taxation principle?

While this proposal sounds attractive, it has several drawbacks. The first point to note is that it is not always easy to determine who is responsible for the externality. Suppose that Bright Paint began production first, perhaps on a small scale, and expanded output later. In the meantime Pure Water and others established facilities downstream. Who is the damaged party? Is Bright Paint the damaged party after Pure Water and the others established their facilities downstream? In the example of the Fina refinery the company originally built the refinery on an isolated parcel of land. Later, individuals built suburban residences nearby. Who is the damaged party? There is a reciprocal nature to damages in most cases. Consequently, it is often difficult to identify the damaged party.

The second point is more important. A per unit tax can prevent the low-cost solution from being implemented. Let's return to the earlier example but assume that the *higher* cost solution occurs when Bright Paint cleans the water before discharge. In Figure 19-6 MSC_1 is the relevant marginal cost if Bright Paint introduces the filtering equipment and cleans the water before discharge. MSC_2 is the social marginal cost if the downstream firms move farther downstream or elsewhere, and so the lower-cost solution is for the downstream firms to move. What are the consequences if the local government assesses a tax so that Bright Paint must pay a per unit tax equal to the marginal damage cost at the former social optimum because the government does not consider option 2 or 3? In Figure 19-6 the per unit tax is equal to the difference between MSC and MC when Bright Paint produces q^* units.

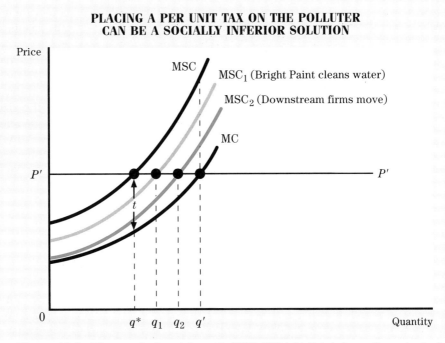

Figure 19-6   The marginal social cost is MSC_1 if Bright Paint cleans the water before discharge into the river. The social marginal cost is MSC_2 if the downstream firms move farther downstream or elsewhere. The lower-cost solution is for the downstream firms to move. If a per unit tax is imposed on Bright Paint for any damages, it will clean the dirty water before discharge and produce q_1 units, a socially inferior solution. Applying the principle that the firm that causes the problem should pay a per unit tax will not always result in the lower-cost solution being adopted. The lower-cost solution is not to tax Bright Paint but for Bright Paint to pay for relocation costs (and other costs) of the downstream firms.

Look at the problem that Bright Paint faces. If it continues production and pays the tax, its marginal cost becomes MSC and it will produce q^* units. However, it prefers the lower-cost solution of cleaning the water before discharge to paying the tax. Therefore, it voluntarily incurs the filter and other costs and produces q_1 units where $P' = MSC_1$. The lowest-cost solution is for the downstream firms to move elsewhere and for Bright Paint to pay for the relocation costs. If the downstream firms move, Bright Paint would equate P' to MSC_2 and produce q_2 units, the socially desirable quantity. However, Bright Paint will not adopt this solution because it would still have to pay a per unit tax since the tax is assessed on discharges of dirty water. In this case imposing a per unit tax on the firm discharging degraded water prevents the lower-cost relocation solution from being adopted.

19-3 PUBLIC GOODS AND PARETO EFFICIENCY

Public goods have special characteristics, and it is these characteristics that create an impediment to achieving Pareto efficiency. A public good exists when the consumption of a good by an individual does not preclude the simultaneous consumption of the good by another. In a real sense the consumption of the good is nonrivalrous. With a public good an external effect is inevitable because the good is nonexcludable. In contrast, private goods are those goods whose consumption by one consumer prevents consumption by another. The consumption of a private good is rivalrous and excludable.

Let's consider some examples. If you purchase a new car or new shoes, no other individual can drive your new car or wear your shoes simultaneously. When you receive utility from wearing your shoes, someone else does not receive more utility simultaneously. Now consider the classic example of a public good, national defense. Suppose the citizens of a country build a sophisticated national defense system with elaborate radar and missile defenses. Such a defense system has two features. The services are nonrivalrous and nonexcludable. The fact that I receive benefits from national defense does not preclude other citizens from receiving the same benefits. All citizens consume the benefits of the system simultaneously. Therefore, the services are nonrivalrous. Second, the services are nonexcludable because the defense against an incoming missile benefits one and all. To take another example, all farmers in an area benefit from a cloud-seeding program. Cloud-seeding is a public good for the farmers because it is nonrivalrous and nonexcludable.

> The services of a public good are nonrivalrous and nonexcludable.

Some goods are nonrivalrous but are excludable. A television signal has some characteristics of a public good. My consumption does not preclude others from receiving the signal. Yet, cable systems are able to exclude those who do not pay for their service. Here, the service is nonrivalrous but excludable.

Many but not all the goods supplied by governments have the characteristics of a public good. Governments provide police and fire protection, public gardens, programs for mosquito elimination, tuberculosis screening and treatment, and other public health services. These programs are typically nonrivalrous at least to some degree. If I receive police protection, so does my neighbor. A mosquito prevention program simultaneously benefits many inhabitants. Consumption is nonrivalrous and nonexcludable. Because of this nonexcludability property, there is an inescapable free rider problem in the delivery of public goods. Each prefers that someone else pay for a pure public good while everyone experiences the benefits from it.

Our discussion of a public good assumes that the good is nonrivalrous and nonexcludable. These features require a modification of the condition for Pareto efficiency in product mix. Let's assume that consumers A and B have separate demand functions for Y, a private good supplied by a competitive market, and for X, a pure public good. Because X is a pure public good, a unit decrease in X decreases the utility of both consumers since X is nonrivalrous. For example, suppose that the economy can produce five more units of Y by producing one less unit of the public good, and so MRT $= -5$. Assume that consumer A remains indifferent by consuming one more unit of Y for one less unit of X and that consumer B remains indifferent by consuming two more units of Y for one less unit of X. Collectively, consumers A and B require just three more units of Y for one less unit of X for each to be indifferent. However, the economy can produce five more units of Y by producing one less unit of the public good. Therefore, we can say that the utility of at least one consumer will increase if the economy produces one less unit of the public good. Therefore, the product mix is not Pareto-efficient. If there is a public good, Pareto efficiency in product mix requires

$$\Sigma MRS = MRT \qquad \text{(Pareto Efficiency in Product Mix with a Public Good)} \quad \textbf{(19-3)}$$

With a public good the marginal rates of substitution are summed for all consumers in the economy because consumption is nonrivalrous and the sum is equated to the marginal rate of transformation.

The Optimal Quantity of a Public Good

The special characteristics of a public good raise two questions: What is the optimal quantity of a pure public good, and how will the public good be financed? To answer the first question, we must derive the demand function for a public good. What is the willingness to pay by members of society for each quantity of the public good? Then, we must consider the marginal cost function of providing the public good. Chapter 3 derived the marginal willingness to pay function of each consumer for different quantities of a good. These functions are the individual demand functions of consumers and have negative slopes reflecting the decreasing amounts a consumer is willing to pay for additional units of a good. Each consumer has a marginal willingness to pay function for a public good that shows how much he or she is willing to pay for successive units of a public good. Because consumer tastes and incomes differ, so too will the positions of their marginal willingness to pay functions. Figure 19-7 shows the inverse demand functions of consumer 1 (D_1) and of consumer 2 (D_2) where consumer 1 is willing to pay a higher price for each quantity of the public good than consumer 2 is.

If this were just an ordinary private good, the kind of good discussed in Chapters 2 and 3, we would simply sum the demand functions horizontally to derive the market demand function. In the case of a pure public good we have to proceed more cautiously because a public good is nonrivalrous.

To derive a function that shows the total value for different quantities of the public good, we must find the total value that consumers are willing to pay for another unit of the public good. Because each demander consumes the same quantity of the good simultaneously, the inverse demand functions of both consumers must be summed vertically for each quantity of the public good to find out what society is willing to pay. The summation is vertical because both individuals can consume the public good simultaneously. Figure 19-7 shows the vertical sum for ΣD. For example, let's consider the quantity X' in Figure 19-7. Consumer 1 will

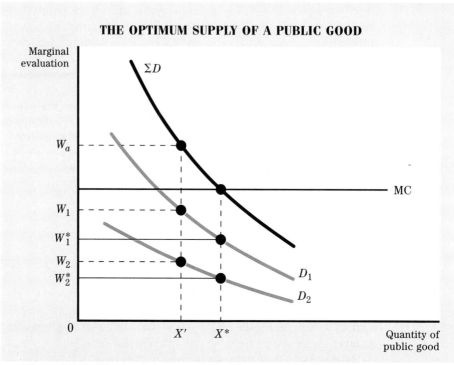

Figure 19-7   The vertical summation of the marginal willingness to pay functions for consumers 1 and 2 (D_1 and D_2) determines the community's inverse demand function for different amounts of a public good. The optimal provision of a public good is X^* where the community's demand function intersects the marginal cost of providing the public good.

pay W_1 and consumer 2 will pay W_2 for the X'th unit. The maximum amount that both consumers are willing to pay for the X'th unit is W_a on the function labeled ΣD. The ΣD function shows the maximum amount that both consumers will pay for each quantity of the public good.

In Figure 19-7 the marginal cost of supplying the public good is MC. The optimal quantity of the public good is X^* units where ΣD intersects the marginal cost function. The sum of consumer and producer surplus is maximized if the quantity of the public good is X^* units. Consumer 1 is willing to pay W_1^*, and consumer 2 is willing to pay W_2^*, so that $W_1^* + W_2^* = \text{MC}$.

Financing a Public Good

While it is comparatively easy to find the optimal quantity of the public good once the demand for and the marginal cost of providing a public good are known, it is less clear how to finance a public good. Consider a city that is thinking of providing a public park. How large should the park be? To determine the optimum size of the park, the city needs to know the marginal willingness to pay function of all potential users. To find the demand function for the park, the local government could simply ask each resident how much each would be willing to pay for parks of different sizes. The trouble with this approach is that everyone has an incentive to underestimate the value of the park and in this way hopes to free-ride on the contributions of others. If individuals expect that the amount they will have to contribute to finance the park depends on their stated valuation of the benefits, then each will understate the benefits. Sometimes municipalities conduct elaborate surveys to estimate the value of a public good to potential consumers. If consumers believe that the results of the survey will not affect the contributions of each one, it may be possible to obtain truthful answers. There still remains the basic question of whether most consumers can even give an accurate answer about frequency and type of use of a pure public good except based on experience. Therefore, the accuracy of estimates based on survey techniques is an open question.

Could we turn over the responsibility of providing a pure public good to the private market? The inability to exclude demanders makes it difficult, if not impossible, for private firms to provide the optimum quantity of a pure public good. Each demander avoids paying while hoping others will contribute to the provision of a public good. The free rider problem is a serious one for a pure public good, and this is probably the most important reason why governments supply these goods.

If a competitive market existed to supply a public good, each firm would have to find a way of requiring payment by consumers. Each firm or firms in the market would have to charge different prices for the same quantity of the public good. Consumer 1 would be required to pay a higher price than consumer 2 because of the different marginal valuations. If one firm incurs the cost of finding out what each one should pay, another competitive firm could copy the pricing policy and not incur the cost of finding out. So, a free rider problem of another form would appear. If a single firm receives a license to supply the public good and has information about the marginal willingness to pay functions, it will behave as a price-discriminating monopolist and charge different prices. The main defect in this solution is that a price-discriminating monopolist would raise prices and equate aggregate marginal revenue to marginal cost and produce less than the socially optimal quantity of the public good.

Because of these difficulties, public goods are likely to be undersupplied compared to private goods when produced in competitive markets.[5] A private market is unlikely to provide the optimal scale of a pure public good. It is for this reason that governments supply public goods and often use general tax receipts to finance such projects. When the government finances the public good out of general tax funds, the revelation problem may be less severe because the revelation of the

---

[5] For an extensive discussion of the role of government in supplying public goods, the reader is referred to Joseph E. Stiglitz, *Economics of the Public Sector*, W.W. Norton, 1988.

marginal willingness to pay is unrelated to the financing of the public good. Consequently, the government may be the preferred supplier since it can secure more accurate information about the willingness to pay than a private firm can.

SUMMARY

- Departures from Pareto efficiency can occur if a monopoly exists in a product market, if significant third-party effects exist, and if the market supplies public goods.
- Private markets can resolve the externality problem when transaction costs are negligible and property rights exist.
- Firms will produce the optimal social output independent of the assignment of property rights if transaction costs are negligible. When transaction costs are significant, a market system may not produce the socially preferred output.
- Pure public goods are nonrivalrous and nonexcludable. Private markets are unlikely to provide the optimal quantity of a pure public good.

KEY TERMS

Relative prices and relative
    marginal costs with monopoly in
    a product market
Positive and negative externalities
Marginal social cost
Internalizing an externality
Transaction cost
Public good

Pareto efficiency with a public good
Product mix inefficiency of
    monopoly
Marginal damage cost
Social surplus
The Coase theorem
Defining property rights
Nonrivalrous and nonexcludable

REVIEW QUESTIONS

1. List some impediments to Pareto efficiency. Explain how each one affects the Pareto efficiency conditions.
2. If a regulated natural monopoly produces an output where $P = AC_L$, so profits are zero, will the economy be Pareto-efficient in product mix? Explain.
3. Draw a diagram showing when it is Pareto-efficient for Bright Paint not to produce any output. What is the lowest per unit tax that will induce Bright Paint not to produce any output?
4. A familiar saying is, "Everyone's property is no one's property." What does this mean?
5. At the Graduate School of Business a joint student-faculty committee works on a wide range of problems and recommends policies for the school to adopt and that affect all MBAs. How would you describe the policy of the GSB? Is it a private or a public good? What problems might appear if it is a public good?

6. In the accompanying figure there are four consumer demand functions for good X. Draw a graph and indicate what the market demand function is if X is (*a*) a private good and (*b*) a public good.

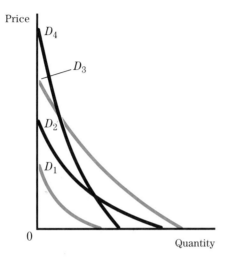

7. Is the temperature in a house a private or a public good? Explain your answer.
8. Show the optimal quantity of a pure public good when marginal cost increases with the quantity produced.
9. Every citizen should pay some amount to maintain a program of flu vaccination. Every citizen should pay some amount to keep the Public Broadcasting System operating. Do you agree or disagree with both these statements?

EXERCISES

1. The social cost of monopoly occurs because the monopolist does not produce at the minimum point of its long-run average cost function. Carefully describe the social objections to monopoly.
2. Assume that a monopolist has constant long-run average and marginal cost functions. Suppose that it can engage in perfect price discrimination and therefore leaves no consumer surplus. With the aid of a graph show the output of a monopolist. Are Pareto efficiency conditions satisfied?
3. When there is a positive externality, the marginal cost function of firm A shifts downward when the output of firm B increases. What is the appropriate per unit subsidy to offer firm B when there is a positive externality?
4. This question applies to Table 19-1. Suppose that Bright Paint has an unencumbered right to pollute with up to five units of paint. What is the maximum amount Pure Water is willing to pay Bright Paint if Bright Paint produces the socially optimal output?

5. This question applies to Table 19-1. Suppose that Pure Water is willing to pay Bright Paint $7 for each unit not produced by Bright Paint. What output will Bright Paint produce?

6. Propose a market experiment that would tell you whether transaction costs are small or large. (*Hint:* Think of the consequences of assigning property rights.)

7. Suppose the social marginal cost, MSC_1, is less if Bright Paint cleans the water before discharge than if the downstream firms move farther downstream. Under this condition is it at all necessary to impose a per unit tax to reach the social optimum output for Bright Paint?

SUGGESTED ANSWERS TO SELECTED EXERCISES AND PROBLEM SETS

Chapter 1

1. Knowing the position of the demand function tells you nothing about the incidence of a shortage. To determine whether a shortage exists, you would have to know the position of the supply function and the market price.

2.   a. Let the initial price be P_1. The price after the increase is $P_2 = 1.75P_1$. Q_1 is initial quantity demanded, and Q_2 is quantity demanded after price increases. Total revenue is $R_1 = P_1Q_1$ before price increases, and $R_2 = 1.52R_1$. Substituting $R_2 = P_2Q_2$ and $R_1 = P_1Q_1$ into $R_2 = 1.52R_1$ yields

$$\frac{Q_2}{Q_1} = 1.52\frac{P_1}{P_2} = \frac{1.52}{1.75} = 0.869$$

Therefore, quantity decreased by 13.1 percent.

   b. The expression for the price elasticity is

$$E_P = \frac{\Delta Q}{\Delta P}\frac{P_1 + P_2}{Q_1 + Q_2}$$

Substituting the respective expressions, we have

$$E_P = \frac{0.869Q_1 - Q_1}{1.75P_1 - P_1}\frac{P_1 + 1.75P_1}{Q_1 + 0.869Q_1}$$

$$= \frac{-0.131Q_1}{0.75P_1}\frac{2.75P_1}{1.869Q_1} = -0.257$$

Therefore, demand is price-inelastic since E_P is between -1 and zero. Revenue is higher at the higher price.

4. This statement does not distinguish between a movement along a supply function and a shift in the supply function. Imposing a tax on the product shifts the supply function upward. For any Q, suppliers are now willing to supply the same quantity only if the price is higher

by the per unit tax. The supply function becomes $S'S'$ after the tax is levied. Because the supply function shifts upward and to the left, the equilibrium price increases to P_2 and the equilibrium quantity decreases to Q_2. See the accompanying figure.

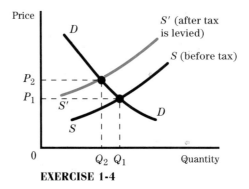

EXERCISE 1-4

Chapter 2

1. A fall in the price of beef relative to the price of fish makes the budget line flatter. You consume just a few more pounds of beef and more pounds of fish. See the accompanying figure.

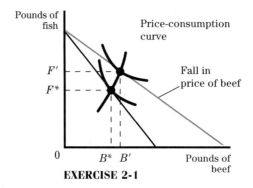

EXERCISE 2-1

2.   a. To calculate the price elasticity, the price of X must change while income and other prices are constant. Income and the price of Y are constant between 1988 and 1989, while the price of X decreases from \$110 to \$90. Arc price elasticity is $E_P = -(10/20)(200/190) = -0.53$, and so demand is price-inelastic.

  b. If all prices and income are constant, a quantity change would have to be due to a taste change. Prices and income are constant in 1987 and 1990, but quantity demanded of X increases from 80 to 100 units.

  c. Consider the years 1988 and 1989. The price of X decreases, but the price of Y and income are constant. You can determine what happens to quantity demanded of Y.

  d. There is no year where the price of Y changes and the price of X, income, and the consumer's tastes all remain constant.

3. The demand for X will be zero if $-P_X/P_Y < $ MRS when $X = 0$. The consumer purchases only Y. It becomes positive when the price of X falls. The inequality is reversed when the

consumer purchases only X. The budget constraint then becomes $P_X X = I$, and so the demand function is $X = I/P_X$. The demand function for X is shown in the accompanying figure.

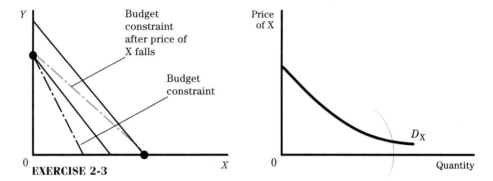

EXERCISE 2-3

4. The consumer purchases Y and X in fixed proportions. Let's say that he selects Y, and so $Y = hX$; that is, for each unit of X, $Y = hX$ units of Y are consumed, where h is a constant. Therefore, the budget constraint of the consumer becomes $P_X X + P_Y hX = I$, and the demand for X can be expressed as $X = I/(P_X + P_Y h)$.

6.   a. The two goods in the utility function are spending on other goods (S) and days of leisure (L). The budget constraint is $S = D(365 - L)$, where D is the daily wage. As days of leisure increase to 365, income and spending on other goods decrease. The budget constraint of the consumer is line aa in the accompanying figure. In the initial equilibrium the consumer works 210 days and has 155 days of leisure.

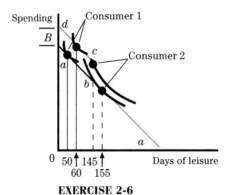

EXERCISE 2-6

b. Under the bonus system the worker qualifies for the bonus if workdays equal or exceed 220 days, and so leisure equals 145 or fewer days. The budget constraint becomes *abcd* with the bonus system.

c. Without the bonus, consumer 1 is a workaholic and consumes only 50 days of leisure. With the bonus, days of leisure increase to 60. So a flat bonus increases leisure. For consumer 2 days of leisure decrease from 155 to 145. The bonus system has both incentive and disincentive work effects.

d. In the two situations, days of leisure change in opposite directions, and so you cannot predict that the average days of work will rise to 220.

8. The utility function of a family depends on spending on other goods (S) and spending on education (E). Assume that all families in each district are alike but that families differ across districts. If a family spends over $100 for education, the district receives a lump sum of $50 per child.

a. Currently, each family spends $500 per child on education. The budget constraint of the family is *abcd* and becomes *abefg* under lump sum grant 1. Given spending on other goods, the family can now spend $50 more on education because of the state grant. See the accompanying figure.

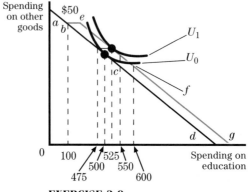

EXERCISE 2-8

b. Under lump sum grant 1 the family cuts back on private spending on education to $475, and so total spending increases to $525 with the state grant. Therefore, a lump sum subsidy induces the family to spend more on other goods. Consequently, total spending on education does not rise by $50. Draw the indifference curves for a family in a different district that is currently spending less than $100 per child and show how the subsidy will either not affect family spending or increase family spending to $150. In this case total spending on education will increase by more than $50. Therefore, you cannot tell whether spending per child will increase on average by $50 because of the state subsidy.

Using a similar analysis, you should be able to analyze the effects of lump sum grant 2 and answer Exercise 8c.

Chapter 3

1. The first experiment indicates that X is a superior good. Therefore, the consumer's demand function should slope downward to the right. Yet, the second experiment indicates that the consumer's demand function has a positive slope. Therefore, the model of consumer behavior cannot explain this behavior.

3. The equation for the slope of a consumer's demand function is

$$\frac{\Delta X}{\Delta P} = \frac{\Delta X}{\Delta P}\bigg|_{U=c} - X\frac{\Delta X}{\Delta I}$$

Since the slope of the demand function is -1.2, $X = 3$, and $\Delta X/\Delta I = 5$, this implies that $\Delta X/\Delta P|_{U=c}$ is 13.8. This is impossible because the substitution effect is always negative.

5. If the substitution effect of the two consumers is the same, the income effect is larger for the wealthy consumer and the wealthier individual's demand function is more elastic.

7.   a. Since the expected wealth of the two occupations is virtually the same, a risk-neutral individual will be indifferent.
   b. The expected utility of the first occupation is

$$EU_1 = 0.6U(W^* + \$133{,}000) + 0.4U(W^* - \$50{,}000)$$

$$EU = 0.5U(W^* + \$180{,}000) + 0.5U(W^* - \$20{,}000)$$

   c. An individual who selects occupation 1 is risk-averse.

Chapter 4

3. The slope of the full price budget constraint equals

$$-\frac{P_X + wt_X}{P_Y + wt_Y}$$

Assume that $P_Y = 0$ for leisure and $t_Y = 1$, and so the full price budget constraint becomes

$$Y = \frac{wT + V}{w} - \frac{P_X + wt_X}{w}X$$

Then, t_Y/P_Y is larger for leisure than for good X. A rise in w increases the full price of leisure by more than the full price of X. So, the full price budget constraint becomes flatter as it shifts outward and the consumer substitutes toward good X.

4. Solving the time constraint for T_w gives

$$T_w = T - C_X - t_X X - t_Y Y$$

Substituting T_w into the budget constraint and collecting terms yields

$$Y = \frac{wT + V - wC_X}{P_Y + wt_Y} - \frac{P_X + wt_X}{P_Y + wt_Y}X$$

when $X > 0$. If $X = 0$, then the consumer can purchase

$$Y = \frac{wT + V}{P_Y + wt_Y}$$

units of Y because she does not incur C_X unless she purchases X. If the consumer buys only X, she can purchase only

$$X = \frac{wT + V - wC_X}{P_X + wt_X}$$

units of X. The number of units of X is equal to full income less the cost of traveling to the store, C_X, divided by the full price of X. The slope of the budget constraint still equals the ratio of the two full prices. The accompanying figure shows the full price budget constraint.

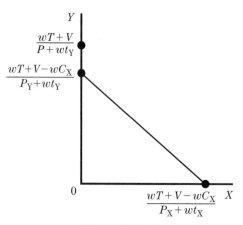

EXERCISE 4-4

5. Because the cost of time of shoppers has increased by relatively more for females, manufacturers are introducing more branded goods that help consumers economize on shopping time. If information supplied by manufacturers through branding is a substitute for information obtained from salespeople, then consumers will demand less information at stores and will purchase from discount and other stores that offer brand names but less service and avoid higher-service department stores.

Chapter 5

2. To determine which factor increases and which decreases, calculate the ratio of the marginal physical product to the price of a factor. For factor A we have 40/$20 = 2 units per dollar, and for factor B we have 60/$300 = 0.2 units per dollar. The last dollar spent on factor A produces more output. Therefore, the firm should hire more units of factor A and fewer units of factor B.

3. Two expansion paths cannot cross. Let the expansion path be ee when the wage is w and let the other expansion path be $e'e'$ when the wage is w'. Because of the difference in wage rates, the slopes of the two isocost functions differ. When the two expansion paths cross, the slope of the isoquant is the same; however, the slopes of the two isocost functions are different at that point. Therefore, the expansion paths of a firm that minimize the cost of producing each rate of output will not cross. See the accompanying figure.

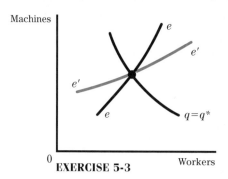

EXERCISE 5-3

4. The marginal rate of technical substitution $\Delta T/\Delta F = -\frac{1}{20}$. The isocost line is

$$T = \frac{C}{P_L} - \frac{\$175}{P_L}F$$

where P_L is the rental price of land, T is an acre of land, and F is a ton of fertilizer. It will be profitable to substitute fertilizer for land if the price of an acre is greater than

$$-\frac{1}{20} < -\frac{\$175}{P_L} \quad \text{or} \quad P_L > \$3,500$$

6. Given the prices of the two factors, the isocost line for a given total expenditure is aa' in the accompanying figure. The firm has 100 computers and 30 workers. When the company receives a subsidy of 10 percent for every extra computer that it purchases, the isocost line becomes steeper since the rental price of a computer falls relative to labor. The firm's isocost line becomes abc.

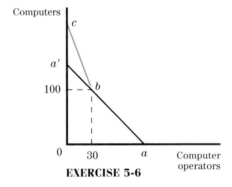

EXERCISE 5-6

Chapter 6

2. a. The completed table is:

$q_1 + q_2 = 9$	AVERAGE COST OF PLANT	SUM OF VARIABLE COST, $V_1 + V_2$	SUM OF TOTAL COST, $C_1 + C_2$
$q_1 = 4, q_2 = 5$	$AC_1 = 90, AC_2 = 15$	86	436
$q_1 = 3, q_2 = 6$	$AC_1 = 112, AC_2 = 16$	81	431
$q_1 = 2, q_2 = 7$	$AC_1 = 158, AC_2 = 20$	105	455

b. The sum of the averages is $AC_1 + AC_2$. Minimizing total cost requires that

$$q_1AC_1(q_1) + q_2AC_2(q_2) = F_1 + V_1(q_1) + F_2 + V_2(q_2)$$

be minimized.

3. a. The necessary condition for minimizing total cost is that marginal costs be the same at both plants. Plant 1 produces q_1^* and plant 2 produces q_2^*. See the accompanying figure.

b. Suppose plant 2 is closed by a strike. The firm must increase output at plant 1 to meet requirements. The increased cost incurred at plant 1 because production increases is the area under the marginal cost function of plant 1 from q_1^* to total requirements. The cost saving because plant 2 reduces production to zero represents the area under the marginal cost function of plant 2 from q_2^* to zero. The shaded area equals the cost increase.

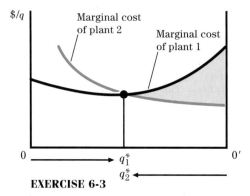

EXERCISE 6-3

5. There are two ways to satisfy the order. One way is to produce q_1 units in September and incur an inventory cost of h per unit. If one more unit is produced in September, the total marginal cost is $\Delta C(q_1)/\Delta q_1 + h$. Another way to satisfy the order is to produce q_2 units in October. If one more unit is produced in October, the marginal cost is $\Delta C(q_2)/\Delta q_2$. Minimizing total cost requires the marginal cost of production in September plus h to equal the marginal cost of production in October, or

$$\frac{\Delta C(q_2)}{\Delta q_2} + h = \frac{\Delta C(q_2)}{\Delta q_2}$$

The quantities to be produced in September and in October can be determined from the accompanying graph.

c. Since the cost function is the same for both months, equality of marginal production costs would require the same amount to be produced only if $h = 0$.

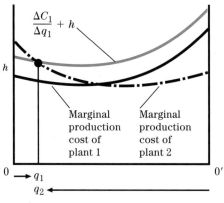

EXERCISE 6-5

d. An increase in h reduces the quantity produced in September and increases the quantity produced in October. The increase in h increases the total marginal cost of producing another unit in September but does not affect the total marginal cost of producing another unit in October.

6. First, short-run marginal cost does not go through the minimum point of the short-run average cost function. Second, average cost does not become infinite as q approaches zero. Finally, average variable cost does not reach a minimum at the quantity where the straight line from the origin is tangent to the variable cost function.

Chapter 7

1. The price elasticity of demand of a firm depends on its market share, the supply elasticity of other firms, and the price elasticity of market demand. In the short run other firms will increase the quantity supplied when the price increases, but not as much as in the long run when they can adjust all factors of production. The elasticity of supply measures the percentage increase in the quantity supplied for a given percentage increase in price. This means that the elasticity of supply of the other firms is larger in the long run than in the short run. As consumers learn of alternative sources of supply, the price elasticity of market demand becomes more elastic in the long run. Both factors will make the firm's demand function more elastic in the long run than in the short run.

3. Agree. In the long run the firm determines the quantity where price equals long-run marginal cost. A second-order condition for a profit maximum requires the long-run marginal cost to be increasing. In addition, a firm will produce in the long run only if $\pi \geq 0$.

7. While the farmer has incurred costs to raise the young calves, these costs are sunk. The farmer must look forward and decide if the price that will be received for the calves in the future exceeds the average variable cost incurred while fattening the calves. If the expected price is less than minimum average variable cost, the farmer will decide to shoot the young calves. This behavior is consistent with profit maximization if the price is less than minimum average variable cost.

Chapter 7 Problem Set: Should Your Company Honor a Contract?

1. Your three options are fulfill the original contract, don't fulfill the original contract or sign the new contract, and fulfull the new contract. The loss incurred from fulfilling the original contract is

$$L_1 = (P'' - b)q_c - F - T \quad \text{where } b > P''$$

2. If the firm does not fulfill either contract, its loss is

$$L_2 = -F - (P' - P'')q_c$$

The second term represents the penalty assessed because the original customer pays P' in the marketplace.

3. If the firm fulfills the new contract, the loss is

$$L_3 = -F - T + (P^* - b)q_c - (P' - P'')q_c$$

4. You will fulfill the new contract if the losses are smaller, or

$$L_3 > L_2$$

$$-F - T + (P^* - b)q_c - (P' - P'')q_c > -F - (P' - P'')q_c$$

$$-T - (P^* - b)q_c > 0$$

If you decide not to fulfill the original contract, then you should select option 3 if the franchise tax is less than the difference between total revenue and total variable cost. T and $(P^* - b)q_c$ are under your control and are determined by your decision. F, P', and P'' do not affect this decision, and F is a bygone. The penalty is incurred under option 2 or 3, and so it cannot affect the decision. If $L_3 > L_2$, then you will need to decide whether it is better to fulfill the original or the new contract.

5. You will fulfill the original contract if

$$L_1 > L_3$$

$$(P'' - b)q_c - F - T > -F - T + (P^* - b)q_c - (P' - P'')q_c$$

$$P' > P^*$$

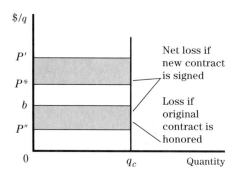

CHAPTER 7: PROBLEM SET

This condition will be satisfied because $P' > P^*$. See the accompanying figure. The firm will fulfill the original contract. Notice that F, T, and b have no bearing on this decision. F is a bygone, and you must pay T whether you fulfill the old or the new contract. Likewise, bq_c is irrelevant because you will incur these costs whether you fulfill the new or the old contract.

Chapter 8

3.   a. There are two facts to account for. First, why do the large and the small firms have the same per unit costs? Second, why do relatively more small firms drop out of the market when market demand decreases?

Assume that the supply functions of the two types of firms are different and that small firms are less efficient than large firms. The supply functions of all large and all small firms are shown in the accompanying figure. S_s is the supply function of small firms, and S_l is the supply function of large firms. Because there are external pecuniary diseconomies of scale, both types supply more units at higher prices. In recessions the price falls from P^* to P' and Q' units are supplied by large firms. No small firm is willing to supply any quantity at the low price of P'. When demand decreases, small firms drop out of the market. This would not be true if both supply functions had the same vertical intercept. When demand increases, the price increases to P^* and both small and large firms supply larger quantities.

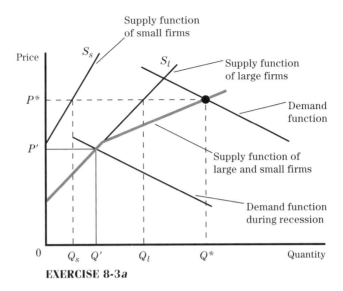

EXERCISE 8-3*a*

Although the supply functions of the two types of firms differ, both have the same average cost because the price of a scarce factor of production is bid up so that neither type of firm earns profits. An increase in the demand for the product increases the earnings of owners of the scarce factor.

b. If large firms supply 15 percent less at every price because of emission controls, then the supply function of large firms shifts to the left by 15 percent. The total supply function will also shift to the left but not by 15 percent because small firms are unaffected. Given the demand function, the leftward shift in the industry supply function increases the price to P'. See the accompanying figure, in which the price increases to P' and the quantity supplied by small firms increases from Q_s to Q_s'. The quantity supplied by large firms decreases from Q_l to Q_l'; however, the decrease is less than 15 percent. If the price did not change, large firms would decrease the quantity supplied by 15 percent. However, the price increases, and so large firms reduce the quantity supplied but by less than 15 percent.

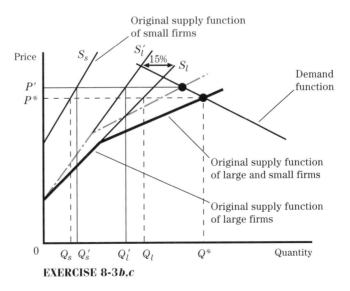

EXERCISE 8-3*b,c*

c. As the figure for Exercise 8-3*b,c* shows, small firms are willing to supply a larger quantity because the price increases. Therefore, total industry output cannot decrease by 15 percent.

11. There are two sources of supply in this problem, the domestic industry and the foreign source. Because there are external diseconomies of scale, the supply function of the domestic suppliers has a positive slope. Foreign suppliers are willing to provide an indefinite quantity at the price of P_w. The supply function of domestic and foreign producers is the heavy line in the accompanying figure. The equilibrium price is determined by the world price of P_w. At this price the domestic industry supplies Q_D and the difference between quantity demanded and Q_D is equal to imports, Q_I. See the accompanying figure.

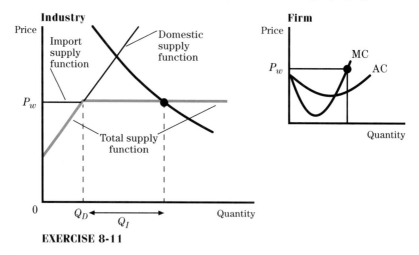

EXERCISE 8-11

12. a. The quantity of imports is reduced by 20 percent. No longer is the supply of imports perfectly elastic at the world price. Only 80 percent of the previous level of imports can enter the domestic economy, and once this occurs the only way to increase the quantity

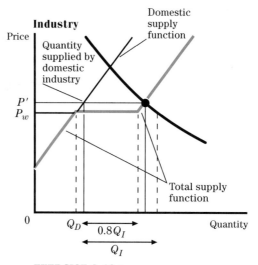

EXERCISE 8-12*a*

supplied is for the domestic industry to supply more. However, the domestic industry will supply more only if the price increases. The new total industry supply function is the heavy line in the accompanying figure. Because the equilibrium price increases from P_w to P', the quantity supplied by the domestic industry increases. Imposing an import constraint raises domestic prices, increases the earnings of the scarce factor of supply, and harms consumers.

b. The price elasticity of demand is -1, and the quantity is to be reduced by 20 percent. Let Q be the original quantity and P be the original price. Then, the new quantity will be $0.8Q$ and the new price will be $(1 + t)P$, where t is to be determined. Substituting these expressions into the formula for the arc elasticity yields

$$-1 = \frac{Q - 0.8Q}{P - (1 + t)P} \cdot \frac{P + (1 + t)P}{Q + 0.8Q}$$

$$= \frac{0.2Q}{-tP} \cdot \frac{(2 + t)P}{1.8Q} = \frac{0.2(2 + t)}{-1.8t}$$

Solving for t yields $t = 0.25$. The import duty must increase price by 25 percent for the total quantity consumed to decrease by 20 percent. See the accompanying figure.

c. Because the total quantity consumed decreases by 20 percent and the domestic price increases by 25 percent, the quantity supplied by the domestic industry increases. Therefore, the total quantity imported must decrease by more than 20 percent.

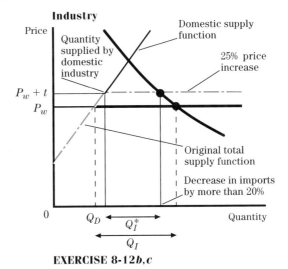

EXERCISE 8-12*b,c*

Chapter 9

3. Currently, the competitive price is P_c. The marginal cost of production of the new firm is lower and is $0.8P_c$ because of the invention. The question asks: What is the smallest value of the price elasticity of demand at the monopoly price at which the monopolist can set the price so that MR = MC?

If the monopoly price of the new firm is greater than P_c, it cannot sell any units at this price. On the other hand, the profit-maximizing monopoly price can be either equal to or less than P_c if the market demand function is sufficiently elastic. Marginal cost is $0.8P_c$, and marginal revenue is

$$MR = P\left(1 + \frac{1}{E}\right)$$

To find the required price elasticity where the monopoly price just equals P_c, we must have

$$MR = MC \qquad MC = 0.8P_c$$

$$MR = P_c\left(1 + \frac{1}{E_P}\right) \qquad P_c\left(1 + \frac{1}{E_P}\right) = 0.8P_c$$

Solve this equation for E_P to get $E_P = -5$. So, if the price elasticity is -5, marginal revenue is $0.8P_c$. The profit-maximizing monopoly price is 20 percent greater than the marginal cost of the monopolist. If the price elasticity is less than -5, say, -10, then the profit-maximizing price will be less than P_c and no competitive firm will produce at this price. See the accompanying figure.

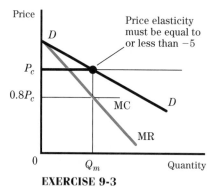

EXERCISE 9-3

4. If there are many firms in the domestic industry instead of just one, placing an import quota on the foreign firms will not affect the market price. While the shape of the supply function of the foreign firms changes when the quota is imposed, the demand function and the modified supply function still intersect at the competitive equilibrium price of P_I, and so the price does not change. The cost functions of a representative firm are shown in panel a in the accompanying figure. The supply function of the domestic and foreign suppliers is S_LabS_L before the quota is imposed. After the quota is imposed, the supply function of domestic and foreign producers becomes S_Labc. At P_I foreign suppliers will supply their quota equal to the distance ab. With a quota only domestic suppliers are able to supply

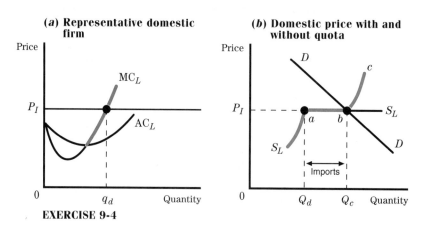

EXERCISE 9-4

more units at prices above P_I. The equilibrium price remains at P_I after the government imposes the quota because there are many price-taking domestic firms in the market.

When the domestic industry is competitive, the price will not change when the quota is imposed. If the price in an industry increases when a quota is imposed, this indicates that the domestic firms have monopoly power.

5. a. The regulated price is determined where the marginal cost function of the monopolist intersects the demand function. When the regulated price is determined in this manner, the firm's demand function becomes horizontal to the market demand function at the regulated price and then is the market demand function at lower prices. See the accompanying figure. When the regulated price is R^*, the demand function facing the regulated firm is the horizontal line at R^*. The firm will equate R^* to marginal cost and produce Q^*. Area 1 is equal to the firm's profits—the difference between R^*Q^* and the area under the marginal cost function. If there is competitive bidding for the right to become a monopolist, the winner of the auction will pay a sum equal to area 1.

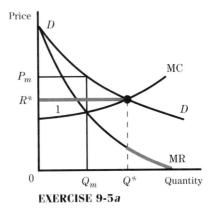

EXERCISE 9-5*a*

b. If the demand function intersects the marginal cost function when marginal cost is greater than average cost, the firm will earn profits and will be willing to bid a positive amount. If the demand function intersects the marginal cost function where marginal cost is less than average cost, the firm will incur losses and therefore will not be willing to bid anything. If the firm bids a positive amount, it implies that average cost is increasing. If it does not bid anything, average cost is decreasing. If it bids a positive amount, marginal cost is increasing. If it does not bid, marginal cost may be either decreasing or increasing, but it is less than average cost. See the accompanying figure.

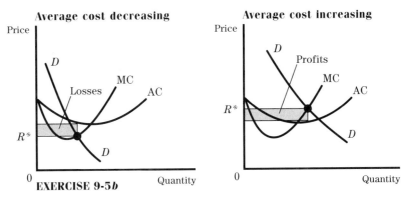

EXERCISE 9-5*b*

Chapter 10

1.   a. If the firms have different cost functions, then an arbitrary 15 percent output reduction will not minimize the cost of producing whatever output the cartel decides to produce.
   b. The quotas should be determined so that marginal cost is equalized across firms.
   c. To reach a consensus among the members when side payments are not possible, the cartel may simply take the easiest way out and assign a 15 percent output reduction to all firms.

3. The solution for firm 1 is

$$q_1 = \frac{a - bq_2 - c}{3b} \quad \text{and} \quad q_2 = \frac{a - bq_1 - c}{3b}$$

If the two equations are added, we have

$$q_1 + q_2 = \frac{2}{3} \frac{a - c}{b} - \frac{q_1 + q_2}{3}$$

$$\tfrac{4}{3}(q_1 + q_2) = \frac{2}{3} \frac{a - c}{b}$$

$$q_1 + q_2 = \frac{a - c}{2b}$$

The duopolists produce the monopoly output. This example shows how critical is the assumption that each firm makes regarding the quantity reaction of a rival. Under the Cournot assumption, price decreases with an increase in the number of Cournot competitors. If a rival matches the quantity increase, the monopoly output is produced.

4. With Bertrand competition a tiny price cut increases the firm's market share from 50 to 100 percent. Suppose that two Bertrand competitors try to cooperate. How might they credibly commit to cooperation? Each could build a plant with a rigid capacity equal to 50 percent of the market at the monopoly price. By building a plant with a rigid capacity, each Bertrand competitor is signaling the opponent that it will not be able to expand output. Therefore, a price cut will be self-defeating.

5. False. Clearly, two firms sharing the market represent an oligopoly. If a hundred firms of the same size are in the market, then each accounts for only 1 percent of the market and the industry behaves like a competitive industry.

Chapter 11

1. A firm cannot live a quiet life if the capital market operates at a low transaction cost. Then, a management that does not maximize profits is subject to a takeover. If impediments are placed in the way so that the capital market cannot replace an inefficient management, then a protected management can deviate from wealth maximization.

2. During a recession the demand for the firm's product declines and the profit function shifts downward. The profit constraint may no longer be binding, and the firm becomes subject to the discipline of the capital market. See the accompanying figure.

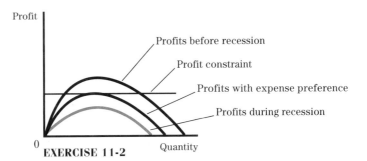

EXERCISE 11-2

5. When the regulator commits to a fixed price, the firm will earn profits by being efficient in production. Therefore, the firm's management will have a greater incentive to be cost-efficient. Any increase in profits will not be taken away by the regulator through a lower regulated price. The danger is that the regulator's commitment may not be binding if the firm's profits rise by too much.

Chapter 12

1. A price-discriminating monopolist will never sell in a market where demand is price-inelastic because marginal revenue [MR $= P(1 + 1/E)$] is negative when $0 > E_P > -1$.

2. **a.** If marginal cost is decreasing and the firm expands into the foreign market, the price in the domestic market decreases. The horizontal summation of the marginal revenue functions intersects the marginal cost function where marginal cost of producing the last unit is lower. See the accompanying figure. The summation of the marginal revenue functions intersects the downward-sloping marginal cost curve when the firm produces Q^* units. The firm allocates Q^* to the two markets so that marginal revenue in the markets is equal. When the firm enters the foreign market, it should reduce price in the domestic market if marginal cost is decreasing.

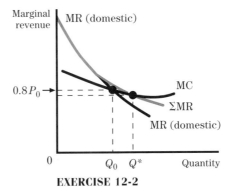

EXERCISE 12-2

b. If the price elasticity of demand is -10, marginal revenue of the last unit sold in the domestic market is

$$\text{MR} = P_0\left(1 + \frac{1}{-10}\right) = 0.9P_0$$

Therefore, the marginal cost of producing the last unit in the domestic market is $0.9P_0$. Since the first unit can be sold in the foreign market as only $0.85P_0$, the first unit sold abroad will *not* cover its marginal cost. The firm should not enter the foreign market.

3.   a. A firm will export some of its output if the marginal cost function intersects the flat segment of the horizontal summation of the two marginal revenue functions. Marginal revenue of selling each unit in the foreign market equals P_w since the firm can sell as much as it wants at this price. The horizontal summation of the marginal revenue functions is the domestic marginal revenue function until P_w is reached. From then on, the marginal revenue function is horizontal at P_w. See the accompanying figure. If the firm's marginal cost function is MC*-MC*, it will sell only in the domestic market at a price of P^*. If the marginal cost function is MC'-MC', the firm will sell in both markets. It produces Q' and sells Q'' units in the domestic market at a price of P'.

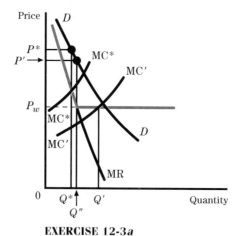

EXERCISE 12-3a

   b. When the world price falls, the flat segment of the horizontal summation of the two marginal revenue functions shifts downward and intersects the marginal cost function at a lower value of marginal cost. A fall in the world price decreases the total quantity sold by the firm. The price in the domestic market falls, and the quantity sold domestically increases.
   c. If the marginal cost function shifts to the right and becomes MC-MC, the firm pro-

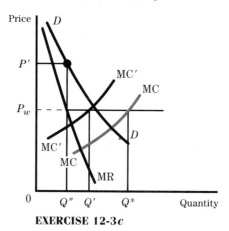

EXERCISE 12-3c

duces Q^* units. The price in the domestic market does not change, and all the increase in production is sold in the foreign market. See the accompanying figure.

8. a. *Policy 1:* The per unit fee equals marginal cost of $c + d$. The entrance fee is equal to area A, and total profits equal A.

Policy 2: Because there is no per unit charge, the consumer determines the number of rides where the demand function intersects the horizontal axis. The entrance fee collects all the consumer surplus or $A + B + C + D + E + F$. The cost of providing the rides equals $D + E + F + G$. Therefore, profits equal $A + B + C - G$.

b. Profits under policy 2 will be greater if $B + C > G$.

c. Suppose that you could limit the number of rides to the quantity where the demand function intersects the marginal cost function c. Then, the entrance fee would be $A + B + C + D + E$ and profits would be $A + B + C$.

10. a. Over a two-day period profits from the old price policy are $2A$. Under the new price policy profits are $A + B + C$ since the consumer purchases the requirements for a two-day period and shops every other day. Profits from the new price policy will be greater if $B + C > A$.

b. Suppose that you raise the entrance fee to $2(A + B + C)$ and allow consumers to purchase as many units as desired whenever they buy. Then, your profits over a two-day period are $2(A + B + C)$.

Chapter 13

2. If the termination of RPM was voluntary, the quantity sold will not decline but the retail margin will. Consumers are now educated, and so they no longer demand special services and the firm no longer wants to supply these services. If the termination occurred because an antitrust case was lost, the quantity sold and the retail margin will decline because the firm can no longer provide special services that consumers are demanding.

3. Proposal 1 makes the retail margin large enough so that the costs of providing the product and pre- and postservices are covered. However, it does not solve the free rider problem. There is nothing in proposal 1 that encourages an individual dealer to supply the special service. The dealer's profits are higher if the service is not provided.

Will proposal 1 encourage the dealer to provide postsale service? Notice that the consumer pays up front for the lessons. The problem here is that there is a short-run profit gain from not delivering the lessons or from delivering lesser-quality lessons. There is an incentive to cheat by promising more than the firm will deliver.

With proposal 2 RPM is designed to solve the free rider problem when a dealer provides presale services. Does RPM solve the problem of postsale services? There is no guarantee that the dealer will provide these services since short-run profits are higher when there is cheating on the lessons.

4. a. Under policy 1, if the firm adopts RPM, first-time buyers will receive the information. Under policy 2 there is a danger that first-time buyers will free-ride by acquiring information from a dealer who sells under RPM but purchase at the other type of dealer. Unless this can be controlled, dealers operating under RPM will suffer losses.

b. Under policy 1 a dealer has a greater incentive to sell to experienced buyers who require less information. So the dealer will earn profits on sales to experienced buyers. Under policy 2 dealers selling under RPM will earn a normal return if the free rider problem is solved and will suffer losses if it is not. Dealers selling to experienced buyers will earn a normal rate of return.

Chapter 14

2. If consumers know the quantity produced by a firm, they can tell if the firm is acting honestly by the amount it produces. A firm could still cheat by producing the profit-maximizing quantity supplied by a firm delivering high-quality output. While profits of a cheater are not as large as they would be if it could produce the quantity that maximizes its profits, they exceed the profits earned when acting honestly.

3. If the number of retailers is limited, the price of the product and franchisee profit will increase until the price premium is large enough so that the present value of honest behavior is equal to the present value of cheating. Therefore, you should limit the number of franchises so that the price premium deters cheating.

5.   a. If a monopolist produces high-quality output, its profit is $A + B$. The present value of profits is $(A + B)/r$.

    b. If the monopolist delivers a low-quality product, it will produce X' units. If the firm cheats, the present value of profits is

$$\frac{A + B + C + D + E}{1 + i}$$

    c. The monopolist will deliver a high-quality product if

$$\frac{A + B}{i} > \frac{A + B + C + D + E}{1 + i} \qquad \text{or} \qquad C + D + E < \frac{A + B}{i}$$

At the end of period 1 the firm receives at least $A + B$ whether it does or does not cheat. Therefore, the *increase* in profits from cheating by producing the lower-quality product cannot exceed the present value of future profits when the firm delivers the high-quality product. Note that a monopolist may produce a high-quality product, whereas a price-taking firm always prefers to cheat when price equals long-run average cost.

Chapter 14 Problem Set:
Integration and Opportunistic Behavior

1. If X acts opportunistically and raises price by P percent, it will earn profits for one period and then be terminated. The present value of profits is

$$\text{PV}_1 = \left[\left(1 + \frac{P}{100}\right)A - A\right]q_c \frac{1}{1 + i} = \frac{PAq_c}{(1 + i)100}$$

2. If Y offers a price premium of k percent, the present value of profits earned by X is

$$\text{PV}_2 = \left[\left(1 + \frac{k}{100}\right)A - A\right]q_c \frac{1}{i} = \frac{kAq_c}{i(100)}$$

X will act not opportunistically if $\text{PV}_1 \leq \text{PV}_2$. This implies that

$$\frac{PAq_c}{1 + i} \leq \frac{kAq_c}{i} \qquad P\frac{i}{1 + i} \leq k$$

3. Given the price premium, the price that Y offers X is

$$\left(1 + \frac{k}{100}\right)A = \left(1 + \frac{P}{100}\frac{i}{1+i}\right)A$$

If r or P is sufficiently large, it will pay Y to produce the part although it is a less efficient producer because the required price premium exceeds the cost inefficiency factor. Y will purchase the part rather than produce it if

$$\left(1 + \frac{P}{100}\frac{i}{1+i}\right)A < \left(1 + \frac{I}{100}\right)A$$

or $$\frac{I}{P} \geq \frac{i}{1+i} \quad \text{or} \quad i \leq \frac{I/P}{1 - I/P}$$

assuming $I < P$. If $I > P$, it will always pay Y to purchase the part.

Chapter 15

2. The probability that a color will not sell is

$$F(P) = \frac{15 - C}{15} = \frac{P}{\$450}$$

since $$C = \frac{\$450 - P}{\$30}$$

The probability that a color will sell is

$$1 - F(P) = \frac{\$450 - P}{\$450}$$

Expected revenue is

$$\text{ER} = P[1 - F(P)] = P\frac{\$450 - P}{\$450}$$

The price that maximizes expected revenue satisfies

$$\frac{\Delta \text{ER}}{\Delta P} = \$450 - 2P = 0 \quad \text{or} \quad P = \$225$$

Since prices are at $30 intervals, the price will be either $210 or $240. By simply substituting $P = \$210$ or $\$240$ into the expected revenue function, expected revenue is found to be $112 at each price. So the firm is indifferent between these prices. At $P = \$210$, $C = 8$; and at $P = \$240$, $C = 7$.

3. Under a two-price policy, the expression for expected revenue is

$$\text{ER}(P_i, P_m) = P_i[1 - F(P_i)] + P_m[F(P_i) - F(P_m)]$$

Substituting the expressions for the probabilities gives

$$\text{ER}(P_i, P_m) = P_i\left(1 - \frac{P_i}{\$450}\right) + P_m\left(\frac{P_i}{\$450} - \frac{P_m}{\$450}\right)$$

$$= P_i\frac{\$450 - P_i}{\$450} + P_m\frac{P_i - P_m}{\$450}$$

Given P_i, the optimal markdown price is derived from

$$\frac{\Delta ER}{\Delta P_m} = \frac{P_i - P_m}{\$450} - \frac{P_m}{\$450} = 0$$

So we have derived the 50 percent decision rule, $P_m = P_i/2$. Substituting this decision rule into the expected revenue equation yields

$$ER(P_i, P_m) = P_i\left(\frac{\$450 - P_i}{\$450}\right) + \frac{P_i}{2}\left(\frac{P_i}{\$450} - \frac{P_i/2}{\$450}\right)$$

$$ER(P_i) = P_i\left(\frac{\$450 - P_i}{\$450}\right) + \frac{1}{\$450}\frac{P_i}{2}\frac{P_i}{2}$$

Expected revenue is maximized when P_i satisfies

$$\frac{\Delta ER}{\Delta P_i} = \frac{1}{\$450}(\$450 - P_i - P_i + P_i/2) = 0$$

Therefore, $P_i = \frac{2}{3}(\$450) = \$300$ and $P_m = \$150$

The firm will charge these prices and sell five colors at $300 and five more colors at $150. Expected revenue is

$$ER = \$300\frac{150}{450} + \frac{1}{450}\left(\frac{300}{2}\right)^2$$

$$= \$100 + \$50 = \$150$$

5. The compensation policy of the firm penalizes a buyer who purchases a fashion line because the probability of not selling all the dresses is higher when there is greater uncertainty. The store buyer will have an incentive to select lines where the price distribution has a smaller variance, and the percentage of dresses sold will be higher.

6. This policy is better suited for goods where there is less uncertainty about the prices that consumers will pay. It should be applied to the sale of paint or hammers rather than to fashion merchandise. Therefore, a store that adopts this policy will offer less fashionable clothing.

Chapter 16

2. If a tax of 33 percent of income in year 2 is announced at the beginning of year 1, the consumer's intertemporal budget constraint becomes $C_2 = 0.67I_2 + (1 + i)I_1 - (1 + i)C_1$. Therefore, the intertemporal budget constraint shifts from dd' to cc'. If consumption in years 1 and 2 consists of normal goods, consumption in both years will decrease and savings in year 1 will increase. In the accompanying figure consumption spending in year 1 decreases from $C_1^{\bullet}$ to C_1', and so savings increase to $I_1 - C_1^{\bullet}$. Consumption spending in year 2 decreases from $C_2^{\bullet}$ to C_2'.

3. An increase in demand for the nonrenewable resource in year 2 shifts the discounted demand function for period 2 from DP to DP'. See the accompanying figure. This means less of the resource is sold in period 1 and more is sold in period 2. Since less of the resource is sold in period 1, the price in period 1 rises from P_1 to P_1' and the price in period 2 increases from $(1 + i)P_1$ to $(1 + i)P_1'$. Although prices rise in both years, the rate of increase is still $1 + i$.

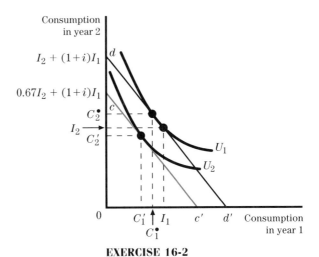

EXERCISE 16-2

6. If P_2 is less than $(1 + i)P_1$, the supply of a renewable resource is augmented in period 2. An increase in i causes the discounted demand function in the second period to shift downward. Since the discounted price is less in the second period than before, the price in the second period will be the same and the price in the first period will be unaffected.

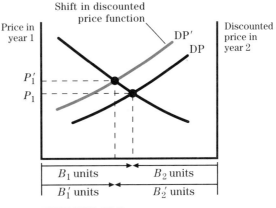

EXERCISE 16-3

Chapter 17

1. An increase in the price of the product shifts the demand for labor to the right. However, this will have no effect on the price of labor if the firm is a price-taking firm in the labor market and the industry hires a small percentage of all workers in the economy.

4. Expert 1 predicts that a general assistance program will eliminate consumers with incomes of less than $5,000 and reduce the percentage of consumers with incomes between $10,000 and $14,999 by 5 percentage points as some of these consumers choose leisure and an income of $5,000. Expert 2 predicts that 4 percent of all consumers whose incomes are between $15,000 and $19,999 will work less, so that they will fall into the $10,000 to $14,999 income class, while 3 percent of all consumers whose incomes are between $10,000 and $14,999 will choose leisure and $5,000. However, the theory of a general assistance program

predicts that a consumer will either be unaffected or will choose leisure. Therefore, the predictions of expert 2 appear not to be based on maximizing behavior of consumers.

10. If the worker who does not want to work many hours treats consumption spending on goods and leisure as close substitutes, the firm will have difficulty sorting workers. In the accompanying figure a low wage–bonus policy does not sort the two types of workers because worker 2's indifference curve $_2U_1$ cuts the budget constraint between points B and C. Therefore, worker 2's utility increases by working more hours and collecting the bonus. The firm is unable to sort workers.

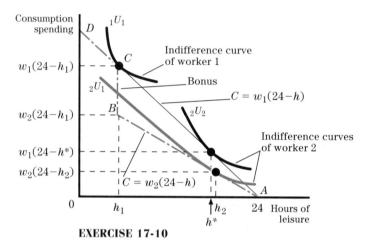

EXERCISE 17-10

Chapter 18

1. Although A has more units of Y than of X and B has more units of X than of Y, the pattern of exchange cannot be determined without knowing the tastes of A and B. The contract curve can pass either above or below the endowment point. In the accompanying figure, A is willing to trade units of X for units of Y and to end up with still fewer units of X and more units of Y.

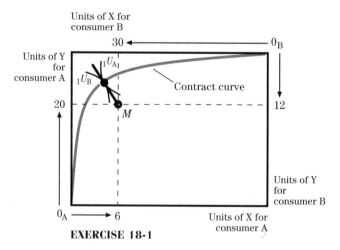

EXERCISE 18-1

7. The assignment of factors will not be Pareto-efficient if the factor price ratios are different in industries X and Y. Industry X has relatively more units of capital and fewer units of labor than it would have if the economy were Pareto-efficient in production. In industry X the slope of *aa* equals the marginal rate of technical substitution along the isoquant X_0. The same is true in industry Y where *bb* is the firm's isocost line and where the slope of *bb* is equal to the slope of the isoquant Y_0. See the accompanying figure.

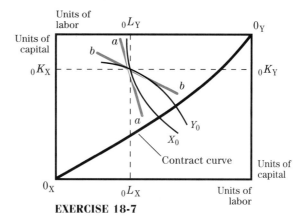

EXERCISE 18-7

9. If the supply of labor increases, the production possibility curve shifts outward. If the economy initially produced only Y or only X, it can now produce more units of Y or of X. The production possibility curve shifts from PP to $P'P'$ in the accompanying figure.

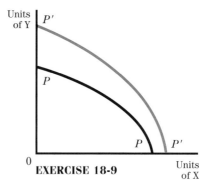

EXERCISE 18-9

Chapter 19

2. If the monopolist can engage in perfect price discrimination, it will produce the same output that it would have produced if the industry were competitive. The monopolist charges the willingness to pay for successive units and will continue to supply units until the price for the last unit equals marginal cost. This is the same rule that determines the output of a competitive industry. Therefore, $P = MC$. Consequently, the economy is Pareto-efficient in product mix since the ratio of prices will equal the ratio of marginal costs. However, the distribution of income is different because the monopolist captures all the consumer surplus and increases profits.

4. If Clean Water is willing to pay Bright Paint $7 for each unit Bright Paint does not produce, Bright Paint has an incentive to reduce output. If it decreases output from 5 to 4 units, its costs decrease by $14 and its revenue decreases by $14, and so it gains $7 from the payment by Clean Water and will not produce the fifth unit. If Bright Paint does not produce the fourth unit, its costs are lower by $10 and its revenues are lower by $14, but it will receive $7 from Clean Water and so it will not produce the fourth unit. If it does not produce the third unit, its cost will fall by $7 and its revenue will decrease by $14, but it will receive $7 from Clean Water and so is indifferent between producing the third unit.

6. To determine if transaction costs are large or small, you must determine whether the assignment of property rights affects the outcome. If transaction costs are small, the outcome should be independent of the assignment of property rights. If transaction costs are large, the assignment should make a difference.

INDEX